Ibn al-ʿArabī on the Mysteries of Purification and Formal Prayer

from the *Futūḥāt al-Makkiyya*

(Meccan Revelations)

Muḥyī Dīn Ibn al-ʿArabī

Translated by

Aisha Bewley

Edited by

Laleh Bakhtiar

Series Editor

Seyyed Hossein Nasr

Great Books of the Islamic World

Library of Congress Cataloging-in-Publication Data

Muḥyī dīn ibn al-ᶜArabī, *On the Mysteries of Purification and Formal Prayer* from the *Futūḥāt al-Makkiyya (Meccan Revelations)*
1. Islamic Law. 2. Sufism. I. Title.

ISBN: 1-56744-775-9 pbk
1-56744-776-7 hbk

Cover design: Liaquat Ali
Cornerstones are Allah and Muhammad connected by *Bismillāh al-Raḥmān al-Raḥīm* (In the Name of God, the Merciful, the Compassionate).

Logo design by Mani Ardalan Farhadi
The cypress tree bending with the wind, the source for the paisley design, is a symbol of the perfect Muslim, who, as the tree, bends with the wind of God's Will.

Published by
Great Books of the Islamic World, Inc.

Distributed by
KAZI Publications, Inc.
3023 W. Belmont Avenue
Chicago IL 60618
Tel: 773-267-7001; FAX: 773-267-7002
email: info@kazi.org /www.kazi.org

CONTENTS

(ORIGINAL CHAPTERS 68 AND 69 OF THE *MECCAN REVELATIONS*)

FOREWORD

God's last plenar revelation to present humanity came in the form of a book, al-Qur'an, which for Muslims is also *the* book and is in fact known also as *Umm al-kitāb* or Mother of All Books. While the peerless majesty of the revelation reduced the first generation of Muslims to silence, the echo of the Noble Book and its encouragement of acquiring knowledge could not but result in a culture which cherished books and honored scholars. This unmistakable emphasis of the Noble Quran on knowledge, combined with the synthetic power of Islam to absorb the learning of older civilizations to the extent that they conformed to the doctrine of unity (*al-tawḥīd*), gave rise to a vast and diversified intellectual life which for the past thirteen centuries has produced millions of works dealing with nearly every field of knowledge from the religious sciences, theology and philosophy to the natural sciences, from law to music, and from poetry to politics.

Islamic civilization was a lake into which flowed streams from many civilizations: Greek, Roman, Egyptian, Mesopo- tamian, Byzantine, Persian, Indian and even Chinese. In this lake the various elements became synthesized into a new body of water which itself became the source for numerous tributaries that have watered the various lands of *D[r al-isl[m*. Furthermore, Islamic civilization created works which had profound influence upon at least three major civilizations outside of the Islamic world: the Far Eastern, the Indian and the Western besides creating numerous masterly works whose influence has remained confined within the Islamic world. Such works in both categories contain a precious message for humanity as a whole and need to be made known by the world at large today.

Most treatises in Islamic civilization were written in the language of the Quranic revelation, Arabic, followed by the only other universal language of Islamic civilization, Persian. But important works have also been written in Turkish, Urdu, Bengali, Malay, Swahili, Berber, and numerous other languages including Chinese and, during this century, even English and French. Nor have all the works in Arabic been written by Arabs nor all the works in Persian by Persians. Numerous treatises in Arabic were written by Persians and later Turks, Indians, Berbers and Black Africans while many books in the Persian language were composed by Indians, Turks and Central Asians. The body of works written within the confines of Islamic civilization belongs to the whole of that civilization and in classical times, in fact, important books became known rapidly from Morocco to India and later Southeast Asia.

The Great Books of the Islamic World series seeks to make some of the most important works produced in Islamic civilization, primarily in Arabic and Persian, available in English so that these treasures of Islamic thought can be appreciated by those who do not possess the facility to benefit from them in the original languages. The audience to which the series addresses itself is predominantly the Western English reading public, but the series is also meant for Muslims themselves who have facility with the English language and also for non-Muslim and non-Westerners who are now becoming ever more knowledgeable in English and who might wish to gain deeper knowledge of the Islamic intellectual universe.

We hope that with the help of God, Exalted is His Majesty, this series will be successfully completed and that by providing a clear and readable translation of some of the great masterpieces of Islamic thought in English, this series will be able to create better understanding of Islam in the world at large and make accessible some of the treasures of traditional thought which, although Islamic in genesis, belong to all human beings who are interested in true knowledge in whatever form it appears. *wa mā tawfīqunā illā bi'Llāh*

Seyyed Hossein Nasr
Washington DC, June, 1997

Editor's Preface

Among the pillars of Islam, it is perhaps the pillar of purification and formal prayer that are most in need of clarification. This the Shaykh al-Akhbar, Ibn al-Arabi (1165-1245 CE) does in this excellent translation by Aisha Bewley. It is an exhaustive explanation of questions the practitioners may have, delving into both the mysteries as well as the divine law ruling on them. References to the Quran and the *Hadith* abound.

In speaking about Chapters 66-72 of the *Futuhat al-Makkiyah* (Meccan Revelations), of which the present volume is a translation of Chapters 68 and 69, Dr. James Morris, an Ibn al-Arabi expert says: "One of the most fascinating and potentially valuable sections of the entire *al-Futuhat*—[these chapters] offer what is almost certainly the most detailed and exacting phenomenology of spiritual experience in the Islamic tradition, presented in terms of an irenic reconciliation of contrasting legal interpretations of the basic ritual practices of Islam (purification, prayer, fasting, etc.)." (http://www.ibnarabisociety.org/articles/mr_introduction.html)

In practicing this pillar, there are those who do not want to delve into such detail or it may be someone who is new to the pillar. For this person we have included in Appendix A the work of al-Ghazzali (1058-1111 CE), "On the Mysteries of Purity and Prayer," from *The Alchemy of Happiness* translated by Jay R. Crook. The sources for al-Ghazzali work here is also the Quran and the *Hadith*.

These two explanations of this pillar show how it can be understood in either the simplest form (al-Ghazzali) or the most complicated (al-Ibn al-Arabi).

Laleh Bakhtiar, Ph. D.
Chicago 2009

Part One: On the Mysteries of Purification

1 Introduction

Look—and you will see the secret of purification clearly, simple for
those who possess wakefulness and cleverness.
How many a pure one there is who is not described by purity when he
is beside the sea of presence (*laduni*), seeking shelter.
If he were to plunge his life into the salt sea when he is not
annihilated in the sea of the Reality, he would not purify (himself).
When a person performs purification with an odd number of stones,
he follows the exemplary *sunna* allying himself to those who have
passed.
If he performs purification with an even number of stones,
he becomes a loser, and parts from those whom he desires
because of inward vice.
If he washes his hands an odd number of times, and does not covet
with what he desires in the original primal nature, then the hand
and wrist are not washed since the sword of trust does not flash
when unsheathed.
When washing the face is done correctly, his modesty is sound,
and it is proper for him to lift the veil whenever he wishes.
If he does not make water touch the locks of his hair and his palms
do not alight on the open part of the back of the neck, then the nose
is not in the bondage of slavery to which others are subject, in a
stage which is contorted.
If he does not see the footstool when washing his feet, he lacks the
meaning of purification for the time and is banished.
When one washes his mouth and is not free of claims, fulfilling what
he lays claim to, and snuffs water up the nostrils, not having
breathed the scent of his arrival, he blows it out leaving his
ruinous pride with it.
He does not neglect his ears in purification if he inclines to good
words, is content and follows.
If he wears overshoes and is traveling, he wipes over them when he

purifies himself and is hidden in its secret
For three days. If he is residing in a place, he wipes them for one day without ending.
There is a secret in wiping which I am not permitted to mention, even if you were to sever my joints and kidneys.
Wiping follows it when there are bandages as is clear for every disciple who does not desire the outward part of nearness.
If pure water cannot be found, he performs dry ablution with his hands using pure earth.
He wipes his face and hands an odd number of times. If he refuses and does it an even number, how excellent is the one who comes!
When a man has intercourse, his purification must cover all just as pleasures have filled his higher parts.
Have you not seen that God addressed His creation when He brought him out from between the breast-bones and back.
That is what harms his purity. If he had been absent with the pure essence, it would not have been harmed.
If a man forgets a pillar, he returns and makes it up, doing what will contain and include it.
If it is not a pillar but he fails to do a *Sunna*, he has not brought the near close nor attained the desire.
That is common to all acts of worship. The one who is ignorant of matters is not like the one with perception.
This is the purification of the gnostics. If you are among their party, you will obtain the select nearness.
Since this is the outward affair, that which is concealed from the eyes is the greatest intoxicant.

1.1 Purification

Know—may God support you and us with a spirit from Him!—that since purification is cleanliness, we know that it has an attribute of transcendence or incomparability (*tanzih*). Purification has both a spiritual and a physical meaning: the purification of the heart and the self from inferior character traits and what is blameworthy; the purification of the intellect from the blemish of opinions and doubts; the purification of the eye from gazing at others; and the purification of the limbs. We know that each limb has a spiritual purification (as well). We mentioned them in *Tanazzutat al-mawsiliyyah* in the chapters on purification. There is also physical purification from impure matters which are considered to be noxious by nature and habit. Both these two purifications (spiritual and physical) are prescribed (by the divine law). (121)

1.1.1. Purification Has Both a Spiritual and Physical Meaning

There are two types of outward, physical purification. We mentioned one type, which is (general) cleanliness. The other consists of the specific actions—in specific places particular to states—which are made obligatory by the divine law. The first kind of purification consists of three types in the divine law: ablution (*wudu*), full bathing (*ghusl*) and dry ablution (*tayammum*). Purification is achieved by three things: two are agreed on and there is disagreement about the third. Agreed on is pure water and dust, whether the dust is separated from the earth or not. That which they disagree about is using the juice of pressed dates for ablution. There is also disagreement about what is taken from the earth which still has the name "earth" applied to it—except for dust, as we mentioned. (122)

Purification can be an independent act of worship as the Prophet said (quoting from the Quran): *"It is light upon light"* (24:35) or it can be a precondition for the correctness of a prescribed act of worship specifically set down by the divine law, the performance of which is only valid by prior purification. The first is like ablution upon ablution (*wudu*), which is *"light upon light."* The second is a means of removing (a state which acts as) an obstacle to performing an act of worship. The act of worship is only valid after purification which (then) makes the act of worship lawful to perform. That is the basis for its being obligatory. (123)

That by which this purification occurs—which both removes the obstacle and permits the act—is water without dispute while pressed dates are in dispute. That which allows a particular act to occur at the prescribed moment, but which does not remove the obstacle (with dispute) is dust. In our opinion, it certainly removes the obstacle at the moment. The Lawgiver deemed it a means of purification. When water is found, there is another rule about dust, as the obstacle returns after it had been removed. There is disagreement on that which is separated from the earth—other than dust. (124)

God said: *"O those who have believed! When you stand up for the formal prayer, then wash your faces and your hands up to the elbows and wipe your heads and your feet up to the ankles. And if you had been defiled, then purify yourselves. And if you have been sick or on a journey, or one of you has drawn near from the privy or you have come into sexual contact with your wives and you find no water, then aim at getting wholesome, dry earth and wipe your faces and hands with it. God wants not to make any impediment for you and He wants you to be purified"* (5:6). (125)

1.1.2. Filth (rujz), Dirt (rijs) and the Exchanging the s With a z

God said: *"He sent down water from heaven for you and He purified you from it and caused to be put away from you the defilement of Satan."* (8:11). The letter *z* in the word "filth" or "defilement" (*rijz*) here replaces the letter *s* for those who read the word *"al-zirat"* with *z*. It is the language of the reading of Ibn Kathir—with *s*—while Hamza reads it with *z*, and the other readings with the letter *sad*. (126)

There was a shaykh named Muhammad ibn Khalaf ibn Saff al-Lakhami to whom I recited the Quran in 568 AH in a mosque known as Qaws al-Haniya in Seville in Andalusia. I recited the word *sirat* using the *s* of Ibn Kathir. He said to me: "One of those who transmit linguistics asked one of the Arabs if they said *saqar* or *saqar* [using the letter *sin* or *sad*]. He replied: 'I do not know what you are talking about, but maybe you are asking about *zaqar*.'" He said: "He increased my knowledge with a third word which I had not known." (127)

Farra said that *rijs* means impurity and there is no doubt that water removes impurity. Purity, according to the divine law removes the defilement of Satan. God says: *"And purify thy garments"* (74:4).

Imr al-Qays said: If one of my traits is abhorrent to you, then separate my garment from your garment and pluck it out. He alludes to "clothing" as (symbolizing) love and union. The Messenger of God said reporting from his Lord: "*Neither My earth nor My heaven contain Me, but the heart of My believing (mumin) servant (abd) contains Me.*" One of His names is The Believer (*al-Mumin*). Whoever takes on its character has purified his heart because the heart is the place of belief (and faith). Therefore it possesses divine vastness and is the place of the Self-disclosure of the Lord. (128)

1.1.3. General and Particular Purification

General purification, which is full bathing, is required because of the annihilation that diffuses one's essence through the pleasure which comes from sexual intercourse. (129)

> I showed her the small stars hiding the glow of the Ursa Major
> and she showed me the moon!

Purification preliminary to another act of worship (the second type referred to above) is the ablution particular to certain limbs which are washed and wiped. It symbolizes known stations and noble divine Self-disclosures. They include power, speech, breath, truthfulness, humility, modesty, listening, and constancy. These are the limbs of ablution, and they are noble stations which result in one drawing near to God.

1.1.4. The Tools of Spiritual Purification

Spiritual purification occurs in one of two ways: either by the mystery of life (water) or on the basis of the configuration of a natural element (dust). Ablution through the mystery of life is to witness the Living, the Eternal: *"The Living, The Eternal"* (2:255), while ablution through a configured element is like a father who is the root of offspring; it is earth and dust. This is only achieved by considering and reflecting on your essence so that you recognize the One Who brought you into existence. He directed you to yourself in His words: *"On the earth are signs for the ones who are certain and in yourselves"* (51:20-21) and in the words of His Messenger: Whoever knows himself knows his Lord. (130)

He directed you to yourself by explaining your constituent parts to you (*tafsil*) and did not refer to you gathered together from separate parts (*ijmal*) so that you might look and deduce. Specifically, He said: *"And certainly We have created the human being from an extraction of clay,"* (23:12)—and he is Adam—*"after that We made him into seminal fluids in a stopping place, secure"* (23:13)—(referring to) the growth of offspring in the womb according to where the sperm settles and the position of the stars. He referred to that as a *"stopping place." "After that We created a clot from seminal fluid. Then We created tissue from the clot. Then We created bones from tissue. Then We clothed the bones with flesh."* (23:14). The body is completed by the constituent parts because the flesh contains the veins and nerves.

In every state there is a sign (*ayat*)
which indicates to me that I am dependent.

Then in this sign He completed the creation of the articulate, rational self which is the human being. He said: *"After that We caused another creation to grow"* (23:14).

1.1.5. The Ranks of the Body and of the Spirit

By making this clear God informs us that our temperament has no effect on our subtle essence. It is obvious even though there is no revealed text (specifically saying this). Clearer than this are His words: *"He Who created thee, then shaped thee in proportion."* (82:7) This is where He mentions "breaking something down into constituent parts." That is, (He refers to) the changes in the stages of human development. He says: *"He composed thee in whatever form He willed."* (82:8) He connected this assembling to volition, His Will. It is clear that if the temperament had pre-determined a particularly designated spirit, He would not have said: *"In whatever way He willed."* (82:8) "Whatever" is an indefinite particle like that of *ma* (whichever). He uses a particle which applies to everything. (132)

The Quran makes it clear to you that "temperament" does not call forth a particular "form." After temperament acquires a form, the form has need of temperament and demands it. Temperament is based on the faculties it contains while the form is solely managed by them. The faculties act like tools which a carpenter or wood-worker uses. For example, when the tools are prepared, finished and mastered through their essence and state, they seek a craftsman to use them for what they have been prepared to do. They are not specific to Zayd, Amr, Khalid or anyone in particular. (133)

When a craftsman comes, he enables his tools by enabling their essence which does not have self-determination. The craftsman (that is, the form) begins to use the tools (that is, the faculties) in his craft and uses each tool for that for which it was prepared. Among them one is perfected and it is that which *". . . was formed"* (*mukhallaqah*) (22:5), meaning its natural disposition has been formed and among others there are those that *"were not formed."* (22:5) So the craftsman (the form) is less than his art to the extent that the tool's (faculties) excellence is less. That is so that he might know that perfection of essence belongs only to God—glory be to Him! (134)

The Real has explained to you the stages of your body and spirit that you might examine, reflect and take note that He did not create you *"aimless"* (75:36), even if the aim may be delayed. (135)

1.1.6. The Aspiration and Intention in Purification

As for the aspiration (*qasd*) (for clean earth or dust for dry ablution) which is (part of) the intention (*niyah*), there is dispute about whether this aspiration is a pre-condition to the validity (of dry ablution). God says: *"Then aim at getting wholesome, dry earth."* (4:43) That is, intend (to use) dry earth which does not contain any impurity (*najasah*) which would prevent its use in this act of worship. He does not say this about purification with water. He referred to pure water, not impure water. In Arabic, impure is defined by that which is added to it. When you say to an Arab: "Give me water," he will bring you pure water. This is what an Arab would understand from it. A Messenger is only sent and a Book only revealed in the language of its people. The Messenger of God said: The Quran was sent down in my language, the clear Arabic tongue. God says: *"We truly have made it an Arabic Recitation so that perhaps you would be reasonable."* (43:3) (136)

For this reason one does not speak of "one's aspiring for" water because it is the mystery of life. It gives life by its essence with or without one's "aspiring" for it to do so as opposed to earth. If there is no "aspiring" for clean earth, one would not be purified because earth is a dense body which does not flow; its spirit is the aspiration. Aspiration is something spiritual (not sensory). One performing dry ablution has need of a special aspiration with the earth or dust but there is disagreement about this. So in reference to water, He said: "*Wash (with water),*" not "perform dry ablution with clean water." (137)

If they say (in the Tradition): "Actions should be accompanied by intention," and that intention (*niyyah*) is the same as aspiring and performing ablution is an action, we reply, in effect: "We accept what you say and we also argue for it." The intention here, however, is connected to the action of performing ablution, not to the water used in the ablution; water is not an "act." For dry ablution, the aspiration is for clean earth or dust. According to this Tradition, ablution requires an intention inasmuch as it is an act, not inasmuch as it is an act done with water. Water here is secondary to action, and the action is the object of aspiring with intention. With dry ablution, the aspiration is for clean earth or dust, and the action done with it would require another intention at the beginning of the act, just as the action with water requires it—ablution, full bath (*ghusl*) and all prescribed acts, require sincerity commanded of them and that (sincerity) is one's intention—with some dispute. God says: *"They were commanded but to worship God as ones who are sincere and devoted in the way of life to Him."* (98:5) Understand that there is some controversy about this sign, and this is a question in which the religious scholars have not fixed precisely the proper path in which to proceed and the truth of its meaning! (138)

It would not be said about water: "*Perform dry ablution* (tayammum) *with water,*" so one needs a spirit from the intention, while water itself is spirit. It gives life by its essence. God said: *"We have made every living thing of water"* (21:30) and *"every living thing"* glorifies with the praise of God. None glorifies except the living. Water is the basis of life in things. For this reason, there is dispute among the scholars of the divine law concerning the intention in ablution, and whether it is a condition for its validity or not. The mystery is what we mentioned. (139)

1.1.7. Abu Hanifa's View

If it is said [as Abu Hanifa said] that the scholar who does not think that there must be an intention for ablution but thinks that one's intention should be made with the full bath because of being in the state of sexual impurity (*janaba*)—although both acts of worship (ablution and full bath) are with water and the mystery of life is in both of them—we reply: that it is because sexual impurity is itself a fluid. The divine law deems that there be purification from it because of its determinative property of being tainted. The mixture of sexual impurity includes a physical ingredient because it comes from blood. Sexual impurity, then, shares with the mystery of life. The two fluids (sexual impurity and water used for purification) oppose each other. The water used for purification is not able by itself to remove the impurity (because both are fluids). Therefore, a person in the state of sexual impurity needs a spirit to support it in the full bath and it needs the help of one's intention. The principle of (making one's) intention—and it is a spirit of "meaning"—and the principle of water are joined together, and together they remove the ruling of sexual impurity through the full bath without a doubt, as is the position of Abu Hanifa and whoever says what he says in this matter. (140).

1.1.8. Hasan ibn Hayy's Opinion

Whoever maintains that the water of sexual impurity is not as strong as pure water because it is not water converted from blood while sexual impurity mixes with the humors and it differs from it by its color and density, is saying that the water of sexual impurity is too weak to resist pure water so it is not necessary to make one's intention known. This is the position stated by Hasan ibn Hayy. (Abu Hanifa and Hasan ibn Hayy) are opposed by some scholars who do not understand water in the way that these two leaders do but whoever follows their school understand it. So occupy your mind with what I have explained to you and prefer which ever one you wish. (141)

1.2. Categories of Water and Categories of Knowledge

After you have realized this, know that there are two kinds of water: (the first is) water that is filtrated to a high degree of clarity and refinement and it is rain water. It is water converted from dense vapors (clouds). Filtration removes any density or solid matter connected to it. This is (similar to) intuitive (*laduni*) knowledge and knowledge of the divine law which comes from discipline, striving (*mujahada*) and refinement. Purify your essence by this for intimate conversation (*munajah*) with your Lord. The other water is that which has not reached this extent of refinement. It is the water of springs and rivers. It springs from rocks mixed with what is in the place from which it springs and the surface upon which it flows. Its taste varies. Some of it is sweet like the Euphrates; some is salty and bitter; and some is bitterly salty. Rain water has one state. It is wholesome, pure, cool, fresh water which is easy to drink. (142)

1.2.1. *Abundant Rain Water and Mystic/Intuitive Knowledge (ilm al-laduni)*

Knowledge of sound rationality and intellect (in the sense of constriction and retention make use of rationality. Sound rationality and intellect are blemished because they change. Knowledge that comes from rationality and intellect are commensurate with the temperament of the person using rationality and intellect. One who uses rationality only sees with the the senses or imagination. The proof of their findings are based on this kind of knowledge. Their statements, therefore, vary about the same thing, or the statement of one onlooker may vary about the same thing at different times due to the difference of their temperaments, dispositions and elemental mixtures which have been with them since conception. Their statements vary about the same thing and about the fundamentals on which their secondary rulings are based. (143)

Intuitive, divine knowledge has one taste. Although palates may vary, it does not vary in (terms of) its goodness. It is good and it makes things good. It is pure and uncontaminated by impurity because it is purified by natural disposition and the effect of springs/sources on it. The Prophets, saints and everyone reporting from God have the same statement on God, no more, no less. They do not differ. They confirm one another, just as the water of the heaven does not become different when it descends. (144)

Let the purity in your heart be like this intuitive knowledge; rely on it. This knowledge is knowledge of the divine law alone. It resembles rain water. If you do not do so (attain to the purity in your heart and rely upon it) you have not been faithful to yourself. Your essence and purification will be according to the place from which your "water" (knowledge) springs. If you discriminate between its sweetness and saltiness, know that you have sound senses. I have not found anyone calling attention to this question. Why give someone sugar to eat with sweetmeat which is already sweet, but in terms of the bitterness of aloe, it is not correct (to say *halwah* is bitter). I have informed you. If you take heed, then examine it! (145)

My friend! Grasp the use of the knowledge of the divine law in your essence and the knowledge of the saints and the people of intellect who derived that from God through discipline, retreat, striving, and detachment from the excesses of the limbs and incoming thoughts of the self! If you do not discriminate between these waters, then know that you have a bad temperament, and are dominated by one of your humors. There is nothing I can do for you unless God corrects your soul by His mercy. (146)

1.2.2. The Mystery of Washing the Hands

When you use some of the water of this knowledge in your purification, knowledge set down by revelation, you purify your attributes and your spirit through it just as your limbs are purified by water and its cleansing. There is no dispute (among religious scholars that) the first act in your purification is washing your hands before putting them into the vessel when you wake up from nighttime sleeping. There is, however, dispute on the obligation of washing them after sleeping in the daytime. The hands are the place of power and disposal. Their purification is achieved by the knowledge of "and no power" (*la awla*) on the left and "except in God, The Almighty, The Powerful" (*wa la quwwata illa billahil-aliyiul-adhim*) on the right. (147)

The hands are the place of grasping and holding, miserliness and avarice. They are purified by expending in generosity, magnanimity and liberality. Sleep at night is your being heedless of knowing the invisible world. Sleep during the daytime is your being heedless of knowing the visible world. This is the source of your character and realization of some of the Most Beautiful Names (attributed by God to Himself). (148)

1.2.3. The Mystery of Washing the Private Parts (istinjah)

In regard to using water and stones (*istinja*) to clean the private parts, combining them is better than using either one alone. They are two purifications: "*Light upon light,*" (24:35) encouraged in the Quran and customs and sayings of the Prophet (*sunna*). You use water in the purification of the private parts from whatever filth is found on them. These two (private parts) are places which are concealed and guarded just as they are the place of the issuing of filth and foulness connected to your inner body. (This is similar to) your base thoughts and deluding doubts (hidden in your mind). It is related in the reliable collection (of Traditions) that Satan comes to a person in his heart and asks him: Who created this? Who created that? Until he (finally) asks: Who created God? The purification of the heart from this filth is that from which the Messenger of God said to seek refuge from when entering and leaving. (149)

The two genitals are private parts, that is, inclinations to matters subject to the whispering of the self which detract from the way of life in its root and branch. The basis of the back part is filth, and it only exists for that. The other two private parts in man and woman are two branches of this root. They possess an aspect which is good and an aspect which is evil: that is marriage and fornication. (150)

Do you not see that when an impurity mixes with a small amount of water, it affects it so that the water cannot be used for ablution? When water mixes with the impurity, the water erases the property of impurity. It is like that when doubts come to weak hearts with weak belief. They are affected. When they come to the sea, they are depleted in it. It is like that with strong hearts, supported by knowledge and the spirit of purity. In the same way, when a Satan of humankind and jinn brings doubt to one well-versed in divine Knowledge—one who is watered from divine Knowledge—being well-versed in divine Knowledge, he turns it around and he comes to know how to turn copper into gold and tin into silver through the elixir of the intuitive knowledge that he received from the divine Mercy which God gave them with the doubt. He recognizes the aspect of Truth in it and prefers it. This is the mystery of spiritual purification of the private parts (*istinja*).

1.2.4. The Mystery of Cleaning with Stones

If the person performing ablution uses stones (*istijmar*) and not water, know that it is the purification of an imitator. The stone is the group, and "*the hand of God is with the group.*" The wolf only eats the one furthest away," and it is what is far from the group and outside it. That is contrary to consensus (*ijma*). The meaning of using stones is to gather stones, the smallest number of which is three or more, using an odd number, since the odd numbered prayer (*witr*) is God's. Your witness is still just one and one demands revenge. The odd seeks stirring-up, which is what Satan casts of doubts into your belief. Stones are gathered to clean the waste arising in the bodily part. (152)

When an imitator finds a doubt in himself, he flees to the group, the people of the *sunna* because "the hand of God," as has been reported, "is with the group," and the hand of God is his support and strength. The Messenger of God forbade separating oneself from the community. For this reason, in indicating the prescribed rule, consensus (*ijma*) occupies the same station as the text of the Book or universally acknowledged *sunna* which profits knowledge. This can be your using stones in this purification. (153)

1.2.5. The Mystery of Rinsing the Mouth

Then he rinses his mouth with good remembrance of God to remove ugly mention from it in the way of calumny, slander and open evil speech. Let your rinsing be by recitation, mending enmity, commanding to good and forbidding evil. God says: "*God loves not the open publishing of evil sayings"* (4:148); *"those who were defiant in the land"* (89:11) and *"no good is there in most of their conspiring secretly but for him who commands charity* (sadaqa) *or one who is honorable or makes things right between humanity."* (4:114) and the like of this. (154)

This is purification of your mouth. I have opened the door for you, so the reward in your ablution, full bath and dry ablution in your limbs proceeds in this manner. It is what God demands of you. We have spoken in detail about this purification in the *Tanazzulat al-mawsiliyyah,* so look there at its prose and poetry. I have flung you onto the Path. (155)

1.2.6. The Eight Limbs of Responsibility in the Human Being

Make use of this purification fully in everything obliged of you. Every obligated thing in you is entrusted to all acts of worship: purification, formal prayer, purifying alms (*zakat*), formal fasting (*saum*), obligatory pilgrimage (*hajj*), striving (*jihad*), and all other actions set down by revelation. Everything you are obliged to use in these acts of worship are according to what its reality demands. *"And God places not a burden on any person beyond what He has given him"* (65:7) and *"Our Lord is He Who gave everything its creation then He guided it."* (20:50), that is, makes it clear how to use it. (156)

The bodily parts charged by the revelation are eight. They are not more although they are less for some people. They are: the eye, ear, tongue, hand, stomach, genitals, foot and heart. There are no additional ones in the human being. They are, however, lacking in some individuals of the human species like those who are blind, mute, deaf and disabled. Whatever remains of these obliged parts in you has its appropriate responsibility because of its mere existence. (157)

1.2.7. The Book Mawaqi an-nujum (Stations of the Stars) and the Circumstances in Which It Was Written

Part of the instruction of the Lawgiver is teaching about the obligations connected to each of these limbs. They are like tools for the responsible self charged with managing this body. You are answerable for establishing justice in them. When the Messenger of God cut the thong of his sandal, he would remove the other one so as to be equitable to both of his feet. He did not walk wearing only one sandal. We have explained these limbs completely as well as their lights, *karamat*, stages, secrets and Self-disclosures in our book called *Mawaqi al-najum* (Stations of the Stars). To the best of our knowledge, no one in the path before us has organized it. We wrote it over the course of eleven days during Ramadan in the city of

Almeria in 595 AH. The book needs no master. Indeed, the master is in need of it because among masters, there is the high and the higher. This book is in a higher station than what most teachers possess. There is no station beyond it in this divine law by which we worship. Whoever acquires it should rely on it by the success granted by God. It has great benefit. I was only moved to acquaint you with its stage because I saw God twice in a dream and He told me: "Counsel My servants." This is the greatest counsel that I have given you. God gives success and guidance is in His hand, and we possess nothing in the matter. (158)

The Messenger of God once confirmed the liar Iblis when he met him. The Messenger of God asked him: What do you want with me? Iblis said: So that you know, Messenger of God, that God created you for guidance although you possess nothing of guidance in your own hand, and that He created me for misguidance although I possess nothing of misguidance in my hand. He did not say anything further, and then left. The angels came between him and the Messenger of God. (159)

1.3. True Happiness Is Happiness and In Between the Outer and the Inner

Now that I have informed you of what will benefit you, know that God addresses the human being in his totality, without specifying his outer more than his inner, nor his inner more than his outer. Those who are dedicated to inviting people to religion—for the most part—invite to knowledge of the outer rules of the divine law but are heedless of the rules set down by revelation relating to their inner self except for a few who are the People of the Path of God. These people investigate both outer and inner. There is no rule confirmed by the divine law in regard to their outer parts, but that they see that that rule has a relationship to their inner (as well). That is how they take all the rules of the divine law. They serve God with what He has prescribed for them outwardly and inwardly. They win where most lose. (160)

A third group arises who are misguided and misguide. They take rules of the divine law and use them inwardly, but nothing is left of the rule of the divine law outwardly. They are called the *batiniyya,* and they have different schools. Imam Abu Hamid [al-Ghazzali] mentioned some of their schools in his book, *Mustazhiri,* in which he refutes them. He clarified their errors in it. Happiness is found with the people of the outer, and they are the opposite of some of the people of the inner. The greatest happiness, however, is found with the group who join the outer and the inner. They are the men of knowledge of God and His rules. (161)

1.3.1. The General Matters About Worship and "the Door of the House"

I hoped that God would let me live long enough to write a large book in which I could deal with all the questions of the divine law in its outer positions and I do so here. When we have dealt with the prescribed question in the outer rule in full, we will follow it with its inner rule in the human being, so that (it will become clear how) the rule of the divine law flows between the inner and the outer. Even if this is the goal and desire of the People of the Path, God has not opened the understanding of any of them to enable recognition of the weight of a rule inwardly. (162)

In this book, we direct ourselves to the general aspect of acts of worship. They are the obligatory: purification, formal prayer, purifying alms, fasting, pilgrimage, and articulating "... *there is no god but God* (*la ilaha illa l-Lah*)." I was concerned with these five because they are the bases of Islam on which Islam is built. They are like the pillars of the house. Faith is the source of the house and its totality and the door of the house by which it is entered. This door has two parts, and they are the articulation of the two bearing witness. The pillars of the house are four obligatories: formal prayer, purifying alms, fasting and pilgrimage. (163)

1.3.2. The "House" Which Protects from the Evil of Hellfire

We concentrated our concern on the setting up of this house so that we might dwell in it and be protected from the bitter cold and heat of the breath of hellfire. The Messenger of God said: "The fire complained to its Lord, saying: 'O Lord! Part of me consumes the other.'" He gave it permission to release two breaths: one breath in the winter and one in the summer. The poisonous winds and heat are from its breath, and cold and bitter cold are from its breath. People therefore use houses to protect them from the heat of the sun and the cold of the air. (164)

An intelligent person must erect a house for himself to shield him from these two breaths on the Day of Rising because on that day hellfire will come running to the standing place: "*When they were cast down into it, they would hear it sighing while it is boiling*" (67:7) and "*. . . and about to burst forth with rage*" (67:8) towards the enemies of God. God will protect those in a house like this from its evil and assault. (165)

Since purification is a precondition for the validity of the formal prayer, we devoted a book to it which we put before the book on the obligatory prayer. We followed it with purifying alms, then formal fasting, then the obligatory pilgrimage. This will be enough about the acts of worship in these books. We will deal with the main points of the questions under their outer names to be found in the divine law. Then I will proceed to the inner meaning of the same questions until I have dealt with them. God supports and gives aid! (166)

1.3.3. Clarification and Exposition: The Rules of Purification

Before discussing the pillar of purification, there is the word *tahara* itself. We mentioned this in the beginning of the section on outer and inner. Let us begin, God willing, with its rules: we will look at its obligation, for whom it is obligatory, when it is obligatory, and at its actions, and what it is done with, what breaks it, and description of the things for which it is done, as scholars of the divine law do in their books. Let us look at the inner and outer aspects of purification. We will indicate it outwardly so that the reader will not have any need to consult the books of the religious scholars. What we mention will be enough for him. (167)

We will not pay attention to the proofs which the religious scholars use for establishing the rulings: from the Book, confirmed practices and sayings of the Prophet (*sunna*), analogy in the schools of those who advocate deduction to pursue the general meaning, they look between what the text has mentioned about something and what the text has passed over in silence. We will not deal with the fundamental principles of jurisprudence in that, nor with the general proofs. As for the common people it is not their duty to have to consider the established proof. We will keep in mind the major categories of branches of the pillars and the position of the people concerning them as to what is obligatory and what is not obligatory. (168)

1.4. The Obligation of Purification and for Whom and When It Is Obligatory

First of all, we say that all Muslims, without dispute, agree that purification is obligatory for whomever the prayer is obligatory when the time for the obligatory prayer comes. It is obligatory for anyone who has reached the age of puberty and is sane. People disagree about whether Islam is a precondition for its being obligatory. That is the outer rule. (169)

As for the inner in that, which is inner purification, we say that the inner aspect of the obligatory prayer—its spirit—is to prepare to have "an intimate conversation with God" since He said in a sacred Tradition (*hadith qudsi*): I have divided the obligatory prayer in half between Me and My servant, etc. He mentioned intimate conversation: The servant says such-and-such and God says such-and-such. When the servant desires to engage in intimate conversation with his Lord in any act, it is incumbent on him to purify his heart from everything which brings him outside conversation with his Lord in that act. When he is not described by this purification at the moment of his conversation with Him, he does not speak with Him and displays bad manners. Thus it is more fitting that he be cast aside. In dealing with its acts, I will mention the categories of the rulings of this purification, God willing. (170)

1.4.1. Purification of the Heart and the Limbs

There is consensus on the position of scholars that it is obligatory for the one who has reached puberty and is sane, while they disagree about being Muslim. So our view is also that this purification is obligatory for the one who has understanding. He is the one who undertakes the command and prohibition from God and what God casts to him in his secret. He discriminates between the thoughts of his heart (which are from God), from himself, from the visit of the angel or from the visit of Satan. That is the human being. When he reaches this extent of recognition and discrimination, and understands what God desires of him and hears the word of God—"the heart of My servant encompasses Me"—then it is obligatory for him to use this purification for his heart and for each limb connected to it in the legal definition. (171)

The purification of the eye inwardly, for example, looks at things through the principle of admonishment so one's eyes will not follow distractions. The like of this is only attained by someone who has fully achieved the use of prescribed purification in all its places. God says: *"Truly in this is a lesson for those imbued with insight."* (3:13; 24:44) He granted that to the eyes. It is our insight (inner sight, *basair*) which takes a lesson. He mentioned "eyes" (sight) because they are the means which lead inwardly to what the lessons learned by insight teach. It is like that with all the limbs. (172)

1.4.2. Are the secondary rules of the Divine Law addressed to the unbelievers?

As for the position of scholars about whether one of the preconditions for this purification being obligatory is being Muslim, their position is about whether the secondary rulings of the divine law are also addressed to the unbelievers. So when a hypocrite performs ablution, is he performing an obligatory act or not? It is a disputed issue, and applies to all prescribed rules. (173)

Our school is that all people—believers, unbelievers and hypocrites—are obligated and addressed by the fundamentals and secondary rulings of the divine law. They will be punished on the Day of Rising for (both) the fundamentals and secondary rulings. For this reason, the hypocrite will be *". . . in the lowest, deepest reaches of the fire"* (4:145), which is the inward domain of the fire. The hypocrite will be punished by *". . . the fire of God, that which is kindled eternally, that peruses the minds"* (104:6-7), since he displayed the form of the outer prescribed rule in this world by articulating the phase bearing witness (*shahada*) and making a display of confirming the Messengers of God and outer actions, while inwardly not having *"an atom's weight of belief."* This sets them apart from the unbelievers, and thus they are called hypocrites. God says: *"Truly God is One Who Will Gather the ones who are hypocrites and the ones who are ungrateful altogether in hell."* (4:140). He mentioned the place. The hypocrites will be punished in the lowest level of hellfire while the unbelievers will receive their punishment in both the highest and the lowest. (174)

1.4.3. Punishment in Hell Has Degrees and Classes

God has arranged ranks and classes for punishment in hellfire for particular deeds with particular limbs in a known proportion which He does not exceed. The fire absolutely does not rise over the place of the belief (*iman*) of the believer (*mumin*). He has no portion of the fire *"that peruses the minds."* (104:7) Even if his faith leaves him there, its protection will pervade the locus within him. It would rather depart from him in order to protect him, and it would repel from him as much of God's punishment as God willed, just as it departed from him in the world when he fell into disobedience. (175)

The Messenger of God said about the believer who drinks wine, steals or commits fornication: he does nothing of that while he is a believer—at the time that he is committing that act. He said: Belief leaves him at that moment (when in the state of the act). People interpreted this Tradition in other than its proper aspect because they did not understand what the Lawgiver meant. They interpreted belief as acts and claimed that he meant the act. The Prophet clarified what he meant by that in another Tradition. He said: When the servant fornicates, belief leaves him until it is like a shadow over him. When he stops, then belief returns to him. (176)

1.4.4. Disobedience and Belief Do Not Join

Know that the divine wisdom in that is that when the servant begins the disobedience, an act that the servant believes in its being in opposition and a disobedience, he exposes himself, through performing the act, to the descent of God's punishment and chastisement being inflicted on him. He believes that the act demands that a punishment from God fall upon him. He therefore removes the belief that is in his heart so that it becomes like *a canopy* for him. When affliction from God descends in search of him, it is received by belief. Belief repels the affliction from him because nothing can stand up to belief; it (belief) prevents the punishment from reaching him as a mercy from God. There is no further clarification required after the clarification of the Messenger of God. (177)

For this reason, we say that the believing servant would never commit an act of disobedience and rebellion that is not mixed with obedience. It is because he believes in its being a disobedience. He is among those who: *"Know they not that God is He Who accepts remorse from His servants and takes charities."* (9:105).God says: *"And that God, He is The Accepter of Repentance, The Compassionate?"* (9:105) Repentance is a return and its meaning is that He turns to them with mercy. God finished the sign with His words: *"And that God, He is The Accepter of Repentance, The Compassionate."* (9:105) Scholars say that when God says: *"Know they not"* it is inevitable. Nothing can stop Him. (178)

1.4.5. Belief Is the Source of Inner Purification

Since belief is the source of inner purification, dispute about it is inconceivable; it is not possible to have disagreement about it as there is about outer purification except from a subtle aspect according to which the rule of the outer is in the inner and the rule of the inner is in the outer purification. From that aspect, we ask from that subtle aspect: Is the precondition for inner purification the articulation of belief so that the tongue articulates what the heart believes or not? If he does not articulate his inner belief in the world of the unseen, he would be a hypocrite, just like an outer hypocrite in the visible world. (179)

For instance, a believer believes in the obligation of the daily prayers but perhaps he does not pray or purify himself while the hypocrite performs the formal prayer and purifies himself although he does not believe that it is obligatory for him in his heart. He does not believe it, and he does not do it to follow the words of the Messenger who prescribed it for him. This is the meaning of that when you examine it closely so that the rule flows in both the outer and inner aspects of the form, for example, as it is in the outer form. There is both disagreement and consensus on this so know that. (180)

2 The Acts of Purification

As for the acts of purification, the Book and the customary mention them and clarify which acts are obligatory, customary and recommended. For this reason, purification has preconditions, pillars, attributes, number and specific limits. (181)

2.1. Intention Is a Precondition for the Validity of Purification

One of its preconditions is intention: that is the aspiration to do it in order to draw near to God when you begin the act. There are people who believe that it is a precondition for the validity of that act and that the act is only valid with the existence of that precondition, and that the obligation is only satisfied through it. Therefore it is obligatory and must exist. That is our position. We say that it is part of both outer and inner purification. In our view, it is especially obligatory for the inner self because intention itself is one of the attributes of the inner. Its jurisdiction in the purification of the inner self is stronger because it is ruling in the place of its dominion. The outer is extraneous to it. To our knowledge, there is no disagreement about it in the inner, while there is disagreement about that in the outer. Intention has already been discussed, and that is adequate. (182)

Others believe that it is not a precondition for validity. What we have mentioned about purification of ablution with water is adequate. (183)

2.2. Washing the Hands Before Putting Them in the Ablution Vessel

Religious scholars of the divine law disagree about washing the hands before putting them into a container from which one wants to perform ablution. They take four positions. One says that washing the hands is definitely customary. Another says that it is recommended for whomever is unsure about the purity of his hands. Another says that washing the hands is obligatory for someone who rises from sleep before putting them in the vessel from which he desires to perform ablution. Another says that it is obligatory only for the one who rises from a night sleep. This contains the positions of the scholars in my knowledge concerning this question. Each one has a proof by exposition which demonstrates his position. This book of ours is not the place to present their proofs. (184)

2.2.1 The Inner Aspect of the Rule of Washing the Hands

Inwardly, washing the hands is their purification from what the Lawgiver obliged that they abandon. There are two categories: one of them is what is obligatory and one of them is what is recommended. The required (*wajib*) and obligatory (*fard*) are the same in our opinion. They are two expressions which carry the same meaning. There is no difference in our opinion whether you say the Lawgiver made something required or obligatory. (185)

2.3. What Is Obligatory Be Left and What Is Recommended to Be Left

We say that he must abandon anything the hand possesses which the divine law judges to be usurped, stolen or that betrayal has played a part in it as well as everything which the Lawgiver did not permit. The distinction in these states is clear. It is therefore necessary to purify the hands from all of these things. I will mention how the hands are purified in its place, God willing. This purification is, therefore, obligatory for them. (186)

As for recommended purification for the hands, it is to forgo what the hands possess of worldly things but only those worldly things from which they are permitted to abstain. The divine law recommends that he cast them from his hand out of desire for what is with God. That is the simple life (asceticism, *zuhd*). It is a transaction because God will give him compensation for what was left aside by him. Leaving aside is better than temporary asceticism. This is a matter of consensus in all religions and creeds based on revelation and reason. People agree that the simple life in this world, leaving all its trivial things, and removing what one has of it, is more appropriate according to a rational person. This is recommended in the purification of the hands and it is customary. (187)

As for those who believe it is recommended to purify the hands when someone is unsure about the purity of his hands—that is setting aside property which he has because of a doubt about whether or not it is permissible. He does not retain it. This is scrupulousness, not asceticism. Even if an aspect of it is lawful, it is preferred to leave it because avoiding the forbidden is better. You are answerable if you retain it, and will not be asked about leaving it because of a doubt that you have about it. So by doing so you are closer to its reward. This is first in the recommended purification because in the preferred purification first is leaving what is permitted to be left. (188)

2.3.1. The Night Is Unseen and the Day Is Visible

As for their disagreement about the obligation of washing the hands after sleep, some oblige it absolutely and some restrict it to night sleep. Know that night is unseen because it is a veiled place. For that reason: *"And We made the nighttime as a garment."* (78:10) The day is visible because it is the place of manifestation and movement. For that reason: *"And We made the daytime for you to earn a living,"* (78:11), that is, seeking provision here. The abundance which is sought is both increase and honor. It is increase of virtues. A person may amass what is not his provision. It is abundance because one accumulates what is not only one's daily sustenance. The human being's daily provision is not what he amasses. It is that by which he is nourished. (189)

Know that sleeping is in the world of the unseen. If the sleep is in the night, it is the unseen of the unseen. Its property is stronger. Sleep by day is unseen in the visible, and its authority is weaker. Do you not see that *"it is He Who made the nighttime a garment for you and sleep a rest"* (25:47), and it is rest without a doubt. It is stronger when it occurs at night. One is more deeply immersed in it than daytime sleep. The unseen is the root, so the night is a root and the visible is a branch; the day is a branch. *"And a sign for them is the nighttime. We pluck the daytime from it and that is when they are in darkness!"* (36:37) So the day is stripped from the night. Since the night veils things and does not make the realities of their forms clear to the eyes, it is like ignorance because ignorance of a thing is when its rule is not clear. Whoever is ignorant of the divine law regarding a thing does not know its rule. (190)

2.3.2. The Sleeper in His State of Sleep and the Ignorant in His State of Ignorance

When a sleeper is in a state of sleep, he does not know anything of his outer affairs in the visible world with respect to people. Sleep is pure ignorance, except in the case of the one whose eye sleeps while his heart does not sleep, like the Messenger of God and whoever God Will of his heirs at present. The day illuminates things so that the forms of their essences are clear. It manifests to those conscious of God harmful matters to be protected from and what does not protect him; the day is like knowledge because knowledge explains the rule of the divine law in things. (191)

The one who sleeps in the day is described by ignorance because of his sleep, since sleep is the opposite of knowledge. Perhaps he will stretch forth his hand while he has no knowledge—or perhaps his foot. He may destroy something which, had he been awake, he would not have destroyed. Therefore the divine law obliges that he obtain purification by knowledge when he awakens from the sleep of ignorance. By his being awake, he knows the rule of the divine law in that. *"He was not aware"* in his ignorance at the time of sleep where his hand wandered, and whether or not it was permitted for him to possess something or not, like usurped plunder and its like. It is as we mentioned. It is as the opponent makes allowances for where his hand passes the night. Both of the two (sleep of ignorance and the sleep of night) share the word "sleep." (192)

The Lawgiver mentioned someone "who spends the night" because most sleep is in it and He always considers that which is predominant. He stipulated this principle in sleeping at night. Consideration of sleep in general is more fitting than consideration of night sleep. The one who considers night sleep, because he mentioned "someone who spends the night," says that when man sleeps in the day and a man or a group of people see the sleeper moving his hand or his foot and that movement might lead to breaking a jar or something else, or puts his hand over the mouth of a small suckling child and harms him or stops his breathing so that he might die, we think that those who are present and awake should prevent that by removing the child who is near to him or the jar, or whatever the light of day and his wakefulness disclose to him. A knower is like that with an ignorant man. When he sees him doing something in which he is ignorant of the rule of the divine law concerning it, he informs him or puts the divine law between him and that act. (193)

Therefore, washing the hands is obligatory in our opinion, and it must be an inner washing for the one who is heedless (the person who sleeps by day) and the ignorant (the person who sleeps by night). As for considering purity before putting the hand into the vessel, it is by knowledge and the act required of us. Knowledge is water, and the act is washing. Purification is achieved with both of them. Washing one's hands before putting them into the ablution (*wudu*) vessel is the good intention he affirms in himself in that act: he aims for the presence of Truth where his happiness lies when he begins the act. This is the meaning of washing the hands before putting them into the ablution vessel in inner purification. (194)

2.4. Rinsing the Mouth and Sniffing Water Up the Nostrils

Religious scholars disagree about rinsing the mouth and sniffing water up the nostrils. There are three positions. One says that they are both customary. One says that they are both obligatory. One says that rinsing the mouth is customary while sniffing water up the nose is obligatory. This is their outer rule. (195)

2.4.1. The Essence of the Rule of Rinsing the Mouth and Sniffing Water

As for its inner rule, part of it is obligatory and part of it is customary. In rinsing the mouth, the obligation in it is to say: *"there is no god but God"* (*la ilaha illa Lah*). By saying it, your tongue is purified of polytheism (*shirk*) as is your breast. Its letters are from the breast and the tongue. It is like that with every obligation which God has obliged you to articulate when He has not delegated it to someone other than you so that it is no longer obligatory for you, like a communal obligation (*fard al-kifaya*). It is like a man who sees a blind man at a distance who is about to fall into a pit which will result in injury or death if he falls into it. It is his specific obligation to call to him to warn him about the peril in a manner which he will understand since he cannot reach him. If another man does that before him, that obligation falls from him and it is no longer his obligation. (196)

When he rinses his mouth inwardly by this or its like, he obtains good and speaks good. It is beautiful discourse and the true tongue. Sincerity of the tongue is purification from lying. Openly speaking good is purification from open evil speech, even if there is a recompense in His words: *"Except by him who had been wronged."* (4:148) Remaining silent about it, however, is better. *"Commanding the good and preventing evil"* is purification from their opposite. The like of this is the obligation of rinsing the mouth and its being customary. It is the same for snuffing water up the nostrils. (197)

2.4.2. The Nose in Arab Tradition Is the Symbol of Might and Pride

Know that the inner meaning of snuffing water up the nostrils refers to the usage of the word "nose" in the custom of the Arabs. It is the place of arrogance and pride. Because of this, the Arabs say in a curse: May God force his nose (to the ground). Also: he agreed in spite of himself (in spite of his nose). *Ragham* is earth. That is to say: May God pull you down from your pride and arrogance to the station of abasement and insignificance. That is designated by earth. God made the earth *". . . submissive to you"* (67:15), using an extensive form of the noun, so it is the most humbled of the humbled. The humble walk on it. The servants are the humble, and they walk *"so walk in its tracts. "* (67:15) For this reason, the Quran referred to it using the intensive form. (198)

2.4.3. Scattering Water or Using the Rules of Humble Worship

You will only remove pride inwardly by using the principles of servanthood, humility and poverty. For this reason, it is prescribed to expel water when snuffing it up the nostrils. He is told: take water into your nostrils and then blow it out. Water here is the knowledge of your servanthood. It (water, knowledge) expels pride when you use (water, knowledge) in place of your pride. It is blowing out the water. Part of it is obligatory, and using it inwardly is obligatory without a doubt. As for its being customary, its meaning is that had you abandoned it, your ablution would have still been valid. Its appropriate to not sniff water into your nostrils in the inner sense if you leave your treatment of your servant or whom one under your command. This is the inner meaning of "Lord, bestow on me such and such"—or with someone who is less humble and you show pride and leadership because of an advantage you envisage, the divine law made it permissible for you to do so. It was permitted not to do this act as a part of your purification but if you do it, it is most excellent. However, in this place its requirement is overridden. (199)

For this reason, we said that it can be customary and it can be obligatory, since we know that if the people of a city were to join together to abandon something customary, it is obliged to fight them. If one person abandons it, he is not fought. The Prophet did not invade a city when he came to it by night until it was morning. If he heard the call to obligatory prayer (*adhan*), he held back and did not attack. When he did not hear the call to obligatory prayer he would recite: "when we descend in the courtyard of a people: *"How evil will be the morning daybreak of the ones who are warned!"* (37:177) (200)

2.4.4. Every Outer Rule of the Divine Law Also Has an Inner Meaning

There is nothing among the rules of the obligations, customary and recommendations of the divine law but it has a principle in the inner realm or it increases according to the opening the servant receives in that, be it obligatory, customary, or recommended. That must be. Accept this in all the prescribed actions of worship. The outer is distinguished from the inner by this. The outer acts on the inner, but there is no prescribed matter in the inner which acts on the outer. It falls short of that. The inner relates to meanings and the outer to physical-sensory acts. One moves from the physical-sensory (outer) to the meaning (inner), and one does not move from the meaning (inner) to the sensory (outer). (201)

3 On Ablution

3.1. Definition of Washing the Face

There is no disagreement that washing the face is obligatory. Its principle in the inner is self-examination and absolute modesty before God. That is so that you do not extend the limits of God. The formal scholars disagree about the definition of washing the face in ablution in three areas: the gap which is between the beard and the ear, that part of the beard which hangs down, and washing the beard. As for the gap, some say that it is part of the face and some say that it is not part of the face. As for that part of the beard which hangs down, some say that it is obligatory to pass water over it and some say that it is not obligatory. As for making water penetrate the beard, some say that it is obligatory to make it penetrate it and some say that it is not. (202)

3.1.1. The Inner Significance: The Rule of Washing the Face in Religious Law

Washing the face is absolute without respect to defining the command in it. Part of it is obligatory and part is not obligatory. As for the obligatory part, it is modesty before God, knowing that He sees you when He forbids you or misses you when He commands you. As for the customary, part of it is modesty before God in that you cover your private parts in retreat. It is more fitting to be modest before God although you know that there is no part in you but that He sees it. The rule is in your act since you are obliged to do what we mentioned, and transmission has reported that. It is like that with looking at the private parts of your wife. It is permitted for you, but modesty in it is better and more fitting. The obligatory falls away in it, that is, modesty in the like of His words: *"God is not ashamed before The Truth."* (33:53) What he specified of it is obligatory for you, and what He did not specify for you is customary and recommended. If you wish, you can do it, and that is more fitting. But if you wish, you would not do it. (203)

The human being observes his acts, abandons outer and inner acts, and watches the effects of his Lord in his heart. What is meant is the "face of his heart." The "face" of the human being—and of everything—designates its reality, essence. One says "the face of things" and "the face of the rule." By this "face," one means the reality of what is named and its essence. God says: *"Faces on that Day will be ones that beam, ones who look towards their Lord. And faces on that day will be ones that scowl."* (75:22-24) The faces preceded by "human" are not described by the attribute of "supposing." Supposing belongs to a human reality. Modesty is all good, and modesty is part of belief. Modesty only brings good. (204)

3.1.2. The Limit Between the Duty of the Face and the Duty of Hearing

As for the gap which is between the beard and the ear, it is the limit which divides the ear and the face. It is the limit between what is obliged of man in purifying his face and his act in hearing. Acting within that is keeping the limit within what is defined. It is more fitting for the human being to use modesty in his hearing as he uses it in his sight. (205)

It is also part of modesty to lower the eye to things God has forbidden. He says to His Messenger: *"Say to the ones who are male believers to lower their sight"* and *"say to ones who are female believers to lower their (f) sight."* (24:30-31) The inner aspect of these two verses addresses the soul (*nafs*) and the intellect (*aql*). Similarly modesty before God is indispensable so that one not listen to what it is not lawful to hear: slander, evil words from one who says what we should not say, and what it is not permitted to verbalize. That gap between the beard and the ear is the place of doubt. The form of doubt in that is that he says: I listened to him in order to respond to him and to the individual who slandered. This is part of an understanding of the self. His talk is part of the edge of the beard so it is surely an excuse. In other words, when a person is rebuked (for listening), he excuses himself saying the above and things like is: I listened only to verify what he said with my own ears so that I could prevent him from slandering. The allusion is to the edge of the beard. For the person who has no beard, it would be the place of the cheek. (206)

Whoever thinks that it is obligatory must wash it based on what God says: *". . . those who listen to the saying of the Quran and follow the fairest of it. Those are they whom God has guided."* (39:18) That is—He has clarified the good of that from the ugly for them—*"and those are those who possess the kernels,"* that is—they understand what We meant. It is like the kernel of a thing which is protected by its shell. Whoever does not think it obligatory for him washes if he wishes, or leaves it if he wishes is like the one who listens to one he cannot refute from someone with power and fears to cross him regarding it. If he can stand up and leave the place, turning away, that is like his washing if he liked. If he prefers to remain there because of something which he sees and supposes is there, he sits and does not leave. This is according to those who do not think that it is obligatory for him. (207)

3.1.3. *Washing That Portion of the Beard Which Hangs Down*

As for washing that portion of beard which hangs down and having water penetrate it, they are non-essential matters. The beard is something which appears on the face. It is not part of the face and is not included in the definition of face. It is similar to questions which appear to you in your essence which are outside your essence. In them, you have the principle of the non-essential. If you are specifically told to purify yourself from the non-essential, that is the position of those who say that it is obligatory to wash the beard. If its purification is not specifically incumbent upon you, then its purification is recommended or you can leave it since it was not specifically incumbent upon you. However, this has a general shortcoming. That is the position of the one who says that it is not obligatory: it is the school of later scholars. (208)

We have clarified for you in earlier parts that the inner principle in these matters is different from the outer principle which consists of what is obligatory, customary and recommended. The obligatory must be done, whether it be in act or non-act. Other than the obligatory it contains what resembles the position of the obligatory in obedience, and it is more fitting to do it than not do it. That is true of all acts of worship. (209)

3.2. Washing the Hands and Arms in Ablution Up to the Elbows

Religious scholars agree about washing the hands and forearms with water in performing ablution, but they disagree about including the elbows in the washing. Our position accords with the consensus about the act. Consensus in principle is inconceivable. Some say that it is obligatory to include them in the washing, and some say that it is not. None of those who say that it is obligatory disagree that it is recommended to include them in the washing. (210)

3.2.1. *The Inner Significance of This*

After affirming the outer principle which entails worship of God, I will speak about washing the hands and the elbows, and with them the wrists. Washing them symbolizes generosity, magnanimity, munificence, altruism, gifts and returning trusts to their owners—he is the one for whom there is no bias—just as one washes them along with the forearms up to the elbows to preserve and to strengthen and assist because " *the believer is compassionate toward his brother."* When the Messenger of God washed his arms in ablution, he passed the elbows until he reached his upper arm. This and its like are among the attributes of the hands. The definition of the extent of hands varies. Its greatest extent is to the armpits, and its minimum is to the division which is called the forearm. So the elbows remained. (211)

Inwardly the elbow is the means by which the servant is at ease and with which the self is familiar. The human being, in the fundamental basis of his character: *"Truly the human being was created fretful."* (70:19), fearing the dependency which his reality accords him in respect to his lack of ability to be independent. Therefore he leans toward what benefits him. Whoever thinks that including the elbows in the washing is obligatory thinks that God made this means a wisdom from Him in His creation since He knows the weakness of their belief. The person does not want the wisdom of God to be neglected by one who is on a path of reliance on secondary causes because that would undermine his dependence on God. (212)

3.2.2. The Elbows or Seeing Causes With Which the Self Is at Ease

Whoever thinks that it is not obligatory to wash them (the elbows) sees a stillness of the self in regard to secondary causes and that he is not in the station of reliance on God now despite finding a discernment in secondary causes. Anyone who would argue that it is not obligatory would prefer the inclusion of the elbows in washing. Also, a discernment of the secondary causes is preferred by everybody, even if their determinations differed about them because God fortified wisdom with their presence. (213)

3.3. Wiping the Head: The Disagreement of Scholars on the Amount It Is Obligatory to Wipe

Religious scholars agree that wiping the head is one of the obligatory parts of ablution but they disagree about the extent of it which is obligatory. Some say that wiping all of it is obligatory, and some say that only wiping part of it is obligatory. They also differ about the definition of "part." Some say that it is obligatory to wipe a third, some say two-thirds, some say a fourth, and some say it is not defined. Some of these mention the definition which the hand wipes. Some say that wiping it with less than three fingers does not satisfy it, and some say that there is no definition of "part" except regarding what is wiped, and not what does the wiping. (214)

The source of this dispute is the existence of the *bi* in His words: "... *and wipe your heads*" (*bi-ruusikum*) (5:6). (215)

3.3.1. The Inner Significance of the Rule of Wiping: The Head Is the Closest Member to the Real (al-Haqq) Because It Is Above

As for the inner meaning of wiping the head, the head in the place of leadership; that is, upper and elevated. The word "head" is derived from the word "leader" of the people, that is, their master who has leadership over them. Since it is the highest part of the body (as seen with the outer eye) and all of the body is under it, it is called the head just as a leader is above those led in rank, and it has the upward direction. God described Himself with being "above" because of His nobility. He said: *"They fear their Lord above them"* (16:50), and He said: *"He is The One Who is Omniscient over His servants."* (6:18) The head is the nearest limb of the body to God due to its being above. (216)

3.3.2. The Site of the Intellect Is the Crown of the Head

It has figuratively another noble quality by which it heads all parts of the body. It is a place which joins and supports all the sensory and spiritual-intellectual faculties. Since it has this position, it is called "head" (*ras*). God made the intellect the noblest of what is in the human being, and He placed it in the highest place of what is in the head. It is the crown. He made it part of what is in the direction of being above. (217)

3.3.3. The Head Is the Place of All the Outer and Inner Faculties

Since the head is the site of all the outer and inner faculties, and each faculty among them has authority, power and glory, that results in might over others. This resembles the castle of the king which rises over all common dwellings. God designated different places for these faculties in the head so that they fill the entire head: high, middle, front and back. As we said, each faculty has its own might, power and pride as well as being in the position of leadership. Therefore all of it must be wiped. That is the conclusion of those who say that it is obligatory to wipe the entire head. It must be wiped with humility and contentment with God. When the wiping is comprehensive, each faculty has a particular wiping in respect to its claim. It prevents it by what is particular to it in the wiping. Wiping therefore includes the entire head. (218)

Whoever thinks that the head has a head over it, as governors are in respect to the sultan, refers the matter to it. The one who rules them sees that every governor has a governor higher than him who has more power than than him. It is like the conceptual faculty which has power over the imaginative faculty. It leads it, even though the imaginative faculty has power. Those scholars who think this say that part of the head can be wiped. It is to run the hands over the top part of the head. (219)

3.3.4. *The Servant Standing in the Place of Humility, Not in Pride*

Our companions disagree about this "part." Each gnostic speaks according to the perception God has given him into the ranks of these faculties. He is ranked according to what he sees and considers. He wipes in this act of worship—which is humility and removal of arrogance by servanthood—because it is through the purification of the act of worship in which he seeks to reach his Lord. This is because the one who prays is in the station of intimate conversation with his Lord. That is the arrival that is sought by purification. (220)

When a mighty leader comes to the One who gave him that might and leadership, he withdraws from his leadership and his might is abased before the might of the One to whom he has come. He is the Master who brought him into existence. He stands before Him as one of His servants stands who is subject to his leadership, through seeking wages in the station of aliens. This servant stands in the place of abasement, not with the attribute of familiarity. Anyone whose thought is dominated by the leadership of some of the faculties over others, must wipe that part for the sake of the connection which he seeks in this act of worship. (221)

For this reason, wiping the head is not prescribed with dry ablution because placing dust on the head is a sign of separation, and it is a great misfortune. If a bereaved has lost his beloved to death, he places dust on his head. Connection and not separation is the goal of this act of worship. For that reason, wiping the head is not prescribed with dry ablution. Therefore wipe it according to what we have mentioned here and what we have informed you. The details of the leadership of the faculties are well-known with the [Sufis]. I do not need to mention it. (222)

As for the part of the hand with which he wipes and the disagreement (of religious scholars) about that, act on it as you act with the wiped area. It is the same. The means of removing this leadership vary in amount. The site of that is the hand. Some remove it by the attribute of force, and some remove it by politics and desire. It is as a man's hand strokes the head of the orphan to heal brokenness through kindness and compassion. This refers to part of the hand and all of it in wiping, so know that. (223)

3.3.5. Temporal Power and Whether It Has an Effect on the Compelled

There is disagreement among scholars regarding this obligation beause of the existence of *bi* in His words: ". . . *and wipe your heads*" (*biruusikum*). Some apply that to partial wiping, some make it stress wiping, and some say that wiping includes the entire head. If the *ba* in this place refers to temporal power, it either has an effect on the object of power—and that is the position of the Mutazilites and others—or it does not have an effect on the amount in any aspect and is extra, as the Asharites say. Therefore its authority falls away. Eternal power includes wiping the entire head; temporally limited power does not make its wiping partial. The extent of consideration of the stress—as it is extra for the sake of stress—is that it is the "acquisition" about which the Asharites speak. It is His words in another place in His Book when He ascribes acquisition and action to the creature. For this reason, they made the *ba* redundant in the meaning, and it is called (a word of) stress. (224)

3.3.6. Linguistically the Arabs in Their Speech Count the Redundant With the Redundant

Do you not see that the Arabs counter the redundant with the redundant in their words when they intend stress. The speaker uses it to stress his words in his answer. The speaker says: Indeed, Zayd is standing or: Zayd is not standing. The one who hears replies: Zayd is indeed standing; Zayd is not standing. In reply to: Zayd is not standing, he says: Zayd is indeed standing. He confirms what the speaker negated and negates what the speaker confirmed. If the speaker stresses his answer, he says: Zayd is standing (with the definite article) and brings in the *lam* to confirm the affirmation of standing. The responder puts the *ba* opposite the *lam* to stress the negation of what the speaker confirmed. He says: Zayd is not standing (with *ba*). The like of it is called "redundant" because the words stand independently of it. (225)

However, if the speaker intends the opposite of the partitive and uses that particle for stress, the intention of the particle is not the stress by that particle, even though the form is outwardly the same. The meaning differs. Consideration belongs to the intention of the speaker who uses that form. (226)

3.3.7. The Source of Difference in the Creation of Actions

When we are ignorant of the meaning for which God created strengthening in the one who does some acts, we find that in ourselves and do not deny it. It is "the movement of free choice." Similarly, God put in us a barrier to some outer actions, and we find that in ourselves, like the movement of someone who trembles without any choice in it. We do not know whether that strengthening which we find in ourselves derives from a temporary power in us which has an effect on that source which exists from our strengthening or whether it is from the volition created in us so that the strengthening is an effect of the volition, and not the effect of temporary power. There disagreement among the people of speculation regarding this question. (227)

3.3.8. There Must Be Disagreement With Every Speculative Question

Because of it, the human being is individually obligated by the strengthening that he finds in himself and he does not know precisely by his intellect what that strength derives from—is it because he has power or because he has choice, even if he is compelled in his choice? However, because of that power that he finds in himself, it is valid for him to be obligated. For this reason, He says: *"And God places not a burden on any person beyond what He has given him."* (65:7) He gave it an existent matter, and it is not said that He gave it nothing. We do not see anything He gave it—without dispute—except for the strengthening which is its capacity. *"God places not a burden on a soul beyond its capacity."* (2:286) (228)

We do not know from what this strengthening and capacity is derived. Does it belong to one of them, that is, to divine Will or temporally originated power, or to something extra in them or which belongs to both of them? This is only recognized by unveiling. It is not possible for us to express the truth of this issue because unveiling—which lifted the disagreement about this issue for us—would not lift the intellectual dispute about this issue. How can disagreement be removed from the world while the question is intelligible? There must be disagreement about every question which is intelligible due to the difference of nature in speculation. (229)

3.4. Wiping the Turban

You are now acquainted with wiping the head and what is in this path. There remains the rule about wiping over the turban and the rule involved in that. (230)

3.4.1. The Inner Significance of Wiping the Turban

Some religious scholars permit wiping over a turban and some forbid that. Some forbid it because of the difference that is indicated by the sign and do not understand the turban to be part of the head. The covering of the head is an incidental matter. Those who permit that do so because of the tradition reported in Muslim, which is the Tradition which was mentioned. Abu Umar ibn Abd al-Barr said that it the Tradition was defective (*malul*). (231)

As for the inner principle of wiping over the turban, know that accidental matters are not contradicted by the roots and do not affect them. That which you must consider is the necessary cause of the recentness of that accident. It is either part of what is independent of it or it is that whose non-existence will bring harm, so it is not independent of it. If it is independent of it, it has no authority in removing the authority of the root. If it is not independent of it and harm is acquired by its non-existence, its authority is that of the root and it has the same position. If a part of the root remains, that part which remains must not be regarded. It must be so. What remains of the root is represented by this non-essential matter whose non-existence would bring harm. This is our position in it. (232)

For that reason, it is related in the Traditions which we mentioned that it is an effect according to some scholars that wiping is achieved by wiping either the forelock or the turban. Water touches the hair, so it acquires the principle of the root in the school of the one who says that one can wipe part of the head. If he wears the turban for adornment, he could not wipe it as opposed to the one who is ill and wraps the turban around his head because of his illness. What is reported does not conflict with the text of the Quran on this question. (233)

3.4.2. The Non-Essential Which Distracts from the Root Establishing the Means for Someone Divested of Means

For the People of the Path, when there is a non-essential which maligns the root word—like performing a secondary cause just in order to disengage from secondary causes or strutting and showing arrogant leadership during war (other meanings of the word *arad* but not its essential meaning)—it is best to give an example in order for the listener to understand. What needs to be understood is what we desire and want in this act of worship. If arrogance had an effect and showed itself to one's state of servanthood and one were to forget his Lord's Magnificence and His Majesty, and if He protected the person from this state of arrogance so that the person not show arrogance, one needs to fling off magnificence from the "self." Arrogance is not permitted in this station because it maligns the root (essence). (234)

If there is no effect on his self, but it is an external matter for the eye of the enemy (while in himself, he remains in humility and spiritual poverty), then he may show the form of pride outwardly (because of the circumstances of the state in respect of the abode), but it still does not affect the root. It is like that with the principle of wiping over a turban in our opinion. Know that! (235)

3.4.3. Casting Means from One's Hand Is One of the Actions of the Hand

You have learned the inner aspect of wiping the turban. The same applies to wiping over the turban with part of the hand. If that impairs your taking the cause for your reliance on God with your heart, then do not do that. Do it only as long as it does not lead to greater distance from God, even if it does not effect your reliance on Him. Therefore wipe with part of your hand, and that entails no harm for you. The cause drives away some of the actions of the hand in meaning. It has many uses with different meanings in prescribed matters and rules—taking, expansion [in spending] and balance. (236)

God says: *"And make not thy hand be one that was restricted to thy neck as a miser nor extend it to its utmost expansion as a prodigal so that thou shalt sit, one who is a reproacher, one who is denude"* (17:29) which refers to extravagance. Similarly the Quran praises people in a similar way. God says: *"And those who, when they spend, neither exceed all bounds nor are they tight-fisted but had been between that; a just stand."* (25:67) It is balance and equity in spending. He said: *"And cast not yourselves by your own hands into deprivation."* (2:195) Here it is miserliness. All that is ascribed to the hands. For this reason, we said that the hand has many acts. If it had not been for the existence of multiplicity, it would not have been valid to talk about apportioning the hand because that which is one is not divided. (237)

3.5. The Times the Head Is Wiped: Is it good to repeat the wiping of the head?

In regard to repeating the wiping of the head, we still need to fix the number of times that the head is wiped. Is it excellent to repeat it or not? Some say that there is no excellence in that and some say that there is. This repetition is recommended in all the actions of ablution for all of its limbs, although it is strong regarding some limbs and weak in other limbs, that is, repetition. There is no disagreement about the obligation of a single time when it includes the entire limb. (238)

3.5.1. There Is No Repetition in the World Because of the Divine Vastness

As for our position regarding the fundamental principle of repeating the wiping of the head, there is no repetition in the world because of divine Vastness. We forbid this expression, but we do not forbid the existence of likes arising from the resemblance in the form. We know absolutely that actions resemble one another in form, even if each of them is not the same as the other. Our position is that we examine the rule of the Lawgiver in that. Since number is by likes, we number by likes as we say after the formal prayer: Glory be to God thirty-three times. We do not forbid the like of this. Multiplicity occurs in the act of ablution to stress the removal of the authority of acts of heedlessness. Its authority has a quick effect on the human being. This means there is excellence in repetition. Excellence is increase. When someone who performs ablution adds a rule because of heedlessness or forgetfulness so that he has to repeat it, increase is not then valid. (239)

What we consider to be valid is that repetition contains excellence because it is *"light upon light"* (24:35) according to what the Lawgiver clearly defined in rules. It is related in the Book and the customs that the likeness of the light of God is a lamp in a glass in a niche—to the end of the sign.

He said at the end of it, *"light upon light"* that is, He comes in light upon light like the two proofs. The three rest on the one proven. The Messenger of God said that ablution on top of ablution is *light upon light*. There is no difference between the arrival of ablution on top of ablution and the arrival of the second handful of water upon the first in ablution. The repetition of the action by the doer obliges the repetition of the reward and the Self-disclosure. As for all the limbs, repetition is established. There is dispute only about the head, the ears, and the feet. We have indicated what is necessary of that. (240)

3.6. Wiping the Ears and Renewing Water for Them: The Disagreement Among Religious Scholars About Wiping the Ears

People disagree about wiping the ears and renewing water for them. Some say that it is customary and some say that it is obligatory. Some say that water is renewed for them and some say that water is not renewed. Does one wipe them on their own, or are they wiped with the head, or wiped with the face, or wiped with what is in front of them of the face, or wiped with what is behind them of the head? Each of these positions has those who advocate it. (241)

3.6.1. *The Inner Meaning of the Rule of the Ears: Listening to the Best Words: The Remembrance of God in the Quran*

As for the inner rule, the ears are an independent limb which demand that the water be renewed. One wipes by listening to the best words. That must take place. There is disparity as regards what is the best. There is the beautiful and the most beautiful, and the most beautiful is remembrance of God in the Quran so that one combines two good acts. There is nothing higher than listening to the remembrance of God in the Quran, like every sign which indicates none other than God. This is the remembrance of God in the Quran. (242)

Not every sign of the Quran contains mention of God. It also contains prescribed rules, tales of the Pharaoh and stories about what they said and their disbelief, but still the greatest reward is in it since it is the Quran—when one listens to the reciter when he recites it, or when a man listens to himself when he recites it. However, the remembrance (*dhikr*) of God in the Quran is better and more complete than the account of the words of the one who disbelieves in God, which the Quran also contains. These words are inappropriate (for God's remembrance). (243)

3.6.2. *The Outer and Inner Parts and the Unequivocal and Ambiguous Parts of the Quran*

As for the outer part of the ear and the rearmost area behind it, it is the outer rule of that remembrance of God in the Quran, as well as what is hidden and secret of it, what is understood of it and what is unknown. The unspecific words are sound in respect to God for God. They are what is behind the rearmost part of the ear so that you would submit to the intent of God for them as soon as the ear hears them recited. What is known, like the unequivocal verses with respect to God and the phenomenal beings which they indicate is what is front of the outer part of the ear. What God means by them is known and so the rule is according to knowledge. Act according to what we have pointed out to you in these details. It is more fitting that the ruling about the ears be like that of rinsing the mouth, sniffing water and blowing it out. (244)

3.7. Washing the Feet

Know that whether the purification of the feet is by washing or wiping and whether or not there is a choice, the number of washings is like that of the wiping of the head which we have already mentioned. (245)

3.7.1. Is the Purification of the Feet by Washing, by Wiping or Is There a Choice?

Scholars agree that the feet are included among the limbs for ablution. They differ about the form of their purification, and whether it is achieved by washing, wiping or if there is a choice between the two. Whichever of the two is done, the other falls from him and the obligation is performed. This is when there are no leather socks on the feet. Our position is that there is choice, but that doing both is better. There is no position but that there is someone who believes it. Wiping is based on the literal text of the Book and washing is based on the what is customary. The probable intent of the sign is to turn away from its literal meaning. (246)

3.7.2. The Inner Significance of the Feet

As for the inward rule in that, know that hurrying to congregational obligatory prayers, numerous steps made to go to mosques, and remaining firm when the battle is fierce is part of what purifies the feet. Let the purification of your feet be by what we mentioned and its like. Do not move among people with calumny; do not walk proudly on the earth; be moderate in your gait. Some of these are obligatory, that is, these acts—and is in the position of washing the limb for ablution just once—the foot and others. Part of it is customary, and what is beyond the obligatory—and that is walking to do what the divine law prescribed for you but did not oblige you. (247)

What is obligatory for you is for you to move your feet to the place of obligatory prayer. The recommended and the customary—whatever you wish to call it—is like moving your feet to the mosques from near and far. That is not obligatory. The obligation in that, according to some people, is a mosque, but not a specific one, and a congregational prayer, but not a specific one. This is the inner significance of washing your feet. (248)

3.7.3. That by Which the Feet Are Purified

Know that washing contains wiping in one perspective. Whoever washes includes wiping in it, as the light of the stars is subsumed into the light of the sun. Whoever wipes does not wash except in the school of the one who believes and quotes the Arabs that wiping is a word for washing so they are synonymous. The sound meaning in the inner principle is that wiping is used in actions which the elite must do and washing in what the common must do. This is the most illustrious path. (249)

For this reason, we believe in choice according to the moment. He may be striving for a particular virtue in a certain need of a person. That is in the position of wiping. He may go to the king for a need which is common to all the subjects and their needs, so that person then becomes one of the common. This is the position of washing in which wiping is included. (250)

3.7.4. Clarification of God's Words, "and your feet": Our Position Is That the fatha on lam Does Not Remove It from What Is Wiped

As for the reading in His words: "... *and your feet*" (5:6) with *fatha* on the *lam* and the *kasra* (*arjulakum* or *arjulikum*), it is because of the letter *waw* (and), which joins the feet to what is wiped when the genitive (*kasra*) is used, and to the washed when the *fatha* is used. Our school is that the *fatha* on the *lam* does not remove it from what is wiped. This *waw* may be the concomitant *waw*, the *waw* of connection, and would be in the accusative. You say: Zayd and Amr stood, and: water and wood are the same, and: you do not have a crumb of stew, and: I passed by Zayd and Amr, and you mean that he was with Amr. It is like that for the one who recites, "... *wipe your head and feet*" with a *fatha* on the *lam*. (251)

The proof of the one who speaks of wiping is stronger in this sign because the speaker is connected to washing in the proof which it designates. It is the *fatha* on the *lam*. The one who speaks of washing with *kasra* on the *lam* does not share it with it. Some of our companions make the elite dominate the common, and some of them make the common dominate the elite. All of that is general. (252)

3.7.5. Proceeding With The Real (al-Haqq) According to the Authority of One's State

Our position is different from that. We proceed with the truth according to the state. We are common when it is common and elite when it is elite. We do not originate a rule. Whoever originates a rule, originates lordship in himself. Whoever originates lordship in himself is lacking in his servanthood accordingly. When he is accordingly lacking in his servanthood, then he is lacking in God's Self-disclosure to him. When he is lacking in God's Self-disclosure to him, then his knowledge of his Lord is lacking. When his knowledge of his Lord is lacking, he is ignorant of Him—glory be to Him and may He be exalted—according to the deficiency in his knowledge. If a rule of that which he lacks appears in the world, or in his world, he does not recognize it. For this reason, our position is that we do not originate any rule at all. (253):

3.8. The Sequence of the Acts of Ablution : The Disagreement of the Scholars on the Actions of Ablution

Scholars disagree about the order of the actions of ablution according to the order in the sign. Some say that the order is obligatory and some say that it is not. This is in the prescribed actions. As for the order of the prescribed actions along with the actions of the customary, they disagree about that in the case of what is customary and what is recommended. (254)

As for the inner significance in that, there is no order. You act in that according to what is specifically demanded of you in the moment. If what is related to your head is demanded of you, you do it and begin with it. It is like that with the rest of it. The same applies, whether it be customary or obligatory. The rule belongs to the moment. (255)

3.8.1. The Inner Significance of the Rule: The Rule of the Occasion in the Order of Acts

Some say that continuity is obligatory when remembered and in the absence of an excuse, it is nullified when there is forgetfulness, or when it is remembered and there is an excuse—if the time which has passed is not excessive. Some say that continuity is not obligatory. All of this is from the actual order of the sign. By the and (*waw*) in things, it inclines to immediate connection, although it may include some slackness in things. It may add so that it is two actions together. This is not permitted in ablution unless he plunges in a river or people throw water on him all at once over every limb. (256)

Our position about the inner significance of continuity is that it is not obligatory. The same applies with order. We act in that according to what the moment demands. We have mentioned the like of this issue in the *Risalat al-anwar.* (257)

3.8.2. Actions on the Path Are According to the Occasion

Our actions on this path are according to the rule of the moment and what it accords. If acts of negligence are written for the human being, he cannot have continuity when that exists. It is, however, hour by hour. It is not decreed for the human being to watch God in secret and openly with every breath. Continuity in general is only acquired when one expends effort to make himself be present and watchful in all his actions. (258)

God says: *". . .those who, they are ones who continue with their formal prayers."* (70:23) By that, He means that whenever its moment comes, they perform it, even if there are other matters which occur between the two formal prayers. For this reason, constancy is acquired in a particular act connected to definite moments. As for it accompanying breaths, that is one of the special privileges of the Highest Assembly: *"They glorify Him nighttime and daytime. They never decrease."* (21:20) This is continuity. If some of the people acquire it, it is very rare. (259)

3.8.3. The Messenger of God Used to Remember God At All Moments

As for the words of Ayisha: "The Messenger of God used to remember God at all times," we do not doubt it. If she meant by that that all his outward actions were not indifferent, but they were always obligatory or recommended, that is possible. It is evident from his rank. He is the teacher of his Community through his actions and lack of action so that they can imitate him. He always remembered God. As for his inner self, she had no way of knowing it except by his reports. In spite of this, we believe that it is conceivable. And so if he was present in a property of the revelation in all his doings, in this fashion, then he would be one of the ones who achieved continuity in his worship. (260)

3.9. Wiping Leather Socks

As for wiping over the two shoes, religious scholars differ about it. Some of them say that it is absolutely permitted, and some say that it is absolutely not permitted, like Ibn Abbas and one transmission from Malik. Some say that it is permitted to wipe shoes on a journey, but not while at home. (261)

3.9.1. The Inner Significance of the Rule: Purification is Incomparability; The Real is the Goal of Incomparability

As for the inner rule in wiping over the two shoes, know that it is a matter which occurs to the person when it is troublesome for him to remove, as the removal of shoes is troublesome for the wearer. The jurisdiction of purification moves to it, so he wipes it. (262)

Then purification is an incomparability. The Real is the one who proceeds to being the incomparable through incomparability, just as He said: *"Glory be to thy Lord, the Lord of Great Glory, from what they allege about Him."* (37:180) Might is inaccessible so He mentioned that His essence is inaccessible. (263)

3.9.2. The Incomparability of Those Who Know God Is Knowledge, Not Action

The Real is incomparable in essence in Himself. None of His created beings can say He is to be incomparable through incomparability, so the incomparability of the *"ulama"* of God, the Real, is rather knowledge, not action. If the incomparability of the created beings of their god were actions, then God (who is incomparable), would be the place for an effect of this practice. So understand this allusion because it is of extreme fineness and beauty. (264)

God does not accept the incomparability of His servants from their acts. Only the ignorant among the servants sees incomparability as action. The one with knowledge sees it as knowledge. When he speaks of it, he speaks based on recognition of what the matter is in itself. It is His word and His remembrance. The effect of his act is in his knowledge of the incomparability of his Creator by speech and remembrance. He is brought out from power to action. Sometimes that has an effect on the self of the listeners who do not believe that God has that attribute of incomparability. (265)

3.9.3. *The Servant Is a Veil Over the Real*

The servant is a veil over the Real because people generally perceive outward effects, that is, secondary causes which the Real determines. For this reason, the servant says: I did, I made, I fasted and I prayed, and he ascribes all his acts to himself because of the veil which covers the acts of the Creator—they are created by Him and from Him—He is their Causer. (266)

As the shoe becomes a veil between the one performing ablution and bringing the ablution water to the foot—the principle of purification moves to the shoe, so the human being's incomparability of His Creator is purification and making pure when, in the heart of the matter, he cannot bring the effect of that incomparability to God since He is incomparable in His Essence. Therefore the rule that incomparability moves to the human being, the incomparable who is a veil over his Creator inasmuch as actual incomparability has an effect on the incomparable, the human being accepts it as the shoe accepts purification by prescribed wiping. The servant is the one who transcends himself from the ignorance to which the self of the ignorant is subject when he ascribed to God that which is not fitting for Him and which His essence does not accept. (267)

3.9.4. *The Witnessing of the One Who Says: "Glory be to Me"*

God states in sound Tradition that He is "the foot of the servant by which he walks." The senses would see the servant walking with his own foot so when he wears a shoe—which is the servant's essence—the rule of purification is transferred to it. "Only your own practices return to you." The thing connecting the rule is the shoe. (268)

Another aspect of this topic is the absolute permissibility of wiping whether on a journey and when not. When one is not a traveler, the incomparability which returns to you so you say: "Glory be to Me!" in this state, as has been related from the people of God. The place of witnessing of the one who says: "Glory be to Me!" is this station which we mentioned. (269)

The journey is the incomparability which moves from your uttering while teaching to the hearing of the listener who hears. It therefore has an effect on the soul of the learner who acquires that knowledge. Let him purify his place of a kind of ignorance which he has in that matter. The extent of its transference from the teacher to the learner is called a journey because through this teaching, he achieved for himself what the issue is so he purified his place. (270)

3.9.5. The Circumstances Specify What Is Unclean

Another aspect of this subject is the custom and normal usage of wearing shoes and things which have the same meaning like *jurmuq* (a covering worn over leather socks) and *jawrab* (woolen stockings) which are worn and veil the goal of ablution from reaching the foot. One of the names of the foot is *qadam*. This is part of what strengthens footness in the foot since, linguistically, the foot is also used to designate constancy. It is said that so-and-so has an earlier foot in this matter meaning he has an old established basis in this matter. Similarly, the foot also shares such a meaning, that is, the application of this phrase linguistically. One says: a swarm of locusts, that is, a portion and a group of locusts. (271)

If someone says: The foot is warmed by the shoes, he knows absolutely that he by means the particular well-known body limb. Contextual circumstances and the indications of adjectival phrases show what had been previously ambiguous because of similar meanings. Therefore the principle of purification moves to the shoe after it had been connected to the foot, but when the shoe is worn, he purifies what he can reach of it when it is not forbidden in the rule and inherently. (272)

3.9.6. The Relationship of Attributing "foot" and "hastening" to God

It is like that when the foot is ascribed to God in the Tradition: The Compeller places His foot in hellfire. It may occur to some of the religious scholars that "foot" is not ascribed to God in the same way as it is ascribed to the human being or to anyone who has a foot and that what is meant by that is something else. They ignore the feet of the embodied spirits. God removes this illusion from the speaker in what He ascribes to Himself like hastening is swiftness in walking. With the attribute of foot preceding, foot is attached to the one who walks on two feet, not to whoever crawls on his belly and with the realization: *"There is not like Him anything.*(42:11)—always with that. (273)

3.9.7. *God is the One Who Is Not Known*

We do not describe Him and we do not relate to Him what He does not relate to Himself or use to describe Himself. He only ascribed hastening to Himself since it is known that it means "advance" which includes the quality of running. Its principle is based on what is not appropriate to His Majesty. He is not the unknown who is not known. It is not said that He is the indefinite pronoun "it" which is not known. He said: *"and they will not comprehend Him in their knowledge."* (20:110) (274)

3.9.8. *What Is Understood by "foot" and "hastening"*

We do not say that by the relationship of the foot He meant His specified source as the "extremists on incomparability" claim and to which they confine themselves. He used "haste" to confirm "footness" and establish in it the station of the foot's shoe in order to remove the ambiguity of the common meaning. Then He transferred the incomparability to hastening from the foot. The one who speaks of incomparability is occupied with the incomparability of the foot. When haste comes, incomparability moves to it as the principle of the purification of the foot moves to the shoe. The servant therefore disconnects his Lord from the ordinary well-known haste, and it is according to what befits His Majesty. The servant cannot describe Him with it since God has more knowledge of Himself and has affirmed this attribute for Himself. Whoever refutes its relationship to Him is not a believer. However, that which he must do is to assign knowledge of it to God, that is, knowledge of the relationship. (275)

As for the intelligibility of haste, He did not address the people of the language except with the tongue that they understand so haste must be intelligible. However, the form of the relationship is unknown. It is like that with all the temporal attributes by which He describes Himself. (276)

3.10. The Permissibility of Transferring Purification

What we desire by what we have mentioned is only to permit moving purification from one place to another by a sort of resemblance and relationship. We speak of permissibility, not of obligation. Obligation is contrary to permissibility. The one who has shoes on can remove his shoes and wash his feet in accord with the divine law or he can wipe them with water according to what his position demands, and there is nothing which forbids him to do so. It is like that with this intelligent person—he may remain with his connection of the foot and not move to haste and remove it from this foot according to what was previously understood, since it is clear that the foot is not related to God in the way that our feet are related to us in every aspect. For this reason, wiping is not obligatory, it is permitted. (277)

3.10.1. Those Who Permit Wiping Shoes on a Journey But Forbid It When One Is in Residence

As those who permit wiping over the shoe on a journey but forbid it when one is resident at home, that is because incomparability is an act. It only has an effect in the receptive listening learner. Incomparability therefore journeys from the knower who is learned to the learner upon the journey through articulation and speech, through expression or indication from the teacher to the learner. (278)

3.10.2. Those Who Forbid It Absolutely

As for those who forbid it absolutely, the reality of incomparability belongs to God. He is incomparable by His essence. The servant is never incomparable. Even if he is incomparable from one thing, he is not incomparable from another thing. Part of his reality is that he does not accept incomparability absolutely. Since the servant has this attribute, his incomparability is not permitted because he is opposed to knowledge. Incidental matters have no effect on realities. The servant's acceptance of the effects of incomparability indicate the lack of incomparability from effecting him. This is an aspect which prevents the permissibility of wiping on the shoe and similar items if you understand. (279)

3.11. Conclusion on Wiping Over Shoes

What is indicated by the two shoes is two configurations—that of the body and that of the spirit. Each configuration has a purification appropriate to it. (280)

3.11.1. Defining Wiping Over Leather Boots and Similar Items: Religious Scholars Disagree About the Definition of Wiping Over Leather Boots

Religious scholars disagree about the definition of wiping over leather boots. Some say that the obligatory amount in that is wiping the upper part of the leather boots, and anything more than that is recommended—wiping the lower part of the leather boots. Ali ibn Abi Talib said: If the way of life had been by opinion, it would have been more fitting to wipe the lower part of the leather boots rather than the upper part. I saw the Messenger of God wiping the upper part of his leather boots. (281)

Some of them say it is obligatory to wipe both the tops and bottoms of them. Some say that it is only obligatory to wipe the tops of them, and the one who says this does not make it recommended to wipe the lower part. Some say that it is obligatory to wipe the lower part. Some say that it is obligatory to wipe the lower part and that wiping the upper part is recommended. That is the position of Ashhab. (282)

3.11.2. The Inner Significance in That

Know that incomparability that is designated here by the purification of wiping is either connected to God, as we previously stated, or to the servant. Thus the division is limited. There is only the servant and the Lord, the Creator and the created. We have a higher and lower expression in this question. The attribute of height belongs to God because He raises the degrees of His essence. God says: *"Glorify the Name of thy Lord, The Lofty."* (87:1) There is nothing in the Quran more likely to be related to wiping the top of the leather boot than this sign. The attribute of lowermost is ours.(283)

It is also like that with with wiping of their outsides and insides, and there is a proponent for obligatory being a wiping of the outside only. God has the rule of the outward and the inward. Perhaps the Real has a property of outwardness and inwardness and perhaps He has a property in the outwardness of "breaking the natural order" while the rule of the inward is in the norms or natural order itself. It is most of the signs which indicate God *"for a people who understand"* (and see inward truths in customary outward reality). (284)

3.11.3. The Ranks of Incomparability

Sometimes incomparability is connected to the Highest in reality. That is the limit of the obligation in that, while the application of incomparability to the servant is recommended inasmuch as his action in it returns to him. This is the position of the one who thinks that it is obligatory to wipe the upper part of the boots and recommended to wipe the lower part. (285)

3.11.4. Outer and Inner Incomparability of God

Sometimes incomparability is connected with The Real, The Manifest and The Hidden. He is one who sees that there is only God in existence because of the dominion of witnessing and divine self-disclosures upon him. Therefore he sees God as both the manifest and the hidden so incomparability only occurs there on The Real because incomparability is related to non-existence, not existence. He is the one who obligates the wiping of the upper part of the two leather boots and their lower part. (288)

3.11.5. The Incomparability of God Because He Is Perfect in His Essence

Sometimes incomparability is connected with God by His perfection in His essence, and it is not recommended that creation be incomparable because of the essential imperfection which it possesses. If he were to transcend it, he would fall into lying. He sees that had the possible been incomparable in any way from any aspect by an attribute of perfection on which it is based, in respect to that attribute it would have been independent from God and set itself up against Him. It is impossible for creatures to have an attribute by which they are independent of God. From all aspects: *"It is you who are poor in relation to God. And God—He is Sufficient, Worthy of Praise."* (35:15) He therefore denies the recommendation of wiping the lower part of the leather boots. He said: there is none incomparable except God, the High, Who is manifest to His servant by the attributes of Majesty. This, as we said, is the school of the one who thinks that one wipes the tops of the leather boots, and that it is not recommended to wipe the lower part. (287)

3.11.6. The Obligation of Incomparability from the Name the Hidden

Sometimes the obligation of incomparability is connected to His Name, The Hidden. One says that The Hidden is a place in which it is hard to discover the attributes of Majesty which befit it since it is hidden. It is obliged to God in His Name, The Hidden, as incomparable from the effect of the veil which deems that the hidden is not perceptible. God is too high and majestic to be contained by a veil. It is therefore obligatory to see Him in respect of His Name, The Hidden as incomparable. This is the reasoning of those who oblige wiping the lower part of the leather boots, like Ashhab. He considers that it recommended to wipe the upper part, which it is the name, The Manifest. (288)

3.11.7. The Recommendation of Incomparability from the Name the Manifest

His Name, The Manifest, is His self-disclosure for the sake of His servants. Its incomparability is from being confined to that form. However, the incomparable which does not bring him out of knowledge is that He is the source of that form. God has more knowledge of Himself than can be understood about Him and than every knower of Him can know except Him. He said about Himself that He is the One who Self-discloses to His servants in that form as Muslim mentioned in his *Sahih* collection. (289)

His incomparability in that is that He is not limited to a form and form does not limit Him. He Self-discloses in whatever form by which He appears to His servants. Part of this reality which He has in Himself is that He mentioned to us about our creation after *"He composed thee in whatever form He willed."* (82:8) Thus He also self-discloses to His servants in whatever *"form in which He willed."* Here is the divine mystery through which He informs you so that you will thereby know Him. Therefore, the one who transcends this position for his purification is an incomparable that is preferred over a permanent Self-disclosure in this particular form of the establishment of the form in yourself, so understand! This is the rule of The Hidden within the boundary of this area. (290)

3.11.8. A Type of Locus for Wiping Which Is Over Any Sock or Stocking Which Covers the Foot and The Disagreement of the Religious Scholars on Wiping Over Socks

Know that those who speak about wiping the shoes agree about wiping them without doubt while they disagree about wiping socks. Some absolutely forbid it and some absolutely permit it. Some permit it when they have a particular attribute, either by density and thickness so that the water of wiping does not reach the foot, or when it is lined by leather in which it is possible to walk. (291)

3.11.9. The Inner Significance of That Rule

As for the hidden meaning in that, leather boots were already mentioned, so the rule about socks remains. It is confirmed that the sock is like the shoe in its attribute of veiling because the servant is a veil over his Creator. For this reason, it is related: "Whoever knows himself knows his Lord." He is the proof of it, the prover and the proven. Even if they are connected by a particular aspect, they are opposites which are not joined. (292)

3.11.10. When the Saint (wali) Is Shown the Remembrance of God

In what preceded, we mentioned that the sock indicates the foot when partnership is removed from the phrase "the foot" to which it is applied. It is like that with haste. That was already mentioned. It is, however, a stocking. If it veils the foot, it is not as strong as the sock since it allows penetration. The water pierces and penetrates its pores quickly. Leather boots are not like that. (293)

Its inner rule is that some of the servants of God have a stronger proof of God than others. They are in the position of the sock, as it is established in the Tradition reported from God about the attribute of the saints of God. More than one person informed me from the one who told him that it reached him that the Messenger of God was asked: "O Messenger of God! Who are the saints of God? The Messenger of God said: 'Those who, when they are seen, God is remembered.'" Abu Nuaym reports it in his book, *Hilyat al-awliya*. (294)

That is since we said that it is part of what is seen in them of the strength of indicating God by infatuation, being enamored with His remembrance and what they have of humility, utter obedience, and utter spiritual poverty upon every breath on God. When people want to be incomparable (the socks, the *awliya*), they can only be incomparable by God's incomparability (foot) because they only mention God because of what was given them of states of truthfulness before God. (295)

3.11.11. The Malamati

If the sock is lined with leather, it is the Malamati who veils himself and his state with respect to God from the lower world lest they (the lower world) perceive the rank and authority of his relationship of sainthood with God, just as the sock is veiled from the earth lest the earth reach the sock and strike it by means of the leather which intervenes between the earth and the sock. It is the attribute by which the seeker of blame is veiled from the lower veiled earth by permitted things. They only perceive this attribute from him by which he is not distinct from the common believers. Beyond this attribute, he is in the station of sainthood with God. He stays over the sock, at the side of The Highest with God with no barrier between him and his Lord. (296)

3.12. Permission Originates from the Form Appropriate to the Essence

I have opened the door of interpretation to you in the divine law. It is that the permission originates from the form whose authority is manifest in the sensory to which is appropriate to your essence, or in respect of God, it is that which directs you to God. This is the meaning of interpretation: You transverse the valley when you cut through it and pass out of it. (297)

3.12.1. The Description of What Is Wiped

One who argues for the permissibility of wiping over a sock agreed about a sound sock. However, they differ about a torn sock. Some say that it is permitted when the tear is small without defining that. Others limit the small tear to the size of three toes width. Some permit it as long as the name sock can still be applied to it, even if the tear is very great, and that is the soundest position in my opinion. Others forbid wiping when the tear is in the front of the sock, even if it is small. (298)

That which I say is that this question has no basis and no text is found about it in the Book or the confirmed sayings and actions of the Prophet (*sunna*). It is more fitting to ignore it and not to concern ourselves with it. The truth in that is a matter of dispute among the scholars of the divine law which requires discussion. The truth in that for us is with the one who permits it as long as it is called a sock. (299)

3.12.2. *The Inner Significance of the Rule: The Hidden Is the Outer. It Is a Wondrous Mystery for The One Who Finds It*

It is that we say that sock is called sock (*khuff*) from concealment because it completely veils the foot. When it is torn and some of the foot shows, what shows of it is wiped when the sock is wiped. That is as long as it is called sock. This condition must exist, and there is a wondrous secret in it for the clever one who hits the mark—The Hidden is The Manifest. Imr al-Qays said: He concealed them from their tunnels, that is, He made them emerge and appear. (300)

3.12.3. *The Manifestation of the Divine Law Veils the Reality of the Rule of Unity (tawhid)*

We said to wipe what was manifest of the foot because we are commanded in the Book of God to wipe the feet. If some part of the foot shows, we wipe it. As for the hidden, the manifest of the divine law is a veil over the reality of the rule of Unity which relates everything to God. Purification in the divine law is connected to the unity which relates everything to God and that is that you associate purification with unity in that you see in unity a rule of God in His creation not like sagacious policies a rule of the created beings. (301)

3.12.4. *The Divine Law Is the Rule of God Not the Rule of the Intellect*

The divine law is the rule of God, not the rule of the intellect as some of them suppose. Therefore, the vision of purification in the divine law is seen as being from God, the One, the Real. For this reason, we must not attack the rule of a religious scholar who struggles to understand an issue of the divine law because the divine law is what God has decreed. He has decided that that rule is the divine law of God by his affirmation of it. It is a question into which all the people of the schools are falling into forbidding since they do not keep in mind that which we have mentioned even though they know it. They fail, however, to keep it in mind. By so doing, they display improper manners toward God while those who have good manners among the servants of God obtain that. Whoever errs in making a religious ruling based in the divine law by himself has erred about God in what He determined as rule. (302)

3.12.5. The Error of the Position Which Ascribes Each and Every Act to God

When the divine law is torn, it becomes manifest in some issue as one of the properties of unity which would remove a property of the divine law completely, transferring the rule to a purification of that Unity which is effecting a removal of a rule of the divine law just as one who relates all acts to God, from every perspective, does not concern himself with what becomes manifest as a consequence whether contradictory or harmonious. The like of this unity must be incomparable in order to purify this effect. It is a tear with respect to the divine law and removes the rule of God as one cannot wipe when the name of "sock" has vanished. If the tear is such that there still remains something called "sock," then the rule is as we mentioned about wiping the sock and wiping what appears of the foot. It is to clarify in that particular unity the prescribed direction in this question. It is that we say: "*God created you and what you do*?" (37:96) Acts are God's creation even though they are ascribed to us. They are not ascribed [to God] from all aspects. It does not effect the wiping, and the rule in that is as we confirmed it. (303)

The people of our path differ greatly regarding this question in the same way as people differ about wiping over leather boots. As for the one who limits the tear to three toes width, he regarded the manifestation of unity (*tawhid*) in three stages. It is the rule of the divine law in the human being in the realm of meaning, senses and imagination. If unity pervades these three realms, he did not permit wiping, and the rule is transferred from wiping (the torn sock) to wiping or washing the foot. In the same way, the incomparability of one's self transfers from the likes of this unity when the rule of the divine law ceases in which case its rule is the rule which applies when the name "sock" ceases. (304)

3.12.6. The Manifestation of God's Oneness in Three Stages: The Disagreement Among Scholars About the Time of Wiping

They differ about the time for wiping. Some of them say that the time in it is three days and nights for the traveler, and one day and night for those at home. Others say that there is no time in it and he can wipe it as long as there is no impediment like sexual impurity. (305)

3.12.7. The Inner Significance of the Rule: The Meaning of the Traveler Wiping for Three Days and Nights

As for the inner meaning in the position of the one who says there is a time limit, we have discussed the wiping of leather boots in the section of the knower and the learner, that it is a journey where the matter journeys from the teacher to the learner. When the Messenger of God taught people their divine law, he would repeat the statement three times so that it would be understood, because he was commanded to make things clear and transmit. This is the meaning of the traveler wiping for three days. (306)

As for the time limit of a day and a night for the one who is at home, he has nothing in himself to do but establish that command. He does not repeat it to himself because it is clear to to him and he has certainty in himself. He has certainty about it but he does not have enough certainty to teach another that so let it be repeated to another three times so that one would be certain that he has understood. (307)

3.12.8. The Meaning of No Time Limit in Wiping

The one who does not argue for a limit considered the primordial natures of the learners. Some understand it the first time, and some only understand it after detail and repetition time after time until they grasp it. He does not specify the number of times in the state of his teaching someone else who is in the rank of a traveler, and he does not look at it in himself when he is in the rank of being at home. In himself, he can conceive of the existence of uncertainty in what appears to him, and that will be explored many times, so there is no time limit. (308)

3.13. Major Impurity (Janaba) Is Exile and the One in a State of Major Impurity Is in Exile

As for the rule of major impurity in the removal of the boots, major impurity is exile. The one in the state of major impurity is an exile. When an alien matter occurs in the heart which lessens the divine law, one must not examine that with the intellect without the proof by the divine law. It is like when the thought of a Brahman who rejects the divine law occurs to him. He does not accept the proof of the divine law about the invalidity of this position which has occurred to his mind. It is the place of contention. He must move from deduction by the divine law to deduction by what the proofs of speculation accord, whether that happens to him at home or on a journey. (309)

3.14. Preconditions for Wiping Over Leather Socks

Some say that one of the preconditions of wiping is that the feet be pure with the purity achieved by ablution. Some say that part of its precondition is only that they be pure of impurities. I say that, but the first statement is more cautious. Another precondition remains that the boots are not worn over other boots. Some say that it is permitted to wipe them both, which I say, and some forbid it. The same applies to the rule regarding over shoes. (310)

3.15. The Inner Significance in the Rule: The Incomparability of God over "Hastening"

As for the inner rule in that, intelligible purity inwardly is incomparable as we confirmed logically and in the divine law. This purity particular to the feet is legal purity. God described Himself as hastening towards the one who comes to him walking. Walking and haste are among the attributes of the feet. Whoever disconnects God from haste, has denied God in what He described Himself even though the intellect does not accept this relationship to Him in respect to its proof, belief accepts it while it rejects anthropomorphism by His words: *"There is not like Him anything"* (42:11) and by logical proof. (311)

3.15.1. *"Divine Haste" from the Viewpoint of Faith and Logic*

Faith does not interpret divine haste by increased divine responsiveness to the servant and its stress, nor other than that of the types of interpretations of incomparability. The "extremist on incomparability" who interprets that interprets it as increased divine responsiveness with a generous reward to the servant when he comes to his Lord running with the types of worship in which there is walking, like moving to the mosques, moving in circumambulation of the Kaba and moving to circumambulate, to festivals, to pilgrimage, to visit the sick, to fulfill people's needs, to bury the dead and every type of worship in which there is movement to a near or far place. God says: "*O those who have believed! When the formal prayer is proclaimed on the day of congregation, then hasten to the Remembrance of God.*" (62:9) (312)

3.15.2. *The Incomparability of God Is to Remove from Him Whatever He Has Described Himself With*

The ablution of purification is the attribute of God since He hurries, and the purification which is cleanliness is the incomparability of the Real lest there be removed from Him what He Himself attributed to Himself. As for the attributes of the possibles with which He does not describe Himself, His incomparability is from being described by something that belongs to the intellect. The intellect is under the jurisdiction of the divine law since the divine law speaks about the attributes of the Real with what He says. Someone who is a believer cannot refute that. That which is spoken and described by that attribute can be accepted; that is, it is possible that it could be accepted and it is conceivable that the means of its accepting could be unknown. The intellect is obliged to accept the prescribed description, even if it is ignorant of how the attribution could be accepted. (313)

For this reason, our position regarding purification of the feet is the purity of the linguistic meaning of purification which is cleanliness and incomparability from impurity. Nothing obliges us to take the position of those who discuss the minor rules in issues concerning the purification of ablution. As for wearing boots over boots, it is God's description of Himself with haste. Haste is an attribute of moving, and moving is an attribute of the foot. Moving may be with haste, or it may be without it. Since this is the case, haste is one of the attributes of moving. Another matter comes between haste and the foot is: it is moving. It is like the sock over the sock, and discussion about it has preceded, so understand. (314)

3.15.3. When the Purification of Wiping Over Leather Socks Is Broken: That on Which There Is Agreement and That on Which There is Disagreement

There is agreement that the things which invalidate purification are all those things which invalidate ablution. The chapter dealing with that will come later. Scholars disagree about removing the boots, and whether or not that breaks one's purification. Some say that purification is invalidated and ablution should be renewed. Some say that the purity of the feet in particular is invalidated and so they must be washed, based on the prior disagreement about continuity. Some say that removing the boots does not affect the purity of the feet. That is what I say. If ablution is renewed, that is more circumspect. It does not effect his entire purity unless he does something to break it as will be mentioned. (315)

3.15.4. The Inner Significance of the Rule: Incomparability Flows Through What Is Described

As for the inner rule of whoever says that the entire purification is invalidated, it is the diffusion of incomparability onto the object of attribution. When the object of attribution accepts transcendence or incomparabilityitself, it accepts all in which incomparability is conceivable. It is like that if he invalidates the incomparability of what is in respect to the object of attrition—invalidation flows in all the attributes being the attributes of incomparability. (316)

3.15.5. The Divine Law Does Not Deny His Every Quality

Whoever says that the purification of the foot in particular is invalidated, it is that the divine law removes a specific attribute from God. Therefore it does not oblige the removal of every attribute demanding similarity because God Himself is incomparable to *"having a son"* but is not incomparable Himself from hesitating in a matter which He intends to do. He is not incomparable Himself from anger. (317)

3.15.6. Negation of God Having a Material Son

Some say that he retains his purity and the removal of the boots does not have any authority nor effect, the purification with which he is described when he donned his boots. He says that even if God Himself is incomparable to have a son, the attribute still remains His. He says: *"Had God wanted to take to Himself a son, He would have favored from what He creates of what He wills."* (39:4) The principle of the matter remains by His words: *"of what He wills."* This is like His words: *"Were it not for a preceding prescription from God."* (8:68) And His words: *"The saying near Me is not to be substituted."* (50:29) This refutes the one who says that God brought the possible into existence by its essence, not by an ascription of will or previous knowledge. That which is sound is what the Lawgiver said. That ascription is not an additional existential matter, so know that. (318)

3.16. Outer and Inner Rulings About Water in General

At the beginning of this book there was some discussion about the difference between rain water and spring water. We gave an adequate clarification of that. We will now mention in these sections the rulings of which divine law scholars have on the outer aspects and how that relates to inner purification. (319)

3.16.1. That on Which the Religious Scholars Agree and Disagree Concerning Water

Scholars agree that all waters are pure in themselves and they purify what is other than them—except for sea water about which there is disagreement. Similarly, they agree that anything which alters water but is not separate from it generally does not remove the attribute of purification from brackish water—except for brackish water. Ibn Sirin disagreed about it. There are those who believe that all that is called water is generally pure and purifying, whether it is sea water or brackish water. (320)

They also agree that water whose color, taste or scent—or all of these—has been changed by impurity is no longer good for purification. If neither the water nor any of its attributes has been changed, it retains its basic purity and purifying quality, and whatever impurity falls into it does not affect it. However, I recognize that there is dispute in this question in the case of a small amount of water in which a small impurity falls when none of its attributes have been changed. (321)

3.16.2. The Inner Significance of the Rule: Water Is the Life Which Enlivens Hearts

As for the inner rule in what we mentioned, know that water is the means by which hearts are brought to life. It brings purity to every heart of ignorance. God says: *"Is he who has been lifeless and We gave him life and We made a light for him by which he walks among humanity like he who is in the shadows and is not one who goes forth from them?"* (6:122) This is a metaphor for disbelief and belief, knowledge and ignorance. (322)

3.16.3. Sea Water Is Created from the Attribute of Divine Anger

As for sea water in which there is a separate dispute, it was created from the attribute of anger. Expulsion and distance result from anger in respect to the one who is the object of anger. Purification leads to nearness and arrival. This is the reason for the inner dispute. As for the outward reason, it is that the taste has changed. Anyone who thinks that the anger of God can lead to nearness to God and reaching Him, thinks that one can perform ablution with sea water—and I believe that. (323)

3.16.4. Vastness in the Knowledge of God's Oneness

Whoever has extensive knowledge of God's Oneness and is not bound by the manners presented in the divine law is not angry for God or himself, and does not think that one can perform ablution with sea water because it is created from anger. He fears that it will generate anger in himself. The attribute of anger established it while his state does not accord that. God's Oneness bars him from anger because in respect of him, there is no one with whom He is angry because of the divine unity of the source with Him in all actions ascribed to the knower. This is because had there been one with whom He was angry, there would be no Oneness. What obliges anger is action, and there is no Doer but God. (324)

3.16.5. The One With Proper Manners (*adab*) Is the One Who Stands Without Judgment

This question is one of the most obscure questions for [the Sufis]. If, at the moment of speech, we have our recognition of the places of divine manners (*adab*) which are prescribed for us, then we take on the divine characteristics. One of them is the anger with which He describes Himself in His Book. He says: *"And God was angry with him and cursed him"* (4:93) and *"and the fifth that the anger of God be on her."* (24:9) The Prophet's sayings and actions reports that on the Day of Rising: God will be angry with a rage whose like He has not had before and the like of which He will not have afterwards. (325)

3.16.6. *Anger Arises from the Soul While Mercy Exists in the Heart*

For this reason, the one who is not angry only sees God, and his state dominates him. This is the station of bewilderment. Woe to him if he is angry here! Woe to him if he is not angry in the world to come! He is overcome by every state in this world and the world to come. The anger of God is sounder, more saving and better for man. He must have the prescribed manners in it. Since anger is an intrinsic part of human nature like cowardice, envy and avarice, God clarified for him how it is used when it occurs in the servant and he is described by it. Submission has places and positions which are prescribed for those with manners to cling to without delay. The people of states have withdrawn from it. Lack of submission has places and positions, and the one with *adab* is the one who stands without rule until the Real Lawgiver gives a ruling. He is the Best of Judges. When He decrees, the one with *adab* stands where he is ordered to stand, no more, no less. (326)

3.16.7. *The Servant Is Compelled in His Choice*

Anger is an inner attribute in the human being which may or may not have an effect on the outer. The state dominates, and some states are higher than others in force and dominance on the one it is based on. He combines the existence of mercy for the object of wrath in his heart and the rule of God's wrath outwardly and in his senses. The people of the path of God look to which of the two paths is higher and truer. Some of us say that wrath based on the self is higher, and some of us say that the existence of mercy in the heart and dispatching the rule of God's anger outwardly is higher. (327)

3.16.8. *Living Water and Natural Substances Mixed With It*

The servant has no free disposal at all in it. The servant is managed. He is according to what is set up in him and desired of him. The human being does not have any authority in either leaving or not leaving something. He is compelled in his choice when he is a believer. We stipulated that anger belongs to God. As for the anger of other-than-God, human nature demands anger and pleasure. The Messenger of God said: "I am a man. I become angry as men become angry and I am pleased as men are pleased." We act by it in state and character. Praise be to God for that! (328)

As for the inner rule on brackish water as opposed to other things which change water and whose penetration does not dominate it, know that God did not disconnect water from anything which changes it which does not pervade and dominate it except for brackish water. He says, describing the people of the Garden who are "in it are rivers of unpolluted water: *"In it are rivers of water which will never spoil."* (47:15) One uses these words for water (*asin* or *ajin*) when it has been changed. That is water stored in cisterns. Every water which is stored changes after a long period of time. (329)

When knowledge is exposed to what the lives of the hearts have of natural disposition, it is a matter which affects it. That is like the knowledge that God is merciful. When the servant sees His Mercy towards the servants of God he sees it in himself through his compassion and kindness which establishes its pain in him, the servant therefore seeks to remove that pain which he feels in himself by mercy towards that to which creatures show mercy. This natural matter establishes kindness in the servant towards it and that depends on God's mercy. So, by analogy, the mercy of God is changed with him to his mercy. He should not purify himself for the worship of his Lord by the like of this divine Mercy which has been altered with him. The reason for that is that God has not described Himself by kindness in His mercy. God tells you that you should not make your nature rule your divine life. (330)

3.16.9. Knowledge Which Dissolves Doubts in the Vast Ocean

Those who think that ablution can be done with brackish water do not discriminate. God has described Himself in places with what human nature demands. All flows in one way. It is more fitting than in what we first mentioned. We do not add anything to the rule of God in what He mentioned about Himself. (331)

3.16.10. The Light of Belief in Which the Lights of Knowledge Are Incorporated

As for the inner rule about "a little knowledge," when a misleading doubt comes to it and effects change in it is, then, that it is not permissible for him to use that knowledge. It is changed. It is not reliable, even if he recognizes that knowledge is directed to God. It is not in his power because of the weakness of the recognition of that exact aspect. In that, he turns to the knowledge which destroys doubt. That is the knowledge which he takes from belief on the path of the divine law and acting according to it is a vast knowledge which does not accept doubt. It directs belief to its proper place, so it is knowledge after it was ignorance and doubt. (332)

The lights of knowledge are incorporated in the light of belief as the lights of the stars are incorporated in the light of the sun. Its path is also clear in making doubt knowledge because it removes its authority and the light of belief shows him the aspect of the truth in it. He sees that doubt is non-existent. Non-existence has no effect or trace in existence. Know that! (333)

3.17. Water Mixed With Impurity When None of Its Attributes Has Been Changed: The Disagreement of Scholars About Water Mixed with Impurity When None of Its Attributes Are Changed

Know also that the light of belief here designates the command of the divine law, so cling to what I tell you and command you, whether or not you find intellectual proof for it. It is like believing that God has haste, laughter, smiling and wonder without "how" or connection with the intelligibility of that in language. We do not know the relationship because we rely on His words: *"There is not like Him anything."* (42:11) This sign is the root of incomparability for its people, and its leads to connection for its people. (334)

Religious scholars disagree about water with which impurity is mixed when none of its attributes has been changed. Some say that it is pure and purifying whether it is much or little. I say that. However, I say that it is purifying and not pure in itself because we know absolutely that impurity is mixed in it. However, the divine law passes over that. I do not know this statement from anyone even though it is logical, and we do not have a proof in the divine law that it is pure in itself even if it is pure. (335)

3.17.1. Water Is Pure in Itself

They argue against us by saying that the Messenger of God said: God created water pure until something makes it impure. We said that he did not say that it was pure in itself. He said that it is pure. That which is pure is the water and the earth which purifies something else. (336)

As we said, we know absolutely that water can carry impurity logically. However, the Lawgiver did not grant it an effect in man's purity and did not call it impurity. The Lawgiver meant to acquaint us with the reality of the matter. It is that matter is pure in itself always in every aspect as long as impurity does not rule it. That means that impurity is not its attribute. The parts of impurity are adjacent to its parts. When it is difficult to separate the parts, for instance, like urine and the parts of water, and there are more parts of impurity than parts of water, one of its attributes is changed. The divine law forbids performing ablution with it according to the definition related in the divine law. When the parts of water dominate the parts of impurity, none of its attributes have changed. The Lawgiver did not consider it nor give it authority in using it for purification. (337)

3.17.2. The Four Rules About Water

We know absolutely that the one doing purification uses water and impurity together in his prescribed purification. Authority belongs to the divine law in the use of things, not to the intellect. The divine law did not mean that it is pure without impurity except in respect to what we mentioned of the absence of inter-penetration of essences. It is an logical matter. It only remains that they are adjacent. The divine law took note of that proximity in one place and did not interpret it in another place. For that reason, one cannot do purification with it in the place which it did not designate. It did not say that there is no impurity in it. (338)

The rule of water, according to what we mentioned, is that it has four types: when it is mixed with impurity and when it is not mixed with impurity. It can be pure and purifying; pure but not purifying; neither pure nor purifying; and purifying but not pure. (339)

3.17.3. The Disagreement About a Little and a Lot of Water

Pure (*tahir*) and purifying (*mutahhar*) is the water with which impurity is not mixed. That which is pure but not purifying is the water which is mixed with that which is not impure when the name 'water' is removed from it like the water of saffron, etc. Water which is neither pure nor purifying is the water which has had one of its attributes changed by impurity. The one with this rule refers to the Tradition which is our proof. The Lawgiver said: "Nothing makes it impure." How can the one who uses it as proof here consider that while he does not consider it in the manner which we believe—namely that it is purifying but not pure? That binds him by necessity, and he has no proof in the divine law to which to refer. The fourth is purifying but nor pure, which we are speaking of now. It is water which is mixed with impurity while none of its attributes are changed. Some say that there is a difference between a little and a lot of water. They say that if it is a lot, it does not become impure. If it is a little, it becomes impure, and they do not define it. They simply say that it is impure, even if none of its attributes are changed. (340)

These people differ about the definition between a little and a lot. The dispute about the definition itself is well-known among the schools, but is not a sound text of the divine law. The Traditions which speak about it are like the Traditions of the two *qullah* and the Tradition about the four *qullah*, and they disagree about the definition of *qullah*. Many secondary questions branch out from this point, like water coming to the impurity and impurity coming to the water and urine going into unmoving water and other matters. (341)

3.18. The Inner Significance of the Rule: When the Incomparable Divine Knowledge Is Mixed with the Knowledge of the Attributes in Which Ambiquity Can Be Imagined

People have many positions about that, and this book is not the place for them. We did not intend to deal with all the rules in the branches of questions connected to purification. We intended their matrices in order to deal with the inner rule in them. We have about eighty sections in this book about them, God willing, section by section. I will do this, God willing, with all the actions of worship which we intend to mention in this book: obligatory prayer, alms, fasting and pilgrimage. God is the Supporter. There is no Lord but Him. (342)

The hidden meaning in what we mentioned in this section is that water which is mixed with impurity and which has none of its attributes changed is knowledge of the divine which must be incomparable from the attributes of the human being. If the knowledge of the divine is mixed with an understanding of the attributes which we imagine to have a relationship between Him and His creation, there occurs to the knower, based on (the presumed shared relationship) that there is some sort of impurity. He strives to understand the attributes in which multiple meanings occurred with the knowledge which compels incomparability from the perspective of intellectual proof and from: *"There is not like Him anything. And He is The Hearing, The Seeing"* (42:11), from sensory proof (*dalil al-sam*). Then the understanding of the divine stays in its root after the purification of incomparability done by intellect and the divine law, even though we still attribute to Him the likes of these attributes which presume similarity, because not one of His attributes has altered, so all of that is affirmed for Him—with the realization of there is nothing like unto Him. (343)

3.18.1. The Many Proofs and the Doubt Which Assails One from Them

As for the principle of little and much in that and the dispute of people about impurity if the water is a small amount, littleness and much in pure water refers to the substantive proofs of the knowers of God. If one has a single proof, and a doubt comes upon him in his knowledge of the incomparability of God in any aspect and it effects his proof, his knowledge departs just as this pure and purifying water vanishes. If one has many proofs of one proven thing, and a doubt consumes it, when it enters one of his proofs, he does not pay any attention to it, but relies on the rest of his proofs. This doubt does not affect his knowledge. It affects a particular proof, not all proofs. This is the meaning of much water whose rule is not changed by impurity. (344)

3.19. Water Mixed with Something Pure Which Enters and Dominates It When It Changes One of Its Three Attributes

As for the one who speaks about not mentioning any definition in that, even if the water is corrupted, he refers to the divine Unity of the source, not the divine Unity of the proof. He says that if this doubt enters knowledge in a time in which it can be conceived—and the time is very short—perhaps he will die in that moment while he does not have other proofs in mind because of the brevity of the moment, so it is invalidated with him. There are many areas of this subject which we do not need to mention. This is enough of what is desired. (345)

3.20. The Inner Significance: Knowledge of God by Means of Reflection Is Pure and Not Purifying

As for water mixed with something pure which penetrates and dominates it so that it changes one of its three attributes, it is pure and not purifying with all, except for some Imams. In their view, it is purifying as long as it is not altered by cooking. (346)

3.21. Water Used for Purification: The Disagreement of the Scholars About Used Water

As for the inner rule in that (knowledge of God by means of reflection), it is that when knowledge of God in respect of the intellect, which has acquired it by means of reflection, is mixed with a description which the divine law reports, that knowledge of God is pure in itself, but it is not purifying by what it indicates of the attribute of connection. It is like their statement about the description of the Word of God being "like a chain on stone." He uses the letter *k* of the attribute. All the divine law is outward and what it brings is accepted. The intellect cannot be free of its proof in negating connection and affirming what the divine law brings without interpretation. (347)

Some think that it is pure in its basic root as long as it is not cooked. By cooking, he means a natural matter. It is that that attribute is not taken from the Lawgiver who reports it from God. He takes it from his understanding and investigation by a sort of analogy about its possibility and nature. It is pure and purifying, so know that. (348)

3.21.1. The Inner Significance of the Rule: Whether Using Water Changes Its General Description

Divine law scholars disagree about water which has been used for purification, and there are three positions. One says that it is not permitted to purify oneself with it. Others say that it is permitted to purify oneself with it and I say that. Some say that it is disapproved to perform purification with it, but it is not permitted to perform dry ablution when it is present. There is a fourth position which is odd, which is that it is impure. (349)

3.22. Attributing God's Oneness to the Essence After Using It in the Oneness of Actions

As for the inner rule in that, know that the reason for this disagreement is that the general name of water must be applied to that water or not applied. If someone thinks that it is applied, its use effects its application, and it is not permitted, or disliked, according to how strong it is with him. As for the one who says that it is impurity, it is a statement which is not considered, even if the one who stated it is one of the respected. He is Abu Yusuf. (350)

3.23. Absolute Oneness of God Is Only for God

Know that the knowledge of God's Oneness is absolute purity. When it is used in the unity of actions, after this use, it returns to the unity of the Essence. Those who know God differ with this dispute about used water. There are gnostics who say that God does not accept this unity in respect to His Essence, so it is not used after that in knowledge of the Essence. Some gnostics say that He accepts it because we have not confirmed an extra source. Relationships are not by a matter of existence. Knowledge of God's Oneness retains its root of purity. (351)

3.24. The Agreement About the Purity of Water Leftover by Muslims and Livestock

As for the one who says that it is impure, only God has absolute unity. When you use this unity for the unity of every unit in a manner that makes it distinct for others, then it acquires the principle of possible being. This is the meaning of impurity. The like of this unity must not be ascribed to God, because His being distinguished from His creation in His unity is not by sharing as possibles being distinguished from each other by their special attributes, and that is their unity. (352)

3.25. The Inner Significance of the Rule: Belief Is Life and Life Is the Source of Purification

divine law scholars agree about the purity of the leftover water of Muslims and livestock, but they differ about what is other than that. Some say that every animal is pure and some make exceptions, and there are many differences about the exceptions. (353)

3.25.1. As Belief Is the Acceptance of Reality (al-Haqq), It Increases Knowledge of the Real

As for the inner rule in that (belief is the acceptance of Reality): faith is life), the leftover water of Muslims and every animal is pure. Belief and modesty are the source of purification in the living, and the believer. By life, there is glorification of God by the living. By belief, there is acceptance of what the divine law brings which the intellect finds impossible, but is not impossible for the believer without a doubt. The Prophet said: Whoever knows himself knows his Lord. No knowledge remains for the servant after his recognition of himself which is his leftover. Every animal shares with the human being, the believer, in the proof. Leftover water is like that. By this amount which remains, he recognizes his Lord. (354)

As for the people who disagree about the exceptions, they look at the believer and not at the animal inasmuch as it is animal and not believer. It is according to what this one who makes an exception sees. The rulings and details of it are long. We made the condition of the believer rather than man alone since belief gives from gnosis of God of what the animal and man give, and more than what man perceives in respect to his humanness or his animality. That comes from his being a believer. For this reason, we said that the leftover water of the believer is more complete in gnosis. (355)

3.26. Purification by Leftover Water: The Disagreement of Religious Scholars

Religious scholars disagree about purification using leftover water and take five different positions. Some say that it is absolutely pure, and we say that. Some say that it is not permitted for a person to use the leftover water of a woman. Some say that it is permitted for a man to use the leftover water of a woman as long as she is not in the state of sexual impurity (*janaba*) or menstruating. Some say that it is not permitted for either of them to purify himself with what remains from his companion, but that they can begin together. Some say that it is not permitted at all. Some say that it permitted for a man to use a woman's leftover water as long as she has not put her hand in it. (356)

3.27. The Inner Significance of the Rule: A Man Has a Degree Above Women in the Glorious Gnosis of God

As for the inner rule in that, know that man has a degree above woman. When an indication of knowledge of God is used—with respect to what the gender of the person, nothing else—the one who thinks that the increase of degree in the proof is better than the one who does not have this degree, who is diminished in knowledge to that extent. Therefore, the view that does not permit purification with that said that instead it indicates a particular knowledge about the divine and that knowledge is the knowledge of affecting and affected and this is found in every active and passive thing. Thus, it is not permitted that the likes of this to exist in the knowledge of God and the heart will not be purified with it from ignorance of God. (357)

3.28. Taking an Aspect of the Proof Is Increase in Recognition of the Proven

The one who permits sublimity of the knowledge of God that He has created us, says that gnosis of God is too glorious since He is our Creator and the Creator of all possibles. When our dependence on Him is affirmed and the fact that He is independent of us is established, we are not concerned with what we have missed of knowledge of Him. These are the two positions about permissibility and the lack of permissibility. (358)

3.29. Exile from the Homeland of Femininity

With this consideration, we are concerned with what remains of the various positions like beginning together although beginning together is increase in knowledge of God. The knowledge is not limiting time (because they begin together). It is similar to halting or like looking at two indications in regard to what they share. This is only for the human being. (359)

The similitude of a woman performing purification with a man's left-over water is that he gives what the woman gives and more. The similitude of a man preforming purification with the leftover water of a woman while she is not in the state of sexual impurity is that he is in exile from the abode of femininity which is the abode of the passive. The feminine shares being passive and being acted upon by him, as he is acted upon by his Creator, with her being similar to the man, which diminishes her femininity. As to being in a state of menstruation, as it is an attribute which prevents intimate conversation with God during the obligatory prayer and the goal of knowledge of God is nearness. The state of menstruation is distance from God in respect to intimate conversation with Him. Recognition of this attribute is the recognition of being veiled from the name, The Distance. (360)

3.30. Ablution with Date-wine: The Disagreement of the Scholars About This

As for the position of the one who says: as long as a woman has not put her hand in it, purification with it is permitted. However if she had finished using it, purification is not permitted. Know that the gnostic, just as he knows that his essence is passive in its very creation by God, he does not know if his acts will please or anger God. When a responsibility falls on him, he does not have complete knowledge. He has used the knowledge of having been acted upon and this impairs the purification of this knowledge. That is, if she had finished using the water, it is not permitted for purification. Then the person discovers that he has been effected from the divine Side as with His Words: "*I respond to the call of the caller when he calls.*" The call from the caller gives to the one called the response. This is the meaning of being acted upon. This is the reality of the words: "as long as she did not finish with it." (361)

3.31. The Inner Significance of the Rule: The Proof by Religious Law Is the Proof by Reason

Divine law scholars disagree about ablution using date wine. Some of them permit it but most scholars forbid it. I say that it is forbidden because of the absence of a sound Prophetic report about it which we would accept as proof. If the Tradition had been sound, his statement would not be a text about ablution with it. The Prophet said about it: Good dates and pure water. The opinion is that date-wine combines dates and water, and so it is called date-wine. The water is pure before the mixture. If his statement about it is sound that it is a pure drink, it is not a text about performing ablution with it. That must be the case. It may be possible to use it to purify garments of impurity. God has only prescribed dry ablution with earth in particular for us to be purified for the formal prayer when there is no water. (362)

As for the inner rule in that, a gnostic may base himself on legal proof. Legal proof is based on logical proof. Legal proof is a branch of logical proof which is the root science. One who only knows legal proof is weak in the knowledge of what the divine law established as proof of divinity. If the divine law calls it "pure water and good dates," that is a mixture of two proofs, and an imitator cannot distinguish between the two proofs. (363)

Whoever grasps this mixture of logical evidence permits using it as proof, and so he permits ablution using date-wine. If he is ignorant of the logical evidence which that mixture contains, he does not permit its use, and he does not have an inner eye in establishing this secondary ruling. Therefore, he does not permit ablution using date-wine. He calls it a drink, and he removes the name "water" from it, so understand! "*God speaks the truth and guides to the Path.*" (33:4) (364)

3.32. Things Which Invalidate Ablution Is All that Lessens the Proofs

The principle of what is in the inner aspect, that is, a factor invalidating ablution is that it designates all that lessens intellectual and legal proofs in knowledge of God. As for intellectually, that comes from doubts which come, and as for the divine law, that comes from the weakness of the path reaching it. It is lack of trust in transmission or rare texts. That is part of what weakens the report. (365)

3.33. Invalidating Ablution by an Impurity Leaving the Body

Whatever removes you from knowledge of God's Oneness, and His Most Beautiful Names and what God is obliged to have, and what it is impossible or improbable logically that He have (unless a common tradition mentions it in Book or the Prophet's confirmed sayings and actions (*sunna*), all of that impairs the purity of the heart in knowledge of God—His Unity and His Names. We will mention this in detail with the outer aspects of ablution, God willing. (366)

3.33.1. The Inner Significance: A Word Which Issues from the Tongue Affects Belief

Divine law scholars disagree—developing three different positions—about what invalidates ablution by an impurity which leaves the body. Some people consider only what emerges from whatever place it emerges and in whatever aspect it emerges. There is dispute among these people on matters. Some people consider two exits: front and back, whatever emerges, in whatever aspect it emerges in health or illness. Others consider what emerges and the exit and the attribute in which it emerges. That is what I say. (367)

3.33.2. Hypocrisy Is the Manifestation of Belief With the Lips While There Is Nothing of It in the Heart

As for the rule of these schools in respect of inner meanings, the one who considers what emerges by itself—and he is the one who looks at the expression issuing from man—he is the one who has it effect the purification of his belief. It is as if he were to say, swearing in his oath: I am free of Islam if it is such-and-such or if it is not other than such-and-such. If he is truthful in his oath and does not break it, he does not return soundly to Islam. It is as the Prophet said: It is like someone who utters a word which will anger God in order to make people laugh: he does not think that it will reach what it reaches. By it, he falls into the fire for seventy years. He did not consider any unbeliever or believer would emerge from it. (368)

3.33.3. The One Who Knows the Real and Unjustly Denies Him

Anyone who considers the two exits (of excretion), they are the hypocrite and doubter. Nothing that leaves them profits them in the world to come. The product may be impurity, like disbelief in speech, and it may be other than impurity, like belief. The like of this comes from the two exits, the hypocrite and doubter, because the two exits are unclean and they do not profit what is pure—like the manifestation of belief while there is none of it in the heart. It is His words, when they said: *"We believe in some."* (4:150) It is like the emergence of the pure, that is, that which is not impure: *". . . and we disbelieve in others,"* and it is like the emergence of what is impure. God said about them: *"Those, they are in truth the ones who are ungrateful."* (4:151) Hypocrisy therefore affects purity. (369)

3.34. The Rule of Sleep Invalidating Ablution: The Disagreement of Scholars About This

As for the one who considers what emerges, the two exits, and the attribute of its emergence in purification, like its emerging in illness, that is like the one who imitates in disbelief, or in health, he is the one who knows the sound truth and rejects it and does not believe. God says about those who recognized the truth and deny what they had of it: *"And they negated them although their souls confessed to them."* Then He mentioned the cause and said: "*. . . out of injustice and self-exaltation. So look on how had been the Ultimate End of the ones who make corruption.*" (27:14) (370)

3.35. The Inner Significance of the Rule: The Two States of the Heart Which Remove Purity

Scholars disagree about sleep taking three positions. Some say that it invalidates ablution, so they oblige ablution for both a little and a lot of it. Some say that it does not invalidate ablution so ablution is not obliged on account of it unless you are certain about having invalidated it, and that is the factor which invalidates ablution and not sleep. Doubt has no effect in purity, and the divine law does not regard doubt in this place. This is what I say. Some say that there is a difference between a little light sleep like a nap for which ablution is not obliged and a heavy sleep for which ablution is obliged. (371)

Know that the heart has a state of heedlessness which is light sleep, and a state of death and being asleep to wakefulness and attention to what God has obliged him to do in the way of study, proof, remembrance of God. These two states remove the purity of the heart which is knowledge of God. We said something to alert the heedless and the traveler in that:

O sleeper! How much repose
 while you make claims? Be aware!
God looks after you in what you ask for,
 even if you are asleep to Him.
Your heart, however, is unmindful
 about that to which He calls and alerts you.
He brings you down in the world of phenomenal beings
 whenever you are dead to Him.
Look at yourself before your journey
 if it increases you in ambiguity. (372)

3.36. The Ruling on Touching Women: The Disagreement of Scholars About This

Religious scholars disagree about touching women with the hand or other physical limb. Some say that anyone who touches his wife without a barrier or kisses her without a barrier must perform ablution whether or not he experiences pleasure. Those who take this position differ about what is touched. Sometimes they say that they are the same in obliging ablution and sometimes they make a distinction between them. Also the one with this position distinguishes between touching female relatives and one's wife. (373)

3.36.1. The Inner Significance: When Desire Touches the Heart

Some say that one is obliged to perform ablution when the touch is accompanied by pleasure. There are further details with those who say this. Some say that touching women does not invalidate ablution. I say that. It is more cautious to perform ablution because of the disagreement which there is in this question, both the toucher and touched. (374)

As for the rule of touching in the heart, women designate and indicate the appetites. When the appetite touches the heart, and appetite is mixed with it, and it is mixed with appetite, and it comes between the heart and what it must have of watching God, then ablution is invalidated. If it does not come between it and watching God in it, he still is in a state of purity. The purity of the heart is "presence with God." One is concerned whether appetite is connected to the permissible or the forbidden when he believes that the forbidden is forbidden and the permissible is permissible. Then it does not affect his purity. (375)

3.37. Touching the Penis: The Disagreement of Scholars About Touching the Penis

If he believes that the permissible which is permissible by text is forbidden, or that the forbidden which is forbidden by text is permissible because of appetite in respect of resorting to an Imam's position who thinks that, knowing that the Lawgiver confirmed the rule of the religious scholar and confirmed the action of the heart when he acts by it, and yet before the occurrence appetite, he already knew about the position but did not act by it or state it, he is resorting to it because of appetite which has touched his heart. The like of this affects his purity, so he must perform ablution without dispute among the people of hearts. As for the outward, we have a view in this question and in it we parted from formal scholars. (376)

Scholars disagree about that, taking three different positions. Some say that he does not perform ablution because of it, and that is what I say. Being cautious in ablution in every question has differences. Caution refers to the place of consensus and agreement whatever he is capable of. Some say that one performs ablution because of it, and people distinguish between touching it in a state of pleasure or with the inside of the hand, or touching it with the outside of the hand or without pleasure. They make that distinction. (377)

3.38 The Inner Significance of the Rule: the Reason for Bringing Beings into Existence: Essence + Will + Command

Know that God has only made the reason for bringing possible beings into existence the Will and the divine Command. Because of this, one includes will in the definition of the command. God says: *"Our saying to a thing when We wanted it is that We say to it: Be! Then it is!"* (16:40) He used will and the command, and he did not mention a third thing called "power." He brought out His words: *"God is Powerful over everything."* (2:284) for it is the source of His word to things, *Be!* when He wants them to be. (378)

3.39. Intercourse Is The Cause for the Manifestion of Offspring

There is no doubt that the hand is the place of power. Since intercourse is the reason for the manifestation of products, whoever relates power to Him in bringing the possible into existence which is manifested—and it is touching the penis with the hand—either neglects divine Power in the word *Be* or he does not neglect it. If he neglects it, his purity is invalidated when he relates the existence of the child to intercourse. If he is not heedless, he remains in purity. (379)

3.40. Ablution on Account of That Which Fire Has Touched: The Disagreement of the Companions About This

The Companions of the Messenger of God disagreed about ablution on account of that which fire had touched. Other than the very first generation do not disagree that one performs ablution after eating camel meat. Ablution is an act of devotion and an independent act of worship even though purity is broken by eating camel-meat. Performing the formal prayer with previous ablution is permitted although he is a rebel if he does not perform ablution after eating camel-meat. (380)

3.41. The Necessity of Ablution on Account of Camel Meat: The Inner Significance of the Rule

This is a statement which none that I know before us has made. If he intends to remove the impediment, that is more cautious. Scholars differ about ablution on account of camel-meat. Some say that ablution for it is obliged, and some say that it is not obliged. (381)

The fire which man finds in himself is that which cooks one's insides because of matters which happen to him which are not in harmony with his natural instinct. He may receive that with submission, contentment or patience with God in it, as God called Himself 'The Patient' by His words: *"Truly those who inflict torment on God and His Messenger"* (33:57), and he gave them a respite and did not take them to task. The Prophet said: A person is not more patient in harm than God, which is forbearance on His part. When the servant is like this, it does not effect his purity. (382)

3.42. The Touch of Satan in the Human Heart

If he is angry, it affects him, especially camel-meat. The Lawgiver called them Satans. That is the call of Satan in the heart. It invalidates his purity because the place of the impulse is the heart, and so it is purified of it by the call of the angel. Camel-meat is the impulse of Satan because Satan is created from "*. . . smokeless flame of fire.*" (55:15) Smokeless fire refers to the fire's flame. The Lawgiver, as we said, called the camels satanic and forbade people to pray in their resting-places. The only reason for that is that they are satanic and they are distant. Prayer is the state of nearness and intimate conversation. We considered the inner rule of ablution because of camel-meat and how purity is invalidated by this. Even if its impulse is to good, evil is hidden in that food unless it is perceived by a knower with precision who recognizes how divine commands come to the hearts. (383)

3.43. Laughter in the Obligatory Prayer Invalidating Ablution: Human States Vary

Know that some oblige ablution because of laughing in the prayer and some forbid it. I say it is forbidden. The inner aspect in that is that a person's states with God vary in his obligatory prayer during his recitation when he is one of the People of God who reflect on the Quran. One sign may sadden him so that he weeps, while another sign may make him rejoice so that he laughs. Another sign may warn him, so that he neither laughs nor weeps. One sign may give him knowledge and another sign may cause him to ask forgiveness or supplicate. His purity remains in its original state. (384)

3.43.1. The Person Whose States Do Not Vary

We have seen those whose states always include laughter—both in the obligatory prayer and otherwise—like al-Salawi and those like him—may God profit us by him! and like Abu Yazid Tayfur ibn Isa ibn Sharushan al-Bistami. Abu Musa al-Daybuli related from him that he said: I laughed for a time and I wept for a time. Now I neither weep nor laugh. (385)

3.43.2. The One Who Is Heedless of His Recitation

If someone is heedless in his recitation, its contemplation and intimate conversation with his Lord because of his shop, diversions and similar things which remove him from presence with God in his obligatory prayer, that laughter of his inwardly in the obligatory prayer is in the school of the one who says that it invalidates his purity, and because of this state which he has, his purity is invalidated and he must renew the purity of his heart. (386)

3.44. Performing Ablution After Carrying the Dead: One Thing Is Joined to Another by a Relationship

A group of scholars have that position, but most scholars forbid that. I say that it is forbidden. As for the inner rule in that, it is connected to the knowledge of relationship. A thing is only joined to another thing when there is a relationship between them. Abu Hamid al-Ghazzali said that he dreamed of some of the people of this affair as a crow and a dove in the Haram. He saw that the relationship between them was distant and was amazed. Neither of them recognized the intimacy of his companion. He pointed to them and they went up, and then each of them rose. He recognized that the ascent joined them. (387)

3.45. The Story of Shaykh Abu Madyan with a Merchant

A merchant used to say to our Shaykh, Abu Madyan: Whenever you see a poor person who needs something I would like you to inform me of it so that I can supply that. One day a naked pauper came to him who needed clothing while the station and state of the Shaykh in that was lack of reliance on other than God in all his affairs in respect to himself and others. The shaykhs have agreed that his trust for himself was sound as was his trust for others. Abu Madyan remembered the merchant's wish and took the pauper to the merchant's shop to take some clothes from him. A man came up to him whom the Shaykh did not know and asked about his way of life. He was an idolater. He recognized the relationship and turned to God in repentance for that thought. He turned, and the man had left him and he did not know where he had gone. (388)

3.46. There Are Two Types of Death: Death to People, Death to God

Then I was informed of his story and I know that in the land of Islam there are basically not two religions. So I knew that God had sent that person to him away from his thought to warn him. By him, God taught us that He can create within the breaths of the world. It is like that with the one who carries the dead. There is a relationship between them which is death. Death can be to phenomenal beings and death can be to the Real. The one who is dead to The Real performs ablution and the one who is dead to beings keeps his ablution. (389)

3.47. Invalidating Ablution by Losing Consciousness: Intellect + Belief + Existence of Transmitted Text = Knowledge of Truth and Unveiling

Religious scholars agree that the departure of consciousness breaks purity. The inner rule in that is that the rule of consciousness ceases in divine matters on which there is a text of the divine law with multiple transmissions, in which there is no probability of doubt, he is in the most perfect purity because the purity of belief with the existence of the text accords true knowledge and unveiling. When his consciousness ceases through a doubt, his purity is broken and he must resume looking at another proof or remove that doubt. (390)

3.48. The Acts for Which This Purity Is Conditional: Ablution Is a Precondition for the Obligatory Prayer

Scholars agree that ablution is one of the preconditions for the obligatory prayer but they disagree about whether it is a precondition of soundness or a precondition of obligation. By ablution I mean prescribed purity. It is the condition of obligation with us, and purification is an independent form of worship, while it may be a precondition or obligation. It may also be recommended and customary (*sunna*) in another act of worship. (391)

3.48.1. Purification of the Heart Is a Precondition for Intimate Conversation with God

The inner rule in that is that purification of the heart is a precondition for intimate conversation with God or contemplation of Him. It is both a precondition for soundness and a precondition of obligation. The reason for that is that we are in the place of obligation, and and must believe in God and what comes from Him, and in the Messenger and the Messengers. This is an indication that the matter is not limited except that He is the High and Higher, and: *". . .above possessors of knowledge is One Who is Knowing."* (12:76) He is *". . . exalter of Degrees"* (40:15) and *"We exalt in degrees whom We will."* (6:83) (392)

3.48.2. Belief Is the Purification of the Heart from the Veil

Sometimes knowledge is a precondition for the soundness of belief and a precondition of obligation and sometimes belief is a precondition for the soundness of the knowledge of unveiling and a precondition for its obligation. Belief, however, contains purification of the heart from the veil, and knowledge is the purification of the heart from ignorance, doubt and hypocrisy. Your heart is therefore purified by two purifications. By that, you ascend in both worlds, and by it, you obtain the knowledge of the two handfuls. God has obliged us to believe in Him and His Names, and His angels, His Books and His Messengers. *"We do not distinguish between any of His Messengers"* although we know that God has preferred some of the Messengers and Prophets over others. He forbade us to have any preference between the Prophets through analogy or speculation. The servant does not impose anything on God. (393)

3.49. Purity For the Funeral Prayer and for the Prostration of Recitation: The Disagreement of Scholars This

The people of knowledge disagree about purity for the funeral prayer and for the prostration of recitation. Some say that it is one of its preconditions, and some say that it is not a precondition. That is what I say. (394)

3.50. Purification of Belief Is a Precondition for the Validity of Every Prescribed Act

As for the inner aspect of all of that, we say that every prescribed action which is not preceded by the purity of belief is not valid since it is deficient. The existence of belief is obligatory in every prescribed action. The one who says that ablution is not obligatory for the funeral prayer and the prostration of recitation does not think that belief has to be present in supplication for the dead or prostration for recitation. Basic belief is enough when he begins the action. This is the reason for the lack of response. Whoever thinks that purification is a precondition, it is the answer, and it must occur in what he prays for. (395)

3.50.1. Purity for Touching a Copy of the Quran: Is Purity a Precondition for Touching the Quran

The people of knowledge disagree about purity and whether or not it is a precondition for touching a copy of the Quran. Some people oblige it and some people reject it [as a precondition]. I say that it is not a precondition, although doing that with purity is better. (396)

The inner rule in that is: is the proof respected by the respect of the proven? We say yes, the proof is respected by the respect of the proven.

Others do not oblige that, for the proof is the opposite of the proven and they are not combined. If the proof is respected, it is by another matter, not by its being a proof of something respected. The copy of the Quran is a proof of the word of God. We are commanded to respect it and to touch it with purity out of respect for it. (397)

3.51. The Universe Is Taken as Proof of God

Know that we take the universe to be a proof of God. We overlook the fact that what is called the "universe" contains both the praiseworthy and blameworthy. We take Pharaoh and his like among those who are arrogant as a proof of the existence of the Maker because it is His workmanship. One is not obliged to respect him. Rather one is obliged to hate him and not to have respect for him. We take Moses inasmuch as he is His work as a proof of the existence of The Maker. It is agreed that his identity in the proving rests on the particular. We are obliged to respect and revere him from one aspect, not from the aspect of his being a proof. For this reason, we revere the copy of the Quran since the Lawgiver ordered us to respect and revere it, and not because it is a proof. It has another respect since it is a proof, and we justify respect for it in any given moment. We say of it that it is the Word of God, even if we write it with our hands. (398)

3.52. The Obligation for Someone in the State of Major Impurity to Perform Ablution When He Wishes to Sleep, Eat, Drink or Resume Intercourse

Religious scholars disagree about what we mentioned in this interpretation. Some say that it is obligatory while some say that it is recommended, and that is what I say. As for the inner aspect of that, it is bringing the intention to that which breaks his legal purity by an appetite which distracts him from seeing God when it is strong. When he wants to sleep, he intends to give the eye its due, then that is the purification of the one in major impurity. If he wants to sleep, major impurity has invalidated his purity. It is exile from the abode of belief which he should have had present with him had it not been for the strength of the power of appetite which annihilated him to himself and to what is other than him. It is like that when he wants to resume intercourse: he intends by this intercourse a believing child who will follow the Messenger of God and who will do much remembrance of God. It is like that when he wants to eat or drink: he intends to give the self its due. This intention in what we mentioned is purification. (399)

3.53. Ablution for Circumambulation: Circumambulation of the Kaba of the Heart Which God Encompasses

Know that some people consider ablution to be a precondition for circumambulation while other people do not consider it a precondition. I say that, although it is better that circumambulation is done with purity. The inner rule in that is that whoever thinks that circumambulation of the House is related to God as the Throne is related to the settling of the All-Merciful, and thinks that the angels encircle it and they are the pure, good, noble ones, considers ablution to be a precondition for circumambulation of the Kabah of his heart which encompasses God, may His Majesty be exalted. He said: "Neither My heaven nor My earth contains me, but the heart of My servant contains Me." It is His descent in His theophany to the heart of His servant. We clarified it in *Mawaqi al-najum* in "The Stage of the Essential Descent from the Sphere of the Heart." (400)

3.54. As the Real is Absolute, No Precondition Limits Him

Anyone who thinks that God is not limited to what He ascribes to to Himself and that the benefit of the one who is obligated is intended by that, does not consider purity to be a precondition for circumambulation. As for the heart, lack of the precondition of purity at the moment when the intellect looks at the affirmation of the divine law in the first gnosis is either in the beginning or when he descends to it by instructing the one wants to recognize God by speculative proofs. (401)

3.55. Ablution for Reciting the Quran: Disagreement Among Scholars About This

Scholars disagree about ablution for recitation of the Quran. Some say that it is permitted for those who are not in purity to recite the Quran. I say that. Some say that it is not permitted to recite the Quran without purity, and that is better without a doubt. It is like that with all we have mentioned that it is permitted to do in our view and that of others without ablution. It is better to do any of that in ablution. (402)

3.55.1. The One Who Recites the Quran Represents the Real and Varieties of Recitation of the Quran

As for the inner rule in that, the reciter of Quran represents God in translating His words from Him and one of His attributes is The Sacred, *al-Quddus*, meaning The Pure, *al-Tahir*. When the servant represents God in His Words by his recitation, he must be outwardly pure by the prescribed ablution, and inwardly by belief, presence, reflection and the like of that. He must precede the recitation of God with it in the beginning, and then he recites it translating from God in what He recites and utters. (403)

Either he transmits in his recitation for the one present with him to remind him, or he translates it with his tongue so that he will hear it and obtain the reward for hearing. Similarly, if the Quran had been in his hand from which he recited, the eye would have taken its due of looking at the word of God inasmuch as it is written, as the hearing takes it inasmuch as the tongue utters it. It is like that if he had placed the Quran in his room and run his hand over the letters. These limbs would receive their portion of that. It was like that when Shaykh Abu Abd Allah ibn al-Mujahid, Abu Abd Allah ibn Qassum and Abu 'l-Hajjaj al-Shuburbali were reciting. I did not see any of our shaykhs who preserved the like of this recitation except for these three. (404)

4 On the Full Bath

4.1. Rules Concerning the Purification of the Full Bath: General Obligatory Purification with Water for All Parts of the Surface of the Body

This full bath prescribed in this chapter is general purification by water which includes all of the outward body without dispute and whatever one can make water reach in the body, even if it is not outward, with dispute—for instance, putting water in the mouth and the like. This will be mentioned. The causes which necessitate this purification will be mentioned. Some of them are obligatory, some customary and some recommended. (405)

4.1.1. Inner Purification of the Self

As for the interpretation of this purification, it includes the purification of the self from all that it is commanded to be purified of in the way of outward actions which are connected to the self (by way of the channels of its attributes, not from its attributes themselves). We said the channels of its attributes, for its attributes cling to the self in the root of their creation and do not part from it. One of our companions considered them the same as its essence. They are the attributes of the self—like avarice, miserliness, slander and every blameworthy description. (406)

4.1.2. Concerning the Blame which Commands Us to Purify Ourselves from It

The blame which we are commanded to be purified of is not the same as the attribute. It is the channel itself. Man is not purified of avarice, but is purified of using avarice in useless things of this world and the forbidden. He is purified by avarice itself according to the principle which purifies its use. He is purified by avarice in seeking knowledge and acquiring causes of good and sound actions and avarice for all the causes of happiness. The source of avarice cannot depart. By one aspect, it is the happiness of greedy, and by another aspect it is the misery of the greedy. For this reason, we spoke of the channel, not of the attribute itself. On this basis, we take all of the attributes to which blame is connected. Blame is connected to their channels, not to their sources. (407)

4.1.3. Inner and Outer Purification in Washing: Judgments of Purification Inner and Outer

The general purification of the inner and the outer in this washing is connected to the channels of the attributes. The only one who knows the channels of the attributes is the one who knows noble qualities. So he is purified by them, and he knows best qualities, and is purified by them. There is nothing hidden of them which he does not perceive as being received from the Lawgiver. It is every action which pleases God. By it, he is purified of every action which does not please Him. Therefore he is purified of it. God says: *"He is not well-pleased with ingratitude from His servants; and if you give thanks, He will be well-pleased with you."* (39:7) For this reason, we presented opposite sections in this book—like repentance and leaving it, scrupulousness and leaving it, and asceticism and leaving it, in the coming sections, God willing, and there will be several sections. (408)

This purification is also obligatory, like purification by paying the purifying alms (*zakat*), for example. It is obligatory full bath. It is also like giving to poor relatives which is recommended. It is like preferring the poor people of the religion more than other relatives, which is also recommended. Such is the principle of this purification in all of the inner and outer of man: in knowledge and ignorance, disbelief and belief, polytheism and unity, affirmation and invalidation. It is like that in all the prescribed actions—he purifies them of opposition by agreement. (409)

4.1.4. The Prescribed Washing

This is the meaning of obligatory and non-obligatory washing. I will mention the details of the questions of this purification which proceed according to the course of the principles which what we will mention of them in the outer rule of the divine law in washing with water. The secondary branches of this purification cannot be numbered or contained in a book, even if we were to clarify the method of taking them, so take them according to that plan if you desire to be among the servants of God who are devoted to His service and whom He created for Himself and is pleased with them, so they are pleased with Him. May God place us among those of knowledge who act and not come between us and using actions, words, deeds, and states which please Him! (410)

4.2. Full Bath After Washing the Dead: Interpretation of the One Who Thinks That It Is Not Obligatory to Perform the Full Bath After Washing the Dead

As for the prescribed full baths, some are agreed to be obligatory while there is dispute about the obligation of some. Some are agreed to be recommended, and there are many such full baths, like washing after contact with the genitals, washing after the knowing emission of sperm, full bath from its emission without knowledge, like someone who discovers sperm and does not remember having a wet-dream, a full bath on Friday for the Friday congregational prayer, a full bath for becoming Muslim, the full bath for assuming pilgrim sanctity, full bath for entering Mecca, full bath for standing at Arafah, and full bath for washing the dead. As for the interpretations of these washings, I will mention them before I mention the principles of the prescribed questions in washing with water and their interpretations. (411)

Since it is prescribed for the corpse to be washed and he has no action, then someone else is obliged to wash him as a warning for the washer that he is in the hands of his Lord in his purification in his success, behavior in obedience and what happens of the actions of his Creator towards him and with him. He is like the corpse in the hands of the washer. He does not see his washing in this respect by his washing the corpse. He sees that God purifies him and sees him as a tool which God uses for that action as the washer sees water as a tool in washing the corpse since if it had not been for water, the name "washer" would not have been valid for this one who washes. The water is not imagined to have any claim inasmuch as it washes the corpse. Water does not move to him and does not intend to wash him. The washer intends to wash the corpse with water. (412)

4.2.1. *Interpretation of the One Who Thinks the Full Bath Is Obligatory*

Similarly, the washer does not see in his intention that he intends to wash the corpse with water. He sees himself as a tool by which God intends to wash the corpse with water. God is the Purifier, not him or the water. God purifies the corpse by the washer and the water. A person like this does not perform a full bath for washing the dead. This is the interpretation of the one who thinks that full bath after washing the dead is not obligatory. (413)

4.2.2. *The Rule Regarding the Full Bath Because of Washing the Dead*

As for the one who washes the dead and does not see that in his washing, God is The Purifier, and claims that the action is his and ascribes it to himself and thinks that had it not been for him, this corpse would not have been purified, he must wash himself and purify himself of this claim by directing himself and being present with God anew and remembering what he neglected of God's purification of the corpse using his hands. Anyone who thinks this is obliged to wash himself after washing the dead. (414)

As for the ruling of full bath after washing the dead with water in the outer aspect of the divine law, my view is not to say that it is obligatory. If, however, he washes because of that, it is better and more fitting without dispute. (415)

4.3. *The Full Bath for Standing at Arafah: Standing at Arafah With Humility*

Since standing at Arafah is done with the attribute of humility, need, supplication and entreaty by nakedness from stitched clothing, and the place in which the pilgrim stands is called Arafah, we know that the interpretation is that it is the stopping place (*mawqif*) of the knowing who are the gnostics of God. God says: *"Only those of His servants who dread God are knowing."* (35:28) He says: *"Thou seest their eyes overflow with tears because they recognized The Truth."* (5:83) God willing, discourse of this sort will come in the book on the pilgrimage. (416)

4.4. Gnosis of God by Means of Logical Reflection: The Purification of the Heart from Connection to Other Than the Lord in Gnosis of the Lord

When the one designated as a knower sees that he is stripped of stitched garments, he crosses to the formation of proofs and their order to acquire knowledge of God by means of speculation by thought through organizing and forming premises. The form of knowledge of his Lord purifies him of that: like the tailor who sets out to cut out the shirt and put it together. The form of the shirt purifies him. It is said that the divestment of stitched clothes will bring knowledge of your Lord by divine or sovereign self-disclosure. Cast away intellectual speculation from yourself in this stopping place and on this day in respect to forming premises, and occupy yourself with acquiring knowledge of your Lord from divine favor and sovereign giving from the Giver who gives in order to bless. He is the One who casts knowledge into yourself in any case, whether or not you look at the formation of premises. Behave toward Him with divestment—it is more fitting for you. Do not start formulating premises by speculation in knowledge of God. That is darkness in gnosis. Only the one with sight sees it since there is no relationship between what you formulate of that and what His Essence deserves. (417)

How can the one who seeks this state from Him in that noble station and great weighty witnessing he not be washed inwardly and in his heart from connection to other-than-God in his knowledge of his Lord? The dirt and impurity of seeing others is removed from him by knowledge of God by God instead of his knowledge of himself since there is no proof of Him except Him. (418)

This is because knowledge compromises one object, while you in knowledge (Arafah) comprise two objects. For this reason, the one with this witnessing acquires two knowledge when he leaves Arafah and heads for Muzdalifa, it is a gatheredness which brings him another knowledge the object of which is God—as the object of knowledge in Arafah is the Lord. This is the one object which you acquire in this day—it is your knowledge of your Lord, not of yourself. You recognize God by God. It is God by whom you are washed and He gives that knowledge of Him. The objective of the washer is the same as yourself in its claim to knowledge of its Lord by itself by means of affectation in acquiring it. Where is the proof in relationship to the proof? How far from the mark! By His might, if you recognize Him, you only recognize Him by Him, so understand! This is your full bath for standing at Arafah if you stand. God supports and inspires. (419)

4.5. Full Bath for Entering Mecca: Entering Mecca Is Coming to God in His Presence

Know that entering Mecca is coming to God in His presence. There must be renewal of the purity of your heart from what it has acquired of acts of heedlessness from the time of assuming pilgrim sanctity at the appointed place outwardly with water, and inwardly with knowledge and presence. The purification of the outer is achieved through the full bath with water, and it is worship and cleansing. The purification of the inner, which is the heart, is clearing oneself in seeking loyalty. There is only loyalty to God by being free of creation in respect of looking at them by yourself instead of by God. (420)

4.5.1. Constant Presence with God and Full Bath When Entering Mecca

Anyone one has the state of constant presence with God does not wash to enter Mecca except for the outer full bath with water to perform the confirmed sayings and actions of the Prophet (*sunna*). As for the inner, it is only in seeing the Kaba or House. He purifies himself with a special modesty to witness His own House. It is like that with circumambulation around it. Those who do circumambulation are like those encircling the Throne, glorifying the praise of their Lord. As it is the Kaba or House of

God and without intermediary since God created this world, the hand of a creature has not done anything to acquire it. (421)

4.5.2. The Divine Name by Which the One Circumambulating Is Purified

Let the divine Name by which He is purified by the Name, The First, among the Most Beautiful Names. It is one of the attributes of the House, so correspondence is obtained. He said: *"Truly the first House to be set in place for humanity is at Bekka, that which is blessed,"* that is, blessing was put in it for My servants, *"and a guidance for the worlds."* (3:96) Whoever sees the House and does not experience divine increase in himself has not obtained anything of the blessing of the House, for blessing (*baraka*) is increase. God has not connected it to him. That indicates that his goal was not sound. Hastening to offer food to the guest is customary. (422)

Therefore let him wash first and not put it second because of his earlier full bath for pilgrim sanctity. It is a particular purification connected to the contemplation of the House and its circumambulation. There is no relationship between it and full bath for pilgrim sanctity except by a certain aspect. If he claims that he is purified by this purification and finishes his circumambulation while his inner aspect is lacking, God has not put blessing and guidance in it. It is clarification, that is, clarifies for him that which he is increased in the way of knowledge from his Lord. Blessing was only put in the House so that its Treasurer might give it to the one doing circumambulation of it, who comes to Him for the bestowal of blessing, nearness, concern and the clarification which is guidance in complex matters in states and obscure divine questions in knowledge of God which are connected to that Chosen House. It is the place of the Right Hand of God—acknowledged, taken as the direction of formal prayer, prostrated to. (423)

4.5.3. Blessing and Guidance in the House of God

This House is God's repository of blessings and guidance. The Lawgiver gave an indication by mentioning the treasure which is in it. What treasure is greater than what God has mentioned of blessing and guidance since He made them the same as the House? Its treasure is the One who is related to it, and He is God. (424)

4.5.4. The Fruits of Circumambulation in the Heart of the Doer

Let the one coming and doing circumambulation look at his heart when he is finished with his circumambulation. If he finds increase of knowledge of his Lord and clarification in his knowledge which he did not have before, then he knows the soundness of his full bath for entering Mecca. If he does not experience anything of that, he knows that he is not purified and he has not come to his Lord or done circumambulation of His House. It is impossible that one come to someone rich and noble and enter his house and not experience his hospitality. If he does not find increase, he has not added to his washing with water and his coming to the stone pillars. He has toiled and failed in his heart. He only has the reward of outer actions in the world to come in the Garden. It is what the ordinary believers acquire. When he visits, he visits the stones, not the source. When he returns to his country, he returns with hidden yearning. May God put us among the people of hearts, the people of God, and His elite by His might, Amen! If the afflicted one recognizes the lack of increase and what he had been deprived of, he will have the reward of someone afflicted in the world to come, when he was forbidden gnosis in this world. (425)

4.6. Full Bath for Pilgrim Sanctity (*Ihram*): Purification of the Limbs and Purification of the Inner Self

The interpretation of purifying the limbs from what is not permitted for the one in pilgrim sanctity is that he does it—purification of the inward from all that is beyond that. As he leaves it in the senses in the way of family, property and children, and comes to the House of God outwardly. He only turns with his heart to what he turns. Nothing can enter his heart or occur to him of what he has left behind him by his repentance and return to God. For this reason, it is the full bath of pilgrim sanctity by what it forbids him outwardly and inwardly. If he does not have this state, he is not inwardly one in pilgrim sanctity. (426)

4.6.1. If the Doorman Sleeps, the Door Remains Without a Guardian

If the doorman sleeps and is neglectful, the door remains without a guardian. The thoughts of the self and Satan are not experienced by the one who prevents them from entering his heart. He says: *Labbayk* (here I am). He says this with his tongue and imagines that he answers the call of his Lord coming to Him, while he actually answers the call of himself or Satan who calls him in his heart: Oh so-and-so! He says: At your service! The thought speaks to him according to what issued from the self of the one with the thought or from Satan, and what it has brought him of which was not prescribed for him to turn to in that state. He says: At your service. The one with this thought says to him: Welcome to the House of the one who will give you deprivation, failure and clear loss. He rejoices that he has made him a deity and said to him: *Labbayk.* (427)

"Had it not for the grace of God on you and His mercy" by the inward tongue and state and what preceded of intention, *"for what you had muttered,"* by the existence of your hearts turning to what you left behind physically, *"certainly would have afflicted you a tremendous punishment."* (24:14) So God forgives you for what yourselves chatter about and what Satan makes occur to them in that state by the concern for the outward *Labbayk*, and no more. They are not given in their hearts what He gives to those in pilgrim sanctity who are the people who have washed themselves inwardly. (428)

4.7. Full Bath When Someone Becomes Muslim: Islam Is Submission and Belief s Inner Purification

It is customary, indeed a duty. A full bath when becoming Muslim is prescribed and related in Prophetic tradition. As for its inner interpretation, Islam is obedience. When a person manifests outer obedience, he is an outer Muslim. He must obey inwardly as well so that he becomes an inner Muslim as he is one outwardly. Here the inner purification is by belief in Islam. God said in respect to a group who said: *"Say to them: You believe not. But say: We have submitted, for belief has not yet entered into your hearts."* (49:14) It is beneficial inner purification which saves one from being endlessly in the Fire. (429)

4.8. Full Bath for the Friday Formal Congregational Prayer

The inner interpretation is purification of the heart for being joined to its Lord and joining the spiritual strength to Him for intimate conversation with Him by lifting the veil from the heart. For this reason, some utter the opinion that the Friday congregational prayer is valid and established by two. That is what I say. God said, "I have divided the prayer into two parts between Me and My servant." He did not mention a third. "The servant says such-and-such and I say such-and-such to him." (430)

4.9. Full Bath for Friday Is Purification of the Heart for Its Meeting with the Lord

The one who seeks this state must purify himself for it with a special purification. I say that each state which the servant has with God has a particular purification. It is a station of arrival. For this reason, two bending forwards are prescribed for the Friday obligatory congregational prayer. The first is from the servant for God by what he says, and the second is from God for the servant by what He informs him in His answer to the words of His servant or what the Higher Assembly informs him according to what the servant says in his prayer. However, the Friday prayer is according to what is prescribed to be recited out loud in it. That must be. God says to the Higher Assembly: "My servant has praised Me," or what the servant says in the way of answer, praise, entrustment and glorification. (431)

4.9.1. Is the Friday full bath for the day or for the obligatory prayer?

The interpretation is purification by before-time for daily time of the seven days which are the days of the week. God has prescribed an obligatory right on every servant to wash every seven days. He washes on Friday for the day, not the prayer, and the purification for the Friday prayer is purification of state. This is purification of time. (432)

4.9.2. Friday Is the Day of Eternity

Scholars disagree (about the ruling of the full bath of Friday). Some say that the full bath is for the day, Friday. That is our position. If it occurs before the Friday congregational obligatory prayer and he also intends to wash for the Friday prayer, that is better. Some say that it is for the Friday noon prayer on Friday. It is the best without dispute, to the extent that he had omitted it before the prayer, he would be obliged to wash as long as the sun had not set. (433)

Since we said that the servant is gathered to God on this day in time, the relationship of this day to the presence of God is what before-endless-time contains of temporal determinations by specifying God's objectives in bringing beings into existence at different times which are accompanied before and after. Now *"to God belongs the command before and after"* (30:4), so know that! It is something very fine indeed. (434)

Anyone who washes for the Friday prayer, joins a full bath for the state and for time. Whoever washes for Friday after the prayer has isolated it and lessened that which is called congregational. It is clear that it is prescribed both for Friday and for the Friday noon obligatory congregational prayer. That is the most correct view. It is not unlikely that that was intent of the Lawgiver in it. (435)

4.10. Full Bath After Menstruation

Our position on that will come and we will clarify it. As for its interpretation, constant bleeding is an illness and the servant is commanded to make his worship sound so that no illness enters it. Anyone who has a fault in any of his acts of worship should purify himself from that fault and remove it so that he serves God as a pure servant without taint of any fault or illness in his worship or servanthood. (436)

Menstruation is an impulse of Satan, so there must be full bath after it. God says: *"Of the disgraceful actions of Satan."* (5:90) Therefore the heart must be purified from the call of Satan when it comes to the heart and seizes it inwardly. Its purification is by the call of the angel. The call is the sign, or one of the signs of the concern of God for this heart inasmuch as He turned it away and removed the impulse of Satan. The call of the angel is used in that, and it is the purification of the heart. That is designated by "the two fingers," and both of them are mercy. They are related to The Merciful. If it had not been that God was merciful to His servant by that satanic call, he would not have acquired the reward of resisting it by change in turning from it to acting by the call of the angel. He has two rewards. For this reason, we said that they are related to the name, The Merciful. (437)

4.11. What Life Is Greater Than the Life of the Hearts With God?

If Satan goads him, he strives against himself not to do what he inclines toward. He therefore receives the reward of the striver. If he acts and then turns in repentance following the action after striving, Satan helps him in a previous amount by the action. The action occurs from him and he sees that it is from Satan and he believes and confirms that, as Moses said: *"This is the action of Satan. Truly he is a clear enemy, one who leads astray."* (28:15) He turns in repentance after the actions occurs. By repentance here, I mean regret. It increases the pillars of repentance. It is related that repentance is *tawba*. He has the reward of a martyr when the action occurs from him. The martyr is alive and not dead. What life is greater and more complete than the life of the hearts with God? (438)

What life is greater and more complete than the life of the hearts with God in whatever action it is? Presence with belief in the occurrence of opposition brings the action to life by the life of presence and it asks forgiveness for him until the Day of Rising. This comes from the concern of the Name, The Merciful, to which "the two fingers" are related. Satan hastens to double the good of the servant while he is not aware of it. Avarice blinds him and the evil and sin of that rebellion diminishes him. This is part of God's device with Satan. (439)

4.12. The Form of God's Deceiving Satan

Had Satan known that God would make the servant happy by that call from Satan with a special happiness, he would not have cast any of that to him. This is the divine device which He uses in respect of Satan. I have not seen anyone speak of it. Had it not been for my knowledge of Satan and my recognition of his ignorance and eagerness to incite to opposition, I would not have spoken about this since I know that if it had not been for this barrier, he would not avoid the call of opposition. This is what caused me to mention it because Satan does not understand it by that veil he has in his eagerness for the misery of the servant and his ignorance of the fact that God turns to this particular servant. Every deceived one is deceived by God inasmuch as he is not aware. The one who is not deceived may be aware of that device. (440)

4.13. Full Bath On Account of Semen Which Emerges Without Pleasure

They differ about the necessity for the full bath because of semen which emerges without pleasure. Some say that it is obligatory, and some that full bath is not obligatory for it. That is what I say. The interpretation of major impurity is exile, and exile is only by separation from the homeland. The homeland of the human being is servanthood. When he leaves his homeland and enters into the confines of lordness, he is described by one of the attributes of mastery over the people of his homeland and his peers and does not experience pleasure because of that. He does not give the attribute of mastery its due. The pleasure of the perfection of the perfect is basically not accompanied by pleasure. Perfect joy does not resemble any other joy. When he does not give the attribute its due, he is obliged to wash. It is an admission of what how much he falls short in respect of that divine attribute. From here a full bath is obliged by the one who obliges it for the emission of sperm while awake without pleasure. Anyone who thinks that when the servant in his exile is described by the attribute of perfection which is fitting for the One who is necessary of existence by Himself, it has no rule in him because he is not its place, does not oblige a full bath for him. (441)

In the like of this there remains the jurisdiction of the words of the Prophet: water is from water. It a specifying of what is abrogated as one of them thought. (442)

4.13.1. Full Bath on Account of Sperm Which the Sleeper Finds When He Wakes Up

The gnostic may experience contraction or expansion in a certain state and not recognize its cause. It is a grave matter among the people of the path, for he knows that it is because of heedlessness on his part in watching his heart in its sanctified enlightenment, and the lack of the penetration of his inner eye in the relationship of his state which brings him that attribute. Submission to the events of fate is obliged of him until he sees what the result of that will be for him in the future. (443)

4.14. Complete Presence with God in the Knowledge of Relationships

When he recognizes it, he is obliged to wash himself with complete presence with God in the knowledge of relationships so that he is not ignorant of what comes to him from God in the way of the sanctified enlightenment of making-pure and what the Name is which brings him that, what the Name is which brings it from Him, and what the divine Name is which rules him in the state. These are three: the name of the summoner, the name of the summoned from, and the name of the person coming to him. There is no way for there to be a relationship connecting us to the Essence of God or connecting it to us. *"There is not like Him anything. And He is The Hearing, The Seeing."* (42:11) We are connected to His Names and take on their character and realize them. God gives success. (444)

The Prophet said: When the genitals meet, then a full bath is obligatory. Scholars disagree about this question. Some say that the full bath is obliged on account of the encounter of the genitals, and some say that the full bath is not obligatory by the encounter of the genitals, and that is what I say. (445)

4.15. On the Full Bath Because of Meeting of the Genitals Without Penetration

The interpretation in that is that when the servant crosses his limit and enters the limit of lordness and his Lord lets him enter the limit with Him by what he is described with among the attributes of the possibles, he is obliged to purify himself from that. The incomparability of the servant is that he does not leave his possibility and that the Necessary-by-Himself does not enter His possibility. He does not say that it is permitted that God do such-and-such or it is permitted that He not do so. That demands the probable, and God has absolute necessity. That which must be said is that it is permitted that movement exist from the mover and it is permitted that it not exist. Movement requires the probable. If the knower of God is like this, he must wash, and it is purification from this knowledge by the knowledge which is not included under possibility. This question will be dealt with, God willing. (446)

4.15.1. Distancing in Relation to the Servant and in Relation to the Lord

We have established that sexual impurity is exile, and here it is the exile of the servant from his homeland which he deserves. It is only servanthood or exiling an attribute of the Lord from its homeland. He is therefore described by it or described as a certain possible by it. Purification is obliged in this question without dispute. (447)

4.16. The 150 States Which Oblige the Full Bath

Know that this one full bath mentioned in this chapter is divided into 150 states. The full bath is not obliged for the servant in his heart from every state among them. We will mention all their sources to you, God willing, in ten sections. Each section contains fifteen states so that you might recognize how to receive them if they come to the heart of the servant, because they must come to every heart among the common and the elite. God gives support and inspires. There is no strength except Him.

They are:

Section 1: The divine kingdom, divinity, might, guardianship, faith, standing, yearning, loyalty, darkness, magic, common and elite mercy, safety, purity and the kingdom.

Section 2: Pride, covering, form, character, innocence, sincerity, affirmation, refuse, good counsel, love, force, gift, provision, opening and knowledge.

Section 3: Expansion and contraction, exaltation, raising degrees, lessening the balance, polytheism, justice, obedience, pleasure, contentment, abasement, voices, vision, fate and equity.

Section 4: Kindness, testing, raising the veil, immensity, forbearance, gratitude, ascension, preservation, appraisal, increase, limits, passion, dissension, sainthood, and transfer of property.

Section 5: Kinship, entering joy, severance, deceit, drawing on, calculation, majesty, nobility, watchfulness, answer, wideness, wisdom, lovingness, sending forth and nobility.

Section 6: Testimony, swearing by the truth, entrustment, strength, rigidity in everything, victory, praise, ennumeration, beginning, repetition, charity, speech, forgiveness, the command and the prohibition.

Section 7: Morals, property, rank, increase, belief, life, death, revival, self-subsistence, ecstasy, looking up, unity, sensing eternity, power and capacity.

Section 8: Advance, delay, the first and last abode, hiddenness, lifting the veils, altruism (*ihsan*), return, revenge over-looking, restriction, marriage, eye-service, fabrication, lying.

Section 9: Compassion, possession of kingdom, miracles, terms, exaltation, declaring great, fraud, gatheredness, independence, transgression, sufficiency, generosity, lying, rejection, politics and laws.

Section 10: Forbidding, guidance, benefit, harm, light, innovation, going on, heredity, guidance, intimacy, injury, favor, enthusiasm, resistance and spying. (448)

Know, may God support us and you with a spirit from Him! that all that we mentioned in these sections—and it does not include every state which we did not mention fearing it would take too long—obliges a person to purify his inner self and his heart of them in the school of the People of God and His elite among the people of unveiling, without dispute among the people of tastes in that. Nonetheless the one who purifies himself of most of them needs an ample knowledge of the manner of purification from what we mentioned. Some of them may purify others.

4.17. Rubbing the Entire Body with Hands in the Full Bath: The Disagreement of Scholars About This

We will now return to our goal of presenting the rulings of this purification, which is full washing with water, and its inner interpretations and rulings. We mentioned what obliges ablution and when it is obligatory, so there is no need for us to mention those areas which are common to both purifications. (449)

Some divine law scholars disagree about rubbing the entire body with the hand. Some say that it is a precondition for the completion of purification and some say that it is not a precondition. As for our position, it is bringing water to the body so that it encompasses all of it, whatever makes it arrive. (450)

4.18. Thorough Examination of the Purity of the Inner Self

The inner interpretation in that is a thorough examination of the purity of the inner realm because of its concealment of the love of praise among people through the good they display. So he employs whatever can remove this attribute. If there any barrier which prevents the purification of the inner from being complete, then purity is not obtained. (451)

4.19. The Intention in the Full Bath: Intention Is the Spirit of the Action

Scholars disagree about the condition of the intention in the full bath. Some scholars consider it a precondition, and that is what I say. Some of them do not make it a precondition. Its inner interpretation is that it must be a precondition for the purification of the inner. It is the spirit and life of the act. There must be an intention in the inner act. It was already discussed at the beginning of the book, outer and inner. (452)

4.20. Rinsing the Mouth and Sniffing Water Into the Nose in the Full Bath: The Disagreement of Scholars About Rinsing the Mouth and Sniffing Water into the Nose

Divine law scholars disagree about rinsing the mouth and snuffing water up the nose in full bath. Some say that it is obligatory and some say that it is not. That which we believe in that is that since ablution is contained in full bath, it has its ruling inasmuch as he performs ablution in his full bath. It is related that the Prophet did not rinse his mouth or snuff water up his nose in his full bath except in ablution. I have not seen anyone else speak of the like of this in their dispute about that. (453)

4.20.1. The Ruling About That

The ruling in it, in my opinion, refers to the ruling of ablution. For us, there must be ablution in full bath from sexual impurity. We look at two states in this question: one state for the one who has intercourse and completes it has two ablution in his full bath. If he has intercourse and does not complete it, he has one ablution. Our school is that the meeting of the two genitals without entry does not oblige full bath but obliges ablution. Abu Said al-Khudri and other Companions and al-Amash stated that. The precondition of the order and immediacy in ablution and its interpretation has already been discussed. (454)

4.21. What Breaks This Purification of the Full Bath

It is invalidated by sexual impurity, menstruation, constant bleeding in the woman and the meeting of the genitals. There is no dispute about menstruation and no dispute about emission of sperm with pleasure while awake. There is dispute about other than these two. Some earlier people do not think that the woman has to perform a full bath if she finds liquid from a wet-dream with pleasure. (455)

4.22. The Obligation of Purification after Intercourse: Opinion of the Scholars About This

Some say that it is obligatory with or without entry when the genitals meet. Some say that it is obligatory when sperm is emitted, and that is what I say, and when sperm is emitted without intercourse. A group of the people who follow the literal text say that purification is obliged only by entry. (456)

Its inward interpretation is that intercourse is applied by the effector to the effected by a sort of giving. The effected must be present and aware in respect to that effector among the divine Names, and so purification is not demanded of him. If he is not, then purification is demanded of him. That effector gives the sleep of the heart. This divine name must effect knowledge of one of the phenomenal beings or a knowledge connected to God. In both cases if may be as when he sees himself doing intercourse and does not take by God. It is as charity falls into the hand of The Merciful while the asker takes and God is The Giver. So God is both The Giver and The Taker, so he must not have to do any purification inwardly. (457)

The purification of things is by The Real. If a person withdraws from seeing this and sees that he himself takes the knowledge which God has placed in his heart, then he is obliged to purify himself of seeing himself. It is like that when someone has intercourse by a question which He teaches him by state or words. If it is with presence, he has no purification obliged and he is still in his purity. If he sees himself teaching another by state or words, he is obliged to purify himself of seeing himself. That must be. The men of God in this path move by God and are still by God by witnessing and unveiling. The common do so by presence, belief and faith in what has come about "*the command being in His Hand*" and "*the forelocks of His servants and every animal being in His Hand.*" [cf. Quran 11:56] (458)

Scholars disagree about the description considered in the emission of sperm obliging full bath. Some say that it is by pleasure, while others say that it is by the emission itself, whether or not there is pleasure. (459)

4.23. Natural Pleasure of the Self and Divine Pleasure

The interpretation in this section about pleasure from the one who enjoys it is either that it is from the self or it is divine. If it is natural and from the self, then full bath is obligatory. If it is not from the self, that knowledge, which is in the position of sexual impurity, is either connected to God or connected to a certain phenomenal being. If it is connected to God and its pleasure does not come from the self, he does not need to purify himself. If it is connected to phenomenal beings, then he must purify himself, whether or not there is pleasure. (460)

The meaning of our statement, "divine pleasure," is that the pleasure of perfection is not the pleasure of the person in the state of sanctified enlightenment. The pleasure of perfection in the servant is that he is a pure servant who is not described by exile from his homeland inwardly, even had God placed on him any of the attributes of mastery He wished from His presence. That does not drive him out of his homeland. If it is like that, he does not have sexual impurity since he has no exile and he is still in his homeland. It is the limit of perfection, while purification is recognition of imperfection. (461)

4.24. Someone in the State of Major Impurity Entering the Mosque: The Gnostic Is Always with God

Some say that it is absolutely forbidden and some say that it is forbidden except in the case of someone who passes through it and does not remain, and some say that it is permitted for all. I say this. The interpretation in that is that the gnostic, inasmuch as he is a gnostic, is always with God. The Prophet says in a Tradition: "All the earth was made a mosque for me." The one in the state of sexual impurity does not cease to be on the earth. When he is on the earth, he is in the universal prescribed mosque which is not limited by the conditions of the mosques known by custom. (462)

4.25. The Entire World is Traveling with Souls

Residing is not valid for the gnostic, nor for the entire world, high and low, in his state. He is always traversing with his breaths. Those with knowledge of God see this passage. Those who are not knowers of God imagine that they reside and that existence is different from that. In every breath God brings into existence. He acts and does not invalidate a single breath which is described as abiding. It is as He said: *"Every day He is on an affair."* (55:29) and He said: *"We will attend to you at leisure, O you two dependents"* (55:31) And he said: *The balance is in His Hand: He lowers it and raises*. (463)

4.26. On Taking on the Character of Another: Whenever He Ceases in This, He Cannot Be of That Character

Whoever takes the prohibition in that is dominated by seeing himself as not being a pure place since as he has not taken on the character of the divine names. If he had taken on their character and not been annihilated to taking them on, he has not taken on their character. We believe that whenever someone who takes on the character of the names is not annihilated to his taking on their character, he has not taken on their character. The meaning of him taking on their character is that they rest on him as the one with character depends on that whose character he has. Another may mould him so that in that, he takes on the character of the divine names. That is because the servant is commanded and God does not command himself. Taking on character is obedience to the command of God by the strength and help of God. (464)

4.27. It Is Good Manners for One Impressed by Another's Character to Consider this State Obligatory

Part of good manners is that the one who takes on character sees that he has taken on character and is obligated and that "the Real is his hearing and his sight." Has not God established the source of His servant in the pronoun in his hearing and his sight? Where does this servant go when the source exists? Its goal is to be a limited form in the substance of absolute existence. After this, he has no rank except non-existence, and non-existence does not accept form, so understand! (465)

4.28. Someone in the State of Major Impurity Touching a Copy of the Quran

Divine law scholars disagree about someone in the state of sexual impurity touching a copy of the Quran. Some people say that it is permitted for one in sexual impurity to touch the Quran, and some people forbid that. (466)

4.28.1. All the World is Unfurled and in Existence: the World Is a Written Book

All the universe is the words of God in existence. God said in respect to Jesus: *"His Word that He cast to Mary."* (4:171) He said: *"yet the Words of God would not come to an end."* (31:27) He said: *"To Him Words of what is good rise and He exalts an act in accord with morality."* (35:10) 'Words' is the plural of word. God says to a thing when He desires it: *Be*! and that thing is clothed in taking form and it exists. Existence is a parchment unfurled, and the universe is a written book in it, rather an inscribed book because it has two directions: one direction seeks height and the divine Names, and another aspect seeks the low, and it is nature. For this reason, we preferred the name 'inscribed to 'written'. Each aspect of the inscribed is written. I say on that:

Phenomenal being is wondrous in its transformation
for any who looks at it: inscription and embellishment.
Look at it! You will see wonders in it
since every aspect of the inscribed is written.
Existence has a secret which bewilders the looker.

Phenomenal being is inscribed and the parchment is
unrolled. (467)

4.28.2. The Sources In Existence Are a Written Book

The matter (that is, existence), as we said, is unrolled, and the sources in it are a written book. It is the words of God which do not run dry. Its house is filled, its roof is raised, its sanctity is protected and its command is heard. Where will this servant go while he is part of the sum of the letters of this copy of the Quran? *"Would you call to any other than God if you have been ones who are sincere? Nay! To Him alone you would call and He would remove that for which you had called to Him."* (6:40-41) Do you call upon the associate himself? No, by God, that is only because you believe him to be a divinity. You call on God, not on that form. For this reason, your call is answered although the form possesses neither help nor harm. (468)

4.28.3. "Your Lord has decreed that you should worship none but Him."

Look at His words: *Say: Name them.* (13:33) If they name them, they have the same name. They do not call their object of worship a stone, a tree or a star. He carves it with his hand and then he worships it, so he does not worship its essence. The form comes from his action. If they call them "god," you will recognize that "god" is a servant. This is the realization of the truth of the business in itself. The sign which comes in it indicates what we believe by His words: *"And thy Lord has decreed that you worship none but Him!"* (17:23) In our opinion, it means this is a rule. With the one who has no knowledge among the scholars of forms of the realities, it has the meaning of command. There is a vast distance between the two meanings in respect of realization. (469)

4.28.4. "Worship God as if you see Him"

Muhammad said: "Worship God as if you were seeing Him" in the Tradition when Gabriel asked the Prophet about altruism (*ihsan*) in the presence of a group of the Companions. The Prophet replied: "It is that you worship God as if you saw Him." He said "as if." You know that the imagination is the treasury of sensory things and that God cannot be perceived by our senses, and we only intellectually understand His existence. He said "as if" in order to bring us under the power of sight. By illusion we connect Him to sensory thing and that brings us near to those who worship Him in what they carve. (470)

4.28.5. The Honor of the Letter of Resemblance Which Is kaf (meaning "like")

Therefore reflect on what we have indicated! The matter is only as the Lawgiver confirmed. He confirmed in one place what He denied in another. The knower among us confirms what God confirmed in the place in which God confirmed it and he rejects what God rejected in the place in which God rejected it. There is only pure belief. Only take acceptance from the power of your intellect, and see how noble is the letter of likeness which is "as if." (471)

> "As if" is our Sultan. Look for news of it.
> There is news of it with the report.
> "As if" are letters which have power in phenomenal being
> if you know that knowledge is in the glance.
> It is the Imam in which we act,
> and no human character opposes it.

4.28.6. The Heart Is a Copy of the Quran Containing the Worlds of God

There is no doubt that the People of God make the heart like the copy of the Quran which contains the Word of God, as the heart contains God while the heaven and the earth are too narrow for that. Similarly we are commanded to free the heart from the impurity of others in it. We saw that the Quran contains the word of God and it is His attribute. The attribute is not parted from the one it describes. Anyone who disconnects the attribute, disconnects the described. Anyone one considers the proof of a certain matters, considers the proven which is that matter. Each of the two schools must put the Quran above being touched by someone in sexual impurity. (472)

4.28.7. The Prohibition Against Traveling to the Land of the Enemy with the Quran

We are forbidden to travel with the Quran to the land of the enemy. The copy of the Quran is called the Quran since it is manifested in it. He did not forbid those who carry the Quran [within them] to travel to the land of the enemy, even though the Quran is in their hearts, memorized and preserved, like what is in the copy of the Quran. That is because it is hidden inside of them. Have you not seen that the Prophet was "not stopped from reciting the Quran by anything which was not sexual impurity by the manifestation of the Quran when the letters are recited by which it is articulated and which God has informed us are His Words." He said to His Prophet: *"Then grant him protection so that he may hear the assertions of God."* (9:6) So the Messenger of God recited it to him. (473)

4.28.8. The One in the State of Major Impurity and Who Is a Stranger, Neither Touches Nor Recites the Quran

That is neither fitting for the one in the state of sexual impurity to touch nor recite the Quran as he is exiled from what God demands of him. Distance by the realities and limits never has nearness in it. After an interval, the one who has it draws near to the matter whose nearness he desires. As the Lord is not a servant, so the servant is not a lord because in himself he is a servant, just as the Lord is a Lord by His Essence. The servant is not described by any of the attributes of God with the meaning by which they describe God, and God is not described by what is the reality of the servant. The one in the state of sexual impurity never touches a copy of the Quran by this interpretation and he should not recite it in this state. (474)

4.28.9. The Servant Must Only Display Pure Worship

The servant must only display pure worship. All of him is in the state of sexual impurity, so he does not touch the Quran. He takes on character and the Hand of God touches the Quran. God related from Himself about the servant: "When He loves him, He is his hand by which he strikes." Look at this intense nearness and this unity! Where is he after the realities? By God, only God recognizes God, so do not tire yourself, speculator! Go with God however He goes and take from Him what He acquaints you with from Himself and do not use analogy and thus become bankrupt. Rather despair—and know that the Hand of God is pure in its root and it purifies as does the purification of water which is used in worship. Take note of what I have acquainted you with in this section! (475)

4.28.10. The Recitation of the Quran by Someone in the State of Major Impurity: The Opinion of Scholars About This

Divine law scholars disagree about that. Some people forbid recitation of the Quran by someone in the state of sexual impurity limited and unlimited. Some people permit that. As for the heir, I believe that he does not recite the Quran in the state of sexual impurity to follow the one from whom he inherits. *"Surely in the Messenger of God there has been for you a good, fair example."* (33:21) Nothing except sexual impurity stopped him from reciting the Quran. However, the circumstances applies in our view. It is disapproved to mention God in recitation except in perfect purity. He performed dry ablution to return the greeting, saying: "I do not like to mention God except in purity." Some people permit the one in the state of sexual impurity to recite the Quran limited and unlimited. I say it is unlimited, but I disapprove of it, in order to imitate the Messenger of God. (476)

4.28.11. The Interpretation of That Imitation of the Messenger Demands That Reciting the Quran in the State of Major Impurity Be Forbidden

The one imitating the acts of the Messenger of God forbids unlimited recitation of the Quran in the state of sexual impurity. We have informed you that sexual impurity is an exile, and exile is the removal of the person from his homeland in which he was raised and in which he was born. It is forbidden for whoever is exiled from his homeland to be described by the divine Names in the state of his exile. God says: *"Experience this! Truly thou, thou art the mighty, the generous"* (44:49), as he claims himself to be, so he is in exile from his homeland. He has a claim. (477)

4.28.12. The Quran Is Only Called the Quran by the Comprehensive Reality It Has

That which I say about this question to the people of realization is that the Quran is only called Quran by the comprehensive reality which it possesses. It joins what God reports about Himself and what He reports about His creatures and servants which he tells about them. When one in a state of sexual impurity wants to recite he must either look and be present in what God translates to us by His words—if it is what His servants say—or he looks in it inasmuch as he translates it. If he looks in respect to the one translated from recites—and it is by the first—he does not recite until he is inwardly purified. The form of the purification of his inner self is that God is his tongue by which he speaks as God is his hand in touching the Quran. Then it is God who recites His words, not the servant in sexual impurity. (478)

4.28.13. The Quran Is Recent In Respect to Its Coming, Timeless in Respect to Its Descent

In it the gnostic has what God recites to him of the attributes of His essence which were not reported from any of His creation. Since He speaks to His servant by this Quran, He only intended its acceptance by that information. Its acceptance is only by the heart. When faith accepts it, it is not prevented from articulating it. The Quran was sent down for our sake, and for this reason, it has recently come while its descent is timeless since it is the attribute of the speaker who is God. (479)

4.28.14. "Nothing Except the State of Major Impurity Kept the Messenger of God from Reciting the Quran"

It was reported about the Messenger of God, may God bless him and grant him peace, that "nothing except sexual impurity prevented him from reciting the Quran." That was not the words of the Messenger of God. It was the statement of a relater who was not with him in all his moments. The result is that he says that he did not hear him reciting the Quran in the state of sexual impurity, that is, outwardly. The one who recites the Quran is only obliged to recite it aloud in what is prescribed to be aloud, like the instruction of the teacher and like the prayer said out loud. The prohibition is not validly reported from the Messenger of God in that and it is not related. Tradition does not forbid it. (480)

4.29. The Rule on Bleeding: There Are Types of Bleeding for Women

Know that there are three types of blood: menstruation, constant bleeding (false menstruation) and lochia. All these are particular to women and have no authority in men. The interpretation in that belongs to the self. Femininity dominates it. God called the self 'reproachful' and 'at rest' (both feminine), so He made the soul feminine. Neither the heart nor the spirit has any portion in this blood. (481)

4.29.1. Lying Is the Menstruation of the Self

We say that the People of the Path among the predecessors and a group of others who share with the people of God in disciplines and in strivings who are intelligent, have agreed that lying is the menstruation of the self. Therefore, truthfulness in this is the purification of the self from this menstruation. (482)

4.29.2. Interpretation of Menstrual Blood

The blood of menstruation only emerges with health, and constant bleeding or false menstruation only emerges with illness. It emerges because of a fault. This one has a certain evaluation and that has a certain evaluation. The interpretation of that is that the menstruation of the self which is lying—and as we said, it is the blood which emerges in health—is lying against God. God says about it, "Who could do greater wrong than someone who invents lies against God . . . or who says: *"It was revealed to me, when nothing is revealed to him?*" (6:93) The Messenger of God said: "Whoever intentionally tells a lie against me should take his seat in the fire." He said: "Intentionally," and that is when it emerges in health. (483)

4.29.3. Interpretation of the Blood of Constant Bleeding

As for the one who has a doubt, that is not the case. This person lies while he recognizes that he is lying. The one in doubt is truthful in himself even though he lies in the heart of the matter. As for the interpretation of constant bleeding, it is lying because of a fault, but it does not prevent prayer or intercourse. This shows you that it is not a harm. Menstruation is a harm because the man is harmed by intercourse during menstrual blood, but he is not harmed by it during blood that is the result of constant bleeding. If it results from an illness, it is this bleeding. If it indicates the false—which is non-existence—it still has a rank in existence which is its articulation. That which is meant by it is repelling harm from whatever it should be repelled by that lying, or attracting prescribed benefit which must appear with this in it and because of it. It is nearness to God to the extent that, had he been truthful in this abode, it would have become distant from God. Can you not see that the woman who bleeds constantly is not prevented from praying in spite of the flow of blood? (484)

4.29.4. Interpretations of Lochia

Lochia blood is the same as menstrual blood. When it lasts longer than the determined time of menstruation or deviates from the description which menstrual blood has, it no longer comes under the ruling of menstruation. Meticulousness about lochia blood is more to the point than meticulousness about menstrual blood without lochia. God kept it in the womb and then released it only in order to make the birth canal slippery out of compassion for the mother. Through that, the birth of the child is made easy for the woman. The birth of the child is pure growth, emerging in God's creation in the natural form and confirming His sovereignty by which He holds the atoms together. Because of this intention, lochia blood has a special description like someone who seeks help by maintaining the remembrance of God by the maintaining of those who remember God with a particular description. Lochia blood has a time and a period in the divine law just as menstrual blood does. Constant bleeding has no definite period at which it ceases. (485)

4.29.5. The Maximum and Minimum Days of Menstruation and the Minimum Days of Purity: The Opinion of Scholars About This

Scholars disagree about this. Some say that the maximum of the days of menstruation is fifteen, some say ten and some say that the maximum of the days of menstruation is seventeen. As for the minimum days of menstruation, some say that there is no limit, and that is what I say, and that the minimum of menstruation, for us, is a minute. Some say that the minimum is a day and a night, and some say three days. As for the minimum days of purity, some say ten days, some say eight, some say fifteen, some say seventeen and some say an hour. I say that. Its maximum has no limit. (486)

4.29.6. The Time of the Lying of the Self Is the Intention; There Is No Limit to It

The time of the lying of the self is the intention. It extends as long as the self extends until one is purified of that by repentance. There is no limit to its maximum or minimum. Similarly, the time of purity generally has no limit. There is no limit to truthfulness although places in the divine law deem it to be praiseworthy or blameworthy. Its basic root is praise. Lying is also deemed to be praiseworthy or blameworthy in various places although its basic root is blame. One must therefore be truthful all of the time. One must avoid lying ways. This would be lying because of a fault, and that resembles the blood of constant bleeding. (487)

4.29.7. Lochia Blood, Its Minimum and Maximum: Opinions of the Scholars About the Limit of Lochia Blood

Scholars disagree on this question. Some say that there its minimum has no limit, and I say that. Some say its limit is fifteen days. Some say eleven and some say twenty. As for its maximum time, some say sixty days, some say seventeen, some forty and some say thirty days for a boy and forty days for a girl. It is more appropriate in that to refer to the states of women. There is no established custom to refer to in it. (488)

4.29.8. There Is No Time Limit for the Intention

There is no time limit for the intention, as we said concerning menstrual blood. Menstrual blood is the same as lochia blood, and we have already considered it. The Messenger of God, may God bless him and grant him peace, said to a menstruating woman, "You have your lochia," using this expression. (489)

4.29.9. Blood Which a Pregnant Woman Sees: The Disagreement of Scholars About This

They disagree about that and whether it is menstrual blood or the blood of constant bleeding. The rule of each is according to what he believes. (490)

4.29.10. Pregnancy Is an Attribute of the Self

Pregnancy is an attribute of the self when it is filled with the matter which it finds. It manifests that in another aspect which is lying. That may arise from a habit it has as one of them said:

> A man only lies because of his humiliation,
> bad habit or lack of good manners (491)

He said: "his humiliation" for kings do not lie. He said, "from lack of good manners" since there is the tradition, "When someone tells a lie, the angels withdraw thirty miles from him because of the foul odor which that brings." When one lies about something which it is not permitted to lie about, he shows bad manner with the angels. The angels are harmed by whatever harms the descendants of Adam, and man is harmed by a foul odor. It is the same with the angels because of the closeness of the resemblance between the generation of angels and the generation of the spirit of man.

4.29.11. Yellow Discharge and Cloudy Discharge and Whether or Not It Is Menstruation: The Disagreement of Scholars About This

Scholars disagree about yellow discharge and cloudy discharge and whether or not they are considered to be menstruation. Some say that they are menstruation during the days of menstruation. Some say they are only menstruation if there is a trace of blood. Some say they are not menstruation, and that is what I say. (492)

4.29.12. Lying by a Doubt and Pure Lying

When one lies because of a doubt, that person is not someone who lies intentionally. It is better that he leave it if he recognizes that it is doubtful. It is only called a doubt because it resembles the truth from a certain aspect, and resembles the false from another. It is better to abandon the like of this unless that is accompanied by repelling a harm or acquiring a benefit of the religion or this world, as opposed to the pure lie which is for its own sake. The man of intelligence never falls into this at all. The lie which is in the position of the blood of constant bleeding should consider the best interest of the religion and the best interest of this world in it. (493)

4.29.13. *On What Menstrual Blood Prevents in Its Time: Menstruation in Its Time and Lying in Acts of Worship*

Know that menstruation in its time prevents the obligatory prayer, fasting, intercourse and circumambulation. Lying in intimate conversation is that you are outwardly in the obligatory prayer while inwardly with other-than-God—the forbidden and the like. Its consideration in the obligatory fast is that the fast is a restraint, but you have not restrained yourself from lying as the menstruating woman does not refrain from eating and drinking. It is obligatory lying provided by the divine law. Its interpretation in circumambulation of the House—which resembles the best of forms—a circle—is unlimited lying. It is to persist in lying. (494)

4.29.14. *The Intention of the Believer in Intercourse*

Its interpretation in intercourse is that the intention of the one who believes in it is the child. When the premises are false, the result emerges from a false source. The result can be true and it can be like our premises. Harm reverts to the one who has intercourse. He says in the time of lying: "You do not have God present in your thought." It is bad manners with God, a lack of modesty before Him and boldness towards Him. How can the servant be bold to a Master and not embarrassed before Him in spite of his knowledge and realization that He sees him: "*Knows he not that God sees*?" (96:14) (495)

4.29.15. *Intimate Contact with a Menstruating Woman: The Opinion of the Religious Scholars About This*

Scholars disagree about the form of intimate contact with a menstruating woman. Some people say that it is permitted with the menstruating woman above the waist-wrapper. Some people say that one only avoids the place of blood in the menstruating woman, and I say that. (496)

4.29.16. *Lying and Belief Are Not Joined Together*

We said that menstruation is the lying of the self. The Messenger of God was asked: "Can a believer fornicate?" He replied: "Yes." He was asked: "Can a believer drink?" He said: "Yes." He was asked: "Can a believer steal?' He replied: "Yes." He was asked: "Can a believer lie?" He said: "No." When you see your self as another self doing what is inappropriate, then insist that in its actions, it must avoid telling lies against God and His Messenger. "The one who grazes around the sanctuary is about to fall into it." (497)

4.29.17. Lying Against People Leads to Lying Against God

Whoever accustoms himself to lying is gradually drawn on by nature until he lies against God. Nature will rob him. God says: "*And had he fabricated against Us some sayings, truly We would have taken him by the right hand and then We would have severed his life-vein.*" (69:44-46) So He warns His servants in the strongest possible terms against forging lies and ascribing them to God. This is the rule about everyone who lies about God. It is related that the one who lies in his dream will be obliged to knot together two barley-corns of fire, by a relationship which has come from an unsound composition. It is not joined in the heart of the matter. Similarly, he cannot knot together these two barley-corns. This is an obligation which is not possible. God will only punish him on the Day of Rising by doing it, nothing else. (498)

4.29.18. Intercourse with a Menstruating Woman Before the Full Bath After Actual Purification: The Opinion of Religious Scholars About This

God says, "*Come not near them until they become pure.*" (2:222) or it is read, "*they become pure.*" Whoever says it is permitted reads "pure." Whoever says it is not permitted reads "purified," which is probable. My position is the first. Some say that that is permitted when they are pure by the maximum period of menstruation according to their school. Some say that it is permitted when she washes her genitals with water, and I say that. (499)

4.29.19. Casting Knowledge Into the Self of the Student

It is the knowledge which the teacher casts into the self of the learner when he has a recent false claim by the levity of his self. He can give him knowledge connected to formation which will not lead him to the use of one full bath. So it is refuted by two intentions and so he has a reward twice over. If he does not repent from that claim, but does not utter it in the state, then he is pure of place by heedlessness in that moment. If the thought occurs to him to retract that claim, he is in the position of a woman who washes her genitals after seeing purity. If she does not wash, it is as he repents from that claim by the action of that thought, which is like the woman washing after purity. (500)

4.29.20. Someone Who Has Intercourse With a Menstruating Woman: Does He Make Expiation? The One Who Gives Wisdom to Unsuitable People

Some say there is no expiation for it, and I say that. Some say there is expiation. (501)

There is no doubt that the scholar who gives knowledge to other than its people has wronged it. If someone thinks that this action requires expiation, its expiation is that he look into the one who is worthy of the useful knowledge in the sight of God. He thirsts for that and he sets out from himself to teach it and to cool the heat of thirst and puts it in its place and with its people. So the expiation in that is for the excess of the first. The one who does not think that that has expiation, says that he repents and asks forgiveness, and that he does not have to seek to teach anyone as expiation.

4.29.21. *Ruling on the Purity of a Woman With Constant Bleeding: The Opinions of Scholars About This*

Divine law scholars disagree about the purity of the rule of the woman with constant bleeding. Some say that she only has one purification when she knows that her menstruation is finished, and she does not have to do ablution or full bath. Her rule is the same as the rule of the woman without constant bleeding. That is what I say. Another section are those who say that she only has one purification and that she has to do ablution for each prayer. That is more cautious. Some say that say she does a full bath for each prayer. Some say that she joins two prayers together with one full bath. (502)

4.29.22. *Lying at Times Is Lawful and Truth Prohibited*

In our school, the woman with constant bleeding does not have to purify herself since the woman with constant bleeding is pure. It is like that with a person who lies for a prescribed benefit, where it is permitted according to the divine law. Indeed, he would be rebellious if he told the truth in that situation. He does not have to repent for that lie. So it is as if the blood of constant bleeding is not the same as menstrual blood, although they share in being blood. The prescribed lie which is lawful is not the same as the forbidden lie which occurs, even those they both share in being lies. That is to say something about a matter which it is not actually the case. (503)

Some think that repentance is due to the fact that the name "lie" is applied by reality, whether it is permitted or obligatory, like Habib al-Ajami in his story with Hasan al-Basri when al-Hajjaj was seeking him to kill him. The story is famous. He said that there is repentance for it as one says about the full bath of a woman with constant bleeding because they share in the name "menstruation" "constant bleeding" is derived from menstruation. (504)

4.29.23. *Intercourse With the Woman With Constant Bleeding: The Opinions of Religious Scholars About This*

Divine law scholars disagree about that, taking three positions. Some allow it, which is what I say, some do not allow it, and some do not allow it unless it lasts for a long time. (505)

4.30.24. *Teaching Does Not Prevent the One Who Learns from Him from Lying*

Teaching does not prevent the one who learns from lying except for a prescribed reason and cause. That does not detract from his good reputation. The like of this occurred among the great perfected men. (506)

5 On Dry Ablution

5.1. The Linguistic and Legal Meanings of Dry Ablution

Dry ablution is to aspire for clean dust. That dust is part of what is called earth, be it soil, sand, stone or arsenic. The one who makes a distinction between any of these and their likes does not permit dry ablution with what is separate of them from the earth, except for soil itself, because a text has come on that and the earth, whether or not it is separate from the earth. (507)

5.2. The Purification of the Servant Is Fulfilling What Is Obligatory for the Servant

The aim is to the earth since it is abased, and it is to aim for servanthood absolutely because servanthood is humility. Worship is part of it. So the purification of the servant is by fulfilling what is obligatory for the servant to have of humility, need and stopping at the rules of his Master and His limits and obeying His commands. The one who distinguishes whether it is earth only performs dry ablution with earth. That is because man was created from earth. We are its sons. That is also because it retains poverty and need, as the Arabs say, "The man's hand is dusty" when he is poor. (508)

5.3. When Water Is Present, Dry Ablution Is Invalid and So When the Divine Law Brings Something of Divine Knowledge, the Imitation of the Intellect in that Matter Is Invalid

Earth is also the lowest of the elements. So the servant stops with his reality inasmuch as his formation was pure from every impurity which would bring him out of this station. This is only when he cannot find water. Water is knowledge, and by knowledge gives life to hearts, as water gives life to the earth. It is like the state of the imitator in knowledge of God. In our opinion, the imitator in knowledge of God is the one who limits his intellect in looking into his recognition of God in respect of reflection. So as when the one performing dry ablution finds water or is able to use it, dry ablution is invalid, that is also the case when the divine law brings something of divine knowledge: the imitation of the intellect by its speculation is then invalid in knowledge of God in that matter, especially when it does not conform in the proof—he refers the proof of the intellect back to the divine law. So he has both divine law and intellect in this matter, so know that. (509)

5.4. On Dry Ablution Taking the Place of Ablution: The Opinions of the Religious Scholars on This

Divine law scholars agree that dry ablution takes the place of lesser purification. They disagree about major purification. We do not say that it replaces anything. We say that it is prescribed purification specific to conditions mentioned by the divine law. It has come from a divine law prescribed by the Prophet not from the Mighty Book, that teaching is a replacement. So there is no difference between dry ablution and every prescribed purification. We said prescribed because it is not linguistic purification. The details in this section will come, God willing. (510)

Some say that this purification means purification of earth in place of greater purification. Some say that it is not a replacement for the greater one. The expressions of lesser and greater purification is related to general purification in washing all of the body and particularly some of the limbs of ablution. Lesser impurity is what obliges ablution and major impurity is everything which obliges full bath. (511)

5.5. The Inner Interpretation: Every Impurity Which Detracts from Belief Obliges Full Bath

Every impurity which detracts from belief obliges full bath with water, which is renewing belief by knowledge if he is one of the people of speculation in logical proofs. So he believes by logical proof. He is like the one who finds water who can use it. If he is not one of the people of strenuous endeavor and is an imitator, he must purify himself with belief from that impurity which removes belief from him by using the sword or good opinion. He is the one who performs dry ablution with earth when water is absent or when he cannot use water. (512)

5.6. Imitation in Belief

This is according to the school of those who think that dry ablution takes the place of major purification. They think that there is dry ablution on account of the state of sexual impurity. As for the school of those who think that the one in the state of sexual impurity does not perform dry ablution, like Ibn Masud and others, they are those who do not think that there is imitation in belief. Rather there must be recognition of God and what He obliges, permits and makes lawful by logical proof. A group of the theologians stated that. (513)

5.7. Analogy in the Rules of the Divine Law

As for dry ablution taking the place of lesser purification, it is because something detracts from a particular question, not from belief, due to the absence of a text in the Book, confirmed sayings and actions of the Prophet (*sunna*) or consensus regarding that. Similarly, as he is permitted to perform dry ablution in this lesser purification as a substitute, analogy is permitted to him in rule in that question by a cause which joins this question which has no articulated rule and another question whose rule is articulated in the Book, the confirmed sayings and actions of the Prophet or consensus. (514)

5.8. Understanding (*Fiqh*) the Creed (*Din*) Is Not Analogy Through Rules

Our position in our statement is that dry ablution is not a substitute, but rather a prescribed specific purification for a particular situation which was prescribed by the one who prescribed the use of water for this particular worship. That was by God Almighty and His Messenger. So it is not a substitute. It comes from deriving the rule in that question from a text related in the Book or in the confirmed sayings and actions of the Prophet. The rule enters into this question in the content of the words which are understanding of the way of life." God said: *"It may be that they become learned in the way of life."* (9:122) Analogy is not required in that. (515)

The example of that is a person who strikes his father with a stick or whatever. The people of analogy say: We have no text on this question. But God said: *"Thou shalt not say to them a word of disrespect nor scold them."* (17:23) We said: Since the prohibition is related about saying *"a word of disrespect,"* which is insignificant, then striking with a stick is far worse. So by the lesser, the Lawgiver indicates the greater and thus there must be an analogy based on it. Saying *"a word of disrespect"* and striking with a stick are both harmful, so we make that analogy of striking with the stick about which there is nothing, and connect it to the articulated statement about saying a word of contempt. (516)

We said that we do not give a rule about anything contrary to the Lawgiver in which He can obligate, nor make rule, especially not in this sort of thing. Were it not that other than this was related in the words of the divine law, we would not oblige this analogy nor state it, nor join it to saying a word of contempt. We judge by what has come. That is the words of God: *"And kindness to the ones who are one's parents."* (17:23) It is a comprehensive statement, and from this comprehensive and general statement, we derive the rule about all that is not kind. Striking with a stick is not the commanded kindness in the divine law which must be shown in our behavior towards our fathers. So we only judge by the text and do not have need of analogy. (517)

5.9. The Creed (din) Is Complete: It Is Not Permitted to Add or Detract From It

The religion is complete, and it is not permitted to add to it as it not permitted to decrease from it. Anyone who strikes his father with a stick is not kind towards him. Anyone who is not kind towards his father has rebelled against how God has commanded that he treat his parents. Anyone who refutes the words of his parents does something which is not pleasing to his parents which he cannot do. It is affirmed that disobedience of parents is one of the major wrong actions. This is why we said that purification with earth, which is dry ablution, is not a replacement. Indeed, it is prescribed just as water is prescribed. It has a particular description in action, and it is clear that we only do it in certain circumstances and not always. Ablution and full bath are not like that. There must be a substitute in the place of the substituted. This is what occurs in the place of the substituted in the action. *"And God says The Truth and He guides to the way."* (33:4) (518)

5.10. The One Who Is Permitted to Use This Purification (Dry Ablution): Dry Ablution for the Sick and Traveler When They Have No Water

Divine law scholars agree that dry ablution is permitted for someone who is sick and the traveler when there is no water, or in our opinion, when it cannot be used although water exists due to an illness he has which he fears will worsen or that he might die. A text is related on that. (519)

5.11. Who is a traveler and a sick person?

The traveler can investigate the proof. He is traveling through his premises and his instruction until he has a result in the form of a ruling in the desired question. The ill person is the one whose natural form does not give him investigation into proofs because he knows the evil of his natural form and his incapacity to reach the goal from reflection. It is obligatory for him to avoid investigation. He is commanded to believe by imitation. (520)

5.12. Who is the imitator, the speculator, and the one with (in the state of) unveiling?

We said earlier that the imitator in belief is like the one who performs dry ablution with earth because earth does not have the cleanliness in purification that water does. However, we called it purification in the divine law, that is, earth, as opposed to water. The one who looks believes first by imitation. He wants to investigate the proofs and to look into what he believes. He has no doubt that he acquires knowledge by the proof into which he investigates. He emerges from imitation to knowledge, or he acts on what he imitates. That action results for him in knowledge of God. He distinguishes between the truth and the false with sound insight, not mere imitation in it. It is the "knowledge of unveiling." God said: *"O those who have believed! If you are Godfearing of God."* (8:29) It is the same as what we said. He said: *"So be Godfearing of God and God teaches you"* (2:282) and He said: *"The Merciful. He taught the Quran. He created the human being. He taught him the clear explanation."* (55:1-4) He said: *"We had given mercy from Us and We had taught him knowledge which proceeds from Our Presence."* (18:65) (521)

5.13. The Journey of the Intellect Through Logical Investigation

It is related that "the scholars are the heirs of the Prophets," and he called them men of knowledge. "The Prophets do not bequeath dinar nor dirham. They bequeath knowledge." Taking knowledge is by strenuous effort. Travel is an act. As the intellect travels with its logical insight in the world, so the one with action travels with his action. They share in the result. He added the one with action is based on insight into what he knows so that doubt does not enter into it. The one with speculation is not lacking in doubt entering into its proof. So the one with action is more entitled to the name "knower" than the one with speculation. There will be discussion on travel which permits and does not permit doing the traveler's prayer in this book, God willing. (522)

5.14. The Sick Person Finding Water but Fearing to Use It: The Opinion of the Religious Scholars About This

Divine law scholars disagree about a sick person who finds water but fears to use it. Some say it is permitted for him to perform dry ablution, which is what I say, and that he does not have to repeat the obligatory prayer. Some say that he does not perform dry ablution when there is water, and that a sick person and fearful are the same in that. Some say that they perform dry ablution and then repeat the obligatory prayer when they find water. Some say that he performs dry ablution and then he finds water before the time is gone, he does ablution and repeats the obligatory prayer. If he finds it when the time has gone, he does not repeat it. (523)

5.15. Imitation in Creeds and Imitation in Rules

The sick person is the one whose natural form does not accord investigation. He is ill even with the existence of proofs, although he fears destruction and leaving the religion if he looks into it by his incapacity. We saw that a group of them left the religion by investigation when their natural form was faulty, although they claimed that they were based on sound knowledge. They are as God said: *"They assume that they are doing good."* (18:104) If someone like this desires to be saved, he accepts creeds by imitation, as he takes rules. He should imitate the people of the Traditions rather than others. This imitation of the prophetic Tradition is based on knowledge of God in which there is no interpretation and is free of specific incomparability and has no similarity. This is because most of the common people are not aware. This is the interpretation of the sick person who finds water and fears to use it. (524)

5.16. The Ruling About the One Who Is Resident and Lacks Water: The Opinion of Religious Scholars About This

Some say that he is permitted to perform dry ablution, and I say that. Some say that the one resident who is healthy is not permitted to perform dry ablution when there is no water. (525)

5.17. Residence By a Contract Which Binds One

Then he understood that the one resident is the one who is based on the bond which connects him to his fathers and educators, consulted himself and was independent. Does he remain on that bond of his or investigate the proof until he recognizes the Truth? Some say that what his fathers and teachers taught him is enough for him and he should occupy himself with action. Investigation might make him bewildered so that he is not safe. He is the one who says that there is dry ablution when water is lacking. We already stated that water is knowledge because they (both, water and knowledge) share in giving life. This one who is resident is lacking a proof in reality. He does not see the relationship between God and His creation. So creation is not a satisfactory guide to knowledge of the essence of The Real. His remaining with what he has of imitator is more fitting. (526)

5.18. Lack of Imitation in the Contract and Lack of Study of the Evidence

Whoever says that he is not permitted to perform dry ablution, even if there is no water, says that he does not imitate, even if he does not look into the proof. When belief is mixed with the confusion of the hearts, he clings to it and finds it impossible to return from it. He does not know how to acquire nor how it is. It is necessary knowledge which he has. He emerges from the principle of what imitation gives although he is not one who investigates nor one with a proof. Most people are like this in their creeds. The lack of water in respect of this one is that he does not feel secure that investigation will make him fall into doubt which may bring him out of belief. (527)

5.19. The One Who Finds Water but Is Prevented from Going Out to It Out of Fear of the Enemy: The Opinions of Religious Scholars About This

Scholars disagree about the one who in this state. Some say that he is permitted to perform dry ablution, which is my position, and some say he does not perform dry ablution. (528)

5.20. Imitation and Discernment Into the Gnosis of God

Fear comes from investigating the proof in order to look into it so that it will lead him to knowledge by the proven. He is ignorant of the proof itself being a proof. He imitates someone in this being a proof of a certain matter which concerns him and which requires investigation and thought in what he is required to accept as a proof of the knowledge of God. If he is the first, then he continues with his imitation in knowledge of God. It is the one to whom it is said: "Perform dry ablution." Whoever says that he is not permitted to perform dry ablution, says that this fear does not oblige him not to look. He must look. (529)

5.21. The One Who Fears the Cold in Using Water: The Opinion of the Religious Scholars About This

Scholars disagree about the one in this state. Some say that he is permitted to perform dry ablution when he thinks it probable that he will become ill if he uses water. Some say that he is not permitted to perform dry ablution. My position is the first. (530)

5.22. The Sufi is the Child of the Moment

The Sufi is the child of the moment. If his moment is health, he is not ill nor very ill, so he does not perform dry ablution. Illusion does not demand that knowledge be eliminated. Fear here is illusion, so he does not remain with imitation and must look into the proofs. Anyone who says that it is not permitted for him to perform dry ablution, even if its moment is fear, is not sound. Fear is a defect and an illness. He must remain with imitation. (531)

5.23. The Intention in Purification by Dry Ablution: The Opinion of Religious Scholars About This

Scholars disagree about the intention in the purification of dry ablution. Some say that he needs to have an intention and some say that he does not to have one. I say the first. God said to us: *"They were commanded but to worship God as ones who are sincere and devoted in the way of life to Him."* (98:5) Dry ablution is worship and sincerity is the same as intention. (532)

5.24. Belief and Intention

Belief comes from necessary knowledge or from good opinion of a scholar or a parent so he does not need an intention. The pre-condition of intention exists in him. It is at the beginning of the action in connecting it to what is prescribed. The one whose belief system has this strength is not an actor that he needs an intention. The Will of God, who is the Creator of this action, is enough here. He does not engender anything except from the connection of His Will to bringing it into existence and it is only by Him. God said: *"Our saying to a thing when We wanted it is that We say to it: Be! Then it is!"* (16:40) This action is engendered in the servant, and there must be the principle of what we mentioned in it. The exception is an unbeliever submitting to Islam. This requires intention because he did not have anything of nearness to God through the specific revelation of Islam. Rather, he had believed that Islam was disbelief and that entering into it would distance him from God. (533)

5.25. The One Who Does Not Find Water: Is It a Condition That He Seek It? The Opinion of Religious Scholars About the One Who Does Not Find Water

Scholars disagree about the one who does not find water. Some say that it is a condition that he seek after it, and he must do that. Some say that it is not a condition that he seek after it. That is what I say. (534)

5.26. The Imitator Is Not Obliged to Seek for the Proof of the One He Follows

The imitator is not obliged to seek for a proof either in the branches or in the fundamentals. That which the imitator is obliged to do when he does not know the question through the principle governing the event is that he should learn it from the people of remembrance of God. He must ask for an opinion. God said: *"So ask the People of Remembrance if you have not been knowing."* (16:43) The one who thinks that seeking water is a condition is the one who seeks the proof from the questioned person for that which he gives an opinion. He asks whether it is from the Book or confirmed sayings and actions of the Prophet (*sunna*), or he asks him to tell him that this is the rule of God or the rule of His Messenger. If he says to him, "This is my opinion as the people of opinion have it in their books,'" he is forbidden to follow him in it. God is only worshiped by what He has prescribed in the Book or the confirmed sayings and actions of the Prophet (*sunna*). God is not worshiped by anyone's opinion. (535)

5.27. The Arrival of the Moment of Obligatory Prayer Is a Precondition for This Purification: The Opinion of the Religious Scholars About This

The people of knowledge, may God be pleased with them, differ about the condition of the arrival of the moment of obligatory prayer for this purification. Some say that it is a precondition, which I say, and some say that it is not a precondition. (536)

5.28. The Moment from the Legal and Inner Aspects

For us, the moment specifies the connection of when the divine law tells the responsible individual what he is obligated to do, outwardly and inwardly. Inwardly, it is divine Self-disclosure which comes suddenly upon the heart. In the path, that is called "attack." (537)

5.29. The Definition of the Hands Which God Mentioned in This Purification: The Disagreement of the Religious Scholars About This

God Almighty said: Perform dry ablution: *"Then aim at getting wholesome, dry earth. Then wipe your faces and your hands."* (4:43; 5:6) The people of knowledge, may God be pleased with them, differ about the definition of the hands in this purification. Some say that it is the same as their definition in ablution. Some say that you only wipe the palms. Some say that it is recommended to wipe to the elbows although the obligation is the palms. Some say that the obligation is to the shoulders. I say that the least amount of what is called "hand" in Arabic is obligatory. Whatever is more than the least of what is called 'hand' I consider supererogatory. (538)

5.30. The Human Being in Respect of His Essence and His Inclination

Earth and dust are the basis of the human organism. It is the realization of his servanthood and abasement. Then the impediment of pretension occurs. The Messenger said about it: He is created upon His form. For us, that is his predisposition which God created in him and by which he can acquire the divine Names by what his reality accords him. There is disagreement about what is meant by "the form" and the conscience. There is no text on the subject. By this relationship, he is proud, high and arrogant. He is therefore commanded to purify himself of this arrogance with earth and dust. It is the reality of his servanthood. He is purified by seeing the basis of his creation from which he was created. (539)

God Almighty says about the one who is like this when he presented the cure of this thought produced by arrogance: *"So let the human being look on of what he was created."* They are offspring. *"He was created of water, that which gushes forth,"* (86:5-6) and it is *"a despicible water."* Power and giving are part of what he says he lays claim to, yet he is basically formed with incapacity and miserliness. These are among the attributes of the hands. When he makes this claim and sees that he has apparent pride and generosity, nobility and giving, he is told: "Purify yourself of these attributes by looking at your intrinsic formation of weakness and miserliness." God Almighty said: *"And whoever is protected from his own stinginess,"* (64:16; 59:9) and He said: *"And when good afflicted him, begrudging."* (70:21) When he looks at this root, his "soul" is cleansed and purified of pretension. (540)

5.31. The Number of Times the One Performing Dry Ablution Strikes the Earth: The Disagreement of Scholars About the Number of Times One Strikes the Earth

Scholars disagree about the number of times the one performing dry ablution should strike the earth. Some say once. Some say twice. Among those who say twice are those who say there is one blow for the face and one for the hands. Some say there are two blows for the hands and two blows for the face. Our school is that the one who strikes once has performed it and there is no objection to someone striking twice. The Tradition of one blow is more confirmed, so I prefer it. (541)

5.32. The Unity (*Tawhid*) of Actions and Wisdom of Causes

The unity of actions and wisdom of causes is turning to that by which this purification exists. Whoever is dominated by unity (*tawhid*) in his actions says it is one blow. Whoever is dominated by the wisdom of the cause which God has set there and to which He has related the action while freeing him of it as He said: "*God created you and what you do*" with affirmation and negation, says that it is two blows. Whoever sees that in every action says that there are two blows for each limb. God knows best. (542)

5.33. Bringing Earth to the Limbs of the One Who Performs the Dry Ablution: The Disagreement of the Religious Scholars About This

Scholars disagree about that. Some say that it is obligatory. Some say that it is not obligatory, but it is obligatory for the hand to reach the limb of the one who performs dry ablution after he strikes the earth or dust with his hand. The outward meaning is to make it reach the limb according to His word: *from it*. (543)

5.34. Purification of the Self by Abasement Which Is Its Origin

We said that when the self is purified by the abasement—which is its basis—from the might to which it lays claim, then it is not obligatory to make earth reach the limbs. If we had moved abasement to the place of might, it would have prevented the acquisition of abasement in that place because that which is in the place has more strength to resist that which comes to remove it. If they had shared in the same place, two opposites would have been joined, and it would not be proper to remove one of them more than the other. (544)

5.35. The Self Is Turned Towards the Presence of Might

The sound position in that is that the self is turned towards the presence of might. From the light of might it obtains that which leads it to make its claims. It is said to it. "Turn your face towards your abasement and weakness from which you were created. If you still have the lights of this might, you are you." So he stops with them and it may be that he will continue to possess that. When he looks at the abasement and weakness of the self, the lights of might depart from it by the Essence. So it is in need of its Creator and abased under His power. For this reason, some say that it is not obligatory to make earth reach the limbs of the one who performs dry ablution. Some say that the word here refers to partition and that earth must reach the limb. He says that the attribute is not independent, so it must have something on which it is based, and that is none other than man's reality. His attribute must be abasement and then his purification is sound. This person says that it is obligatory to make earth reach the limb of the one who does dry ablution. (545)

5.36. That With Which the Purification Is Done: The Disagreement of the Religious Scholars About This

Scholars disagree about the definition of earth. Some say that dry ablution is only permitted with pure dust itself. Some say that it is permitted with whatever rises on the surface of the earth—sand, pebbles and dust. Some say the like of this and add whatever is generated from earth—like lime, arsenic, gypsum, clay and marble. Some make it conditional that the dust be on the ground. Some say the dust of garments and brick. As far as we are concerned, it is permitted to do dry ablution with all that is in the earth which the name "earth" designates. If it is separated from the earth, that is only permitted with dust itself. (546)

5.37. Rules in the Divine Law Follow Names and States

It was previously stated that the name "earth" leaves it when it is moved, and it is called arsenic, stone, sand or dust. Since the text used the word "dust," we found that this name accompanies earth. When it is separated from earth, we do not find anything except it (that is, dust). Therefore, we are obliged to do dry ablution with dust, whether or not it separated from the earth. The rules of the divine law follow names and states. The principle changes when the name and state change. (547)

5.38. What Breaks This Purification: The Agreement and Disagreement of the Religious Scholars About This

Scholars agree that dry ablution is invalidated by all that invalidates ablution and purity. They disagree about two matters. One of them is when one wants to pray an obligatory prayer with the same dry ablution with which he prayed another prayer. Some say that desiring to perform the second prayer invalidates it. Some say that it does not invalidate it, and that is what I say. I think it better that he perform dry ablution again because our school is that dry ablution is not a substitute for ablution. It is rather another type of purification which the divine law stipulates with particular conditions. It is not considered to be a substitute. We said that the principle follows the state and the principle changes as the states and names change. (548)

5.39. As for Each Self-disclosure (*tajalli*) There Is a Purification so for Each Obligatory Prayer There Is a Dry Ablution

As a Self-disclosure is not repeated, so this dry ablution is not repeated. Each Self-disclosure has a purification, and each prayer has a dry ablution. Whoever looks at the self-disclosure itself, inasmuch as it is a self-disclosure, not inasmuch as it is a Self-disclosure in such-and-such, says that one can pray as much as he likes with one dry ablution, like someone in ablution. There is no difference. It is our statement:

Until when the splendor of His face appears to the eye
and to me, come quickly then. It is only that splendor. (549)

5.40. Finding Water When One Has Performed the Dry Ablution: The Imitation of the Intellect and the Imitation of the Divine Law in Divine Matters

Some say that finding water invalidates dry ablution. Some say that what invalidates it is minor impurity. (550)

5.41. Whether This Purification Makes Permissible All That One Does With Ablution: Does dry ablution permit more than one obligatory prayer?

We said that the imitator has a proof established for him in a particular divine question which contradicts what his imitation of the divine law accords him. That proof does not dislodge him from his imitation. It dislodges him from imitating the proof of the intellect by which the divine law is confirmed for him, and it is not this particular proof. If the same impurity appears to him in his belief in his imitation in that question, by that he knows that the Lawgiver did not intend this apparent meaning in this question. The existence of his unforeseen proof that occupies the position of water calls his attention to that. The problem is like that if you examine it closely.

Scholars disagree about whether more than one single obligatory prayer is permitted with dry ablution. Some say that it is permitted, and this is our position. It is more suitable, as far as we are concerned that it is not permitted. Some say that it is not permitted, and there is disagreement on the secondary rulings on that. (551)

5.42. Repetition of the Self-disclosure

We have already discussed the repetition of a self-disclosure. Discussion on the matrices of the questions of dry ablution is complete. It is brief and succinct regarding the positions of scholars regarding it. *"And God says The Truth and He guides to the way."* (33:4) (552)

6 On Impurities

6.1. Purification from Impurity: The Opinion of Religious Scholars This

Know that there are two types of purification. One is purification whose meaning is not intelligible. It is purification from ritual impurity which prevents obligatory prayer. The other is purification from impurity whose meaning is intelligible. It means to be clean. Is it a precondition for the validity of the obligatory prayer like the purification of someone who has a ritual impurity or not? Some say that being pure of impurity is an absolute obligation while it is not a condition for the validity of the obligatory prayer. Some say that it is obligatory, like purification from ritual impurity which is a precondition for the validity of the obligatory prayer. Some say that it is a confirmed practice of the Prophet. Some say that removing it obligatory when one remembers but is not when one forgets it. (553)

6.1.1. The Inner Aspect of Purification from Impurity

Know that there are two purifications in our Path. The meaning of one purification is not intelligible. It is purification from ritual impurity. Ritual impurity is an attribute of the self, so how can the thing be purified of its reality? If it had been purified of its reality, its source would have been negated. If its source were negated, for whom then would worship be necessary? There is only God. For this reason, we said that purification from ritual impurity does not have an intelligible meaning. As far as we are concerned, the form of purification from ritual impurity is that God is your hearing, your sight, and all of you in all your acts of worship. He affirms you and negates you. You are you in respect to your essence and you are Him in respect to your movements and perceptions. (554)

6.1.2. The Worshipper Is Obliged, the Lord Acts

You are obligated in respect to the existence of your source, the place addressed by God. He acts with you since you have no action when ritual impurity does not affect the action itself. It has an authority in the action since it is part of what God obliged in the way of movement and non-action. God only does it by the existence of that which moves and is still since the servant only exists by God. God is exalted above movement and stillness. He is the place of His effect in himself. The servant must be in-time so that he can be a locus for the effect of God. (555)

6.2. The Incidence of Creation and the Effect of The Real Purification from Impurity

The servant is obliged to purify himself of ritual impurity (*hadath*, in-timeness = *huduth*). The formal prayer itself, which is outward action, is not valid coming from him because he has no effect. Because of his source, he is a cause for the manifestation of a divine effect in him. By being purified from looking at the action through his in-timeness, the actions validly belong to other than him (although the source exists for the validity of the action which the essence of God does not accept). (556)

6.3. The Various Types of Impurities: Types of Impurities About Which the Religious Scholars Agree and Disagree

Purification from impurity is not like that. Impurity consists of inferior qualities, and their meaning is intelligible. It is cleanness. Purification from impurities is therefore purification by noble qualities and by removing inferior qualities from the self. It is the purification of the self, whether or not worship is intended by that. If worship is intended by that, it is abundant favor upon favor and *"light upon light."* If it is not intended, it is only abundant favor. Noble qualities are sought for themselves. The highest of their stations is to use them as worship to purify oneself from impurities and to remove impurities from the self. We stated that they are blameworthy qualities. We say that it is not a condition for the validity of worship. God made it an independent act of worship desirable in itself, so it is like all obligatory things. It is obligatory when it is remembered, and it falls away when it is forgotten. It means that whatever you remember is obligatory, like the obligatory prayer. God said: *"Perform the formal prayer for My Remembrance."* (20:14) We will now discuss its individual rulings. (557)

6.4. Primary Death or Lack Which the Possible Has

Scholars agree that its sources are four: carrion with blood, which is not aquatic; the flesh of pigs however it has died; blood from a non-aquatic animal, separated from the living or dead when it flows a lot; and human urine and feces, except for the nursing child about which they disagree. (558)

Know that there are two deaths: basic death which is not from previous life in the one who is described by death, and that is the words of God Almighty: *"How is it you are ungrateful to God? You had been lifeless then He gave you life."* (2:28) This is basic death. It is the non-existence which the possible has when its source is known by God while it has no existence in itself. Then God Almighty said: *"Then He gave you life."* The other is incidental death, which is the death which comes unexpectedly to the living and removes its life. It is the word of God Almighty: *"After that He will cause you to die."* (559)

6.5. Incidental Death Which Happens to the Living

This is incidental death and it is what is meant in this question. Then another attribute is added. He said, "with blood" which is flowing blood. He says any animal which has a flowing spirit, that is, which flows in all its parts. This does mean the one whose life is the same as himself that all existents have. Then he added another attribute: "Which is not aquatic" that is, the land animal. The animal which is on the land is not the sea animal. This is because "the sea" refers to knowledge. He says: I do not mean the animal that exists in the knowledge of God for there is disagreement about that. I mean the animal whose source has appeared and who lives by air. All of these preconditions confirm its undisputed impurity. If one of the preconditions is lacking, there is no agreement. (560)

6.6. The Life of the Servant Is Incidental, Not Essential

Since the life of the servant is incidental and not essential, he must not glorify it and have pretensions. When he has pretensions and says "I" and withdraws from contemplation of the One who brought him to life, incidental death appears to him, meaning: This is your root. He is returned to his root, but he is not pure because of false claims and forgetting the One who gave him life. We looked into the cause which necessitates this claim. It is because it is a land-animal. We said, "What does it being a land animal mean?" He said, "Its life is from air (*hawa*). We know that passion (*hawa*) is what destroys him as God Almighty said: He forbade the lower self passion (*hawa*)." (79:40) All that vacillates between two airs must die as our friend, Abu Yazid Abdur-Rahman al-Fazazi said:

Passion (*hawa*) is sound
    and air (*hawa*) is ill.
It is impossible that my state be sound
    through the two of them. (561)

He recited it for himself in Tlemcen in 590. Whoever has all these preconditions in him is impure by the agreement of the scholars.

6.7. The Attribute of the Flesh of Pork

As for the interpretation of the flesh of pigs, its flesh is the place of blood life. Meat is solid blood. The attribute of porkness is fixed passion for filthy things which make the self malignant. These are blameworthy qualities. When life leaves that flesh, it is impure. That is because it is generally agreed that the one with blameworthy qualities is absent from the principle of the divine law in him which is his spirit. In respect to it, he is dead. (562)

God said: *"And the recompense for an evil deed is the like of an evil deed."* He did not limit it in any aspect. He attached it to blameworthy qualities. Then He said about the one who did not do it: *"Then whoever pardons and makes things right, his compensation is due from God."* (42:40) He informed us that it is a noble quality to forgo paying back the evil deed. Because of this, we said, "for whatever reason it has died" since sacrificing it would not cause it to be pure. (563)

6.8. The Repayment of Evil Is Evil, but Pardon is Better

The Messenger of God spoke to the man who sought retaliation from the one who killed his client and the Messenger of God asked him to forgive him or to accept blood-money. He refused. The Prophet said: "Take him." When he took him, the Prophet remarked: "If he kills him, he will be like him," and he meant the words of God: "The repayment of a bad action is one equivalent to it." The man heard about that so he returned to the Prophet and did not kill him. Ugliness and beauty are built on this question. It is a very great question into which people delve. This section is not the place to unveil the reality of that, even though we have mentioned it in this book. (564)

6.9. The Land Animal Is the Existent Source In Itself or Itself

The third category of impurity which is agreed upon is blood itself from the land animal, when it is generated from the living or the dead and there is a lot of it, that is, an excessive amount. We have informed you that the land animal belongs to a source of existence of its own. It is not that which exists in the knowledge of God like the sea-animal, even if it lives by air. Blood is the root from whose heat that vapor emerges by which that animal has life. It is the animal spirit. Since blood is a root in this impurity, it is more appropriate to call it impurity than what is generated from it. (565)

6.10. The Human Being's Impurity When He Is Often Heedless

That which produces pretension in the servant is might. Man is formed and based on it since he is the place of gathering for the universe and the opposites of all existent things without exception. Then he is oblivious to divine concern in that and the basic death which God alerted us to when He said: *"You had been lifeless."* (2:28) He also said: *"Surely I have created thee before when thou wert nothing."* (19:9) and He said: *"Has there approached the human being for awhile, a long course of time, when he would be nothing remembered?"* (76:1) Therefore scholars agree that it is impure when there is a lot of it, that is, when there is a great deal of heedlessness about this station. If there is not a lot of it, there is no agreement about the ruling regarding it. (566)

6.11. The Perfect Human Being Represents God on the Earth

The fourth category is human urine and feces. As far as its interpretation is concerned, know that when someone has a noble rank and high station, his minor error is great. Whoever is low in station, abased in rank, his great error becomes small. Man is noble in station and high in rank. He is the representative of God and the teacher of the angels. He must purify the one who keeps his company and make pure those who mix with him. When he neglects his reality, he is occupied with his nature. Pure foods and drinks accompany him. He takes those that are good by his nature, not by his reality. He expels what is bad of them by his nature, not by his reality. The good is impure, and it is blood, and the bad is impure, and it is urine and feces. It is better that he does not acquire bad odors. They are from the world of breaths, and their impurity is in respect to their nature. It is like that with all animals. (567)

6.12. Dead Animals Which Have no Blood and Dead Aquatic Animals: The Position of Scholars About Dead Animals Without Blood and Dead Aquatic Animals

However, the realities and spirits of animals do not have the height of nobility and station which the reality of man possesses. His error is great, so they all agree, without any disagreement, that the like of this is impure. They disagree about urine and feces of other animals, even though all comes from nature. The one who keeps nature in mind, says that it is impure. The one who keeps the station of nobility and inferiority in mind says that the urine and feces of man are impure and does not overlook it because his station is immense. He overlooks whatever is below him among the animals. I have clarified the reason for the dispute and agreement for you. Praise belongs to God: "*God says The Truth and guides to the path.*" (33:4) (568)

6.13. Life Generated from Blood

Scholars disagree about these two dead things. Some say that they are pure, which is what I say. Some say that the dead water animal is pure and the dead land animal which has no blood is impure except what is generally agreed to be pure since it is not carrion, like the vinegar worm and what is generated in foods. Some say that both the dead sea animal and the dead land animal are impure except for that which has no blood. (569)

6.14. The Rule on Parts of That Which They Agree to be Carrion: The Position of Religious Scholars About Parts of Carrion Like Hair and Bones

We have previously informed you in this purification about the interpretation of blood. Some say that which has no blood is pure. That is being clear of pretension because pretension occurs in the life which is produced by blood, not by the life which all existents have by which they glorify God's praise. That life is basically pure because it is from God without any cause which might veil it from God. Some say that the dead sea animal is pure, even if it has blood. It is in the knowledge of God, and things have no authority in the knowledge of God. Rules are connected to them when they appear manifest in their source form, which is when they emerge from knowledge to sensory experience. The rest of their dispute is interpreted in a similar way in this question. (570)

6.15. Sudden Death Which Removes Life

Scholars disagree about the parts of that which they agree is carrion, although they agree that meat is a dead part of something dead. We have clarified the interpretation of meat in pig-flesh. They disagree about the bones and the hair. Some say that they are carrion, and some say that they are not carrion. I say that they are not. Some say that the bones are carrion but that the hair is not. (571)

Since the death referred to in this question is sudden death which removes the life which is in this place, we looked at what is called "life." Some consider life growth, and say that they are carrion. Some consider life sensation and say that they are not carrion. Some distinguish and say that bones feel, and so they are carrion, and hair does not feel and so it is not carrion. The one who thinks that growth is by food and sensation is by the animal spirit so they are both carrion, considers that life comes from growth and from sensation. Some think that growth is by its Lord, not by food, and that its perception of sensory things is by its Lord, not by the senses. He does not look at the means since he is annihilated in looking at the root which is his Creator. If he sees that God is his hearing and sight and that He is the source of his sensation, then it is not valid at all that it be carrion for him, whether he considers life as a consequence of growth or from sensation. (572)

6.16. Using the Skins of Carrion: The Position of Scholars About Using the Skins of Carrion)

Some say that they are used, whether or not they are tanned. Some distinguish between tanned and untanned, and disagree about their purity. Some say that tanning purifies them. Some say that tanning does not purify them, but that they are used when they are dry. Those who believe that tanning purifies, agree that tanning also purifies that which is sacrificed, that is, animals which one is permitted to eat. (573)

They disagree about that which is not slaughtered. Some say that tanning only purifies that which is slaughtered, and that tanning is a substitute for slaughtering in bringing about purification. Some say that tanning is used to purify all dead animals except for pigs. Some say that tanning purifies all dead animals, pigs included. (574)

6.17. The Position of Shaykh al-Akbar About This

That which I believe and say is that one is permitted to use the skins of all dead animals and that tanning purifies them all, and I do not exclude any dead animal. (575)

6.18. Its Inner Interpretation: Accepting Outward Judgments Without Interpretation

We have acquainted you with that which is called "carrion." It is not forbidden to use its skin. It is using the outward. Anyone who accepts rules outwardly without interpretation or turning from the outward rule which the phrase indicates has no impediment in that. The one who utters what some of the phrases indicates similarity has no proof against us. We said that they do not support the outward. It is what the outward brings in the way of similarity, because "like" and the adjectival "as" are not in the outward. That error in the question is only due to interpretation. When the expression has this sort of relationship with a clear expression which does not allow interpretation, then its connection to it is like the relationship the dead has to the living. Since we did not find any impediment from the Lawgiver against using it, we remained on the fundamental position, which is found in the words of God: *"It is He Who created for you all that is in and on the earth."* (2:29) He did not separate the pure from the impure, so we do not make any rule about its purity if we use it unless it has been tanned. Then it is pure. (576)

6.19. The Possible Expression Is Judged by Its Apparent Meaning

Its interpretation is that in the probable phrase which comes from the Lawgiver, we judge by the outward but we do not state conclusively that that is indeed what is meant. If it happens that we find another text on that which we can make a rule with, the probability which comes from that other expression is removed. The first expression is then purified of that probability. If it has a second report, like tanning for this skin, then we join the purification which it has in itself to the second report, which directs it to one of its probabilities with definite rule. We use it as we would have used it before it was pure in respect of our using it, not in respect to our using it from a particular aspect. That report may remove it from the outward sense in which we applied it to another probability. For this reason, we said in respect to its use, not in respect to its use in a particular aspect since others have thought that it is not to be used to all. (577)

6.20. The Blood of Aquatic Animals and a Small Amount of Blood from the Land Animals: The Position of the Religious Scholars About the Blood of Land and Aquatic Animals

Scholars disagree about the blood of the sea animal and about a small amount of blood from a land animal. Some say that fish blood is pure and then some say that it is impure as blood is basically impure. Some say that a small amount of blood and a large amount are the same in the ruling. Some say that one overlooks a small amount of blood. (578)

6.21. The School of Shaykh al-Akbar on Blood

That which I believe is that the prohibition is recommended for every type of blood which flows from every animal and it is forbidden to eat it. As far as its impurity is concerned, I only make rules about the impurity of forbidden things based on a text from the Lawgiver about its impurity in general, or an amount which a text states is impure. The text does not say to avoid another text in any case. One needs the connection. Therefore not every forbidden thing is impure. If we avoid it, we do not avoid it because of its impurity. Its being impure is a rule of the divine law. It may be neither intellectually dirty nor offensive. (579)

6.22. Its Inner Significance: The Judgment About the Thing Which Is Self-Necessary

The rule about the thing which is self-necessary does not have the existence of its source nor its amount as a precondition for it. It is the same whether its source is existent or non-existent. The rule about it is the same in either case, whether that rule be that it is pure or not pure. That does not affect the fact that it is in the knowledge of God or that it exists in its source. (580)

6.23. What Is Understood by Possibility

Do you not see that in the case of the possible, its existence may outweigh its non-existence or its non-existence outweigh its existence? That does not detract from the principle of its possibility. The possibility is necessary by its essence as the impossibility of the impossible is necessary by its essence and as the necessity of the necessary is necessary by its essence. The intelligibility of the necessity is applied to that which is necessary by itself. It is like that with the principle of the possible and the impossible. Their principle does not change, even if their ranks vary. (581)

6.24. The Ruling on the Urine of Animals: Positions of the Scholars on Animals' Urine

The people of knowledge disagree about the urine and dung of all animals except for man, and there is a further exception about the urine of suckling infant. Some say that they are all impure. Some say that they all pure without exception. Some say that their rule follows that of their flesh. If something it is lawful to eat, its urine and dung are pure. If something is unlawful to eat, its urine and dung are impure. If something it is disliked to eat, its urine and dung are disliked. (582)

6.25. Things Are Basically Pure, Impurity Is Non-Essential

Purity in things is basic, and impurity is an incidental, non-essential matter. We remain with the root as long as that non-essential does not occur. This is our position. The servant is pure basically in his servanthood because he is created in the true natural state. That is affirmation of servanthood to the Lord. God Almighty said: *"When thy Lord took from the Children of Adam—from their generative organs—their offspring and called to them to witness of themselves: Am I not your Lord; they said: Yea!"* (7:172) The Messenger of God said about this sign: When God created Adam, He took them from his back and brought them forth from him like atoms. He then made them testify against themselves. (583)

6.26. The Most Holy Created the World With His Name the Absolutely Pure

Similarly, knowledge is pure in its relationship to the known. This is the case, whatever prohibition appears in any matter and any knowledge, and so we stop there. Similarly, life is essentially pure and purifying. All that is other-than-God is alive, so whatever is other-than-God is basically pure. He created all the universe by His name, The Pure. (584)

6.27. There Is Nothing That Does Not Glorify God

We said that "what is other-than-God is alive." There is 'nothing', and the thing is the most indefinite of indefinites, but *"There is not a thing but it glorifies His praise."* (17:44) There is only glorification from that which is alive, even if God has taken away our hearing so that we do not hear the glorification of inanimate objects, plants, and animals without intellect. He has also seized our sight so that we do not perceive the life of inanimate objects and plants unless it was someone for whom God breaks the norm patterns of things through a miracle, like the Messenger of God and whoever was present among the Companions when God made them hear the glorification of the pebbles. The miracle occurred in the fact that they could hear it. In the beginning of our affair, God let us hear stones glorifying and uttering phrases in remembrance of God. (585)

6.28. The Human Being Is Alive by Three Types of Life

All existent things are alive and have two lives: a life which can be perceived by the senses and a life which cannot be perceived by the senses. Some are alive by one life which is not perceived by the senses. Some of them are alive by three types of life—and that is man. He is alive by the basic life which cannot be perceived normally; he is also alive by the life of his animal spirit—and it is that by which the senses exist; and he is also alive by his rational self. (586)

All the world is therefore pure. If a divine impediment happens to it which is called impurity, then we judge that place to be impure according to the definition determined in the divine law in respect to that particular relationship. Impurity in things is therefore a non-essential relationship. The greatest of all impurities is associating a partner with God. God Almighty said: *"Truly the ones who are polytheists are unclean, so let them not come near the Masjid al-Haram after this year."* (9:28) The idol worshiper is impure in his source. When he believes, his source is pure. This is the source of idolatry and the source of belief, so understand! (587)

6.29. Only the Pure Issues from the Pure

Only the pure issues from The Pure. Therefore we said that impurity is a non-essential accidental relationship. Non-essential accidental relationships are non-existent. Therefore, impurity has no root in the source because the sources are basically pure outwardly. There are secrets here, and it is only possible to mention the very tip of them to their people. This book will fall into the hands of those who are the people of these secrets and those who are not. Whoever understands that to which we allude has obtained an immense treasure which he can spend for whatever remains of this world and the world to come, that is, without any end to its existence. God is the Support. *"He taught him the clear explanation."* (55:4) (588)

6.30. The Rule on a Small Amount of Impurity: The Position of Scholars About This

The people of knowledge differ about a small amount of impurity. Some say that a little of it and a lot of it are the same. Some say that one overlooks a small amount of it. They also disagree on what is meant by a small amount. Some say that a lot and a little are the same except in the case of blood, which we have already discussed. (589)

6.31. The School of Shaykh al-Akbar with Respect to a Small Amount of Impurities

As far as we are concerned, a lot and a small amount are the same except for that which can be broken up. Whether or not an impediment to perform the obligatory prayer in that results or not is not considered. That is another rule entirely. The details about that have been related in the divine law. One stops at that and does not exceed them. The fact that it is impure does not oblige that the obligatory prayer be invalid in it. The divine law may overlook some of that in one place and not overlook it in another. Circumstances have an effect in that. The Messenger of God removed his sandals because of the blood of a mite on them, but did not invalidate his obligatory prayer and he did not repeat what he had already performed the obligatory prayer. (590)

6.32. A Little and a Lot of Bad Qualities Are the Same

As for its inner interpretation, blameworthy qualities, ignorance and bad opinion in some places, be they great or small, are the same. The People of God have stories and sayings about that. Details have come down about the disagreement on what is pure which are interpreted accordingly. The details have already been mentioned. However, we will deal with the inner aspects of its interpretation. (591)

6.33. The Rule About Sperm: The Position of the Scholars About the Sperm

Divine law scholars disagree about sperm, and whether it is pure or impure. Some say that it is pure and some say that it is impure. (592)

6.34. Natural Formation in Things Issues from the Presence of Sanctification (*taqdis*)

Taking-form is natural and unnatural. There are two distinctions between them. If we like, we can interpret them, and if we like, we do not interpret them. As far as we are concerned, there is no distinction between natural taking-form and unnatural taking-form. Natural taking-form is in respect to a particular aspect which is known with the People of God and there is a text on it in the Quran. It issues from the Presence of Purity and the name, The Pure. There is an aspect other than that particular one, and it issues from its like. It is also what we call the world of creation and the world of command. (593)

6.35. The World of Creation and the World of Dominion

All that exists with a created cause other-than-God is: "the world of creation." All that does not exist by means of a created cause is "the world of command." In reality, all is the world of the command. However, we cannot remove causes from the world. God has put them there and there is no way to remove what God has put in place. (594)

6.36. Whoever Veils Himself from His Lord Is Not Pure

I say that whoever is veiled to his Lord by his self is not pure. When the emission of sperm dominates, man is absorbed in his pleasure. Indeed, the entire animal is annihilated to its Lord by the principle of what emerges from it. This is sperm, and sperm is not pure. For this reason, we are commanded to purify ourselves of it, that is, a general purification of all the parts of the body, because it issues from between the loins and chest. Anyone who bears in mind that natural taking-form is only undertaken by God, deems that it is pure because the state descends on him. It is blood which is confined, and so its bloodness is changed.

Therefore the ruling changes and is more appropriate. As far as we are concerned, sperm is pure unless it is mixed with something impure of which it cannot be purified. Then we deem it impure because of what has happened to it. As its root and source was blood, had it remained in its basic form of bloodness when it emerged, we would deem it impure by the divine law. (595)

6.37. The Places From Which Impurity Is Removed: The Places From Which Impurity Must Be Removed

As for the places from which impurity is removed in the divine law, that consists of three things: garments, the bodies of those obligated, and mosques. (596)

6.38. Inner Garments Are Attributes

Inward garments are attributes. The garments of the inward are its attributes. Imr al-Qays said to Unayza:

> If I have troubled you with creative sperm,
> then remove my garment from your garment and
> unravel it. (597)

He means what he wears of the garment of her love in his heart. God said: *"The garment of God-consciousness,"* that is better. (7:26) As far as I am concerned, He is referring to the circumstances as He said: *"The best ration is God-consciousness"* (*taqwa*). (2:197) whether or not you understand what He means here by piety.

6.39. Bodies Are the Forms of the Hearts and Mosques Are the Homelands of Conversation with God

Bodies are interpreted as the hearts and the spirits. Mosques are interpreted as the places of intimate conversation and their divine states.(598)

6.40. Concerning What Removes These Impurities from These Places: Earth, Stones and Liquid

Divine law scholars disagree about pure—purifying water which removes impurities from these three places. We say that all that removes the thing itself can be used to remove it—earth, stone, or liquid. Color is considered regarding whether or not the thing remains if it has a color which the eye can see. One does not consider whether the smell remains when the source has gone. This is due to another knowledge which we have. (599)

6.41. The Knowledge Which Piety Produces

The result of piety is knowledge as God Almighty said: *"So be Godfearing of God and God teaches you"* (2:282) and He said: *"If you are Godfearing of God, He will assign you a Criterion between right and wrong."* (8:29) That knowledge is what removes impurity and purifies these three places which we mentioned. Inwardly, they are the attributes, the hearts and states which we called clothes, bodies and mosques. (600)

6.42. The Relationship Between Stones and Hearts

Scholars also agree that stones remove impurities from the places of excretion. In the divine law, this is called *istijmar*. As far as I am concerned, *istijmar* is not valid using only one stone. That would be contrary to that which is termed *istijmar*. *Jamra* is a group. The least number for a group is two. The interpretation which is agreed upon here is that God has effected a relationship between stones and hearts in certain matters. *"After that your hearts became hard so that they were as rocks or harder in hardness."* (2:74) Hardness is something of which one must be purified. It is one of the impurities of hearts for which they can be punished or pardoned. (601)

6.43. Stones From Which Rivers Gush

"And truly of the rocks there are some that rivers gush forth from them." (2:74) They are the knowledge of the hearts which are copious, extensive, full of many known things. They gush forth when they are spoken by men of knowledge in order to give instruction in different fields. (602)

6.44. Stones Which Gush Water

There are stones *". . . that split open so water goes forth from them."* (2:74) They are hearts which are overcome by states. Outwardly, those who have those states utter them according to how much they have split and how much knowledge they contain. People then profit by that. (603)

6.45. Stones Which Fall Down Out of Fear of God

"And truly there are some that get down, dreading God." (2:74) When hearts fall down, they resemble stones when they fall. It is their descent from their self-importance to their servanthood, and the like of that in their basic incapacity and helplessness. We have said that water removes and purifies impurities from these places. Stones are the springs of this water. Its principle in removing impurities from the places of excretion is the same as the principle of what emerges from it. This is interpreted as knowledge, as it is fear of that which is one is purified of. Fear is one of

the qualities of the knowers of God with whom God is pleased. Pleasure with God is demanded of them. God Almighty said: *"Only those of His servants who dread God are knowing."* (35:28) He said: *"God is well-pleased with them and they are well-pleased with Him. That is for him who has dreaded his Lord."* (98:8) (604)

6.46. Knowledge Is Pure and Purifying

Knowledge is pure and purifying, especially the knowledge which results from piety. Other knowledge, even if they are pure and purifying, do not have the same strength as this knowledge which we are alluding to. The fear with which stones are described is that which leads to them falling down. That is humility and abasing oneself from the elevation given by God. When He described them as falling, we knew that He meant the stones which are in the mountains. The mountains are the pegs by which God made the field of the earth still. When He made them pegs, that bequeathed to them the glory of the high position. These stones fell down out of fear of God when they heard God said: *"This is the Last Abode that We will assign to those who want not self-exaltation in the earth nor corruption. And the Ultimate End is for the ones who are Godfearing."* (28:83) Will is one of the attributes of hearts. It descends from its height, even if it is by God, and falls down out of fear of God. It is on its guard lest it not have a portion in the world to come to which it will move. By the world to come here, I mean its ultimate happiness. For this reason, it is pure, purifying. (605)

6.47. The Theophany of God on Hearts

As for the special usage of purifying the places of excretion with stones—and the places of excretion mean those from the dense (that is, feces) is excreted, and the subtle (which is urine)— know that God has two self-disclosures in the hearts. The first self-disclosure is in dense things, and it is His self-disclosure in the forms which the eye and imagination perceive—as one sees God in a dream, and he sees Him in a form which is like the forms which are perceived by the senses. He said: *"There is not like Him anything,"* so by this knowledge, you remove from your heart the inclination to limit God by those forms in which He gives a self-disclosure in your sleep or in your imagination in your acts of worship. This is because His Messenger, may God bless him and grant him peace, *"did not speak from erroneous opinion."* He did not speak from whim. He said: Worship God as if you were seeing Him. He said, *"as if,"* and it grants the realities. (606)

6.48. The Theophany of the Imagination

The Messenger of God asked the one who had said: "I am truly a believer," "What is the reality of your belief?" He said: "It is as if I am looking at the Throne of my Lord appearing distinctly." He used "as if" and "seeing." The Messenger of God said to him: "You have recognized it, so cling to it." He testified to his recognition. This is the other Self-disclosure. The Self-disclosure of the imagination is so much more subtle than the Self-disclosure of the senses that it cannot even be estimated. For this reason, it is quickly transformed from one state to another. Whatever the inward part of man is like here, his outward will be like that in his formation in the world to come. (607)

6.49. The Market of the Manifestation of Forms in Heaven

It is related that there is a market in the Garden. There is no buying or selling in it, but it is the place of the self-disclosure of forms. Whoever desires a form, enters it as does the inner part of man right now. (608)

6.50. The Knowledge of Fear Purifies the Heart From Ascription

When the worshiper makes his Object of worship be as if he saw Him, it is as if he were placing Him in his heart in the same position as the one he sees with his eye—even though there is an exterior form there. It is like it is in the Self-disclosure of the dream. The imagination then limits it, although God has no limit by which He is confined. The knowledge of fear purifies it, and it is the stones which we mentioned in the definition of limits. By fear, the heart is purified of the like of this connection and limitation since *"There is not like Him anything."* (42:11) (609)

6.51. Liquids and Solids Remove Impurities

This is the interpretation of the agreement of scholars about the stones which purify the places of excretion. They differ about things other than what we mentioned upon which there is agreement. These are other liquids and inanimate things which remove impurities from the places which we mentioned. Some say that every liquid and inanimate object which is pure, no matter what place it is in, removes the impurity itself. I say that. Some say that it is absolutely prohibited except for that for which there is agreement—water and *istijmar*. We have discussed them. (610)

They disagree about purification using bones and dry dung. Some people forbid it and some people permit cleaning oneself with other things which are pure. Some people exclude that which is respected food, like bread. It has come that bones are "the food of our brothers among the *jinn*." (611)

6.52. Cleaning Oneself (*istijmar*) Using Bones and Dry Dung: The Position of Scholars About Cleaning Oneself Using Bones, Dry Dung and the Like

Another group exclude using in *istijmar* that which would be extravagant, like gold and ruby. As far as things which would not be extravagant, they do not limit anything. Had they faulted it by another intelligible matter, that would have been better. However, one must investigate things like this. If the gold is minted and has on it the Name of God or one of the Names given to Him in the language of a certain people and one fears that it might be one of the Names of God in that language, or there is a form on it, one avoids doing *istijmar* with it for this reason, not because it is gold or ruby. (612)

Some people limit purifying to stones alone. Some people permit *istijmar* using bones and dung, even if it is disliked in their opinion. Some permit *istijmar* with every thing, pure or impure. Tabari alone has this opinion, contrary to the majority. (613)

6.53. The Inner Import of What We Mentioned: Purification of Blameworthy Qualities

It is valid to purify oneself of blameworthy qualities and ignorance by anything which is sound—by a good quality, another inferior quality, a noble knowledge whose known is noble, or a lesser knowledge which only has the effect of purification in the place. It is permitted to use that to remove this impurity. This is the aim of al-Tabari in his unique opinion, which is not the opinion of the community. (614)

6.54. Interpretation About Removing What Is Removed

Some make provision for removing the remover and not what is removed. They follow the divine law and the details about that in the divine law. This is according to what they understand from the Lawgiver in their understanding of the religion of God. People are created differently in understanding God. It is the place of striving. The impurity itself is only removed by that which dominates his understanding of what the divine law intends, and what is better. This applies both in the outward and inward rule, and there is no need for details. (615)

6.55. The Property by Which These Impurities Are Removed

These are: washing, wiping, sprinkling and pouring water on the impurity, as has come down in the Traditions about the bedouin who urinated in the mosque. People shouted at him, and the Messenger of God told them to leave him alone until he had finished urinating. Then the Messenger of God called for water and poured it on the spot. This state is not called washing, wiping or sprinkling. For this reason, we added pouring although scholars do not use this expression and include this action under "washing." The term "washing" is enough for them, and they have no need of "pouring." We think that it is clearer and more fitting to use the expression "pouring" because the relater of the Tradition mentioned it as "pouring", and he did not call it 'washing'. (616)

6.56. The Many Ways Water Is Used in Purification

Know that these ranks only vary with the difference of types of impurities as a lightening for this community. That which is intended is to remove the impurity itself, be it existent or imaginary. Whatever will remove illusion or these attributes themselves is used to remove it. There is a more general use under which the particular use is included. It relieves one of using the particular, if you understand. It is like washing which is the most general. It is adequate for all. The Lawgiver poured, washed, wiped and sprinkled (splashing). Traditions have come down on all of that, and their place is the books of jurisprudence. (617)

6.57. Purification Is General and Particular for All Sinful Characteristics

If we find a blameworthy quality which we can use to remove all blameworthy qualities, we will use it. It is like the washing which encompasses all the attributes which remove impurities themselves and their illusion. It is better and easier, even if you have to ask pardon for that. One looks at each blameworthy quality and looks at the attribute which will remove the thing itself. Then you use it to remove that quality and nothing more. This is the assessment of this book. (618)

6.58. The Wisdom of the Divine Law

There are vast differences in this book regarding wiping, sprinkling and the number of times. This is not the place for that unless God makes an opening and lengthens my life. We will write a book on the interpretation of all the rules of the divine law in all forms and the differences of scholars regarding it in order to join the two paths and to disclose the wisdom of the divine law in the two formations and the two forms, that is, the outward and the inward. It will be a comprehensive book for the people of the outward and the people of the interpretation in the inward and their counterparts who examine relationships. God is the Support. There is no God but He. (619)

6.59. On the Rule of Politeness When Cleaning Oneself and Entering the Lavatory: Prophetic Traditions on Cleaning Oneself and Entering the Lavatory

There are numerous traditions and commands related on that: like the prohibition against doing *istinja* with the right hand, touching the penis with the right hand when urinating, not speaking for a need, and seeking refuge when entering the lavatory. There are many of them. Some say that all of them are treated as recommended. Most of the religious scholars say that. (620)

6.60. The Inner and Outer Law for Traveling and Journeying

As far as the interpretation is concerned, they are all obligatory. The authority of the inward in the commands of God is not the same as the outward. God only looks at a man's heart. Therefore a person must keep his heart constantly pure because it is the place at which God looks. The divine law looks at the outward part of man and supervises him in this abode, the abode of obligation, more than it does with his inner self. (621)

6.61. In the World to Come

It will be the reverse of that in the world to come. There the secrets will be tested. Here the divine law also supervises the inner in specific actions which the divine law obliges be done, specific actions which the divine law recommends, specific actions which the divine law gives one the choice to do or not to do, specific actions which the divine law forbids, and specific actions which the divine law dislikes. The principle in leaving actions is like that. (622)

6.62. The Position of Religious Scholars About the Rules of Politeness in Cleaning Oneself

They disagree in these manners about facing the *qibla* for defecation and urination, and turning one's back to it. They have three positions in that. Some say that it is not permitted to face the *qibla* at all for defecation or urination in any place. Some say that it is absolutely permitted, which is what I say, but it is better and more appropriate to avoid that. Some say that it is permitted in an erected structure, but not permitted in the desert. Each group has a proof from a tradition on which it relies. divine law scholars have mentioned that in their books. (623)

6.63. The Inner Significance of That: God Is In the Direction of Obligatory Prayer

The Prophet reported that God is in the direction of formal prayer for the one who prays, and that when a man prays, he faces his Lord. Some understand from that the known direction of formal prayer is related to God in the state of obligatory prayer in particular. Some understand by that that what is intended by that relationship is that it is not permitted to face the direction of formal prayer when going to the lavatory because of bad manners. Some people understand that what is meant is the state of the one who prays. He is permitted to face the direction of formal prayer in the lavatory since he is not praying a particular prayer with a known description. (624)

6.64. The Spirit of Obligatory Prayer Is Presence with God

Some think that it is the spirit of the prayer which is constant presence with God and intimate conversation with Him, so all his actions are prayer. He does not prohibit facing the direction of formal prayer in the lavatory since he is constantly in the spirit of prayer. They are the people of constant presence with God. God Almighty indicated them when He said: *"They are watchful of their formal prayers."* (70:33-34) As for the one who only has the thought of presence with God occur to him at the moment he needs to go to the lavatory, that then is a satanic thought on which he does not rely. He avoids facing the direction of formal prayer. As far as we are concerned, if someone has this state it must be part of the work of Satan. God said: They are *". . . the disgraceful actions of Satan, so avoid them."* (5:90) (625)

6.65. Buildings and Cities Are a State of Association

As for the one who thinks that you can face the direction of formal prayer in an erected structure but not in deserts, erected structures and cities are the state of gatheredness. That resembles the gatheredness of the divine Names. There is nothing which is not connected to a divine Reality by which it is intelligible. The non-existent is connected to disconnection. Therefore, the one with this state always sees his Lord in respect to that reality. Buildings and cities show him that, so he can face the direction of formal prayer, and that is due to the place. (626)

6.66. Choice on the Part of the Servant Is a Limitation of the Vision of the Divine Reality

As far as the desert is concerned, he is alone, so there is nothing to prevent him from avoiding the direction of formal prayer for the lavatory. He shows correct manners and does not face it out of respect for the what the Lawgiver said. Only his own choice confines him in seeing a divine Reality in the desert. The servant does not have any choice with his master. God Almighty said: *"And thy Lord creates whatever He wills and chooss."* (28:68) Whatever the cities and built structures choose, *"not for them had there been a choice."* in whatever is not chosen for them. They cannot choose. They stop at the rules of the divine law. The One who legislated the divine law is God. This is the manner in which one deals with all the reports coming about facing the direction of formal prayer or turning one's back to it in the lavatory and the prohibition in that. (627)

6.67. General Statement on Purification: Purification from Intelligible and Unintelligible Impurity

We have put in this chapter sections on purification which are arranged according to the basic principles. The comprehensive statement on purification is that purification has an intelligible meaning, being that which will remove it, whatever it may be among controversial or existential proofs. The goal is to remove it, not what removes it, as long as that which removes it does not effect impurity in the place. Then the impurity would not have been removed. (628)

As for the impurity which is not intelligible, its purification is based on a text given by God Almighty or His Messenger in that. If God wills, He will acquaint you with its meaning and relationship. In respect to you, it is removing it by precise knowledge. If it is not that, it is called worship. It is the general meaning in all obligations. It is the comprehensive cause. *"And God says The Truth and He guides to the way."* (33:4) (629)

Part Two: On the Mysteries of the Formal Prayer

1 The Mysteries of the Five Formal Prayer

1.1 Introduction

How many a person there is who prays and has nothing
of his formal prayer except seeing the *mihrab*,
trouble and work,
While another person obtains constant intimate
conversation when he prays the formal prayer and attends!
How much greater it is since the secret of God is before him!
If he follows the leader (*imam*), he reaches the utmost point.
The pilgrim sanctity (*ihram*) of the prayer occurs when you say
"*Allahu Akbar*," although a person is the same,
whether in pilgrim sanctity or out of it.
One leaves its pilgrim sanctity by the greetings (*salam*)
if you follow his sublime return in the Night Journey.
There is a limit between these two stations and there are
secrets of the Unseen which are neither sensed nor seen.
Whoever sleeps through the moment of the obligatory
prayer is alone, unique in time, a pole which is straight.
If forgetfulness and negligence occur in the obligatory
prayer, The Merciful reminds him, compelling him to
do what he forgot.
If he is mounted, heading for the source,
the formal prayer is decreased by half
Except for the dawn and evening formal prayers because
of a secret which is hidden in the morning and evening.
Guard the *shaf* and the *witr*, and you will win
by what brought victory to the first Muslims.
There are twenty-seven degrees between the obligatory
prayer said alone and that said in a group, even if the
one who prays is repeating it.
So do not forget the Festival (*id*)—be present at its
formal prayer when the luminous sun and splendor arises.
Set out early before noon on Friday, and you will come first
in the racetrack of the High.
If an eclipse of the sun or moon occurs, it is the veil

of the existence of the self. Look out, young man!
Whoever prays for water changes his cloak. Thou dost change
states. Perhaps you will be content.
These are the acts of worship which are purely for the goal.
If man has only that, he strives. (1)

1.1. The Ascription of the Formal Prayer to God, Angels and Human Beings

May God support you with the spirit of obligatory purity! Know that the formal prayer is ascribed into three, and to a fourth in two senses: a comprehensive meaning and a non-comprehensive meaning. The formal prayer is ascribed to God by the comprehensive meaning. The comprehensive meaning is mercy. God described Himself as Merciful (*rahim*) and He described His servants as merciful, He said: "*The Most Merciful of the merciful.*" The Messenger of God said: God shows mercy to those of His servants who are merciful. God says: "*He is the One who prays blessings for you.*" He described Himself as praying, that is, showing mercy to you since He brought you out of darkness to light. He said: "From misguidance to guidance and from wretchedness to happiness." (2)

The formal prayer is also ascribed to the angels. It means mercy, asking for forgiveness and supplication for the believers. God says: "*He is the One who prays blessings for you, and His angels.*" The formal prayer of the angels is what we have mentioned. God said in respect of the angels: "*And ask for forgiveness for those who have believed.*" (40:7) They say: "*So forgive those who have repented and have followed Thy way and guard them from the punishment of hellfire.*" O God! Answer the angels' excellent supplication for us! The formal prayer is ascribed to man as meaning mercy, supplication, and specific actions which are known in the divine law as we shall presently mention. The human being has all three of these ranks which are called the "formal prayer" (*salah*). God commands us: "*Perform the formal prayer.*" (3)

The formal prayer is also ascribed to all that is other-than-God among all creatures: angel, human being, animal, plant and mineral—according to what is imposed on it and assigned to it. God says: "*Hast thou not considered that God is glorified by whatever is in the heavens and the earth and the birds, ones spreading their wings?*" (24:41) Each knows its proper prayer and glorification. Prayer is therefore ascribed to all. Glorification (*tasbih*), in Arabic, is a form of prayer. (4)

1.2. Supererogatory Formal Prayers During a Journey

Abd Allah ibn Umar, who was an Arab, did not perform supererogatory prayers while on journeys. Someone asked him about that and he said: If I had been a glorifier, I would have done it. God Almighty says: *"The seven heavens glorify Him and the earth and all that is in and on them. There is not a thing but it glorifies His praise."* (17:44) He addressed Muhammad, the master of unveiling, when he saw what you do not see: *"Hast thou not considered that to God prostrates to Him whoever is in the heavens and whoever is in and on the earth and the sun and the moon and the stars, the mountains, the trees and the moving creatures, and many of humanity?"* (22:18) Look at the understanding of Abd Allah ibn Umar when he realized that God intended to make things lighter for His servants by reducing half the formal prayer for them. Therefore he did not perform supererogatory prayers since he wished to be consistent with God's intention in that. This is a spiritual comprehension. (5)

As for someone who performs supererogatory prayers on a journey, he thinks that what God intended to reduce was the formal prayer, not to reduce the supplicative prayer which a person does of his own accord. When the traveler does it in full, two bows (*rakat*) of it are obligatory and the rest is supererogatory. God only imposed two cycles on him as stated by the Messenger of God. The one who performs supererogatory prayers thinks that only the formal prayer is reduced and not the voluntary prayer, and that is why he performs supererogatory prayers on a journey. The Messenger of God used to perform supererogatory prayers while riding his camel. By this, the one who takes this position knows that what is meant is to reduce the formal prayers and he follows the Messenger of God in performing supererogatory prayers while traveling. God says to us: *"Surely in the Messenger of God there has been for you a good, fair example."* (33:21) (6)

1.3. The Formal Prayer

Know that the formal prayer, which include the obligatory ones and the confirmed voluntary prayers of the Prophet (*sunna*), are eight, just as there are eight obligated limbs in the human being and The Essence has eight attributes. These eight are: Essence, Life, Knowledge, Will, Speech, Power, Hearing and Sight. The obligated human being is an essence which is alive, knowing, with will, speaking, ability, hearing and seeing. The obligated limbs, that is, those by which the human being does or does not do what he is obliged to do, are eight: the ear, eye, tongue, hand, belly, genitals, foot and heart. (7)

The eight formal prayers which are prescribed as obligation and confirmed *sunna* (practices and sayings of the Prophet) are: the five daily formal prayers, the *witr* (odd number) after the night formal prayer, the Friday noon congregational, formal prayer, the two Festival formal prayer, the recommended eclipse prayer, the recommended prayer for rain, the recommended *istikhara*, and the recommended funeral prayer. (8)

1.4. The Prayer For the Messenger of God

As far as the supplication for the Prophet is concerned (within the formal prayer), it is a supplication. The Messenger of God taught us how to bless him, that is, how to make supplication for him. He commanded us to ask God to give him mediation (*al-wasila*) and the praiseworthy station. If God Will, we will mention the details of all these supplications in this book, complete with their conditions. However, I will not mention all the details concerning them as that would take too long. I intend to mention these sections according to the matrices as we did in obligatory purification in order to deal fully with them, God willing. (9)

1.5. The Rank of the Formal Prayer in the Foundations of Belief On Which Islam is Based

Formal prayer occupied the second rank of the foundations of belief on which Islam is built according to a sound tradition from the Messenger of God. He said: "Islam is built on five: the testimony that there is no god but God, establishing the formal prayer, giving the purifying alms, formal fasting in Ramadan and the formal pilgrimage. The Companions knew that the Prophet kept the proper order when he included the "*waw*" (and) of likelihood. For this reason, when one of them quoted this Tradition from the Companions and said: The obligatory pilgrimage and obligatory fasting in Ramadan, it was rejected. He was told: Formal fasting in Ramadan and the formal pilgrimage. Fasting comes first. We know that he meant to keep the proper order and alerted us to the fact that when something is transmitted from the Prophet, one only transmits exactly what he said. There are scholars who think that one can transmit the Traditions uttered by the Prophet by its meaning. (10)

The formal prayer, "*salah*," is the second of the foundations. It [the word *salah*] is derived from [the word] "*musalli*" which refers to the one who follows the one who comes first in a race. The first of the foundations is the bearing witness to the Oneness of God and the Messengership of Muhammad (*shahada*). That which comes second is the formal prayer. He put the purifying alms after the formal prayer because offering the purifying alms is purification, so it is in harmony with the formal prayer. The formal prayer is not accepted by God without purity. Giving the purifying alms is the purification of one's property. God says: *"He who makes it pure prospers"* (91:9), that is, the soul which He "fashioned." He means that the one who has purified it by obeying the commands of God has prospered. The preconditions for the formal prayer include purity of garments, body, the place where the formal prayer is performed and whatever is on it. Formal fasting comes after the purifying alms. The formal pilgrimage remains last. (11)

We have discussed the bearing witness (*shahada*) to the Oneness of God (*tawhid*), and we have discussed obligatory purification, without which the formal prayer is not valid. We will discuss the formal prayer, God willing, in this chapter, beginning with the formal prayer and what is necessary for it. After that, we will mention the formal prayers which certain circumstances demand. We ask help and support from God! (12)

2 The Times of the Formal Prayer

2.1. Definition of "Time"

In dealing with "times" (*awqat*), I do not intend to speak only about the times of the formal prayers. I mean the "moment" inasmuch as it is a moment, whether it pertains to an act of worship or something other than that. When we have acquainted you with its meaning and interpretation, we will discuss the times prescribed for acts of worship. (13)

The "moment" designates determination in a matter which will not admit of the existence of a source which is not determined: it is the obligation. In the same way we determine or apportion "first," "middle" or "end" to a circular form while it does not intrinsically actually accept firstness, middleness or lastness. We assign any of that to it by the principle of obligation and determination. (14)

The "moment," then, is a determined obligation in time. Time is circular as God created it in the beginning. It is like a ball. The Messenger of God said: "Time revolves as was its form on the day that God created it." He mentioned that God created it in a circular form and that the moments in it are determined. (15)

2.1.1. The Creation of the Starless Sphere

When God created the Starless Sphere (*al-fulk al-atlas*) and it revolved, the day had not been determined in it and it did not manifest itself at all. It was like the water of a jug while it is still in the river before it is in the jug. Then He assigned twelve portions to it which each have specific times. He called them (zodiacal) castles in that sphere. It is the words of God: "*By the heaven possessing the constellations.*" (85:1) They are these set portions. A person can stand still while this sphere revolves around him. This person has an eye with which he looks at these portions by signs which have been given to him regarding them. He distinguishes some from others by those signs which indicate them. He looks at one of the portions, that is, one of the signs. (16)

Then the sphere revolves with that particular sign at which this person is looking and it withdraws from him while he is still standing in that place until it once again returns to him. Thus he knows that the sphere has completed one rotation in respect to him—not in respect to the sphere. We call that rotation a day. (17)

2.1.2. The Creation of the Sun in the Fourth Heaven

After that, in the fourth of the seven heavens, God created a luminous star, immense in size. It is called the sun. When the human being looks at that sphere from behind the veil of the earth which he is on, it rises for him. The place of rising is called the East (*mashriq*) and the rising is called sunrise (*shuruq*) since that luminous star rises from it and illuminates the atmosphere where this viewer is. He follows the movement of that star with his eye until it is parallel with him. That summit is called levelness. Then the star begins to descend from its levelness with this person, and it goes to his right. This is not in respect of the star itself as we have said. The beginning of its withdrawal from levelness in his eye is called noon and evening. (18)

He continues to follow it with his eye until the body of that star vanishes. Its disappearance is called sunset (*ghurub*). The place where the eye sees that it has vanished is called the West (*maghrib*). The atmosphere becomes dark for him. The period of the illumination of the atmosphere from the rising of that star to its setting is called daytime since light is ample in it. It is derived from the river (*nahr* = river; *nahar* = daytime) which has ample water in the stream in which it flows. Then the human being remains in darkness until the star which is called the sun rises from the place called the East. This is for the one who looks at it from that place. However, it rises from another place next to the place from which it rose the day before. This is called "a degree." The period of darkness in which you remain from the setting of the sun to sunrise is called night. The day joins daytime and night together. The places from which this star rises every day are called degrees. (19)

Then he looks at this luminous star called the sun which moves in those determined portions in the Encompassing Sphere degree by degree so that it is divided by sunrise into days. Whenever a span of one of those portions is completed, the span of another portion begins until the twelve portions are completed. The beginning of the span of each portion up to its end is called a month. The span of all these portions is called a year. (20)

2.1.3. Time Is an Imaginary Matter

It is therefore clear for you that night, daytime, day, the month and the year are referred to as moments (*awqat*). That becomes more defined in that which is called hours, and whatever designations are smaller than that. All of that has no existence in itself. These are merely relationships and ascriptions. That which exists is the source of the sphere and the star, not the moment and time. They are determined in them, that is, the moments are determined in them. It is clear to you that time designates an imaginary matter in which these moments are assigned. The moment is an imaginary portion in an existing source, which is the sphere and the star. The movement of that sphere and star is intersected by the portion allotted to it in an imaginary sphere which has no real existence, and which is called time. (21)

I have therefore explained to you the reality of time which God made a container for discrete beings which fall under this determined sphere to which the specification of moments is assigned. This is so that it can be said: "Such-and-such was created, and such-and-such appeared in such-and-such a moment." *"Then We blotted out the sign of nighttime and We made the sign of daytime for one who perceives that you may look for grace from your Lord and that you may know the number of years and the reckoning."* (17:12) (22)

2.1.4. Before-Time Belongs to the Creator and Time to the Creature

Now you know the meaning of time (*zaman*) and the moment, interpret it, that is, dissect it and divide it until you achieve recognition of before-time (*azal*) which is the attribute of your Creator. You attribute before-time to Him as you attribute time to yourself. By this relationship, your time is then a non-essential relationship with no reality in its source and you are a limited creature. Before-time is further and yet still further from being a limit to the existence of God in your words and the words of the one who says: "God spoke in before-time," and "He said in before-time." and "He determined such-and-such in His before-time." By illusion, the speaker imagined a period of time in it even as you imagine a period of time in respect to yourself. This arises from the judgment of illusion, not from the judgment of intellect and sound perception. (23)

The meaning of the expression "before-time" designates the negation of firstness in respect to God. That is to say, there is no beginning to His existence. He is the source of the First. Glory be to Him! It is not by a firstness which has any authority over Him so that He could be contained by it and effected by it. There is a distinction between what your illusion accords you and what you intellect gives you. It is not necessary to say more than this about this matter. (24)

2.1.5. God Determines Things Before Time But Does Not Bring Them Into Existence Before Time

God—glory be to Him! determined things before-time. It is not said: "He exists in before-time." That is impossible from two aspects. He brings into existence since He exists. He does not bring into existence that which is existent. He brings into existence that which is not described by existence in itself. It is non-existent. Therefore, it is impossible that the existent which was non-existent be described as existing in before-time. It exists from an existent which brings it into existence. Before-time designates the negation of firstness in respect of the One who is described by it. It is impossible for the world to exist in before-time when its existence comes from One who brings it into existence: God Almighty. (25)

Another aspect is that it is impossible to say that the world exists in before-time because that which is understood by the term "before-time," is negation of firstness. God is described by that and so it is impossible to use "before-time" to describe the existence of the world. That would lead to saying that the existence of the world which is derived from God is not derived from God because firstness is denied Him since it [the world] exists in before-time. It is therefore impossible for the world to be described with the negative attribute, before-time. It is not impossible for the One described by it—and He is God—to say that He created creation before-time with the meaning of "determined" (*qaddara*). Determination derives from know- ledge. However, it is impossible if "created" has the meaning "to bring into existence." The action is not in before-time. (26)

2.1.6. *Affirmation of Determination Before-Time and In Time*

Determination in before-time is established for you as determination in normal time is established for you. Time is illusory. It has no existence. Similarly before-time is a negative attribute which has no existence. It is not the same as God, and it is only God. It is not an existential matter which is other than The Real. The Real is a container for it. He contains it since it is an adverb describing Him, and we contain time since it is an adverb for us in the manner which we have mentioned, so understand! Now that I have informed you of the meaning of the "moments," we will explain what is meant by the times of the acts of worship. The times of the formal prayers are included among acts of worship. (27)

2.2. The Times of the Formal Prayers

2.2.1. *Specified and Unspecified Times*

There are specified times of the formal prayer and unspecified times. The unspecified time occurs when someone remembers a forgotten formal prayer and when one wakes up having overslept. The time for that formal prayer is when he remembers it, if he has forgotten it, or when he wakes up, if he was asleep. The specified moment has two divisions: a pure division and a shared division. The pure one is the middle of the wide time for all formal prayers, the end of the time of morning (*subh*), and the beginning of the time of noon (*dhuhr*). In these moments, there is no partnership with any other formal prayer as opposed to the situation at the end of the other formal prayers. (28)

The shared is the moment which is between two formal prayers, like noon and afternoon, and other formal prayers in spite of the well-known dispute regarding that among scholars of the divine law. We will discuss that in its proper place, God willing, when we speak about the times of all the formal prayers individually in detail. (29)

2.2.2. The Formal Prayer is Established in Rank in Relation to the Testimony of the Oneness of God (tawhid)

In its interpretation, we say that the one who performs the formal prayer (*musalli*) is the one who comes second after the leader in the race. The formal prayer is second in rank, coming after the bearing witness to the Oneness of God. God said: "I have divided the formal prayer into two parts between Me and My servant." During the formal prayer, He made him second in the divine portion. He mentioned the formal prayer in general. He did not limit that to the formal prayer rather than the voluntary one. We said that the moment is specified—and it is interpreted as the formal prayer—and unspecified—which is interpreted as the voluntary prayer. (30)

2.2.3. The Gnostic is the Master of the Moment

The gnostic is the one who is constant in his formal prayer, and in his intimate conversation in the presence of his Lord in all his movements and stillnesses. He has no specified or unspecified moment. He is the master of the moment. Whoever does not witness this, acts according to whatever reminder his Lord grants him of presence with Him. (31)

However, since the gnostic, who is constantly present, does not differentiate between moments (because he experiences increase and overflowing favor in them, both in what is obligatory of that presence and what is voluntary from himself) he is imperfect in his station and perfect in his state, because he is accompanied by constant presence. Presence in states is not presence from a particular cause. Presence from a particular cause belongs to the perfect human being. (32)

The first of the people of presence (the gnostic who does differentiate between moments) does not distinguish between reasons because he is utterly submersed in the state. It is like an unknown pleasure which a person experiences when he does not know what has caused it. The second of the people of presence is perfect and constantly present by virtue of causes. It is like the one who experiences pleasure by what the pleasure actually is. He always enjoys the pleasure in relishing knowledge, intercourse or anything which agrees with his predisposition. The one who has a taste of that knows the distinction and difference between them. The names of God Almighty vary in the hearts of the "Friends of God" (saints, *awliya*) according to the varieties of gnoses which occur with signs and breaths. In each and every breath and time he discovers a knowledge which he did not have regarding his Lord. This is the result of what that breath and time grant him from the self-disclosure of that particular name. (33)

2.2.4. *The Moments of the Gnostics in Their Spiritual Prayers*

Since we have divided the moments into pure and shared, know then that "the moment" in this path is what you have in your state, whatever that may be—good or evil, recognition or ignorance. It is not dependent. It is like that with moments of time according to what God causes to happen in them in respect to each person. (34)

The pure moment is every name which comes to you free of any partner in its authority. The shared moment is every name which has two or more aspects. The first category is like "The Living." It belongs purely to life. Similarly, "The Knower" belongs purely to knowledge. The second category is shared as the moment is shared. This is like the name "The Wise." One of its aspects is related to The Knower, and another is related to The Manager. The Wise makes two judgments: a judgment about the proper places of things and a judgment about putting them in their actual places. There are many people with knowledge who do not put a thing in its proper place, and there are many people who put things in their places out of mere conformity rather than due to knowledge. (35)

The Wise is the one who knows the places of things and puts them into their places according to his insight. Whoever has wisdom as his moment is in a shared moment. Whoever is in a name which can only indicate one matter—like The Powerful and names like that—is in a pure moment. These are the inner moments of the gnostics in their formal prayers. It is like their outer moments in the formal prayers which their bodies perform. (36)

3 The Time of the Noon Formal Prayer

3.1. The Formal Prayer is Prescribed at a Specific Time

God Almighty says: "*Truly the formal prayer has been—for the ones who believe—a timed prescription*" (4:103), that is, it is obligatory at specific moments, whether those moments are wide or narrow. It must be specified because He says: "*A timed prescription.*" Whoever performs an formal prayer outside of its specific moment— whether he forgets it or remembers it—will never perform that formal prayer or clear himself of it. He has not performed the formal prayer since the moment is one of the preconditions for the validity of the formal prayer. He should do a lot of supererogatory prayers after he repents. In our opinion, he does not make it up after the moment (which is a precondition for its validity) has gone. (37)

The moment for the one who forgets is when he remembers and the moment for the one who sleeps through it is when he wakes up. He must perform it then. That is not called "making it up" (*qada*) in the expression used by the religious scholars except as one says linguisticaly. There is no difference between the one offering the formal prayer and the one who is making it up according to that linguistic term. Everyone who offers the formal prayer performs what he is obliged to do. When he does what he was specifically ordered to do by God, he fulfills its performance. (38)

3.2. The Disagreement of the Religious Scholars About the End of the Wide Time of the Noon Formal Prayer

Scholars of the divine law agree that the moment of the noon formal prayer is that moment which immediately follows the time in which it cannot be performed, which is noon. There are two points of disagreement: when the widest time in which it is permitted ends, and the moment which is the most preferred time in which to perform it. Some say that the end of its widest time is when the shadow of a thing is the same length as the object. Some of those who say this say that the time which is the end of the time of the noon formal prayer is the beginning of the time of the afternoon formal prayer. Some say that it is only the end of the time of the noon formal prayer. They say that the beginning of the time of the afternoon formal prayer is when the shadow is twice the length of the object. Between these two, the noon formal prayer is not in its proper time. (39)

As far as its preferred time is concerned, some say that the beginning of the time is better for the one who performs the formal prayer alone and for those who performs it in groups unless there is intense heat. Some say that the beginning of the time is absolutely better, alone or in groups, in cold or heat. Each person has a particular proof, but this is not the place to deal with them. (40)

3.3. Levelness and the Acts of Worship of the Gnostics

The interpretation about the time of the noon formal prayer is that of levelness (the meridian). It is when the servant stands in one place, reflecting, without giving preponderance to any side in what he does. That is, levelness of intention which he makes when he intends to perform an act of worship (whether it designates the performance of what is demanded of him—because of his servanthood and the fact that he is a subject) or whether that designates what is demanded of him in performing the due of his Lord and Master. He is in a state of levelness without any predominance at all. When the sun begins to descend, then that descent dominates him so he worships God by the servanthood which lordship demands. This is due to the blessings which come to the servant from the moment when the sun rises until it is level above him. He worships Him out of thankfulness for this blessing. (41)

Then he looks at its descent with the eye of separation as it seeks to leave him and lower the veil over him. He worships Him in abasement, poverty, contrition, and desire for witnessing. He continues to watch the sun fearfully until it sets. At sunset, he fearfully watches its traces at the evening formal prayer and the supererogatory prayers after that until the twilight and its traces vanish. He remains in the darkness of the night, asking, weeping, imploring, observing the stars of the night since they take their light from the light of the sun. He asks and implores until dawn rises. Then he sees the coming and acceptance of his supplication. Therefore he worships Him out of thankfulness for that. He sees the traces of acceptance, so he performs the formal prayer of morning. He continues to watch fearfully with remembrance until the rising sun is clear. (42)

When it becomes white and the alteration which had come between his eye and the whiteness leaves it as a result of the earth's atmosphere [lit. vapors] which are natural breaths, then he stands up to perform the formal prayer to honor and offer his thankfulness until the sun is level. He continues in his worship of joy and thankfulness until the sun is level. Then he returns to the worship of steadfastness, need and anticipation of separation. As long as he is alive, he is between these two types of worship. That is because he heard the Messenger say: "You will see your Lord as you see the sun." He takes note of that in his worship in his obligatory and supererogatory prayers, in thankfulness and poverty, between blessing and affliction, hardship and ease. (43)

The believer is the one whose fear and hope are equal. He calls on his Lord out of fear from the time of the sun's descent until twilight passes, and out of desire for the rest of the night until dawn rises, until sunrise, until noon, desiring that there should not be any veil after that. The actions of worship of the gnostics are like that, so understand! (44)

3.4. The End of the Widest Time of the Noon Formal Prayer

The end of the widest time for the noon formal prayer is the end of the authority of the divine name particular to that moment. That is the name, The Manifest. The beginning of noon is under the authority of the divine name, the First. This is the manifestation particular to the prescribed act of worship. This extends until the shadow of a thing is the same as the length of the object. This is the end of the time. The authority of the divine name is like that when this servant concerns himself with it in its particular worship in this moment. He completes it when he encounters it. That is to say that this divine name has no authority particular to it in that moment whose effect is not manifest on this servant. Then the rule of this divine name is finished in this servant, so he leaves the time of the noon formal prayer and enters the time of the afternoon formal prayer. It is under the authority of another name. There is an imaginary distinction between the two names. It cannot be divided intellectually and does not exist. It is an inter space between them. (45)

The Messenger of God said in a well-established Tradition: "The time of the formal prayer has not gone until the time for another formal prayer has come," that is, in the four formal prayers. When the time for the morning formal prayer is gone, the time for noon formal prayer has come until the sun begins to decline. This is different from noon, afternoon, evening and night, so know that.(46)

3.5. The Four Temporal Quarters of the Day

The day is twenty-four hours long. Each quarter is six hours. From sunrise to noon is one-fourth of a day—six hours, but the place of formal prayer is not determined by the principle of specification. We spoke about the principle of specification in relation to the one who forgets and the one who was asleep. The moment is what specifies that the formal prayer occurs at that moment. It is specified in the divine law for the one who forgets when he remembers and for the sleeper when he wakes up whether it is in that moment or in another moment. For this reason, we were very precise in speaking about that, and discussed the principle of specification. (47)

My view in all that I present here is that I do not mean to use one expression rather than another one which will indicate its meaning unless I intend to demonstrate a particular meaning. I do not add a single letter unless it is for the meaning. I do not pad my words in achieving my aim. If the reader imagines that there is padding, then the error is entirely his. It is not mine. (48)

From midday until sunrise of the following day is a time which is accompanied by specific formal prayers which are prescribed in it. When they occur, they occur in their specific times. (49)

3.6. The Four Quarters of the Human Being

Similarly the human being is divided into four quarters. Three of the four quarters worship God by specific actions like the three-quarters of the day. The quarters of the human being are: his outward, his inward, which is his heart, his subtle aspect of self which is his spirit, and his nature. His outward, his heart and his spirit never cease to perform the worship basically connected to them, whether he rebels or obeys God. (50)

The last quarter is his nature. It is like the time from sunrise to noon. By his nature he acts in what he is permitted to do. There is no objection to that. If he wishes to join it to the rest of his three-quarters in acts of worship, he does what he is permitted to do by the divine law. He concentrates on it with belief. That is like someone who supplicates from sunrise and its light until the beginning of noon, that is, when the sun is level. That is not forbidden, although it is not a time when any of the five prayers is obligatory, so understand that! (51)

3.7. The First Is the Best and Highest of Things

We have mentioned the disagreement about the most desirable moment to perform the formal prayer. All, or rather, most people, are in agreement regarding the beginning of the time. However, they disagree about states. Know that the beginning is the best and highest thing since it does not come from anything. Things come from it. If it had come from something, you could not apply firstness to it. (52)

Similarly, the servant strives to worship his Lord in respect to the firstness of his Lord, not in respect to the firstness of his source. The firstness of his source comes from many others first before it, meaning causes. God is the first cause whose firstness has no cause. When the gnostic worships Him in that firstness which is disconnected from any prior firstness, then the worship of this gnostic is applied to every creature which God has created from the very first creation until the time of this gnostic's existence. This is the firstness which effects the bringing into existence of beings. He has worshiped Him in the desirable moment, whether he worships Him with a particular attribute from his obligated limbs—like the one who prays alone—or worships Him with all of his limbs as in the group-prayer, or in the time of heat, that is, the intensity of his fear, striving, the burning of his yearning, ecstasy, and distracted love and attachment, or in coldness, that is, in the state of his knowledge—the ice of certainty and his coolness in any state. Firstness is better for him. God commands us to be "*those who compete with one another in good works.*" He praised this state. He says: ". . . *are those who compete with one another in good works and they are ones who take the lead.*" (23:61) (53)

3.8. The Divine Command Implies Caution About What Is Formal and the Prohibition of What is Forbidden

The forerunner who worships at the beginning in the times of worship is more prudent. This is what is desired of the servants in the state of obligation. Because of this, the divine Command is treated with caution and care when it is unconnected to states which are understood as necessarily permitted or recommended. The same applies to a prohibition of something forbidden when it is free of anything which would make it to be considered disliked. He does not cease to carry out the command and prohibition according to what we have stated—unless it is connected to some circumstances which removes it from the principle of the obligation in the command and the principle of the forbidden in the prohibition. (54)

3.9. The People of Gatheredness and Existence Are the People of the Divine Law and the Reality

So, my brother, the general interpretation of the times is clear to you as well as the interpretation of the desirable time. We have acquainted you with the schools of the divine law scholars in regard to joining two acts of worship: outwardly in your senses and inwardly in your intellect. We are among the people of gatheredness and existence. When you seek the path to God by what God has prescribed, then God is the One who prescribes your end. When you seek Him by what your self gives you by purity and affiliation to its world in disconnection from the natural principle which rules it, your end will then be affiliation to the spiritual world. This is the origin of the development of the roads by which and on which the spirits travel so that God is their goal. This is if God gives him enough room in his fixed term. If he dies, he will never reach that. (55)

We have devoted an absolute retreat for this path which is not limited to the part upon which the believer acts. He increases in belief. The one who is not a believer—the unbeliever, the atheist, the idolater and the hypocrite—can act on it and by it. If he fully carries out his actions on it and by it, then he obtains knowledge of what the matter really is and that may be the reason for his acceptance of the existence of God if he is an atheist, of the unity of God if he is an idolater, the acquisition of belief if he is an unbeliever, and his being made sincere if he is a hypocrite or a skeptic. (56)

Whoever enters that retreat and performs these conditions, as we have confirmed, will obtain the fruits which we mentioned. As far as I know, no one has dealt with this before me unless that happened and no report of it reached me. Access to God is not denied. "*He gives wisdom to whom He wills.*" (2:269) I know that none of the People of the Path are ignorant of it if they are in possession of complete unveiling. However, they did not mention it, and I did not see any of them pointing it out except in limited retreats. If it had not been that I was asked about it by our friend and brother, Abu-l-Abbas Ahmad ibn Ali ibn Maymun ibn Ab al-Tawzari, then al-Misri, known as al-Qastallani, who now resides in Mecca, it would not have occurred to me to clarify it. It is possible that something like this happened to some of those before me, but they did not point it out since no one asked them about it. (57)

4 The Time of the Afternoon Formal Prayer

4.1. The Disagreement of Legal Scholars On the Beginning of the Time of the Afternoon Formal Prayer

Scholars of the divine law disagree about the beginning of its time as well as the end of the time of the noon formal prayer and about the end of the time of the afternoon formal prayer. Some say that the beginning of the time of the afternoon formal prayer is the same as the end of the time of the noon formal prayer. That is when the shadow is the same length as the object. There are two conflicting statements about this. Some say that the two formal prayers share that moment, and that its extent is that in which four cycles can be prayed if you are at home and two cycles if you are shortening the formal prayers. Some say that the end of the time of the noon formal prayer is the time which is the beginning of the afternoon formal prayer. It is not a divisible time. (58)

An established Tradition has come about Gabriel leading the Prophet in the formal prayer. On the second day, he prayed the noon formal prayer in the time in which he had prayed afternoon formal prayer on the first day. In another established Tradition, the Messenger of God said: "The end of the time of noon formal prayer is as long as the time for the afternoon formal prayer has not begun." He says in another established Tradition, "The time of a formal prayer has not gone until the time of another formal prayer has come." (59)

The first Tradition accords partnership in time, and the other two Traditions gives a time which is not divisible and has no partnership. The statement here is stronger than action because action makes it difficult to know the exact time. One says what his reflection gives him while the words of the Prophet are contrary to what the Companions said and judged from the prayer of Gabriel, with the Prophet. The words of the Messenger of God are explained by the action which the transmitter explains. Accepting the words of the Messenger of God is what God has commanded us to do. God Almighty says: "*And whatever the Messenger gives you, take it.*" (59:7) (60)

4.2. The Disagreement of Scholars Is a Mercy to the Worshippers

Therefore it is desirable that there be no conceivable dispute in this question and others like it. However, God made this dispute a mercy for His servants and a widening for what they are obliged to do in the way of worship. The religious scholars of our time hinder people and make things narrow for those who follow the scholars even though the divine law makes it easy for them. They say to the follower of the Hanafi school, "Do not seek the indulgence of al-Shafii." It is the same with all of them. This is among the most serious of damaging things in the way of life. It is oppression. God says: *"There is no compulsion in the way of life."* (2:256) (61)

The divine law has confirmed the judgment of the religious scholars (*mujtahid*) for himself and whoever follows him. The religious scholars of our time reject that and claim that it would lead to toying with the religion. This is sheer ignorance on their part. By God, the matter is not as they claim, although they confirm that they themselves are not religious scholars who exercise personal judgments in legal matters (*mujtahidun*) and that they have not obtained the rank of scholars who can exercise personal judgments in legal matters (*ijtihad*). They do not move from the Leaders who were founders of their schools of law. They travel this road. They make themselves liars when they say that they do not have the predisposition for the ability to exercise personal judgment on legal matters which they deny their followers. That itself is only the result of an exercise of personal judgment on a legal issue. We seek refuge with God from blindness and disappointment! God only sent His Messenger as a mercy to the worlds. What is a greater mercy than relieving this grave distress and all too common business? (62)

4.3. The End of the Time of the Afternoon Formal Prayer

As for the end of the time of the afternoon formal prayer, some say that the end of its time is when the shadow is twice the length of the object. Some say that the end of its time as long as the sun has not become yellow. Some say that the end of its time is one cycle before sunset, and that is what I say. (63)

4.4. Stopping Between Two Stations and "Now" Is Between Two Times

This interpretation was previously mentioned in the interpretation of the time shared between divine names in respect of one of the people of God who takes on their character, and the time which is not shared. It is absolutely applied to all the formal prayers. All that remains is us to discuss is the interpretation of the "now" which is indivisible and the yellowing. The time which divides the two times is the meaning which divorces two names between which there is no understood partnership. It manifests the authority of each of the two names in isolation. (64)

It is the definition of the one standing still in our view. When the human traveler (*salik*) moves from a station which has ruled him, and whose quality, taste and character he has acquired, to another station, he wants to acquire that station as well. Between the two stations is a pause, a place of standing. The authority of that pause is outside of the authority of both stations: the authority of the station from which he has moved and the authority of the one to which he wants to move. The traveler is given recognition in that pause between the two stations—and it is like the "now" between the two times—of the correct behavior: inward and outward of the station to which he is moving and how he should behave with God. When that becomes clear for him, he enters under the authority of the station to which he moves with knowledge. (65)

4.5. The Stations of the Path of Sufism

The stations in this path are like the types of actions in the the divine law—formal prayer, poor-due, fasting, pilgrimage, struggle (*jihad*) and others. As each of these actions has a knowledge particular to it, so each station has correct manners: inner and outer manners particular to it. Muhammad ibn Abd al Jabbar al-Niffari clarified that in his book called the *Mawaqif wa 'l-qawl* (stopping places) where he discussed most of that. It is a very noble book which contains the sciences of the correct behavior: inward and outward manners of the stations. He discusses stopping places (*mawqif*) by the name of the seeker who stops. He talks about moving to the stopping place of knowledge—which is one of the stopping places in this book, and says: "The stopping place of knowledge: He stopped me in the stopping place of knowledge and said to me: 'My servant! Neither knowledge nor your character has any fruit which will direct you to other-than-Me!' He said: 'He said to me: "The night is Mine. It does not belong to the Quran which you recite. The night is Mine. It does not belong to praise and honoring."'" (66)

He continued until he had dealt with all the stopping places in which God stopped him. He enters that station after recognition, and he recognizes the proper behavior: inward and outward manners with God in that station. The Messenger of God said: "God taught me correct behavior: inward and outward manners, so my manners are excellent." This is the time which is between the two formal prayers. The people of direct experience (*dhawq*) among the people of God stop in it and have the correct behavior: inward and outward manners of the formal prayer which must be performed on that day. It is like that in the formal prayers of each day. (67)

4.6. The Yellowing of the Sun By Way of Secrets

The yellowing is the limit of the end of the time of the afternoon formal prayer. As for its interpretation, know first of all that the yellowing is a change which occurs in the eye of the onlooker. He imposes it on the light of the sun, deeming it to be the result of the vapors of the earth which come between the eye and the perception of the pure light of the sun. Its interpretation is what occurs in the self of the servant in respect of the divine name, The Real, from accidental thoughts of the self about that principle. He relates it to God by an aspect which is not pure, and he relates it to himself by an aspect which is not pure. The like of this occurs in the path with someone who has correct behavior: inward and outward manners and someone who does not have it. (68)

As for its occurring in someone who has correct behavior: inward and outward manners, he is someone who recognizes in himself that the light does not turn yellow nor change, and he knows that the judgment which belongs to the divine name is purified and the self has no judgment with it. That judgment may be connected to the name of a defect in the divine law or by custom. So he disconnects the presence of God Almighty from that judgment being related to Him. It is related, however, to the Will of God. He says: "When I was ill, He healed me." This is a well-known defect. He relates the illness to himself since it is a defect which he possesses. He relates the healing to God since it is goodness. (69)

This is his intention, so the outward articulation removes the principle of the divine name which made him ill. Since the Friend of God [Abraham] knew this, he called on the divine name which made him ill when he said: My Lord "*. . . from Whom I am desirous that He will forgive me my transgressions on the Day of Judgment.*" (26:82) He said that he had erred. This reflects his correct behavior: inward and outward manners since he ascribed illness to himself and he did not ascribe it to the authority of the divine name which made him ill. He only intended to show correct behavior: inward and outward manners with Him and to avoid ascribing something they normally consider to be a fault to the authority of a divine name. It is understood from this admission that authority belongs to the divine name. That is what is generally meant by the divine name. (70)

This gnostic combines two types of correct behavior: inward and outward manners in this question: the manner of ascribing illness to himself and the manner of admitting that the illness itself is the judgment of the divine name without being explicit about it. It is implicit and included when he said: "Lord, forgive me my error on the Day of Judgment." He did not mention what the fault is on the Day of Judgment. He says: "the Day of Repayment." (71)

It is the same when he said: "*And none but Satan caused me to forget to remember it.*" (18:63) That is what Joshua, the servant of Moses, said to Moses, peace be upon both of them. In reality, the divine name which ruled him made him forget. He ascribed it to Satan because of his good manners with that divine name which made him forget to inform Moses about the life of the fish when God desired to complete what He knew about the number of steps which He had decreed that he had to walk to cover that distance. By them, he passed by the place where Khidr was, *"So they went back following their footsteps"* (18:64), that is, they followed their tracks until they returned to the place. They found him there. It was a warning from God and a lesson in good manners since he passed the limit when he ascribed knowledge to himself, even though he was the person with the most knowledge on the earth in his time. (72)

If he had really been in possession of knowledge, he would have known the proof of God which occurred when the fish took *"And it took its way into the sea in a wondrous way."* (18:63) He did not know that although Joshua knew it and then God made him forget to acquaint Moses with it. That was in order to show Moses that he had passed over the limit in his claim since he did not ascribe that to God in His knowledge of His creation. This story contains something connected to the interpretation of the yellowness which enters into the light of the sun when he spoke about killing the boy. He said: *"We desired."* He used the pronoun to refer to both the divine name and himself because of what that killing contained of mercy for the parents and for the boy. Moses himself had killed an innocent person, and that was not in retaliation for another life. It was an outward injustice, and therefore he shared the pronoun between himself and God. Yellowness comes in when this action is outwardly attributed to God. This is alteration since the name Khidr shares with God because of good manners. He said: *"And I accomplished that not of my own command,"* that is, God taught me good manners toward Him. (73)

4.7. "Now" Is the Division Between the Two Times

Now I have explained to you the interpretation of the time and the yellowing of the sun. Pursue it when you find the meaning of the time which divides those two sides. The yellowness which enters pure light comes from His name, The Light. It is like His words: *"God is the Light of the heavens and the earth"* (24:35). He did not apply to Himself the name of Absolute Light which cannot accept any relationship. He said: *"The Light of the heavens and the earth,"* and so He taught us what He meant here by light. (74)

He transmitted the principle of teaching and information about relationship to the absolute Light. He limited it by the heaven and the earth, and therefore it is not absolute. When He placed it in a relationship, it descended from the degree of absolute light to the attribute. He says: *"The parable of His Light,"* that is, the attribute of His light in relationship to the heavens and the earth "... *is as a niche*," and so on, until He mentioned the lamp, the substance and where the quality of the lamp is. In this fashion, it comes from the attribute of the light by which the heavens and the earth are illuminated. (75)

God instructed us in good manners in this sign (*ayat*) regarding looking at His names when we use them to refer to Him in any relationship and when we apply it to Him without any relationship. He says: "*God guides to His Light whom He wills*." He related light to Himself, not other. He made the light related to the heavens and the earth as a guide to recognition of His absolute Light. He made the lamp a guide to His light which is limited by relationship. He completed that by His words: "*And God propounds parables for humanity*." Then He forbade us to do anything like this, and said: "*Ascribe not partners with God. God knows and you know not*." (76)

4.8. God is a Comprehensive name: Do Not Make Likenesses of Him

God (Allah) is a comprehensive name which joins together all of the divine names and contains all of their meanings. Likenesses are made with one particular name. If we were to make likeness with God which is an all-inclusive name, we would not be able to make a likeness about the object of the likeness. The likeness is particular, and the object of the likeness is absolute. That would certainly be ignorance. Therefore we are forbidden to make a likeness in this manner without specifying a particular name about which one can make a likeness. It is valid to make a likeness about that particular name as He said in this sign: "God (Allah)." God said (and He did not make a likeness for the name God, but used another name), "*the Light of the heavens and the earth*." He made a likeness of the lamp to the name "the Light" which is relative. Proceed like this then, and do not make any likeness of God. I have not done that. Understand then! May God give you understanding of the places of His discourses and place us among those who have good manners with what we recognize of His manners. He is al-Latif, The Subtle to those He loves. (77)

5 The Time of the Evening Formal Prayer

5.1. The Disagreement of Legal Scholars on the Time of the Evening Formal Prayer

Our scholars disagree about the time of the evening formal prayer and whether or not it has a wide time like the rest of the formal prayers. Some say that it has one moment which is not wide. Some say that its moment is indeed wide, and that it is what is between the setting of the sun and the disappearance of twilight. That is my position. (78)

5.2. The Evening Formal Prayer is Odd Numbered

The inner interpretation of that is that the cause of this disagreement lies in the fact that the evening formal prayer is odd/singular. The odd/singular has one as its root, and, therefore, it must have one time because of its affinity with oneness. For that reason, it is related that when Gabriel led the Messenger of God in formal prayer, he prayed the evening formal prayer at the same time on both days, at the beginning of the obligatory time. This is because the angel is nearer to singularity than the human being. The evening formal prayer is the odd one of the daytime formal prayers as the Messenger of God informed us. That was before God increased us with the odd number [of cycles] (*witr*) prayer of the night: "God has increased you with a prayer in addition to your formal prayer," and he mentioned the odd number prayer. "So offer the *witr* prayer, you people of the Quran!" He made it like the formal prayers, and commanded that it be done. For this reason, some consider it an obligation outside of the formal prayers and above the *sunna*. The one who leaves it out has acted wrongly. How excellent is this view and understanding! (79)

5.3. The Odd Number of the Day and Night Formal Prayers

When the Prophet saw that God had prescribed the odd number of cycles night prayer and added it to the formal prayers, one of which is the evening formal prayer, the odd one of the daytime prayers, he said: "God is singular and loves the singular." He mentioned the evening as formal prayer as being the odd one of the daytime formal prayers and he mentioned the *witr* as being the odd of the night prayers. He said: "God is singular and loves the singular." That is, He loves the singular for Himself.

that is, prescribed two odd prayers for us so that it would be even since oddness is impossible in respect to the creature. God Almighty says: "*And of everything We have created mates.*" (51:49) Therefore, oneness is only proper for God. (80)

Then the Messenger of God saw that God had prescribed the *witr* of the night prayers in order to make the odd daytime prayer even. This was so that He—glory be to Him!—should be isolated with the reality of oddness which does not accept evenness. In the heart of the matter, there is no other god to make the oddness of God Almighty even as the *witr* of the night prayer makes the odd daytime prayer even. It is part of what God refers to when He says: "*We created a pair of everything.*" (51:49) He created two odds, so each of them makes the oddness of the other even. Because of this, the Messenger of God did not join it to the supererogatory prayer. He said: "He has added a prayer to your formal prayer," that is, to the obligatory ones. Then he commanded his community to perform it. (81)

5.4. The Evening Formal Prayer Has Two Times Like the Other Formal Prayers

When the Messenger of God was questioned after Gabriel led him in the formal prayer, and they asked him about the times of the formal prayers, he prayed with the people for two days. The first day he prayed at the beginning of the times. On the second day he prayed at the end of all the five formal prayers, and the evening formal prayer was one of them. Then he said to the one who had asked: "The formal prayer is between these two." Therefore he gave evening formal prayer two times like the rest of the formal prayers and connected it to the even [number of cycles of] formal prayer even though it is an odd [number of cycles]. It is, however, an odd which is used to make the *witr* of the night prescribed prayers even. Its moment is wide like the rest of the formal prayers. We must rely on that. That was behind the leadership of Gabriel, so we must accept it. (82)

The Companions would take that which was the more recent. That which was more recent came from the action of the Messenger of God. When he performed the formal prayer, the Prophet would persist in offering the formal prayer at the beginning of the times. That does not indicate that the formal prayer does not have two times and that which is between the two of them. He clarified that and was explicit about it. He was only obliged to convey and clarify. This is an interpretation and an explanation. "*God guides to the truth and the straight way.*" (83)

6. On the Time of the Night Formal Prayer

6.1. The Disagreement of Legal Scholars on the Time of the Night Formal Prayer

The divine law scholars disagree about its time in two places: the beginning of its time and the end of its time. Some say that the beginning of its time is when the redness of twilight vanishes. That is my view. Some say that the beginning of its time is when the whiteness vanishes which comes after the redness and twilight. There are two twilights, and this is the cause of the dispute. The first twilight is true. The whiteness which comes after it is the second twilight, and there is some uncertainty about it. It is the same uncertainty about the false dawn at the end of the night. It is quite long. The lawgiver considered it to be part of the night. When it appears the morning formal prayer is not permitted nor does the one who intends to fast need to stop eating. Uncertainty arises because it is like the spreading dawn in which the morning formal prayer is performed and after whose appearance the person fasting is not permitted to eat. (84)

That which I think is most likely is that it is like the spreading dawn at whose appearance the morning formal prayer is performed, and that is due to the fact that it is connected to sunrise by redness. It is not cut off by darkness as the false dawn is cut off. It is like that with the whiteness which is at the beginning of the night and which is joined to the redness. When the redness vanishes, the whiteness remains. If there had been a little darkness between the whiteness and the red as there is between the spreading dawn and the redness of the glow of the morning formal prayer, we would have joined it to the false dawn and eliminated its authority. This is—and God knows best—because a person who waits for the whiteness to vanish at the beginning of the beginning of the time of the night formal prayer makes a distinction. (85)

However, it is established that the Prophet performed the morning formal prayer in the whiteness after the red twilight vanished. We stop at that. It is up to the Prophet to interpret the whiteness and redness which are at the beginning of the night in a different manner than our interpretation at the end of the night. This is in spite of the fact that it is derived from the effects of the sun in its rising and setting. God Almighty says:

"And by the morning, when it sighs." (81:18) I consider that its best interpretation is that it is the long dawn since it is cut off as is the breath of the one who stops for breath. After that, his breaths are continuous. (86)

As for the end of its time, some say that it is up to a third of the night. Some say that it is up to a half of the night. Some say that it is until the rising of dawn, and that is my position. I have seen a statement—and I do not know who said it or where I saw it—that the end of the time of the night formal prayer is up until the time when one goes to sleep, even if he stays awake until the rising of dawn (87).

7 Correspondence Between the Three Ranks of the World and the Three Ranks of the Formal Prayer

7.1. The Interpretation of the Beginning and the End of the Time of This Formal Prayer

Know that God apportioned the world into three ranks. God also divided the times of the formal prayers into three ranks. He put the world of the visible (the world of the senses and the outwardly manifest) in the position of the daytime formal prayer. So the person speaks with God according to what the visible world and the senses give him of the proof of God and the names which he sees. The Messenger of God said: "God says on the tongue on His servant, 'God hears whoever praises Him.'" that is, in the formal prayer. The servant is designated as the representative of God. This comes from His name, The Manifest. God is manifest by the form of the person who says: "God hears whoever praises Him." It is the same about what God said to His Prophet Muhammad about the bedouin. "Give him protection so that he can listen to the Words of God," although he only heard sounds and letters from the mouth of the Prophet God said: "That is My speech," and He related it to Himself. God is manifest in the visible form by the form of the one who recites His Words. Understand then! (88)

He also made the world of the unseen. It is the world of the intellect. It is in the position of the night formal prayer and the night formal prayer after twilight vanishes up until the time of the rising of dawn. The one who prays speaks with his Lord in that formal prayer according to what he is given by the world of the unseen, the intellect, and reflection in the way of proofs and indications of Him—glory be to Him and may He be exalted! It is special. The special proof is the gnosis which the people of the night recognize. It is the formal prayer of the lovers, the people of secrets and hidden knowledge, those surrounded by veils. They are given knowledge which befit this moment in this world. It is the moment of the ascensions of the Prophets, the Messengers, and human spirits to see the divine Signs in the imaginary world (*alam-i mithal*). It is the time when the spirit draws near. It is the time when God descends from the station of sitting on the Throne to the nearest heaven for those who ask for forgiveness, turn in repentance, ask of Him and make supplication. It is a noble time. Whoever performs this formal prayer in a group or congregation, it is as if you had stood up for formal prayer for half of the night. There is a fragrance in this Tradition for whoever says that the end of its time is up until the first half of the night. (89)

God—glory be to Him!—also made the world of imagination and the inter space which is the gradual descent of meanings into sensory forms. They are not part of the world of the unseen because of the sensory forms they possess. They are not part of the visible world since they are pure meanings and their manifestation by these forms in an accidental matter which occurs. It belongs to the one who perceives them, and it does not belong to the meaning in itself. It is like knowledge in the form of milk, the religion in the form of a chain, and belief in the form of a handle. (90)

Among the formal prayers it is the time of the evening formal prayer and the time of the morning formal prayer. They are two moments which are neither part of the night nor the day. These are the two inter spaces between day and night since the time of the night and the day are circular. For this reason, God Almighty says: "*The night winds up the day and the day winds up the night*" (39:5). Whoever winds the turban hides part of it by the appearance of another part. It is as He says: "*the night enshrouds the day*" (7:54), that is, covers it. Similarly the day enshrouds the night. The one who prays at this moment speaks with his Lord by the proofs of God in the Self-disclosures, their variety and transformation in forms which he is given in the world of the interspace. This has come down in sound reports. (91)

7.2. The Quality of the Interspace of the Evening and Morning Formal Prayers and the Difference Between Them

However, the quality of the inter space of the evening formal prayer is that the servant leaves the visible world for the unseen world. He passes through this odd inter space, and in it, he comprehends the secrets of the unseen world which receives the visible world. This is like the senses which give form to the imagination, after which the imagination grasps them by the faculty of reflection. Then it attaches them to intelligible things since the imagination makes their form subtle in spite of its denseness in the senses. It is made to alternate by this inter space. The cause lies in the oddness of the evening formal prayer. The action which the odd has is that which makes the form subtle in reality so that it can be accepted by the world of the unseen and the Intellect. This is because the intellect does not accept forms of density and the unseen does not accept the visible. Therefore, its forms must become subtle in the Inter space so that the unseen world can accept it. (92)

It is like that with the inter space of dawn. You leave the unseen world for the visible world and the senses. You must pass through the inter space of the imagination. That is the moment of the morning formal prayer, from the rising of dawn until sunrise. The pure intelligible meanings which belong to the night are made dense by the imagination in its inter space. They are clothed in density by the power of the imagination after they were subtle. This is by means of a relationship which exists between them and the senses. At that moment, a dense form appears in the senses after it had been a subtle unseen form of the spirit. This is the effect of the inter space. It turns the sensory to the intelligible at the end of the night and it returns the sensory to the intelligible at the beginning of the night. (93)

7.3. The Intelligible, Imaginary and Sensory Forms

One example of that is that the form of the circle has a subtle intelligible form in the intellect. When the imagination looks at it, it gives form to it by its faculty. It gives it detail and makes it dense after it had been subtle in the intellect. Then it directs the limbs to build it by combining brick, mud, lime and all that might occur to the imagination of the architect in building. He sets it up in the senses as a dense form which the eye sees after it had been a subtle intelligible thing which could be fashioned in any form. That faculty leaves it in the senses because it has acquired a certain limitation. Throughout the entire day it remains limited by that form according to the length of the day. (94)

When the day has no end—like the day of the world to come—the period of duration of that form will never end. If the day comes to an end like the day of this world and its separate days (a day which lasts twenty-four hours, a day which lasts a month, a day which lasts a year, a day which lasts thirty years, or any other duration), then its form remains limited by that period for the length of his day. It is called its "life" up until the designated time when the amount of the evening formal prayer comes. Then the Inter space makes its form subtle and removes it from the world of the senses and conveys it to the world of the intellect. It reverts to the subtleness from which it came. Such is the movement of this "circular wheel." (95)

If you understand these meanings whose secrets are now clear to you, then you comprehend the knowledge of this world, the knowledge of death, the knowledge of the world to come, and the times specific to each place and their rules. May God give us and you understanding of His wisdom and place us among those whose feet are firm in His gnosis! (96)

7.4. The Three Parts of the Night and the Three Worlds of the Human Being

The night is composed of three thirds and the human being has three worlds. There is the world of the senses, which is the first third. There is the world of the imagination, which is the second third. There is the world of meaning, which is the last third of the night of his formation. In it God descends. He said: "The heart of My servant contains Me." He said: "God does not look at your forms," and that is the first third, "or your actions," and that is the second third, "but He looks at your hearts," and that is the last third. This covers the entire night. (97)

Whoever says that the end of its time is the first third designates the third of the senses. Whoever says that its end is up to the first half (and that is the middle third), designates the world of the imagination because it is the place of action in making subtle or dense. Whoever says that it is until the rising of dawn designates the world of meaning. Everyone speaks according to what the matter seems like to him. All agree that the rising of dawn is the end of the time of the night formal prayer. The manifest is that the end of the time extending to the rising of dawn belongs to the place of consensus and agreement about the end of the time by the rising of dawn. That which we have stated was also stated by Ibn Abbas, that is, the end of its time being until the rising of dawn. (98)

8 The Time of the Morning Formal Prayer

8.1. The Disagreement of the Legal Scholars on the Preferred Time of the Morning Formal Prayer

All agree that the beginning of the time of the morning formal prayer is the rising of dawn and that the end of it is sunrise. They disagree about the preferred time. Some say that the glow is better. Some say that the darkness is better. That is my position. (99)

8.2. The Vision of God: Is It By the Eye or By Knowledge

Know that some understand the words of the Prophet and the words of God Almighty about the vision of God to be in reference to knowledge and the intellect and not to actual eyesight (and there is a group of thinkers among the people of the *sunna* who state that). He is in the position of the one who thinks that darkness is better. The one who considers it likely that the Tradition in the divine law about seeing refers to eyesight which does not limit the divine Presence while the eyesight is not limited by direction, is in the position of the one who thinks that the glow is the time for the morning formal prayer. When there is still the length of time necessary for his cycle before sunrise, he can perform the salutations at the end of the formal prayer when the edge of the sun appears. (100)

The wonder is that the one who believes that the seeing which is related in the divine law is in reference to knowledge and not to sight, thinks that the glow is morning. Most of those who think that the seeing on the Day of Rising is in reference to eyesight and not to knowledge, think that the darkness is morning. (101)

This is the best way of interpreting this moment. It is the most sublime and universal. There are other interpretations, but what we have mentioned contains them all. Those interpretations which we have omitted do not contain the reality which we mentioned. This is why we were content with it. "*God speaks the truth and guides to the path.*" (102)

9 Rules About the The Times of the Formal Prayer

9.1. The Times When the Formal Prayer Is Imperative and the Excuse [for Not Praying]

9.1.1. The Disagreement of Legal Scholars on the Imperative and the Excuse

Some people confirm the times when the formal prayer is imperative and the excuse for not performing it and some people reject it. The dispute between them is well-known. (103)

9.1.2. The Ascription of Action to God or to the Servant

The inner interpretation in that is that the one who ascribes actions to God rejects excuses and the one who confirms that the servant acts by acquisition or character confirms it. (104)

9.2. The Times When the Formal Prayer is Imperative According to Those Who Affirm It

9.2.1. The Four Imperative Cases

The divine law scholars agree that they apply the times when the formal prayer is imperative and the excuses for not performing it to four categories: the menstruating woman who becomes pure at those times or who menstruates at those times—and those moments are not continuous; to the traveler who remembers the formal prayers in these moments when he is resident or the one who is resident who remembers them while he is traveling; the child who reaches puberty at that moment; and the unbeliever when he becomes Muslim. They disagree about someone who has fainted. Some say that he is like the menstruating woman and does not have to make it up. Others say that he must make it up if it is less than five formal prayers. (105)

9.2.2. The The Interpretation of the States When It is Imperative

The inward interpretation of the menstruating woman who becomes pure in the imperative time is the one who turns in repentance by necessity. The woman who is pure and then menstruates is the truthful person who lies by necessity. The interpretation about the one who is on a journey or resident is that he is traveling with his thoughts or his remembrance of God. Then he remembers what he missed at the time of the journey and what he did not obtain when he was resident when he sees an imperfection in his journey. He then knows that he forgot that at the time of his journey. The one who was resident remembers what he missed while resident while he is on a journey. This comes from inner and outer good manners with God. It is like their words, "Sit on the rug and be careful of expansive joy (*inbisat*)." This is due to the flaws which he saw in his journey. He knows that it is the result of whatever good manners he neglected when he was at home. God Almighty says: *"Certainly we have met fatigue from our journey."* (18:62) Before that, fatigue had not touched him. This was in order to make him remember the proof of the fish. (106)

The interpretation of the child who reaches puberty, then, is like the servant who is under restriction. When God is his hearing, sight, hand, power and limbs as is related, he emerges from that restriction. When this state reaches him while he is under the authority of a divine name, then which has authority over him? The name whose authority he was under or the name to which he moves? The moment is shared. (107)

The same applies to the interpretation of the unbeliever who becomes a Muslim in a time when the formal prayer is imperative. The unbeliever possesses the veil and is dominated by jealousy. Jealousy for God is not valid. Jealousy in God is valid, and jealousy about God is valid. The fact that there is no other dominates him, especially if he recognizes the meaning of *"He is The First and The Last, The One Who is Outward and The One Who is Inward."* (57:3) There are only these states. He is all since He is their source. Who is jealous? For whom is he is jealous? About whom is he jealous? (108)

Tell me! Tell me! I am free in God, so I do not do it.

As for the interpretation of the one who faints, he is the master of the state, whatever its judgment may be—if he regains consciousness in this moment or if the state seizes him in this moment. It is the name The Controller, which rules him in that moment. (109)

9.3. The Times in Which It is Forbidden to Offer the Formal Prayer

9.3.1. The Five Times in Which It Is Forbidden to Offer the Formal Prayer

There are five times in which it is forbidden to perform the formal prayer (in both agreement and disagreement): sunrise, sunset, noon, after the morning formal prayer, and after the afternoon formal prayer. (110)

9.3.2. The Truly Real Is the Sun of Existence: When He Appears in Theophany There is Bewilderment and Annihilation

The inner interpretation of that—and *"God has the most sublime example!"* (16:60)—is that the sun is the truly Real and the formal prayer is intimate conversation. When God gives a Self-disclosure, there is stupefaction and annihilation. Neither speech nor conversation is valid. This divine Station is such that when He makes you see, He does not let you speak. When He lets you speak, He does not let you see unless the Self-disclosure is in a form which combines speech and witnessing. When the one who sees is overwhelmed in himself, conversation is not valid. This is because the Messenger of God said: "Worship God as if you were seeing Him. Even if you do not see Him, there is no doubt that He sees you." You know, therefore, that the servant vanishes in the witnessing since The Witnessed takes possession of him. There is no conversation then. (111)

9.3.3. At Noon the Shadow of the Possible Vanishes

At noon, your shadow withdraws from you in you. Your shadow is your reality. Light lines upon all sides of you and floods over you. You do not have any specific matter to which to prostrate. The sun is behind you as well as in front of you, on your right, on your left, and above you. It does not attract you from any of your sides because you are light from all sides. The formal prayer is light, so lights rise in lights, and the formal prayer is not prayed for them. (112)

9.3.4. Distraction by the Embrace of the Beloved

As for the time after the morning formal prayer until sunrise, that is the moment when you leave the world of the inter space for the visible world. The time of the formal prayer is only obligatory in the senses, not in the inter space. It is the same after the afternoon formal prayer. Distraction by the embrace of the Beloved annihilates him to speech, since the pleasure of that embrace is free and unrestrained and envelops him. So that annihilates him from perception. (113)

9.4. The Formal Prayers Which Are Not Permitted During These Times in Which It is Forbidden to Offer the Formal Prayer

9.4.1. The Positions of the Legal Scholars About Offering the Formal Prayer in Forbidden Times

Some say that all of the formal prayers are not permitted in these five times. Some say that it is any formal prayers beyond the obligatory ones, whether it be a confirmed custom of the Prophet (*sunna*) or supererogatory. Some say that it is only the supererogatory ones and not the *sunna* ones. Some say that it is only the supererogatory prayers after afternoon and morning formal prayer, and both the *sunna* and the supererogatory prayers together at sunrise and sunset. As far as we are concerned, these moments belong to the formal prayers for the person who has been asleep and the forgetful one when he remembers. It is also for making up supererogatory prayers when he had neglected them in the moment allotted to them. (114)

9.4.2. Divine Conversation and Its Divisions and the Source of Its Interpretations

The inner interpretation in this is that divine Conversation between God and His servant has four divisions. One is conversation inasmuch as He sees you. Another is conversation inasmuch as you see Him. Another is conversation inasmuch as He sees you and you see Him. The last is the conversation of some of the people who speculate about beliefs by means of proofs. You do not see Him by knowledge in belief nor do you see Him by eyesight in belief, and He does not see you by sight or knowledge in belief when one denies His knowledge of parts. However, you see Him by knowledge of the incorporation of the part in the whole. (115)

This is our belief, and it is not the belief of the people of the *sunnah*. He—glory be to Him!—*"has knowledge of everything."* He says: *"Knows he not that God sees?"* (96:14) The Prophet is reported as saying in a sound Tradition, "He sees you." We have informed you about the source of the interpretations in these divisions. You recognize your division. When someone recognizes his division, then he confirms his conversation or transforms it. (116)

10 On the Call to Formal Prayer and the Declaration to Perform the Formal Prayer

10.1. Introduction

10.1.1. In the divine law, the Call to the Formal Prayer Announces That the Time of Formal Prayer Has Come

The call to formal prayer s the notification of the arrival of the time of formal prayer and the call to gather together for the formal prayer in the mosque. The declaration to perform the formal prayer (*iqama*) is the call for divine Conversation. (117)

10.1.2. The Reality of the Call to the Formal Prayer Is Announcing divine Theophany

The inner interpretation in that is that the call to formal prayer is the notification of divine Self-disclosure so that the essences can purify themselves in order to see Him. The declaration to perform the formal prayer is to stand up for His Self-disclosure when the day arrives when people stand up for the Lord of the worlds. (118)

10.2. The Description of the Call to the Formal Prayer

10.2.1. The Four Forms of the Call to Formal Prayer

There are four descriptions of the call to formal prayer. The first description is the double saying: "God is Greater," (*allahu akbar* called the *takbir*), fourfold bearing witness to the Oneness of God (called the *shahada*), and the rest of it double. Some people of this opinion think that the bearing witness is first double in a low voice and then double a second time in a high voice. This call to formal prayers is the call to formal prayer of the people of Medina. (119)

The second description is the first recitation of "God is Greater" (*Allahu akbar, takbir*) four times, the fourfold bearing witness (*shahada*), and the rest of the call to formal prayer double. This is the call to formal prayer of the people of Mecca. The third is the first recitation of "God is Greater" four times and the rest of the call to formal prayer double. This is the call to formal prayer of the people of Kufa. The fourth is the first recitation of "God is Greater," four times, the bearing of the witness of the Oneness of God three times, and the two "Come to. . ." three times. One begins with the *shahada* and continues to: "Come to success" and then repeats it again this way three times. These four statements are recited in order three times. This is the call to the formal prayer of the people of Basra. (120)

10.2.2. Aspects of Interpretation in the Different Calls to Formal Prayer

The inner interpretation in that is that doubling the recitation of "God is Greater" is for the Great and the Greater. Reciting it four times is for the Great and the Greater, and whoever makes himself great in himself and in the senses, legitimately, and illegitimately. Doing the bearing witness four times is for The First and The Last, The Manifest and The Hidden. Doubling what remains is for you and for God Almighty. Repeating the four statements three times in order (and, as we said: it is the school of the people of Basra), is that the first time is the notification of the visible world, the second is the notification of the world of the divine Kingdom (*jabarut*), and the third is notification of the angelic world (*malakut*). According to Abu Talib al-Makki, the second is for the world of the *malakut* and the third is for the world of the *jabarut*. (121)

10.2.3. Causes Are Waymarks and Signs Set Up for the Will of God in Creation

To be precise, that is when the human being looks with his actual eye and his inner eye at the causes which God Almighty made, waymarks and signs of what He desires by His formation and creation of things, and He had prior knowledge that He would give them existence together. The proof indicates that the existence of some of them depends upon the existence of others. He hears the praise of God Almighty about whoever exalts the waymarks of God. That exaltation of them comes from consciousness of God (*taqwa*) in the hearts. God says in His Mighty Book, *"Whoever holds the waymarks of God in honor, then it is truly from hearts filled with God-consciousness* (taqwa)." (22:32) Then He says: *"God is Greater."* (122)

Even if it is great in itself because of what it indicates, and great since God commanded it to be exalted, He is still greater than it. This is "greater" in comparison. It is the Arabic pattern *afal*. When he finishes it, this man who has articulated it is unveiled to the insignificance of causes in themselves and how much they are in need of the One who brought them into existence by their possibility. The need of effects is the same. He sees with the eye and unveiling when the covering is removed from his eye. They glorify their Creator and exalt Him. (123)

10.2.4. Everything Glorifies Its Creator

God says: *"There is nothing but that it glorifies His praise."* Glorification is speech connected to that thing. It is not glorification by state. For that reason, He says: "You do not understand their glorification" because of the variety of what glorifies Him. This is unless someone hears it. "*Truly He has been Forbearing*" (17:44) since He does not punish nor hasten punishment for the one who says that it is glorification by state: "*Forgiving*" (17:44). He veils their speech from hearing unless God breaks the normal pattern in granting a miracle to someone. (124)

It is related that the pebbles glorified in the palm of the Messenger of God in the presence of the Companions who were present there. The pebbles continue to glorify. The miracle only occurred when they actually heard it. He said: "But you do not understand their glorification" so as to refute the one who said that it is glorification by state. Methods of proof may be tortuous. Whoever says that it is glorification by state was proved false by God when God says: "You do not understand." (125)

10.2.5. Exaltation of the Waymarks and Sacred Places of God

As for the words of God Almighty, "*Whoever holds the sacred things of God in honor, then that is better for him with his Lord*" (22:30), it is better for him than the one who exalts the waymarks of God. He made "better" (*khayr*) a comparative. It is to distinguish between the exaltation of the waymarks and exaltation of the sacred places of God. The sacred place of God is essential, so He demands exaltation because of its essence. This is not like the exalted causes. The one who looks at the proof does not seek the proof for itself. He moves from it in order to reach what is proven. (126)

This world possesses a proof of God because we move from it to Him. We must not take The Real as a proof of the world, for then we would pass from Him to the world. This is not valid. How sublime are the words of prophethood when the Prophet said: "Whoever knows himself, knows his Lord." God Almighty says: "Do they not look" at such-and-such? He mentioned various creatures so that we would take them as proof of Him and not remain with them. This is the distinction between the sacred places of God and the waymarks of God. (127)

10.2.6. God Is Absolutely the Great Without Limitation

The second time, he says: "God is greater" to exalt the sacred place of God. It does not have comparative meaning. That is quite well-known linguistically. It means: "God, The Great." It is not comparative. He is The Great, The Placer of Causes, and He commanded us to exalt them. Whoever has no essential greatness is affected by the principle of extinction. The Great is absolute without limitation or comparison. He is God. (128)

This is the second recitation of "*Allahu akbar*" (*takbir*) in the call to the formal prayer. It belongs to these two forms. If the recitation of *"Allahu akbar"* is fourfold, the single recitation of *"Allahu akbar"* is doubled according to the definition which we mentioned in the senses and the intellect, that is, as the tongue exalts Him by the articulation of comparison, so the intellect exalts Him. When he says: "God is Greater" with the tongue, it is as if we were saying, "God is Greater!" with the intellect. That is to say, He is Greater by the proof of the senses and the proof of the intellect. Then he also doubles the other *takbir* in the senses and the intellect. He says: "God is Greater," that is, The Great. This is not by means of comparison in the senses. God is Greater, The Great. This is not by means of the comparison of the intellect, respect, and the divine law. This is what is seen by the one who recites the *takbir* four times in the call to the formal prayer which is a public announcement. (129)

10.2.7. Testimony to Divinity

Then he says: "I testify that there is no god but God. I testify that there is no god but God" in a low voice which he can hear. He is then in the position of the one who formulates the proof first in himself. After that, he gives it expression and says it openly before his adversaries or in order to teach someone the proper course of that proof. That is because this caller to formal prayer testifies in this bearing witness that he sees the causes veiled from the gnosis of God which are given the power of speech. They are veiled from perceiving the matter for what it is due to ignorance, and they are veiled from what the majesty of God demands in relating everything to Him. This is due to the veil of heedlessness. (130)

The ignorant man says: *"I am your lofty lord"* (79:24) or he is scornful, which is a sort of ignorance, or he says: *"I knew not of any god for you other than me."* (28:38) He may be lying and know that he is lying because he is scornful and thinks but little of his people. They obey him. He says: "I have blessed so-and-so. I have power over so-and-so. I have taught so-and-so the knowledge which he has and the Quran. If it had not been for me, he would not have known any of what he knows." Yet he hears God say, *"Is then He Who creates as one who creates not? Will you not then recollect?"* (16:17) And He says: *"O humanity! Worship your Lord Who created you and those who were before you."* (2:21) They are the causes in which you exist. (131)

He says to the one who thinks that we exist by causes, not in them: *"Then ascribe not partners to God while you know."* (2:22) He brought the causes in existence and brought you into existence in them, not by them. Then he says: "I bear witness that there is no god but God," that is, there is no Creator except God. He therefore rejects the divinity of all that claims it for itself which is other-than-God. He affirms it for the One who deserves it, even if he laid claim to it with God as the idolater does. He testifies that it belongs to God in the intellect, the divine law, senses and meaning. All of this is with himself. It is like that one who first formulates the proof. Then he says it aloud so that others will hear: the student, the pretender, the ignorant one, and the one who is heedless of the words of God Almighty—"The Merciful, He taught the Quran," and other signs. He said: "*He created the human being. He taught him the clear explanation.*" (55:3-4) He cuts off any authority that causes might have. This is the meaning of the bearing witness, making it double and making it fourfold. (132)

10.2.8. Testimony to the Message of Muhammad Is Testimony to the Oneness of God

It is the same when he says: "I bear witness that Muhammad is the Messenger of God." When he sees what the proof gives him by unification, he sees it by knowledge, not by means of nearness. This is due to the fact that the human being does not know that saying that and looking into the recognition of that will bring one closer to God by his intellect. His portion is to know that he is ennobled by the attribute of knowledge above the one who is ignorant of that. Openly saying it as well as every proof of the like of this knowledge contains an aspect of instruction for the one who does not know. It is also a deterrent for the stubborn. All of it ennobles this self over the self which does not have that because the intellect has no power to grasp anything of nearness to God. (133)

The Messenger came from God. He told him to say that and to look at that, and to hide it in himself and to conceal it. He also teaches and deters others when he openly declares it. This is in the path of nearness to God. Even though it is knowledge, it is also worship. When the believer with knowledge speaks or recites the call to formal prayer as does the caller, "I bear witness that Muhammad is the Messenger of God," he utters it both as knowledge and as worship, whereas the common man says it as imitation and worship. (134)

Doubling this second bearing witness of the message and making it fourfold has the same principle as that of the bearing witness to the Oneness of God. It has the same ranks which we have already mentioned. If it is three like the call to formal prayer of the people of Basra who repeat the four statements in order each time, then it is because he says it as knowledge the first time, teaching the second time when he says it aloud, and worship the third time. It is all knowledge, instruction and worship, so understand! The only difference among the people of Basra, Kufa, the Hijaz and Medina is in regard to doing it three times. All of that is *sunna*. The human being chooses to give the call to formal prayer in any manner he likes among these four. Our position is like the various transmissions regarding the eclipse prayer and other things. (135)

10.2.9. Saying "Come to . . ." Twice Is a Call to Come to Conversation with God

After the double bearing witness, God told us to say: "Come to formal prayer" twice. We call ourselves by one of them and we call others with the second one. The first time it means, "Devote yourselves to conversation with your Lord. Purify yourselves and come to the mosques." The second time he addresses whoever is in the mosques: "Purify your hearts and be present before your Lord. You are in His house. You desire to speak to Him." (136)

It is the same when he says: "Come to success" with the same two explanations and interpretations of the two times. He speaks to the one who is outside and to the one who is in the mosque, to himself, and to others: "Devote yourself to doing that which will save you from His punishment by His bliss, and from His veil by His Self-disclosure and vision of Him." He says in the second one: "Devote yourself to that which will make you continue in your bliss and the pleasure of your contemplation." God is more entitled to the recitation of "*Allahu akbar*" than that which prevents you from turning to it. (137)

10.2.10. God Is More Entitled to the Recitation of God Is Greater (takbir) Than That Which Prevents You from Turning to It

Then he says: "God is Greater. God is Greater" to himself and to others, to whomever is waiting for the formal prayer—like the one who is inside the mosque, and whoever is outside of it, engaged in his business. He says: "God is Greater than that in which you are involved," that is, more entitled to exaltation than that which prevents you from turning to that which you are commanded to do in the way of formal prayer, success, and going on in the "Come to formal prayer. Come to success." (138)

He does not make the second fourfold, so it is not like the first. The second recitation of "*Allahu akbar*" (*takbir*) and the two expressions of "Come to. . ." aim for nearness. The intellect cannot perceive it on its own. It belongs especially to the divine law. Because of this, neither "Come to" or the *takbir* is uttered four times. It is double since he addresses himself and others, and whoever is in the mosque and whoever is not. (139)

10.2.11. The Call to the Formal Prayer Concludes with Absolute Oneness of God

Then he says: "There is no god but God," and seals the call to formal prayer with absolute bearing witness of the Oneness of God since the call to the formal prayer contains several matters, including actions which are related to the servant, and it might occur to the lower self of the one called that he is not called upon to do that. Action has a reality. The caller is also like that. It is feared that he will ascribe the action to himself as a quality as some of them think. God did not make it one of the proofs of His Oneness except by making creation belong to Him alone. He says: "*Is then He Who creates as one who creates not? Will you not then recollect?*" (140)

It is the divinity hidden in the self of every person. It is the hidden polytheism which is forgiven. He seals the call to the formal prayer with Oneness of God and does not utter it two, three or four times. This is the absolute Oneness which the Prophets brought from God by God. It is the best statement uttered by the Messenger of God and the Prophets before him. He informs all the listeners that there is no god but God. He unifies by seeking absolute Oneness. In all four schools, it is prescribed that he does not add anything to the Oneness in each call to formal prayer. (141)

10.2.12. The Spiritual Reward of the Morning Formal Prayer

As for the spiritual reward (*tathwib*) in the call to the formal prayer of the morning formal prayer—and it is—"formal prayer is better than sleep"—some people say that it is part of the prescribed call to formal prayer and interpret it. Some people say that it comes from what Umar did, and so they do not interpret it. As far as we are concerned, we say that it is the divine law, even if it did come from what Umar did. The Prophet confirmed it when he said: "Whoever makes a good *sunna*, there is no doubt that it is a good *sunna*." Then it must be interpreted as the divine law. According to this interpretation, it is part of the *sunna* of the call to formal prayer unless your position is that the *sunna* is only that which was done in the time of the Prophet which he recognized and confirmed, or that which he actually made *sunna*. Someone who holds this opinion only calls "*sunna*" something which fits this description. This is not really a dispute. (142)

10.2.13. The Addition of "Come to the best action"

As for the one who adds, "Come to the best action," it was done in the time of the Messenger of God. It is related that it was called out in the Battle of the Ditch when people were digging the ditch. The time of formal prayer came and it is the best thing, as the Tradition relates. So it was called out, "People of the Ditch! Come to the best action!" The one who puts it in the call to formal prayer does not err. He imitates. If this tradition is sound or he makes a good *sunna*, he has the reward of whoever performs it. The one who objected to it only did so out of fanaticism. How just is the one who says it! We seek refuge with God from the dangers of the servants! (143)

10.3. The Ruling of the Call to the Formal Prayer

10.3.1. The Position of the Scholars About the Call to the Formal Prayer

Some say that it is obligatory and some say that it is a confirmed *sunna*. Among those who say that it is obligatory is the one who thinks that it is a general obligation. Some say that the call to formal prayer is obligatory for mosques where the formal prayer is performed in a group. Malik's school maintains in one transmission which has come from him that it is a confirmed Tradition of the Prophet. He did not think that it was either obligatory or strong *sunna* for the person who is on his own. Some say that it is obligatory for each individual. Some say that it is obligatory for each individual and for groups, both on journeys and when one is resident. Some say it is only on a journey. Some say that it is *sunna* for the one who is alone and for groups, although it is a confirmed *sunna* for the group. (144)

All agree that it is either a confirmed *sunna* or an obligation for cities. That was stated by our shaykh, Abu Abd Allah ibn al-As al-Dallal in Seville. I heard him say that more than once. He said: "When the people of a city agree to abandon the call to formal prayer or abandon a *sunna*, one is obliged to attack them." He took his proof from the established Tradition that when the Messenger of God was raiding some people, he would wait until morning. If he heard the call to formal prayer, he would not attack. If he did not hear the call to formal prayer, he would attack. (145)

10.3.2. It Is the Duty of the Human Being to Call Himself and Others to God After the divine law is Established

The inner interpretation in that is that it is the duty of everyone to call himself and others to obey God after the divine law is set forth. The Messenger of God said to Malik ibn al-Huwayrith and his companion, "When you are on a journey, recite the call to formal prayer and the declaration to perform the formal prayer." This is a Tradition. The human being has been traveling with his breaths ever since the day when God created him. He is traveling in this world and the next. It is not valid that he should ever be stationary. Had he remained stationary for more than one single breath, the action of the divinity regarding this world would have been invalidated. God—glory be to Him!—is engaged in some affair in creation at every breath. It is His effect in each existent source with a special quality. God has made us see it, both fine and great. How precious and mighty with God is the one who possesses this! Whoever misses guarding and watching his breaths in this world and the world to come has certainly missed a great blessing. (146)

10.4. The Time of the Call to Formal Prayer

10.4.1. The Formal Prayer Is Not Called Before Its Time Except for the Morning Formal Prayer

Scholars agrees that the call for the formal prayer is not given before the time except in the case of the morning formal prayer. There is some dispute about that. Some say that it is permitted to recite the call to formal prayer for it before dawn, and some forbid it, which is my position. As far as I am concerned, the call to formal prayer before its time is remembrance of God which takes the form of the call to formal prayer. It is not actually the call to formal prayer as regards notification that the time of the formal prayer has arrived. (147)

Bilal used to recite the call to formal prayer at night. The Messenger of God said: "Bilal's call to formal prayer does not stop you from eating and drinking," that is, in Ramadan and for the one who desires to fast. Bilal recited the call to formal prayer, they would continue to eat and drink until Ibn Umm Maktum recited the call to formal prayer. He was blind and did not recite the call to formal prayer until someone told him, "It is morning. It is morning." (148)

As far as I am concerned, the call to formal prayer is only obligatory after the time of the formal prayer has arrived. Some say that there must be two calls to formal prayer: a call before the time and a call after it. Abu Muhammad ibn Hazm said: "There must be a call to the formal prayer after the moment." (149)

10.4.2. The Moment Has Authority

The inner interpretation of that is that it is actually calling the selves to God from God, and it is a call from phenomenal beings in respect to heedless or ignorant people who are under the jurisdiction of the divine names or divine Management even though they are unaware of it. Because of this, we said: "in the heart of the matter." (150)

Know that the power of the moment must be specific for the one who is under its judgment. It is the divine name particular to that moment. One can only call to it through obligation after the proper time has come. Then he can be one of those who call to God by the inner eye. It is the call in each moment which is particular to what that moment demands. (151)

If he calls him by other than his moment, then the human being will fall into ignorance. He is calling him by that which will remove him from the power of its jurisdiction which the listener is anticipating in himself. Therefore, there must be a call for him after the time has come so that it will be set down by the one who is the master of the moment among those divine names. Think! Is thankfulness valid for you before the arrival of the moment of the authority of the name, the Blesser? When your moment is blessing and its moment is present with you, then you are called upon to be thankful to the Blesser. (152)

10.4.3. The Interpretation of the Difference in the Call to Formal Prayer for the Morning Formal Prayer Before Its Time

Dispute arises concerning the morning formal prayer because the listener does not know what the lawgiver intended by that remembrance of God. It is a call for the master of the moment. This is different from the other formal prayers. Since night is the place of sleep and people sleep, he prescribed the other call whose purpose is to wake up those who are asleep. It is a call for alertness and a preparation for the arrival of the morning formal prayer at the beginning of its time. It is a call of selection and stimulation of desire. It is made in the form of the call to formal prayer which is prescribed for the formal prayer, that is, we call you for the sake of the formal prayer so that you might remember and get ready for it. (153)

When its time comes, one is obliged to announce the arrival of the time since the listeners do not know about the arrival of the beginning of the time. It is hidden from most people. Most of them do not know and they learn by the call to formal prayer which is prescribed for the arrival of the time that the time has actually come. (154)

10.4.4. The One Who Is Heedless As to Which divine name Has Jurisdiction Over Him

It is like that with the judgment about the interpretation of the one who is heedless about which divine name has jurisdiction over him. The caller calls him from the sleep of heedlessness since he is under the jurisdiction of a divine name which directs him and he has no strength nor power except by Him. When he awakens from the sleep of his heedlessness and remembers with his intellect, then he recognizes which name is the ruler of the moment. He obeys it according to what the reality of that name demands in respect of this person. God Almighty says: "Let those with inner cores [intellects, lubb] remember." He says: "*And remind, for truly the reminder profits the ones who believe.*" (51:55) (155)

10.4.5. The Call to the Formal Prayer Before the Morning Formal Prayer is Remembrance of God in the Form of the Call to the Formal Prayer

We believe that the call to formal prayer before the morning formal prayer is remembrance of God and a call in the form of the call to formal prayer. It is not the actual call to formal prayer which is prescribed in order to announce the arrival of the time. The Prophet said: "Bilal calls at night." He did not say, "recites the call to formal prayer." Similarly they said "call" about Ibn Umm Maktum in a doubtful place. He was blind and did not call until he was told, "It is morning. It is morning," that is, you are near morning. The relater said: "Between the call of Bilal and the call of Ibn Umm Maktum was the length of the time that one descends [from the minaret] and the other ascends." He termed it "call" because of this capacity, that is, the call of the formal prayer of Ibn Umm Maktum. Eloquence in Arabic is that the phrases correspond, and he previously said that Bilal called at night. (156)

The Tradition of Ibn Umar strengthens what we believe: "Bilal recited the call to formal prayer before the rising of dawn." Ibn Umar called it a call to formal prayer since he recognized the state. The Messenger of God told him to go back and call, "The servant is asleep," so that the people would know that the time for the formal prayer had not yet come. The call to formal prayer is prescribed for the arrival of the formal prayer. Since he recognized that Bilal intended to recite the call to formal prayer, and that those who heard might pray the formal prayer outside of its time, he commanded him to tell people that he erred in his call to the formal prayer. (157)

For this reason, some of the callers to formal prayer at night use supplication, reminding, recitation of signs of the Quran, stern warning, and composing ecstatic poetry to remind you of death and the world to come while you are in this world. This is in order to teach people. When they hear the call to formal prayer, some of them intend remembrance of God as we have stated. It is also to awaken people who are asleep, and not for the actual arrival of the time. It is like that with the interpretation of the different states of the people of God. They must have signs which they use to distinguish between the states given by the given names, so understand! (158)

10.5. On the Preconditions of This Act of Worship

Some scholars say that it has eight preconditions which they enumerate. The first is whether or not it is a precondition that the call to formal prayer be done by someone who is resident there. The second is whether or not it is a precondition that the caller not talk while he is reciting it. The third is whether or not it is a precondition that the caller be in a state of purity. The fourth is whether or not it is a precondition that the caller face the *qibla* [the Kaba in Mecca]. The fifth is whether or not it is a precondition that the caller be standing. The sixth is whether or not it is disliked for the call to formal prayer to be done by someone while mounted. The seventh is whether or not it is a precondition that he have reached puberty. The eighth is whether or not it is a precondition that he not take any wages for the call to formal prayer or that he take wages. (159)

10.5.1. The Disagreement of Religious Scholars About the Preconditions of the Call to the Formal Prayer

Scholars of the divine law disagree about these conditions and their proofs in respect to analogy and comparison of sound and weak Traditions. Our school is that the call to formal prayer is valid both when these preconditions exist and when they do not exist. It is better to recite the call to formal prayer with the eight preconditions if there is agreement about them, and but none of them are an impediment. (160)

10.5.2. The One Who Calls People to God When the Caller Is Before God (The States and Stations of Those Who Call People to God)

As for the interpretation of that in all of the preconditions which we mentioned, know that the caller may be the divine name by which God calls to God. It is the very same as the caller who undertakes to perform it before God in whatever state to which he calls. It may be another of the names, so it is not a precondition of the call to formal prayer that he reside there if there is difficulty in it. (161)

10.5.3. Speech Is a State Which Demands Calling to God

The one who calls to God may talk while he calls to God when the state demands that from him and it is something which he cannot delay—whether it is due to good manners or by an obligation specifically incumbent on him. He should not say that which would lessen the understanding of the listener which would make him cease to be a caller for him. This is the interpretation of the second precondition. (162)

10.5.4. Calling to God in State and Word

The caller may call by his state which is purity, and this is more excellent, or he may call by that which he does not possess in his state. This is also good in every aspect as Hasan ibn Abi-l-Hasan al-Basri said. He was one of the people on the sublime path of God. They say that had one of them not warned another in order to warn himself, none of them would ever have warned anyone. Someone who does a reprehensible action must forbid the reprehensible. If he does not do so, he has two wrong actions. Know that! This is the interpretation of the third precondition. (163)

10.5.5. Calling to God While Aiming for This World

If the caller intends God by his call, that is better. If he intends the world by that, that still does not prevent him from calling to God. However, the first is more excellent. It is hoped that the other will benefit the one who hears the call. He calls him, and he is happy because of his call. This is the position of facing the *qibla* for the call to formal prayer, which is the fourth precondition. (164)

10.5.6. Undertaking the Rights of the Call or Not Doing So

If the caller is standing up, undertaking the rights of that to which he calls, that is better than his sitting down, refraining from that in his call. That is the interpretation of the fifth precondition. (165)

10.5.7. Calling to God and Presence With the Servanthood of the Self

When the caller calls, is he present with servanthood and abasement, or is he involved in looking at the might of his ego (*nafs*) and its pride and conceit? This is the one who gives the call to formal prayer while mounted. This is the interpretation of the sixth precondition. (166)

10.5.8. Calling to God and Reaching Gnosis of Him

Should the caller call before he has arrived at recognition of that to which he calls such as the call of the imitator who at first does not call until he has recognized the One to whom he calls? It is the precondition of having reached puberty for the call to formal prayer. It is the interpretation of the seventh precondition. (167)

10.5.9. The Wage for the Call

Is it a precondition for the caller to God that he does not receive any wage for his call? We consider that it is better that he does not take it, but if he does take it, he is allowed to do so. The station of calling to God demands a wage. There is no Prophet who called his people but that it was said to him, "*Say: I ask of you no compensation for this but that whoever willed should take himself on a way to his Lord*" (25:57). He affirmed the wage for his call and asked God for it. He did not ask the one he called for it. The Messenger of God did not ask us for any wage for conveying the call except love for his relatives. It is love for the People of the House and his relatives and that they be shown generosity for his sake, whoever they may be. (168)

The Messenger of God said: "What you have learned of the Book of God [Quran] is better." This is in the Tradition in which a healing talisman was made for a man stung by a scorpion. It was made from the Opening Chapter of the Quran and the man was saved. The Messenger of God said: "Divide it up and assign me a share of it," that is, the sheep which they received as a wage for that. The human being calls the servants of God by his admonition and reminding. If he takes a wage, he is allowed to do that. It is an action which demands a wage according to the testimony of every Messenger, even if he does not take it from people, and asks God for it. So he can do that. (169)

The reason that the Messengers left that and asked for their wage from God is that God is the One who employed them to convey the message. Therefore God Almighty should pay the wage, not the person who is called. The one who made the talisman took the wage from the stung man because the stung man employed him to do that. For that reason, the Prophet said: "Assign me a share of it." He is the one who told the maker of the talisman that which he used to make it for this man. One should not look at what is near to this in the Tradition of Barira when he said: "It is charity for her and a gift for us" because it reached its place. This is the eighth precondition. (170)

10.5.10. The Wage of the Slaves and the Wage of Those Who Know God

Know that this wage is the wage of divine Favor which the Master assigns to His servant. The servant does not deserve a wage from his Master in whatever He employs him to do. He owns him and he is His property. However, his Master is kind to him for He gives him a wage for his work. Its secret is that He created him in His form. Our servants, our brothers, understand! (171)

As for those who know God, The Great and Majestic, their wage is the contemplation of their Master when they return to Him after having conveyed what they were commanded to convey. They are made sorrowful by separation from that absolutely pure witnessing and by the contemplation of phenomenal beings. He promised them that when they return to Him, they will have increase in contemplation. That is why they informed people that their wage was due from God. (172)

10.6. The One Who Repeats Exactly What is Said When He Hears the Call to Formal Prayer

10.6.1. The Disagreement of the Religious Scholars About How to Respond to the Call of Formal Prayer When It is Heard

Scholars of the divine law disagree about this. Some say that he says the same as the caller to the formal prayer says: verbatim, until the end of the call. Some say that he says the like of what the caller to formal prayer says except when he says the two, "Come to. . ." Then the listener says: "There is no power nor strength except by God." I say that it is the first one. It is more fitting even though it is confirmed that the Messenger of God said: "No power. . ." in that. I say that, but I do not make it a precondition that the listener go along with the caller word for word. However, if he likes, he can say exactly what the caller to the formal prayer says after each statement, or if he likes, he can say the like of that when he is finished. (173)

This concerns the caller to the formal prayer who recites the call from the minaret or at the door of the mosque or inside the mosque. This is when the beginning of the time comes before the people in the mosque know that the time for the formal prayer has come. This is the caller for whom the call to the formal prayer is prescribed. As for the callers to formal prayer in the mosque who are among those who hear the call to formal prayer, they perform remembrance of God in the form of the call to formal prayer. The listener is not obliged to repeat it. He is in the position of the listener who hears what the caller has recited. It is not prescribed for us nor are we commanded to say what the listener says when he says what the caller recited. (174)

10.6.2. Calling to God With Insight

The inner interpretation in that is that God Almighty said in what the Messenger said: "I call to God with insight, I and whoever follows me." There is no doubt that the caller calls to God. He said: "And whoever follows me." That is the one who is not a Prophet and calls as the Prophet called. He calls the servants of God to the Oneness of God and to action which entails obedience to Him. He is in the position of the one who hears the caller and who is commanded by the lawgiver to repeat the like of what the caller says: and neither add to it nor detract from it. (175)

Similarly, the one who calls to God must call by His the divine law which is sent down and articulated. He does not add to the call of the Messenger of God. These are his words: "God has made flourish a man who heard a word from me and then learned it by heart and performed it as he heard it. Many a conveyer has put something into the vessel of a listener." (176)

10.6.3. Transmitting the Meaning of Hadith

This is a matter about which people disagree, that is, about transmitting this report according to meaning. What I consider to be sound is that it is not permitted at all to do that unless the transmitter makes it absolutely clear that he is transmitting the meaning. He transmits to us his understanding of the words of the Messenger of God. We do not worship God by someone else's understanding except in traditions about which there is agreement and the Quran. This does not include the non-Arab who does not know Arabic. (177)

He transmits the meaning. If he transmitted exactly what the Messenger said: we might well understand the like of what he understood, or more or less, or even the opposite of what he understood. It is better to transmit the Tradition as we transmit the Quran. (178)

10.6.4. The One Who Calls to God Does Not Add to What the Messenger of God Brought Until God Acquaints Him with That

The one who calls to God does not add to what the Messenger of God brought us of reports about unseen matters unless God acquaints him with something of the unseen which God has taught him. He can call by it as long as it does not remove what the divine law confirmed by multiple transmission, that is, in a way which has useful knowledge. That is necessary. According to this definition, the interpretation about reciting exactly what the caller to the formal prayer recites extends to such an extent that had the listener said: "Glory be to God!" when the caller recites, "God is Greater," he would not have obeyed the command of the Messenger of God. Whoever does not obey the command of the Messenger of God has not obeyed the command of God. God says: "Obey the Messenger," and He says: "Whoever obeys the Messenger has obeyed God." The Messenger of God commanded us to say the like of what of the caller to prescribed prayer says: even if this listener says something better. (179)

It is the same if he were to say, "God The Great." He did not recite the same as the caller to formal prayer recited unless the caller actually said: "God The Great." There is disagreement about the one who recites the call to formal prayer with this expression. Some permit that, and so the listener is obliged to say the same. Had the listener said: "God is Greater," he would have uttered the prescribed call to formal prayer which is transmitted by multiple Traditions. There is a great difference between "God the Great" and "God is Greater." (180)

10.6.5. One Must Transmit Traditions As Their Speaker Said Them

One must transmit Traditions as their speaker said them—except in cases of necessary—that is, a translation for the one who does not speak the language. As for the Quran, one must transmit the written text and confirm its articulation as it is related. After that, it can be translated so that there will be no dispute. There may be commentary within the translation which is not part of the recitation. As for something other than the

Quran, one must transmit the meaning with the closest expression which conforms to the meaning, just as one does with prophetic Traditions. (181)

10.7. The Declaration to Perform the Formal Prayer

10.7.1. The Ruling of the Declaration to Perform the Formal Prayer According to Legal Scholars

The declaration to perform the formal prayer has a judgment and a description. People disagree about its judgment. Some people say that it is a confirmed *sunna* for each individual and for groups, even more so than the call to the formal prayer. Some people say that it is obligatory. This is the school of some of the people of literal interpretation. If they mean that it is one of the obligations of the formal prayer, then the formal prayer would be invalid if it were omitted. If they do not say that, the formal prayer is valid and he is a rebel if he omits it. I saw some of them who say that the formal prayer was invalid if it were omitted. Some say that omitting it intentionally invalidates the formal prayer. This is the school of Ibn Kinana. (182)

10.7.2. The Declaration to Perform the Formal Prayer for the Sake of God and the Declaration to Perform the Formal Prayer by the Command of God

The interpretation of that in judgment is that the declaration to offer the formal prayer which is for God is an obligation and must be done. As for the declaration to offer the formal prayer which God has commanded us to undertake, we are in that declaration according to our states. If the state accords that it is an obligation, we consider it an obligation as He says: "*Perform the prescribed way of life and be not split up in it.*" (42:13) He said: "*Perform the formal prayer*" and "*Lay down the balance with equity.*" (21:47) This is the definition of the obligation. If the balance overweighs on the side of fulfilling it, it is better. You have obeyed the command of God. The balance need not overweigh in order to be described by the declaration to offer the formal prayer, that is, performing that which is the definition of the obligation. After that, the balance is overweighed. The one who makes the balance lighter has not reached performance as it is defined in weighing so that he would acquire the obligation as does the one whose balance overweighs. (183)

We only praise the one who overweighs because he has established the balance, not because he has overweighed. Then we praise him again for the overweighing. Therefore, the one who overweighs is praised from two aspects, so know that! His praise for establishing that is more sublime since it is obligatory praise. The praise for overweighing is supererogatory except for the one who considers that to be obligatory. It is the Messenger's words about settling what one owes: "When you weigh, give overweight." He commanded him to overweigh and confirmed it in word and deed. If the matter is not an obligation by the state, it is still based on that. (184)

This is the interpretation of the judgment of the declaration by a useful aspect in the religion of God. Whoever grasps this Book and acts by what we have confirmed in it, we have not confirmed any matter which is not prescribed. Praise be to God. If we did not undertake some proofs out of fear of being too lengthy, we still did not depart from the Quran and *sunnah* in it by the praise of God. It is as Junayd said: "This knowledge of ours is limited by the Quran and the *sunna*." (185)

10.7.3. The Description of the Declaration to Perform the Formal Prayer According to the Legal Scholars

As for the description of the declaration to perform the formal prayer, since people say that the recitation of "*Allahu akbar*" (which is at the beginning is double and the rest is single and the rest is single and the recitation of "*Allahu akbar*" at the end of the declaration is double. Some people consider it like the declaration except the declaration is all double. Some people choose between the double and the single. Some people say that it is all double, and that the first recitation of "*Allahu akbar*" is agreed to be based on the Oneness of God of the last "*la ilaha illa Lah*." (186)

10.7.4. The Interpretation of the Description of the Declaration to Perform the Formal Prayer

As for the interpretation of the one who doubles, that is, adds to the one, it belongs to the same ranks which we mentioned about the call to formal prayer. It is the same. We will not turn to another interpretation because it has come in the outward divine law as the articulation of the call to the formal prayer and no other articulation, except for the statement of the declaration to perform the formal prayer itself (*qad qamati s-salat*). It has the declaration while the call to formal prayer does not. This is the statement, "The formal prayer has been established." It is a communication in the past tense although the formal prayer is in the future. (187)

It is good news from God to His servants and to whomever comes to the mosque to wait for the formal prayer, or is on his way to it, or is performing ablution for it, or is intending to perform ablution for it before he actually begins it (when he intends to pray with that ablution). If he dies in any of these situations, he has the same reward as someone who performed the formal prayer, even if he did not actually perform it. He used the past tense to confirm that attainment. If it is attained by action, he has the reward of attaining by action. The reward of attainment which someone acquires who dies in these situations before the formal prayer is due to the fact that it is related in a Tradition that the human being is in the formal prayer as long as he is waiting for it. He used the past tense for this reason. It is the result of His words: "*Performed the formal prayer. . .*" (188)

The declaration of the formal prayer is the completion of its formation and perfection, that is, it is yours, its formation established, its form complete according to what is prescribed. When you enter it and obtain the second reward, it may be like the first in establishing its formation, and then again, it may not. The one who performs may perform it incompletely and not whole. Therefore it is written for him as incomplete since he performed it contrary to what was written for him before the action. Look at how immense God's favor is to His servants! The cause of that is the words of God Almighty, "*God has the conclusive disputation.*" (6:149) Had He given him the reward for it for it before He did it in accordance with His knowledge of him in it—as far as its being incomplete is concerned—the servant might have said: "If you had let me live, I would have performed it in the most perfect fashion." Therefore God, The Mighty, The Majestic, gave His servant the reward of the most perfect performance. God has praise and favor in that! (189)

11 The Direction of Formal Prayer (*Qibla*)

11.1. Introduction

11.1.1. The Ruling of Turning Towards the Kaba in the Formal Prayer

Muslims agree that turning to the *qibla*, that is, to the Kaba, is one of the preconditions for the validity of the formal prayer. If it had not been that there was a consensus before me regarding this question, I would not have said that it was a precondition. God Almighty says: "*Wherever you turn, there is the Countenance of God.*" This was sent down after it. This is a sign of judgment and has not been abrogated. However, the consensus agrees about this and that His words, "*Wherever you turn, there is the Countenance of God*" (2:215) is the principle for the one who is confused and does not know where the direction of formal prayer is. He performs in whatever direction he thinks is the direction of formal prayer by his own striving. If it is clear to him after he has performed the formal prayer that he has not performed the formal prayer towards the direction of formal prayer, he does not have to repeat the formal prayer, although there is some dispute regarding that. There is also dispute about the one who cannot find any way to purify himself. There is a dispute about whether he performs or not. (190)

There is no dispute that when a person sees the House, he is obliged to turn towards it. If he does not see the House, the scholars disagree about the two topics in this question. One topic is whether the obligation is the eye itself or the direction. The second topic is whether the obligation is to get the correct direction or to try to get it right, that is, being right with the eye or the direction according to the person who makes the eye obligatory. (191)

Some say that the eye is the obligation. Some say that the direction is the obligation. I say that it is the direction, not the eye. Otherwise there would be compulsion. God says: "*There is no compulsion in religion.*" (2:256) By direction, I mean when the Kaba is hidden from the eye when there is a long row of people. Their formal prayer is valid in spite of the severance which occurs as all of them do not turn their eyes to it. This is understood. (192)

11.1.2. The Interpretation of Defining the Direction of Formal Prayer

The interpretation of the delineation of the direction of formal prayer is that the servant is not given any choice. His root and the root of all that is other-than-God is compulsion and coercion. Even the choice of the servant is forced in his choice. This is in spite of the fact that God is the Doer, the Chooser. That is because He said: "*He chooses*" and "*He Wills*." He only does what He already knew. Change of knowledge is impossible. God Almighty says: "*The saying near Me is not to be substituted and I am not unjust to the servants*." (50:29) He says: "*God has the conclusive disputation*." (6:149) (193)

I have not seen anyone who comprehended this divine statement. Its meaning is utterly clear. Because of that very intensity, its clarity is hidden. We have spoken about it in this book and made it quite clear. It is the secret of the degree. Whoever understands this question, does not oppose God in all that He decrees and causes to happen to His servants in them and from them. For this reason, He says: "*He will not be asked as to what He accomplishes but they will be asked*." (21:23) If you had been a person of intelligence, you would have understood from God and this sign would have been enough for you regarding what is meant. (194)

11.1.3. Definition of Things and the Actions of the Chosen Doer

We will now return to the interpretation of this. The formal prayer is going to visit God. It has come in a sound Tradition that the formal prayer is light. The human being has an inward eye just as he has an outward one. He must have unveiling in his formal prayer. Part of the totality which is unveiled to him in his formal prayer is that he is compelled in the choice which he ascribes to himself. Therefore, in this place and in all acts of worship, delineation is prescribed for him in things so that he is under the principle of compulsion in his conduct. This is a root which contains every existent thing. Nothing is excluded from this root when you have keen eyesight. "*He listens and He is a witness*." This applies even in the principle of the permissible. He has no choice in it because it is impossible that it be judged by any other principle than the permissible: obligatory, recommended, forbidden or disliked. (195)

11.1.4. Facing the Kaba With the Eye and Facing Its Direction

For this reason, he is told to face the House in his formal prayer when he sees it, and to face its direction when it is hidden from him. His obligation in trying for that proper direction when it is hidden is to be right in striving, not to be right with the eye. Had it been obligatory to be correct with the eye, the servant would have been commanded to turn to his Lord with his heart in the formal prayer, rather in all of his movements and stillnesses so that he sees only God. We know that it is impossible for creation to recognize the Essence and source of God. Part of the impossibility is to turn to the source of His essence with the heart, that is, it is impossible for the person of intellect to know his Lord in respect of His source. He knows Him from the aspect which the possible has in its need of Him and being distinguished from Him since He is not described by the attribute of things in-time in the same way in which the possible in-time is described by them. This is why we said that it is by direction, not the eye. (196)

11.1.5. The Obligation to Strive, Not To Be Correct in the Effort

Being correct is by trying, not by being right with the eye. For this reason, the striver is rewarded in any case. In our school, one strives in the roots as well as in the branches of judgments. There is no difference between them. As for the words of the Messenger of God: "The striver is both right and wrong," we think that it means in this question that the one who tries to be right is not the same as the one who is right by the eye or the direction. The one who is right is the one says that it is to get the direction correct. The one who is wrong is the one who says that it is being right by the eye. (197)

Being right in direction when it is not cloudy—by day or night—in the desert occurs only according to the principle of agreement. It is better to be right by the eye, not by the principle of knowledge. We do not worship God by meteorological observation or engineering based on observations. One of their inventions is the longitude and latitude of places. In every respect it is without certainty when we ourselves adopt it. It is clear that it is obligatory for the obligated person to strive, not to be right. The one who performs but does not get the direction right does not repeat it when that becomes clear to him after he has completed the formal prayer. (198)

11.1.6. God Is with the Belief of Everyone Who Has a Belief After He Has Striven

The inner interpretation of that is that when you look, you give the glance its proper due. You obtain the incapacity to perceive and you believe that. There is only incapacity. God is with the belief of everyone who has a belief after he has striven. God Almighty says: *"And whoever calls to another god besides God of which he has no proof."* (23:117)Understand! He is according to His servant's opinion of Him. However, the ranks are distinguished from each other. God is vaster, more majestic and more immense than being contained in a single attribute which would grasp Him. The idea of God being with one of His servants and not with another would deny divine Vastness. For that reason, God says: *"And He is with you wherever you have been"* (57:4), and *"Wherever you turn, there is the*

Countenance of God." The countenance of face of each thing is its reality and essence. (199)

If God—glory be to Him!—had been with one or present with one and not with or present with another, the one with whim He is not present would then worship his illusion, not his Lord. God says: *"And thy Lord has decreed that you worship none but Him!"* (17:22) that is, He so judged. It is for His sake that any god is worshiped. Only God is intended by the worship of every worshiper. Nothing in itself is worshiped except God. For that reason, the idolater erred when he set up for himself a worship in a particular means which was not prescribed for him by God. That is why he is wretched. *"And those who take to themselves protectors other than Him say: We worship them not but that they may bring us near to God.'"* (39:3) They admitted it. It is inconceivable in the world that there be anyone nearer than the one who has a whiff of the comprehension of absolute atheism. Those who believe in atheism make a certain attribute inoperative which the affirmer believes in. (200)

Whoever turns his eye to the House when he sees it or in its direction when it is hidden from him and runs to his Lord in his *qibla* as he was told to do in his heart and senses, it seems in his imagination that he is too weak to connect knowledge to it as His majesty demands. When you pray, even if you face God in your direction of formal prayer, it says that God *". . . is One Who Encloses them from behind."* (85:20) He is the Forerunner and the Guide. He—glory be to Him!—is the One whose hand holds the forelocks of all. *"He is the Guide to the straight path"* and the One *"who will drive the wrongdoers to hellfire"* as has been related. *"The entire affair will be returned to Him, so worship Him and rely on Him! Your Lord is not unmindful of what you do."* (201)

11.2. The Formal Prayer Inside the Kaba

11.2.1. The Position of the Religious Scholars About Praying Inside the Kaba

Some absolutely forbid praying inside the Kaba. Some absolutely permit that. Some scholars make a distinction between the obligatory and the supererogatory in that. All of them have some basis for what they say. (202)

11.2.2. The Inner Interpretation of the Prayer Inside the Kaba

After we have confirmed the outward judgment which was set down for us and by which we worship Him, there is the inner interpretation of that. We are not prevented from interpretation after we confirm this. We say that this is the state of the one for whom God is his hearing, his sight, his tongue, his hand and his foot. However, he is in the state of using every limb for that for which it was created. The truthful person is limited in that manner in his transmission. In that is a remembrance for whoever possess a heart. (203)

This state came from the Prophet in a sound Tradition and that Tradition was confirmed by unveiling as the state of supererogatory prayers and their result. For this reason, the Messenger of God performed supererogatory prayers in the Kaba when he entered it as has been related. He would pray the formal prayers outside of the House. It is exactly the same as when he did supererogatory prayers while mounted wherever his mount faced. "*Wherever you turn, there is the Countenance of God.*" (2:115) (204)

We know that the matter in itself may be as we see and witness. This is that which the contemplation of this station accords. He sees Him hearing others as he sees Him hearing Him. The miracle which this person obtains is unveiling and discovery. It is not that God is his hearing. God is exalted above unforeseen accidents. This is one of the most precious of divine questions. (205)

11.2.3. God Is Existence and by Him Source-Forms are Manifested

Whoever has this judgment outwardly permits all the prayers, obligatory and supererogatory, inside the Kaba. All that is other-than-God cannot leave the Hand of God. He brought them into existence. Rather, He is their existence and their existence is derived from Him. Existence is not contrary to God nor does it leave Him to be given from Him to them. This is impossible. He is existence, and the sources are manifested by Him. (206)

Someone said in the presence of the Messenger of God:

> By God! Were it nor for God, we would not have been guided nor would we have given charity nor performed the formal prayer.

The Messenger of God, was delighted by that and confirmed the truth of what he said. (207)

We are by Him and belong to Him as is related in sound Traditions. If we look at our essences and our possibility, we leave Him and our possibility seeks us by speculation and need of Him. He brings our sources into existence by His generosity from His existence. This is the interpretation of His words, "*And from wherever thou hast gone forth, then turn thy face in the direction of the Masjid al-Haram.*" (2:149-150) From wherever you go out to pray, face the the Masjid al-Haram (in Mecca). It indicates that from wherever you go out to existence, from whatever time you leave non-existence for existence. Its interpretation is by whatever aspect you leave God for your possibility and contemplation of your essence, turn you face towards the Sacred Mosque. Return by the glance and facing the direction of formal prayer, for you are in need of that from which you came. You have no "where" except Him. (208)

So look there and you will find that He encircles you even though He is that to which you turn. He joined the absolute and the limitation. You suppose that you have left Him, but you have only turned to Him. He encompasses you from behind you. Wherever you turn among the divine names and states, turn your face, your essence, towards Him. Do not turn away from Him. The "countenance or face" of a thing is its essence and source. Turning from God is to fall into non-existence. It is pure evil even as existence is pure good. Labid said:

> Everything except God is false.

The Messenger of God said: "It is the truest sign that the Arabs have uttered." There is no doubt that the false designates non-existence. (209)

11.2.4. Perform the Formal Prayer Wherever the Formal Prayer Catches You

As for the outward judgment of this sign, it is that the formal prayer is permitted inside the Kaba since no prohibition or ban against that has come. It is related and established: "*Wherever the formal prayer catches you, pray,*" unless that is in a particular place which the divine law mentioned, and that is not because of their sources, but due to an attribute which is based on them. They forfeit that capacity because of that attribute. (210)

He said: "*From wherever you go out,*" that is, when you go out from the Kaba or any other place, and you want to perform the formal prayer, "*then turn your faces towards it.*" When you perform the formal prayer, do not turn your face in any direction except that in which the Kaba is located. Your direction of formal prayer is there. Do not turn away from it. It is the same when you leave it. Your direction of formal prayer is only to that part of it to which you turn, whether you see it or whether it is hidden from your eyes. It is not in your capacity to face all of its essence because its essence is great and your essence is small in size. The formal prayer inside of it is like the formal prayer outside of it. There is no difference. You turn to it while you are inside of it. You do not turn or direct your attention by illusion to any part of it which is behind you when you are in it. Turning to the rear in the formal prayer is not something which has been related to us. Facing has been related. We only deem a person responsible for the judgements which have been articulated. (211)

11.2.5. Commanding a Thing Does Not Necessitate the Prohibition of the Opposite

In our opinion, commanding something does not necessitate the prohibition of the opposite of that thing. He did not say anything about that. If he actually states that and you do not do something which God has commanded you to do, then you have rebelled against Him. If the command to do something had also been a prohibition of its opposite, then the human being would have two or more errors according to the opposites which that commanded thing has. No one says this. The human being is punished for not doing what he was commanded to do, and for doing what he was commanded to not do, and nothing more. He has burden and one evil deed and he is only repaid with its like. This question has been adequately discussed, outwardly and inwardly, in regard to God, creation, and the divine law. "*God speaks the truth and guides to the path.*" (212)

12 Covering the Private Parts

12.1. Introduction

12.1.1. Covering the Private Parts (awra) in General

Scholars agree that covering the private parts is an obligation. There is no dispute about that. It is an absolute obligation — in the formal prayer and at other times. We will presently discuss what the definition of that is in respect to men and women. (213)

12.1.2. The Divine Secret Must Be Concealed

The inner interpretation of that is that every person of intellect is obliged to cover the divine secret. If it had been uncovered, the one who has neither knowledge nor intellect would have lost respect for the most protected and precious divine presence because of that uncovering. The reality of the "private parts" is inclination. For this reason, they said: "Our houses are exposed (*arwa*)," that is, inclining, about to fall. They said this when they were called to war. God showed that they were liars when He said: "*. . .are exposed. But they were not exposed. They want only to flee.*" (33:13) He means they want to flee from that to which you call them and they incline away from it. His glance inclines to one direction. (214)

Similarly, the person of knowledge must conceal the secrets of God from the ignorant in statements like: "*There is no secret conversation of three, but that He is their fourth,*" (58:7) and "*We are nearer to him than the jugular vein,*" (50:16) and "*I am his hearing, sight and tongue.*" When the ignorant person hears that, it may lead him to understand that it means incarnation or something clearly defined. That is forbidden, so he must veil the fond inclination which God has for the hearts of those with knowledge, and what God has of inclination in His words. He does this by what His majesty demands of absolute rich independence of the worlds. It even applies to what He said on the tongue of His Messenger: "I was hungry and you did not feed Me. I was ill and you did not visit Me. I was thirsty and you did not let me drink." (215)

So he veils the knowledge of this from the ignorant and does not add any commentary to what God Almighty said. God also veils it when He says: "If such-and-such a person is ill and you visit him, you find Me with him." This is more obscure than the first. In this statement, He gives those who know God yet another knowledge of Him which they did not have. That is because in the first one, He—glory be to Him—made Himself the same as the one who is ill and hungry, and He made Himself a visitor of the ill as He is with him. Whoever visits a sick person, God is with him. Where is the One who made Himself the same as the ill? Every word of that is true, and "every truth has a reality." (216)

As for the veil which the common person has in that, it is that He said to him: "*You find Me with him.*" The state of the sick person is always need. He is compelled to the One who has healing, and that is only God. The remembrance of God dominates him along with his means. He wants Him to drive away what has descended on him. This is not the case with healthy people. God said: "I sit with the one who remembers Me." This is sound. The common person is content with it while the knower has what he knows of that according to the extent of his knowledge. This is the secret of divine Inclination in respect to the common person. (217)

12.2. Covering the Private Parts in the Formal Prayer

12.2.1. The Position of Religious Scholars About Covering the Private Parts in the Formal Prayer

Scholars disagree about whether or not it is a precondition for the validity of the formal prayer. Some say that covering the private parts is one of the *sunna* of the formal prayer. Some say that it is among the obligations of the formal prayer. (218)

12.2.2. The Interpretation of the Private Parts in the Formal Prayer

As for the interpretation of that in the self, we have informed you about what is meant by "private parts." In this question, it is affirmed that the one who performs speaks with his Lord and that God has divided the formal prayer into two parts, shared between Him and His servant. Whoever tends to think that God is the One who performs by the actions of His servant, that is, the servant's outward actions in the formal prayer (as it is confirmed that God says on the tongue of His servant, "*God hears whoever praises Him*" when he rises from the bowing forward although it is certainly the servant who says it, and as he paid the man to listen to the words of God while the Messenger of God was reciting, he says that covering the private parts is one of the obligations of the formal prayer. He means that the like of this does not appear among the common people. He refers to the meaning and secret which the knower recognizes. The common person accepts it as it is related, "*No one is reasonable among them but the ones who have knowledge.*" (29:43) (219)

Whoever thinks that there is no rank between the common person and the knower, and that there is only what the text itself says and what has reached the listener (and the language would not change even if their ranks were different) for him, it is one of the confirmed practices of the Prophet of the formal prayer that the private parts be covered, not one of the obligations. "*God speaks the truth and guides to the truth.*" (33:4) (220)

12.3. The Definition of Private Parts

12.3.1. The Position of the Religious Scholars About the Definition of a Man's Private Parts

Some say that for men the private parts are the genitals. Some say that for men it is from the navel to the knees. In our opinion, it is only the genitals. (221)

12.3.2. The Interpretation of the Definition of Private Parts for the Self

The interpretation of that in the self is what is disliked and foul in the human being is the reality of the private parts. They are a place for the reasons we have mentioned, which is the forbidden. That which is beyond the genitals is what is next to them, from the navel above to the knees below, which is the position of doubtful things. One must be careful about them through fearfulness. Someone who grazes around the forbidden place is on the verge of falling into it. (222)

12.4. The Definition of a Woman's Private Parts

12.4.1. The Positions of the Religious Scholars About the Definition of a Woman's Private Parts

Some say that a woman's entire body is considered to be a private part except for her face and palms. Some say that, and add that her feet are not private parts. Some say that all of her is private. Our view is that the private parts of women are only her genitals as God Almighty says: "*They took to stitching together for themselves from tree leaves from the Garden.*" (20:121) It was the same for Adam and Eve in covering the genitals. They are the private parts. If a woman is commanded to cover herself, this is also our position. However, it is not inasmuch as she is private. That is a judgment of the divine law which has come regarding covering. It does not demand that the thing be veiled because it is a private part. (223)

12.4.2. The Interpretation of the Definition of the Woman's Private Parts

The interpretation of that in the soul is feminine, and the thoughts of the soul are all private parts. As for the one who makes an exception for the face, palms, and feet, that is because the face is the place of knowledge. If you do not recognize the face of a question, you do not know it. When the face of a thing as you are commanded to uncover the face of what you are commanded to know. The face is therefore not covered for being a private part. It is not a private part. (224)

As for the hands, which are the palms, they are the place of generosity and giving. You are commanded to ask, and the giver must extend his hand with that which he gives. Therefore, the hand is not covered. When the one who owns the blessing which you seek bestows it on you out of generosity, you must take it. Generosity and liberality are commanded by the divine law. It is related that the upper hand is better than the lower hand. Both the hand of the asker and the giver extend. The giver must extend it and the asker must grasp it. (225)

It is not obligatory to cover the feet. They are not private parts because they carry the entire body and convey it from place to place. Whoever has the principle of circulation is excused from veiling and covering. He must appear and emerge by necessity. It is very far indeed from being private parts which must be covered. (226)

13 Clothing in the Formal Prayer

13.1. Introduction

13.1.1. The Agreement of the Religious Scholars about Clothing in the Formal Prayer

Scholars agree that a person can make use of a single garment in the formal prayer. (227)

13.1.2. The Interpretation of the Single Garment

The interpretation of that is the self which unifies in the formal prayer. He is the one who does not see himself in it. He sees that God makes him stand and sit. He is like a corpse in the hands of the one who washes it. This is the meaning of a single garment. (228)

13.2. A Man Who Performs the Formal Prayer with His Belly and Back Uncovered

13.2.1. The Disagreement of the Religious Scholars About a Man Who Performs the Formal Prayer With His Belly and Back Uncovered

Some people believe that the formal prayer of the man who performs the formal prayer with his belly and back uncovered is permitted. Some people believe that his formal prayer is not permitted. (229)

13.2.1. The Interpretation of a Man With His Belly and Back Uncovered

The interpretation of the soul is that it has an outward and inward aspect. It is the action of the heart in the formal prayer and the action of the limbs. When the outward and inward matter of the man is unveiled to him during his formal prayer, he does not see himself performing it. This is in the same position as the one who says that the formal prayer is invalid. In this view, the one who has this unveiling invalidates the relationship to the formal prayer actually taking place through him. Whoever acquires this unveiling and insists upon it, the man is deemed to be "praying," to this extent and to this extent his formal prayer is permitted. (230)

13.3. Clothing Which a Woman Can Wear in the Formal Prayer

13.3.1. *The Position of the Religious Scholars About the Clothing a Woman Can Wear in the Formal Prayer*

It is generally agreed to be a chemise and head covering. If she performs the formal prayer uncovered, some say that she must repeat it within the time or after it, and some say that she must repeat it within the time. Some say that the servant girl can pray with her head and feet uncovered. Some say that it is obligatory that she cover her head. Some say that it is recommended that she cover her head. (231)

13.3.2. *The Interpretation of the Clothes Which a Woman Can Wear When Performing the Formal Prayer*

There is no difference between the servant girl and the free woman in the interpretation of the self in that. All is the property of God. There is no freedom from God. When freedom is ascribed to creation, it is their leaving the bondage of others, not the bondage of God. No creature has any means of controlling their hearts nor having any authority in them. This is the meaning of freedom in this view. We have already discussed the single garment, so there still remains the interpretation about covering the head. (232)

Know that in the interpretation the woman represents the self and the head is leadership. The self loves to manifest its leadership in the world since it is veiled from its Master's leading it. It seeks to disclose itself to others like it. For this reason, it is said that the last thing to leave the hearts of the truthful is love of leadership. It is the presence of its Lord in the formal prayer. There is no doubt that the chief in the presence of the King is in the place of the need. When he goes out to whoever is below him, he manifests his leadership over him. For this reason, the owned servant is ordered to cover her head in the formal prayer. (233)

13.4. Wearing Unlawful Clothes When Performing the Formal Prayer

13.4.1. *The Position of the Religious Scholars on Performing the Formal Prayer in Unlawful Clothes*

Some say that the formal prayer of such a person is permitted, and that is our school, even though I dislike that he do that. Some say that it is recommended that he repeat it within its time. As far as we are concerned, he is a rebel by wearing clothes which are not lawful for him, even though his formal prayer is permitted. For us, he is among: *"They have mixed acts that are in accord with morality with others that are bad deeds."* (9:102) (234)

13.4.2. The Interpretation of Performing the Formal Prayer in Unlawful Clothing

The interpretation of this in regard to the self is that in every place, the human being is not provided with protection in all his states and success in all his affairs. He is successful in that in which he is successful and he is disappointed in that in which he is disappointed. It is like the one who recites the remembrance of God with his heart and his tongue, and while he is in that state, he wrongfully strikes someone with his hand although it is forbidden for him to hit that person. However, that does not detract from his remembrance as that remembrance does not remove his wrong actions or judge that he has done something forbidden. The remembrance does not make it unlawful either. For this reason, we think that the formal prayer offered in an illegally appropriated house is valid. However, it is a misdeed from one aspect, and it is rewarded from another. (235)

14 Being Free of Impurity When Performing the Formal Prayer

14.1. The Position of the Religious Scholars About Being Free of Impurity When Performing the Formal Prayer

Some say that it is one of the obligations of the formal prayer, and that the formal prayer is only valid when that impurity is removed. Some say that it is a *sunna*. I have already discussed it in the section on purification. Some say that removing the impurity is an absolute obligation. Part of his belief is that he is not obliged to say that removing it is a precondition for the validity of the formal prayer. He performs the formal prayer and his formal prayer is valid, but he rebels since he has that impurity on him in the formal prayer. (236)

14.2. The Interpretation of the Principle of Being Free of Impurity During the Formal Prayer

The interpretation of that in the self is as follows. The one who insists that its removal is obligatory deems that the impurity necessitates distance from God while formal prayer demands nearness inasmuch as it is conversation. Whoever thinks that nearness dominates distance removes this ruling. Whoever thinks that distance dominates nearness does not consider the formal prayer valid. It is more fitting that you say that the states of the formal prayer vary and that all of it belongs to God, and that whatever comes from him is for God. "*God does not wrong the weight of an atom*" (4:40). His formal prayer is therefore accepted, whether he performs the formal prayer with the impurity or does not pray. It is better to remove it without any disagreement regarding that, whether it is a small amount or a lot. Its position is that a person is not present with God in every state since he naturally has heedlessness and weakness, so know that! Success is through God. (237)

15 THE PLACES IN WHICH ONE PERFORMS THE FORMAL PRAYER

15.1. INTRODUCTION

15.1.1. THE POSITIONS OF THE RELIGIOUS SCHOLARS ON THE PLACES IN WHICH IT IS PERMITTED TO PERFORM THE FORMAL PRAYER

Some people believe that the formal prayer is permitted in every place in which there is no impurity. Some of them made exceptions to that in seven places: the dung hill, the slaughterhouse, the graves, the middle of the road, the bath-house, the watering-places of camels, and on top of the Kaba. Some only exempt the grave and the bath house in that. Some only mention the grave. Some disagree about praying in these places, but think that it does not actually invalidate the formal prayer. (238)

15.1.2. THE INTERPRETATION OF THE PLACES IN WHICH ONE DOES NOT PERFORM THE FORMAL PRAYER

As regards the interpretation of the self, God Almighty says: "*He is with you wherever you are.*" (57:4) The one who performs the formal prayer is speaking with his Lord. He says: "*Those who are constant in their formal prayers.*" (23:9) Ayisha said about the Messenger of God: "From what I know of his states he used to remember God at all times." Places have no effect on the veiling of the heart except in the case of the people of states. The effect in that belongs to heedlessness or ignorance for the common people and to the state among the people of states. (239)

These forbidden places are all incompatible with purity. We have already discussed purification and its interpretation. This leaves the formal prayer on top of the House of God. This is due to the fact that you are commanded to face it during the formal prayer. When you are in this state, you do not turn toward it and so you do not pray the formal prayer. You do not turn to the direction of the Sacred House. Whoever allows that, traces back the main aspect in the interpretation to the essence. There is no doubt that you, by your essence, are in the direction of the Sacred Mosque. You are on top of it, and all the earth is a mosque. (240)

15.2. Synagogues and Churches

15.2.1. The Position of the Religious Scholars About Performing the Formal Prayer in Synagogues and Churches

People disagree about synagogues and churches, that is, about offering the formal prayer in them. Some people disagree with that and some people permit it. Some people make a distinction between those in which there are images and those in which there are none. (241)

15.2.2. The Interpretation of Performing the Formal Prayer in Synagogues and Mosques

The interpretation of the self in that is as follows: Does God speak to two people in the same rank? As far as we are concerned, that does not befit divine Vastness. God Almighty says: *"For each among you We have made a divine law and an open road."* (5:48) This is a commentary or an indication. If we offer formal prayer in these places, it comes from our divine law, not theirs, so understand that! God is the One who gives inspiration. (242)

15.3. Performing the Formal Prayer on Velvet-like Carpets and Other Things Which Are Normally Used for Sitting On

15.3.1. The Position of the Religious Scholars About Performing the Formal Prayer on the Earth, Carpets and Other Things

Scholars agree about offering the formal prayer on the earth. They disagree about performing the formal prayer on velvet-like carpets and other things which are placed upon on the earth. Most of them allow prostration on the mat and other things like it which are produced by the earth. They dislike prostration on other than that. (243)

15.3.2. The Interpretation of Performing the Formal Prayer on the Earth on Carpets

As for the interpretation of the self in that, God Almighty says: "I have divided the formal prayer into two halves, between me and My servant." He affirmed you in the formal prayer and did not deny you. He has the highest, most disconnected attribute while you have the lowest, most sinking attribute. All descends from you to the earth of your servanthood or what it demands. It lessens what you are commanded to do. He calls you a servant in the formal prayer. Servanthood is abasement. God Almighty said when He describes the earth, "He made it submissive to us, so we walk in its tracts." It is under our feet. That is utter abasement—the one on whom the lowly walks. (244)

Since it has this position in abasement, He commanded us to place on it the noblest outward thing which we have—that is the face. We rub it in the dust. Doing that mends the brokenness of the earth which comes to it when the lowly servant walks on it. The face of the servant and the face of the earth are joined in prostration. Its brokenness is mended. God is with those whose hearts are broken. The servant in that station with that state is nearer to God than in all the other states of the formal prayer since he is acting for something else, not for his own sake. That is in order to mend the brokenness of the earth which comes from its abasement under the feet of the abased. (245)

Take note of what I have pointed out to you! The divine law did not omit anything. It indicated it by a gesture. Whoever knows it, knows it. Whoever does not know it, does not know it. For this reason, only the people of unveiling and existence know these secrets of these matters. The entire world speaks to them and informs them of their realities. (246)

15.3.3. Ibn Arabi in Cairo in 603 AH

Abu 'l-Abbas al-Hariri related to me in Egypt in 603 AH that he was walking with Abu Abd Allah al-Qarbaqi in the small market of Wardan. He had purchased a small potty for his young son who was with him. They met some people in a certain place while he still had the new potty with him. There were some righteous men of God with him. They wanted to reach something and asked for a condiment to have with their food. They all agreed to buy a certain amount of sugar. They said: "This potty has not been touched by any filth. It is still new, in its original state." They filled it with sugar and sat down to eat until they were finished. The people left and the owner of the potty took it and left with Abu 'l-Abbas. (247)

Abu 'l-Abbas said: "By God! I heard this with my own ear, and Shaykh Abu Abd Allah al-Qarbaqi heard it as well. The potty said: 'After the "Friends of God" have eaten from me, shall I then be a vessel for filth? By God, that shall not be!' It leapt from his hand and fell to the ground and broke." He said: "A state overcame us because of what it said." (248)

When he told me that, I said to him, "You have lost sight of the real intention of the admonition of the potty. The matter is not as you claim. There is many a potty which has been eaten from by those who are better than you and afterwards used for filth. My brothers, it told you that after God has made your hearts vessels for His gnosis and Self-disclosure, you must not then make them vessels for others. God would not forbid your hearts from being a vessel for Him and then let them break like that. Be with God!" He said to me: "We did not think about what you have just told us." (249)

16 On the Words and Actions of the Formal Prayer

16.1. Action Incompatible with the Formal Prayer

Some of the preconditions of the formal prayer are words and some are actions. As for actions incompatible with the formal prayer, they are all the permitted actions which are not the actions of the formal prayer with the exception of killing a snake or scorpion during the formal prayer. They disagree about that. They agree that the insignificant action does not invalidate the formal prayer. (250)

16.2. The Interpretation of Actions Incompatible with Performing the Formal Prayer

The interpretation in the self is that is the scorpion of passion and the snake of appetite which come to the one who speaks with his Lord. Should he kill them or let them go on their way which the lawgiver specified for them? The gnostic knows that it is impossible to kill them. He loves what is with his Lord by passion, and he desires constant conversation with Him by His appetite. This one thinks that they should not be killed. The one who thinks that they should be killed is the one who thinks that they come between him and his conversation with his Lord. (251)

16.3. Words Which Are Incompatible With the Performing of the Formal Prayer

As for words, they are those which are not part of the words of the formal prayer. There is no disagreement among scholars about their invalidating the formal prayer if someone speaks intentionally. However, the scholars disagree about that in two places. The first regards someone who speaks absent mindedly, and the other is when someone speaks intentionally in order to put the formal prayer right. Some—and it is a rare position—say that the one who speaks intentionally in the formal prayer in order to save a life or for some great matter, continues with what he has already completed of his formal prayer, and that it is not invalidated. This is the school of Awzai. Some say that the intentional speech to put the formal prayer right does not invalidate it. Some say that any speech invalidates it, unless it comes from forgetfulness. Some say that any speech at all invalidates it, intentional or forgetful. (252)

16.4. The Interpretation of Words in the Formal Prayer

The interpretation of this is that the one who performs the formal prayer consigns with his Lord. When he consigns with someone else for His sake, he is still engaged in conversation with his Lord. When he speaks to someone else and it is not for the sake of his Lord, then he leaves the formal prayer. Forgetfulness is not considered except in the case of the one who is dominated by seeing the veil. God only speaks to His servant from behind a veil as God Almighty says: "*And it had not been for a mortal that God should speak to him, but by revelation or from behind a partition.*" (42:51) (253)

The nearest veil is the form in which the Self-disclosure occurs. This is the nearest veil. It is not the form and it is not other than it. Whoever is distracted by the form from the relationship which is not form, or distracted by what the form is from the relationship which is form, forgets in both states. The principle in the interpretation is like the outward principle in the dispute which occurs between the scholars, so understand! (254)

17 The Intention in the Formal Prayer

17.1. Introduction

17.1.1. The Intention Is a Precondition for the Validity of the Formal Prayer

Some say that it is a precondition for the validity of the formal prayer. The scholars agree about it except for one rare opinion. (255)

17.1.2. The Interpretation of the Intention in the Formal Prayer

The interpretation of the self in that is that the servant may intend conversation with his Lord, and that may also come to him unexpectedly. Moses went out to fetch fire and his Lord spoke to him even though he had no intention in that instance. The root in all actions of worship is that their beginning comes from God. They are not intended by responsible people except for rare instances like the sign of the veil and other things about Umar ibn al-Khattab. (256)

This does not at all prevent the intention. It is taken into account inwardly. The reality grants that there is nothing outside or from which God is absent that you could intend in any matter. All has the same relationship to Him. Whatever I intend, He is with me wherever I am and in whatever state I am in. The intention is only the direction of nearness to God. The connection of the intention is a particular state with God which you intend from a particular state with God to which you aim from a particular state with God from which you emerge by Him from Him to Him. (257)

States vary. The one who takes into account the variety of states says that the intentional is obligatory. In this manner, the various types of divine laws vary. The one who takes presence into account and does not look at the state is the master of the state. He does not recognize the intention, for he is in the source. God Almighty says in respect to the one who has this state (and this is by way of indication, not commentary), "*So with what are you going off?* " (81:26) and "*Fear not. Truly I am with both of you. I hear and I see.*" (20:46) (258)

17.2. The Intention of the Leader of the Formal Prayer and the One Following the Leader

17.2.1. The Positions of the Religious Scholars About the Intention of the One Following Coinciding With the Intention of the Leader of the Formal Prayer

Scholars of divine law disagree about the intention of the leader and the one who follows the leader, and whether it is a precondition of that that the intention of the one following agree with that of the leader in the formal prayer, that is, in specifying the formal prayer. Some say that it is obligatory, and some say that it is not obligatory. Each one has a proof, and this is not the place for it. (259)

17.2.2. The Interpretation of the Intention of the Leader of the Formal Prayer and the One Following

The interpretation of the self in that is that it is valid, that it not be obligatory since it is an unseen matter. Following the leader is only by what the senses connect to it in the way of hearing and seeing. For this reason, the Prophet gave details about what it contained in following the leader. He mentioned actions which are perceived by the senses, by whatever means they are perceived. He did not mention the intention. That is an action of the heart. It is an obligation whose recognition cannot be obtained. (260)

Whoever knows that divine vastness makes it impossible that God repeat the same Self-disclosure to a person or give a Self-disclosure to two people in the same form knows that the intention of the first following is not attached to the intention of the leader except inasmuch as the formal prayer possesses actions. "Every person has what he intends." The intention of a self-disclosure is an indebting favor from The Giver of the Self-disclosure to the one who receives it. The intention from the recipient of the Self-disclosure is knowledge and enjoyment of that self-disclosure. (261)

18 The Ruling of the States in the Formal Prayer

18.1. All Acts of Worship Are Based on States Which Are Considered by the Lawgiver

Know that the formal prayer contains words and actions, and their judgment is based on states. All acts of worship are based on states, and they are considered by the lawgiver. The judgment is applied to the responsible person from the state which he has. Therefore, the lawgiver took them into account when he considered the responsible person. (262)

Someone asked Malik ibn Anas, "What do you say about the water-pig?" He thought that it was forbidden. They said: "Isn't it a sea creature?" He said: "You have called it a pig," and he did not add anything to that. (263)

It is the same with wine which it is forbidden to drink. When it becomes vinegar, the name of wine leaves it since the state has departed which necessitated the name "wine." It is called vinegar by another state which has come upon it. The essence is the same, but the judgment moves from the forbidden to the permissible. The outward and the inward are the same in this. The interpretation is in the divine law for the one who understands it. (264)

19 The Recitation of "God is Greater" in the Formal Prayer

19.1. The Position of the Religious Scholars About the Recitation of "God is Greater" in the Formal Prayer

There are three different schools among scholars of the divine law regarding the *takbir* in the formal prayer. Some believe that all of them are obligatory. Some of them believe that all of them are not obligatory. This is the opposite of the first. Some believe that only the recitation of "God is Greater" after which everything but the formal prayer is forbidden (*takbir al-ihram*) is obligatory. (265)

19.2. The Interpretation of the Recitation of "God is Greater"

The interpretation of the self in that is that "God is Greater" is obligatory for every state. However, one of the conditions is that the human being see himself. If he sees only God and does not see that other-than-God has any source, the *takbir* is not obligatory because he is not based on anyone, and so nothing is obligatory for him. The *takbir* is only intelligible when there are others or the determination of the existence of others. (266)

The speaker sees that only God is Seeing, Seen, and the act of seeing. There is no more comprehensive state in annihilation (*fana*) than this one. If he sees Him in respect of His most beautiful divine names, the *takbir* is obliged in respect to their relationships, that is, from the relationship of some to others. The name The Living, has a controlling presence over all the names. The name The Knower has a more general connection than the names The Transformer and The Powerful. There must be a *takbir* proclaiming Him greater than it. The realities of the names demand it by their rivalry. (267)

If one looks at the divine names in respect to that which joins them— and He is the One who is named by them— they are set down by the theologian as a proof for the source of the named. If they have realities in themselves which are connected to the disconnection or to others, he does not think that the *takbir* is necessary. (268)

Whoever makes a distinction between formal prayer and other forms of worship, thinks that only the recitation of "God is Greater" after which everything but the formal prayer is forbidden is obligatory. By it, he informs himself that he is detained or barred from acting in whatever would bring him out of this particular form of worship called the "formal prayer." These are the various schools in the interpretation. Praise be to God! (269)

19.3. The Articulation of "God is Greater" in the Formal Prayer

19.3.1. The Position of Religious Scholars On the Description of the Reciting of "God is Greater" in the Formal Prayer

Scholars of the divine law disagree about the description of the *takbir* in the formal prayer. Some say that it is only permitted to say "*Allahu akbar*." Some say that it is permitted without any definite form, but the letters of the *takbir* must be in it. They are: *kaf, ba* and *ra*. Some permit the *takbir* with the meaning, like "more glorious" and "more immense." (270)

Our position is that it is better to follow the *sunna*. The Messenger of God said: "Perform the formal prayer as you have seen me performing it." All that is transmitted to us is this articulation: "*Allahu akbar*." This comes from many independent transmissions. (271)

19.3.2. The Interpretation of the External Form of the Formal Recitation of "God is Greater"

The interpretation in that is that the divine law does specify one particular articulation in spoken worship rather than another expression which has the same meaning, but that it desires to set it apart by that expression in the meaning which those who know God have. It sets it apart from any partnership which might occur in it. It is better for us to imitate and observe the meaning in which the distinction occurs. We know that meaning or we do not know it. If we do not know it, we bring it according to the knowledge which it contains. We do not make an arbitrary judgement about the context of another expression. (272)

God commanded His Prophet when He said: "*Say: 'Lord, increase me in knowledge!'*" When the knower is wise, he does not turn to any other matter which is close to it in meaning unless that is for a particular attribute. He takes that into consideration and does not turn away from it in word or action. The one who turns away from it is forbidden the benefit of that distinction. There is no doubt that he is described as being in conflict. (273)

20 On Directing Oneself in the Formal Prayer

20.1. Introduction

20.1.1. Quality of Directing Oneself in the Formal Prayer and Position of Religious Scholars

Some say that it is obligatory. Some say that it is not obligatory. Its form is that one says after the *takbir*: "*Truly I have turned my face to He Who Originated the heavens and the earth—as a monotheist and I am not of the ones who are polytheists.* (6:79) "*Say: Truly my formal prayer and my ritual sacrifice and my living and my dying are for God, Lord of all the worlds. No associates are to be ascribed with Him and of this was I commanded and I am the first of the ones who submit.*" (6:162-163) This is in the Traditions. Some say that he should glorify, even if he does not use this exact articulation. Some say that he should combine glorification and directing oneself. (274)

20.1.2. The Interpretation of Directing Oneself with the People of God

As for that which I believe, it is that there is the directing oneself in the night prayers of *tajahhud*, not in the formal prayers. Between the *takbir* and the recitation in the formal prayers, he says silently: "O God! Put distance between me and my errors as You have put distance between the East and the West! O God! Cleanse me of my errors as the white garment is cleansed of dirt, O God! Wash me of my errors with snow, water and hail." This is what he chose, and it is the *sunna*. Our position is that we stop there and act by it even though we do not make it obligatory since God did not make it obligatory. It is better to follow the *sunna*. (275)

The interpretation of this with the people of God is as follows: directing oneself (*tawjih*) from one state to another is from God, by God, to God, with God, in God, for God, on God. He begins from God, help is by God and support. The end and finish is to God. Company and watchfulness is with God. Desire is in God. Nearness for His sake is for God. Trust and reliance is on God. Then the expressions in directing oneself are interpreted as well as the supplication between the *takbir* and recitation. (276)

Water is life. "He made every living thing of water," that is, that which gives it life. My heart is given life by Your remembrance and my limbs by obedience to You so that they only act in it. They are witnesses. This is verified on the Day of Rising when they testify against you. The testimony of the limbs is related in the Quran. (277)

The interpretation of coolness is the coolness of certainty like the coolness of the fingertips in the sound Tradition. He acquires knowledge with certainty by it. It cools what the Chosen servant experiences of the heat of yearning for the high rank with the Glorified Most High, One in knowledge of God. Snow is the snow/joy of the heart which is its delight with what God has given it of His Self-disclosure and witnessing. (278)

20.2. Moments of Silence in the Formal Prayer

20.2.1. Three Moments of Silence in the Formal Prayer

The first silence is after the recitation of "God is Greater" after which everything but the formal prayer is forbidden (*takbir al-ihram*) and before the recitation. The second silence is after the recitation of the Opening Chapter. The third silence is when he finishes the recitation and before bowing forward (*ruku*). This is outside of the times of silence when he stops at each sign in order to reflect on what he has recited. This third silence is for the one who recites more of the Quran than the Opening Chapter. If he stops with the Opening Chapter, there are only two moments of silence, so know that. (279)

20.2.2. The People of God's Interpretation of the Silences of the Formal Prayer

Its interpretation according to the people of God is that there are people who dislike the leader to have silences while some of them recommend it. There is no doubt that the silences are the part of the *sunna*. God says: "I have divided the formal prayer into two parts between Me and My servant." The Prophet said: "Worship God as if you were seeing Him." The one who offers the formal prayer prepares for conversation with his Lord and puts Him before his eyes in his direction of formal prayer. The heart of the matter is like that, but without definition or connection. It is as befits His Majesty. The one who performs the formal prayer turns to his Lord in his *qibla*. That is related from the Prophet. (280)

Intimate conversation (*munaja*) is the form called *mufaala*. *Mufaala* is the action of two doers in certain places where something takes place between them. When the servant says: "Praise be to God, the Lord of the worlds," God hears this statement from the servant. When the servant finishes the sign, he must listen while he is a witness. He is silent so that he can hear what God will say to Him, may His Majesty be exalted in that! It is good manners: inward and outward with God. He must not interrupt Him while He is speaking. This is part of the good manners of conversation. It is better to have good manners with God. God says: "My servant has praised Me." There are some servants of God who hear that statement with their ears. Even if you do not actually hear it, then listen for it and believe it because he reported about that. In the same way, He speaks to you in every sign according to what the sign demands. (281)

Part of good manners is attentiveness to what the speaker says to you when he is speaking with you. If you interrupt him while he is speaking, you have bad manners. This is universal for everyone who speaks. The business between the speaker and the listener is to obtain some benefit. You should know that the one who has no manners is not taken by kings as a table companion, a companion for night talk, or as an intimate. (282)

20.3. Reciting "In the Name of God, the Merciful, the Compassionate" (*basmala*) in the Beginning of the Recitation of the Formal Prayer

20.3.1. The Position of the Religious Scholars About "Seeking Refuge" and the Recitation of "In the name of God, the Merciful, the Compassionate" in the Formal Prayer

Scholars of the divine law disagree about the recitation of "In the name of God, the Merciful, the Compassionate" when beginning the recitation in the formal prayer. Some people forbid it both silently and aloud—except for the Umm al-Quran—that it is in the formal prayers, although they permit it in the supererogatory ones. Some say that it should be recited silently with the Umm al-Quran in every cycle. Some say that it should be recited, and that it should be aloud in what is recited aloud, and silent in what is recited silently. (283)

I say that seeking refuge from God from the accursed Satan at the beginning of the recitation in the formal prayer and at others times is obligatory. This is by a divine Command which comes in the words of God Almighty: *"So when thou hast recited the Quran, seek refuge with God from the accursed Satan."* (16:98) It is better to recite the *basmala* in the recitation in the formal prayer, obligatory or supererogatory, with the Opening Chapter and with the other chapter than to leave it out. The obligation for the one who offers the formal prayer is to recite what is easy of the Quran. God specified what He desired of the Quran in the formal prayer, and it is that which is easy. It was known after it was not known. That is the Opening Chapter. If it is easy for one to recite the *basmala,* he recites it. If it is not easy to recite it in the Opening Chapter and other places, there is no objection if one does not do that.

The Opening Chapter must be in the formal prayer. If someone does not recite the Opening Chapter, it is not the formal prayer which God has divided between Him and His servant. For us, the *basmala* is a sign since it has come from the Quran. It is also part of a sign in Chapter of the Ant within the letter of Solomon. God knows best. (285)

20.3.2. The People of God's Interpretation of "In the name of God, the Merciful, the Compassionate" (basmala)

The interpretation with the people of God is that you eat from that over which the name of God has been mentioned, and you do not eat from that over which the name of God has not been mentioned. The Quran is the speech of God. It is related, "When the leader seeks to feed the one behind him, let him relish it." He called it food, and made the relationship of that "eating." This is why we used the sign of eating in the obligatory. Whoever recites the Quran and believes that it is the Word of God, has said that God speaks, even if this particular name has not been reported, so understand. May God give you understanding of the places of His speech! (286)

20.4. Recitation in the Formal Prayer and What Is Recited of the Quran in It

20.4.1. Position of Religious Scholars on the Ruling of Recitation in the Formal Prayer and the Amount Which Is Recited In It

Some people oblige the recitation of the Quran. In fact, most of them do. Some people do not think that the recitation is obligatory. Some people think that it is obligatory to recite the Opening Chapter in the formal prayer. If it is omitted, then the formal prayer is not complete. (287)

Then they also disagree about what part of the Quran is recited in the formal prayer. Some oblige the recitation of the Umm al-Quran in the heart, if the person knows it by heart, and that is my position. Beyond that, any more of the Quran is based on timing. Some oblige it in every cycle. Some oblige it in most of the formal prayer. Some of them oblige it in half of the formal prayer. Some of them oblige it in one cycle of the formal prayer. Some of them oblige recitation of the Quran no matter what the sign is. There are those who limit it to three short signs or one long sign—like the sign of the religion. This is in the first two cycles. As for the last two cycles, some people recommend glorification instead of recitation. In general, most agree that the recitation in the formal prayer is recommended for the entire formal prayer. That is my position. (288)

20.4.2. The People of God's Interpretation of Recitation of the Quran in the Formal Prayer

The interpretation of the people of God is that the one who performs the formal prayer speaks with His Lord. Intimate conversation consists of words, and the Quran is the Word of God. The servant is incapable of recognizing from himself what he should say to his Lord in the intimate conversation to which he is summoned in the formal prayer. Therefore, his Lord taught him how to speak with Him and what to say to Him when He said: "I have divided the formal prayer into two halves, between Me and My servant." Then He said: "The servant says: 'Praise be to God, the Lord of the Worlds.'" This is a report from God which is His instruction to the servant about what he should say to Him. God says: "My servant has praised Me" in this Tradition. It is not mentioned that the one who offers the formal prayer should speak to Him with anything except His own words. (289)

God then specified the Umm al-Quran for him. He only consigns with Him with His own words and by the most comprehensive of His words. This is the Umm al-Quran. After that He taught us how to speak with Him—glory be to Him!—and what to say to Him in the formal prayer with the recitation of the Umm al-Quran. This is a sound Tradition from the Messenger of God which he related from his Lord to comment about what is easy of the Quran. When a comprehensive command comes from the Prophet and he mentions a particular aspect which explains that comprehensive thing, those with knowledge and good manners do not go beyond what the speaker said when they comment about that comprehensive matter. The speaker is God Almighty. They must stop there. (290)

God prescribed conversation by divine speech for the state of standing in the formal prayer more than any other of its states because of the existence of the attribute of self-subsistence (*qayyumiyya;* standing = *qiyam*) since the servant stands (*qaim*) in the formal prayer. God attends to every self for what it has earned. Here is great knowledge when the servant attends to the words of the Lord and has no speech with his Lord except with his Lord's words while he is standing. For whom does he translate, and from whom does he translate and who is the translator? What does the self based on it earn? Who is the servant so that the Master—may His Majesty be exalted!—should say, "The servant says such-and-such and God says such-and-such" were it not for divine Solicitude and the favor of the Lord? (291)

If it is said: "We have understood what you have pointed out about the attribute of standing, but then rising from the bowing is standing which has no recitation in it," then we say that rising from bowing is prescribed as a division between it and prostration. One can only prostrate from a standing position. If he had prostrated from bowing, it would have subjection from subjection. Subjection from subjection is not valid since it is like leaving the same thing which he is entering. Humility only comes from elevation. When humility appears from the humbled self, that is not humility. That is humiliation and not humility. For example, the non-existence of existence is the same as existence. (292)

For this reason, he divides the two prostrations by a rising in order to make a break between the two prostrations so that they are distinct from one another by the division which separates them. Then he knows that there is another matter, even if they share the same form. It is like His words: *"And they will be given from there ones that are alike."* (2:25) We do not doubt the reality of *"la ilaha illa Lah"* inasmuch as it is *"la ilaha illa Lah."* The form is manifested in thirty-six places in the Quran. The master of tasting knows that its judgment varies in tastes in each individual place in which it appears. If you understand this, it is like the resemblance of the cycle in the formal prayer. Each cycle has a flavor and taste which another does not have, no matter what it is. There is no doubt that when two likes are separated by the opposite, they are distinct from one another. (293)

Part of the good manners with kings is that when they are greeted, they are greeted with a bow (and it is bending forward) or by placing the head on the ground (and it is prostration) out of respect for them. When they turn towards a person or they are eulogized, the eulogizer stands up. When someone speaks to them in their presence, he does not speak while seated or in any other state. This is the recognized good manners for the one who is below The King while he is with The King. How much more so it is with the one who is His servant and does not admit of freedom! (294)

As for the Quran, it is intelligible on the tongue and it is known for being designated as "comprehensive." The formal prayer is a state in which the servant is joined to his Master. It is also a state which joins God and His servant since God divided it between Him and His servant in the formal prayer. The relationship occurred between the Quran and the formal prayer. He should not recite anything in it except the Quran. Standing erect is like the letter *alif* [Arabic *a*] among the written letters. It is the root of the articulated letters, and all of the letters appeared from it by its stopping in its articulations which rise from the chest to the lips. It gathers the sources of the letters. The sources of the letters are its ranks and stages when it is expelled and travels from the heart (which is the world of the unseen) to the visible world. Standing joins the types of positions and their roots—bowing, prostration, and sitting, although sitting has an aspect which resembles standing because it is half of standing. (295)

It is still more fitting to recite the Quran standing since it gathers all. Standing is the straight movement. Straightness is what the servant asks God for success in doing. The servant says: *"Guide us to the straight path"* since God Almighty says to him: "*So go straight as thou wert commanded.*" (11:112) (296)

What we mentioned in general that the obligation of the recitation of the Umm al-Quran in the formal prayer is stipulated in one cycle since that is the least amount to which the name "formal prayer" can be applied in the divine law. This is the *witr* (the odd number prayer). The Messenger of God performed the *witr* with one cycle. Or it is preferred over other signs of the Quran. Then the stipulation for the one who offers the formal prayer to recite the Umm al-Quran while standing is either by obligation or by precedence. In that, we will clarify the form of the recitation of the knowers of God which they use in their conversation in the formal prayer. (297)

20.5. The Description of This State

20.5.1. The One Who Performs the Formal Prayer Is the Second in Derivation and In Respect to the Testimony of the Oneness of God

Know that the one who offers the formal prayer is a second as we have confirmed by derivation. Although he is a second, it is not by anything real. That is in relationship to the testimony of the Oneness of God in belief. That is the duality of belief (*iman*), that is, its manifestation in two places: the place of testimony and the place of the formal prayer. Similarly, we make it three with the obligatory poor-due or alms (*zakat*) and whatever is more than this. For this reason, God mentions increase in belief when He says: "*Which of you has this increased in belief?*" (9:124) It is one source while it is manifested as multiplicity in places. It is like the One manifested by many individual things. In itself, it is not multiple. Don't you see that when a rank leaves it, that rank has neither authority or source? (298)

In the same meaning, God says about those who say: "*We believe in some and we disbelieve in others.*" (4:150) "*Those, they are in truth the ones who are ungrateful.*" (4:151) He completely denied them belief since they denied it from one rank. They are more suited to the name of "ungrateful," which is the veil. The basic ingrate (*kafir*) is the one from whom God is veiled. This person recognizes belief and then veils it, saying: "We believe in some." Therefore he deserves the name ungrateful more than the one who does not recognize it. (299)

20.5.2. The Firstness of God Does Not Accept the Second

The firstness of God does not accept the second. God says: "I have divided the formal prayer between Me and My servant." He mentioned Himself and He mentioned the servant. Here He did not mention firstness for Himself or for the servant. He mentioned the separation between Himself (with the pronoun) and His servant (plainly stated). This is the limit by which the servant must be distinguished from his Lord. God Almighty put Himself first in the division and said: "Between Me." He delayed the division of the servant and said: "and between My servant." He related the servant to Him in order to inform him that he is His servant, and not the servant of his passion (*hawa*). He says: "*Have you seen the one who takes his passion as his god*?" (45:23) So he considers him to be a servant of his passion, although in the heart of the matter, he actually worships his Lord—glory be to Him! (300)

The servant has no will with his Master. He acts according to what is desired of him. God—glory be to Him!—must necessarily exist be His essence. The servant is the one who derives existence from Him while his root is non-existence. God gives him advancement in this rank since the division is only intelligible when it takes place between two matters. The two matters here are the Lord and the servant. (301)

20.5.3. Advancing the Servant in the Word Before the Word of the Truly Real

After God had put Himself first when He said: "between Me," next to that He advances the servant who speaks before the words of God. God Almighty said: "The servant says: 'Praise be to God, the Lord of the worlds.'" He puts the words of the servant first. Then He said: "God says. . ." and so He put His words after the words of His servant. That is in order to make it clear to us that He has command in His word, "between Me." He comes before, and He comes after when He says: "God says." He is The First and The Last. Firstness is established for the servant in speech so that he will realize that the divine firstness in His word "between Me" does not demand the acceptance of a second. This person might imagine that he is second, and He made him first in speech in the conversation. (302)

We have informed you that the goal is specification of the ranks, not the productive organization. He—glory be to Him!—does not beget in His word "and between My servant." He is not begotten in His words, "God says: 'My servant has praised Me.'" Had the intellect perceived Him in reality by its speculation and proof, and recognized His Essence, He would have been produced from the intellect by its speculation. He—glory be to Him!—is not produced by intellects as He is not begotten in existence. He does not beget by His bringing creation into existence because there is no relationship between it and the existence of God. The intelligible relationship between the father and the child is that each premise only produces what is consistent with it. The only relationship between God and His creation is creation's need of Him in bringing-into-existence. He is Rich, Independent of the worlds. (303)

As it is affirmed that the firstness of the servant in speech does not make God second, so the firstness of the servant in speech does not make God second since there is no number in firstness. That which is opposite the servant is God. He is the One to whom He speaks. (304)

20.5.4. God Does Not Speak by Phrases But by Presence

He does not turn aside to remember other. Whoever sees other in his formal prayer is stripped of seeing God in it, or his seeing in God, or a seeing which issues from God. This is what Abu Bakr al-Siddiq said: "I have not seen anything but that I saw God before it." The one who offers the formal prayer and does not have this state which we mentioned among the types of witnessing, simply does not perform the formal prayer. If he does not offer the formal prayer, he does not consign, and God does not consign by what is articulated in this state. He consigns by presence with Him. (305)

The one who says: "*Praise be to God, the Lord of the worlds,*" when he is not with God, has the tongue of the servant, but does not have his source and reality. Then God says: "The tongue of My servant has praised Me," not "My servant who is ordered to consign with Me." When the speaker is present in his words, God says: "My servant has praised Me." He brings back to him what departed by the favor of God. When the servant is present, his presence includes the presence of the tongue and all of the limbs because the source gathers them together. If his source is not present, none of his limbs or any other part of him stands up. (306)

Since God called His servant first in the declaration to offer the formal prayer, "Come to formal prayer!", the servant begins with the recitation of "God is Greater" after which everything but the formal prayer is forbidden (*takbir al-ihram*). If he remains in his state in which everything but the formal prayer is forbidden until the end of the formal prayer and is truthful and fulfills the agreement, God will repay him for it. He says: "*so that God may give recompense to the ones who are sincere for their sincerity.*" (33:24) He says: "*Live up to the compact with Me. I will live up to the compact with you.*" (2:40) He is not forced. If the servant does not fully meet his concentration on God in his formal prayer, and his family, his shop, or whatever desires he has are present with him, then his affair is left up to God. He does with him according to what His knowledge of him demands. (307)

The servant says: "*Allahu akbar*" in the recitation of "God is Greater" after which everything but the formal prayer is forbidden (*takbir al-ihram*) in imitation since he specifies a particular state which is called formal prayer. He said "*Allahu akbar*" since my Lord has specified a particular state. He is in all states; rather, He is all states. Rather, all states are in His hands and none of the states leaves them. He proclaims Him greater than the like of this judgment of illusion, not the judgment of the intellect. Illusion possesses an authority over man as intellect possesses an authority. He made it the recitation of "God is Greater" after which everything but the formal prayer is forbidden (*takbir al-ihram*), that is, a *takbir* of prevention. He utters that phrase of "God is Greater" (*takbir*). No phenomenal being shares with Him in the like of this greatness. (308)

20.5.6. In divine Conversation There is Only One as in Love

On the basis of the reality which we are telling you about, how can he associate with the One who is his source, since He has told him that He is his hearing, sight, tongue, hand and foot. The thing does not share with itself. There is only One. He is the One who proclaims great, The Great, and He is greatness. There is only Him, may He be exalted, disconnected and pure from being proud by any pride of which He is the source. Then the gnostic stands before God with this description and does not see other than his Lord in his standing or his *takbir*. He listens to the call of his Lord when He says: "Come to formal prayer" in the declaration to perform the formal prayer, that is, turn yourself to My conversation, after he has been told: "*And your garment, purify it.*" Then the one who offers the formal prayer in this station bestows the robes of praise on God and seeks blessing by that. He knows that God will answer his action as we say to the people of the religion, "Put this garment on me for the blessing (*barakah*)." Then he puts the clothes on him. (309)

God says in what we mentioned: "My servant has extolled Me," that is, put the robes of praise on Me. In reality, God—glory be to Him!—extols Himself by the tongue of His servant even as He told us that He says on the tongue of His servant, "God hears the one who praises Him." Look at how noble the rank of the one who performs the formal prayer is! God described him as putting the robes of praise on his Master. Where is the one who offers the formal prayer who has this state? How far from the mark they are! (310)

Rather people employ their tongues for bad manners and lack of knowledge of the One who calls them and the praise which they are told to seek. They answer only with their outward parts, while they let their hearts go to their desires. They are: "*Those who offer the formal prayer and are heedless in their formal prayer.*" This does not concern their outward formal prayer when they answer His call. They set up their outward parts as a proxy for them in the *qibla* to obey the command of God. God calls them to this station when the knower of God comes and articulates the recitation of "God is Greater" after which everything but the formal prayer is forbidden (*takbir al-ihram*) as we mentioned. He does not see himself as worthy to speak with his Lord except after he has renewed his purification since He said: "*and your garment, purify it.*" The garment is interpreted as the heart. The Arabs say:

Remove my garment from your garment, unravelling it.

It is said in a commentary on His words, "*And your garment, purify it,*" that "purify" is a command to shorten his garment. Ali ibn Abi Talib, may God be pleased with him, said in this meaning:

Your shortening the garment is true. It is cleaner,
more enduring and has more cautious awareness. (311)

20.5.7. Purify the Heart for Intimate Conversation

There is no doubt that the servant is obliged to obey his Lord. By his essence, he is incapable of the exaltation which the majority of his Lord demands. It is a divine Instruction that the servant should purify his heart since it is the garment of his Lord which contains Him in His words, "The heart of My servant contains Me." The like of this garment is the one who is ordered to purify it in this station. Then the gnostic sees that when he purifies his heart for conversation with his Lord by himself and not by his Lord, he adds filth to his filth. It is like the one who washes impurity from his garment with his urine because it is a liquid. The purification which is sought here is being free of oneself and returning the entire affair to God. God says: "*To Him is the return of the command so worship Him*" (11:123). (312)

For this reason, we consider it invalid for him to speak to Him in the formal prayer with anything except His words since it is not proper that there be anything of people's words in the formal prayer. It is related in a Tradition that the formal prayer in which there is anything of people's words is not proper. It is glorification. This is a Tradition. Then this statement was strengthened by what was commanded when the words of God were sent down: "*Glorify the name of your Lord, The Great.*" The Prophet said to us: "Put it in your bowing." When He revealed the sign: "*Glorify the name of your Lord, the Most High,*" the Prophet said: "Put it in your prostration." (313)

We embrace the Quran in our states: standing, bowing, and prostration. The one who offers the formal prayer does not mention anything in his formal prayer except what was set down for him by the tongue of the Messenger of God. We recognize that *"nor speaks he for himself out of desire. It is but a revelation that is revealed."* (53:3-4) We do not call all divine speech the "Quran" even though we know it is the Word of God. The Quran is the Word of God, but not all of divine Speech is contained in the Quran. All are His Words. We only speak to Him with His Words in the formal prayer. (314)

20.5.8. The Supplication of Directing Oneself According to the Gnostic

The purification which He—glory be to Him!—commanded is like in His words, *"And your garment, purify it."* Between the recitation of "God is Greater" after which everything but the formal prayer is forbidden (*takbir al-ihram*) and recitation of the Opening Chapter, the gnostic says in obedience to this command in his formal prayer, "O God! Put distance between me and my errors" (the impurities connected to his garment) "as You put distance between the East and the West." The reason for that is that when God calls the knowing servant to speak with Him, He singles him out for the place of nearness to Him. If He were to show him his errors in the place of nearness (and his errors are in every distance from that place), the servant would then be in the place of nearness (and his errors are in every distance from that place), the servant would then be in the place of distance, far from what God demands of nearness. Therefore he asks God to come between him and seeing his errors before he begins the intimate conversation. This is so that they will not appear in his heart in this place which is the place of nearness. For that reason, one of them said: "The definition of repentance (*tawba*) is to forget your wrong action." If coarseness appears in the place of clear purity, it becomes coarse. I have not seen anyone who achieved this station except for a certain king in his station with creation. He did not want any of his errors to he shown to him by imagination or recollection. (315)

The making a likeness of: "You put distance between the East and the West," contains a precious, abundant, and mighty knowledge. But here he meant the distance between two opposites since two opposites are not joined together. The knowledge which we refer to is concealed in these two opposites when they are joined in any principle—like white and black joined together in a color, and like the in-time and the out-of-time when they are described by any necessity. Although the East is far from the West in the senses, each of them sees the other opposite it. It is far by the two places in the senses, and it is far by sunrise and sunset in meaning. Sunset is opposite sunrise. The place of sunrise is the East. It is very far from the place of sunset which is the West. He did not say, "as You put distance between black and white." Colors can be joined together. (316)

Look at how wise this instruction is! How true! How fine! He shows good manners toward God since he seeks distance from his errors by striving and seeking in that place for himself. He would be in the position of the one who turns the King's attention towards him in order that he might come to see him. When he comes to him, he asks him at the beginning for that which would be good for himself. This is bad manners. He must seek from God what befits that state when he asks for preparation to speak with his Master. Therefore he seeks distance from errors, and does not seek that they fall away. (317)

20.6. The Explanation of the *Tradition* of the Supplication of Directing Oneself

20.6.1. Cleansing of Errors

Then he says: "O God! Cleanse me of my errors as the white garment is cleansed of dirt." That is because He, The Majestic and Great, said to him, "*And your garment, purify it.*" Therefore, he used the expression "garment" in his supplication to inform God that he has learned by using His Words. This is good manners since he leaves his knowledge for his belief, that is, I only call on You by what You commanded me to do of purification of the garment for Your conversation. O Lord, attend to that purification! I have no power nor strength except by You. Every attribute which does not befit Your majesty is an error. This occurs when the servant oversteps his limit and steps out of his proper place and acts outside of his own arena. He is like the one who walks in land that has been illegally appropriated. When the servant steps into other than what his Master has commanded him, he is called mistaken and in error. That action and movement is called an error. The servant is the servant and the Lord is the Lord. (318)

20.7. The Rest of the Supplication

20.7.1. Washing Errors with Snow, Water and Hail

Then he says: "O God! Wash me of my errors with snow, water, and hail." Undertake to wash away my errors! He related the washing to Him. He says: "Thou dost order me to say, 'There is no power nor strength except by God.' Thou dost order me to speak when Thou didst said: '*Thee alone we worship and we seek help only from Thee alone*' that is, in Thy worship. If Thou dost not take charge of me with Thy power and help when Thou dost command me to purify my essence to speak with Thee, how then shall I speak to Thee in a state which Thou hast made impure? Thou hast said: '*We have made every living thing of water.*' (21:30) (319)

"So wash my errors with water," that is, "bring my heart to life for changing evil actions into good actions by repentance and right action." The life in this state comes from bringing water onto impurity and dirt to purify it. Whatever dirt there is becomes clean, and whatever impurity there is becomes pure. Its dirt and impurity is not by its essence. It is by a judgment of the divine law by which this place is singled out. When it is joined to water by bringing water to it, it belongs to another judgment of the divine law which is called cleanness and purity. The ugly become beautiful and the evil becomes good. One seeks to act like this and not to remove the source. The removal of that judgment is sought. The source exists when it is joined with water. (320)

He said: "snow." When a man's heart is joyful about anything, it is said that the heart of the man is joyful (*thalija; thalj*=snow) that is, he is in something which gives him joy. He says: "O Lord! If you do the like of this washing, my heart will be happy since it is pure for what pleases Thee by what pleases Thee. Therefore its sorrow is turned to joy." (321)

20.7.2. There Is Only God and I!

He said: "Coolness." This is what puts out the embers of burning which exist in the heart when its Lord calls it to speak with Him while it is in a state which is not suitable for standing before its Lord: He wants to put that fire out, so he uses the expression "coolness" from "hail" (*bard, barad*). In one transmission, it has "cold water." It is used that way in Arabic as we have related it. Their poet said:

> My camel is riderless. That will cool some livers
> and make some people weep. (322)

He is saying: "There are people who have fire and flame in themselves from envy and enmity while I am alive. When they see my camel riderless, they will know I am dead. The fire they had when I was alive will become cool for them. My friends who loved my life will weep. The attribute of these will move to those, and those to these." This is as the abasement, weariness, fatigue, exhaustion, and trouble of the "friends" (*awliya*) in this world in the pursuit of their Lord's obedience will move to the wretched tyrants in the fire. The joy of the tyrants and the leisure of the people of wealth in this world will move to the people of happiness, the people of the Garden in the world to come. (323)

That which the poet mentioned in his sign is the state of an existent thing. Every existent thing must have a friend and an enemy. God Almighty says: "*Do not take My enemy and your enemy. . .*" He made them His enemies as He said about the repayment of them: "*That is the repay-*

ment of the enemies of God." God has enemies, so how is it with the species of this world! It is like that with friendship. God has "friends" as does every existent thing. The knower of God who is occupied with Him is the one who says: "There is only God and me." All is annihilated in the presence of God. He is more worthy and He is truly the "friend" (*wali*) since this state pervades creation and The Real. God is an enemy to the unbelievers as He is a friend to the believers. They are His servants, His enemies. So what do they have in their competition and envy of one another? (324)

When the gnostic asks God for this purification after the recitation of "God is Greater" after which everything but the formal prayer is forbidden (*takbir al-ihram*), then he begins directing the self. (325)

20.8. To Complete the Most Perfect Formal Prayer in Directing Oneself

20.8.1. The One Who Knows God Relies on the Most Perfect Formal Prayers in the Sight of God

We mentioned this because the knower of God is intent on the most perfect prayer with God in states of words and actions, even if that is not considered obligatory. The "friends" of God are more entitled to the form of perfection in their acts of worship because they speak to the One who has the perfection which can actualize the answer. That is made obligatory for them by their gnosis and witnessing. (326)

20.8.2. Turning the Face by the divine law (sharia)

At the beginning of directing oneself, the servant says: "I have turned my face." The servant relates his face to himself from the divine law which gives him that. This is through good manners: inward and outward with God. He is present with God since He is his tongue by which he speaks. He is called to this relationship by the words of God Almighty, "Between Me and My servant." He affirmed him although in reality, it is related to the Master. The gnostic servant who has good manners is the one who turns to his Master since nothing should be ascribed to the servant. He is ascribed and nothing is ascribed to him. When the Master ascribes Himself to him, it is in order to honor and instruct as when He said: "*your God*" and the like of that. He related the action of directing himself to himself since he knows that God has related action to the servant. He says: "The servant says: 'Praise be to God.'" Words are a type of action. (327)

The man of knowledge always proceeds with God according to His designs. He said: "*He created the human being. He taught him the clear explanation.*" (55:4) He informs him about the places and how one should be in them. If the human being had been left to himself, he would have reverted to the non-existence from which he emerged. He gave him existence and what it requires and He is The Manifest in him by Himself through what He manifests of actions by him. First He gave His servant a known existent, and last He gives him something known in existence and intelligible in determination. He is The Manifest by what appears from Him in him, and The Hidden by what is hidden from him which comes from Him. (328)

Then He limits him by these limits and frees him by them. He says to him: "You are not Him. He is The First and The Last, The Manifest and The Hidden." He makes the servant go on in the state of his existence according to his possibility as long as he remains in it. It is not valid that he leave it. Actions are ascribed to him so that he can obtain tranquillity of heart since he has no valid claim in it. He says: "*To Him is the return of the command.*" (11:123) and He says: "*Is then He Who creates as one who creates not? Will you not then recollect*?" (16:17) For this reason, the man of knowledge related directing oneself. The face of the thing is its essence and reality, that is, I have set up my essence upright as Thou hast commanded me. (329)

20.8.3. "Originator of the Heaven and Earth"

Then he says: "To the One who exploded the heavens and earth into existence." It is His words, "*We unstitched them*" (21:30), that is, the One who distinguished my inward from my outward and my unseen from my visible. He separated the spiritual faculties in my essence as He separated each of the heavens from one another. He inspired every heaven with whatever celestial faculties He placed in each. He says: "and the earth," and so He separated my limbs. He gave the eye a domain, the ear a domain, and all of the limbs each a domain. It is His words: "*And ordained its subsistence within it.*" (41:10) It is the knowledge given by the senses which nourish the human intellect. This comes from what reflection reconstitutes in order to recognize God and recognize what God has commanded to be recognized. (330)

This and things like it is what the human being of knowledge has in mind by directing oneself when he says: "*I have turned my face to He Who Originated the heavens and the earth.*" (6:79) This is a vast ocean. If we had begun to mention what the gnostic obtains which causes him to say: "*He Who Originated the heavens and the earth,*" no book would be able to contain it. Tongues would have become exhausted dealing with the interpretation of only one of its heavens. (331)

20.8.4. ". . . A MONOTHEIST (HANIF), AND I AM NOT ONE OF THE IDOL WORSHIPPERS. . . "

Then he said: "a *hanif, a monotheist*," that is, inclining. "*Hanf*" is inclination. He says: "inclining to the presence of God from my possibility to the necessity of the existence of my Lord. Being above non-existence is valid for me. I go on in pure good." This is the meaning of his word "*hanif*." (332)

Then he said: "I am not" in this inclination "among the idolaters." He says: I do not incline by my own bidding as the virtuous servant said: "*And I accomplished that not of my own command*." [Khidr, Quran 18:82] God taught me how to turn to Him and with what to turn to Him and from what to turn to Him and in what state I should be when I turn to Him. All of these must be recognized by those who know God in directing oneself. If they are not like this, they are not the people who direct oneself, even though they may use the very same words. (333)

He casts idolatry out of himself. Even if the servant ascribes the action to himself, he is not a partner in the action. He singles out what he can validly possess of that action while God is singled out for what he has of that action. The servant does not share with his Master in his servanthood. The Master is not a servant, and the servant is not a master of the one to whom he is a servant. This is because he is His servant. (334)

20.8.5. ". . . MY FORMAL PRAYER, MY PRACTICES, MY LIFE AND MY DEATH. .

Then he said: "My formal prayer, my practices, my life and my death," and he related all to himself. These actions can only validly appear by means of the servant. It is impossible that these things be related to God in respect to their sources being brought into existence as they are related to the servant since he is in the place where their sources are manifested. He is the one who performs the formal prayer. The one who moves is actually the moved, not the One who causes the movement. In reality, he is moved. It is not valid that God be moved as it is not valid that the moved be the causer of movement in himself since we see that he is still. (335)

You must know that and then you will recognize that what you relate to yourself is part of what you cannot validly relate to your Lord intellectually. What you relate to your Lord cannot validly be related to you in the divine law. "My practices" here means my worship, that is, my formal prayer and my worship. He says: "my abasement and my life my life and my death," that is, the state of my life and the state of my death. (336)

20.8.6. ". . . TO GOD, THE LORD OF THE WORLDS. . ."

Then he said: "to God, the Lord of the worlds," that is, to God. The bringing-into-existence of all that belongs to God, not to me. That is to say, the manifestation of that in me is for the sake of God, not for the sake of whatever good falls due to me because of that. God says: "*And I created not jinn and human kind but that they worship Me.*" (51:56) He made the cause refer to His presence, not to me. The first purpose is not for our own good. It is rather preference for the presence of God in that which must be preferred. It is a teaching and an admonition for us from God. Rabia said: "Is He not worthy of worship?" (337)

The man of knowledge is the one who worships God for God. The one who has no knowledge is the one who worships Him since he hopes that God will give him prosperity through that act of worship. For that reason, we are told to say, "to God, the Lord of the worlds," that is, He is the Master of the worlds and their Owner and the One who puts them right. He made rules for them and clarified them so that He would not leave them in confusion. God Almighty says concerning the indebtedness of His servant: "*And found He thee one who goes astray, then He guided thee,*" (93:7), that is, you were confused and He made the path of guidance clear for you from the path of misguidance. Here the way of guidance is recognition of that for which He created you. Your worship should be based on that. Then you will be "*on a clear sign from your Lord.*" (338)

20.8.7. ". . . He has no partner, and I am commanded to that, and I am commanded to that, and I am the first of the Muslims. . . "

He said: "*He has no partner, and I am commanded to that, and I am commanded to that, and I am the first of the Muslims,*" meaning that the only divinity meant by that worship is God. He created me for its sake. I do not associate myself in it because of the reward I obtain in it. God has promised that for the one who is like this. One of them believed that the reward is present in the state of this worship and he rejects the one who does not say that. This person is of no consequence at all. He is one of the great theologians, but he is not among those who know God by tasting (*dhawq*, direct experience). He is one of the famous people of speculation. He refutes what Rabia al-Adawiyya said. (339)

We do not take into consideration our differences which the people of formal knowledge unless it is regarding the transmission of the judgments of the divine law. All are equal in that. One considers the one who disagrees about it by objecting to the path by which it has arrived or by what is understood by the Arabic language. As for other than this, it is not taken into consideration except for a dispute among fellows. This operates in every rank of those who know a particular knowledge. (340)

He said: "I am commanded to that" referring to all of it and to every part of it according to what is appropriate for that part. There is no need to mention it in detail since what it contains will be clear for you *"if you have a heart or listen while you see."* (50:37) Then he says: "I am among the Muslims" that is, among those who obey His commands in His words, *"I am commanded to that."* (341)

20.8.8. " . . . O GOD! THOU ART THE KING!"

Then he says: "O God! Thou art The King!" That is God Almighty when He calls him to stand before Him. That is because only kings call people to stand before them. He singles out this name in directing himself rather than others. For this reason, we are required to cross our hands while standing because it is the place where the servant stands before The King. (342)

Then he says with the most special attribute: "There is no god but Thee." He did not say: "There is no king but Thee," out of good manners before with God. God has affirmed kings in the earth when He says: ". . . *and assigned kings*." (5:20) He denied that there is any other god in the world except Him, either by reality or by the principle of appointment. Therefore, the servant says in directing himself: "There is no god but Thee." If he had said: "There is not king but Thee," He would have been denying what God has affirmed. Whatever God affirms is not denied. When He negates something, it cannot be affirmed at all. The expression of this directing oneself is transmitted from God. If these are the words of God, he verified what He affirms and denies. If it is from the expression of the Prophet it is still part of the station of good manners with God since he did not deny what God affirmed. Even if there is no king except God, God has affirmed kings. (343)

This is the meaning of: "There is no god but You" after his words, "Thou art The King." There seems to be a lack of connection. Since divinity contains kingdom, and kingdom does not contain divinity, he used an expression whose meaning indicates the existence of The King who is named even though he does not use the phrase: "God is King." Not every king is God. (344)

20.8.9. "THOU ART MY LORD AND I AM THY SERVANT"

Then he says: "Thou art my Lord and I am Thy servant." He put his Lord first and himself later. He related himself to his Lord by the particle of address because he is before Him. Look at the good manners in these words! He says to Him: "Thou art my Lord and I am Thy servant and Thou hast divided the formal prayer between Thee and the servant. I stand before Thee with this particular servanthood." It is the state of intimate conversation and no other state. The states of the servant vary with the variety of what the Master calls him to, even if he is servant in every state. (345)

20.8.10. "I HAVE WRONGED MYSELF AND I ADMIT MY WRONG ACTION"

Then he says: "I have wronged myself and I admit my wrong action, so forgive me for all my wrong actions. None forgives wrong actions except Thee." He says in these words what he said before the supplication of direction. That is the supplication which we put after the *takbir* when he asks to put distance between himself and his errors. He says: "I have wronged myself by what I have acquired of errors and I have admitted that in Thy presence before speaking with Thee, so forgive me my wrong actions," that is, veil my wrong actions for my sake because only Thou canst veil them. Do not let them see me so that they can come to me and then I should act wrongly by them. Do not let me see them so that they might please me and I would then do that and become a wrongdoer because of it. It is his words: "Put distance between me and my errors as Thou hast put distance between the East and the West." (346)

He says: "If Thou dost veil it from me by this distance, then I will not see it and so I will be free to accept that to which Thou hast summoned me. If Thou makest me see my wrong actions and do not veil them, when I see them, then shame and consternation will prevent me from understanding what Thou dost desire of me in that to which Thou summoned me." He did not mention having them fall away from himself. He is not striving for his own portion. What he asks is that they be veiled from him in this state. This is why the one who knows God remains with his repentance when he recalls his wrong action, it then produces the effect of the estrangement of opposition within him. Even if that is not held against him, the state still accords that. (347)

Then he says: "Guide me to the best character. None guides to the best character except Thee." This is the position of his words in the supplication: "Wash me of my errors with water, snow and coolness," that is, give me success in using noble qualities in this place as it is proper that I should use them in showing good manners towards Thee when I speak to Thee and learn from Thee. Give me understanding of what Thou hast brought me in Thy words, and understanding of what I say to Thee in Thy words. All of that is part of good character. In my actions, it is by exterior forms and my standing before You outwardly and inwardly as Thou hast told me to do. None guides to the best character except Thee. (348)

In other words, Thou art the One who gives success in that. I have no power to do that. It is only specified by Thy power and Thy information about it since this is part of what cannot be perceived by striving. It is by what Thou settest down and clarified since Thy value is not known and what befits Thy majesty is not known and we cannot draw analogies between our behavior with Thee and the behavior of servants with kings. Thou sayest that "there is nothing like Thee." Good manners are that which Thou demandest of us in our behavior with Thee. We only know it from Thee. (349)

20.8.11. "Guide me to the best character. None guides to the best character except Thee."

Then he said: "Turn aside its evil from us. None turns aside its evil except Thee." He begins by instruction: 'Acquaint me with how I must behave with Thy Majesty. Secondly, by application, when I leave what is not good by Thy Power since the entire affair is in Thy Hand. Thou teachest the servant and he does not behave badly in what Thou hast taught him. Therefore, turn aside evil character from me by knowledge and application." (350)

20.8.13. "At Thy service and assistance"

Then he says: "At Thy service and assistance," that is, answering Thee and assisting that to which Thou hast called me by Thy words on the tongue of the doorman: "Come to formal prayer." Here I am. I have come in answer to Thy call. At Thy service! and to help in what Thou desirest that I accept. (351)

20.8.14. "All good is in Thy hands"

Then he says: "All good is in Thy Hands" since it is pure good. It is pure unadulterated existence which comes neither from non-existence nor the possibility of non-existence. All good is in His Hands. (352)

20.8.15. "And evil is not to Thee"

Then he says: "And evil is not to Thee." He says that evil is not ascribed to Thee. Pure evil is non-existence, that is, the non-existence of good is not ascribed to Thee and does not befit Thy Majesty. He used the *alif-lam* [the definite article] to include the various types of evil, that is, absolute evil, and evil limited by particular forms. All of this is not to Thee, that is, what Thou callest evil or is evil should not be ascribed to Thee out of good manners and reality. The strongest proof that the opponent has in this question is His Words, may He be exalted! *"And we would not have been guided if God had not guided us"* (7:43), and His words: *"And whomever God causes to go astray, for him there is no one who guides."* (13:33). (353)

20.8.16. Misguidance and Guidance; Misery and Happiness

Know that misguidance designates confusion and ignorance of the affair and the Straight Path of the Truth. God says: *"God misguides whomever He Will,"* that is, whomever He acquaints with the path of misguidance and so he is misguided in it. Whoever He acquaints with the path of guidance is guided in statements like *"There is nothing but Him"* (42:11) and *"glory be to your Lord, the Lord of might, above that which they describe"* (37:180), and *"they have not valued God with His proper value"* (6:91), and *"He has no equal"* (112:4). (354)

The sound intellect is guided by it when it hears the like of this from God. For this reason, He said: *"We are nearer to him than you, but you do not see"* (56:85), and *"We are nearer to him than the jugular vein"* (50:16), and *"whoever comes to Me running, I come to him rushing,"* and the like of these statements. The sound intellect is confused in reports like these and it wanders tracklessly. This is the meaning of "He misguides," that is, He confuses the intellects with the like of these statements which come from God on the tongues of the Messengers. They are true, but how they are true is not known. The intellect cannot be guided to what God means by that from that which is not fitting in what is understood by it. (355)

Then the intellect sees that God only spoke to us so that we would understand Him. What is understood from these matters is impossible for Him—glory be to Him! from every aspect which the servant understands by a connection in-time, either by means of a meaning in-time or by means of the senses. The intellect cannot possibly accept this discourse, so it is bewildered. Then the servant emerges from bewilderment. It is only possible for him to leave it though divine concern. It is not possible to leave bewilderment solely by what God has given the intellect of divisions of the power by which God supports it. The prover is bewildered in the proven due to the immensity of the proof. (356)

After this, the divine law brings matters which the intellect has judged to be impossible by its proof and yet the divine law affirms phrases which indicate the necessity of what is deemed to be impossible. It accepts that out of belief but does not know what it is. This is the confused person who is called "misguided." It is related that he said: "Increase me in bewilderment in Thee," that is, send down to me that which the intellect deems impossible from all aspects so that it will recognize its incapacity to perceive what is proper for Thee and Thy majesty in the way of attributes. (357)

As for the happiness and wretchedness by which one designates things in which you experience pain and bliss, that is a general quest for the servants in respect of the senses and the sensory. That which we are dealing with is another matter which refers to the gnosis of the realities.

20.8.17. "I ask Thee to take charge of me"

Then he says: "I ask Thee to take charge of me and I turn to Thee in repentance," that is, the beginning is by Thee, not by myself. It is our statement that man exists by other than Himself. He said: "I turn to Thee," that is, the source of my existence reverts to Thee. I am not it. Thou art in it. It has only taken existence from Thee while Thou are the source of existence. In the root of my essence I am from non-existence. Neither principle nor state is altered for me in my possibility. I continue. (359)

20.8.18. "Thou art blessed and exalted"

Then he says: "Thou art blessed," that is, Thou hast blessings (*barakah*) and increase, not me. He says: "Thou! Existence is Thine. Then Thou hast clothed me in it when I was not. Blessings and increase are in existence when they appear by two relationships: it appears by me, and it is Thy existence, and it is related to Thee, and it is Thy source." Then he says: "Thou art exalted," that is, Thou art too High to be manifested by other-than-Thee. Existence related to Thee is none other than Thy He-ness. This is the meaning of his words: "Thou art blessed and exalted." (360)

Then he says: "I ask Your forgiveness and I turn to Thee in repentance." He says: "I seek veiling from Thee in my being described by existence so that I do not withdraw from my reality and lay claim to existence. It is not me, it is Thee, and I am not Thee. I am according to what I have by my essence. The sphere of manifestation is from me in me by what Thou hast described me with of existence. I do not have any manifestation in Thee by what I have of possibility in my reality. (361)

Then he says: "I turn to Thee," that is, return to Thee from what I have been described with of existence since Thou art the source of existence and I am described by it. Therefore it returns to Thee. It is my words: "I turn to Thee." What the servant says of supplication and directing himself to God between the *takbir* and the recitation is finished. Now, if God Almighty wills, we will deal with the recitation of the Opening Chapter on the tongue of those who know God in the state of the formal prayer, not in any other state. (362)

21 The Interpretation of the Recitation of the Opening Chapter of the Quran in the Formal Prayer

21.1. Having the Meaning of the Opening Chapter in Mind When Reciting It in the Formal Prayer

Know that when the knower of God begins to recite in the manner which God has commanded the Quran to be recited, he seeks refuge since he recites, not since he performs the formal prayer. I have informed you that God says such-and-such in the recitation of the servant as an answer according to the demands of the sign which he recites. When you recite the sign, you must call to mind in yourself what that sign gives according to your understanding. The answer will be in harmony with what you call to mind of the meanings of that sign. For this reason, the lowest of the ranks of the common comes in the answer since the common person and the foreigner who does not know Arabic have no knowledge of the meaning of what they recite. God speaks to them as is related in the Tradition. If you isolate something, when you call it to mind, God makes the answer conclusive for you, so do not miss this value in the recitation! The ranks of those who know God and people in the formal prayer are distinguished by it. (363)

21.2. Seeking Refuge with God and Its Rank in the View of the Gnostics

When a person finishes directing himself, he says: "I seek refuge with God from the accursed Satan." This is Quranic text. It is related in sound a Tradition, "I seek refuge with God, The Hearing, The Knowing, from the accursed Satan." God Almighty says: *"When you recite the Quran, seek refuge with God from the accursed Satan."* (16:98) When the gnostic seeks refuge, he looks at the state which obliges him to seek refuge. He looks at the reality of that with which he seeks refuge, and he looks at that from which he must seek refuge. He seeks refuge according to that. (364)

The one who is dominated in his state by the fact that everything from which he seeks refuge is in the hand of his Master, that all he seeks refuge with is in the hand of his Master, and that he in himself is the servant of the place of management and being turned about, seeking refuge from his Master by his Master. It is his words "I seek refuge from Thee with Thee." This is the seeking refuge of the Oneness of God. By it, he seeks refuge from fusion. God Almighty says: "*Experience this! Truly thou, thou art the mighty, the generous*" (44:49), and He says: "*Thus God sets a seal on every heart of one who increases in pride, haughtiness.*" (40:35) He says: "True pride and greatness is My cloak and might is My wrapper. Whoever struggles against Me, one of them breaks him." (365)

Whoever is below this degree in seeking refuge, seeks refuge from what is not suitable with what is suitable in action or attribute. This is a universal question, and the state specifies the individual cases and then the judgment proceeds according to that. It is related in a Tradition, "I seek refuge with Thy pleasure from Thy wrath," that is, with what pleases Thee from what angers Thee. Here the servants leaves his own portion by establishing the proper respect of his Beloved. He is God. Then he has what his self has in this. He said: "With Thy remission from Thy punishment." That is for himself. He looks to which of the two ranks is higher in that. (366)

Some look at what the majesty of God demands since a possible cannot reach and it is not in the reality for a possible to accept the exaltation which the majesty of God demands. That is impossible in the heart of the business. This person thinks that it is only for himself since that returns to him. Whoever looks at His words: ". . . only to worship Me," says that I am obliged in respect of my Lord what my power can reach. I only act for my Lord, not for myself. The lawgiver set down the types of seeking refuge for these two people. Whoever thinks that his existence is the existence of his Lord because it is not his inasmuch as it is existence, says: "I seek refuge with Thee from Thee." It is the third rank. The source of the servant is confirmed in this rank. (367)

21.3. Seeking Refuge With God from the Accursed Satan

When the one who recites the Quran seeks refuge in the recitation of the Quran, The Obligator—who is God Almighty—teaches him how to seek refuge, with Whom to seek refuge, and from whom to seek refuge. He said to him, "*So when thou hast recited the Quran, seek refuge with God from the accursed Satan.*" (16:98) He gave him the comprehensive name and mentioned the Quran to him and did not single out any particular sign. Because of that, He did not single out any particular name. He used the name God. Therefore the one who recites looks to the reality of what he recites or looks at what he must seek refuge from in that sign, and mentions it in his seeking refuge. He looks at which of the names of God he should seek refuge with. Whichever name it is, he specifies it by mentioning it when he seeks refuge. (368)

The one who recites the Quran sits with God since the Quran is remembrance, and the one who remembers sits with God. Moreover, the formal prayer is the state of intimate conversation with God, so he is also in a state of nearness upon nearness. It is like light upon light. It is more proper to seek refuge with God here and to seek refuge from Satan because he is the distant one. One says: "*birun shatunun*" (a very deep well) since its bottom is distant. Distance is opposite nearness. In the state of his nearness, he seeks refuge from what would distance him from that state, so there is nothing more fitting than the name "Satan." (369)

Then He described him as "accursed" (*rajim*). If it has the passive meaning (*maful*), then its meaning comes from the stoned (*marjum*) Satan, that is, with meteors, which are burning lights. God Almighty says: "*We have made to appear pleasing the lower heaven with lamps*." (67:5) The formal prayer is light and God stones him with lights. Therefore the formal prayer is part of what keeps Satan far from the servant. God Almighty says: "*Truly the formal prayer prohibits depravity and that which was immoral*" (29:45) because of the fact that one puts aside everything but the formal prayer. (370)

If it has the active meaning, it is because of the blameworthy thoughts, evil calls and whisperings with which he stones the heart of the servant. For this reason, when the Messenger of God stood up to pray in the night and did the recitation of "God is Greater" after which everything but the formal prayer is forbidden (*takbir al-ihram*), he would say, "God is very much Greater. God is very much greater. God is very much greater. Praise be to God abundantly. Praise be to God abundantly. Praise be to God abundantly. Glory be to God morning and evening. Glory be to God morning and evening. Glory be to God morning and evening. I seek refuge with God from the accursed Satan, from his puffing, his spitting and his pricking." Ibn Abbas said: "His pricking is what he whispers during the formal prayer, his spit is poetry, and his puffing is what he casts of doubt in the formal prayer," that is, forgetfulness. For this reason, the Prophet said: "The prostration of forgetfulness is to spite Satan." The one who offers the formal prayer is obliged to seek refuge with God from the accursed Satan by freeing his heart to seek the protection of his Lord. (371)

Since the one who offers the formal prayer does not recognize what evil thoughts and whisperings Satan will bring him in the formal prayer, he cannot specify what will repel it. Therefore, he used the name "Allah" which contains the meanings of the names since this name contains the reality of every name which repels every thought that should be repelled. The state of the one who performs the formal prayer should be like that when he seeks refuge if God gives him success. (372)

21.4. In the Name of God, the Merciful, the Compassionate

After seeking refuge, he says: *"In the Name of God, The Merciful, The Compassionate."* When he says it, God says: "My servant has mentioned Me." One must act in accordance with this in *"In the Name of God, The Merciful, The Compassionate."* Mention it, and connect the *ba* to this action if this tradition is sound. If it is not sound, then recite, *"In the name of God."* That is clearly manifest in *"Recite! In the Name of your Lord"* (96:1). (373)

This obligates you. They say that you do not perform any action but that its origins came before it. If they are deferred, then you will be too weak to act. This, for us, is not a satisfactory explanation since it is a judgment of grammar. The Arabs do not rationalize or offer pretexts. I think that the *basmala* is connected to His words: *"Praise belongs to God"* by His names. God is only praised by His names. However, that does not make it necessary for us to force ourselves to surmise in the Quran except in case of necessity. There is no necessity here. (374)

The words of the Messenger of God are sound from God, the Blessed, the Exalted, that when the servant says: *"In the Name of God, The Merciful, The Compassionate"* in his conversation in the formal prayer, God says: "My servant has mentioned Me." There is no dispute. This Tradition is related like that. Abd Allah ibn Ziyad ibn Saman related from Ala from his father from Abu Hurayra that the Prophet said: "When you perform the formal prayer and do not recite the Umm al-Quran in it, then it is like a three-month miscarriage, incomplete." It was said to Abu Hurayra, "We are behind the leader." He said: "Recite it to yourselves, for I heard the Messenger of God say, 'God Almighty says: "I have divided the formal prayer into two parts between Me and My servant, and My servant has what he asks for. When he begins the formal prayer with 'In the name of God, the Merciful, the Compassionate,' My servant has mentioned Me."' The servant says: "Praise be to God, the Lord of the worlds," and God says: "My servant has praised Me." The Tradition will come in detail, word for word, God willing, as we mentioned the phrases of the the supplication for directing oneself to God right up to the end of the Opening Chapter. Muslim mentioned this Tradition from the Tradition of Sufyan ibn Uyayna from al-Ala from his father from Abu Hurayra. He did not mention the *basmala* in it. (375)

21.5 When the Knower of God says: "In the Name of God"

When the knower of God says: *"In the Name of God, The Merciful, The Compassionate,"* he connects the *ba* to what there is of the meaning of action in "praise." As we said: he says that God is only praised by His Most Beautiful Names. He mentioned three of those names. There is the name "Allah" since it is comprehensive and is not derived. It is described and does not describe. In relationship to the names, it is as the Essence is to the Attributes. He mentioned it first since it indicates the Essence as all the names are guideposts in language, even if one does not have the power to inform because it describes the rank of the name "The Sultan." Since it only indicates the absolute pure Essence inasmuch as what it is in itself without relationships, no derivation can be conceived of in this name. This is why it is called the *basmala*. It is the name with God, that is, your words, "In the name of God." It is like the *abdala*. That is Abd Allah (servant of God). It is also the same with the *hawqala*. It is power (*hawl*) and strength (*quwwa*) with God. (376)

After he says: "In the name of God," the servant says: "The Merciful, The Compassionate" since "The Merciful, The Compassionate" is a compound name like Balbakk (*bal* + *bakk*) and Ramhurmuz (*ram* + *hurmuz*). He calls Him that since it is one of His names, not because of those who are shown mercy or because of the connection of mercy to them. It is because it is an attribute of His, may His Majesty be exalted! Other-than-God does not have any mention at all in the *basmala*. (377)

21.6. The Recitation of the Gnostics in the Two Books

Whenever a divine name occurs which is not preceded by a phenomenal being which demands the name nor followed by a being which the name demands in the sign, then the gnostic looks at that name. It indicates the Essence named by it, and the attribute intelligible from it or the derivation which the being demands. This is different from the divine name which comes after a phenomenal being, or has a phenomenal being which comes after it, or is between the two beings. When a being comes after it, that being is its result, is connected to it and seeks it. It issues from it. If you reflect on it, you will find it as in His words, "*The Merciful. He taught the Quran. He created the human being.*" (55:1-3) (378)

When the being comes first and the divine name comes after it, He is The First and The Last is the opposite of The First as He said: "Fear God! and then "God will teach you." Consciousness of God manifested the object of the consciousness. That is God. In the first example, the name manifested the source of the human being. In the same way in "and God will teach you," teaching manifested the divine name which is Allah. (379)

When the phenomenal being falls between the two divine names, the being belongs to the first by the principle of the result, and to the last by the principle of the premise as the "worlds" occurred between the "Lord" and the "Merciful." When He says: "*Praise be to God, the Lord of the worlds,*

The Merciful, The Compassionate," it is like *"Be Godfearing of God and God teaches you"* (2:282). *"Teaches you"* occurred between the two names. The name God preceded it and the name God came after it with two different meanings. The first name effected in it the quest for instruction, and teaching was accepted by the second name. (380)

It is like that when the divine name occurs between a divine name which precedes it and a being which comes after it like the name "Lord" between "God" and the "worlds" when He says: *"Praise be to God, the Lord of the worlds."* It is also like that when it comes at the end of *surah al-zumar*, or between a being which precedes it and a divine name which is after it like His Words, *"The worlds, The Merciful, The Compassionate, Master. . ." "The Merciful, The Compassionate"* is preceded by the word *"worlds"* and after it comes *"The Master of the Day of Judgment."* The source of the *"worlds"* manifested *"The Merciful, The Compassionate"* by their need for the two mercies: the general mercy and the particular mercy, the necessary mercy and the mercy of pure graciousness. (381)

"The Merciful, The Compassionate" demands *"Master of the Day of the Judgment"* in order to manifest that He is The Sultan of The Merciful, The Compassionate since He is The Master. The mercy from the presence of the king is the mercy of might and gracious bestowal accompanied by rich independence. This is different from the mercy of the one who is not a king—like the mercy of the mother to her child because of the pain she experiences for his sake in herself. She herself is his mercy, and she works for her child while she is veiled from the knowledge of that by her child. Kindness towards her child is obliged on her by causality, it is not hers. Mercy to her child occurs naturally as opposed to the mercy of the King. It is from might and rich independence of the particular person in his flock who is shown mercy. (382)

It is like that when a divine name occurs between two divine names like His words: *"He is God, The One Who is the Creator, The One Who Fashions."* (59:24) The name *"Creator"* occurs between the name "God" and the name *"The One Who Fashions."* Similarly, the name *"The One Who Fashions"* is between *"The Creator"* and *"The Giver of Form."* This is tremendous. The Creator is an attribute of God and an actual description of The Fashioner. (383)

This style proceeds when the gnostics recite the two books—the Quran and the Book of the entire unisign. It is "a written book" whose pages are scattered. Existence is in it. Their remembrance proceeds in that manner. (384)

It is the same when a phenomenal being occurs between two things. The first has a son, and the second one after it has a father in whatever is understood of that. For this reason, God says about the words of the servant, *"In the Name of God, The Merciful, The Compassionate,"* "My servant has mentioned Me." This mention is not limited by anything because of the difference in the states of those who recite the remembrance, that is, the motives of the remembrance. Desire can provoke one to remember. Fear can provoke one to recite remembrance. Exaltation and glorification can provoke one to recite remembrance. God answers the lowest of the ranks of the knower. This is the one who recites with his tongue and does not understand with his heart because he does not reflect on what he says. When the reciter knows with the tongue and does not know what he mentions, his reflection or remembrance of his recitation is God's answer to him according to the knowledge he obtains about what he recites. Therefore, reflect on what we have written for you! (385)

21.7. "Praise be to God" on the Tongue of Gnostics

Then he said: "God Almighty said: 'When the servant says: *"Praise be to God, the Lord of the worlds,"* in the formal prayer, God says: "My servant has praised Me."'" The gnostic says: *"Praise belongs to God,"* that is, the ends of praise return to God. The meaning of the "ends of praise" is that every praise with which a phenomenal being is praised rather than God, its end result returns to God by two paths. One path is praise of phenomenal being by what that being has of praiseworthy attributes which demand praise, or by the praiseworthy effects it has which are the results of praiseworthy qualities which it has. No matter what aspect it has, that praise returns to God since God is the One who brought those attributes and qualities into existence. They do not belong to that being so the end result of praise returns to God. (386)

The other way is that the gnostic looks and sees the existence which possible things make use of is the source of the manifestation of God in them. He is the One to whom praise is connected, not beings. Then he looks at the place of the *lam* in His words, "to Allah" (*lil Lah*) and he sees that the Praiser is the same as the Praised, no more and no less. He is the Praised Praiser. He denied praise to phenomenal beings as being a praiser and denied it as being praised. From one aspect, being is praised and not praising, and from another aspect, it is neither praising nor praised. As for its not being praising, we have made that clear. Praise is an action, and actions belong to God. As for its not being praised, the praised is praised for what he has, not for someone else has. Being has nothing, so it is not praised at all as is related about the like of the one who makes a display of what he does not own, even as the one who wears my garment lies. (387)

When the gnostic says: *"Praise belongs to God, Lord of the worlds,"* he brings to mind all that we mentioned and what the name "Lord" gives

Him of permanence, setting things right, instruction, kingdom and mastery. The name "Lord" demands these five qualities. He calls to mind what the world accords him of evidence of God Almighty. The answer of God when He says: "My servant has praised Me," is only for the one who praises Him by the lowest rank because He takes into consideration the weakest one who does not have a portion of knowledge of Him. This is because of His generosity and a mercy to him. This is because the knower knows from his question or recitation what he has understood of meanings in that recitation. God answers him according to what happens to him. It is included in what is addressed to Him by His common servant with little knowledge or the non-Arab who has no knowledge of what is indicated by what he recites. Understand then! God gives inspiration. (388)

21.8. "The Merciful, the Compassionate"

Then he said from God: "The servant says: '*The Merciful, The Compassionate,*' and God says: 'My servant has extolled Me,' that is, by the attribute of mercy from which both of these two names are derived. He did not say in what. His mercy is general. This is because the common person only recognizes God's mercy to him when it conforms with his desire, even if it is harmful for him; or what is in harmony with his nature, even if his healing is concealed in it. (389)

The gnostic is not like that. divine mercy may come to the servant in something disliked like drinking a remedy whose taste and smell is disliked by the sick person even though healing is hidden in it. When the gnostic says: "*The Merciful, The Compassionate,*" he has present in himself what is indicated by these words inasmuch as The Real is described by them and inasmuch as the object of mercy seeks it by his knowledge of all that. He also has present in his heart in his heart the universality of the single mercy which is apportioned among His creation in the abode of this world—human and *jinn,* obedient and rebel, unbeliever and believer. It embraces all. He sees that even if the reality of this single mercy had not granted that God provides for His servants by it—inanimates, plants, animals, men and *jinn* (and it is not veiled from the unbeliever and believer, obedient person and rebel), he would still have recognized that its essence demands that inasmuch as it is mercy. (390)

Then the revelation came after this one mercy stating that this one mercy flows throughout the world. Its reality demands that the mother bestow affection on her child in all animals. This is one of a hundred mercies. God—glory be to Him!—has stored up ninety-nine mercies for His servants in the world to come. When His judgment and decree are carried out by this one mercy on the Day of Rising, and the Reckoning is finished and people descend into their homes in the two abodes, God—glory be to Him!—will add ninety-nine mercies to this mercy, and it will be a hundred. He sends it down on His servants without limit in the two abodes. Mercy flows and encompasses everything. It encompasses some of them by the principle of necessity, and it encompasses others by the principle of gracious bestowal. (391)

Divine mercy therefore encompasses everything in its place and in the source of its thingness. The hot is blessed by bitter cold and the cold by burning fire. If the same had come to each of these two states, it would then punish, When the people of the Garden look down at the people of the fire, it increases them in bliss upon their bliss because of their victory. If the people of the "fire" had looked upon the people of the "gardens," they would have been punished by this equality because of the deviation they possess in it. For this reason, He repaid them with its opposite from the sum of the hundred mercies. The principle in this world is the mercy of this world as you know it. Now (that is, in the world to come) it is one of the total hundred, so what do you think? This is enough. (392)

This is the manner in which the gnostic says: *"The Merciful, The Compassionate"* in the formal prayer. He recognizes that by which God will answer him. (393)

21.9. "One Who is Sovereign of the Day of Judgment (din)

Then God says: "The servant says. '*One Who is Sovereign of the Day of Judgment,*' and God says: 'My servant has glorified Me.'" Another variant has "My servant has trusted in Me." This is a general answer and a general response. We have confirmed what is meant by it. When the gnostic says: *"Master of the Day of Judgment,"* He does not restrict himself to the world to come alone by the Day of Judgment. He sees that *"The Merciful, The Compassionate"* does not part from the *"One Who is Sovereign of the Day of Judgment."* It is the attribute of them (The Merciful, The Compassionate). Repayment is both in this world and the world to come. Similarly, it appears by what is given of the establishment of the punishments and the appearance of pollution/corruption in the land and sea by men so that *"He causes them to experience some of what they have done so that perhaps they would return and repent"* (30:41) from it. This is the same as repayment. The day of this world is also the Day of Repayment. God is the One Who is Sovereign of the Day of Judgment. (394)

Therefore, the gnostic sees that acts of expiation take effect in this world, and that the human being in this world is not safe from a matter which might constrict his breast and pain him in the senses and intellect even to the extent of a flea-bite or stumble. Pains are limited in time but the mercy of God Almighty is not limited by time. It encompasses everything. Some of it is obtained and delivered by means of gracious bestowal. The root of taking it is bestowal. Some of it is what is taken by means of divine Obligation in His words: "Your Lord has written mercy for Himself." He said: "I will write it." People take it as repayment. Some of the obligated creatures obtain it by bestowal in any case, so understand that! (395)

Every pain in this world and the next is expiation for things which have taken place, and they are limited in time. It is expiation for the one who has experienced pain from him, whether he is young or old, provided that he understands pain. He must grasp what the sensation of pain is. This perception is only perceived by the one who has it unveiled to him. The suckling child does not understand pain even though he feels it. His father, mother and others who love him and do not love him feel pain and understand the pain which they see in the suckling child in any illness which afflicts him. That is expiation for the one who understands pain. If it is more than that, the one of intellect has a mercy as well as the expiation. He is rewarded then. There is a reward for every living thing (lit. everything with a moist liver). Every liver is moist because it is the house of blood, and blood is hot and wet, the nature of life. (396)

As for the child, when he understands pain and seeks to flee from the causes which occasion it and tries to avoid it, he has expiation in it for that which he has done which has caused pain to others—animals or other human beings, or refusing to do what his mother or father asks him to do, or refusing what someone else asks him to do. The one who asked him has pain because his need was refused. When this small child experiences pain, that pain which he has is a repayment and a expiation for the pain which the asker experienced when he refused to do what he asked him to do. Or he may have injured an animal—like hitting a dog with a stone, killing a flea or a louse, or walking on an ant with his foot and killing it. It can be anything else like that which he might do, intentionally or unintentionally. The secret of this matter is wondrous! It operates in all existent things to the extent that the human being can experience the human being from the existence of clouds. His breast might be constricted by them. It is expiation for things that he did and has forgotten or still remembers. (397)

The people of unveiling see all of that realized in His words: "*One Who is Sovereign of the Day of Judgment.*" God says: "My servant has entrusted to Me" or "glorified Me" or both of them. Glorification refers to the presence of God by what his Essence demands and what the relationship of the world to Him demands. Entrustment is in respect of what the relationship of the world to Him demands and nothing more. He is their Protector by the power of management which is entrusted to Him.

For some other people, He says: "My servant has glorified Me" in intention. The servant might join both intentions so that God will combine both answers for Him—glorification and entrustment. This half of the Opening Chapter is all purely for the presence of God. The servant does not share in it at all. (398)

21.10. "Thee only we worship and to Thee alone we pray for help"

Then God says: "The servant says: '*Thee alone we worship and to Thee alone we pray for help.*' and God says: 'This is between Me and My servant, and My servant has what he asks for.'" This sign includes the asker and the Asked, the One addressed. It is the *kaf* of "*iyyaka*" (Thee alone) in both of them. "We worship" and "we ask for help" belong to the servant. He is the worshiper and the one who is asking for help. When the servant says: "*iyyaka,*" he unifies God by the letter (pronoun) of direct address. He gives it direction, but not by way of definition. It is in obedience to the words of the Prophet to the one who asked him about the good and beautiful in the form of instruction. The Prophet told him: "It is that you worship God as if you were seeing Him." Therefore you must turn to Him with the pronoun of direct address. It is the *kaf,* or the letter *ta* with the *fatha* for the masculine and *kasra* for the feminine. The pronoun used can be feminine because the Essence is feminine. (399)

This is a witnessing of the imagination. It comes from an inter space. This sign comes as an inter space in which sharing between God and His servant occurs. The previous part of the Opening Chapter was purely for God, and the rest of it is purely for the servant. This is the one sign in which there is partnership. It is alone without having anything joined to it to make it plural since the Object of worship is One. He makes himself plural by the *nun* of the plural in worship and the desired help because "the worshippers" from "servant" are many and each of the worshippers seeks help. The goal of acts of worship is One. The eye owes worship, as does the hearing, the sight, the tongue, the belly, the genitals, the foot and the heart. For this reason, he says: "*We worship and we seek help*" with the plural *nun*. (400)

If the person of knowledge looks at the parts of his world while the jurisdiction of the formal prayer encompasses all his stations, both outward and inward, he does not isolate any one part from another. He stands with all of them, he bows with all of them, and he sits with all of them. All of his world is concentrated on the worship of his Lord and seeking help from Him in His worship. He used the *nun* of the plural in "*We worship and we seek help.*" The tongue speaks for the whole as one person speaks for a delegation in their presence before the King. The servant knows that God sent down this sign to isolate Himself so that none is worshiped except Him.

When God bound the servant by the *nun*, it is because He wants him to worship Him with all of himself, outwardly and inwardly, with his faculties and limbs, and to seek help according to that. If the person who offers the formal prayer is not like this and his entire world is not concentrated on the worship of his Lord, then he is a liar in his recitation when he says: "*Thee alone we worship and to Thee alone we pray for help.*" God looks at him and sees him turning away in this formal prayer or sees that he is preoccupied with thoughts about his shop or business. In spite of this, he still says: "we worship." He is lying. God says to him, "You have lied in your allusion to all of you being engaged in My worship. Did you not turn your eye away from your *qibla*? Did you not listen to what the people there were saying? Were you and your heart not conscious of what they were saying? Where is the truth in your words, 'we worship' with the *nun* of the plural?" (402)

The gnostic has all of this present in his thoughts, so he is ashamed to say, "*Thee alone we worship*" in his conversation with Him in the formal prayer lest it be said to him, "You have lied." The one who has this state must concentrate himself on the worship of his Lord so that God will say to him, "You have spoken truly since you recite with all of your being fixed on Me in your worship of Me and seeking My help." (403)

21.11. What Is Intended by Recitation of the Quran Is to Reflect On Its Meaning

We will now relate what our shaykh, Muhammad ibn Khalaf ibn Saf al-Lakhami, related to us from on the teachers among the righteous. A young boy used to recite the Quran with him, and he noticed that he was quite pale. He asked someone about his situation and was told that this boy would stand up the entire night reciting the Quran. He said to him, "My son, I am told that you stay up the entire night reciting the Quran." He said: "It is as you have been told." He said: "My son, tonight keep me present in your *qibla* and recite the Quran to me in your formal prayer. Do not forget me." (404)

The youth said: "All right." In the morning, he asked him, "Did you do what I told you to do?" He replied, "Yes, teacher." He said: "Did you finish the whole Quran last night?" He said: "I could not recite more than half of the Quran." He said: "My boy, this is excellent. Tonight place before you whomever you wish among the Companions of the Messenger of God Recite it to him and be careful!" They heard it from the Messenger of God so do not make any mistakes in your recitation." He said: "Teacher, God willing, I will do that." (405)

In the morning, the teacher asked him about his night. He said: "Teacher, I could not manage [to recite] more than a quarter of the Quran." He said: "My son, tonight recite to the Messenger of God upon whom the Quran was sent down. Recognize the one to whom you are reciting." He said: "Yes." In the morning he said: "Teacher throughout the entire night I could not do more than one thirtieth (*juz*) of the Quran." He said: "My boy, tonight let your recitation of Quran be in the presence of Gabriel who brought it down on the heart of Muhammad. Take care! Recognize the value of the one to whom you recite!" (406)

In the morning, he said: "Teacher, I could not do more than such-and-such," and he mentioned a few signs of the Quran. He said: "My son, tonight turn in repentance to God and prepare! Know that the one who performs the formal prayer speaks intimately with his Lord and that you are standing before Him reciting His words to Him! Look at your portion of the Quran and His portion! Reflect on what you recite! That which is desired is not to join the letters together and relate words to one another. Reflection on the meanings of what you recite is what is desired in recitation, so do not be ignorant!" (407)

In the morning, the teacher waited for the youth but he did not come to him. He sent someone to ask after him. He was told, "This morning he is ill. You should visit him." Therefore the teacher went to him. When the youth saw him, he wept and said: "May God repay you with good from me, teacher! I had not recognized that I was a liar until last night. When I stood in my place of formal prayer and had God Almighty present and I was before Him, I recited His Book to Him. I started the Opening Chapter and came to His words: '*Thee alone we worship*,' and I looked at myself and I did not see that I was truthful in saying it. I was therefore too ashamed to say: "*Thee alone we worship*" before Him when He would know that I was lying. I saw myself as heedless and oblivious with my own thoughts, neglecting His worship. (408)

"I remained repeating the recitation from the beginning of the Opening Chapter to His words, '*One Who is Sovereign of the Day of Judgment*.' I could not say: '*Thee alone we worship*' since it was not sincere in me. I remained ashamed to lie before God Almighty so that He would hate me for it. I did not do a single cycle until dawn. My liver is crushed and bruised, and I am only traveling to Him with a state which will please Him." Not a second had passed before the youth died. When he was buried, the teacher went to his grave and asked him about his state. He heard the youth's voice from the grave, saying to him: "Teacher! I am alive with The Living. He did not take me to account for anything." The teacher returned to his house and took to his bed. He was ill from the effect which the state of the youth had made on him and he soon followed him. Whoever recites *"Thee alone we worship"* with the recitation of the youth has indeed recited it." (409)

21.12. "Guide us on the Straight Path"

Then God says: "The servant says: '*Guide us on the Straight Path, the path of those Thou hast blessed, not those against whom Thou art angry nor those who are misguided.*'" God says: "This is for My servant, and My servant has what he asks for." When the gnostic says: *"Guide us"* he has the divine name "The Guide" present. He asks Him to guide him on the Straight Path, to make it clear for him and to give him success in walking on it. It is the path of two types of Oneness of God: Oneness of Essence and Oneness of rank. It is divinity with all its inseparable attributes of the judgments of the divine law which are the right of Islam in his words "except by the right of Islam, and their reckoning rests with God." He has present in himself the Straight Path which his Lord is on inasmuch as He leads the one who walks on it to his happiness. (410)

God Almighty related that the Prophet Hud said: "My Lord is on a Straight Path." When the gnostic walks on that straight path on which the Lord is and has witnessing, God is in front of him. The servant follows God on that path. He is compelled. How can he not follow and be compelled when his forelock is in the hand of his Lord who drags him to Him? God says: *"There is no creature crawling but that He takes it by the forelock. My Lord is on a Straight Path."* (11:5) All that crawls, both high and low, is included under the domain of this sign through abasement and servanthood. People in that include the unveiled person who sees the hand on the forelock and the believer. This includes every crawling creature in general, with the exception of men and *jinn*. Only righteous men and *jinn* are included among them. (411)

If all the men and *jinn* had been included, all would have been on a Straight Path, the path of God, since He is the Lord. He says: may He be exalted! *"There is not a thing but it glorifies His praise."* (17:44) He says about men and *jinn* in particular, "We shall deal with you, men and *jinn*!" This is in order to threaten them and provoke their fear since they do not place their forelocks in His Hand and they are left to their own will and not His in what He commands and forbids. For this reason, He says: *"The path of those Thou hast blessed,"* meaning those to whom God has given success. They are all of the men of knowledge and the righteous men and *jinn*. This is like the Messengers, the Prophets, the "friends," and the righteous believers. The Straight Path is only given to the one God has blessed—Prophet, truthful one, martyr, righteous and every crawling creature which He takes by the forelock. (412)

When the gnostic is present and attentive in his recitation, he places his forelock in the hand of his Lord in the unseen of His He-ness. Those who are headed for the "fire" are among those who are outside. They are the object of the exception of God when He says: "Not of those against whom there is anger," that is, those with whom God is angry since He called them when He said: "Come to formal prayer," but they did not answer. *"Nor of those who are astray,"* and with the conjunction He excepted those who are confused. They have a better state than the one who is the object of anger. Whoever does not recognize his Lord as Lord and associates something with Him in His divinity which does not deserve to be god is among those who are the object of anger. (413)

When the servant has this and its like present in himself when he recites, the angels say: "Amen" and the inward part of the human being, which is his spirit shared with the angels in their formation and purity, says: "Amen," that is, safe with the good that exists. The reciter calls with the tongue and then listens to his heart. He hears the recitation of his spirit reciting the Opening Chapter of the Quran which coincides with the recitation of his tongue. The tongue speaks, believing in its supplication, that is, the supplication of his spirit by reciting His words, *"Guide us."* (414)

If his "Amen" coincides with the "Amen" of the angels in an attribute in harmony with purification and sanctification by noble, good essences, God answers him after he says: "Amen," with these two tongues. When he rises, God is his tongue in God's recitation of His own words. When he says: "Amen," the divine names say "Amen." The names are what manifest The One by whom this servant has character, "Amen." Whoever has his "Amen" coincide with the "Amen" of the names of his Creator, he is all truth. (415)

We have clarified for you the manner of recitation in the formal prayer. Proceed in it according to your capability and the speed of your movement. You will see more. *"There is not any of us but he has a known station. And truly we are ones who are standing in ranks. And truly we are the ones who glorify."* (37:164-166) (416)

22 Actions of the Formal Prayer

22.1. The Recitation of the Quran in the Bowing Forward (ruku) [of the Formal Prayer]

22.1.1. The Position of the Religious Scholars About Recitation of the Quran and Glorification in the Bending Forward (ruku) [of the Formal Prayer]

Some forbid recitation of the Quran when bowing in the formal prayer and some permit it. That which they agree about is the recitation of the glorification in the bowing. They disagree about whether there is a defined statement about it or not. Some say that there is a limit in that, and that is that he says in the bowing, "Glory be to your Lord, The Great" three times, and "Glory be to your Lord Most High" three times in prostration. Among those who say that are those who think that it is obligatory and that the formal prayer is invalidated when it is left out, or that the minimum in that is three times. Some do not say that it is obligatory. This is the view held by most scholars. Some say that the leader must say it five times in order to give the one behind him a chance to say it three times. (417)

22.1.2. Bending Forward [in the Formal Prayer] By Way of Secrets

In the area of secrets, I say that when the one who offers the formal prayer stands before his Lord in the formal prayer, he has a relationship to The Self-subsistence (*qayyumiyya*). Then he moves from it to the state of bowing which is humility. It is like that with prostration. This attribute must not belong to God. The Prophet set down what he understood of the words of God when it was sent down on him: *"Glorify the name of your Lord, The Sublime."* (56:74) The Messenger of God said: "[Recite] it in your bowing (*ruku*)." Then God Almighty sent down, *"Glorify the name of your Lord, The Lofty."* (87:1) The Messenger of God said: "[Recite] it in your prostration." They are connected by the word of God, "glorify." God and the Messenger of God commanded us to make it part of the formal prayer. (418)

He said: "Disconnect the immensity of your Lord from humility." Humility is to God, not by God. It is impossible that the attribute of humility be based on Him. One relates it to the name "Lord" because it demands the ruled. It is one of the three matrices. It is a name which recurs often and appears many times in the Quran, more than the rest of the names. The matrices of the names in the Quran are three: Allah (God), the al-Rahman (The Merciful), and Rabb (Lord). (419)

When glorification is connected to this name, it is not connected to it in relation to the glorifier himself. He said: "Glory be to my Lord, The Great." He is connected to it in relation to the right of every glorifier because the knowledge of it is separate from every knower. One person may believe in it differently from the manner in which another person believes. Every person glorifies his Lord which he believes is the Lord. How many people do not believe what another believes about the Lord! That person with one belief thinks in what he relates to his Lord that the belief of the other person is impossible and he does not think that He can possibly have this attribute and declares that the other person is a unbeliever because of that. Had he glorified Him absolutely with the belief of every creed, this person would have glorified the one whom he believes has failed to disconnect Him. For this reason, every glorifier relates Him to what his belief demands. (420)

22.1.3. *The Portion of the Gnostic Is to Glorify Him With the Tongue of Every Glorifier*

The portion of the gnostic is to glorify Him with the tongue of every glorifier and to regard the immensity of God and disconnect it from having humility based on it and to proclaim Him High above prostration. In his prostration, the servant seeks the root of the formation of his bodily frame which is water and earth. When he stands, he seeks the formation of his spirit. God says of them: "*And you will be among the lofty.*" (3:139) The state of bowing becomes a middle space between standing and prostration. It is in the position of the derived existence of the possible. It is a space between the Necessary of non-existence by Himself and the possible by Himself. By itself, the possible is non-existent, and non-existence is not derived since there is none who derives any benefit from it. The existence of the Necessary of existence is by itself. A state of space appears, and it is the existence of the servant. It is the position of bowing. One does not say that this derived existence is the source of the possible, nor that it is other than the source of the possible. It is not said that it is the same as God nor that it is other-than-God. It has two relationships which the gnostic recognizes. (421)

In the state of bowing an inter spatial state which divides the two matters occurs to the gnostic. It is the intelligible meaning by which the Lord is distinguished from the servant. It is also the intelligible meaning by which the servant be described with the descriptions of the Lord, and the Lord can be described by the descriptions of the ruled. This is not by attribute. It is description, not attribute. We said: "description, not attribute." One understands from the attribute an extra matter and an extra source which is added on to the source of the one who is described. The description, however, can be the source of the described with a particular attribute which does not have an existent source, so understand! (422)

22.2. The Supplication in the Bending Forward (*ruku*) [in the Formal Prayer]

22.2.1. The Positions of the Religious Scholars About Supplication in the Bending Forward (ruku) [in the Formal Prayer]

They disagree about supplication in bowing although they agree about the permissibility of extolling God in it, and that it is an obligation for the one who thinks that it is a precondition for the validity of the formal prayer. Some of them dislike supplication when bowing. Some permit it, and that is my position. They also disagree about supplication during the formal prayer. Some say that it is not permitted to make supplication in the formal prayer using anything other than the phrases of the Quran. Some permit that. (423)

22.2.2. The Position of the Religious Scholars About Supplicating in the Formal Prayer

I say that since the meaning of the formal prayer is supplication, it is valid that supplication be one of its parts. That is by means of calling the whole by the name of the part. As for the one who dislikes the recitation of supplication when bowing, the state of the inter space has two aspects: one aspect belongs to God and one aspect belongs to creation. Whoever sees in his bowing the aspect which seeks God, dislikes the recitation of supplication when bowing but does not make it forbidden since phenomenal being may be described by the attribute of self-subsistence. God Almighty says: "*Men are supporters of women.*" Whoever is dominated by the aspect which seeks creation when bowing says that supplication is permitted in bowing. The *sunna* has brought that, and it is the school of al-Bukhari, may God have mercy on him! (424)

It is like that with the one who prefers that you not offer supplication in the formal prayer with anything except the phrases of the Quran. He sees that God Almighty has prescribed different supplications in the Quran. Therefore, turning from them to expressions of people arises from the antagonism of the ego (*nafs*). Such is its nature that it does not agree with its Lord. Sound manners (*adab*) lies in that. As I only speak to Him in the formal prayer with His words, so we only call upon Him by what He has sent down and prescribed for us in the Quran or the *sunna* to say in the formal prayer. Whoever recites supplication in the formal prayer in any fashion has his heart dominated by the fact that there is only God and there is no speaker but God, either by the actions he does (as it has come that God says: "God hears whoever praises Him" in the formal prayer on the tongue of His servant) or other matters. (425)

22.3. The Sitting Back on Your Knees (*tashahhud*)

22.3.1. *The Position of the Religious Scholars on the Sitting Back on Your Knees (tashahhud) [in the Formal Prayer]*

Scholars disagree about the obligation of the *tashahhud* in the formal prayer and what is preferred in it. Some say that it is obligatory. Some say that it is not obligatory. (426)

22.3.2. *The Word for Sitting Back on Your Knees (tashahhud) Means "to Summon Present*

I say that since in reality the meaning of the sitting back on your knees (*tashahhud*) is "to summon present." You do that by witnessing—and it is presence. The human being is commanded to be present in his formal prayer. Therefore, there must be *tashahhud*. It is more fitting and more excellent. Since the witness speaks with knowledge of what he sees as opposed to the judge, presence or summoning present is not valid without the witness knowing what his witnessing means. He only has with him present what he knows of God. He is not asked to do more than that. (427)

People say different things about Allah (*al-Lah*). Since statements vary, then the person of intellect is alone in his knowledge of his Lord, he must base himself on one of these statements which result from his reflection, and they vary. The one with sound intellect is the one who abandons what his speculation gives him about God as well as the speculation of others among those who have opinions through mental speculation. He refers to what the Prophets said: and what the Quran articulates. He believes it and keeps it present with him in his formal prayer, and in movements and stillnesses. It is more fitting for him than the one who is present with God Almighty with his own thoughts. (428)

Some people have erred in this. That is because this person thinks that the divine law is not established in people until the existence of God, His Unity, the possibility of sending Messengers and prescribing the laws of the divine law have been established for him intellectually. By this, he prefers to be present with God in his formal prayer by this knowledge. The matter is not like that. Even if his intellect is sound in establishing the existence of God and His Unity, the possibility of prescribing the divine law and confirming the lawgiver by the proof which he brings, he still knows that the lawgiver has described Himself with things that our intellect stops short of. If we had attempted to reflect on them with our intellectual capacity, we would not have accepted them. (429)

Then we saw that those descriptions which came from the Prophet about God and His gnosis are demanded by acts of worship. Acts of worship are nearer in relationship to His gnosis than the recognition given by logical proofs which is distinct from it. We see that we are present with God in our *tashahhud* and formal prayer by the divine Gnosis which we take from the lawgiver in the Quran and the *sunna* by multiple transmissions. We think that this is better than presence with Him based on the opinions of intellects. We will look at what is related of *tashahhud* in the formal prayer, and we will proceed in the same manner which we used to discuss directing oneself to God, recitation, and what is said in bowing and prostration. (430)

22.3.3. *The Words to Recite When Sitting Back on Your Knees (tashahhud) [in the Formal Prayer] Related from Umar ibn al-Khattab*

In that we have the *tashahhud* of Umar. It is: *At-tahiyyatu lillahiz-zakiyatu lillah. As-salamu alayka ayyuhn-nabiyyu wa rahmatullahi wa barakatuh, as-salamu alayna wa ala ibadillahis-salihan. Ash-hadu an la ilaha illallah wa ash-hadu anna Muhammadan abduhu wa rasuluh.* (Greetings belong to God. Pure actions belong to God. Peace be upon you, O Prophet, and the mercy of God and His blessings. Peace be upon us and upon the righteous servants of God. I bear witness that there is no god but God and I bear witness that Muhammad is the servant of God and His Messenger." One group of people have adopted that. (431)

22.3.4. *The Words to Recite When Sitting Back on Your Knees (tashahhud) [in the Formal Prayer] of Abd Allah ibn Masud*

The *tashahhud* of Abd Allah ibn Masud is: *At-tahiyyatu lillahi wassalawatu wat-tayyibat. As-salamu alayka ayyuhan-nabiyyu wa rahmatullahi wa barakatuh, as-salamu alayna wa ala ibadillahis-salihan. Ash-hadu an la ilaha illallah wa ash-hadu anna Muhammadan abduhu wa rasuluh.* (Greetings, prayers and good words belong to God. Peace be upon you, O Prophet, and the mercy of God and His blessings. Peace be upon us and upon the righteous servants of God. I bear witness that there is no god but God and I bear witness that Muhammad is the servant of God and His Messenger." Most people use this one since its transmission is well-established. (432)

22.3.5. The Words to Recite When Sitting Back on Your Knees (*tashahhud*) [in the Formal Prayer] of Ibn Abbas

The *tashahhud* of Ibn Abbas is: *At-tahiyyatul-mubarakatus-salawatut-tayyibatu lillah. Salamun alayka ayyuhan-nabiyyu wa rahmatullahi wa barakatuh, salamun alayna wa ala ibadillahis-salihin. Ash-hadu an la ilaha illallah wa anna Muhammadan abduhu wa rasuluh.* (Blessed greetings, formal prayers and good words belong to God. Peace be upon you, O Prophet, and the mercy of God and His blessings. Peace be upon us and upon the righteous servants of God. I bear witness that there is no god but God and that Muhammad is the servant of God and His Messenger)." A group of them have adopted it. All of them are *hadith*s which have been transmitted from the Messenger of God. (433)

22.3.6. The Words to Recite When Sitting Back on Your Knees (*tashahhud*) [in the Formal Prayer] from the Gnostic Is in Three Spheres

When the gnostic says the *tashahhud* with this very *tashahhud*, either he is in a state of contraction, awe and majesty arising from a divine name, or he is in a state of intimacy, beauty, and expansion arising from a divine name, or he is in a state of watchfulness and presence because his essence is in a state of balance by the acts of worship which he is obliged to do in the formal prayer. He fills up each of his faculties in the formal prayer, and each of his limbs in the formal prayer with the forms which befit it which God has demanded that they have in his formal prayer in respect to each limb and faculty. He fills them whether he is in a state of awe or intimacy. It is the most perfect state. The matter is contained in three stations: the station of majesty, the station of beauty, and the station of perfection. (434)

22.3.7. The The Words to Recite When Sitting Back on Your Knees (*tashahhud*) [in the Formal Prayer] with the Language of Perfection

He testifies in the *tashahhud* with the language of perfection. It is the first *tashahhud* for the wayfarer. He says: "Greetings belong to God," that is, the greetings of every greeter and everything greeted by it in the entire world. All the divine relationships belong to God, that is, they are for the sake of God, the Comprehensive name which encompasses all their realities. That is because every greeting in the world is connected to a divine Reality, whatever it may be. Whenever a person does not encompass all the divine Realities with his intention and his heart as he joins the expression of greetings to his faculty, other than the one reality prescribed for him in his greeting designated for him by in respect to his divine law, then he is not pure in himself in the perfection of his formal prayer. He says: "pure actions" belong to God. He says: "Purified prospering greetings," that is, that from which good grows for the one who says it, from the divine Realities which bring these greetings into existence according to what their names demand. (435)

Then he says: "Peace be upon you, O Prophet," with the definite article, *alif-lam*, of the generic noun, not the previously defined. His peace upon the Prophet is like his greetings in universality and comprehensiveness, that is, it includes every peace. This proclaims that the servant has moved from the contemplation of his Lord in respect to an absolute sense or a state which he had in his prostration to the contemplation of The Real in the Prophet. When he advances to him with presence, he greets him, addressing him directly and openly stating his prophethood. He did not greet him by referring to the message. Prophethood in respect of the essence of the Prophet is more general and nobler. In it is included what he has and what he has been commanded to convey to his community from which he is a Messenger. He recognizes what he should use to address the Messenger of God in that presence and which of it would announce distance without the vocative since he has a state of nearness. For this reason, he used the letter of direct address [second person]. (436)

After supplicating for peace upon him, he added divine Mercy since it contains both the bestowal and the necessary mercy. He ascribed it to God since He provided him with safety from all the attacks made against his station. He added the blessings which are related to He-ness. Blessings are increase. He was commanded to say, "Lord, increase me in knowledge." It is as if this one who is praying was saying in the greetings to him, "Peace be upon you and the mercy which necessitates increase of your knowledge of God which is the noblest of all states with God." It is as like "pure actions" (*zakiyat*) in greetings, He made a relationship between the obligatory poor-due (*zakah*) and blessings (*barakah*). It is because of this that God Almighty put blessings (*barakah*) in the obligatory alms (*zakat*) which is charity (*sadaqah*) since it is connected to the obligatory poor-due (*zakah*). There is no gap in existence. God replaces it and fills up his hands with the blessings of knowledge and other things of sensory reward in the Abode of Generosity whose value cannot be compared with what he spent. (437)

Then he says: "Peace be upon us and on the virtuous servants of God." He greets himself and his species with the general peace as he greeted the Prophet. God Almighty says: "*When you entered houses, then greet one another. . .*" (24:61) Entering each of the states of the formal prayer is like the rooms/houses in the house which encompasses all. ". . . *with a greeting from God.*" (24:61) He made you a messenger to yourself from Him with this blessed greeting because of what it contains of the increase of good blessing. They are acquired by taste and found to be delicious as if they were exquisite fragrances by a path which is from the breath of The Merciful. (438)

He uses the *nun* of the plural when he says: "Peace be upon us," in order to announce that his greetings of peace reaches every part of him which he addresses by a particular act of worship. He greets them since he is coming from his Lord by his withdrawal from himself when God calls him to speak to Him. He uttered the recitation of "God is Greater" after which everything but the formal prayer is forbidden (*takbir al-ihram*) and this state prevented him from looking at other than the One who called him to Him. For this reason, he greets himself with the *nun* of the plural. (439)

That is because this servant has entered the house of his heart and God is disconnected far above being incarnate in him, even if it contains Him as God says. This is due to what The Majesty of God demands of lack of relationship between the Essence of God Almighty and His creation. He sees the house of his heart empty of all that is other-than-God and God is not greeted with "peace." He is Peace. They were forbidden that because they used to say, "Peace be upon God" in the *tashahhud*. The Messenger of God said to them, "Do not say, 'Peace be upon God.' God is Peace." When he enters his house and does not see anyone in it or he disconnects God from being contained by the house of his heart, nothing remains for him to see except his obligated world which is none other than himself. When one enters a house which is empty of everyone, God has commanded him to greet himself in His words: "*When you entered houses, then greet one another. . .*" Here the servant interprets from God in his peace because He said: ". . . *with a greeting from God*" (24:61), as has been related about, "God hears whoever praises Him." He says that in the formal prayer in the same way, as a representative of God, may His Majesty be magnified and His names pure! because he has no speech in the state of leaving or entering, so the peace is from him on him. It indicates that it is a particular Self-disclosure. It must be so, understand then if you want to want to be among the people of this station in the formal prayer! (440)

Then, without explicitly stating "peace," he added peace on the righteous servants of God. It is contained by the *alif-lam* (definite article) so that his peace flows on every righteous servant of God in the heavens and the earth. He did not leave out any of the righteous as is well-known. There is only the righteous, God says: "*There is not a thing but it glorifies His praise.*" (17:44) Everything which disconnects its Lord is therefore righteous (*salih*). This is one of the knowledges of unveiling and belief. By the *salihun*, he means those who do what is right for them. That is none other than glorification. God reported that they have this attribute. There does not remain anyone, unbeliever or believer, whose particulars are not contained in this sign: "*However, most people do not know*" because they neither hear nor see. For this reason, He did not mention "peace" in this conjunction. The *waw* (and) was enough notice. In it he includes the one who deserves to have peace by means of necessity and the one who does not deserve that by means of necessity. It was hidden so that the undeserving would not be distinguished from the deserving as a mercy from Him to His servants. "*He is The Forgiving, The Merciful.*" (441)

He did not add peace with a conjunction when he greets himself after the peace with which he greets the Prophet in the beginning. Prophethood, that is, prophethood of giving the divine law at a level which is distinct from the level of following. Had he added the expression "peace" on himself with a conjunction, he would have greeted himself in respect of prophethood, as well, since the *waw* gives partnership. The door of prophethood is closed as the door of the message is closed. I mean the prophethood of bringing the divine law. Only the inheritance remains with us until the Day of Rising. The Messenger of God said: "The message and prophethood are cut off. There is no Messenger or Prophet after me." By this, he specified that there is no relationship between us and the Messengers in this station. He specifically had firstness and he had lastness. He brought the second peace with the conjunction on the virtuous servants of God. He is one of the righteous without any doubt from every aspect. He is in the rank which we cannot have. Therefore we began with "Peace be upon us" in our level without the conjunction. (442)

Know that we do not depend upon a transmission from the Messenger of God in the *tashahhud* which he used by his own tongue in the *tashahhud* in the formal prayer when we say, "Peace be upon you, O Prophet." We do not know whether he used this expression or said something else like Prophet Jesus said: "*And peace be on me the day I was given birth and the day I die and the day I will be raised up, living*" (19:33), or whether he did not say any of that and was content with our words, "Peace be upon us, and the righteous servants of God." (443)

If he said the like of what he taught us to say, it has two aspects. One of them is that the one greeted is God. He represents and interprets for Him in that as has been related about "God hears whoever praises Him." The other aspect is that he stands in that state during his supplication in a station which is other than prophethood. Then he addresses himself in respect to the station in which he was established since he is a Prophet. He is present because of the *kaf* of direct speech. He says on his tongue to the station which calls him present, that is, in which his self is present: "Peace be upon you, O Prophet!" with the action of the alien. (444)

Then he says: "I testify that there is no god but God and I testify that is the servant of God and His Messenger." As for the meaning of testimony (*shahada*), it preceded at the beginning of the *tashahhud*. This *tawhid* here is a *tawhid* which the action of the formal prayer generally demands and so does the state of everyone who performs the formal prayer in particular in his own formal prayer. The states of those who perform the formal prayer vary in the formal prayer without a doubt from every aspect: the aspect of judgments, the aspect of stations, and the aspect of taste. Part of the aspects of judgments is that the formal prayer of the Hanafi differs from the formal prayer of the Maliki and the Shafii in some judgments. In the aspects of stations, the formal prayer of the one who relies on trust differs from the formal prayer of the one who does without. Part of the aspects of tastes is that the formal prayer of the one who is constant differs from the formal prayer of the intoxicated in the path of taste. Spiritual sobriety and spiritual intoxication are part of the knowledge of tastes. (445)

Then he connected the bearing witness to servanthood to God and the message. It is added to the belief in the Oneness of God to inform us that "Whoever obeys the Messenger has obeyed God." He "did not speak from passion" and he only had to convey. Conveying is only the state of the scope of the one who conveys it to the one to whom it is conveyed. It is a conjunction by the *waw* (and) of partnership which announces divine Nearness to the Master by what he has of servanthood to God and nearness to the Messenger since the Trusty Spirit [Gabriel] brought it to him from the presence of his Lord. He is nearer in the chain to the Sender than us. The Messenger of God received it from the Spirit by his Lord, not by himself, because gnostics receive what comes to them from their Lord by the tongues and movements of the world by their Lord, not by themselves. Whoever sees his Lord in himself, without a doubt sees Him in others. It is as the people of God said about the state of the one who relies in trust, "Whoever has sound trust/ reliance on himself, his trust/ reliance on others is sound." (446)

We said that he received it by his Lord, not by himself, because if the receiver had received the command and revelation of his Lord by himself, instead of by his Lord, he would have burned up where he stood. This is due to the assailing blows of the power of the lights of the Trusty Spirit Gabriel. Have you not seen that, in spite of the divine Power by which God supported him, how he came to trembling to Khadijah's house? He said: "Wrap me up! Wrap me up! Enfold me!" because his joints were trembling and the spiritual light had penetrated to the passages of his essence so that even the pebbles could hear it. (447)

Therefore, he began bearing witness to the Oneness of God and Messengership of Muhammad when he connected it with the conjunction to his name since all praiseworthy qualities are joined in it, that is, that which deserves the conjunction with the letter of partnership. Then he said: "Servant of God," and he mentioned him with the servanthood of election to give notice that he is free from all that is other-than-God and that this servanthood is sincere and purely for God. There is no portion in it for any phenomenal being. Then he joined the message onto servanthood and onto God by He-ness. He increased him in servanthood with two prerogatives which are: prophethood and the message. He conveyed the message rather than prophethood since the message includes prophethood. If he had mentioned prophethood alone, we would have been obliged to mention his being singled out with the message. It needs to be mentioned so that we know his special attributes and we distinguish between him and those among the servants of God, the Prophets, who do not have the stage of this message. This is the recitation in the final sitting position of each two cycle formal prayer (*tashahhud*) of perfection. (448)

22.3.8. The Words to Recite When Sitting Back on Your Knees (*tashahhud*) [in the Formal Prayer] by the Tongue of Beauty

As for the *tashahhud* by the tongue of beauty, it is the *tashahhud* of Abd Allah ibn Masud which we have already quoted. It is the same as the previous one except for that which is particular to it and that is what I will mention. It is that the one with this station says with his tongue, "formal prayers and good words." He said "formal prayers" because of the universality of what they indicate in things of The Merciful, supplication and its different varieties among the states. All of them are supplications. *"He it is Who gives blessings to you and His angels."* (33:43) He connected good things to it by the means of connecting attributes. It is an attribute connected to formal prayers and based on it since they give joy [*tayyaba*] to the self. (449)

In this recitation in the final sitting position of each two cycle formal prayer (*tashahhud*), he also especially mentioned the relationship of servanthood to He-ness, not to God. It is a noble station in respect to the Messenger of God since he reports that the Prophet was in the station of looking at his Lord in respect to what His Essence demands and it is not encompassed by knowledge. It is not recognized at all by the attribute of permanence. It is only one. It is not valid that it be two because it is impossible that there be separation established in respect of His Essence. There is no relationship between God and His creation. *"There is not like Him anything."* (42:11) How could it be valid that He resemble anything or that anything resemble Him? This is different from the first tongue. The relationship of servanthood was to God, not to He-ness. It is when he looks at it in respect to the demands of the possible. It is not that by which Ibn Masud testified in the *tashahhud*. (450)

22.3.9. The Words to Recite When Sitting Back on Your Knees (*tashahhud*) [in the Formal Prayer] by the Tongue of Majesty

As for the *tashahhud* of majesty, he added to what the *tashahhud* contains. Greetings are described as "blessed," that is, greetings which have blessings in them. He omitted the "pure" as Ibn Masud omitted it. Both of them bear in mind the sharing which occurs in increase. Umar considers what the purifying alms contains of "making pure" along with the existence of increase which shares with blessings in it. He was content with "pure things" for that reason. A group of the scholars of formal knowledge, who know nothing at all about the knowledges of tastes and the places of disagreement regarding the words of the Messenger of God rejected "pure words" as part of the *tashahhud*. (451)

In this language, he did not use the letter of the conjunction in the description of greetings. He also used "peace" in the indefinite. This is the recitation at the final sitting of each two cycle formal prayer (*tashahhud*) of Ibn Abbas. That is because he took into consideration the special properties of the state of each person who performs the formal prayer. The names of God are like the possibles. They are endless. Each possible has a particular description, so it has a name from God which is particular to it from the name which is particular to the attribute which distinguishes it from other possibles. This is one of the noblest of the knowledges of the people of God. It is mentioned in the supplication of the Prophet: "O God! I ask Thee by every name with which Thou hast named Thyself or Thou hast taught any of Thy creation and which Thou hast kept to Thyself in the knowledge of Thy unseen world." As for the names which are generally numbered, they are 99: one hundred less one. There is no valid text which specifies exactly what they are, nor is it related from the Prophet that he said: "They are such-and-such." (452)

Therefore Ibn Abbas put "peace" in the indefinite so that each person who performs the formal prayer can take from the name which gives to him and in which God consigns with him. He greets the Prophet of God from us and he greets us and the righteous servants of God. Similarly he did not repeat "I bear witness." He left it out and did not bear witness to his [Muhammad's] servanthood or message with an independent testimony. His bearing witness to the Oneness of God was enough, and he was content with the *waw* (and) and what that has of the capacity to share. That is like the words of God Almighty: "*God bears witness that there is no god but He, as do the angels and those imbued with knowledge*" (3:18). He did not connect them by mentioning the actual testimony in order to honor them. If He had, He would have separated them from His testimony to Himself by mentioning there is no god but Him. He also dropped the expression of servanthood since the message contains it. (453)

22.4. Recitation of The Prayer For the Prophet When Sitting Back on Your Knees (*tashahhud*) in the Formal Prayer

22.4.1. *The Disagreement of the Religious Scholars about the Formal Prayer for the Prophet When Sitting Back on Your Knees (tashahhud) in the Formal Prayer and Seeking Refuge*

They disagree about the supplication for the Prophet in the *tashahhud*. Some say that it is obligatory, which is my position. Some say that it is not obligatory. Similarly, they also disagree about seeking refuge from the four things which one is commanded to do while saying the *tashahhud*. That involves seeking refuge from the punishment of the grave, the punishment of hell, the temptation of the Dajjal (Antichrist), and the trial (*fitna*) of life and death. Some say that it is obligatory and some forbid that it be obligatory. I say that it is obligatory. Even if there has not been a command to seek refuge from them, it is better to imitate the Messenger of God since he used to seek refuge from them. This is because God Almighty says: "*You have a good model in the Messenger of God.*" He [Muhammad] said: "Offer the formal prayer as you saw me doing." How much more it is when his command to do that has reached his community! (454)

22.4.2. *Supplication and Blessings on the Best of Mankind*

The supplication for the Prophet in the formal prayer and other places is a supplication from the servant who is asking for blessings for Muhammad secretly, behind his back. It is related in a sound Tradition from the Messenger of God: "Whoever makes supplication secretly, the angel says to him, 'and you have its like.'" Another variant has, "Twice its like." The Messenger of God prescribed that and God also commands it when He says: "*O those who have believed! Give your blessings to him and blessings of peace and invoke peace for him.*" (33:56). This refers to the Tradition from the angel about whoever of his community blesses the Messenger of God. He commands us to ask for peace on the Messenger of God when God says: "And ask for much peace upon him." He intensifies it with the verbal noun. It is possible that by that, He means the peace which is mentioned in the recitation said in the final sitting position of each two cycle formal prayer (*tashahhud*). It is also possible that He means the greetings and salutations (*salam*) of the formal prayer by that,

that is, when you finish the prayer on the Prophet you say the *salam* to conclude your formal prayer. The one who says that it is obligatory connects it to this possibility. (455)

22.4.3. Seeking Refuge from the Four Trials

As for seeking refuge from the punishment of the grave, the grave is the first of the stages of the world to come. He, therefore, asks God that he should not encounter the punishment of his Lord in the first step he takes in the world to come in his grave. As for seeking refuge from hell, it is seeking refuge from distance. The meaning of "hell" is that whose bottom is distant. The one who performs the formal prayer is in a state of nearness. He is near to being separated from this state which brings him near, so he seeks refuge with God that he should not depart to a state which will make him far from God. Rather, it should be to nearness to another state of the religion. (456)

Seeking refuge from the temptation of the Dajjal (Antichrist) is because of what he manifests in his claim to divinity and the matters which he suggests which break normal patterns—like bringing the dead to life. There are other things which are confirmed by reports in transmission. He offers those signs as a proof of the truth of his claim. It is a problem which is utterly obscure because it detracts from what theologians have confirmed about the knowledge of prophethoods. Every proof becomes invalid with this temptation. What temptation is greater than one which detracts from the proof which obliges happiness for the servants? May God makes us among the people of unveiling and existence, and join together the intelligible side and the witnessed side for us! (457)

As for the trial of life and death, the trial of life is the temptation of the Dajjal (Antichrist) and whatever tempts the human being away from his religion in which his true happiness lies. As for death, part of it is what occurs in the death-throes and the succession of satans who appear to him in the form of his past ancestors, relatives and brothers. They say to him: "Die a Christian, or a Jew, or a Zoroastrian, or an atheist," in order to come between him and Islam. Another part of it is what there is in the state of being questioned in the grave. That is when the angel says to him, "What do you say about this man?" pointing to the Prophet. (458)

The dead person does not see the angel show respect for the Messenger because the trial is meant to distinguish between the one who is true in belief, and the unbeliever and the doubter. The believer will say:"He is Muhammad, the Messenger of God. He brought us the clear signs and guidance, so we believed and confirmed." The hypocrite or the doubter who doubts the prophethood of the Prophet is from God, and thinks that it is simply something like a spiritual faculty, sees the lack of respect that the angel has for the Messenger in that question since he said: "What do you say about this man?" and not "What do you say about the Messenger of God?" The doubter says: "If he had really possessed this value, which he claimed to have in his message, this angel would not have spoken about him in this manner." Then he says: "I do not know. I heard people saying something and I said the same as they said." By doing so he will be very wretched indeed in an unimaginable way! This is part of the trial of death and the grave, so know that! This concludes a rough abridgement about the recitation said in the final sitting position of each two cycles of the formal prayer (*tashahhud*). (459)

22.5. The Salutations (*taslim*) at the End of the Formal Prayer

22.5.1. *The Disagreement of Religious Scholars about the Salutations (taslim) at the End of the Formal Prayer*

They disagree about the *taslim* in the formal prayer. Some people say that it is obligatory, and that is my position. Some say that the greeting which terminates the formal prayer is not obligatory. There is also disagreement among those who say that it is obligatory. Some say that one offering of greeting is obligatory for the one supplicating on his own and for the leader to say. Some say that two are obligatory. Some say that one is obligatory for the leader to say and two for the one following the leader. The one who voices this opinion has also stated that the one who follows the leader recites three greetings which terminate the formal prayer: one for the end of the formal prayer, the second for the leader, and the third for the one who is on his right. (460)

There is no text on which to base oneself for its number or prohibition, so reflection demands that one add a fourth recitation of greeting which terminates the formal prayer to the third. If you follow the leader is there is anyone on your left? The leader recites two or three greetings which terminate the formal prayer (*taslim*) if there are people on his right and left. If there is no one on his left, he recites the *taslim* twice: once for ending the formal prayer and the second for the one who is on his right. It is confirmed that the Messenger of God recited the *taslim* twice. There is nothing in the Tradition which necessitates leaving the formal prayer comes after the *taslim*. (461)

22.5.2. *The One Who Prays Is Speaking with His Lord, Absent from All Others*

Know that the reciting the greeting: "Peace be unto you," is only valid for the one who performs the formal prayer and is speaking with his Lord in the formal prayer, withdrawn from all that is other-than-God: phenomenal beings and those who are present with him. When he desires to leave the formal prayer and move from that state to the state of contemplation of beings and the group, he greets them with the *salam* of arrival since he had withdrawn from them in his formal prayer to his Lord. If the one who performs the formal prayer is still with beings and the group when he is in a group, how then can he greet them if he is like this? He is still with them. Is not this person ashamed when he sees that he was with God when he utters the *salam* for the formal prayer. (462)

The *salam* of the gnostic is articulated because he moves from state to state. Then he recites two "peace be unto you," (*taslim*): one for that from which he moves and one for that to which he goes. However, the one who is with God during his formal prayer does not greet the one from which he moves. God is Peace, so He is not so greeted. (463)

22.6. What Is Said by the One Who Rises from the Bowing Forward (*Ruku*) [in the Formal Prayer] and During the Bowing Forward (*Ruku*)

22.6.1. The Praise (tashih) Contains the Most Perfect Supplication

When the gnostic who joins the most perfect formal prayers raises his head from bowing, he says: "God hears whoever praises Him" representing his Lord—glory be to Him!—and translating from Him. It is from the words of his Lord, the Blessed, the High. Then he is silent. Then he says to answer himself on his own tongue, "O God, our Lord! Praise is Yours!" That is because it is related in a sound Tradition from the Messenger of God that when the leader says: "God hears whoever praises Him," say "O God, our Lord! Praise is Thine!" God says: "God hears whoever praises Him" on the tongue of His servant. For this reason it is recommended for the one supplicating to be silent a bit in order to separate His words, "God hears whoever praises Him" and His words, "O God, our Lord! Praise is Thine in quantity as great as the heavens and in quantity as great as the earth, and in quantity as great as what is between them, and in quantity as great as Thou wishest!" or anything from the people of praise and glory. The most fitting of what the servant said is, "All of us are Thy servants. Nothing prevents what Thou gavest and none gives what Thou forbiddest. The earnestness of the earnest gives no profit from Thee." (464)

As he says in bowing after he says: "Glory be to my Lord, The Great, and by His praise," three times if he is alone or following an leader. If he is an leader, he says it five times so that the one following can say it three times. Then after this glorification, he says: "O God! I have bowed to Thee. I have believed in Thee. I have surrendered to Thee. My hearing, sight, brain, bones and sinews are submissive and humble to Thee." Know that when the servant bows, he informs you that he is in a state of inter space between standing and prostration. (465)

The gnostic says after glorifying his Lord: "O God! I have bowed to Thee, that is, because of Thy might and highness in Your greatness, I have humbled myself to honor Thee." He says: "I bow to Your Self-subsistence which is Thine alone. When I stood before Thee, I only stood to obey Thy command since Thou hast said: '*Stand for God.*' So I stood. I am humble in my bowing because of any thought which might occur to me while I am standing that I might stand for myself. By my bowing, I confess before Thee that I have bowed to Thee. He says that it is by Thy support that I have verified this. It is not by my own power or strength. I have no power nor strength except by Thee since the hearts are in Thy hand which is the place of belief. I have surrendered to Thee. My obedience is to Thee. If it had not been for Thee, my states with Thou in my worship would not have changed. Thou art the One who prescribed that for me on the tongue of Thy Messenger in action and word. He performed the formal prayer, reminded and then commanded us: 'Offer the formal prayer as you have seen me do.' It was Thou who spoke. '*Nor speaks he for himself out of desire.*' (53:3) We know that he was commanded because he commanded us. That is Thy command, not his command. Thou hast said: '*Whoever obeys the Messenger has surely obeyed God.*'" (4:80) (466)

Then he says: "My hearing is submissive to Thee in whatever Thou tellest me in my intimate conversation with Thee in Thy own words." Then he says: "My sight" using the *waw* of partnership. There is only humility. It is as if were saying: "My sight is submissive to Thee from modesty in Thy presence since I know that Thou seest me in the state of my bowing before Thee. Thou art in my *qibla* as Thy Messenger reported to me. He ordered me to make Thee seen in my formal prayer as if I saw Thee. O Lord! If I make a likeness in myself in order to see Thee, I cannot deny my knowledge that Thou seest me. The cause of my modesty before Thee is only my knowledge that Thou seest me, not that I see Thee. Not a single atom in the heavens or the earth escapes Thee, Thou who 'perceivest the eyes while the eyes do not perceive Thee!'" (467)

He says: "My brain, my bones and my sinews. Thou putest a faculty in all that I have mentioned. My organism is based on that and my form is fixed so that by these faculties, I can obtain the going-on of this form which is obligated to perform what Thou hast commanded in obtaining gnosis of Thee. Perhaps something will happen to my brain, bones and sinews (which are described by humility to Thee) which will be a cause for that and so it will be perceived. That might entail vanity and pride. Therefore each of these faculties is obliged to be submissive to Thee by freeing itself of any strength or power in causality. (468)

22.6.2. *When the Gnostic Raises His Head from Bending Forward (ruku) [in the Formal Prayer]*

When the gnostic raises his head from bowing, he represents his Lord and hears himself say with God's words, "God hears whoever praises Him." When he had bowed, he said: "Glory be to my Lord, The Great," and he had said that every praise and eulogy with which He praises Him from the beginning of the formal prayer. Then he answers his Lord by his Lord by the presence of himself since it is by his Lord as He supports him in power and strength. He said: "O God, our Lord." He omits the letter of the vocative since the one who performs the formal prayer is in the state of nearness and the vocative announces distance. The caller remains and it is because he goes on in the answer of his Lord. He says: "Praise is Thine," that is, complete praise by what is Thine and from Thee. There is no praiser nor praised except Thee. Thou hast the ends of every praiser in the world and everyone who is praised. It is his words: "In quantity as great as the heavens and in quantity as great as the earth and in quantity as great as what is between them and in quantity as great as what Thou hast wished from everything after that." (469)

He says: This includes every part of the celestial and terrestrial world, what is between them, and whatever is possible to which Thou mightest give existence while it remains a source-form in non-existence. Every part of it is known by the principle of existence, and determination has particular praise of Thee in respect of its source, its isolation, and its being joined to other than it in major and minor joining. I praise by its tongue and the tongue of every praiser who praises Thee for Thyself and praises other-than-Thee for Thee. This praiser by these tongues has all that it demands of the divine Self-disclosure and sensory rewards for his nature and structure. He praises him by tongue and heart, inward and outward. (470)

His words are "the best of what the servant has said," that is, what a servant like me is obliged to say. There are those like me belonging to a Master like Thee. Thou hast no like, and all of us are Thy servants. He says: "I represent my likes—they are all of the possibles, existent and non-existent, from whomever speaks by Thou art in his knowledge from presence and whoever speaks by himself from absence. I represent them in Thy praise by my knowledge of Thee which Thou gavest me. Thou hast made them ignorant of what befits Thy majesty. None can bar what Thou hast given of predisposition to accept a particular self-disclosure and particular knowledge. "None can give what Thou hast forbidden" if Thou dost not grant general predisposition. There is no master except

Thou to give what Thou dost not give. "The earnestness of the earnest one does not have any profit from Thee" that is, by whatever portion he has in the world of power, rank, property and jurisdiction by other-than-Thee in his knowledge, not in the heart of the matter. That has no profit with Thou in the world to come when the covering is removed. (471)

22.7. Prostration in the Formal Prayer

22.7.1. *Offering Praise (tasbih) in Prostration*

When he prostrates and glorifies his "Lord Most High and by His praise" as was previously stated, he says after his glorification in the prostration, "O God! I have prostrated to Thee, I have believed in Thee, I have surrendered to Thee. I have prostrated my face to the One who created it and opened my hearing and sight. Blessed is God, the Best of Creators! O God! Put light in my heart, light in my hearing, light in my sight, light on my right, light on my left, light in front of me, light behind me, light above me, and light under me. Give me light and make me light." (472)

The gnostic says: "My face has prostrated," that is, my reality. The face of the thing is its reality for which He created it, that is, determined it from His name, the Manager, and brought it into existence by His name, The Powerful, The Creator, The Fashioner. He opened its hearing by what He made it hear in "*Be!*" and He took the contract and then the obligation. He opened its sight by what that is, made it perceive in order to reflect on seen things. That is in respect to this organism and its likes. He also brought the heavens and the earth into existence and separated them from one other after He had stitched them together, in order to make them distinct from each other. The effector and the effected appear by the existence of giving-form. Blessed is God, the best of Creators fixing source-forms so that His word is valid "for a people who reflect." (473)

Then he asked for light in every limb, the light of the heavens and the earth whose likeness is *"a lamp in a glass* (the station of purity) *in a niche* (the station of being veiled from passions)." He is not touched by what people say about it through their thoughts. *"It is kindled by olive oil shining"* by nearness. It is the principle of support from the tree. It furnishes it while it belongs neither to the East nor the West in the station of equilibrium. It does not incline one way to turn to the East so as to have complete knowledge of it—nor to the West. It does not know its rank. *"Light upon light,"* existence upon existence—the existence of the generosity of source upon the existence in need. Then he asked Him to put light in every limb. Dispelling is light. Every limb has a claim by what God gave it in the creation of the faculty which He built in it and in which He created it. Since the Messenger of God knew about that, he asked God to place knowledge and guidance in him which dispels darkness. The call of everyone who makes a supplication in this world is connected to this supplication. (474)

In the end, he said: "Make me Light." He says: "Make me Thee." He is the Light of the heavens and the earth. Then God Almighty says: "I am his hearing, his sight, his foot, his hand and his tongue" in what he hears, sees, speaks, touches and runs. He says: "Make me light so that whoever sees me in the darkness of the land of his outward and the sea of his self and inward will be guided by me." He gave him the Quran and he gave him understanding of it. This gift is one of the highest gifts in rank. It is one of the most radiant of ranks. Its meaning made me withdraw from myself. Thou art my existence so that my eye will see everything by Thee and my hearing will hear everything by Thee. The light of every limb is its perception. It is like that with all that he detailed. However, there is a distinction between lights. For that reason, he made it indefinite in every limb, in himself, and in his essence. He distinguished the light of the left from the light of the right, and the light of above from the light of below. It is like that with the lights of the faculties and limbs. Then after this, set me up in the source of gatheredness and existence so that the lights become one by the oneness of the source. If I am not there, then it is because Thou makest me light. If I am there, it is because Thou hast place me in light by which I am guided in the darkness of my being. (475)

22.8. What Supplications the One Who Performs the Formal Prayer Says Between the Two Prostrations in the Formal Prayer

When the one who performs the formal prayer sits between the two prostrations in the formal prayer, he says: "O God, forgive me and show mercy to me and provide for me and mend me and guide me and give me health and pardon me." The gnostic says: "Veil me and veil for my sake. Veil me from acts of opposition so that they do not recognize where I am and aim for me. Thou hast said that Thy splendor burns up the sources of every thing described by existence, even if it is Thy existence. However, as it effects the attribute of existence in the possible, and it is not described by existence, so it effects the relationship to the possible, even if it is called existent and is an in-time limited by in-timeness. (476)

However, the divine presence is described by as being jealous of its existence in respect of the claim of this claimant. If it had not been for the claim which issued from him, he would not have been subjected to authority. It must be like that. When the veils are lifted, the splendor burns up what the eye perceives of creation, that is, the natural. The world of command is lights. It hardly burns. Rather, it rises in degrees in the greatest light. The world of command does not have any claim. The world of creation is burned up and becomes ashes. It is not connected to non-existence. It remains ashes unless it is reverted to it. Then all becomes non-existent except the claim of the transfer of the source which does not have a claim. (477)

He says: "Show mercy to me with the mercy of obligation which is only acquired after the mercy of bestowal by the success Thou gavest me in obtaining the mercy of obligation so that I exist. Thy mercy encompasses everything." Therefore the gnostic seeks the mercy of bestowal in the source of the necessary through success in right action which demands that special mercy. Therefore, the gnostic wants to take it from the source of bestowal which Iblis and his followers among the jinn and men seek. However, this gnostic is described as being protected and secure from wrong action, opposition, and the disappointment which necessitates deprivation. (478)

Then he says: "Provide for me," that is, from the food of gnoses by which my heart is given life, as Thou hast provide me with the food of the bodies by which my natural body and form goes on." Then he says: "Mend me." Mending only takes place after brokenness. Linguistically, it means to be shattered. The shattered one is broken after mending. It is the brokenness of the gnostics. The servant is broken in his basic root by his possibility. Then God mends him, that is, He connects him to necessity, but to other-than-Him. When He brings him into existence with this meaning, gnosis of himself and his Lord breaks him, and so he returns to his possibility. This is brokenness after mending. Mending only takes place after brokenness. For this reason, we said that it is shattered linguistically when he says: "Compel," that is, acquaint me with my compulsion in my choice. The servant is compelled in his choice. You only desire what God, the Lord of the worlds, desires. God says: "I am with those who have broken hearts for My sake." (479)

Then he says: "Guide me, make clear to me what we should be fearful of and give me success in the clarification when I translate from Thee to Thy worship since Thou hast given me all the words I need to confirm my inheritance from Thy Messenger: "I have been given something which no Prophet before me was given." Then he mentioned it and said: "I was given all the words." (480)

Then he says: "Give me health, free of the sicknesses of the hearts which are their desires, not the sicknesses of the bodies. Thou art utterly near to the one whose body is ill. Thou hast said to me in sound tradition which goes back to Thy Messenger, that Thou hast said: "When I was ill, you did not visit Me." I say to Thee, "How can Thou be ill when Thou art the Lord of the unisign?" He related that Thou hast answered, "My servant so-and-so was ill and you did not visit him." Thou hadst promised him: "Thou wilt find Me with him." Who art Thou with Him? Glory be to Thee! He is not wretched. Thou dost not make Thy servant ill but that Thou visitest him. Whoever wants to find Thee, let him visit the sick. Glory be to Thee with a glorification which only Thou dost deserve! (481)

Then he says: "Pardon me." He says: "Give me much of Thy good and little of Thy affliction," that is, little of what should be little and much of what should be much. There is only Thee pardoning my error. I ask Thee to veil it from me so that it does not reach me and then I would be described by it. Pardon (*afw*) is one of the words which have opposite meanings. It is applied both to much and to little. Be my representative, O Lord! I cannot move to what Thou hast command me to do of right action since I am chronically ill with the desire to move. (482)

22.9. The Raising of Hands in Supplication (*Qunut*) in the Formal Prayer

22.9.1. The Disagreement of the Religious Scholars about the Raising of the Hands in Supplication in the Formal Prayer

Religious scholars disagree about the raising the hands and supplicating while standing in formal prayer. Some say that it is recommended to be recited in the morning formal prayer. Some say that it is according to the practice of the Prophet (*sunna*). Some say that *qunut* can be recited in every formal prayer. Some say that there is only *qunut* in Ramadan. Some say that *qunut* should only be recited in the last half of Ramadan. Some say that it is in the first half of Ramadan. It is a supplication which is made by the one who performs the formal prayer. Some of them think that it is before bowing. Some think that it is after bowing. Some people think that the *qunut* is only in time of hardship. That is what I say. As far as I am concerned, it is recommended. (483)

There is a special supplication which is transmitted which describes the raising of the hands while standing in formal prayer (*qunut*) of the odd number prayer (*witr*). There is also a special supplication which describes the *qunut* of the morning formal prayer. It is not firmly established. One can use whatever supplication he wishes according to his state. However, one must avoid curses and abuse in the *qunut*. One should ask for the good of this world and the next and whatever will bring one near to God. This is like what the Prophet said in the *qunut* of the *witr*: "O God! Guide me among whomever Thou hast guided, and give me health among those to whom Thou hast given health, and take charge of me with whomever Thou hast taken charge of. Give me blessing in what Thou givest, and avert evil from me which Thou hast decreed. Thou hast decreed and no one compels Thee. The One Thou hast taken as a friend is not abased and the one Thou hast guide is not misguided. Thou art Blessed, High." This is a teaching from the Prophet about how to supplicate to God in our *qunut* and in every supplication. (484)

22.9.2. Explanation of the Supplication When Raising One's Hands

The gnostic looks to what he knows to use in supplication or what is like it. He asks God to guide him among those whom He has guided. If one stops with the phrase itself, he is asking for the future to be in the past. The future is not in the past unless one aspect joins them together. The gnostic looks and finds that it is non-existence which joins the past and the future together. Existence is only valid for the present state. Existence belongs only to God. The existence of the state is an existence of essence. Non-existence is not valid in it. It is constant, and the people of the Arabic language describe it with this. It exists between the two ends of non-existence in which existence is not at all possible. That is the past and the future. It is the source of the servant. He is described by non-existence. It limits him by the past (which is non-existence) and the future (which is non-existence). Guide me to the future as Thou hast guided me to the past! There is no distinction in non-existence. For this reason, he should say: "Guide us among whomever Thou hast guided," and the like of this. (485)

Then guidance is obtained, and it is the source of the existence of the present state, and the state is a well-known adverb. For this reason, he used "*fi*" (among), and said: "among whomever Thou hast guided." Non-existence is not an adverb because the non-existent is nothing. Non-existence denotes nothing, and nothing is not an adverb. "Other" is something. Therefore one understands his words, "Guide me among whomever Thou hast guided" and supplications like it by the power which grants whatever is in it. Since Thou hast clothed me in the existence of guidance and direction, and there is no questioning in it, let it be in a state which is constant. It is not described by the past and thereby connected to non-existence, nor by the future so that it would not exist. God is disconnected and free of limitation by time in His actions. (486)

The servant who is created is described by "is not" in the past and described by "is not" in the future. In the state of his being described by existence in respect of his essence, he is described by "is." It is as if "was not" had a reality for him which he does not leave. It is his source. It is like that with "is" which belongs to God in existence. Glory be to Him! It is a reality. He is not described by its opposite. Existence is His source. If action were to be stripped away from Him and ascribed to the cause, that should not affect the existence of God. When we realized that the servant is non-existent, and that nothing is ascribed to non-existence, we said:

You defend them and blame them. What about my realization
Tell me what am I to say?
I defend them. Do they know that I defend them?
Tell me what you say.
The servant is precise in his realization when he says
that I speak and he is the utterance.
Is his like to be blamed when justice is My attribute?
Support Me. What do you say and what do We say? (487)

22.9.3. God Said on the Tongue of Pharaoh:I am your Lofty Lord

God said on the tongue of Pharaoh, *"I am your lofty lord"* (79:24) while He—glory be to Him!—is the Most High in reality. God is our Lord Most High. Therefore, God *". . . took him with an exemplary punishment for the last and for the first."* (79:25).The lesson in that is for the one with knowledge. God describes those who know with fear. He says: *"Only those of His servants who dread God are knowing."* (35:28) As God reported, the knower considers from where Pharaoh was taken. This is an attribute of God which appeared on Pharaoh's tongue. He knows that what he said represents God as occurs when the one who performs the formal prayer says: "God hears whoever praises Him." When he withdrew from being a representative in the statement, the attribute sought what it describes and so it returned to God Almighty! Then Pharaoh remained stripped of it even though he had not put it on at all with himself. God has put a seal on every proud arrogant heart that pride will enter it because that attribute is only appropriate for the One who is not limited. He is the Most High. He is higher than limitation. (488)

Pharaoh was repaid when he withdrew from this station when God made him an exemplary punishment for the last and the first, that is, He stopped him in his limitation. He does not have this attribute. The first belongs to the past, and it is the statement: *". . . thou takest another god other than me."* (26:29) The last belongs to the future; it is *"I am your lofty lord."* (79:24) In our opinion, they are the reason why he was made an exemplary punishment for the first and the last. In the first, he showed what God had taught him when He punished him for the absolute quality to which he laid claim. He punished him with the limitation. *"Nikl"* means fetter. When we saw that God said *"nakal"* (punishment), we knew that it is the opposite which is stripped away. It is the absolute. (489)

In one place God says: *"Call to Me,"* (40:60) and in another place He tells us that the matter is decided and that *"The saying near Me is not to be substituted"* (50:29) and what He already knows, for he is a phenomenal being and caution will not save him from the decree. I wrote these lines to clarify the excellent riddle in them:

When I said: "God!" He said: "Why do you call?"
 If I do not call, He says: "Why don't you call?"
Whoever is dumb and speechless has won pleasures
 and has been given rest from a God who hears! (490)

Basically, there is no silence at all in the world. Silence is non-existence and speech is constant since the benefit of speech occurs when the listeners understand what is intended. States are understood, and so they are speech. There is no existent thing but that it has a certain state. Its state is the source of its speech because the one who understands and looks at it, does not have it at that moment. No tongue is more eloquent than the tongue of states. Connected states convey knowledges which come by means of expressions. Expressions are part of states as far as we are concerned. The word "speech" is applied to expressions in technical language. For the gnostic of God, all of existence are the words of God and they never run out. [cf 19:109] Understand then what the servant must recognize of that when he hears speech or when he speaks. He must distinguish between that in which the servant represents God and that in which God translates for the servant. That is distinguished by the attribute. The attribute demands the described. Only the one who has it accepts it. If speech contains an attribute which is only appropriate for the servant, then the servant has it, even if God describes Himself with it. All speech is interpreted like that no matter who says it, whether it is by expressions or by states. (491)

This is the meaning of His words, "In that is a lesson for whoever fears." He is the knower. That contains an indication of what preceded in the story, and that which preceded in the story in his words, *"I am your lofty lord,"* and "God made him an exemplary punishment for the last and the first," that is, this claim obliged that he be seized and that the attribute seek what it describes. That is God. Pharaoh remained denuded of it, so he did not have anything to protect himself from being seized. God says of Himself, "I was hungry and you did not feed Me" representing a hungry servant whom you did not feed. The attribute seeks what it describes, and that is the servant. In that way, the gnostics understand the realities. (492)

22.10. Raising the Hands (*Qunut*) in the Formal Prayer

22.10.1. The Judgment of Raising the Hands (Qunut) in the Formal Prayer

Scholars disagree about raising the hands in the formal prayer, that is, its judgement and about the places in which one raises them, and the extent to which one raises them. As for the judgement, some say that raising the hands is *sunna* in the formal prayer. Some say that it is obligatory, and those people fall into different categories. Some oblige that only in the recitation of "God is Greater" after which everything but the formal prayer is forbidden (*takbir al-ihram*). Some oblige that in the beginning, coming down to bowing, and rising from bowing. Some oblige that in these two places and in prostration. (493)

As for the places in which the hands are raised in the formal prayer, some say that it is only in the recitation of "God is Greater" after which everything but the formal prayer is forbidden (*takbir al-ihram*). Some say that it is in the recitation of "God is Greater" after which everything but the formal prayer is forbidden (*takbir al-ihram*), bowing and rising from bowing. Some say that he raises them in prostration and in rising from prostration. This comes from the Traditions related by Wail ibn Hagar. Some say that it is when he stands up from the two cycles. This is from the transmission of Malik ibn al-Huwayrith from the Prophet. As for myself, I saw the Messenger of God, in a true dream. He commanded me to raise my hands in the formal prayer in the recitation of "God is Greater" after which everything but the formal prayer is forbidden (*takbir al-ihram*), in bowing and when rising from bowing. (494)

As for the extent to which the hands are raised, some say that it is up to the shoulders, some say to the ears, and some say to the chest. Each position is based on a transmitted Tradition. The firmest of them is up to the shoulders. The Tradition about the ears is firmer than the Tradition about the chest. That which I believe in this question is that in the Traditions related about that which recount his actions, it is not related that he commanded that. He said: "Perform the formal prayer as you saw me performing it." It is known that the formal prayer contains obligations and *Sunna*, so it is not understood from this Tradition that all of the actions of the formal prayer are obligatory which would be contrary to the consensus of what is understood by this. We should offer it and raise our hands in the knowledge of the Prophet without specifying whether it is obligatory or *sunna*. This is as Ali ibn Abi Talib took on the sacred state as the Prophet took it on although he did not know what to do in that state. The Messenger of God confirmed him in that and did not reject it. Therefore we raise our hands in the formal prayer according to the judgment of the divine law in it. We accept it according to that principle. (495)

As for the limit, I think that this action demands that you make a choice. Traditions are related about different limits of action. The one who performs the formal prayer is repaid for whatever state he follows, be it obligatory or *sunna*. The best course is to lift them to the ears. However, they must then be lifted to the chest, opposite the shoulders, and up to the ears. Therefore, he combines the three states. It is like that with the places—all of them are contained in the recitation of "God is Greater" after which everything but the formal prayer is forbidden (*takbir al-ihram*), in bowing, in rising from bowing, in prostration, in rising from prostration, and in standing up after two cycles. That does not harm it. It is related. It is not related that it invalidates the formal prayer, and its opposite has not been related. (496)

It is understood from the Tradition of Ibn Masud and al-Bara ibn Azib, that the Messenger of God raised his hands once in the sacred state. He did not add to it, that is, he did it once and did not do that twice in the sacred state. It is quite possible that when they said that, they meant that he did not raise them again for the rest of the formal prayer. There is no text on this. Increase in established by raising them in bowing, in rising from it, and in other places. Increase from a person who is trustworthy and just is accepted. It is better to raise them in all the places which it is transmitted that he raised them. (497)

22.10.2. *The Interpretation of the Gnostic in Raising the Hands in the Formal Prayer*

As for the gnostic's interpretation of that, raising the hands announces that what he has obtained in them has fallen away when he raises them. God informs him, "When you stand before Me, stand poor, in need. You do not own anything. Throw away everything which you own and stand empty-handed. Put it behind you. I am in your *qibla*." For this reason, he turns his entire being to his *qibla* to announce that his hands are empty. When he drops them, the inside of his palms returns to the back. That is where he threw it from his hand. (498)

Then God gives it to him in every state of the formal prayer whose action demands repayment. If he owns it, he leaves it. He informs God by raising his hands that he has left it in the place in which it should be left. He has turned to the divine Giving seeking, poor, empty-handed. It gives to him, and he raises his hands which are empty. It is like that in all the places which the Messenger of God told him to raise his hands. (499)

He raises them from the door of power and strength since the place of power is in the hands. He raises his hands to God, confessing, "Power is Thine, not mine." My hands are empty of power. Whoever raises them to his chest considers that God is in his direction of formal prayer. Whoever raises them to his ears that God is before him as He says: "He is The Conqueror over His servants." In every lowering and raising he does that. By raising his hands, he says: "I have no power nor strength in every lowering and raising. Power is Thine. There is no god but Thee." (500)

22.11. Bending Forward [in the Formal Prayer] and the Level Position in the Bending Forward

22.11.1. The Position of the Religious Scholars About the Level Position in Bending Forward (ruku) [in the Formal Prayer]

Scholars disagree about bowing and the level position in bowing. Some say that it is not obligatory, and some say that it is obligatory. (501)

22.11.2. The Interpretation of the Bending Forward in the Formal Prayer

The interpretation in that is that humility to God Almighty is necessary in every state, both inwardly and outwardly. When the servant stands in a place in which it is more appropriate to manifest the might, power and greatness of belief, by the might, power and greatness of the believer, then the believer might display some disdain and pride which would be contrary to humility. Only humility is mandatory in that place, although it might be more appropriate to present an attribute which that place demands. God Almighty says: *"And it is by the mercy of God thou wast gentle with them. And if thou hadst been hard, harsh of heart, they would have broken away from around thee."* (3:159) This place demands that he behave in it as He mentioned. (502)

He stated in the other place: *"O Prophet! Struggle with the ones who are ungrateful and the ones who are hypocrites and be harsh against them."* (9:73) This manifests the might of belief by the might of the believer. It is confirmed that the Messenger of God said: "God and His Messenger hate this manner of walking in any place except this." (503)

When you know that places have rules, then act according to what is necessary and you will be wise. It is confirmed that the Messenger of God said to the man to whom he taught the obligations of the formal prayer, "Bow until you are still in the bowing and stand up until you are still in the standing." You are obliged to believe that it is obligatory. (504)

22.12. The Form of Sitting [in the Formal Prayer]

22.12.1. The Position of the Religious Scholars on the Form of Sitting in the Formal Prayer

Some say that he puts his buttocks on the ground, keeping his right foot upright and folding the left foot under, and that the man and woman do the same in that. Others say that he keeps his right root upright and sits on his left foot. Others make a distinction between the middle and last sitting. They say that he keeps his right foot upright and sits on his left in the middle sitting, and he puts his buttocks on the ground, keeps his right foot upright, and folds the left foot under in the final sitting. Each speaker is based on a Tradition and he is repaid for whatever of that he does. (505)

22.12.2. The Interpretation of the Form of Sitting

The interpretation in that sitting is that sitting in the formal prayer is when the servant sits before his Master. He can only sit when his Master commands him. The one who performs the formal prayer is commanded to sit in the formal prayer. The Messenger of God said: "I am a servant who sits as the servant sits." The best state of sitting in the formal prayer is the sitting in which he is nearer to standing before his Master. This is the state of the gnostic. It is a state which the servant must have inasmuch as he is servant. (506)

If the gnostic is in a place where he looks at the root of his gnosis of himself in order to recognize his Lord, it is better that he put his buttocks on the ground at the end of his sitting. That is necessary. It is closer to contemplation of his essence than in the middle sitting. Sitting is something non-essential which comes to him from God, that is, He makes him sit and makes him revert to looking at himself so that he might recognize what he desires to obtain. He is like the alert person because he is summoned to stand up in the third cycle. There is stillness in bowing and prostration. (507)

All the states of movement are in the states of the formal prayer which means that he is stationary in order to fully realize the self-disclosure in it. If he is swift with the least amount of action to which the name "bower" is applied, he will miss a great knowledge which is only obtained by the one who is stationary. For this reason, he is commanded to be still in these places. Haste comes from Satan except in five places which are mentioned in their proper chapter. Hastening to good deeds is prescribed in being stationary and in stillness, and it refers to the good which you have. Therefore there is no contradiction between stillness and haste. (508)

22.13. The Middle and Final Sitting

22.13.1. The Ruling of the Middle and Final Sitting in the Formal Prayer

Scholars disagree about the middle and final sitting. Some say that the middle is *sunna* and not obligatory. A few people say that it is obligatory. The root on which I base myself in all the actions of the formal prayer is that the actions of the Messenger of God are not considered to be obligatory unless the proof indicates that. As for the final sitting, it is the opposite of the middle one. Most people think that it is obligatory, but a few people say that it is not obligatory. Some say that the two sittings are *sunna*. This is the weakest of the positions. The sitting in the *witr* of the formal prayer remains and we will mention it later in this book, God willing. (509)

22.13.2. The Interpretation of the Middle and Final Sittings

As for the middle sitting, its interpretation is that it is non-essential as we have said. One stands up for the third cycle after it. For this reason, whoever forgets it, prostrates for it. They distinguish between it and the pillar of the formal prayer. If he misses it while no command is connected to the middle sitting, it might be considered obligatory. It is a non-essential matter which happens to the one who performs the formal prayer in a state of intimate conversation. It comes from the Self-disclosures of the inter space. He is summoned to greet it when the Self-disclosures begin in it. When he sees that the station calls him to greet, he must sit down as it is obligatory for him in the last sitting which is an obligation. (510)

The wisdom of that witnessing is that the root of the formal prayer demands that it be even for the division between God and the servant which is mentioned in it. The least of that is then two cycles—except for the *witr*. It has a special description which I will discuss in the section on the *witr*, God willing. Since the source of being even is established by the existence of two cycles, the Lord is distinguished from the servant and so the goal is obtained. There must be sitting as occurs in the morning formal prayer and the night formal prayer, two by two, and in the traveling formal prayer. The relater said at the beginning of the obligation of the formal prayer, that two cycles are obligatory. You add to it in the formal prayers which are said at home. Its root form is confirmed in the journey. When threeness and fourness occur in this evenness in the formal prayer when the two things are combined, then the name of the two things is valid for each of them. (511)

Some people say that they are the same thing. Joined to the existence of the first two cycles is the relationship of the thingness of the formal prayer to the servant while the relationship of the thingness of the formal prayer to the Lord is negated. He said that He performs the formal prayer blessings for us, so the two cycles belong to this in the formal prayer of four cycles. He wanted to divide the first two and the last two, so he distinguished between them by the sitting. This is the non-essential thing which he sees, so he sits. If he misses it, he prostrates for it and does not redo the formal prayer as he does when he misses one of the pillars of the formal prayer. (512)

22.13.3. Sitting After the Two Cycles of the Evening Formal Prayer (*Maghrib*)

When someone sits after the two cycles in the evening formal prayer, it belongs to something else. It is not a middle sitting because it does not have two cycles after it. It is in the half of the formal prayer of three and four cycles. That is because it informs us that when the two things are joined, they become one thing. That one thing is the source of the third cycle of the evening formal prayer. It indicates that these two cycles divided between the Lord and the servant have the same meaning because one of the meanings contains the second from all aspects. The other one is not like that since that one contains it by one aspect but does not contain it from another aspect. Two cycles appear after them middle sitting from the aspect which contains it. One cycle belongs to the one being so that it can contain the meaning of the other. The other one belongs to the last so that the meaning of the first contains it. The one aspect which has no brother remains in the position of the *witr* which God added to our formal prayer. It is a single cycle without any second. It is the aspect by which God isolates Himself from us in respect of His essence. (513)

22.13.4. The Connection of Existence Between the Necessary Real and the Possible Creation

The form of that in gnoses is that the servant demands the Necessary of existence because he is possible. He must have something which predominates. Without doubt, the servant contains the Lord by his existence. The cycle of the evening formal prayer is enough for us because it contains the second. The existence of the One who is Necessary by Himself has an aspect which contains the possible. It is the aspect of being God, The Powerful, The Transforming. The divine cycle of the evening formal prayer comes from this aspect. He—glory be to Him! also has an aspect which is His alone which does not imply the existence of the possible at all. This is the richness which is His absolutely. In respect of Him, glory be to Him! one does not oblige the existence of the world from the existence of His essence. That is necessary. If you look at it in respect of what the possible demands, then relationship appear in that. He is The Powerful, so that demands the object of power. He is The Transforming, so that demands the object of the will. The prescribed *witr* which is desired, is the aspect which belongs to God inasmuch as He demands phenomenal beings and phenomenal beings do not demand Him since we do not investigate their essences. (514)

God, The Mighty, The Majestic, says. *"Then truly God is Sufficient for the worlds."* (29:6) "Worlds" here are the proofs of God. So in this sign He is saying that He is Rich above proofs of Him. He removes any relationship between Him and the world, or any aspect which would connect Him to the world in respect of that aspect by which He is Rich over the worlds. That is what the people of speculation call the objective of the proof. God says: "There is no proof of Me which would imply an aspect which is connected to Me and which would limit Me. I am Rich, The Mighty who is not limited by any aspects or proven by any proofs or things in-time." (515)

The proof of God is the existence of God in the source of the existence of the possible which is the possible has inasmuch as its existence is existence which is the same as the existence of God and not inasmuch as it exists from God or that it is in need of God. The possible only needs a possible command, that is, it can acquire it and it is possible that it not acquire it. It is impossible that the possible need the possible. It is also impossible that the possible need the Necessary of Existence in other than the possible. The possible and the Necessarily Existent basically have no need at all. (516)

The Necessarily Existent is absolutely Rich, Independent. The possible is not in need of a possible at all, nor is it in need of other than the possible. The servant does not acquire any of The Real and the servant has nothing of Him. The existence of The Real is outwardly manifest by the possibles and their sources. The possibles always continue to have their root of possibility. They never leave that. The meaning of deduction is proving God by His existence on the proof, not by its proof of Him. They never prove Him. (517)

Someone who looks into this question may imagine that phenomenal being is a proof of God since he looks into himself and forms a proof. He does not know that he is looking at something which reverts to the principle of being described by existence. Existence is what looks. He is God. If it had not been that His essence is described by existence, then by what would he look? Only God looks into God. God gives rise to Himself. He said: "I recognized God by God." That is the school of this group. One times One is One, so understand! (518)

22.14. Crossing the Hands in the Formal Prayer

22.14.1. The Position of the Religious Scholars About Crossing the Hands in the Formal Prayer

Scholars disagree about placing one hand over the other in the formal prayer. Some people dislike it in the formal prayer, but permit it in the supererogatory. Some people think that it is one of the *sunnas* of the formal prayer. This action is reported from the Messenger of God. Similarly, it is also related that he did not do so when the formal prayer is described. It is also related that people were ordered to do that. (519)

22.14.2. The Interpretation of Holding the Hands and Letting Them Hang at the Sides in the Formal Prayer

The interpretation of that with the people of God is that the states of the one who performs the formal prayer before his Lord, The Mighty, The Majestic, vary in his standing according to the different things he says in his intimate conversation. If what he says to Him demands folding the hands, he folds them. If it demands that they hang down, he lets them hang down. Similarly, when the sign demands that he ask for forgiveness, he asks for forgiveness. If it demands supplication, he makes supplication. If it demands exaltation of the sublime presence, he exalts it. If it demands joy, he is joyful. If it demands humility, he is humble. He acts according to what he says. For that reason, it is not necessary that the one who performs the formal prayer keep to one particular attribute in the conversation. This is why he said that there is choice in this question. All forms are both permitted and excellent. (520)

22.15. Getting Up from the Odd Cycle Supererogatory Prayer (witr)

22.15.1. The Ruling of Getting Up from the Odd Cycle Supererogatory Prayer (witr)

A group of people believe that when the one who performs the formal prayer is in the *witr* prayer, he cannot stand up until he has been erect in the sitting. Others say that he does not sit and rises from the prostration. (521)

22.15.2. The Interpretation of That With the People of God

The one who performs the formal prayer, performs the formal prayer according to that to which God calls him. If he calls him to sit while he is in the state of prostration, he sits and then rises. If he calls on him to rise, he rises. That is based on whatever is given to him in himself. We have already discussed this, so look at that interpretation. (522)

As for sitting between the two prostrations, it is so that his prostration will combine prostration from standing and prostration from sitting. When he prostrates from sitting, he learns the secrets of the descent of The Real from the Throne on which He, glory be to Him! sits between the two prostrations, he speaks to The Merciful since He sat on the Throne. When he prostrates from sitting, he speaks to The Real by the name "The Lord" since He descends to His servants in the last third of the night. He gives him a Self-disclosure from these states by that which will increase him in the knowledges which these states give him because of what they contain of remembrance of God, supplication, and forms. Each is according to what he drinks of spiritual knowledge. (523)

22.16. What He Puts on the Ground When He Goes Down to Prostrate

22.16.1. What Parts of the Body Touches the Ground First in Prostration

People disagree about what the one who performs the formal prayer places on the ground when he goes down to prostrate and whether he put his hands before the knees. Some people say that he puts his hands before the knees and some think that he puts the knees first. (524)

22.16.2. The Interpretation on Putting Down the Hands or Knees First

Interpretation of the People of God in that is that the hands are the place of power and the knees are the place of reliance. Whoever relies on his Lord with the power which he finds in himself (like self-restraint with power), says that you put the knees before the hands. Whoever thinks that the hands are the place of giving and generosity and sees that God Almighty says: "*Put forward charity before of your conversing privately,*" (58:13), puts the hands before the knees. (525)

22.16.3. The Interpretation of the People of God in That

The giver must have one of two states—either he gives while he is a healthy avaricious man who fears poverty and expects to live, or he gives being one of those who trust in God and rely on God since the thought of poverty or need does not occur to him because he knows that God knows best what he needs. Whoever is like this puts his knees before his hands. Someone who moves by avarice strives for himself, fears poverty, and expends great effort from himself in giving, puts the hands before the knees. (526)

No matter which of these two states the prostrater puts forward, he acquires the other in his prostration. That is necessary. Whoever relies on trust obtains the attribute of generosity, preference for others, and all the ranks of generosity and giving. Whoever gives to God out of cowardice and anxiety, that giving bears the fruit of the state of trust and reliance on God. That which the lawgiver preferred was to put the hands first. (527)

22.17. Prostration Being on Seven Bones

22.17.1. *Position of the Religious Scholars about How the Prostration in the Formal Prayer Is Done*

Scholars, may God be pleased with them, agree that whoever prostrates on his face, hands, knees and the ends of his feet has indeed completed the prostration. They disagree about when he prostrates on his face and leaves out one of those limbs and whether or not his formal prayer is invalidated. Some say that it is invalid and some say that it is not invalid. They do not disagree that whoever prostrates on his forehead and nose has prostrated on his face. They disagree about the one who prostrates on his forehead and not his nose, and on his nose and not his forehead. Some say that it is permitted to prostrate on the forehead rather than the nose, but if he prostrates on his nose rather than his forehead, it is not allowed. Some say that he is permitted to prostrate on his nose without the forehead and the forehead without the nose. Some say that he can only prostration both of them together. (528)

22.17.2. *The Interpretation of Prostration on Seven Bones*

The interpretation of that is that the seven refers to the attributes to which all of the names revert. They are contained by them. These are: Life, Knowledge, Will, Power, Speech, Hearing and Sight. If one of the attributes or relationships are lacking according to the dispute which we have clarified about them being relationships or attributes, all are invalidated. That would mean that it is not valid that God be God. This is the interpretation of the one who only allows the formal prayer when he prostrates on the seven bones. The bones of this one who prostrates are in the position of these seven to the divine Presence. (529)

In the case of someone who says that the face is necessary, this resembles life among these attributes. It is the precondition for the existence of the rest of the seven attributes or relationships according to what we have clarified. There are people of knowledge who say that hearing and sight refer to knowledge and that knowledge is independent of them. They are two ranks of knowledge—the seen and the heard. Therefore, they are a particular connection to knowledge. He therefore allows the formal prayer if one of these limbs are lacking unless it is the prostration of the face. The face is like life. (530)

Life demands honor and might for itself over the rest of the attributes and names since these attributes are conditional on the existence of life. Might and life are connected like one thing. It is like the connection of the forehead and the nose inasmuch as they are the same bone although the form is different. Some say that what is meant by face is the least thing to which the name "face" can be applied. That would be sufficient so he permits prostration on the nose without the forehead and on the forehead without the nose. This is like the one who thinks that The Essence is an all-encompassing goal. (531)

Some look at the form of the nose and the form of the forehead to see which is the more entitled to the name "face." The forehead dominates. Therefore, even if the nose is the same bone, he does not allow prostration on the nose without the forehead because it is not a special bone. It is more like a muscle than a bone. Therefore it is distinct from the forehead. It is the forehead which is designated in prostration and life is considered in the same way among the attributes. Even if it has might since it encompasses it, knowledge also has encompassment. Therefore they share. He does not think that might has an effect in this matter. (532)

Some say that the Face of God must be inaccessible, mighty. They say that prostration must be on the forehead and nose together. Since the nose is the sense which is the place of breathing, and breathing is animal life, its relationship to life is the best relationship. (533)

22.17.3. The Seven Bones and Seven Attributes and Organizations of the World

The organization of the world is completed by these seven. It is ruled, subject to the divine. The possible does not have any possible reality which demands something more than these seven. There is nothing more exceptional possible than this world because three is nothing more perfect than God in existence. His perfection in His divinity is by these seven attributes which are ascribed to Him, glory be to Him! If one of these attributes or relationships been non-existent and lacking, the rank which brought the world into existence would not be valid, so the world would not exist. It exists, so that rank exists. (534)

There is perfection and it is a logical connection. If the cause is removed, the effect is removed. If the effect had left the intellect, the cause would not manifest any effect in it. Then it would not longer be a cause. It is a cause by its own essence. Therefore when the effect does not exist, then cause does not exist inasmuch as it is a cause. This is not in relationship to the source to which causality is ascribed. God is Rich, Independent of the worlds by His essence. We are speaking about Him inasmuch as He is God. We are speaking about the rank, not about the source. This is as we speak about The sultan inasmuch as he is a Sultan, not inasmuch as he is a man. The only benefit lies in speaking about the realities of the ranks because we understand the distinction between the different sources by them. (535)

22.18. Squatting

22.18.1. *The General Principle Applicable in Questions of the Divine Law*

Abu Talib al-Makki, may God have mercy on him, said: "The celestial spheres revolve by the breaths of the world." Then the effects gives what is within its capacity. If it has nothing more to give, it is finished as a giver. In respect to the going-on of the world, it is the source of its substance which it manifests as being form. As far as the form is concerned, when part of it is non-existent, the world is not necessarily non-existence in respect to its substance. That is, of course, unless the form has no basis. When all of the form ceases to exist, then the world is non-existent in respect to its substance. There are many divine questions connected to this subject. I wish to give a principle in this question which will be applicable for all the questions of the divine law. We say that when the Prophet uses a particular phrase, that phrase is applied to what is understood by it in technical usage in Arabic. If the Prophet specifies what he means by that expression, that attribute becomes the basis for that expression. When the expression comes from the Prophet, it is applied to what is understood from it in the divine law unless another proof in the divine law or a connection to a state indicates whether he means that expression as commonly understood in Arabic or something else. This is constant in all that the Prophet said. Examples of this are the expressions ablution, formal prayer, obligatory fasting, pilgrimage to Mecca and giving the obligatory poor-due, and so on. (536)

22.18.2. *Squatting: Its Form and Ruling in the Formal Prayer*

Now I will tell you what is understood by "squatting" in the language. It is the squatting of the dog and the monkey. Its description is that a man sit on his buttocks with both of them on the ground during the formal prayer while his thighs are upright. This description of squatting is how the dog and wild beast squat. There is no disagreement among scholars that this form is not part of the formal prayer. It has been related that it is forbidden to squat in the formal prayer. We have referred to squatting as it is commonly known linguistically. If the Sharia specifies a particular form outside of what is commonly understood linguistically, we should stop there and know that it is that form which we are forbidden. (537)

A group has stated that the squatting which is forbidden is that a man rests his buttocks on his heels in between the two prostrations and that he sit on the front of his feet. It is related that Ibn Umar used to do what because he had problems with his feet. It is confirmed from Ibn Umar that it is not part of the *Sunna* of the formal prayer for a man to sit on the front of his feet. Ibn Abbas said that squatting on the feet in this manner of prostration was the *Sunna* of our Prophet. (538)

22.18.3. The Interpretation of Squatting

The interpretation of that is that the form of squatting is the form of the alert, prepared person. The servant must be like that in his states. For this reason, Ibn Abbas said that squatting was the *sunna* of our Prophet. The servant must be prepared for the commands of his Master. Me must not cease to watch for them so that when they come to him, they will find him ready to receive what comes to him. Then he will be quick to obey them. The one with this state is praised when God Almighty says. "*Those who compete with one another in good works and they are ones who take the lead from them.*" (23:61) He also says about them: "*Some of them are ones who take the lead with good works.*" (35:32) Whoever seeks haste in matters has a state of being awake, present, vigilant, alert, and prepared. You must know that. (539)

It is inferred then that the prohibition about squatting in the formal prayer refers to being like dogs and wild animals in that. He should do that inasmuch as it is prescribed in an intelligible form which is transmitted to us in an intelligible place. It comes from the linguistic position that squatting involves having both hands on the ground as the dog does. This is not in the prescribed form of squatting. (540)

So we have mentioned some of the actions and words of the formal prayer according to the various sub-branches of the roots. (541)

23 Concerning Different Aspects of the Formal Prayer

23.1. Introduction

23.1.1. Aspects of the Formal Prayer

We have mentioned some of the actions and words of the formal prayer, so now we will move to aspects. This is like the congregational or group formal prayer and its ruling, the preconditions for being leader and who is most entitled to it, specific rules about the leader, the position of the leader in relation to the one who follows him, the rulings particular to them, that in which the one praying behind the leader follows the leader and that in which he does not follow him, the description of following, what the leader does on behalf of the follower, and the things by which the formal prayer of the leader are invalidated and when it includes the follower according to the various details put forth by the divine law scholars and the disagreement of the scholars about that. We will mention the interpretations of all of what with those who know God according to what the Path of God demands of the actions of the hearts and the secrets. This path is with the people of tasting. It is not the path of transmission. (542)

Before we discuss these aspects, we will first mention two Traditions which are connected to the words of the formal prayer and its actions which were discussed in the previous section. They are like the seal. I have put them in the section on states because: "*it was a need of Jacob's inner self which he satisfied.*" (12:68) It is pleasure and knowledge when we teach it. However, "most people did not know." The first Tradition is about when the Prophet taught the formal prayer to the man who asked him to teach him how to perform it. The second Tradition is the description of the formal prayer of the Messenger of God. (543)

23.1.2. The Prophet Teaching the Formal Prayer

The first Tradition is one in al-Bukhari which comes via Abu Hurayra. He mentioned the Tradition of the man who came into the mosque and performed the formal prayer. The Messenger of God said to him: "Go back and perform the formal prayer. You have not performed it." The man said: "Teach me, Messenger of God!" The Messenger of God said: "When you stand up to perform the formal prayer, perform ablution thoroughly. Then face the direction of formal prayer and recite the *takbir*. Then recite what is easy of the Quran for you. Then do bowing until you are at rest in that position. Then stand up straight. Then prostrate until you are at rest in that position, and do that throughout all of your formal prayer." In another version, "Then stand up straight," that is, from the second prostration. (544)

Ali ibn Abd-l-Aziz related from Rifa ibn Rafi in a Tradition that the man said to the Prophet: "I don't know what is required of me." The Prophet said: "None of you completes the formal prayer until he has done ablution thoroughly as God commanded him. He should wash his face and his hands up to the elbows, wipe his head and feet up to the ankles. Then he says: 'God is Greater' and praises and glorifies Him. He recites what God allows him to recite of the Quran and what is easy. Then he recites the *takbir* and bows. He places his palms on his knees until his joints are at rest and relaxed. Then he stands upright until each bone take its due and the back is straight. He recites the *takbir* and prostrates. He puts his face on the ground until his joints are at rest and relaxed. He recites the *takbir*, and raises his head and sits up straight on his buttocks and his back is straight." He described the entire formal prayer like that up to the end. Then he said: "The formal prayer of any of you is not complete until he does this." Nasai related it. This is clearer still. (545)

In another transmission from Rifaa, Nasai reported, "When you do that, your formal prayer is complete. If you leave out something of it, your formal prayer is deficient, but not all of it has gone." At the beginning of it, he said: "When you get up to pray, perform ablution as God has commanded you, recite the bearing witness, and stand and recite the *takbir*. Abu Umar ibn Abd 'l-Barr says that this Tradition is established by the second one. (546)

23.1.3. The Description of the Formal Prayer of the Prophet

The second Tradition is related by Abu Dawud about the description of the formal prayer of the Messenger of God. It came from Muhammad ibn Ata who said that he heard Abu Humayd al-Saidi with ten of the Companions of the Messenger of God—one of whom was Abu Qatada. Abu Humayd said: "I will teach you the formal prayer of the Messenger of God." They said: "Why? By God, you did not follow him more than us and you did not precede us in his company." He said: "Yes, indeed." They said: "Show us then." (547)

He said: "When the Messenger of God would stand up to perform the formal prayer, he would raise his hands until they were opposite his shoulders and recite the *takbir* when every bone was straight in its proper place. He raised his hands until they were opposite his shoulders. Then he did bowing and placed his hands on his knees. He was straight in that and neither lowered nor raised his head. Then he lifted his head and said: 'God hears whoever praises Him.' He would raise his hands until they were level with his shoulders. He said: 'God is Greater,' and lowered himself to the earth, keeping his arms away from his sides. Then he raised his head, folded his left foot under him and sat on it (and he opened out his toes when he prostrated.) (548)

Then he would prostrate saying 'God is Greater,' and get up. He would fold his left foot under him and sit on it until every limb was in its proper place. He would do the same in the other. When he stood up from the second cycle, he would say the takbir and raise his hands until they were opposite his shoulders as he did the takbir at the beginning of the formal prayer. He did that for the rest of his formal prayer until the last prostration which has the *taslim*. He would put out his left foot and sit on his left hip." They said: "You have spoken the truth. This is how the Messenger of God used to perform the formal prayer." (549)

Abu Isa Muhammad ibn Sura al-Tirmidhi said about this Tradition that the Messenger of God would stand upright when he stood up to pray. He would raise his hands until they were opposite his shoulders. When he got up from bowing, he would stand straight until every bone returned to its place. It was like that between the two prostrations. Another version adds: ". . . and then he would say the *taslim*." He said that this Tradition is sound-excellent. (550)

23.2. Concerning the Dispute About the Group Formal Prayer

23.2.1. *The Ruling of the Group Formal Prayer Among the Religious Scholars*

They disagree about whether or not the group formal prayer is obligatory for the one who hears the call to formal prayer. Some say that it is *sunna*. Some say that it is a general obligation. Some say that it is an individual obligation for every legally responsible person. (551)

23.2.2. *The Interpretation of the Group Formal Prayer*

The interpretation of that is that when God ordered the one who performs the formal prayer to say: "*Thee alone we worship*" with the *nun* of the plural, He indicated that every part of him must perform the formal prayer together in the same state. This is why the first recitation in the formal prayer of: "God is Greater" (*Allahu akbar*, *takbir* is called the recitation of "God is Greater" after which everything but the formal prayer is forbidden (*takbir al-ihram*), that is, it makes it forbidden for the servant to use any of his limbs in the formal prayer for that which is not part of the formal prayer. All the actions which he is allowed in the formal prayer are part of the formal prayer. Every action which is permitted in the formal prayer is the formal prayer since the Prophet specified it. The formal prayer is not invalidated by any of that. (552)

There is no doubt that it is obligatory for all of the servant to be present with God Almighty. Each of his limbs must pray in the formal prayer. The least number to which the "group" can be applied is two. God says: "I have divided the formal prayer between Me and My servant into two parts." He also said that "He performs the formal prayer blessing on us." Therefore whoever performs the formal prayer with his Lord without a doubt is in a group without a doubt. God is the Leader and the servant is the one who follows Him since He is the One who makes him stand and sit. The servant is the leader in the intimate conversation since God let him begin by speaking to Him. So there is no one who performs the formal prayer alone. (553)

If he is not present with God in this formal prayer, he has isolated himself in this worship. He is with himself rather than his Lord. This is the one who is alone in the interpretation. That is what he is based on. Even if he is in a group in his world, he is still falls under the ruling of the one who is alone. The other one who is alone is the one who thinks that the formal prayer belongs only to the Lord since he sees Him and is annihilated to himself. He does not see himself praying since he sees that the formal prayer happens from him by his Lord. This is also connected to the person praying alone. (554)

If the servant had been unveiled to that fact that every part of himself in the formal prayer is kept alive by the praise of his Lord in its formal prayer and that every part is annihilated to itself by seeing Him, then he is gathered in the group and has the reward of the one performing the formal prayer alone by every part of him as part as his parts reach. If you like, you could say that he performs the formal prayer in a group and God is the Leader. (555)

There are gnostics whom God sets up in the station of the leadership (*leadership*) and then God is the one following the Leader. That is like his statement: "God does not tire until you tire. He goes with you as long as you go with Him." God Almighty says about this: "*Remember Me, I will remember you*" (2:152), and "whoever remembers Me in himself, I remember him in Myself. Whoever mentions Me in an assembly, I mention him in a better assembly." This is the meaning of the leader and the one who follows the leader. God—glory be to Him—puts you forward in this place and its likes. It is like, "*I answer the call of one who calls when he calls to Me.*"

(2:186) The likeness of His being the Leader to you is "Then answer Me" when He calls them. Then they answer Him in obedience to His call, and He answers them by their answer to Him. Look how noble this Lord is with the absolute richness with which He has described Himself! See how He connects Himself to His servant in all the worship which He has commanded him to do! That is clear overflowing bounty. (556)

23.3. Someone Who Performs the Formal Prayer Alone and Then Comes Upon a Group, or Who Performs the Formal Prayer in a Group and Then Comes Upon Another Group

23.3.1. The Ruling of the Individual Formal Prayer and the Group Formal Prayer)

Know that if you perform formal prayer alone and then come to the mosque, there must be one of two situations—either you performed the formal prayer alone or in a group. If you performed the formal prayer alone, you repeat all the formal prayers with them except for evening formal prayer. A group of people say that you repeat all of them except evening and afternoon formal prayer. One group say that it is all of them except the evening formal prayer and the morning formal prayer. Some say that it is all of them except the morning formal prayer and the afternoon formal prayer. Some say that all of them are repeated. (557)

If you performed the formal prayer in a group, do you repeat it in another group? Some say that you repeat it and some say that you do not repeat it. (558)

Our position in the like of this question is that the group formal prayer is obligatory if he can join it. If he cannot join a group, he performs the formal prayer alone. If he comes upon a group—even if he has already performed the formal prayer in a group, he performs the formal prayer with the group if he hears His call in the declaration to perform the formal prayer, "Come to formal prayer." In both cases, it is supererogatory for him, and he has the reward of the group if he cannot join it. (559)

23.4. The Interpretation of That in the Self

23.4.1. The Interpretation of Repeating the Formal Prayer

The Prophet stipulated that intimate conversation is in the formal prayer. The Messenger of God said: "The coolness of my eye is in the formal prayer." He tells us that he is one of the people who see God in it with a more complete method than seeing that it is following. He said about beauty, goodness, "It is that you worship God as if you were seeing Him." He did not specify any particular worship. God says: "God loves those who turn in repentance." They are those who return to Him often in every state which pleases Him. There is no state nobler than the formal prayer since it joins witnessing and intimate conversation. He says: "*He loves the ones who keep themselves clean.*" (2:222) Purification is one of the preconditions of the formal prayer.

The believer yearns and desires to always remain in the contemplation of his Beloved and to always speak intimately with Him. When the Beloved calls him to that when He says: "Come to formal prayer! The formal prayer is established," then he must of necessity hurry and go ahead to that to which He has called him so that he can enjoy His witnessing and intimate conversation. (561)

The one who has this state thinks that the formal prayers are repeated in the group when the declaration to perform the formal prayer is given and he is summoned to it, no matter whether he performed the formal prayer it alone or in a group. We have clarified the meaning of the one praying alone and the group in the previous section. (562)

23.4.2. The Interpretation on Not Repeating the Formal Prayer

Those who think that the formal prayer is not repeated are gnostics. Those who think that the formal prayer is repeated are the lovers. That is because the gnostics know that repetition is impossible and that the self-disclosure which he had in his formal prayer is not the self-disclosure which he will have in the other formal prayer. This is endless. Since he thinks that repetition and recurrence is impossible because of the divine boundlessness, he does not consider repetition to be valid. (563)

The lover performs the formal prayer the repeated formal prayer while he does not know. The gnostic does not pray by the aspect of repetition as he possesses recognition. Knowledge is the noblest of the stations. Love is the noblest of the states. The one who combines the two stations of love and gnosis says that the Self-disclosure is repeated while the object of the self-disclosure is not repeated. It has firstness in every prayer, obligatory or supererogatory. (564)

23.4.3. The Interpretation of Not Repeating the Evening Formal Prayer (*Maghrib*)

The one who thinks that evening formal prayer cannot be repeated sees that the evening formal prayer is the oddness of the servant, and the *witr* at night is the oddness of The Real. The night *witr* is one cycle, and God, The Majestic, The Great, has oneness. The *witr* of the evening formal prayer is three cycles. It combines the qualities of being even and being odd. It is the beginning of isolation and "God is odd and loves the odd."

The servant does not see his Lord in respect to his evenness. He sees Him in respect to the oddness of uniqueness. God has the oddness of being unique inasmuch as He is essence. When the servant sees his Lord in respect of his unique divine Oddness from that unique divine Oddness, he sees the oddness of the one essence, but not by the unique oddness of the servant. God is only seen by God. If he were to repeat the evening formal prayer, the oddness of the servant would become even and he would never see his Lord as odd. So he says that you must not repeat the evening formal prayer as opposed to any of the other formal prayers. (565)

The one who says that the evening formal prayer is repeated says that it is repeated by the oddness of divine Uniqueness, not by his own oddness. God's oddness remains unique and it does not become even, even by the repetition of the the evening formal prayer formal prayer. There is no doubt that God is distinct from creation in every way. (566)

23.4.4. The Interpretation of Not Repeating the Morning (subh) and Afternoon (asr) Formal Prayer

As for the one who thinks that the morning formal prayer cannot be repeated, the first the morning formal prayer is the obligation. It is the same with the afternoon formal prayer. The first the morning formal prayer and the first the afternoon formal prayer are supererogatory. When man performs the obligation, he is a pure servant with the servanthood of compulsion. In the supererogatory he is servant by choice. The servanthood of compulsion is nobler than the servanthood of choice in respect of him because in the servanthood of choice, he is granted servanthood. God Almighty says: "*They count as a favor to thee that they have submitted. Say: Show not grace to me for your submission. Nay! God has done a favor to you in that He has guided you to belief if you truly have been ones who are sincere.*" (49:17) (567)

Since God has made compared the servant's vision of Him to their seeing the sun, the sun has an increased rank for them, especially for the lovers, since the Beloved compared their seeing it with their vision of Him. When they see it, it is as if they were seeing God, because when they see it, they are reminded of the vision which God has promised them. They do not want the sun to rise on them unless they are described by the servanthood of compulsion. They do not want it to set on them unless they are also in the servanthood of compulsion. They desire the vision of God in the state of compulsion and pure servanthood since its pleasure is sweeter and more complete, as their seeing the sun is more universal and resplendent. (568)

When the sun rises and sets, they want it to say to its Lord, "We left them compelled servants and we came to them and they were compelled servants." This is like what the angels say who ascend in the morning formal prayer and afternoon formal prayer. God, The Majestic, questions them—although He has more knowledge of them—"How did you leave My servants?" They reply, "We left them when they were performing the formal prayer and we came to them when they were performing the formal prayer." The angels who are with them do not leave them and other angels do not come to them at any other time than the beginning of the formal prayer, no matter whether they perform it at the beginning of the time or the end of the time. The angels only leave each man as we have said. (569)

For this reason, the people of belief and the people of unveiling think that when the one who performs the formal prayer wants to recite the recitation of "God is Greater" after which everything but the formal prayer is forbidden (*takbir al-ihram*) in the morning formal prayer and the afternoon formal prayer, he says: "Peace be upon you and the mercy of God and His blessings" because at that moment the angels who were with them leave them and the angels who are coming to them arrive. When they come, they greet the servant, and when they leave, they greet the servant. God gave us this command: "*When you were given greetings with greetings, then give greetings fairer than that or return the same to them.*" (4:86) It is obligatory for every believer in respect of his belief and its reality to answer: "Peace be upon you" at that moment. If not, it harms his belief if he is present. We remember it in that moment. The master of unveiling has a specific knowledge and the believer has an inner eye. (570)

Whoever makes the afternoon formal prayer rather than the morning formal prayer the exception thinks that he can only face the unseen with the servanthood of compulsion since the unseen is the root. It is the He-ness of God. The unseen does not part from He-ness. The morning formal prayer is leaving the unseen for the visible world. He does not care what state of servanthood—by compulsion or by choice —he has in the visible world because the obligation is to pause in servanthood. The visible is the place of claim because it is the place of movement, livelihood, seeing others, and the veils of actions. (571)

Whoever makes an exception for the morning formal prayer rather than the afternoon formal prayer says that he wants to face the name, The Manifest, with the servanthood of compulsion. He does not care by what sort of servanthood he meets the night. He meets it either with the servanthood of compulsion or the servanthood of choice. For this reason, the Messenger of God performed supererogatory prayers after the afternoon formal prayer and did not do them after the morning formal prayer. The one who holds this view says that you can perform supererogatory prayers after the afternoon formal prayer if you like. He says that the night has the unseen and it has the name The Hidden. It has a power which makes me compelled whether I like it or not. The day is not like that. If I face it with the servanthood of choice, its power rules me and makes me compelled. Each group takes a certain matter into consideration in the interpretation of the formal prayers when they think that they cannot be repeated if they have already performed the formal prayer. We have already discussed the one alone and the group. (572

24 The One Most Entitled to Act as Leader of the Formal Prayer

24.1. The Position of the Religious Scholars About the One Most Entitled to Act as Leader (*imam*) [of the Formal Prayer]

The Messenger of God said: "The person among a people who can recite the greatest amount of the Quran should be the leader (*leader*)." A group of people stated that this means the one who knows the most jurisprudence, not the one who knows the most signs by heart. This is a dispute between those who say this and the Messenger of God. I asked those who state this position: "Has this Tradition reached you?" They admitted that it had and said: "We have related it and know it." My position is that of the words of the Messenger of God. Those who state something contrary to what he said have no proof, especially as the Messenger of God said in this Tradition, "If they are equal in the recitation, then the one who has the most knowledge of the *sunna*." (573)

Therefore he made a distinction between a jurisprudent and a reciter of the Quran. He gave the leadership to the reciter of the Quran as long as they are not equal in recitation. If they are equal in that, then one of them is not more entitled to the leadership than the other. Therefore, you must advance to the one who has more knowledge of the *sunna*. He is the one with more knowledge of jurisprudence. (574)

Then the Messenger of God said: "If they are equal in knowledge of the *sunna*, then it is the earliest of them to emigrate. If they emigrated at the same time, then it is the one who has been Muslim the longest. No man acts as the leader where another man has authority or sits in his place of honor in his house without his permission." Abu Hanifa said that people agree that it is a sound Tradition. The sound Tradition is the one on which we rely. (575)

As regards someone who opposes the text by saying that all the reciters knew an equal amount of jurisprudence at that time, this interpretation is refuted by his words, "The one with the best knowledge of the *sunna*." (576)

Know that nothing at all can be placed before the words of God in any aspect whatsoever. If the elite is preceded by something below it, it is not elite. The people of God are the people of the Quran. Their elite are those who recite its letters, whether they be Arab or non-Arab. divine worthiness and election is valid for them. If he also has recognition of its meanings, that is excellence in worthiness and election, but not in respect to the Quran. It is in respect to its meanings. If memorization and knowledge of the meanings have action by it added to them, then it is light upon light. (577)

The reciter is the master of the garden. The man of knowledge is the one who recognizes the varieties of the fruits of the garden, their tastes and the uses of its fruits. The man of action is like the one who eats from the garden. The one who memorizes the Quran knows it and acts by it is like the owner of the garden. He knows what is in his garden, what is good for it, what is bad for it, and he eats from it. The example of the man of knowledge and action who does know the Quran by heart is like the one who knows the varieties of the fruits and their tastes and cultivation, but eats fruits from another garden. The example of the man of action is one who eats from another garden. The owner of the garden is better than the group who have no garden. The rest need him. (578)

24.2. The Interpretation of the One Most Entitled to the Leadership Inwardly

The one who is the most entitled to leadership of the formal prayer is the one whose hearing, sight, hand, tongue and all his faculties are God. If they are equal in this state, then it is the one with the most knowledge of what lordship demands. If they are equal in that knowledge, then it is the one who has the one recognition of servanthood and its requirements. There is no pleasing state beyond the recognition of servanthood which can be in the same station or be above it because they were create for that. God Almighty says: "*I only created jinn and human kind to worship Me,*" (51:56) (579)

In reality, the leadership of the formal prayer belongs to God, The Real, may He be exalted and may His Majesty be magnified! The people of these states are His representatives and viceregent. For this reason, He described them with His attributes, Rather He made His source the source of their attributes. He is the Leader, not them. (580)

24.2.1. Those in Authority in Reality

God Almighty says: "*Whoever obeys the Messenger has surely obeyed God.*" (4:80) He says: "*Obey God and obey the Messenger and those imbued with authority among you*" (4:59), that is, those with command. In reality, those in power have nothing assigned to their power because they command by God as they hear by Him and see by Him. When they say to a thing, "*Be!*" and it is, that is because they speak by Him. This is the meaning in the interpretation of "*those in authority.*" This is why it is obligatory to obey the ruler. The ruler is in the position of the prescribed command of God. Whoever obeys it is saved. Whoever rebels against it is destroyed. (581)

24.3. The Leadership of a Child [of the Formal Prayer] Who Has Not Reached Puberty

24.3.1. The Statements of the Religious Scholars Regarding It

They disagree about the leadership of the formal prayer by a child who has not yet reached puberty if he can recite the Quran. Some people absolutely permit it and some people absolutely forbid it. Some people permit it in the supererogatory prayers, but not the obligatory ones. (582)

24.3.2. The Interpretation of the Leadership of a Child [of the Formal Prayer]

The interpretation of that is that it is said: "Someone yearned (*saba;* child—*sabiy*) for that" when he inclined to it. When the child inclines to the rule of nature and obtaining his desires, he is called "*sabiy*" (child) that is, inclining to his appetites. He has not reached the limit of the intellect which obliges responsibility. Nature is in a rank below that of the intellect. Therefore, it cannot go ahead, nor can the one who inclines to it. Therefore he must fall behind, and the one who falls behind cannot be the leader who is put in front. It conflicts with the ruling in that. Anyone who follows this interpretation does not permit the leadership of the child, even if he can recite Quran. (583)

The one who observes that he is a bearer of the Quran gives preference to the recitation of the Quran, not to the child. The leadership of the formal prayer by a child in respect to the one who follows is because of the Quran. That is why he permits the leadership of the child. God Almighty says: "*We gave him critical judgment while a lad*" (19:12), that is, the authority of the leadership. "*They said: How speak we to one who has been in the cradle, a lad? Jesus said: Truly I am a servant of God. He gave me the Book and made me a Prophet.*" (19:29-30) (which is the station of the leadership) although he was called a child. (584)

Whoever makes the servanthood of the child the servanthood of choice since he is not responsible and thinks that the supererogatory prayer is worship by choice, allows the child to act as the leader in the supererogatory prayer but not in the formal prayer, because of the relationship of choice. (585)

24.4. The Leadership of the Impious (*fasiq*) [of the Formal Prayer]

24.4.1. The Ruling of the Leadership of the Impious (fasiq) [of the Formal Prayer] from a Legal Aspect

Some people absolutely reject allowing an impious person (*fasiq*) to lead the formal prayer. Some people absolutely permit it. Some people differentiate between the one whose impiety is definite and the one who is suspected. They do not allow someone who is definitely known to be impious to act as leader of the formal prayer. If you perform the formal prayer behind him, then you must perform it. If you perform the formal prayer behind someone whose impiety is suspected, it is recommended that you redo it immediately. They also differentiate between the one whom you conclude is impious by interpretation and the one who is impious without need of interpretation. They permit the formal prayer behind the one who is considered to be impious by interpretation, and do not permit it behind the one who is impious without need of interpretation. My position is that it is absolutely permitted. The believer is not impious at all since nothing of belief could stand up when it exists in the place of the rebel. (586)

24.4.2. The Interpretation of the Impious (fasiq) Inwardly

The interpretation in that is that the impious person is one who leaves his real root. That is that he is a servant because he was created for this. He must either be a servant of God or a servant of his passion. He has only left the relationship which he was commanded to have. Therefore his leadership of formal prayer is permitted since the successful one among the servants of God follows this impious person because he sees that he establishes his servanthood in respect of his passion in which his wretchedness lies. By him, he learns how to fulfill the proper servanthood which God has commanded in being a servant to Him. He says: "I should have this attribute in respect to God more than this servant has it in respect to his passion." (587)

Then we see the friends of God following them while they have benefit from that with God, and this following is a cause for their rescue. Therefore his leadership is valid. Abd Allah ibn Umar performed the formal prayer behind Hajjaj and there is no disagreement about al-Hajjaj being interpreted as being impious. Whoever believes in God and says that God is One in His divinity, God is too glorious to call this person impious in reality, even if he is called one linguistically when he abandons a particular command, even if it is little. Acts of rebellion do not affect the leadership of the formal prayer as long as he is not called an unbeliever. As for suspected impiety, far be it from the believer to have bad opinion when he believes that so-and-so is impious by mere supposition. The believer whose belief is pleasing with God does not fall into that. (588)

This is in all of the outward states. As for the inward states, that is up to God or the one God teaches. Then the gnostic rises by seeing the impiety which the divine law blames up to what the language grants. This is in the interpretation, not in the outward principle. This is when man leaves his humanness by leaving the rule of nature over him for the world of purity among the divine Spirits. Is his leadership valid there or not? Some of our companions say that his leadership in the Higher World is absolutely valid, and this is our position. Some of our companions say that he cannot be the leader since he only leaves the authority of his nature by the spirits which are connected to the natural bodies of *jinn* and men. (589)

The cause of their dispute is that everyone who has unveiling experiences what he sees in his unveiling at that moment. The one who is unveiled may see a matter from all its aspects in a moment, or he may see only some of its aspects while God veils from him whatever aspects of that matter He wishes. Then the one with unveiling judges all of it. His unveiling itself is sound, but he errs in making the principle all-inclusive. Then he sees that in respect to his spirit it is one of the angelic spirits and he says: "Even if I have left my nature, I have not left my angelhood by what I have of the world of command." Then he seeks to break through and come out of his spirit as he came out of his nature. He comes out by his lord-like secret. Then the divine names rise for him and he leads them towards his Creator. He is in front of them. Every name has a reality, and this servant joins all these realities together. Therefore, the leadership of the formal prayer is valid for him in that place when he leaves his nature and his spirit. (590)

There is no one who leaves his homeland but that a group of people blame him because that group sees that this servant is worshipping by his totality and it is sound. They call him immoral even though he is excused. Wayfaring (*suluk*) entails dissolution and decomposition until the end. When it ends, then he is re-constructed stage by stage even as he was dissolved, until he is whole and perfect. Then the name "immoral" leaves him every world. This is the interpretation of the leadership of the immoral. (591)

24.5. The Leadership of a Woman [of the Formal Prayer]

24.5.1. The Ruling of the Leadership of a Woman [of the Formal Prayer] From a Legal Aspect

Some people absolutely permit woman to be a leader of the formal prayer for both men and women, and this is my view. Some people absolutely forbid her to act as a leader. Some people permit her to act as a leader for other women, but not for men. (592)

24.5.2. The Interpretation of the Leadership [of the Formal Prayer] of a Woman

The interpretation in that is that the Messenger of God testified that some women are perfect as he testified that some men are perfect, even if there are more perfect men than women. This is prophethood and prophethood is leadership, so it is valid for a woman to be a leader of the formal prayer. The basic root is to permit her to act as a leader. Whoever forbids that without any proof should not be listened to. The one who forbids that has no text. His proof of that includes something else and is shared. Therefore, the proof falls away and the basic root of allowing her to be a leader remains. (593)

Know that man is a world in himself and is multiple in respect of meaning, even if he is small in volume. For this reason, He says: "*Thee alone we worship*" with the *nun* of the plural. He made his limbs and outward and inward faculties follow what rules them and is ahead of them. That is the intellect, the self and passion. Each of them can act as a leader to the group at any one time. All acts of obedience are close to the intellect. Permitted actions are close to the self. Acts of opposition are close to passion. (594)

The intellect is told: "When your self is fed up with following you in immediate matters and imitating you when you are the leader and it advances in permitted matters and becomes your leader, then follow it and pray behind it in order to guard it so that passion will not deceive it. If passion follows it in that state, it might pull it into the forbidden." In places like this, the leadership of the self is permitted. This is the leadership of a woman. The leadership of the intellect is in the position of the Muslim man who is adult, has knowledge, and is legitimate. The leadership of passion is in the position of the leadership of the hypocrite, unbeliever and impious. The leadership of the self is in the position of the leadership of women. (595)

24.6. A Bastard Acting as Leader (imam) [of the Formal Prayer]

24.6.1. The Ruling About a Bastard Acting as a Leader (imam) from a Legal Aspect

They disagree about a bastard acting as leader. Some permit him to be a leader and others forbid it. (596)

24.6.2 The Interpretation of the Leadership [of the Formal Prayer] of a Bastard

The interpretation of that is that the bastard represents sound knowledge arising from an unsound intention which is not pleasing to God. It is a truthful result from an unsound premise. So it is more fitting for a man to seek knowledge of other-than-God than ignorance. When he acquires it, it might provide the one who has it with success and so he would then learn how to worship his Lord. So the leadership of the bastard is permitted. It is following the edict of the man of knowledge who seeks reputation and showing off by his knowledge so that it will be said: "He is a man of knowledge." The basis of his quest is not prescribed, but the obtaining of the knowledge itself is a virtue in the existence of this person. (597)

24.7. A Desert Arab Acting as Leader [of the Formal Prayer]

24.7.1. The Ruling About a Desert Arab Acting as Leader [of the Formal Prayer] from a Legal Aspect

The disagree about a desert Arab acting as leader. Some permit him to be leader and some forbid that. (598)

24.7.2. The Interpretation of the Leadership [of the Formal Prayer] of a Desert Arab

The interpretation of that is that the one who is ignorant of what the leader must know is not suitable for the leadership because the leader is followed. However, this one neither knows nor learns so the one who is like this cannot be the leader because he does not know what is obligatory from what is not obligatory. The one who follows him is misguided. (599)

This is not the same situation as the one performing the formal prayer while following the one performing the supererogatory prayer. When the leader does the supererogatory prayer and the one following has a different intention, still there is no difference in what is obligatory in the formal prayer, no matter whether it is an formal prayer or supererogatory one since it contains obligatory parts and *sunan*. All its pillars are obligatory as well as their *sunan* in the supererogatory prayer and obligatory one. The one is the leader and performs a supererogatory prayer, only does what he is obliged to do of the pillars of the formal prayer—bowing, prostration and others, and their *sunan*. The one who is performing the formal prayer follows him in these actions which are obligatory to perform. The one who intends to perform the formal prayer behind one performing the supererogatory prayer only follows what is obligatory for the one performing the supererogatory prayer, so you must know that! (600)

24.8. Someone Who Is Blind Acting as Leader (*Imam*) [of the Formal Prayer

24.8.1. The Ruling about a Blind Person Acting as Leader [of the Formal Prayer]

Some permit a blind person to act as leader and some forbid it. God knows best. (601)

24.8.2. The The Interpretation of a Blind Man Acting as Leader [of the Formal Prayer]

The interpretation of that is that the blind man is the one who is in confusion, who does not give greater weight to anything in the place of seeing. He does not stand, so he is in doubt. The basis is the principle of the natural form with which he was born. He is a believer when he looks and in his confusion as long as he does not stop or give greater weight to something. His leadership is permitted on the basis of his nature form because the Messenger of God appointed Ibn Umm Maktum to lead the people in the formal prayer in Medina and Ibn Umm Maktum was blind. (602)

24.9. The Leadership [of the Formal Prayer] by Someone Who Is Less Excellent

24.9.1. The Ruling about the Leadership of Someone Who Is Less Excellent from a Legal Aspect

Scholars disagree about the leadership of someone who is less in excellence. Some permit it and some of them forbid it. The Messenger of God performed the formal prayer behind Abd al-Rahman ibn Awf, and there is no dispute about that. He made up what he had missed and said: "You did well." (603)

24.9.2. The Inner Interpretation of That

The interpretation of that is that the excellent person performs the formal prayer behind the one who is less in excellence in order to elevate his spiritual strength and give him desire to seek what is more precious and more sublime. It is based on policy and good teaching. He calls to God Almighty based on insight. God gives opening to the great by the truthfulness of the turning of the small. The small therefore benefits the great from where you are not aware. (604)

When some calamity befalls a truthful disciple and he is worried about it, he presents it to the Shaykh. The Shaykh may not know the meaning of the meaning of that calamity and then the spiritual strength of the disciple may become weakened and fail since only this Shaykh would know how to unravel the problems of his calamity, so God gives that Shaykh an opening in it by the spiritual strength of that disciple and his truthfulness in it. It is God's concern for the disciple and the Shaykh profits by the principle of following even though the Shaykh has a higher station than him. (605)

However, it is not a precondition of every state which a person enters by taste that he encompass all that it contains in detail. We know absolutely that we are joined together in some stations with the Prophets, peace be upon them, while there is still a great distance between us and them in the knowledge of the secrets. They have what we do not have even if we are together in the station. (606)

This is the leadership of the one who is less in excellence, so understand that! Do not deceive yourself and say, "I am the Shaykh of this person. I have more knowledge than him about what teaching demands." You may not have more knowledge than him in its results. We have seen that with our own eyes in certain individuals. Praise belongs to God. (607)

24.10. The Ruling from a Legal Aspect about Whether the Leader [of the Formal Prayer] Says "Amin" or Not When He Finishes Reciting the Opening Chapter

Scholars disagree about that. Some say that he says "*Amen*" and some say that he does not. (608)

24.10.1. The Inner Interpretation of That

If a person puts his ego in the position of a stranger to him, he then addresses it as he addresses the stranger. God Almighty says: "*We have created the human being. We know what evil his soul whispers to him.*" (50:16) Every person discovers this by tasting, and his organic formation demands it. The Messenger of God said to the man who was legally responsible according to the divine law: "Your ego has a right due from you." Thus he related the ego to him, and the thing cannot be related to itself. He made the ego other than the person, and said that it had a right due from him which it sought. (609)

If he is reciting, he must say "Amen" to himself when he finishes the Opening Chapter. If the ego recites, then he must say "Amen." The human being is one in his source and multiple by his faculties. The words of God support this: "*Then of them are ones who are unjust to themselves*" (35:32) and "My servant has hurried his ego to me" about the one who killed himself. Whoever sees this, says that the leader and the one performing the formal prayer alone say: "Amen." (610)

Some of them think that the leader is a single source or that he speaks by his Lord as He said: "He hears by Me, he sees by Me and he speaks by Me." Shaykh Abu Madyan in *Bijaya* used to say: "I have not seen anything but that I saw the *ba* written on it." He indicated this station. It is called the *ba* of relationship. It is also like what he said. Whoever sees this, says that the leader does not say "Amen." (611)

It is better by every aspect to say "Amen." The legally responsible person is ordered to begin with himself when he makes supplication. When he says "Amen," the supplication is "O God! We have trusted in good and that by which we head for Thee." The human being acts according to his state and what he sees. It says in another Tradition: "Say 'Amen' when the leader says it." It says in another Tradition: "Say 'Amen' when the leader says 'and those who are misguided.'" (612)

24.11. When the Leader Recites "God is Greater"

24.11.1. The Position of the Religious Scholars on the Time When the Leader (imam) Recites "God is Greater" (takbir)

Some say that it is after the declaration to perform the formal prayer and when the rows are straight. Some say that it is when the declaration to perform the formal prayer is completed. Some say that it is after the caller to the formal prayer says: "The formal prayer has been established." I say that you can choose in that. (613)

24.11.2. The Interpretation of the Time of the Reciting of "God is Greater" (Allahu akbar) (takbir) of the Leader (imam) [of the Formal Prayer]

The interpretation is that the declaration to perform the formal prayer belongs to standing in the presence of God Almighty. He says: "Come to formal prayer" and the rows are straight like the rows of the angels with God Almighty by which He swears: *"By the ones standing in ranks, ranged in rows."* (37:1) This indicates establishing justice. The managing angel relieves him when God puts him in charge of him in this formation which He alludes to as "the Safe Land." This is because it is a comprehensive matrix (mother) like Mecca which is the Mother of the Cities and the Opening Chapter which is the Mother of the Book. There must be obligatory principles for establishing justice in the acts of worship to which the limbs are called. It is obligatory to concentrate spiritual strength on that outwardly and inwardly. (614)

Whoever thinks this, says the saying of "God is Greater" (*Allahu akbar*) after the declaration to perform the formal prayer and straightening the rows, it is as if he were saying, "God is Greater than having his saying "God is Greater" limited by this description since He encompasses absolutely by every state and aspect. *"He said: Our Lord is He Who gave everything its creation then He guided it."* (20:50) He is *"on a straight path."* When He obligated His servants to walk on a particular path which He specified for them, the one who goes to it is fortunate and the one who swerves from it is wretched. (615)

The one who thinks that one should hasten to good deeds and go ahead to intimate conversation recites the phrase "God is Greater" when he hears "Come to formal prayer" unless he himself is giving the declaration to perform the formal prayer. Then it would not be possible for him to do so until he finished saying, "There is no god but God." Then he recites the phrase "God is Greater." We say that he hurries in order to put the phrase "God is Greater" before the words of the caller to formal prayer, "The formal prayer has been established" in order to verify the truthfulness of the caller to formal prayer in saying, "The formal prayer has been established." This is because he uses the past tense of the verb. He builds his formal prayer on the rule of truthfulness. Therefore he wins the reward of: *"Truly the ones who are Godfearing will be in Gardens and rivers, in positions of sincerity near an Omnipotent King,"* (54:54-55), that is, in veils of vast flowing knowledge. Whenever this becomes little, another one comes because the river is always flowing with likes. (616)

24.11.3. The divine Supplication and the Supplication of Phenomenal Being

Know that the beginning of the declaration to perform the formal prayer of the formal prayer is the recitation of "God is Greater" after which everything but the formal prayer is forbidden (*takbir al-ihram*). It is like the marvel of the end at the establishment of the human organism. When the caller to formal prayer says: "The formal prayer has been established" before the *takbir* of the Leader, he has not spoken the truth. It is permitted linguistically while the knowledge of tastes and secrets does not allow that to be permitted in speech. His action is based on the reality and unveiling. A person's spirit is not under his control. If the leader had died and then the caller to formal prayer said: "The formal prayer has been established," while the leader had not recited: "God is Greater," we would know that he died a liar. He would not be helped by the words of the Prophet: "A man is in the formal prayer as long as he is waiting for the formal prayer." We are governed by the principle of the formal prayer which is expected in this place, and he used the definite article. (617)

There is no doubt that the gnostics are in formal prayer and intimate conversation in their movements and stillnesses. However, that which is demanded in this state is the formal prayer which we have bee commanded to establish from the recitation of "God is Greater" after which everything but the formal prayer is forbidden (*takbir al-ihram*) to the *taslim*. What is between these two is the organization of its limbs so that it is an even creation which is seen by the eye of the one who forms it, especially the one who establishes it by his Lord. It issues from the most perfect forms and the ego has no portion in it. This is the divine Prayer, not the prayer of phenomenal being. (618)

Whoever considers that the declaration to perform the formal prayer recited by the caller to formal prayer or himself is the same as establishing the form of the formal prayer recites "God is Greater" (*Allahu akbar, takbir* after which everything but the formal prayer is prohibited, *takbir al-ihram*) after the declaration to perform the formal prayer. The formal prayer is shared in its formation only in respect to the one who performs the declaration to perform the formal prayer for himself, not the caller to the formal prayer. In his opinion, there is no difference in the beginning of the formation of the formal prayer and the declaration to perform the formal prayer unless the one reciting the declaration to perform the formal prayer—and he is the caller to formal prayer—and the leader act by their Lord in advancing to their annihilation to themselves. Then the formation of the formal prayer is a divine Formation and it does not have the strength of one in its form because the nature of each of these two individuals is separate from the other. God only gives a Self-disclosure according to the recipient. (619)

You must know that the servant who establishes his secret in the presence of his Lord in every state is the one who performs the formal prayer at every moment. Then no matter at which of these two moments he recites "God is Greater" —about which the formal scholars disagree— he is correct. The formal prayer has been established. God confirmed the principle of the person who strives in the divine law which obligates us. His words, "Come to formal prayer" in the declaration to perform the formal prayer are addressed to the limbs since they are occupied in actions other than those specific to this state, and it is addressed to the spirit. Rather it is addressed to all, telling it to leave the state it is in for another state, that is, to advance to it. If you are in the formal prayer, you are among those "*those who, they are ones who continue with their formal prayers.*" (70:23) (620)

24.12. The Opening Chapter with the Leader

24.12.1. The Ruling from a Legal Aspect of the Recitation of the Opening Chapter for the Leader [of the Formal Prayer]

Scholars disagree about reciting the Opening Chapter with the leader. Some say that he does say it with him, and some say that he does not say it with him and bows without having uttered it. Some say that he does not recite the Opening Chapter except when he can. Some say that he only recites the Opening Chapter with him, and the one who says this says that the one who recites this chapter with him has invalidated his formal prayer. (621)

24.12.2. The Interpretation of the Opening Chapter with the Leader [of the Formal Prayer]

Someone who speaks of the first thought says that he does not recite with the leader as does the one who speaks of the moment and the one who speaks of guarding the breaths. As for someone who speaks by what comes first at the beginning, he considers this thought and gives it authority and then makes an intention to recite a chapter or some sign when he begins and then becomes speechless, can complete what he intended. He asks the follower to prompt him and he should do so. He recites with him when he does not speak. (622)

When Ubayy was silent with him, the Prophet asked him: "Why did you not recite with me?" because Ubayy knew the Quran. He considered the first intention to recite, so he wanted to complete it. (623)

When the servant is speechless in the formal prayer, it is one of the most direct proofs of the existence of the source of the servant. By the existence of his source, I mean his constancy because that is not one of the attributes of God. If he performs the formal prayer by his Lord, the one who performs the formal prayer must be with God according to the moment. He does not look at the past or the present. He does not begin or recite with, but he bows when his Lord finishes speaking to him. That is what "is easy for him of the Quran." God Almighty says: "*So recite of it as much as is easy.*" (73:20) He has done it. The creature should not have any effect ascribed to him in the formal prayer. This is the position of Ali ibn Abi Talib. Allowing it is the position of Ibn Umar. (624)

24.13. The Place of the Leader (imam) [of the Formal Prayer]

24.13.1. Position of the Religious Scholars about the Place of the Leader (imam) [of the Formal Prayer]

Scholars disagree about the place of the leader. Some say that he is permitted to be higher than the place of those following. Some forbid that. Some recommend that if it is slight. Our position is that whatever of that they follow, it is better to elevate the leader because he is followed. (625)

24.13.2. The Interpretation of the Place of the Leader (imam) [of the Formal Prayer]

Correspondence in matters is better than lack of correspondence. The rank of the leader is higher than the rank of the one who follows, so he must be higher in that rank. He should be in a higher place because he is in the station of being followed. He must have honor above the one following. That is the place of the one following, and this is why he is called "leader." (626)

He has two states and two states. The first two states is that he is both leader and follower at the same time. He follows the weakest of the followers in his formal prayer, so he follows a leader, while the one following the leader follows him in his bowing, prostration, and all his actions, so he is the leader. The last two states are that by which he is called one who is performing the formal prayer. He is with his Lord in this state and he is an leader to others. He has another state. (627)

The one who considers him to be someone who is performing the formal prayer forbids that he be above those who are praying, even if there are many of them. They are leaders for one another, from the leader to the last row. Whoever considers him inasmuch as he is an leader, thinks that it is better for his place to be higher than the one following the leader. He is according to what he witnesses. (628)

24.14. The Leader's Intention (*niyyah*) to Act as the Leader (*imam*) [of the Formal Prayer]

24.14.1. The Ruling from a Legal Perspective on the Intention of the Leader to Act as Leader (imam) [of the Formal Prayer]

Scholars disagree about whether the leader must intend to act as leader or not. Some say that it is obligatory. Some say that it is not obligatory, and that is my position, but it is better if he does make that intention. (629)

24.14.2. The Interpretation from an Inner Perspective of the Leader (imam)

The one who performs the formal prayer must be occupied with his Lord, not with other than his Lord. God has divided the formal prayer between Himself and the one who performs the formal prayer, so he does not have to intend to be leader. The one who looks at the words of God Almighty: "I have divided the formal prayer between Me and My servant in two parts" without looking at the details which come after this statement in the recitation of the Umm al-Quran, includes the principle of consideration of the follower in this statement, that is, the one who performs the formal prayer, no matter whether he is an leader or follower. "The formal prayer is divided in half between Me and My servant, so he intends to turn to Me, intends to turn towards the *qibla,* intends nearness to Me by this act of worship, intends to be leader of those who follow; and the one who follows intends to draw near Me by this act of worship and intends to follow the leader." Everyone who performs the formal prayer is according to what occurs to him and what God makes him see when he speaks intimately with Him. (630)

24.15. The Position of the Follower in Relation to the Leader (*Imam*) [of the Formal Prayer]

24.15.1. The Circumstances and Position of the Follower in Relation to the Leader [of the Formal Prayer]

The one following the leader is either, one, two, or more. It can be one man, two men, a woman, or a child. As for the one following the leader, when it is an adult male, he puts him to his right. If it is a child, he puts him at this right the same as the man. It is also said that he puts him at his left in order to distinguish the principle of the child from the principle of the man. If it is two men, he puts one at his right and one at his left. If he likes, he can have them stand behind him. (631)

If it is a man and a boy, it follows the same rule as two men. If it is a woman, she stands behind the leader when she is by herself. If there is one man with her, the man stands at the right of the leader and the woman is behind him. If there is more than one person with the woman, the men stand behind the leader and the woman or women stand behind the men. (632)

24.15.2. The Inner Position of the Follower in Relation to the Leader (Imam) [of the Formal Prayer]

It is related in a Tradition that it is recommended to take on the qualities of God. The Prophet said: "It is not for God to forbid you usury and then take it from you." There is no quality with which God has described Himself but that we are recommended to be described by it. This is the meaning of taking on qualities, imitation, and following the leader. This is the leadership itself. In reality, the Leader is God Almighty and those following the Leader are the creatures. (633)

The leader must do one of a certain number of things. He can see himself as one in respect of his unity, what is particular to him, and what distinguishes him from everyone else with God. He can see himself with God in respect to his evenness. He can see himself with God in respect to his uniqueness and then he is three—that is, the third of two. He can see himself as not perfect while others are perfect. He can see himself with God inasmuch as he inclines to his nature—and the child is the one who yearns when he inclines. He can see himself with God inasmuch as he inclines to his nature and not his intellect, and then he is in the position of the woman. He must have his intellect present with his nature. (634)

God Almighty is the Leader in all these states. The right has strength, and both of His Hands are right by nearness and the dropping of strength and force. Being behind belongs to obedience and following. (635)

See then which of the states which we have mentioned you have to in your formal prayer, you who perform the formal prayer! Stand in the station which we have made clear in relation to the leader, then you will have performed the formal prayer. Your true witnessing and leader should be according to how the Prophet described it, not according to any proof of the intellect of that you will have judgment in your intellect, creed and action. If you do not do this, then your worship will be deficient according to how much your intellect introduces into it from your reflection and speculation. (636)

24.16. Someone Who Performs the Formal Prayer Alone Behind the Row [of Those Performing the Formal Prayer]

24.16.1. Making the Rows Straight from a Legal Perspective

Scholars agree that it is desirable to be in the first row. Also it is desirable to keep the line straight and stand close together. There is one rare opinion which says that if you are able to perform the formal prayer in the first row and you do not do so, your formal prayer is then invalid. It is the same with straightening the rows and standing close together. If that is not done, then the person with that view thinks that the formal prayer is invalid. It is also true that some people consider it to be recommended while others consider it to be obligatory, as is the case with the person we mentioned whose position is that the formal prayer is invalid without this attribute. That which I say is that the formal prayer is valid, but that they are rebels. (637)

As for the first row, it is related in sound Tradition that the Messenger of God mentioned racing to it. Then he said about it, "If they can only draw lots for them, then let them draw lots." As for straightening the rows, they called to the same state with God—that is the formal prayer. Therefore they are all equal in this call to the servants. When they turn to that to which they are called, their row should be straight because the One who summoned the group only summoned them in order to consign with them inasmuch as they are an equal group. He did not specify anyone of them more than another. Therefore they must be equal and straight in the row. No one should go ahead or behind of the row with anything which might lead to crookedness. They consign in this way. (638)

24.16.2. The Leader (imam) Is Meant to Represent the Group

The inward form and spiritual strength of those who perform the formal prayer must be straight in respect to their relationship in turning to God Almighty and sincerity to Him in this worship in which He has called them inasmuch as they perform the formal prayer. When God chooses one of them, He calls him the leader, and he speaks to Him for the group by what He wishes to give to the group. He makes him like the one who translates between Him and them. He advances to his Lord, so the group must be still, silent, and wait for what will come to them from their master by means of that leader. This is why it says in the Tradition reported by Jabir that the recitation of the leader is enough for the group. The leader is the one whom God put ahead in order to speak with him. Since the leader is appointed the representative for the group and the divine law has commanded that they follow him in all that he does which is prescribed for him to do, they are obliged to be silent and follow all that the leader does in his formal prayer. (639)

24.16.3. Pressing Together in the Row

As for pressing together in the row, it is so that there should not be any gaps between a man and the one who is next to him, from the first row to the last. The reason for that is that Satan fill in that gap. Those who perform the formal prayer are in the position of nearness to God Almighty, so they must be close to one another so that no gaps remain between them which would lead to each one being far from his companion. The behavior between them in respect to the gaps is contrary to the attribute of nearness to which they are summoned. Those who are distant from God come into those gaps and openings because of the distance which is between two men in the row in the formal prayer. They lessen the mercy of nearness which the one who performs the formal prayer in the row has according to the gap and by the rank of that Satan in distance from God. When the shoulders press together the gaps are stopped and the attribute of distance from God has no place because Satan is the one who is the place of distance from God. (640)

The Satan rejoice when there are gaps in the row and go into them because they see that it contains mercy which God gives to those who perform the formal prayer. They crowd into those gaps in order to obtain some of the mercy by being near to the source of favor. They recognize that they are far from God. These are not the Satan who whisper in the formal prayer. Their place is in the hearts, so they are at the gates of the hearts with the angels. They cast at the ego and put things into the heart to distract it from that to which it was called. One of the things which it casts at it is not to fill the gap between him and his companion for two reasons. (641)

One reason is so that the person performing the formal prayer will be described by opposition which would lead to distance from God. The reason Satan is distant from God is because he opposed God's command. The second reason is for Satan's companions to be able to go into those gaps and get some of the mercy of those who perform th formal prayer. The leader speaks with his Lord and He speaks with him. This is why the plural is used in the conversation of the formal prayer. The leader does not specify himself in the supplication rather than them, He is the tongue of the group. (642)

The one who is unveiled sees all of this and takes from God what He gives him by means of this leader in what God gives him. It is the same whether or not that leader is properly present with God in that to which he is called or not. Everyone who is like this receives it from God, so the leader is fortunate when the follower is like this. As for the one who is not unveiled or present in the formal prayer with his heart are concerned, when someone who is like this is together with the leader in their lack of presence, then the leader is one the leaders of those who are misguided. If he is fortunate, it is by the one behind him. If only the leader is present while the hearts of the group in that formal prayer are not present, then the leader intercedes for the entire group in that formal prayer. He is the intended source of the group and so the goal is obtained. (643)

24.16.4. One Must Choose the People of the Religion (din) and Goodness as Leaders (imam) [of the Formal Prayer]

This is why one must choose the people of the religion and goodness and those who are occupied with God for the leadership, even if they have only a little knowledge. They are more entitled to the leadership than the heedless people of knowledge, because that which is desired of the one who performs the formal prayer is presence with God. The one who performs the formal prayer has no need of knowledge inasmuch as he performs the formal prayer. He recognizes that he is in the presence of his Lord and speaks to Him by what God makes easy of His Quran, and no more than that. He should not be concerned about what is lacking of his knowledge during the formal prayer. If the one who is performing the formal prayer calls to mind contracts and questions of marriage and divorce while he is engaged in intimate conversation, then there is absolutely no difference between him and the one who is heedless of his formal prayer. He should be with God inasmuch as he is in His presence in a particular act of worship to which he has been summoned. That forbids him inwardly what it forbids him outwardly. (644)

As he must not turn his face away from the direction of formal prayer, so he must not look with his heart at anything except the One to whom he is speaking. That is God. As his tongue can only be occupied with the words of his Lord or His remembrance of God which He has prescribed for him and none of people's words are valid in it, so inwardly he is forbidden the conversation of the ego with the one he was buying and selling with, or conversing with his family, children, brothers or the ruler inwardly during the formal prayer. (645)

For this reason, it is not a precondition that the leader have a lot of knowledge. What is desired is that which is fitting for this state. If it happens that that one who has this state of the religion, fearful, watchful and modesty before God, is a firm master with a lot of knowledge, then he is more entitled to go ahead He is better than the one who does not have that. (646)

24.16.5. The Legal Wisdom of Rows in the Formal Prayer

Rows are commanded in the formal prayer in order to remind man that he will stand before God in rows on the Day of Rising in that most terrible place. The intercessors among the Prophets, believers and angels will be in the position of the leaders in the formal prayer. They will be in front of the rows. How many a person there is who in this world is one who follows the leader among the people of the rows, while tomorrow he will be an leader of the rows! Many who are leaders in this world and people pray behind them now tomorrow will be followers. What sighing and grief then! (647)

Their rows in the formal prayer are like the rows of the angels with God. God Almighty says: "*And the angels, ranged in row*" (89:22), and He says: "*And the angels will stand up ranged in rows, they will not assert themselves but he whom the Merciful gave permission.*" (78:38) The leader is the representative of the group. (648)

God commanded us to form rows in the formal prayer as the angels form rows and keep close together in their rows. The angels do not keep close together because of the fear that if there were gaps in the row, the gaps would be penetrated by Satan. These are the angels of heaven, and heaven is not the place or location of Satan. They press close together by the harmony of lights. When they are connected to one another, they come down as a continuous light to the rows of those who perform the formal prayer. Those lights encompass them. If there were gaps in the rows of those who perform the formal prayer which Satan entered, those lights would burn them up. They are like that in al-Kathib (Slipping Heap) in the general visit. They are in rows as they are in rows in the formal prayer. (649)

Whoever leaves gaps in his row and can close it himself and does not do so, is deprived of its blessing there in that place. If he cannot close it, the blessing covers him there. If you perform the formal prayer between two men, then you go close to one man and pull the other one towards you. If he is pulled towards you, that is done. If not, there is no wrong action in that. The one you go close to is the one who is nearest the leader. If there is a gap in the first row and he is able to reach it, he must. If he does not go to the first row in order to complete it, that is, fill in the gap in it, it does not help him at all to press together in the row where he is. The first row is what is specifically incumbent on him, so know that! (650)

24.17. The One Who Performs the Formal Prayer Alone Behind the Row

24.17.1. The Ruling from a Legal Perspective of the One Who Performs the Formal Prayer Behind the Row

People disagree about people who perform the formal prayer behind the row. Some people say that his formal prayer is valid. Some say that it is not valid. That which I believe about the one who does this is that either he can find a way to enter the row or he cannot do so. If he cannot do so, he indicates to one of the people in the row to come back to him. If he does not come back to him because he is ignorant of the reward he would have with God for that, then this man's formal prayer is valid. He has feared God and done as much as possible, and he cannot do more than this in this situation. If he is able to do anything we have mentioned and does not do it, his formal prayer is invalid. The Prophet ordered the one who performed the formal prayer alone behind the row to repeat his formal prayer. This is the Tradition of Wabisa ibn Mabad. (651)

24.17.2. The Inner Interpretation of That

Acts which bring one near to God are only known from God. The intellect does not have any authority in them by any aspect whatsoever. When the Prophet prescribed acts of nearness, they are done according to his prescription. That which he forbade as an act of nearness cannot be made an act of nearness by the intellect. (652)

Now to return to our subject—the one who performs the formal prayer behind the row alone while he can do what we have mentioned is either one of the people of who strive to understand the divine law (and his principle is to permit that action) and his formal prayer is sound by his legal judgment, or he is not one of the people of this kind of reasoning. If it comes from strenuous endeavor, then the formal prayer is valid. If it is not from that, and he imitates the jurisprudent after questioning him, then the formal prayer is valid. If he does it without strenuous endeavor or questioning, his formal prayer is invalid. If is like that with all of the acts of nearness which are prescribed. (653)

As the formal prayer of the leader is valid in front of the group outside of any row, so the formal prayer of the one who performs the formal prayer behind the row alone is valid. The subtlety of the human being has one source. It does not line up with the limbs in the formal prayer and it must not be their leader. It does not accept direction, so it only performs the formal prayer alone. Our outward is a group, so he is one row in himself alone. Every part of him is responsible for worship and none are separate from others. He is a row alone. If some of his limbs are engaged in what is not part of the formal prayer, that occupation in respect to his essence is like gaps in the row.

In the interpretation, a person performs the formal prayer in a row in respect of his whole. In respect to his subtlety, he is alone. It does not go to the rows because it has no bias, and this is the school of the one who says that it has no inclination. As for the one who says that it has inclination, it is connected to the whole of the essence of the one who is performing the formal prayer. This is why the one who permits the formal prayer alone behind the row permits it. We have made our school clear in that in a manner which is supported by the roots of the divine law. (654)

24.18. Does a man or legally responsible person who wants to perform the formal prayer and hears the declaration to perform the formal prayer (iqama) and who hurries to go to the mosque fearing to miss part of the formal prayer, miss a part of the formal prayer or not?

24.18.1. The Ruling from a Legal Perspective on Hastening to the Mosque

Some say that it is not permitted to hurry. One should come with gravity and tranquillity, and that is my position. Some say that it is permitted to hurry out of eagerness for good, but I dislike that. (656)

24.18.2. The Interpretation of Hastening to the Mosque from an Inner Perspective

Hastening to good actions is prescribed. Tranquillity and gravity is also prescribed. In order to combine them, you should hasten to make normal preparations before the time comes, and then you can come to it with tranquillity and gravity. Then you combine haste and tranquillity. (657)

The servant is ordered to hasten to good deeds when he is involved in permitted actions. The one whose state is that he is not involved in the permitted, is in something better still. That is why there has come that which indicates both states together. It is said: "*And compete with one another for forgiveness from your Lord."* (3:133) That is worship. Whoever hastens to it, has hastened to forgiveness. In another state, He said: *"Those who compete with one another in good works."* (23:61) He made it better to hasten to them. They represent him. (658)

There is another aspect. That is that forgiveness is only valid after the necessary good action is performed. Therefore, we hasten to forgiveness in good deeds. The one who hastens in them is the one who hastens to them. (659)

When someone is involved in something other than the permitted, he must either be in the recommended or the obligatory. If he is in the recommended and aware that it is the moment of the obligatory, he hurries to it in the recommended so that he will take care of the causes which make that obligatory thing valid. The meaning of haste here is to set out to the actions which are a precondition for the validity of that obligatory action. (660)

When someone who thinks that the group is obligatory and holds that it is obligatory to complete the row while he is doing an action, hears the declaration to perform the formal prayer while he is coming to the formal prayer, the Prophet ordered him to come to it with gravity and tranquillity. The reason for that is that God is not limited by states. The one who comes to the formal prayer is in the formal prayer as long as he is coming to it or waiting for it. Then the prescribed haste is obtained. (661)

As for haste in movement, it entails bad practices and limiting God. For this reason, the Messenger of God said to the one who crept up while he was bowing until he reached the row (and this was Abu Bakr), "May God increase you in eagerness! But do not do it again," that is, in hurrying movement. He did not say, "May God increase you in haste." Eagerness obliges haste, therefore the Messenger of God informed him that eagerness for good is what is desired. It is the haste which God seeks from His servant, not the movement of the feet. That would announce the limitation of God. God is with the servant wherever he is. You were neglectful at first by delaying it. Then you must make haste in preparation as it is related about one of them, that the time of formal prayer never came over a period of forty years but that he was in the mosque. It is related about someone else that he remained like that for a year. He never missed the recitation of "God is Greater" after which everything but the formal prayer is forbidden (*takbir al-ihram*) with the leader. (662)

He said: "with gravity." This indicates that the servant must behave with God according to what He deserves of majesty, awe, and modesty. These states produce weight in the limbs and establish balance in his movement with God. It happens as God has commanded—with humility and fear. This is the tranquillity which is sought. He said: "Had his heart possessed fear, his limbs would have had fear," that is, that would have flowed in their limbs. Haste with the limbs only comes from the one whose spiritual strength is connected to the direction to which he hastens for the sake of God. It is not connected to God. (663)

The servant must connect his spiritual strength to God so that God The Real will testify for him. When you are like this, your state is awe and stillness. "Only a whispering is heard." God Almighty says: *"Voices will be hushed for The Merciful so thou shalt hear nothing but a murmuring."* (20:108) This is with the name "Merciful" so how is it with the one who does not recognize what name he is going to and walking by? (664)

Whoever has this state at the moment when he is walking and making for something is permitted to hurry. As for the one who witnesses the One who is his goal, he says that it is not permitted. That would entail narrowing the moment. The lawmaker takes not of the one who arrives at the moment. The moment of the one who goes to the formal prayer is when he witnesses his goal. Therefore he must have tranquillity and gravity when he comes, rather than rapid steps. This is out of respect for the sanctity of the moment and in order to give it its due. (665)

24.19. When should one following the leader (*imam*) [of the Formal Prayer] stand up for the Formal Prayer when he is in the mosque waiting for the formal prayer?

24.19.1. The Moment When the One Following the Leader [of the Formal Prayer] from a Legal Perspective

Some say that is at the beginning of the declaration to perform the formal prayer. Some say that it is when he says: "Come to formal prayer." Some say that it is when he says: "Some to success." Some say that it is when he sees the leader, and I consider that to be the best. Some say that there is no special time in that. It is related from the Messenger of God, "Do not stand up until you see me." If this Tradition is sound, then we must act accordingly and not turn away from it. (666)

Our position is that if this Tradition is not sound, then he hurries at the beginning of the declaration to perform the formal prayer. Then our position is that if this Tradition is sound—and I consider it to be sound—then the judgment of the Prophet in this matter is to wait. So we do not stand up until we meet him, as he ordered. It is not like our present state. In the time when the Prophet was alive, it was possible for the command to be abrogated and another judgment brought in its place. Therefore, they would not stand for the words of the caller to formal prayer until they saw the Prophet coming out for the formal prayer. Then they would know that nothing had happened to remove the principle of that to which they were summoned. This is different from the situation today. The principle of standing for the formal prayer remains. Therefore, when he hears the caller to formal prayer giving the declaration to perform the formal prayer, he stands up quickly. If the caller to formal prayer errs when he hears something and imagines it to be the leader and gives the declaration to perform the formal prayer when the leader has not yet come out, there is no blame against the one who does that. He has the reward of hastening to good. He returns to his place until the leader comes out. It is certain that the principle of the formal prayer continues. (667)

24.19.2. The One Who Calls the Declaration to Perform the Formal Prayer (iqama) Is the Doorkeeper of God Who Summons People to Come to Him

The interpretation is that the one who performs the declaration for the formal prayer is the doorkeeper of God who calls the creation to come to God with this state and quality to which it is summoned. They are ordered to come to Him in it, so they hurry to establish it with good practices and calmness as we have mentioned, being present in that to which they advance, and calling to mind that to which they are summoned of recitation, remembrance of God, recitation of "God is Greater," glorification and specific supplication which they do not exceed in this state. When they finish it by the greetings at the end of the formal prayer, they make whatever supplication they like. However, it should be part of what is pleasing to God. They should not curse a Muslim nor cut off relatives. (668)

24.20. Someone Who Recites "God is Greater" (*takbir al-ihram*) Behind the Row Fearing that He Will Miss the Bending Forward(*ruku*) [of the Formal Prayer] with the Leader and Then Creeps Up to the Row While He Is Bowing Forward

Some people dislike someone who recites "God is Greater" behind the row fearing that he will miss the bowing of the formal prayer with the leader and then creeps up to the row while he is bowing. Some people permit it. Some people distinguish between the one performing the formal prayer alone and the group in that, and dislike it for the one who performs the formal prayer alone and permit it for the group. (669)

24.20.1. Part of Performing the Formal Prayer in Full Is That You Can Work to Obtain It

Bowing is to show humility to God Almighty. It is better to hurry to it than walk to it bowing until he enters the row. That is considered either disliked or permitted. Whoever thinks that it is permitted, walks until he enters the row. The Prophet did not invalidate the formal prayer of Abu Bakr for doing that. He made supplication for him and forbade him to do it again. He knew that the prohibition is dislike. (670)

If they said that it is a specific case, we say that his prohibition against repeating it is a specific case because he was told not to repeat it and he did not forbid anyone else from doing that. However, because of the circumstances, we know that he meant anyone who performs the formal prayer according to what he commanded. All that is part of the completion of the formal prayer which you can work to obtain in the formal prayer. Many questions are connected to this rule. (671)

24.21. That in Which the Follower Follows the Leader (imam) [of the Formal Prayer]

24.21.1. The Ruling of the Follower Following the Leader (imam) in the Formal Prayer

There is no disagreement among scholars about the obligation of following him in that which the Prophet commanded him to do in words and actions. They disagree about saying, "God hears whoever praises Him." Some say that it is not obligatory for him to say it with the leader. Some permit him to say it. I think that the first is better by the Tradition which has come. (672)

24.21.2. The Interpretation on Following the Leader (imam) in the Formal Prayer

Since the leader is a representative of God in respect of the one who follows him, he can validly say, "God hears whoever praises Him." He translates from God to those who follow and informs them that God has said that when they praised Him in their recitation and glorification in bowing. He informs from the one who delegated him. If God had established the leader in his station, he would have said: "I hear the one who praises Me." He confirms the source of the servant when he says: "God hears whoever praises Him." (673)

Know that he only worships Him inasmuch as is God, not inasmuch as He is Essence. This is different from the words of Rabia-l-Adawiyya. If it is said: then what do you do with the like of His words: *"Surely God has heard the saying of she who disputes with thee about her spouse.*" (58:1) That is what God said to His the Messenger. He did not say, "I heard," meaning what we mentioned and what you know. Perhaps His Words, "God hears whoever praises Him" is like that, especially when the Prophet says: "God says on the tongue of His servant, 'God hears whoever praises Him.'" (674)

We say that this sign is from Gabriel, the Trusty Spirit, about the command of God to say the like of this, that is, Jibril, tell him, "God has heard" as was said to Muhammad, "*Say: I am only a mortal like you.*" (41:6) He is a man and God is not a man. It is like that with all of the Words of God which are of this sort. If I ascribed it, then it must be to God. Then the word belongs to God by a special rank informing about another special rank. If you like, you can interpret it as the essence, and if you like, you can interpret it by a divine name. (675)

Inasmuch as He is Speaking, God says: "Muhammad, God has heard." By God, here He means the name, The Hearing or The Knowing according to the school of the one who thinks that hearing is knowledge. The first person thinks that hearing is another reality. He does not call it that or other than that. This is what the first one says who thinks that His hearing is His essence. It is like that with all these attributes which are ascribed to Him. (676)

The follower says: "God hears whoever praises Him" with this entire commentary. If that has come down regarding the leader, there has not come down any prohibition in respect to the follower or the one praying alone, especially since man is the leader of the group of his essence. There is no part of him but that it praises God. His tongue tells all of his essence that: "God hears whoever praises Him." This is especially true in the case of the one who has been unveiled to the glorification of His praise by everything. (677)

24.21.3. *Another Section on Following the Leader (imam) [of the Formal Prayer] Where The Leader (imam) [of the Formal Prayer] Is Appointed to Lead*

Following the leader is only valid for the follower when he knows what he follows of the leader's actions, outwardly and inwardly. Most people only know the outward movements of the leader—standing, bowing, rising, prostration, sitting, recitation of "God is Greater" and *taslim*. The intention is hidden. It is one of the actions of the heart which the follower does not see. God has not obliged him to follow him in what he does not know in him. (678)

For this reason, the Prophet said: "The leader is appointed only to be followed. When he recites "God is Greater," then recite it, and do not recite "God is Greater" until the leader has said it. Bow when he bows, and do not bow until he has bowed. When he says: 'God hears whoever praises Him,' then say: 'O God, our Lord, praise is Thine.' When he prostrates, then prostrate, and do not prostrate until he prostrates." He did not deal with the intention nor that which is hidden from the knowledge of the one who is following. He mentioned the outward motions which the senses perceive. It is established that one formal prayer cannot be performed twice in the same day. When someone performs the formal prayer alone and then catches the group and performs the formal prayer with it, one of his formal prayers is supererogatory. Therefore, the leader has a different intention. (679)

By this Tradition, the follower can say: "God hears whoever praises Him," and then say, "Our Lord, praise is Thine" for following the leader. It is established that the Prophet said while he was an leader in the formal prayer: "God hears whoever praises Him. Our Lord, praise is Thine." (680)

24.22. Following the Formal Prayer of Someone Sitting

24.22.1. The Ruling from a Legal Perspective of Someone Sitting Acting as Leader (Imam) [of the Formal Prayer]

Scholars in the legal schools and others agree that the healthy person cannot perform the formal prayer sitting if he is alone or the leader. They disagree about when a follower is healthy and performs the formal prayer behind an leader who is ill who performs the formal prayer sitting. There are three positions regarding that. Some say that he performs the formal prayer sitting behind him, and this is my position. Some say that he is not permitted to be leader if he performs the formal prayer sitting, and if they perform the formal prayer behind him standing or sitting, both his formal prayer and their formal prayer is invalid. (681)

Some of the transmitters of Malik mentioned that Malik said: "No one acts as leader for the people while sitting. If he leads them sitting, then both his formal prayer and their formal prayer is invalid." The Prophet said: "No one after me will lead the formal prayer sitting." This is a very weak Tradition because it comes from ibn Yazid al-Jufi who is not a competent source. In spite of its weakness, the Tradition is transmitted, but the sound established position is that the leader can be sitting. (682)

24.22.2. The Interpretation on the Leadership of the One Sitting from an Inner Perspective

In reality, the leader is the one who holds the forelocks of creation in His hand. The one who performs the formal prayer must either see the leader as a representative of God as He made him or as a follower like himself. If he sees him as a leader, he must follow him in any state that he has. If he sees him as a follower like himself whom God has made his leader and performs the formal prayer sitting by the command of the Prophet to do that, then this is the leader according to the divine law. Whoever puts God in His direction of formal prayer and turns to Him, then without a doubt the leader is hidden from him. (683)

The state of the leader who is ill differs from the state of the follower. When the follower is ill, he performs the formal prayer behind the one who is standing with an excuse. The interpretation of the leader and the follower has already been dealt with. The leader is commanded to follow the formal prayer of the sick person in order to make it light for him and not to be hard on him. Then each of them is commanded to follow him and not to be hard on him. Then each of them is commanded to follow the other. The Prophet specified what we should not turn away from, and he specified that for the one who waits to follow the *Sunna* and stop with the judgment of God and His Messenger. (684)

Since in reality, the Leader is God who is not heedless of the states of His servant in his movements and stillnesses and not distracted from His watching by anything (as He says of Himself: *"And God has been One Who Watches Over everything"* (33:52)), the one who follows, who is the servant, must follow Him in fearful watchfulness and presence. He must not neglect his Master in his formal prayer nor let anything distract him from fearful watchfulness in his formal prayer so that he can properly follow Him in this attribute of watchfulness and the absence of heedlessness. Know that! (685)

24.23. The Time When the Follower Recites "God is Greater"

24.23.1. The Position of the Religious Scholars About the Time When the Follower Recites "God is Greater"

Some say that it is preferred that when the follower recites "God is Greater" (making everything but the formal prayer forbidden) after the leader has finished the recitation of "God is Greater" after which everything but the formal prayer is forbidden, but if he recites this with him, that is permitted. Some say that he is not permitted to say the recitation of "God is Greater" after which everything but the formal prayer is forbidden with him. I take the first position—he recites the recitation of "God is Greater" after which everything but the formal prayer is forbidden after him and nothing else is accepted. Some say that he is not permitted to recite the recitation of "God is Greater" after which everything but the formal prayer is forbidden before the leader. Some say that if he recites the recitation of "God is Greater" after which everything but the formal prayer is forbidden before the leader, it is permitted. Some say that if he recites the recitation of "God is Greater" after which everything but the formal prayer is forbidden with the leader and finishes when the leader finishes, it is permitted, but if he finishes the recitation of "God is Greater" after which everything but the formal prayer is forbidden before the leader finishes, his recitation is not allowed. (686)

If he is considered inasmuch as he is someone who is performing the formal prayer, it is permitted for the recitation of "God is Greater" after which everything but the formal prayer is forbidden to be before the leader, with him, and after him. If he is considered as one who is performing the formal prayer and following the leader, he is not permitted to say that the recitation of "God is Greater" after which everything but the formal prayer is forbidden before the leader. The Prophet said: "Do not recite the recitation of "God is Greater" after which everything but the formal prayer is forbidden until he recites the recitation of "God is Greater" after which everything but the formal prayer is forbidden." He forbade it. If he knows that his prohibition is dislike, he allows it before the leader and with him. If he knows that his prohibition makes it unlawful, he does not allow it. [a]687)

24.23.2. *The Interpretation of the Recitation of "God is Greater" of the Follower from an Inner Perspective*

It is related in a Tradition that when the servant [of God] says: "God is Greater" in any state, God says: "I am Greater." The servant says: "There is no god but Thee,' and God says: "There is no god but Me." The servant says: "There is no god but He. He has the Kingdom and the praise." He confirms the truthfulness of the servant. His name al-Mumin (The Believer) and others come from this. (688)

If God does not say any of that until the servant speaks, the servant is more entitled to follow. The follower cannot precede his leader in any of the words or actions of the formal prayer, even in the recitation of the Opening Chapter. He should not start it when it is said aloud until he finishes it or else he follows in the silences of the leader. He recites what the leader has finished in the silence of the leader. In the silent formal prayer, he recites it according to what he thinks except in the formal prayer after the middle sitting. Then he recites it first. (689)

Some people say that the one who raises his head before the leader has acted badly, and goes back and his formal prayer is still valid. Some people say that his formal prayer is invalid. (690)

24.24.2. *The Interpretation on Raising the Head Before the Leader (Imam) [of the Formal Prayer] from an Inner Perspective*

The Leader is God and Self-subsistence is His attribute. The follower is not permitted to raise his head before his leader. If he does so, his formal prayer is invalid since he is in a state in which he cannot be a proper follower of his like or God. God's self-subsistence in rising from bowing precedes his self-subsistence since all that the servant is established in comes from an divine Attribute whose shadow is what is manifested in the servant. The shadow follows without a doubt. The servant is the shadow as the Sultan is called the Shadow of God on the earth. (691)

This is related in respect to rising because seeking height, rather His height—glory be to Him!—is by merit. That which the follower must do is to follow the leader in every lowering and rising. As for the lowering, the ego may seek it by the false imagination which occurs to the ignorant man. (692)

You must know that God has described Himself with descent and so the descent of God comes before the follower descends and drops to prostration. He does not drop to prostration until his leader precedes him. If he does not find God in his prostration, then to whom is this servant performing the formal prayer descending? When he falls by that action, he only falls to the God who has described Himself as descending from His height to His servant. (693)

The servant says: "O Lord! This is my attribute and I am more entitled to it. Then the necessary call raised me from the station of descent since Thou hast said that Thou hast created me in the form. My self disdains the one who descends the one who descends from the rank which Thou hast given me." The one who sees this and drinks it, follows the leader in all his states and rules. (694)

24.25. What the Leader (imam) [of the Formal Prayer] Takes Upon Himself on Behalf of the Follower

24.25.1. The Ruling from a Legal Perspective of the Recitation of Someone Following a Leader (imam) [of the Formal Prayer]

Our scholars agree that the leader does not take any of the obligations of the formal prayer upon himself from the follower except for the recitation. They disagree regarding that. Some say that the follower recites with the leader in what is silent and does not recite with him in what is aloud. Some say that he does not recite with him at all. Some say that he recites the the Opening Chapter and other parts of the Quran in what is silent and he only recites the Opening Chapter in what is aloud, and that is my position. (695)

Some differentiate between the one who hears the recitation of the leader in the recitation when it is aloud and the one who does not hear him. The follower must recite it if he does not hear him and he forbids that he do so if he can hear him. I believe that it is obligatory for everyone who performs the formal prayer, leader or otherwise, to recite the Opening Chapter. It is best to recite it to himself unless he hears the leader. This is an obligation by the command of God when He says: *"When the Quran is recited, then listen and be silent"* (7:204). He did not specify the one state more than another. (696)

Listening to the Quran is definite and certain according to everyone. If the follower who does not hear does not recite anything except the Opening Chapter, his formal prayer is accepted. The Opening Chapter of the Quran is obligatory for everyone who performs the formal prayer. God divided the formal prayer between Him and His servant and He only mentioned the Opening Chapter. If he does not recite it, he has not performed the obligatory formal prayer which God has divided between Him and His servant. The follower follows the recitation of the Opening Chapter in the silences of the leader, and therefore he combines the sign and the Tradition. If the leader is not silent (and that is disliked for him to do so), the follower should recite it in himself, sign by sign, when he cannot hear the leader, until he finishes. He does not recite it aloud with the leader. (697)

24.25.2. The Interpretation of What the Leader (imam) [of the Formal Prayer] Take upon Himself for the Follower from an Inner Perspective

Since the formal prayer contains pillars, which are the individual obligations, no one can compensate for anyone else in anything. Anything that is not obligatory and rectified by the prostration of forgetfulness, the leader can take upon himself for the follower. This means that when the follower decreases or adds, he does not prostrate on account of his forgetfulness. That is because the obligations are the rights of God, and the right of God should be dealt with first. As for what is other than the obligations, even if they are due inasmuch as they are commanded (and they are of two sorts), there is nothing held against him if he does not do them. (699 sic)

Some of them has a substitute, which is the prostration of forgetfulness. These are actions with which the divine law is concerned inasmuch as there are blessings in them near to the blessings of the obligations. For this reason, God made a substitute for them. Some of them are the rights of the servant which are desirable. If he likes, he can do them, and if he likes, he can omit them, and they have no substitute. If he does them, he receives a reward for them. If he does not do them, there is no harm and he does not obtain that reward which the one who does them obtains—like raising the hands in every lowering and rising deliberately. If he means in himself to lift them or his school is one whose proof demands that and he forgets to do that, then he prostrates for his forgetfulness, not for the raising of the hands. The prostration was only prescribed by God for forgetfulness, not for the thing forgotten. The proof of this is that had he left it out deliberately or by strenuous endeavor, he does not prostrate for that. (700)

This is different from that which has a substitute. It is not obligatory. The formal prayer is invalidated by its deliberate omission or intentionally doing what he is not commanded to do. (701)

They distinguish between the middle sitting, the sitting for rest, the sitting between the two prostrations of every bowing forward, and the final sitting. The ruling in all that varies. Its interpretation is in the Mist, the Throne, the lowest heaven, and the earth, with every sitting that the one who performs the formal prayer performs. The Mist belongs to sitting between the two prostrations. The Throne belongs to the last sitting. The heaven belongs to the middle sitting. As for the sitting on the earth in my assemblies, it belongs to the sitting for rest. (702)

If he has intentionally sat down for rest, then he has intentionally done what was prescribed for him to do and his formal prayer is not invalid. If he sits in the odd number prayer when he means to stand up out of forgetfulness, he prostrates because of his forgetfulness, not because of his sitting. He then has the reward for sitting and the reward for what he forgot by the prostration of forgetfulness which is to spite Satan. He has the reward of the on who damages the enemy of God and his enemy. God says: "*Nor tread they any treading on any ground —enraging the ones who are ungrateful— nor glean any gleaning of ground against the enemy but as an act in accord with morality written down for them.*" (9:120) Satan is one of those who reject. God says about him: "*He refused and grew arrogant.*" (2:34) That which concerns all of that about forgetfulness will come in this chapter if God Almighty wills. (703)

24.26. The Connection of the Formal Prayer of the Follower to the Leader [of the Formal Prayer] in Respect of its Soundness and Validity

24.26.1. The Connection of the Formal Prayer of the Follower to His Leader (imam) [of the Formal Prayer] from a Legal Perspective

Scholars disagree about whether the validity of the follower's formal prayer is connected to the validity of the formal prayer of the leader or not. I say that it is. Some people think that it is connected to it and some people do not think that it is connected. This is why they disagree about when the leader performs the formal prayer in a state of sexual impurity and they learn about that after the formal prayer. The one who thinks that there is a connection says that their formal prayer is invalid. The one who does not think that it is connected says that their formal prayer is valid. That is what I believe. Some people differentiate between when the leader knows that he is in the state of sexual impurity and when he forgets. They say that if he knows that, their formal prayer is invalid. If he has forgotten that, their formal prayer is not invalid. (704)

24.26.2. The Interpretation of the Connection of the Follower's Supplication to that of the Leader (imam) [of the Formal Prayer]

"God places not a burden on a soul beyond its capacity." (2:286) It is not in man's capacity to know is in the self of someone else or to have knowledge of the states of someone else. Everyone who performs the formal prayer acts according to his state with God. For this reason, the divine law only commands us to follow the leader in the rising and lowering which we see in the leader. If someone has the state of the leader unveiled to him, he acts according to his unveiling. If he knows that the leader is not in a state of purity, he cannot follow him from the moment that he knows that. What he has already performed of his formal prayer before he knew that is valid. There is no interpretation about whether the leader does that intentionally or forgetfully. From the moment when the leader has knowledge of that, he is no longer in the formal prayer, and God has only commanded the connection, that is, following, for the one performing the formal prayer. If the leader forgets that he is in ritual impurity, then he is performing the formal prayer and the formal prayer of the follower is valid in the divine law. (705)

If the follower knows that the leader is not in a state of purity and the follower can inform him about the ritual impurity in the formal prayer, he does so, and thus the formal prayer of the follower is not invalidated by that. God says: *"Render not your actions untrue."* (47:33) If he cannot do so, he performs the formal prayer for himself. When he has finished his formal prayer, he informs him about his ritual impurity rather or not the leader has finished. If the leader remembers or appoints him, it is pure. If he does not remember or appoint him, he is according to what his knowledge demands and whatever his school is regarding that. The formal prayer of the follower is valid (706).

25 On the Mysteries of the Friday Congregational Formal Prayer: Introduction

25.1. The Disagreement About Its Obligation

Scholars disagree about the obligatory nature of the Friday congregational formal prayer. Some say that it is an individual obligation. Some say that it is a general obligation. Some say that it is *sunna*. (1)

25.2. The Interpretation of the Self in the Friday Formal Congregational Prayer

This formal prayer does not have anything to do with the Unity of the essence and it has no effect in the man of action who knows it. However, it has the knowledge of the unity of multiplicity. It is like that with the one who thinks that the essence itself demands the existence of the world. This knowledge does not result from what comes from God to the heart of the servant or in His Self-disclosure in this formal prayer. That is because in its existence and reality, it is built on something more than one. It comes from the presence of the divine names. It cannot occur from one person as opposed to all the other formal prayers. They are valid when done by one person. (2)

Every formal prayer except the Friday congregational formal prayer gives what the Friday congregational formal prayer gives inasmuch as it is a formal prayer, from the recitation of "God is Greater" after which everything but the formal prayer is forbidden to the *taslim*, and they accord what the Friday congregational formal prayer does not of the Unity of God which is absolutely rich, independent, and of the knowledge that relationships and attributes refer back to One Source, so know that! (3)

26 Those for Whom the Friday Obligatory Congregational Prayer is Obligatory

26.1. Preconditions for the Friday Formal Congregational Prayer

Scholars agree that it is obligatory for whomever the formal prayers are obligatory. Then they add four preconditions. They agree about two and they disagree about two. The two they agree about are being in good health and male. It is not obligatory for a woman or a sick person. The two about which they disagree are travellers and servants. (4)

Some say that the Friday congregational formal prayer is obligatory for travelers (and I say so) and for servants. A servant must prepare and then if his master stops him, he is one of those who bar from the way of God. Some say that it is not obligatory for either of them. A Tradition is related which says: "The Friday congregational formal prayer is obligatory except for four: an owned servant, a woman or a child." Another version has five and mentions the traveler. (5)

26.2. The Essential Unity of God Without Relationship to Possibles

Since one of its preconditions is that there be more than one person, it is not valid when there is only one. You must know that the intellect knows that there is no relationship between the essential Unity of God and what possibles demand. We have mentioned it and the man of intellect knows it. It is impossible that the intellect understand the existence of the world from this oneness. Therefore he is obliged to perform the Friday congregational formal prayer so that he returns to looking at what the possible demands of the existence of the One who has this Unity. He looks at it inasmuch as the God demands the one who seeks the divinity. This is another recognition which is only valid by the group. It is to organize and arrange the proofs. (6)

The Friday congregational prayer is obligatory for the intellect with which the man of intellect is described. Since the woman is imperfect in intellect and deed, and the intellect in which she is lacking is the comprehension of this essential unity, it is rather an obligation for the man and he combines the knowledge of that unity and the knowledge that He is God. The woman is imperfect in the comprehension of that unity, so it is not obligatory for her to join it and the knowledge that God is God. (7)

26.3. The Human Being Is Compelled in His Choice

Then there is the servant for whom the Friday congregational prayer is not obligatory with the one who holds that position. He is the servant who calls to mind the fact that God compels him in his choice. The reality accords that the servant is compelled in his choice. Since he cannot combine freedom and servanthood, the Friday congregational prayer is not obligatory for him. (8)

If any of those we have mentioned and will mention who are not obligated to attend the Friday congregational prayer are present at it, they perform it. If the points mentioned which are interpreted as impediments to the obligation are present, then the Friday congregational prayer is not mandatory for him. If he leaves it because of a different case, then Friday congregational prayer is mandatory for him, that is, the knowledge of what was not mandatory for him becomes mandatory. His knowledge is like Mary and Asiya who had the degree of perfection. Therefore they were specifically obliged to have the knowledge of the Oneness of the Essence and the knowledge of divine Unity which is the oneness of multiplicity. (9)

26.4. The Principle of Causes and Divestment of the Oneness of God

As for the one who is sick—and he is the one who does not speak of causes or comprehend their wisdom, he does not have the station of health (validity) since he is deficient in his knowledge of God according to what the wisdom of causes would give him. If someone's state does not grant him this knowledge and is divestment is deficient and there is fear for him, he is not obliged to have both knowledge of the wisdom of causes and knowledge of the divestment of Unity from them. (10)

26.5. Every End Has a Beginning and Not the Reverse

As for the traveler, his state demands that the Friday congregational prayer not be mandatory for him. He is between the beginning of the end and the end of the end. He is between "from" and "to." Therefore his state does grant that he join "from" and the "to" which it demands—except for the "from" which is in "to—to—to" etc. The "to" of that has "from" hidden in it. If it had not been for the other "to," it would not have been recognized in the first "to." There is no end but that it has a beginning and not the resign. (11)

Friday congregational prayer is not mandatory [for the traveler] for it inasmuch as it is a source from the first. We say that the one for whom the Friday congregational prayer is mandatory is the one who is with the "from" which is contained in the first "to," the second "to," the third one, *ad infinitum*. If it had not been for the stages and stations in the Path, there would be no comprehension of the end of "from." "To" demands "from," and "from" does not demand "to." (12)

26.6. The Inclination to Nature and Gnosis of Reality

As for the child, he is the one who inclines to his nature. He does not recognize anything but it. He is only a child by that description. It is therefore impossible for him to life his head to recognize its reality by whose knowledge Friday congregational prayer falls to his share. This is our interpretation of why the Friday congregational prayer is not mandatory for a child. (13)

27 The Preconditions for the Friday Congregational Prayer

Scholars agree that they are the preconditions for the Friday congregational prayer are the same as those for the formal prayers. We have already discussed all of them except for the time and the call to formal prayer. They disagree about that as they disagree about the preconditions particular to it. I will now discuss them. (14)

27.1. The Time of the Friday Formal Congregational Prayer

Some say that the time of the Friday congregational prayer time is noon, that is, the time of the noon formal prayer. Some say that its moment is before noon. I say that you can choose between the two times. (15)

27.2. Oneness of the Essence and Oneness of the Action in Bringing Into Existence

God Almighty says: "Have you not seen how your Lord extended the shadow? Then He says: *"After that We made the sun an indicator over it."* (25:45)

He commanded us to look at it. Looking at it is recognizing it, but inasmuch as He extended the shadow. It is the manifestation of the existence of your Source. You do not look at it in respect to the Oneness of His Essence in this station. You look at it in respect to the Oneness of His action in bringing you into existence in the proof. This is the Friday congregational prayer. It is not permitted for the one who is alone. One of its preconditions is that there be more than one person. Whoever takes note of this divine gnosis says that this formal prayer is before noon since he is commanded to look at his Lord in this state. The one who speaks with his Lord and turns to Him in his *qibla*. (16)

27.3. The Shadow Is Extended But the Sun Is the Proof

The pronoun in "to it" seeks out the nearest thing which was mentioned, and that is the shadow. The name "Lord" sought it and its return to the Lord is more direct. God has made a likeness of seeing him on the Day of Rising. He said on the tongue of His Prophet: "You will see your Lord as you see the sun at noon." He meant midday since the shadow is drawn into the person at that moment since the light covers the one who sees. It is the state of his annihilation to seeing himself by the contemplation of his Lord. (17)

Then He says: *"Then We seized it to Us an easy seizing."* (25:46) This is at midday, and then He again extends it when the sun goes down after noon. He recognizes it after the witnessing as he first recognized it before the witnessing. The state is the state. He said that if the time of the Friday congregational prayer is after high noon, it is because at this time recognition of his Lord is firm since He extended the shadow. (18)

27.4. The Shadow Is an Indication of the Sun in Sight, Not Effect

Here the pronoun in "to it" refers to the Lord, "to Him." At sunrise, he sees the shadow extend and looks to see the cause of its extension. He sees that his essence comes between the shadow and the sun and so he looks at the sun. By extending the shadow, he recognizes the effect that the sun has in that. Then the shadow is a guide to looking at the sun. The sun is a guide to the extension of the shadow in the effect. (19)

He cannot grasp this recognition except at noon. Then after that as the sun descends, he sees the shadow extend from him bit by bit. He makes the sun a guide to the extension of the shadow. Its descent is opposite the extension of the shadow. The shadow is like the essence of the sun. Descent by the sun is in the position of the extension of the shadow. That which affects the extension is the descent of the sun. The manifestation of the shadow is the source of the sun by your existence. Your existence in this question is the station of divinity which the essence of God has since He did not bring the world into existence inasmuch as He is Essence. He brought it into existence inasmuch as He is God. (20)

27.5. The Absolute Transcendence Which The Real Must Have

My friend, then look at the station of your essence in respect to your existence and you will see how noble its relationship is! Your existence is the existence of The Real since God only created everything by The Real. As the sun inclines away from you, so your shadow extends. It is recognition of incomparability which is a proof so that you believe it. The sun goes far from you. As it goes far from you, it informs you that you are not like Him and He is not like you unless He veils you from seeing it. That is the absolute disconnection which the Essence of God must have. (21)

When it rises and seeks you up until noon, your shadow rolls out bit by bit in order to inform you that when it is high, it obliterates and annihilates you so that none of your shadow remains at all outside of you. It is the negation of effects through you. This is why the formal prayer is not prescribed at noon when the shadow is annihilated. To whom do you pray or to whom do you turn in your formal prayer when the sun is over your head? (22)

27.6. "People of Medina (Yathrib), you will not be able to stand firm"

For that reason, he said to the people of Medina and those at the same latitude, "face East (that is, in turning to the *qibla* in the formal prayer) and do not face West." Watch the sun when it shines. It rises and annihilated you to yourself and you no longer have any station or any effect. God Almighty said: "*O people of Yathrib! There is no habitation for you, so return.*" (33:13) The Prophet pointed out that it is the noblest station as opposed to descent. The descent of the sun enables man to see his shadow extend. He can look at the disconnection of God in inclination as opposed to sunrise in the proof. The Prophet said: "Look to the East and do not look to the West," that is, take your recognition of God from this proof. It removes the potentiality from sunset. (23)

27.7. The Friday Congregational Formal Prayer Before Noon

Now that this is clear, whoever performs the Friday congregational prayer before noon is correct. Whoever performs the formal prayer it after noon is correct. That which I believe is that the formal prayer before noon is better because it is a time in which no formal prayer is prescribed. One should turn to God—glory be to Him!—with the obligation at all times. The Friday congregational prayer before noon is better even if it happens that it is the time for performing the formal prayer in the case of someone who forgets or sleeps through it when they remember it. It is by the principle of following. The interpretation is that waking up or remembering in whatever moment it may be is different from the Friday congregational prayer which we placed before noon. A time is specified for it as times are specified for the formal prayers. God has indicated the blessing of witnessing Him and company with Him without limitation or making it specific to one thing. He says: "*Truly He is who One Who Encloses everything*" (41:54) and He says: "*He is with you wherever you have been.*" (57:4) Know that. (24)

28 The Call to Formal Prayer for the Friday Congregational Prayer

God Almighty says: "*When the formal prayer is proclaimed on the day of congregation, then hasten to the Remembrance of God.*" (62:9) At the time of the call, the reward ranges from the camel to the egg, which is the time when the leader begins his sermon. Whoever comes from the time of sunrise until the time of the call has a reward according to how early he came. It is a matter of dispute. The camel of the time specifically mentioned hurrying. (25)

As for the call to formal prayer itself, scholars agree that its time is when the leader is at the pulpit. They disagree about whether there is only one caller to formal prayer before the leader or more than one. Some say that there is only one call before the leader, and this is the one which makes buying and selling forbidden. Others say that there are two calls, and others say that there are three. Each has a proof and is based on Traditions. (26)

What I believe in this question is that the call of the Friday congregational prayer is like the call of all the formal prayers. It is not permitted to perform the call twice or to join them together. It is one after the other, otherwise would be contrary to the *Sunna*. (27)

28.1. The Call to Formal Prayer Is God Calling His Servants to His Gnosis

The call is announcement. It is God calling His servants to recognize Him inasmuch as He is the God of mankind, our Lord, and the Lord of our fathers. It is what the Prophet said: "Whoever recognizes himself recognizes his Lord." He mentioned Him with the pronoun attached and did not make an absolute statement. God, The Real—glory be to Him!—cannot be specified by any expression or limited by any matter unless He wants some of His servants to consider Him in respect of what He has singled out and isolated for that state or specified by that expression. When he does not look at these matters by this source, he does not see the correct and desired course of action. (28)

Since Friday congregational prayer is only valid with a group, we know that the call which is the public announcement to and hurry to this particular Self-disclosure must give what is given by the one who is alone. We have made that clear for you. All that remains is the disagreement about the stations of those who look into that, and say that it is one, two or three. We do not think that there is any timing in that other than the fact that there must be one call. If there is more than one, it is permitted. However, it is one after one. (29)

As for one call, he thinks that it is inasmuch as the Friday congregational prayer is simply an formal prayer. The one who thinks that it is two, does so since it is an formal prayer in a group which is not allowed for the one who is alone. As for the one who says that it are three calls, it is because it is an formal prayer in a group on a particular day which does not occur on other days, as opposed to the formal prayers which are prescribed for every day. Whoever takes these three states into account, says that there are three calls. The first says: "Come to formal prayer." The second says: "Come to formal prayer in the group." The third says: "Come to formal prayer in the group on this day." Know that each caller to formal prayer has a state which the other does not know and the scholars take that into consideration. If it is only one, then it is allowed. (30)

29 The Conditions Particular to the Day of the Friday Congregational Prayer

29.1. The Size of the Group for the Friday Formal Congregational Prayer

One of its preconditions is the group. They disagree about the size of the group. Some say that it is one with the leader, and that is my position. I do not care whether he lives there or is a traveler. Some say that it is two in addition to the leader. Some say that it is forty. Some say that it is thirty. Some say that it is twelve. Some do not stipulate any number, but think that it is permitted if it is less than forty, but not permitted if it is three or four. This is one of the preconditions for obligation and validity, that is, by it, the Friday congregational prayer is obligatory and valid. (31)

29.2. The Stages of the Timing in the Friday Formal Congregational Prayer

As for the stages of the timing in the Friday congregational prayer with the leader, it is the portion of the one who recognizes the Unity of God from the unity of himself. He takes the unity of himself as a proof of the unity of his Lord. The poet [Labid] said:

He has a sign in everything that indicates that He is One.

The sign of everything is its oneness since every existent thing must be distinct for other things by a unity which the others do not have. In reality, that oneness is the reality of its I-ness and he-ness. By that, he knows that his Lord has a special attribute in His He-ness which other-than-Him cannot have. (32)

29.3. Proof of Oneness by Evenness

As for the one who says two, he is the one who recognizes His Unity by looking at his evenness. He sees that all that is other-than-God cannot be isolated by itself and that it is in need of something else. It is compounded in its source and in its description with the derived existence which it does not have in respect of its source. (33)

29.4. One as Proof of Oneness

As for the one who says three—and it is the first uneven number, he is the one who thinks that two premises only give a result by connection. It is four in the form and three in the meaning. He thinks that God is only recognized by being recognized by three. He takes the uneven number as a proof of the One. It is nearer in relationship than taking the even as a proof of unity. (34)

29.5 The First and Second Moses' Times

As for the one who says forty, he considers the time appointed for Prophet Moses which resulted in recognition of the words of God in view of what you know about his story which is mentioned in the Quran. It is also like that for the one who obtains gnosis of his Lord by being sincere for forty days. This is the retreat which is known in the Path of the people. They undertake it in order to acquire gnosis of God by what they obtain in it of sincerity without any flaw with God. (35)

As for the one who says thirty, he looks at the first time appointed for Prophet Moses. He knows that it is the limit for gnosis. However, there was a gap in it so ten days were added to mend that gap. In meaning, it is thirty. When thirty days is free of the gap, then the goal of knowledge of God is obtained by the thirty. God Almighty says: "*We appointed thirty nights for Moses*" (7:142). Part of that limit is what took place with the wives of the Messenger of God. What occurred led him to isolate himself with God and leave them. He withdrew from his wives for a month since he knew that the goal is obtained by that amount of time. When the month was over, God addressed him with the sign of choice. He gave his wives a choice. What was desired by that amount of time was what was opened to him. God gives His servant opening according to his goal and the reason which leads him to isolate himself with Him. What led him to isolate himself with Him was to turn over the matter to Him. The result of his retreat was unrestricted. He thinks that its effect in the divine is the effect of divine existence on existent things. It is the most perfect and sublime unveiling in phenomenal being. This is the source of the command to take on the character of the divine names. If not, then what relationship is there between the possible and the Necessarily Existent? (36)

29.6. The End of the Human Being and His Sublime Rank

As for the one who says twelve, he considers the end of man and his sublime rank. It is twelve. He also considers the names of simple numbers rather than compound numbers. That is twelve—from one to nine, and the knot is three. These are ten, hundreds, and thousands. This is twelve. After that, there are only the compound numbers with these roots. It is the addition of the simple numbers, so know that! (37)

29.7. Uniqueness and Oneness

As for the one who does not stipulate any number and says that it can be less than forty but above four—it is one tenth of forty. Forty is the result of ten times four, so it is a tenth of forty. It is as if it descends from forty and rises from four, and does not stop there. He says that gnosis of God is only valid by more than four, and the least of that is five. It is the rank from uniqueness (odd numbers) The first of that is three. It belongs to the servant. It is that from which gnosis of God results for the one who says that Friday congregational prayer is permitted with three people. The one who says that it is more than four, thinks that the second uniqueness is what belongs to God. That which the servant obtains is by his third uniqueness. The result of the uniqueness of God belongs to His Unity because nothing can validly result from His Unity. This is not the case with His uniqueness (unevenness). The first odd number belongs to the servant in respect of the proof. Recognition of the self of the servant precedes the servant's recognition of his Lord. The proof is in agreement with the proven by the aspect which connects the proof and the proven. The odd number only results in the odd number. The first uneven number after three is the unevenness of five. He gave it to God, that is, to the gnosis of God in the fifth rank. The uneven numbers go on to infinity. The stages of fixing the time are clear to you in the different of states which the Friday congregational prayer establishes. (38)

29.8. On the Second Condition: Residence

All the scholars who say that Friday congregational prayer is not mandatory for the traveler agree about residence. Some of them say that there must be a city and a ruler. Some do not stipulate that, but stipulate residence in a village or something like it. (39)

29.8.1. Journey and Residence in the Way of the People of God

The People of the Path of God fall into two categories: one of them are those whose state changes with the breaths while they know that in their hearts. They are the great ones among the People of God, They are those who are constantly travelling. It is impossible for them to reside in a place. They have two aspects in that. There is the one who is firm in the station of closely guarding the breaths and tasting their change and the varieties of the Self-disclosure always in every breath. In this state, his constancy is referred to as residence. In reality, he resides and does not reside from two different points of view. If he has no station, no abiding to make residence one of the conditions of the validity and obligation of the Friday congregational prayer. He is traveling in his residence like the journey of the one with a ship. It is as one of them said about the journey of man through his life: (40)

> You! Your journey is like the journey of the ship.
> People sit while the sail is flying. (Maliki)

There are men of God who are not in this rank. God has established them in one station in what they see in themselves, even if it is impossible in the heart of the matter: "*They are perplexed about a new creation.*" (50:15). By this interpretation, they are among the people of residence. They establish the Friday congregational prayer and think that it is one of the preconditions of the validity and obligation of the formal prayer. (41)

The person who moves through states and sees it and sees that it is impossible to remain in one state in taste and that his journey is like the journey of the person on the ship in what he sees (although the matter is the opposite of what he sees), does not consider residence a precondition. He says that the Friday congregational prayer is mandatory and valid simply by number, not by residence. (42)

30 Two Friday Formal Congregational Prayers in the Same City

30.1. Scholars Disagree about Whether or Not There Can Be Two Friday Formal Congregational Prayer in the Same City

Some permit that and some do not permit it. I say that it is permitted unless there is some reason for which it would not be good to initiate that, in which case it would be better not to do so. Similarly some of them stipulate that the mosque must have a roof, and some do not. No text in the Quran or *sunna* has come about any of these matters. If the group is valid, the Friday congregational prayer is valid. That is all. (43)

30.2. The Interpretation of the Permission to Have More Than One Friday Formal Congregational Prayer in a City

The one city is the essence of the man in the interpretation. He is a city in himself. Rather, he is the entire world. The essence of man is divided into two parts: subtle and dense. It happens that the Self-disclosure to varies from person to person. One receives a Self-disclosure in the name The Manifest in the senses and form, and in the name The Hidden in the meaning and descent. He is commanded to accept both of them in this state. Abu Said al-Kharraz was asked, "By what have you recognized God?" He said: "By joining the two opposites." Then he recited: "*He is The First and The Last, The Manifest and The Hidden*" (57:3). He permits there being two or more Friday congregational prayers in the same city. (44)

He may see God in every name of His which he possesses. Every name has a world which the other name does not have. Therefore, there are many Friday congregational prayers in one's essence since there are many worlds in himself. Each name has an authority and a power in its own world and gathering, yet the city is one. Therefore, he has a city, a ruler, residence and traveling in the same state and the same source. He is called human being. He is a world which is small in size and great in meaning. (45)

30.3. The Interpretation of Forbidding That There Be More Than One Friday Formal Congregational Prayer in a City

There is the one who looks at these various Self-disclosures in the divine names and source of phenomenal being and sees that God who is The First is the same as The Last who is the same as The Manifest who is the same as The Hidden. It is the same with all of the names, no matter which ones they are. The matter is vast in itself because of the variety of the meanings of these divine names and sources of phenomenal being. Even if they are many by relationships, they are one source in existence. This one forbids that there be two Friday congregational prayers in the same city. Every gnostic of God acts according to his moment and what he sees. For this reason, they said: "The Sufi is the child of the moment." (46)

31 The Friday Sermon (khutbah)

31.1. The Scholars Disagree on the Ruling of the Sermon in the Friday Formal Congregational Prayer

Divine law scholars disagree about the sermon in the Friday congregational prayer and whether or not it is one of the preconditions of it and one of its pillars. Most of them think that it is a precondition and an obligation. Some people say that it is not obligatory, and that is my position. In something like that the Messenger of God did not stipulate that it was obligatory and he did not state the opposite of that. It is rather related by many transmissions that he always gave a sermon in it. Obligation is a judgment and leaving it is a judgment. We must not set down that it is obligatory or not obligatory. If that is set down, God has not given us any permission to do so. (47)

Our accurate belief is that we stop and we do not make any judgment about it even though we perform it and we must do so. The Messenger of God always performed the Friday congregational prayer with a sermon as he always performed the Festival congregational prayers with a sermon. We agree that the Festival prayer is not obligatory nor is the sermon in it obligatory. However there was no Festival congregational prayer but that the Prophet performed the it and gave a sermon. (48)

31.2. The Preacher (*khatib*) is the Caller of God and the Chamberlain of His Door

The sermon is prescribed for exhortation. The person giving the sermon is the caller of God, His doorman, and His representative in the heart of the servant. He returns him to God to prepare for intimate conversation with Him. That is why it comes before the Friday congregational prayer. Ayisha, Mother of the Believers, may God be pleased with her, even related that the sermon in the Friday congregational prayer was a substitute for two cycles. The Friday congregational prayer is two cycles like the traveling formal prayer. It is *sunna* before the formal prayer in order to prepare for conversation as the supererogatory prayer is *sunna* before the obligatory one to remind and prepare you. The divine law is concerned with what is obligatory. The supererogatory prayer is *sunna* at the beginning of all the formal prayers. (49)

Do you not see that when night formal prayers were enjoined on the

Prophet, he would begin with two short cycles before he actually began the formal prayer. All of that is to alert the heart about the intimate conversation to which it is called which is obligatory for it, and to witnessing and fearful watching. The formal prayer is what is desired of him and he is desired by it. (50)

31.3. Alertness Before Conversation Is Better Than Becoming Alert During the Conversation

He who thinks that alertness is the basis of the Path, like al-Harawi and others, say that the sermon is mandatory even as ablution rouses one for the formal prayer. Those who think that what is desired is the formal prayer, and that the declaration to preform the formal prayer in it is what alerts the one who is a light sleeper, say that the sermon is a strong *sunna* and must be done, even if there is no text commanding it. The Prophet always applied himself to it. Similarly, it is better to be alerted to intimate conversation before it than to be alerted to it during it. His previous sleep may affect his conversation. (51)

God Almighty says: "*O those who have believed! When the formal prayer is proclaimed on the day of congregation, then hasten to the Remembrance of God.*" (62:9) It may be that here the remembrance of God refers to the sermon. He is commanded to be silent during the sermon in order to listen to what the speaker says. Have you not seen what is said about those who call to formal prayer? "They will have the longest necks." The neck is the breath-passage. He extends it so that it will be heard by raising the voice. Therefore, he is said to have a long neck. When God made me witness the call to formal prayer by my breath, I saw that each word of the report was limited by the senses as far as the eye could see. The callers to formal prayer are the best group who call to God by the command of God and His Messenger. If it had not been for the compassion of the Messenger to his community by the call to formal prayer, if the call to formal prayer was given and the one who heard it failed to answer it when he said: "Come to formal prayer," he would have been a rebel. "He was compassionate and kind to the believers." (52)

He said that "*hasten to the remembrance of God*" here means the sermon because the formal prayer itself "forbids outrageous action (that is manifesting opposition) and the objectionable" (that which the hearts object to [cf. Quran 29:45]. The remembrance of God in it is greater. What it contains (of the words in it) is the noblest of the actions of the responsible person in the formal prayer. It contains words and actions. We have related that one of the scholars interpreted the remembrance of God to which one hurries as the sermon. (53)

31.4. The Disagreement of Those Who Say That the Sermon Is Obligatory and What Is the Definition of What Is Rewarded

Some say that it is the least of what the word "sermon" can be applied to in the divine law. Some say that there must be two sermons. Some say that it is the least of what the name "sermon" (*khutba*) can be applied to in the Arabic language. The one who thinks that there must be two sermons thinks that the speaker must sit between the two sermons. In one of them he stands to praise God in the beginning and to say the formal prayer on the Prophet advise fearfulness of God and recite some of the Quran. He makes supplication in the second one. (54)

31.4.1. The Steps of the minbar and Rising Through the Stations of Wayfaring (suluk)

The interpretation of the climbing the steps of the *minbar* are the stations. Ascending them is ascending in the stations of traveling to God Almighty. The caller has insight – as the speaker sees the group with his eye, he sees with his inner eye. If he is blind, he is in the position of the one who calls to God with insight. This is the imitator. (55)

31.5. Standing While Giving the Sermon (*khutbah*) Is Representing God

As far as the sermon is concerned, in the first one he mentions the praise which befits God and urges things which bring one near to God by proofs from the Quran. The second sermon has supplication and seeking refuge from abasement, poverty, begging and imploring in success and guidance to what he mentioned and commanded in the sermon. When he stands up in the sermon, the first time it is by the principle of representing God in what He warns about, promises and threatens. It is a true standing by a truthful call. The second standing is when the servant stands in the presence of a generous Master seeking Him for help in whatever God said by his tongue in this sermon by way of counsel. (56)

31.6. Sitting Between the Two Sermons Is a Division Between Two Stations

The sitting between the two sermons is in order to divide the station demanded by representation of God Almighty in the exhortation which he gives to His servants on the tongue of this speaker, and the station demanded by the station of asking and desire for guidance to the straight path. (57)

31.7. Action by Way of Obligation and Action by Way of Imitation

Since no text has come from the Prophet making the sermon obligatory or saying what should be said in it outside of his own actions, we cannot properly say what the sermon is in the divine law or the language unless we look at what he did. Then we act as he did by means of following his model, not by way of obligation. God accepts it according to what he knows of it. God Almighty says: "*Surely in the Messenger of God there has been for you a good, fair example.*" (33:21) He says: "*Say: If you have been loving God, then follow me.*" (3:31) (58)

We are commanded to follow him in what he makes *sunna* and obligatory. In that which is obligatory, God Almighty rewards us for two obligations: the obligation of following and the obligation of the action in which the following occurs. In what is *sunna* and not obligatory, we are rewarded for one obligation and a *sunna*: the obligation of following and the *sunna* of the action which is not obligatory. If that action contains obligatory parts, we are rewarded for whatever obligations it contains. This is like the supererogatory prayer and the supererogatory pilgrimage. It is an act of worship which contains pillars, *sunan*, and supererogatory parts. Voluntary charity does not have any obligations in it. We are rewarded in every action according to what that action demands of the good which God has promised the one who does it. You must have the obligation of following, so know that. (59)

31.8. The Three Steps of the minbar of the Prophet and the Three Ranks of the divine names

The gnostic relates the steps of the *minbar* to rising in the divine names by taking on their character. There is a sublime step in them like the Powerful and the Knower, and a step below it like the One with power and "so that We know." The *minbar* of the Messenger of God had three steps. Similarly the names have three ranks. Each step has a rank. Some names indicate The Essence and nothing else. Some names indicate the attributes of incomparability and some names indicate the attributes of the actions. (60)

There is no fourth rank. All of these names appear in the world. The names of Essence are connected to it but their character cannot be taken on. The names of the attributes of incomparability are what purify the presence of God Almighty. The servant can take on their character according to what they accord him which is appropriate for him.

As the servant of God purifies the majesty of God by which the attributes of in-timeness are set up, so the servant is purified by those names when he takes on their character in himself. The attributes of out-of-timeness and absolute richness and independence are established by them. The names of the attributes of actions are those by which the servant unified his Lord so that he does not associate any of His creation in His action, may He be exalted! (61)

There is only what we have mentioned in the divine presence. There is only what we have mentioned in man. There is only what we have mentioned in the possibility. The servant is not a Lord of the one to whom he is a servant. The Lord is not a servant. God has made Himself great! There is nothing which can possibly be more original than this world since it is perfect in its indication of Him and containing what God has related to Himself and to the world. (62)

If you were to say that the Messenger of God said when he supplicated by the divine names: ". . . and what Thou alone hast in knowledge of Thy unseen world," and think that it might indicate another matter, we say that that name must either indicate God or what is other than God, or God and what is other than God by two aspects and two interpretations. There is no third division. All these divisions are contained within these names which we have in respect to their meanings. That man which we do not know either indicates an attribute of incomparability (which exist with us) or an attribute of action (which exist with us) or an attribute whose meaning is understood in things which are in-time like joy and amazement. The end of the business is that the world as proof as well as possibility is like this world. It is endless, and the matter is contained in what exists in the world in respect to the realities. Know that then! (63)

31.9 Silence During the Sermon of the Friday Congregational Prayer

31.9.1. The Ruling About Remaining Silent During the Sermon of the Friday Formal Congregational Prayer

People disagree about silence during the Friday congregational prayer when the leader is speaking. There are three statements. Some say that silence is obligatory in every case and that it is a necessary rule of the sermon. Some say that one can speak during the sermon except when the Quran is recited. Some people make a distinction in that between the one who can hear the sermon and the one who cannot hear it. If he can hear it, he is silent. If he cannot hear it, he can glorify or speak about something regarding knowledge. Most agree that if he speaks, it does not invalidate his formal prayer. (64)

It is related that Ibn Wahb said: "The one who speaks is performing the four cycle formal prayer of noon." As for those who say that silence is obligatory (and that is most people), they are in three groups. One group allows one to return the greeting and bless the one who sneezes during the sermon. Al-Awzai, al-Thawri, and I say so. Some do not permit you to return the greeting or bless the one who sneezes. Some of them make a distinction in this and say that you can return the greeting, but not bless the one who sneezes. (65)

31.9.2. Warning and Reminding Is Prescribed for Listening

It is prescribed to warn and remind. One must listen to what the warner and reminder says. The person giving the sermon is the speaker who summons to God. You must be silent for him when he is speaking in order to see what God will cause the tongue of His servant to say. This person is the representative of God. It is as if God were speaking to His servants. You must be silent and listen except in the things which God has commanded, like returning the greeting and blessing the one who sneezes when he praises God. Whoever thinks that it is God speaking must be silent and listen, especially during the recitation of the Quran in the sermon. If he does not listen, then he must be occupied with what the person giving the sermon is occupied with—remembering God, praising God, exhorting himself, rebuking himself, affirming the blessings of God to him, and recitation of the Quran. All of that which he does should be as He said: "*Voices will be hushed for The Merciful so thou shalt hear nothing but a murmuring*" (20:108). This is how his remembrance of God is when he cannot hear the sermon because he is too far from the speaker or because he is deaf. Then the person must exhort himself. (67)

31.10. Does the one who comes to the Friday formal congregational prayer when the leader (imam) is speaking Perform two cycles of formal prayer or not?

Scholars disagree about whether a person who enters the mosque for the Friday congregational prayer should perform two cycles (two bows, *rakat*) of *sunna* prayer. Some say that he performs two cycles, and that is my position. Some say that he does not perform any. (67)

31.11. Bending Forward [in the Formal Prayer] Is Humility to God

Bowing is to show humility to God. It is always mandatory for the entire world as long as the one who remembers God does not grow heedless. All except the *jinn* and men remember God and glorify His praise. If one of us remembers God while his heart is not fearful and he is not humble when he remembers Him without any respect for the divine presence and does not properly exalt it, the first to hate him are his limbs and all the parts of his body. (68)

It is definitely known that the one who comes to the Friday congregational prayer, will be present when he enters the mosque and sees the person who is giving the sermon. He intends to perform the formal prayer and He remembers God. God has commanded him on the tongue of His translator, the Messenger of God when He said about the one who obeys him, "*Whoever obeys the Messenger has surely obeyed God.*" (4:80) He has been commanded to greet the mosque before he sits down. No prohibition is related which removes this command. However, when he performs his cycle, he does not recite "God is Greater" aloud or recite aloud. He recites that as silently as possible. He does not add anything to the greeting, especially where the leader might hear. (69)

Someone who enters while the leader is giving the sermon is permitted to recite the greeting and no one says that he errs by doing that. The one who enters the mosque is not commanded to initiate the greeting (*salam*). The command is connected to returning the greeting, not beginning it. Bowing when beginning the greeting is better if he permits it since the command has come for the one who enters to perform a *Sunna* before he sits down. The formal prayer is the best place. However, he does not add anything to the two cycles. If he cannot sit down, he does not have to perform the cycles. If he wants to sit down, he must perform the two cycles. If a man is fair, there can be no opposition to a person performing two cycles when he enters the mosque. (70)

31.12. People Disagree on What the Leader (imam) Recites in the Friday Formal Congregational Prayer

People disagree on that. Some people say that the Friday congregational formal prayer is just like all the formal prayers and there is no particular chapter to be recited in it and he recites whatever is easy for him. Some people limit it to what the Messenger of God recited in it according to what is firmly established by transmission. That is the Chapter the Friday Congregational Prayer (Chapter 62) in the first cycle and Chapter the Hypocrites (Chapter 63) in the second. He could also recite The Enveloper (Chapter 88) instead of Chapter the Hypocrites. He could also recite The Most High (Chapter 87) in the first and the Enveloper in the second. I say that there is nothing specific, but that it is better to follow. (71)

31.13. The Difference in the Excellence of the Chapters and Signs of the Quran in Relation to One Another

In regard to the difference in excellence of the chapters and signs of the Quran in relation to one another, the One who consigns is God. The one who consigns is an active participle. The Quran is the Word of God, and all His Words are good. There must be the Opening Chapter. The other chapters are each one stage among 113 stages to God. There are firm traditions which give preference to certain chapters and signs over others in respect to the one who recites them. This is in respect of the reward we have for them. (72)

It is related that the Throne Sign (2:255) is the Master of the signs of the Quran. God has mentioned The Manifest and The Hidden in sixteen places in it. It has come about the chapters that the recitation of Chapter Yasin is worth the ten recitations of the Quran. The recitation of Mulk (67) argues in the grave for the one who recites it. The Chapter Earthquake (99) is worth half of the Quran. The Chapter Those Who Cover Over the Truth (*Kafirun*) (109) is a quarter of the Quran. Chapters the Help (110) and Sincerity (112) are a third of the Quran. (73)

Each of these we mentioned has an intelligence meaning in excellence. The Chapters the Cow (2) and Ale-Imran (3) will come on the Day of Rising with two eyes, two tongues, and two lips to testify for the one who recited them. There are many prophetic Traditions about that. (74)

As for what we know of it from the path of unveiling, I cannot mention it, but Chapter Sad (38) is a fountain of lights. I saw that with direct witnessing. (75)

31.14. The Best Course Is to Combine Imitation and Appropriateness

O leader, if in the Friday congregational formal prayer, you aim for what is proper, then recite Chapter the Friday Congregational Prayer in it and whatever it is established that the Messenger of God recited. God says: "*Surely in the Messenger of God there has been for you a good, fair example.*" (33:21) Recite: "Glorify the praise of your Lord, the Most High" and disconnect God from the actions which appear in this act of worship since He told us about Himself that He performs the formal prayer blessing for us. We glorify Him above the imagination which is conceived by illusion in man when He performs the formal prayer, that blessing "*by glorifying the name of your Lord, the Most High,*" "*When the hypocrites come,*" and "*Has the story of the Enveloper come to you*" are fitting for the threat and promise which the sermon demands. The recitation in the formal prayer is appropriate to what the leader mentions in the sermon. Then he combines imitation and harmony. (76)

32 Taking a Full Bath (*Ghusl*) on Friday

32.1. The Ruling of Taking a Full Bath (*Ghusl*) on Friday

Taking a full bath (ghusl) on Friday is, in our opinion, mandatory for everyone who has reached puberty. The full bath is for the day. If he washes in it for the formal prayer, that is better still. As for the full bath on Friday, some people say that it is *sunna* and some people say that it is obligatory. I think it is obligatory. Of those who say that it is obligatory, some say that it is obligatory for the day (and that is what we say), and some say that it is best if he washes before the formal prayer for the formal prayer. Some say that it is obligatory that it be before the Friday congregational prayer. (77)

32.2. God Chose a Type from Every Species and an Individual from Every Type

The general purification of the inward part of the human being, which is his heart, is by the inward life which it has by gnosis of God. The hearts have life by it as the Friday congregational prayer gives that since God—glory be to Him!—stipulated this particular act of worship in this form. It is part of the greatest guidance to which God has guided this community. It is "a day about which they disagreed and God guided them to the object of their dispute by the truth with His permission." (78)

God chose one sort of every species and one individual of every sort. He chose him as an act of concern for the chosen one or as an act of concern for someone else because of him. He may choose two or three sorts from a species, or He may choose two, three or more individuals of a sort. He chose the believers from the human species. He chose the saints (friends of God) from among the believers. He chose the Prophets from among the saints. He chose the Messengers from among the Prophets, and He preferred some of the Messengers over others. If it had not been that the Messenger forbade it when he said: "Do not prefer some Prophets to others," I would have specified who is the best of the Messengers. However, God taught us that He preferred some over others. (79)

32.3. One Must Not Insert into Creeds that for Which There Is No Text or Logic

Whoever finds a text transmitted by many Traditions or has verified unveiling, must stop there. Whoever has a single sound Tradition should judge by it if its ruling is connected to the actions of this world. If it is a judgment about the world to come, he should not make it specifically part of his creed. He should say, "If this is from the Messenger in the heart of the matter as has reached us, we accept it and all that comes from the Messenger of God what I know and what I do not know." He should only make what is completely definite part of his beliefs. If it is by transmission, it is what is passed down by many routes. If it is from the intellect, it is what is confirmed by logical proof as long as there is no text by multiple transmission which would detract from it. If such a text detracts from it, he cannot join both of them. He believes in the text and then abandons the proof. (80)

The reason for that is that belief in matters has been articulated by the divine law. It is not necessary that the matter which comes be in itself that which belief grants. The person of intellect knows that God wants the responsible person to believe this text, which comes from multiple transmissions, which inform us that the Prophet said it, even if it is contrary to the proof of the intellect. He still has his knowledge inasmuch as it is knowledge. He knows that God did not mean by it that belief must be connected to that known thing by the existence of the text or that it is removed from his knowledge. He accepts this text according to what God means by it. If God teaches him by unveiling what He means by this text—which detracts from the known thing—he accepts it in the place which God has specified in respect to the one who is meant by that address. We are forbidden to display such unveiling to the common people since it would lead to confusion. We should thank God for what He has given us. This is a useful premise in the Path. (81)

God singled out the month of Ramadan from the months and gave it His name. Ramadan is one of His names. Similarly, He singled out Friday from the names of the week—it is Friday. He acquainted the communities with the fact that God has singled out one of these seven days and honored it above the rest of the days of the week. This is the source of the error of the one who makes its excellence like that of the day of Arafah and the day of Ashura. The excellence of that refers to all the days of the year, not the days of the week. For that reason, Arafah may fall on a Friday or Ashura may fall on a Friday, but Friday does not change. It is never Saturday. (82)

The excellence of Friday is intrinsic. The excellence of Arafah and Ashura are matters which occur no matter which day of the week in which they occur. The excellence of that day comes from these states which occur. The comparison of Arafah and Ashura occurs in the comparison between non-essential causes which demand excellence in that type. Similarly Ramadan is more excellent than the rest of the lunar months, not the solar months. The best of the solar months is that day in which the sun is in the house of its elevation. The month of Ramadan can come in all the months of the solar year. That solar month is then honored over the rest of the solar months because Ramadan is in it. It is an incidental matter which happens during its passage. (83)

Friday congregational prayer is not compared to Arafah or anything else. This is why the full bath in it is for the day, not for the formal prayer itself. If it happens that washing on that day is for the Friday congregational prayer, there is no dispute with us that it is certainly more excellent, and the dispute which occurs between the scholars is removed. (84)

32.4. The Best of Days and Times

When God mentioned the nobility of this day to the communities without specifying it, God left them to learn it by their own strenuous endeavor to understand the divine law. The Christians said that the best day was Sunday because it is the day of the sun, and it is the first day in which God created the heavens and the earth and what is between them. He only began its creation in it because it is nobler than the other days, so they make it a holiday and say that it is the day which God meant. Their Prophet did not say anything to them about that and we have no knowledge about whether or not God informed His Prophet of that. There is no report regarding it. (85)

The Jews say that it is Saturday and that: "God finished His creation on Friday and then rested on Saturday, lay down on His back and put one foot over the other and said: 'I am the King.'" To counter this and similar things, God Almighty said: "*They have not valued God as He should be valued.*" The Jews claim that this is part of what was sent down in the Torah. We do not say that they are telling the truth and we do not say that they are lying. The Jews say that Friday is the day which God meant to be the best day of the week. The Jews and the Christians disagree. (86)

32.5. Friday Formal Congregational Prayer Was Brought in the Form of a Polished Mirror in Which There Is a Dot

This community came and Gabriel came to Muhammad with Friday congregational prayer in the form of a polished mirror in which there was a dot. He said: "This is Friday and this dot is an hour in it which will not come upon a Muslim who is praying but that God will forgive him." The Prophet said: "God guided us to that about which the People of the Book disagreed." It is this divine recognition of the mirror. He ascribed guidance to God. (87)

The reason for its excellence is that it is the day in which God created this human organism for whom He created all that He had created from Sunday to Thursday, so it must be the best of times. He created him in that hour which appears as the dot on the mirror. When this dot appeared on the mirror, the multiplication of the like indicated that it does not move as that dot which is in the mirror does not move. It is a specific hour in the knowledge of God. If we consider the multiplication of that in the senses (and we must do so), we say that the hour does not move, as it does not move in the senses. If we consider its multiplication in the imagination without moving it to the senses, then we say that the hour moves in the day. The judgment of the imagination belongs to movement in the form because it is not sensory and determined. It is a meaning in a bodily form of the imagination which resembles the sensory form. So as one meaning moves in the forms of many expressions and different languages at the same time, which the imagination makes alike, so the hour moves in Friday. Both matters are allowed in that. That is only recognized through being informed by God. (88)

32.6. The Specific Hour in Friday Formal Congregational Prayer and the Night of Power in the Year

This hour in Friday congregational prayer is like the Night of Power in the year. God Almighty said regarding this day: "*Humanity had been of one community. Then God raised up the Prophets, ones who give good tidings and ones who warn and with them He sent forth the Book with The Truth to give judgment among humanity about what they were at variance in it. None were at variance in it but those who were given it after the clear portents had drawn near to them because of their insolence to one another; then God guided those who have believed to The Truth about what whey were at variance in it with His permission and God guides whom He wills to a straight path.*" (2:213) This sign was sent down about the disagreement about this day. (89)

Taking a full bath on Friday is to wash oneself of this disagreement so that you are certain in your purity about what God has unveiled to your inner eye. It is the knowledge of the hour which is in this day. The day was obscure and then God acquainted us with it on the tongue of His Messenger, while the confusion remained regarding the hour which is in it. Whoever knows it in every Friday if it moves or knows it in its specific time if it does not move can perform the full bath on Friday to wash himself clean of this ignorance which he had about it. For this reason, it is more general if he washes for the sake of the day.

33 The Obligation of Attending the Friday Formal Congregational Prayer for Someone Who Lives Outside the City

33.1. People Disagree about Whether Friday Formal Congregational Prayer Is Formal for Those Who Are Outside the City

People disagree about the obligation of Friday congregational prayer for the one who lives outside the city. Some say that Friday congregational prayer is not mandatory for the one who lives outside of the city, and some say that it is mandatory for the one who lives outside of the city. They disagree about the amount of distance. Some say that it is a day's journey, but that is a very rare and unusual statement. Some say that it is three miles. Some say that it is the distance in which the call to formal prayer can be heard. I say that the distance is such that when the person hears the call, he can perform ablution, set out for the mosque and walk with tranquillity and gravity and arrive and still catch the Friday congregational prayer. Then the Friday congregational prayer is mandatory for him. He knows that if he does not catch the formal prayer, it is not mandatory for him because he is only commanded to hurry to it after the call. He is not commanded to go to it before that. (91)

33.2. The Place Where Two Kinds of Knowledge (Gnoses) Are Connected and the Station of Bewilderment When Sources Meet

The one outside of the place which gnosis of God grants since he is commanded to that by the proof of "Whoever knows himself knows his Lord," (and it is the connection by the two gnoses), must either go out to gnosis of his Lord inasmuch as He is Necessarily Existent, or go out to the presence of bewilderment and stopping or multiplicity. If he goes out to the authority of recognition of His being Necessarily Existent, Friday congregational prayer is not mandatory for him. If he goes out to what is other-than-this, there is no doubt that Friday congregational prayer is mandatory for him. (92)

34 The Times Reported in Which It Is Excellent to Set Out for the Friday Congregational Prayer

34.1. The Position of People about the First of the Times in Which It Is Excellent to Set Out for the Friday Formal Congregational Prayer

Some say that it is the normal hours from the beginning of the day. Some say that it is parts of the hour before noon and after it. I say that it is parts from the time of the first call until the leader begins the sermon. Whoever comes early before that will receive a reward according to how early he comes which will be greater than the camel, being part of that for which the law-giver did not set a time. (93)

34.2. Drawing Near by the Breath to the Most Glorious Drawing-Near

There are two hurryings. One hurrying is recommended, and it is from the beginning of the day to the time of the call. There is an obligatory hurrying, and it is from the time of the call until you catch the leader in bowing in the second cycle. The reward is specified for the one who hurries to the beginning of the sermon. After that, the reward is not specified because nothing is related in the divine law regarding that. The specified reward is from the camel to the egg and what is between them is the cow which follows the camel, and the ram follows it and the hen follows it and the egg comes last after the hen. There is no specified reward after that. (94)

The egg is from the chicken, and the chicken is formed in it and whatever animal is formed from the egg since the egg is connected to the animal in specifying the sacrifice. The animals intended in the likeness is that whose meat is eaten constantly about whose meat there is no disagreement. By it, the life-strength becomes strong in the person who is nourished. It is as if the one who draws near by it draws near by his life. (95)

Have you not seen the martyrs in the way of God when they draw near by themselves to God in fighting the enemies of God? They have constant life and constant provision and joy in what God has given them.

The martyrs are not called dead since God has forbidden that because God has taken the eyes of creation from perceiving their life as He took their eyes from seeing the angels and *jinn* although they know that they are present with them. We also do not believe that the martyrs are dead as He says: "*And assume not those who were slain in the way of God to be lifeless. Nay! They are living with their Lord.*" (3:169) God's blessing is truthfulness. He affirmed that they are alive since they intended to draw near to God by themselves. (96)

It is related that a certain young man, who was one of the virtuous was at Mina on the Day of Sacrifice, was poor and divested, possessing nothing of this world. He looked at the people who were drawing near to God by sacrificing their camels, cattle and sheep, and what animals they could manage. The youth said: "My God! People have drawn near Thee in this day by what Thou hast given them of Thy blessing. Thy poor servant has nothing by which to draw near except himself, so accept it." As soon as he finished speaking, he left the world and God took him. He takes the martyrs in the way of God. We wrote a line of a poem expressing this.

> I sacrifice a blemished self as a sacrifice for drawing near.
> Have you seen any creature drawing near with faults?

One of them who saw the like of what this young man saw at Mina in the pilgrimage composed this line:

> Animals are sacrificed while I sacrifice my life and blood. (97)

35 Selling at the Time of the Call to Prayer on Friday at the Time of the Friday Congregational Prayer

They disagree about selling at the time of the call. Some say that it is void and some say that it is not void. God Almighty says: "*When the formal prayer is proclaimed on the day of congregation, then hasten to the Remembrance of God and forsake trading.*" (62:9) He commanded us to leave selling at that moment. (98)

35.1. The Interpretation of the One Who Says the Sale at the Time of the Call to Formal Prayer Is Not Void

God Almighty said: "God buys their selves from the believers," The Messenger said about the struggle that it is the struggle with the self (ego) and that is the greater struggle. God Almighty said: "Fight those of the unbelievers who turn you around." Nothing is more of an unbeliever, more ungrateful for the blessings of God, than the ego. There is nothing nearer to man than himself. The struggle with the ego is greater than the struggle of the enemy because man can only go out to the struggle of the enemy after performing the struggle with his ego. There may be showing-off and reputation, and fanaticism in the servant in the struggle with the enemy. Struggling with the ego is an inward matter which only God knows about. It is like fasting among the actions. (99)

It is more proper to sell the self to God when the call for the Friday congregational prayer is given. Then he leaves all his desires and wants and comes to this market and sells himself to God. The like of this sale is not void. This is the school of the one who says that it is not void. (100)

35.2. The Interpretation of the One Who Says That It Is Void

The interpretation of the one who says that it is void is that he says that all the actions of worship are ascribed to the servants except for two. One act of worship is obligatory fasting which He related to Himself. The cause for that is that it is a negative eternal attribute which is only appropriate to God in respect of His essence, not in respect to His being God. All that is other than the essence of God is fed by some nourishment which is appropriate for it to use in making that nourished thing continue. The second act of worship is the formal prayer. He said: "I have divided the formal prayer between Me and My servant. Half of it is Mine and half of it belongs to My servant." This Tradition indicates the validity of what the servant owns. He related half of the formal prayer to Himself and half of it to His servant. Even if he is His servant, he owns that which God has related to him. In respect of what is related to him in the formal prayer, he is not owned. He said that selling to void. (101)

The sale is void because what is ascribed to him in this state cannot be ascribed to God because that would be disputing with God since He related the matter to you. Then would you refute Him! This is bad manners. What person who performs the formal prayer can refute this second portion which He related to the servant and put in his possession during the formal prayer? It is a sale which is void. For this reason, God Almighty says about this state: "*Forsake trading.*" (9:62) He said that what is desired from you in this state is that half of the formal prayer be yours. The successful one is the one who has good manners with God in every state. (102)

36 On the Good Manners on Friday for the Friday Formal Congregational Prayer

Know that three things are part of the good manners of Friday congregational prayer—wearing scent, using the tooth-stick (*siwak*) and wearing good clothes. None of the scholars are in any disagreement about this. (103)

36.1. Scent Is the Knowledge of the Breaths of the Merciful

As for scent, it is the knowledge of the breaths of The Merciful. It is all that comes from God which sweetens the transaction between God and His servant in the state, action and word. (104)

36.2. *Siwak* Is the Purification of the Tongue of the Heart by Quranic Remembrance of God (*Dhikr*)

As for *siwak*, it is all of the remembrance of the Quran by which the tongue of the heart is purified. It is the most complete purification. Sweet divine fragrances are emitted from the attributes of all that is pleasing to God. The people of fragrances among those who are unveiled smell them. The Messenger of God said that the *siwak* purifies the mouth and is pleasing to the Lord and that *siwak* removes the veils between God and His servant so that he sees Him. It contains two immense attributes—purification and the pleasure of God, The Prophet indicated this meaning when he said: "A formal prayer with *siwak* is better than seventy formal prayers without it." *Siwak* directs those who pray to their Lord, not to themselves. It is related that God has seventy veils. Make the relationship between what I have told you and this these Traditions, and you will see wonders. (105)

36.3. Good Clothes Are a Sign of God-consciousness (*Taqwa*)

Good clothes are consciousness of God. God Almighty says: "*The garment of God-consciousness—that is better*" (7:26), that is, the best garment. He says: "*Take your adornment at every place of prostration.*" (7:31). There is no stronger sign of consciousness of God than the formal prayer. The one who performs the formal prayer consigns and sees. He says: "*And pray for help with patience and formal prayer."* (2:45) He said to His servant: *"To Thee alone we pray for help."* (1:5) He put steadfastness and the formal prayer in the same situation in help. (106)

Every person who performs the formal prayer and speaks in his formal prayer with other-than-God in his heart is not the one who performs the formal prayer and speaks with his Lord and sees Him. No servant who is like this would dare come near the state of conversation and witnessing out of fear of God. Those who truly perform the formal prayer are few. There is the one who performs the formal prayer with his outward form—standing, bowing and prostration. He does not perform it inwardly, and yet that is what is desired from him. However, we hope in this place that his outward will intercede for his inward as his inward intercedes for his outward in some states. (107)

The reason for that is that if the outward movements did not have any presence in the inward by which they were established and from which they appear, they would not exist, and would not be manifest in existence. That amount of observed presence in the divine law comes from the inward. It is supported along with the outward action. It can cope with the whisperings which befall the one who performs the formal prayer during the formal prayer so that they do not have any effect in lessening the form of the formal prayer. This is an act of concern from God. *"Truly God is Gentle toward humanity, Compassionate."* (2:143) (108)

Then the beautiful garments of adornment which a person is commanded to have in the formal prayer are not the beautiful garments which a person wears in intimate conversation with his Lord. Part of his adornment is with servanthood. The other adornment is by his Lord since He says: "I am his hearing, his eye, his hand, his foot and his tongue." The servant is established by the pronoun. His adornment by God Almighty is in all his acts of worship. (109)

37 On the Mysteries of Formal Prayer While Traveling

The journey causes the formal prayer to be shortened by a general consensus, and formal prayers to be joined, although there is dispute about that. Scholars agree that it is permitted to shorten the formal prayer when travelling—except for Ayisha who said that the formal prayer can only be shortened the case of the formal prayer for fear since God, the Almighty, the Glorious, said: "*If you feared persecution from those who were ungrateful.*" (4:101) They said that the Prophet shortened it because he feared [the enemy]. They disagree about that in five cases which I will mention, God willing. (110)

37.1. The Journey and Its Categories in the Level of divine Realities

We have made it clear to you in this chapter that travel is a necessary state for all that is other-than-God in the divine realities. It is necessary for whomever is described as existing. This is the journey of the great people in taking on character as God Almighty said: "*Whoever is in the heavens and in and on the earth. Every day He is on an affair.*" (55:29) There is also the Tradition about God descending to the nearest heaven every night in the last third of the night. It is the portion of the night before daybreak. (111)

The great people travel by knowledge and realization. The journey in the divine names is by taking on character. It is the journey of the one whose state is less than the first state. The third journey is in phenomenal beings by interpretation. It is a state lower than the other two states. A journey which joins all these journeys is the greatest of the journeys of phenomenal being. The first one is the greatest and most glorious of journeys. (112)

When God calls the traveler to formal prayer, he shortens the formal prayer of the resident person, according to the difference. As the state of the traveler and the resident are distinct, and as residence is distinct from traveling, so the principle of the travel of the resident is distinct from the principle of the formal prayer of the traveler. (113)

As for what Ayisha says—and it is the statement of God about fear—in every state the servant is commanded to fearfully watch God in every breath to see the judgment of God Almighty in that breath in respect of what God has prescribed for it. Not every one can guard this station with God, so he is constantly in fear. When the gnostic obtains it and fears that the intimate conversation with God will be obscure for him in his breaths, he shortens the conversation particular to that breath. Fear is the reason for shortening it. It is the words of God Almighty which Ayisha followed. I will deal more exactly with that to which we have alluded later. (114)

We said that the scholars disagree about that in five topics. We will mention them and their interpretations one by one—if God Almighty wills—as we have done with all the acts of worship in this book. (115)

37.2. The First of the Five Topics: Shortening [the Formal Prayer]

37.2.1. Legal Scholars Disagree About the Ruling of Shortening [the Formal Prayer]

Divine law scholars disagree about this and have four positions. Some say that it is a specific obligation for the traveler to shorten the formal prayer and that is my position. Some say that shortening the formal prayer and doing it in its complete form are both obligations and he can choose between them as one chooses in the obligation of *kaffara*. Some say that it is *Sunna* to shorten them. Some say that shortening them is an indulgence, and that it is better to perform them in their complete form. (116)

37.2.2. Shortening and Performing the Formal Prayer in Full

Those who think that establishment in change is residence says that it is better to perform the formal prayer in full. Those who take note of change with the breaths, whether or not he is aware of them, says that shortening is an obligation for any individual. Whoever considers both change and establishment, allows a choice in shortening and doing the formal prayer in full according to the master of the moment and its authority. If the master of the moment is change by state and establishment by knowledge, he shortens the formal prayer. If the master of the moment is establishment by state and change by knowledge, then he performs the full formal prayer. Whoever does not take change and establishment into consideration and acts according to the Path, not according to the wayfarer on it, says that it is *sunna* to shorten it. (117)

37.3. The Second of the Five Topics: The Distance Required to Allow Shortening [the Formal Prayer]

Scholars disagree about the distance required to allow shortening of the formal prayer. Some say that it is forty-eight miles. Some say that it is a distance of three days. Some say that it is every journey, near or far, and that is what I say. I consider in it that which is called "journey" linguistically. (118)

37.3.1. The Ranks of Number of Stages of the Path to God

Those who say the distance is 48 miles, say it is four barids of twelve miles each. The distance demands the amount by its essence, and the number demands amounts. The ranks of the number are twelve—no more, no less. They are: one, two, three, four, five, six, seven, eight, nine, ten, a hundred, a thousand. These are the simple numbers, and what is more than them is compounded from them. (119)

When man walks in the Path of God in the four pillars by which his organism is set up (and they are the four humors) he crosses every pillar by these twelve. As for the great, they cross them in the four divine names which are the matrices of all the names. The existence of the world is built on them. They are: The Living, The Knowing, The Transforming, The Powerful, and no more. It is established by these names that He is God. When the servant looks at these four with the four that he has, that then is eight. He looks at his ego and his intellect, and that is ten. He looks at the Unity of His Essence and the Oneness of His divinity, and that is twelve. The barid is complete. This is also seen in the four ranks of His words: *"The First and The Last, The Hidden and The Manifest,"* (57:3), God and creation. In each of these states, the twelve move by which those four barids are established. Therefore he shortens formal prayer for them. (120)

37.3.2. Three Types of Asceticism (zuhd) and Three Days of Travel

As for the three types of asceticism and three days of travel, a day is like what Abu Yazid said when he was asked about asceticism. He said: "It is simple. I only do without for three days. One day I do without in this world. The second day I do without in the world to come. The third day I do without in all that is other than God." Whoever is like this shortens the formal prayer. He has traveled the most perfect journey without any dispute. (121)

37.3.3. The World of the Responsible Person and Shortening the Formal Prayer During a Journey

As for the one who shortens the formal prayers in whatever the name "journey" is applied to, it is necessary linguistically, he does not take note of the distance or nearness. He considers his world of responsible individuals. Whoever of them travels, he shortens the formal prayer. When man travels by his eye to interpretation, he shortens the formal prayer. When he travels by his hearing, he shortens the formal prayer. If he travels by his reflection in intelligible things, he shortens the formal prayer. The form of shortening is shortening his consideration of what his state gives him at that moment. If he gives him all, he acts according to that. This is the position of the Community and they base themselves on it. (122)

37.4. The Third of Five Topics: Their Disagreement about the Type of Journey in Which the Formal Prayer Can Be Shortened

In regard to the third of these five topics, there is disagreement about the type of journey in which the formal prayer can be shortened in journeys which entail acts of obedience and drawing near to God. Some say that it is done in every journey which is called 'journey"—be it an act of nearness, permitted, or act of rebellion. That is my position. (123)

37.4.1. God is the End of Every Traveler

God Almighty says: *"To Him you return."* This is in the sources. This is in the sources and the states. He says: *"To Him the whole matter will be returned"* (11:123). He says: *"Truly will not all affairs come home to God?"* and (42:53) *"There is not a moving creature but He is the One Who Takes of its forelock."* (11:56) All these signs and their likes indicate that the human being is traveling to God, so he shortens the formal prayer. God is the end of every traveler, whether he travels from Him, from himself, or from a phenomenal being, and in Him or in the names of his Lord. God—glory be to Him—is the end of the paths aim for that. (124)

What is the end of the goal of the wayfarer? The wayfarer must be restricted to a goal, and God is only limited by absolute liberation. The unrestricted can be refined. For this reason, He commanded us to shorten in all that is called "journey," no matter whether it is an act of nearness, permitted, or rebellion. Whoever considers or sees His word, *"No indeed! They will be from their Lord on that Day ones who are alienated"* (83:15), and *". . . that this is My straight path, so follow it. And follow not the ways that will split you up from His way"* (6:153), thinks that only the formal prayers in the journey of obedience and permitted action can be shortened since the formal prayer is an act of drawing near to God in which happiness lies. (125)

The first school is more appropriate. Rebellion is only established as rebellion for this traveler inasmuch as he is a believer or follows a school which particularly believes that it is an act of rebellion. He is one of those who mix right action and another wrong action. He travels. No matter what meaning we apply to the principle of rebellion, we say that he does not shorten the formal prayer for traveling in that which does not please God. The one who says this does not see the principle of belief in this act of rebellion in this traveler. He believes that it is an act of rebellion, so he is in act of obedience since the Lord is pleased that he believes that it is an act of rebellion. Belief in principle is stronger than the specific action called "rebellion." It does not prevent him from being allowed to shorten the formal prayers. He is traveling with his belief in it in an act of obedience. The good action counts as ten and the evil action as one. "*If there are twenty of you who are steadfast, they will overcome two hundred*" (8:65). How is it when they are two hundred and the fact of rebellion twenty? The sign which is used as an argument for specifying the Path and the proof is about the one who is not a believer. The one who is not a believer is not called upon to shorten the formal prayer nor to do the full formal prayer because the formal prayer is only obligatory after belief. If all are addressed, then our position is the most suitable in this question. (126)

37.5. The Fourth of Five Topics: The Place Where the Traveler Begins to Shorten the Formal Prayer

In regard to the fourth of five topics, the place where the traveler begins to shorten the formal prayer, some scholars say that he does not shorten the formal prayer until he leaves the houses of the village and he does not do the full formal prayer until he passes the first house. Some say that if it is an extensive village, he does not shorten the formal prayer until he is three miles from it. (127)

37.5.1. The Judgment of the Human Spirit Living in the Body and His Journey from It

The human being consists of both body and spirit. As long as a man's spirit dwells in his body and the world of his senses acts according to his nature, he is a resident and not a traveler and so he performs the full formal prayer. When his spirit travels from his body and leaves it behind by a state of annihilation, he leaves it behind in the first step. When he leaves it behind, the *sunna* is to shorten the formal prayer. The meaning of shortening here is particular to the principle of the formal prayer inasmuch as it is a spirit, not inasmuch as it manages the body. In this state, it withdraws from its body and only the principle of the formal prayer which is particular to it remains. (128)

Some consider that its corporeality has three categories. It is what it contains of length, width and depth. It applies to everything called "body" except among theologians. According to them, the body is length without width, that is, the least object which is "body." In another school, it consists of eight [ontological] substances. They are the least of the bodies. They combine length (as two substances), width (with four substances) – and it is the plane, and depth (as eight substances). It is two planes and four lines. (129)

It is the same whether this spirit has its particular body or has moved from its body in the unseen which manages it to another natural body which it sees. The principle of corporeality still exists, and it is not lessened until it completely leaves it and it is stripped of seeing corporeality, and the spirit remains. Then it begins the formal prayer particular to it. That is the shortened formal prayer. This is the interpretation of the one who says that it is three days. (130)

37.5.2. The Extensive Village Is Encompassing Corporeality

The extensive village is the corporeality which encompasses his body and other bodies. Some of our companions say that it is the one who moves in the unseen from the form of his senses to the form of his sensory, so it is not called "unseen." That form can be spiritual, a form of the names, a form of meaning. or a physical form. Whenever it appears in Self-disclosure in a physical form, it is resident in the body. Therefore he must be the full formal prayer which includes the short and the long form. That is the formal prayer of four cycles. As for the formal prayer of two cycles—and that is the morning formal prayer—it does not include the short formal prayer. One cycle belongs to the Oneness of God and the second cycle belongs to the oneness of the servant. There must be the one who performs the formal prayer and the One to whom he directs it. Therefore the the morning formal prayer is not shortened. As for the three cycles which are the evening formal prayer, the two which are aloud are the evenness of man. The recitation in them is aloud because they are set up as proofs of God. The proof of other than what is proven is not valid. The third cycle is for the existence of the proven—that is God. The recitation is silent in it since He is unseen. There is no way to shorten the evening formal prayer. It is a proof of the servant and his evenness and God and His oneness. (131)

37.5.3. The One Is Only Recognized by the One

There can only be shortening in the formal prayer of four cycles by the existence of two even things in it. It is connected to the the morning formal prayer by the principle of unity in the presence of God and the presence of the servant. It is the statement of the one who says:

There is a sign in everything which indicates that He is One.

He did not say "two" or "two things." He considers the unity of everything inasmuch as it is a thing and inasmuch as it is a sign of the Unity of God so that the One is only recognized by the One. This is why Hasan ibn Hani, the poet of his age, said: "I would give all my poetry to have this one sign." Then he worked on its meaning and what has come on it, but nothing gave the excellent development of meaning which this sign gave. At this moment, I do not remember what al-Hasan did. Had I remembered it at this moment, I would mention it to you in this place so that you would recognize the excellence of this sign. It is inimitable speech. I think that it is only be general agreement that it occurred to the one who uttered it—that was Abu 'l-Atahiya. (132)

37.6. The 5th of Five Topics: The Length of Time In Which the Traveler Can Shorten the Formal Prayer While He Remains in a Place

In regard to the fifth of five topics, the length of time in which the traveler can shorten his formal prayer, Abu Umar ibn Abd 'l-Barr related eleven positions about this question. At this moment I cannot remember them. If you want to learn that, then look in his books. We will mention a little of it. Some say that if the traveler resolves to remain for four days, then he does the full formal prayers. Some say that it is fifteen days. Some say that it is twenty days. Some say that it is when he decides to stay more than four days. I think that the best thing to do is to look at how long the Prophet remained in Mecca until he returned to Medina. He did the shortened formal prayers during that time. (133)

37.6.1. The Day of the Perfect Gnostic Is divine in Breath

If the wayfarer remains in a station with the intention of remaining in it, he does the full formal prayer from two breaths to twenty breaths. The day of the gnostic is his complete divine Breath. If he seeks to rise in every breath and God holds him in it, its authority does not give him what he walks by in his breath and he is not aware of it. If his intention is to travel in every breath, he does the short formal prayer for his entire life. He is in the position of the one who exposes himself to opening and does not have opening although it is joined to him. When he dies, in his death he sees what was hidden from him of the coolness of the eye. Then he knows that he was traveling while he was not aware of it since he did not have opening in his first life and he did not see what other travelers to God saw. (134)

38 On the Mysteries of Combining the Formal Prayer

38.1. That on Which Scholars Agree and Disagree Regarding the Joining of Two Formal Prayers Together

All the scholars agree about joining the noon formal prayer and the afternoon one at the beginning of noon on the Day of Arafah at Arafah and joining the evening formal prayer and night one by delaying the evening formal prayer until the time of night at Muzdalifa. They disagree about delaying any formal prayer in other than these two places. Most people think that they can be joined in the places which allow joining and the states which permit it. Some of them forbid it absolutely except in these two places on which there is agreement. (135)

38.2. A Confirmed Basis Is Not Abandoned for Something Probable

I think that the times are fixed without any dispute and so we do not take any formal prayer out of its proper time unless there is definite text regarding it. We cannot leave a firm root by a matter which is only likely. Only someone who has not smelt any whiff of knowledge would say that. Every Tradition which is related concerning that is only likely, not definite. It is discussed according to its likelihood or soundness, but it is not a definite text. (136)

38.3. Delaying the Formal Prayer to a Shared Time

If you delay the noon formal prayer until the shared time and then join them in that way and do the same with the evening formal prayer and night one, then you have performed the formal prayer within its time. That is the sound method on which you should base yourself. The firm Tradition which is the proper text is that of Anas. He said that if the Prophet set out on a journey before the sun had declined, he would delay the noon formal prayer and then perform it together with the afternoon formal prayer. It is a likely text as we mentioned. If he set out after the sun had declined, he would perform the noon formal prayer alone, and then mount up. He did not advance the afternoon formal prayer ahead to it because it is not its time by agreement. (137)

The likelihood of delaying is strengthened by this and part of it was in the shared time. That is when it is right to put the two formal prayers together. If it is not a wide time, he may perform three cycles of noon formal prayer in it (or less than that) and he will perform the afternoon formal prayer in what remains of the shared time. This is a better and more encompassing position. (138)

38.4. Joining at Arafah and Muzdalifa by Way of Secrets

In regard to joining at Arafah and at Muzdalifa by way of secrets, there is no disagreement that there is joining in gnosis in the Unity of God in His divinity. It is that there is no god but Him. This is only recognized after recognition of that which is the vassal of God. It is joining together two gnoses. This is the joining of Arafah. As for Muzdalifa, it is the place of the nearness and a place of joining. The authority of the name of the place is over the one who alight in it. He must join. Do you not see that the Messenger of God said: "No man must lead another in formal prayer where the latter has authority, or sit in his place of honor in his house without his permission." He granted authority and the leadership to the owner of the house. (139)

38.5. Analogy and the Perfection of the Ranks of Things

This stage is called joining. He has the leadership and authority, so he joins the two formal prayers in them by what its reality grants by general agreement. In these two places, the Prophet also joined, advancing and delaying the formal prayer. There is nothing to connect them in this place so as to perfect the ranks of things for the sake of using analogy. God knew that there would be some of His servants after the Messenger of God who would adopt analogy as a basic principle when they do not find something in the Book and nor in the *Sunna* or consensus. On this day, the Messenger of God agreed to join formal prayers by putting ahead the afternoon formal prayer and delaying the evening formal prayer so that those who are based on analogy could form an analogy. They delay by this delaying and they put ahead by this putting ahead. (140)

38.6. Everyone Who Practices Strenuous Endeavor Holds to That to Which His Strenuous Endeavor Leads

The Prophet confirmed that the judgment of the person who undertakes strenuous endeavor to understand an issue of the divine law is a legal judgment. Therefore the establishment of an analogy on the part of this person through his evidence, investigation and striving is a basic principle in the divine law, and such a legal ruling must not be rejected by someone who does not include analogy in his school, even if he does not use it. The lawgiver confirmed it as a ruling in respect to the one who reached this position as a result of his striving. Whoever moves to reject it has rejected a principle which the Prophet affirmed. It is the same for the person of analogy if he rejects the person who holds to what is outward and literal. He clings to the outward because of his striving. If he rejects him, he has also rejected a principle which the Prophet confirmed. Every striver of this sort must have that to which his striving leads him. He should not turn his attention to the error of the one who contradicts him. That would be bad manners with the Prophet. divine law scholars must not have bad manners with what the divine law affirms. (141)

38.7. The Form of Joining the Formal Prayers

38.7.1. Position of the Scholars in the Form of Joining Formal Prayers in a Journey

People disagree about the form of joining in the journey. Some people think that the first formal prayer is delayed and performed the formal prayer with the second. Some people think that the last one can be brought forward to the first if he likes, and the first can be delayed to the last if he likes. (142)

38.7.2. The Interpretation of Joining by Advancing, Delaying or Both

Whoever thinks that the first formal prayer is delayed, interprets it as gnosis of God. "God was, and there was nothing with Him."[1] The world comes after the existence of God. Its existence is derived from the existence of God. When we want to recognize Him inasmuch as He is the God of the World, we delay His recognition until the moment when we recognize ourselves. When we recognize ourselves, we recognize our Lord. The Messenger of God said: "Whoever recognizes himself has recognized his Lord." Therefore, we perform the first in the time of the second. (143)

Whoever takes existence into consideration in the interpretation puts the last forward to the first. He considers the existence of the source of the servant to be the existence of God. The truth is that the world is by God. His knowledge is from God and He knows God by God. (144)

Whoever considers the matters both together in the interpretation, puts it ahead if he likes and delays it if he likes. Each method has a group. The perfect one among us is in the one who has recognition in every method and every group. If he is in them, he is outside of them. These are the great people. (145)

38.8. The Journey in Which Joining is Permitted

It is agreed that travel is one of the areas which make it permissible to join formal prayers. They disagree about joining the formal prayers in the case of the one who is at home and about the preconditions of the journey which allow joining. Some say that the journey itself permits the joining of formal prayers, and say that it does not matter what journey it is or what sort of journey. Some make it a precondition that it be a type of journey and a particular sort of travel. They refer to the Tradition which says: "If he hastens his journey by it." They consider the cause behind the joining to be haste. As for the type of journeys, we have already mentioned the journey which is an act of nearness, a permitted one or act of disobedience to God. (146)

38.9. The Real Journey Is the Journey of the Breaths: Joining It Not Valid in It

It is only valid to join two formal prayers in what we have mentioned of Arafah and the joining of Muzdalifa. The real journey is the journey of breaths. Joining is not valid in that since joining refers to bringing one of two formal prayers out of its proper time. No one in our Path says that it can be done except for the one who has no gnosis of it by experiencing that. Had the one who says this occupied himself with his outward movements, sight, hearing and limbs, he would have seen that they change at every time. He has no experience because he is heedless about himself. For this reason, God says to us: "*And in yourselves.*" (51:21)? (147)

38.10. Joining the Formal Prayers at Home Without Any Excuse

Ibn Abbas said that when the Prophet joined two formal prayers without any excuse, "He wanted to not make things difficult for his community." This tallies with the words of God, The Great and Majestic: "*He has not placed any constraint on you in the religion.*" (22:78) The Prophet said: "The way of life of God is easy." A group the literalists stated that it is allowed. Others say that it is not permitted to join together two formal prayers without a clear excuse for joining them. (148)

38.11. Constriction in Worship Is Doubling the Responsibility

Joining belongs to the people of the veil. It is compassion to them in responsibility and they are permitted it in order to remove constraint and difficulty. Difficulty in worship is doubling the burden. Action itself is a trouble. When hardship is ascribed to it, it is burdening upon burdening. As for the people of contemplation, they only join formal prayers at Arafah and Muzdalifa and nowhere other than these two places. (149)

38.13. Position of the Religious Scholars about Joining the Formal Prayers Because of Rain

Some permit joining of the formal prayers night or day. Some forbid it during the day and permit it at night. Some permit it when there is mud without rain at night. I believe that if the school of the one who performs the formal prayer is such that he thinks that the formal prayer is only valid in the group and there is no group except that in the mosque, then he can join two formal prayers at night or in the daytime if he is in a group. If his school is such that it permits the formal prayer of the one who performs the formal prayer alone, in spite of the existence of a group, he cannot join them unless he is in the mosque and the leader joins them. It does not matter what school the leader belongs to if the leader is a person who has undergone strenuous endeavor to arrive at an issue, and not an imitator. However, today that person is imitated in all he happens to do. That is what most of the jurisprudents of our time do. (150)

38.14. The Resident Is Veiled from Seeing the Journey

It is permitted for someone who is resident to join formal prayers for he is veiled from seeing his journey. He travels in every breath inasmuch as he is not aware. This is by the difference of states and thoughts, the conversation of the ego, and inward and outward movements. When the excuse of rain is ascribed to that (and it is the knowledge of what is sent down and so it is the knowledge of outward divine law which allows joining), then he is allowed to join formal prayers by what this legal knowledge indicates to him. Therefore he must not turn away from it. Whoever takes difficulty into account, adds mud to it and permits that in the night formal prayers. Whoever does not take difficulty into account, permits that night and day, and does not permit it because of the mud. (151)

39 The Sick Person At Home Joining the Formal Prayers

Some of them permit the sick person at home to join the formal prayers and some of them forbid it. I say that it is the first position because of the tradition of Ibn Abbas. That is a sound Tradition and we have already mentioned it. (152)

39.1. Laziness Is an Illness

Laziness is an illness of the ego. If the illness is laziness and whatever has the same meaning, he is not permitted to join the formal prayers. If his illness is due to the overpowering of states since he fears that that state will overpower him, like the sick person who is afraid that he will faint, then he is permitted to join formal prayers. The state is an illness and speech is health. (153)

39.2. States Are Gifts and Stations Are Acquisitions

The ignorant among the people of our path say that the state controls knowledge. This is because they are ignorant of what the state actually is. The great people seek refuge from states in this world. They are among the greatest veils. For this reason, the people consider the states to be gifts and stations to be acquisitions. As far as the great are concerned, this world is the abode of acquisition, not the abode of states. Acquisitions will elevate you in degree while the state may completely make the one who has it loose his moment so he does not rise by it. It is one of the results of his station which he seeks to hasten in this world. For this reason, states are gifts. If they had been acquisitions, one would have risen by them. The nobility of the state is in the world to come, not in this world. (154)

The nobility of knowledge and the station are in this world. God Almighty commanded His Prophet to seek increase in knowledge. He said to him: "*Say: 'Lord, increase me in knowledge!'*" (20:114) He did not command him to seek increase in state. If the one who made this statement had recognized the nobility of knowledge and possessed sound tasting of it, he would have agreed with God Almighty when He honored those who know Him. He is driven from this attribute with which God described Himself, and the elite of His angels and servants. He has not reached that degree and he begins to shield himself by making the state nobler than knowledge. By God's praise, he is stripped of both knowledge and state. (155)

39.3. Those With Divine States

As for the people of sound divine states, may God be pleased with them, they know that knowledge is nobler than the state. Knowledge is their goal and the state comes between them and that for which they were created. They try to free themselves of it. Part of what will show you is that even if the people of states conceal it, you will see them trying to free themselves of it and remove it from themselves when they are dying. They hope then that they are not the people of states. The state is not a matter which brings one near to God. This world is the place of the means of drawing near. The world to come is the place of nearness. He gives every attribute its authority in its proper place. The authority of the state is in the world to come. The authority of knowledge is in this world. Each is in its place because its honor is more complete. (156)

40 On the Mysteries of Formal Prayer Because of Fear

40.1. Introduction

40.1.1. Disagreement on the Form of the Fear Formal Prayer

People agree that the fear ritual prayer is permitted. They disagree about its form according to the disagreement of the various transmissions about it which come about when the Prophet performed it—except for Abu Yusuf. He has a very rare position and says that the fear ritual prayer is not allowed in the form in which the Messenger of God performed the formal prayer with only one leader. He states that that was only for the Messenger of God. That was particular to him and the fear ritual prayer should be performed with two leaders. Each leader performs the two cycles with a group while the other stands guard. (157)

I think that the leader can choose this form which is established from the Messenger of God. Whatever form he performs the formal prayer is allowed and the formal prayer of all is valid, except for the transmission which says that they must wait for the greetings at the end of it (*salam*). I look at the fact that the leader is followed in it and God has made him follow. The reason that I stop in that being less than certain and definite by means of the meaning is that the Prophet commanded the leader to perform the formal prayer of the sick person and the weakest of the group. (158)

The interpretation that makes this likely is that Abu Bakr followed the formal prayer of the Messenger of God. Tahawi mentioned that. Abu Bakr acted as the leader of the people in the formal prayer while the Messenger of God was among them. The narrator said that the people were following Abu Bakr al-Siddiq, may God be pleased with him, while Abu Bakr was following the formal prayer of the Messenger of God. The meaning of following here is to make the formal prayer short because of the illness of the Messenger of God. This interpretation is not unlikely. The leader in this state is a leader following a leader. The term "leadership" came in the transmission from the Companion. For that reason, I do not prefer the version about waiting for the greeting. The disagreement about the form of the fear ritual prayer is well-known and recorded in the books of Tradition. (159)

40.1.2. God Is with the Servant According to the State of the Servant

God is with the servant according to the state of the servant. "I am with My servant's opinion of Me, so let him think well of Me." No matter what the state of the servant is, God is with him according to how he behaves with Him. God Almighty said: *"So remember Me and I will remember you."* (2:152) If the servant remembers his Lord in himself, God remembers him in Himself. If the servant mentions his Lord in an assembly, God mentions him in an assembly better than it. In this question, the servant is in the position of the leader. The other state is that the state of the servant with God is based on the state of God with the servant. It is as He says: *"He loves and whom love Him."* (5:54) (160)

The people of the path of God are based on that which the realities demand in this question. The love of the servant is only because God loved him, provided him with His love, gave him success in it, and let him act in it. It is like that with all the matters that the servant has which bring him near to God, The Immense, The Majestic. This station warns the People of God against being negligent in it. For this reason, we likened it to the fear ritual prayer. (161)

40.2. The Formal Prayer of the Fearful During Hand-to-Hand Combat

40.2.1. People's Disagreement about the Formal Prayer During Hand-to-Hand Combat

In regard to people's disagreement about the formal prayer during hand-to-hand combat, some people say that he does not perform the formal prayer. Some people say that he performs the formal prayer by making movements with his eyes. That which I believe is that he is commanded to do the formal prayer in that moment as far as he is capable of doing it. That is because every other state except hand-to-hand combat is preparation for struggle and battle. It is not the struggle itself or the battle. Hand-to-hand combat is struggle and battle. It is that which God commanded His servants to be firm in and to *"And pray for help with patience and formal prayer."* (2:45) God Almighty says: *"O those who have believed! When you met those who were ungrateful marching to battle, then turn not your backs to them in flight."* (8:15) Then He threatened the one who is not firm and said: *"And whoever turns his back that Day, but one who withdraws from fighting for a purpose, or one who moves aside to another faction, he will surely draw the burden of the anger of God and his place of shelter is hell; and how miserable the Homecoming!"* (8:16) (162)

God said in that state: *"And pray for help with patience* (and it is to keep the nafs from fleeing in that state) *and formal prayer."* (2:45) He commanded him to perform the formal prayer. It is a specific command to him in order to disappoint the enemy. He made it one of the actions of the struggle. The formal prayer is obligatory and flight in that state is one of the great wrong actions. God commanded him to be steadfast. It is being firm in that state and the formal prayer. He made the formal prayer obligatory for him as He made steadfastness obligatory. He performs the formal prayer it as much as he is able. God says: *"So be Godfearing of God as much as you are able"* (64:16) and He says: *"God places not a burden on a soul beyond its capacity."* (2:286) The Messenger of God performed the odd number formal prayer on his camel, indicating the movements with his head. Therefore it is better to perform the ritual prayer of fear and with the existence of security. Good news is one of the causes of victory. (163)

He performs the formal prayer as much as he is able to in that moment and in that state provided that he does not stop fighting or falter in it. That is the capacity of that moment. The obligated person acts according to his moment, whether or not he is in a state of purity. The one who disagrees with this has no looked closely at the command of God or at what God meant by removing constriction from the obligated person in the religion of God. God Almighty says: *"He . . . . has not made for you in your way of life any impediment."* (22:78) (164)

40.2.2. The People of ijtihad (English?) and the People of Imitation

I say that when this obligated person is in this state in this place, he is either a striver or an imitator. If he is one of the people who strenuously endeavors to understand an issue, there is nothing to say about it. He must act according to what his proof demands and he is forbidden to oppose his proof. If he is an imitator, the best he can do is to follow the one who says that the formal prayer is permitted during hand-to-hand combat, and he can pray it without being in a state of purity. The Quran supports him and the imitator has no proof with which to oppose imitation of the one who says that he performs the formal prayer. He has met his obligation and done what is best. He is one of those who remember God in every moment. He imitates the Messenger of God in the sound Tradition from Ayisha. She said: "The Messenger of God used to remember God at all times." She did not specify any one state instead of another. (165)

40.2.3. The State of Hand-to-Hand Combat Is the State of the Servant with Satan

The state of hand-to-hand combat is the state of the servant with Satan in his whispering and when his ego whispers to him. God is nearer to him than his jugular vein in that state, but he is in a great battle with his companion. When the servant who is in this state looks at this divine proximity, he performs the formal prayer. The one who is in this state must pray. If he performs the entire formal prayer in his battle, he fights it by God. He fulfills the outward pillars as they are prescribed according to the power which he has of inward presence with God in his formal prayer, as the one performing the struggle performs the formal prayer inwardly while in hand-to-hand combat according to what he is able to do by making signs with his eyes and reciting "God is Greater" with his tongue while fighting the enemy outwardly. The whisperings of Satan in that moment do not bring him out of that which God has made it obligatory for him to perform. His purity in that moment is the battle itself—like performing ablution fully on account of disliked things. (166)

When Satan sees his resolution to fight in struggle for God, Satan makes it occur to him that it is desire and greed on his part. He wants to make the action of this servant come to nothing. His intention was sincere when he first began to fight to defend the religion of God and to let the word of God be the upper and the word of those who reject be the lower. Here the unbeliever is the idolater, the one who assigns God a partner. We say this because the people of God recognize what I show them in this statement. Then that fighter is not concerned with this thought. His root is sound and his basis is strong. That is his intention at the beginning. If Satan suggests to him that he leave this action which he has begun due to the soundness of what he whispers to him, what he suggests to him about showing off is false and he answers him with the words of God Almighty, *"Render not your actions untrue."* (47:33) This sign drives away this doubt which has occurred to him concerning abandoning that action. (167)

41 On the Formal Prayer of a Sick Person

Scholars agree that when the sick person still has understanding about his responsibility, he is called upon to perform the formal prayer. He is not obligated to do that part of it which he is not capable of doing—standing, bowing and prostration. They disagree about the form of the formal prayer for the one who is able to perform the formal prayer sitting and about the form of the one who cannot perform it either sitting or standing. (168)

As for the person who performs the formal prayer sitting, some people say that he is the one who cannot stand at all. Some people say that it is the one for whom standing is difficult because of his illness. (169)

Some people say that the form of sitting is to sit cross-legged when you sit instead of standing. Ibn Masud dislikes sitting cross-legged. (170)

As for the person who can neither stand nor sit, some people say that he performs the formal prayer reclining. Some people say that he performs the formal prayer however it is easy for him. Some people say that he performs the formal prayer with his feet towards the direction of formal prayer. Some people say that he performs the formal prayer on his side if he cannot sit. If he cannot pray on his side, he performs the formal prayer lying with his feet toward the direction of formal prayer. (171)

41.1. The Sick Person Performs the Formal Prayer According to His Ability and What Is Feasible for Him

My position is that God has removed constraint from the obligated Muslim in the religion of God. He commanded him to be conscious of God as much as he can. The sick man performs the formal prayer according to his ability and as is feasible for him. Constraint is removed from him which would harm him by aggravating his illness. He does not abandon the formal prayer at all, even if he is not capable of performing all the pillars and all of the preconditions which make the formal prayer valid. (172)

The lawgiver said that he is obligated according to the state which he is capable of doing: "*And God places not a burden on any person beyond what He has given him.*" He lightened for the soul what is more than this. God Almighty says: "*God will make ease after hardship.*" (65:7) This is connected to *"And God places not a burden on any person beyond what He has given him."* It is as if He were saying: if He gives to the self and it performs and then he does it with difficulty, which is hardship in respect to the obligated person, the ease is then in what He said: *"He . . . . has not made for you in your way of life any impediment."* (22:78) How great is His compassion to His servants! (173)

41.2. Illnesses of the Self Do Not Detract from Belief

There are three types of sickness: physical sickness, sickness of the self, and sickness of the intellect. There is no fourth category. The physical sickness is the one about which we have been speaking. That is the type of sickness which the formal scholars recognize. The sicknesses of the self are anxieties which include performing the due of God which is obligatory for the self. The sicknesses of the intellect are misguiding doubts which lessen the proofs of belief and come between the intellect and the soundness of belief. (174)

There can be a sickness of the self while belief exists. Belief in this believer in respect to the ego is in the position of the intellect of the one who is ill with a physical illness. He performs his formal prayer in conversation with his Lord and seeing Him as Umar ibn al-Khattab, may God be pleased with him, prepared the army during the formal prayer. The truthful believer has no conversation except with his Lord. He does not speak with any of the servants of God without seeing the conversation of his Lord in that according to what is fitting. (175)

The believer with a sickness of the ego consigns with his Lord in respect to his belief while he is involved in his anxieties and he is distracted from Him by them. He is still in his anxiety while his belief in God tells him, "Your worry is God and your looking at it is by God. God is existence and the existent. He is worshiped in everything which is worshiped and in everything. He is the existence of everything. He is the goal of everything. He is The Manifest in the manifestation of everything. He is The Hidden in the absence of anything. He is The First of everything and He is The Last of everything." The worship of God in every aspect of every state does not miss the believer. The sicknesses of the self do not lessen belief. (176)

41.3. Sicknesses of the Intellect Lessen Belief

As for the sicknesses of the intellect, they do lessen belief. Belief is connected to two things: it is connected to the existence of God and it is connected to the Unity of God. As for belief in the Unity of God in respect to His essence, that is one of the faculties of logical perception according to the people of speculation, and in our opinion, it comes from our reflection. As for being from remembrance of God and unveiling, it is not from that. Similarly, the Unity of God can be perceived by belief and can be perceived by reflection. The divine law does not present the Unity of the Essence by means of texts about it, even if it refers to it as a whole. For this reason, it is not included in the line of belief. (177)

If the sickness of the intellect comes between you and the soundness of belief in the existence of God, it has come between you and necessary knowledge. When the thinker sees the manifestation of the product, knowledge of the Maker is necessary. If the thinker does not know the reality of the Maker nor His what-ness, and what is necessary, conceivable and impossible in respect to Him until there is logical perception and divine prophetic information, then this is a sickness which has no medicine. (178)

41.4. Lack of Necessary Knowledge

Whoever lacks necessary knowledge is in the position of the sick person whose sickness has emptied himself while he does not know that he is sick or what is in him. He is not called upon by the divine law because he has no intellect. If he has belief or necessary knowledge of the existence of God, the Creator, it negates the sickness which removes the soundness of Unity. He imitates, so he is a believer, or he looks and derives a proof, so he is a man of knowledge. If it comes from analysis and seeking proofs, his sickness is that he does not accept what the Prophet brings regarding the attributes of God which detract from the Oneness of the essence while the Unity of God is sound both intellectually and in the divine law. He performs the formal prayer and performs his acts of worship in spite of this sickness. It helps him since he understands that he has this illness since he is only capable of this degree of the Unity of God Almighty which we mentioned. (179)

The believer with sound belief is the one who worships God as described by the lawgiver. The believer who is sick in his belief is the one who worships God only by what the proof of intellect indicates. I have informed you about a matter which contains the excuse of everyone with an excuse. If Unity is sound, that is what is desired from every existent thing. How much more so when it is related to performing prescribed acts of worship in inward and outward movements. (180)

42 Things Which Invalidate the Formal Prayer

42.1. Introduction

They agree that all that violates one of the preconditions for the validity of the formal prayer, whether it is intentional or due to forgetfulness—like facing the direction of formal prayer or purity—requires that formal prayer be repeated. That is my position, but I also say that there is no excuse when it is intentional. (181)

42.1.1. The Precondition of Happiness and the Precondition of Salvation

The preconditions of happiness are Unity, and by happiness, I mean that one is not eternally in the Fire. These and the preconditions of being rescued from every destructive station of the world to come are those whose existence makes salvation sound. This is without looking at the mercy which encompasses all. The heart of the gnostic is vaster than God's Mercy, even if its existence is from the Mercy of God. The Mercy of God cannot possibly encompass Him for God has not described Himself as being shown mercy. The heart of the gnostic servant contains God and the mercy which encompasses everything. He is the Absolutely Vast. The reason for that is that existence is the existence of God. Take note then, you who are fail to perceive this! (182)

42.2. The Ritual Impurity Which Breaks the Formal Prayer. Does it demand that he repeat the formal prayer or does he build on what he has already performed of the formal prayer?

Does ritual impurity demand that a person repeat the formal prayer or does he build on what he has already done of the formal prayer? Some people believe that he does not build on what he has done—not for ritual impurity or anything else which breaks the formal prayer, except in the case of a nosebleed, and some people say that it is not for a nosebleed either. Some people say that he builds on it for all ritual impurities which break ablution. (183)

That which I say is that everything which breaks the formal prayer is either a ritual impurity which demands purification or one of those things which break the formal prayer and does not demand purification. If it is something which affects purity, he cannot build on it. If it does not affect purity, he can build on it. This is provided that he does not do anything more than absolutely necessary to remove that factor which breaks the formal prayer. If he does more than that, he does not build on it. He repeats the formal prayer. (184)

42.2.1. That Which Breaks Off Conversation and Intervenes Is Witnessing

Does that which breaks off conversation and comes between you and witnessing affect the vision in the world to come such as it is, like the time between the two milkings? Or does it not affect it so that the vision and witnessing is continuous? If the factor which breaks it is a ritual impurity which affects belief, the prescribed conversation which preceded this ritual impurity bears no fruit. This is the position of the one who does not build on it. If the factor which breaks it is seeing a cause and relying on it, he plucks the fruit of the conversation which preceded the event of this causal factor of severance. He is in the position of the one who builds on it without a doubt. (185)

42.3. When Someone performs the formal prayer with or without a barrier and something crosses in front of him, is his formal prayer broken or not?

When someone performs the formal prayer with or without an object in front of him, and something crosses in front of him, is his formal prayer broken or not? Some say that nothing breaks his formal prayer. Some say that his formal prayer is broken by a woman, a dog, or a donkey which crosses in front of him or between him and the object. My position is that the one who crosses in front of him does a wrong action. The one who is performing the formal prayer is commanded to stop him from crossing in front of him and pushing him away as much as he can. If he does not do that and does not push him away, then the one who performs the formal prayer commits a wrong action although his formal prayer is valid in every aspect. The definition of the area which he must keep him from crossing is that which is the place of his forehead in prostration on the earth. If he comes between him and the place of his prostration, he is commanded to push him away and fight him. The one who is performing the formal prayer is not obliged to push him or fight him more than that. Wrong action is attached to the one who crosses in that amount which the Arabs call "directly in front of him (lit. between his hands)" since the Prophet did not make any definition about that. (186)

42.3.1. The Truly Real Is the *qibla* of the Servant in His Formal Prayer and His Life

The Truly Real is the direction of formal prayer of the servant. If anyone passes between God and His servant by himself and not by his Lord, the unhealthy consequences of his action redound on him. The one who is performing the formal prayer—and he is the one who is conversing—must alert him and turn him back from seeing himself in that. He is commanded in a Tradition to give good counsel to God, His Messenger, the common Muslims, their rulers, and all people. He is specifically obliged to give good counsel. If he does not give good counsel, he commits a wrong action. The one who is conversing has a sound conversation in his state in any case even if he acts sinfully. (187)

That which crosses is a thought which occurs to him while he is in the formal prayer which comes between him and his Lord. If he is sound in his formal prayer with his heart, it is impossible that anything contrary to that which he is involved in—be it recitation of a sign or remembrance of God—should cross before him. Other than that cannot find any access to him. If the person performing the formal prayer neglects himself in the formal prayer, and thoughts occur, as they must, and he was present with his Lord at the beginning of his presence, then he does not concern himself with what occurs to him. His formal prayer is valid. He is present with himself as he speaks with his Lord. (188)

He is one of those who consigns with his Lord in everything in the state of his formal prayer, like Umar ibn al-Khattab, or who sees that everything comes from God in the state of his conversation between him and his Lord like Abu Bakr. His inner formal prayer is sound. That result is either because he has will or does not have it. If he does not have will, there is nothing against him. If he does have will, he is either compelled to cross before him in the source of his choice or he actually chooses to do so. The one who chooses to do so does a wrong action, and the one who is compelled does not do a wrong action. (189)

42.4. Blowing During the Formal Prayer

Some people say that it blowing during the formal prayer is disliked. Some people say that the formal prayer must be repeated because of it. Some people make a distinction in that between that which is heard and that which is not heard. You must know that this refers to whether or not it is speech. There is no dispute that it is not good. (190)

42.4.1. Jesus Was Present With His Lord in Every State

Jesus was present with his Lord in every state. His blowing the spirit into the bird did not break his presence with his Lord. His blowing occurred by His permission. How could He give him permission to do that which would veil him from presence with his Lord? That is what is desired of him and of every created thing. God should always be before their eyes and in their secrets as He is Himself. That is consciousness of God on both sides. (191)

Whoever considers that blowing is a substitute for "*Be*" considers it to be speech. Whoever considers that it is not in the meaning of "*Be*" and is a cause, does not consider it speech. He makes His words, "by My permission" effective by the words, "and so it was a bird" and not by His Words, "*and so he blew into it.*" (192)

42.5. Laughing in the Formal Prayer

They agree that laughing while performing the formal prayer breaks the formal prayer. They disagree about smiling. Some people say that it is in the same position as laughter and so it breaks the formal prayer. Some say that it is not connected to laughter and so it does not break the formal prayer. (193)

42.5.1. Laughter Lessens the Awe and the Good Conduct of the Person Who Is Conversing

When one is conversing, laughter lessens awe and good manners. The one who does not have good manners does not consign. If he smiles, it may be because he smiles because of the laughter of his Lord in some event which occurs like the old man of Moses or the story of Hannad. Part of the good manners of the servant is that he smile in events like these because of the laughter of God. If he is not like this, the event gives laughter to himself and so he smiles. This is bad manners and it is not proper for presence. It comes between him and presence. He should renew his repentance and repeat the action. He is in the position of the one who says that smiling breaks the formal prayer. (194)

42.6. The Formal Prayer of Someone with a Full Bladder

Some say that his formal prayer is invalid and must be repeated. Some say that it is disliked. My position is that the prohibition does not indicate that the prohibited thing is invalid. It indicates that the one who does it commits a wrong action. Therefore, the formal prayer of the one whose bladder is full is allowed. He does a wrong action like the one who performs the formal prayer in a house which has been unlawfully appropriated. (195)

42.7. The Inner Secret of the State of the Formal Prayer

The one whose secret is foul in the state of the formal prayer reflects on the evil of what he does or which happens to one when he finishes his formal prayer although he is still a believer. The formal prayer is valid, and he is one of those who speaks evil to himself. That is excused as long as he does not act on it or utter it. (196)

42.8. Someone Who is Performing the Formal Prayer and Returns the Greeting to the One Who Greets Him

A group of them make an indulgence for someone who is performing the formal prayer and returns the greeting to one who greets him, and that is my position. It is remembrance of God, and it is a form of remembrance which is prescribed in the *tashahhud* of the formal prayer. It is a root to which it is referred. Supplication is allowed in the formal prayer although people are mentioned in it as when the one who performs the formal prayer says: "Forgive me and my parents." Some people forbid it absolutely. Some people permit him to return the greeting inwardly. Some people say that he does not return the greeting until he finishes the formal prayer. (197)

42.9. Every Remembrance of God (*Dhikr*) Is Permitted in the Formal Prayer

Every prescribed remembrance is permitted in the formal prayer. God Almighty says: "*And when you were given greetings with greetings, then give greetings . . .*" (4:86). He used the "*fa*" (then) so there is no delay allowed. He did not single out the formal prayer rather than any other time. All remembrance of God which is prescribed by supplication or any other form is a specific command. This is like blessing the one who sneezes and returning the greeting. He can articulate it during his formal prayer and at other times. If it were not obligatory, how could he do it? The obligation is connected to returning the greeting and blessing the one who sneezes when he praises God. (198)

43 On Making Up Missed Formal Prayers

43.1. The Obligation for One Who Forgets or Sleeps Through the Formal Prayer Is to Make It Up

Muslims agree that it is obligatory for the one who forgets and the one who was asleep to make up the formal prayer. They disagree about the one who does it deliberately and the one who faints. I think that the one who forgets and the one who was asleep both must perform the formal prayer they forgot or slept through. If the jurisprudents think that *qada* (making up a missed formal prayer) means that the formal prayer is obligatory for him with the same meaning as performing it, that is my position. If by *qada* they mean the distinction between the one who performs it in his known specified time and who is awake and intentionally rebels and leaves it and the one who performs it when he remembers it makes it up by *qada* there is no harm in that. (199)

If they mean something different by *qada* than what we have mentioned, and that he is not performing the formal prayer but praying it outside its proper time in a different form than what we have mentioned, that is not my position. The one who forgets and the one who is asleep are not called upon to perform the formal prayer while he is asleep or in forgetfulness. That is not its time in respect to them. "*God places not a burden on a soul beyond its capacity.*" (2:286) Had it not been that the Prophet gave the person who forgets and sleeps a time when he remembers and wakes up, that formal prayer would have ceased to be due from them when the time known with those who are awake and remember departs as it is not due from someone who is unconscious. (200)

43.2. The Forgetfulness of the Gnostics

The one who forgets, recognizes that there is nothing in existence except God, His attributes, and His actions. He is the source of existence. The one with this station of gnosis of God must have good manners with God according to what this gnosis demands. It is well-known, and has been mentioned in this book and in the knowledge of the path of God. If this gnostic forgets and has bad manners with God which is given to him by this gnosis, he is not punished for it. If he has an appointed remembrance in respect to the one who does not have this gnosis, He is with God according to what he remembers and decides in respect to that. If it is good, it is good. If it is bad, it is bad. (201)

The reason that he forgot may be that he was involved in forbidden action, permitted action, or recommended action. He is rewarded in his forgetfulness in respect to that recommended action, not in respect to his forgetfulness. He does a wrong action in respect to the forbidden thing, and he has neither reward nor burden in respect to that permitted thing. (202)

If this forgetful person remembers his gnosis, he acts by it according to what its manners demands and what it makes specifically incumbent on him of its rules and good manners of actions and stillnesses in the state of his forgetfulness when he calls them to mind in himself according to the definition which his gnosis in it demands. When he calls it to mind, he calls to mind in himself what it demands of good manners. That is its moment. If he does not do it, then God will punish him for the bad manners which he had in the state of forgetfulness since he did not call it to mind at the time when he remembers. God says: "*So worship Me and perform the formal prayer for My Remembrance.*" (20:14) (203)

43.3. The Sleep of the Gnostics

As for the interpretation of the one who sleeps who recognizes this gnosis, he is the one who is veiled by looking at his nature and what it has of jurisdiction in it without looking at its Maker. This is a particular type of forgetfulness because he leaves action, or the desired action does not come into existence from him in that state. If it is his looking which puts him to sleep in the jurisdiction of his nature inasmuch as its reality intrinsically demands that and he does not remember or witness the One who brought its source into existence, God does not punish for the manners which he lacked and which is demanded of the one who is present with his gnosis. (204)

When this one who is asleep wakes up, he calls God present in himself as the One who brought the source of that nature into existence while confirming its authority which follows the existence of its source like the states. He has good manners by the position of the one who does not sleep in that calling present. If he does not act, he is punished because he did not call it to mind, not because he had slept during it. (205)

The causes which necessitated his sleep are matters in which his portion lies according to what the divine law rules about it. Wrong action is connected to it because of that reason and the judgment of the divine law, not because of his sleep, or reward is connected to it because of that cause, not in respect to his sleep. This is how the sleep of the gnostics and their forgetfulness must be in this interpretation in gnosis of God. (206)

43.4. Corollaries and Considerations of the Instruction of the divine law

Even if the message of the divine law is connected to the outward, its interpretation is in the inward. If the message of the divine law is connected to the inward, its interpretation is in the outward. The man of knowledge continues to look at the lawgiver to see what is the object of the connection of the principle in what he brings in this particular question: is it to the outward like movements, or to the inward like the intention, envy, malice, desiring good for the believers, good opinion and bad opinion? When that which the Prophet addressed is connected to the outward, the interpretation is in what is opposite it or opposite the principle—like the good opinion and the bad opinion. When that which the Prophet addressed is connected to the outward, the interpretation is in what is opposite it or opposite the principle—like the good opinion and the bad opinion. The good action outwardly is opposite this place like the good action with the *dhimmi* inasmuch as he acknowledges his Lord, but does not recognize what is demanded of him. (207)

44 On The One Who Leaves the Formal Prayers Deliberately or the One Who Faints

Scholars disagree about one who deliberately leaves the formal prayer and one who faints while performing the formal prayer. Some people say that he must make it up and some people say that he is not obliged to make it up. The last is my position. Some people say that he is obliged to make it up. I think that it is better that he do so. If it is not written down for him as an formal prayer, it is still written as a supererogatory prayer, so it is a more careful approach. Some of those who says that it is obligatory to make up the formal prayers stipulate a precondition of a certain number. They say that he must make them up if it is five formal prayers or less. (208)

44.1. Knowledge of God from Thinking and Knowledge of God from Unveiling and Taste

As for the one who intentionally abandons that which God has commanded him to do, no *qada* is obligatory for him. He is one of those whom God has misguided in knowledge. He must submit to Islam anew. He declares it openly. This cannot happen to the one who takes his knowledge of God from proof and speculation. He says that all movements and stillnesses are in the hand of God, and God did not put it into myself to perform what He commanded me to perform. He says: in reality: "He is the Commanded and the Hearer and the One who addresses the command." He has insight and it makes him wretched and comes between him and his happiness. It harms him in the world to come, even if he enjoys it in this world. Nothing harms God. This is a frankness about a right which has no benefit. (209)

If it had come from tasting and unveiling, the awe of majesty, the immensity of the station and the Master of the state of taste would have stopped him from being like this and abandoning the right of God while he is sober. He is in the position of the one who curses the ruler when he is not looking at him. When he comes before him, then awe rules his heart and he is quick to obey his command. This sort of knowledge does not help him at all for it comes from a proof. Is the blind man who walks with a staff and not within sight like the one who follows by his eyesight in his path? (210)

44.2. The One With the State Who Is Annihilated by Majesty or Bedazzled by Beauty

As for the one who is unconscious, he is the one with the state who is annihilated by majesty or made to wander beside himself in love by beauty. He has no understanding. God has overpowered him in that stupor in his senses and makes him do whatever He likes. I have been in that state for a length of time and I did not miss any of the outward movements of the formal prayer with the group in the most perfect way that an leader can be. When I recovered and came to my senses in the visible world, those present informed me that I had not missed any of the obligations directed to me which are directed to the one with intellect and remembrance among the people of our path who do not have this state. It is a noble state which is not spoken of as wrong action. (211)

It is related that Shibli was seized by enraptured love and would return at the times of the formal prayers. When he finished the formal prayer, enraptured love would seize him again. When al-Junayd was told about him, he said: "Praise be to God who has not caused wrong action to be said of him!" It is possible that Shibli would perform the formal prayer at that time while he had no knowledge of that. People present decided that he had returned since they saw him perform the formal prayer. This is like what happened to me. They spoke of his outward form, while in the heart of the matter, he had no knowledge. Some of them do return, but we are only speaking about the one who is taken from himself at the time of performing what is outwardly obligatory for him. As for that which is outside that time, that is not the question here. (212)

44.3. The Interpretation of the Precondition of Five Formal Prayers in the Case of Someone Who Faints

Those who stipulate five or less formal prayers do so because each of the five formal prayers is a root different from the other in time and certain attributes. When the five have passed, what is after the five is by an attribute of each of them. They are considered inasmuch as they are roots. The jurisprudent was not inadequate in the like of this. It is a very deep wisdom for the one who recognizes the realities of this path. Whoever recognizes that the reality demands that it not be repeated does not say that. It is the first root. The gnostic acts according to what is opened to him in his moment. (213)

45 The Description of Making Up Missed Formal Prayers

45.1. Introduction

45.1.1. *The Two Sorts of Making Up and Their Rulings*

There are two sorts of *qada*. There is *qada* for the entire formal prayer and *qada* for part of the formal prayer. *Qada* for the entire formal prayer has a description, a precondition, and a time. Its description is the same as the incidentals of actual performance of the formal prayer. However the states vary. This is like the one at home who remembers a formal prayer which he had forgotten on a journey and the resign of that. This is the meaning of the difference in states. Some say that he makes up the like of what he owes and does not take into consideration the moment in which he remembers. Some say that he always makes it up with four cycles, whether it is at home or on a journey. Some say that he always makes it up according to the obligation of that moment, that is, the moment in which he remembers. If he is on a journey and remembers a formal prayer which he forgot while he was at home, he makes it up with the travel formal prayer, and vice versa. I say that that moment is the moment of the formal prayer. (214)

45.1.2. *States and Judgments*

Whoever thinks that the state has authority in the station says what we say. Whoever thinks that the state has no authority because this world does not have the power of a state, acts according to the station and performs the like of what he owes. Whoever thinks that the station which he is in is the basis on which he relies and that another station has no authority in spite of the interpenetration of stations (like joining scrupulousness and asceticism, and joining abandoning, submission, entrustment and reliance, and lack of turning to what is decreed and contentment with the judgment of God in what the moment brings), acts by the most complete and universal way. He is the one who always makes it up with four cycles. (215)

The lawgiver took states into considerations and judgments are directed to them. The essences are the place of states by the principle of following (consequence). Carrion is forbidden for Zayd. When Zayd is compelled by necessity, then that carrion is permissible for him. It is the same Zayd, but the states are different. Therefore the judgments differ. For that reason, the formal prayer missed while he was at home is made up as a travel formal prayer when he is on a journey and remembers. The formal prayer which he missed on a journey is made up as a formal prayer at home when he remembers it while he is at home. (216)

45.2. The Precondition

45.2.1. The Precondition of Making Up the Formal Prayer Legally

The precondition about which they disagree is the order. They disagree about the obligation of performing forgotten formal prayers in order along with the current formal prayer at the time he remembers, and about the order of the forgotten formal prayers with each other when there is more than one. Some people think that the order is obligatory in them when it is five formal prayers or less and he begins with the forgotten formal prayers, even if he misses the current formal prayer. This is held to such an extent that if he remembers it while he is performing the current formal prayer, the formal prayer which he is doing is stopped when he remembers. Some of them said the like of this but they make the obligation of order apply when the moment of the current formal prayer is very wide. They agree that the obligation of order falls away when they forget. Another said that the order is not obligatory, but if the moment of the present formal prayer is wide, then the order is better. (217)

45.2.2. The Moment: Its Judgment and Wideness with Those of Realization

The people of realization give authority to the moment, and nothing else. The moment reminds the one who forgets, so it has authority. We do not consider the moment wide. It is a single time. Wideness in some prescribed moments belongs to certain principles. For the gnostics, the wideness of moments is a likeness inasmuch as it is formal prayer or specific form in worship. That form and that name always accompany it in its moment and in the repetition of that form in different moments. This is how they speak of the wideness of the moment. These are moments. (218)

The one among the gnostics who is not a master of breath says that the moment is wide. They are the people of drink and quenching. The first one has more recognition of the realities and is more unveiled to the fine points of matters. The Self-disclosure and states vary with the breaths. Only a few of the people with knowledge of God among the people of God know that. The senses and nature veil the intellect from what its rank would grant it in the form of looking into the fine points of matters, their subtleties, and their basic elements. (219)

45.2.3. *The Order in Making Up in the Same Moment*

This question has no root to which it refers. The moments of the forgotten formal prayers vary. There is no order in *qada* except in the one moment which is the very moment for two formal prayers together. This is conceivable in the school of the one who says that two formal prayers can be joined. Thus he has a basis to which he refers in his view. (220)

45.3. The Second Missed Formal Prayer: Making Up Part of the Formal Prayer

45.3.1. *Forgetfulness and Knowledge of What the Station Demands*

This omission in making up part of the formal prayer has two causes. One cause is forgetfulness and the second cause is what the follower misses of the formal prayer of the leader.

As for forgetfulness, he knows what the station which he is in demands of his behavior. He forgets one of the aspects which lessen its result in stages and miracles. (221)

45.3.2. *Seeking the Cause and the Soundness of the Results of the Station*

The second cause belongs to the leader who is the divine law which is followed in word and principle. He has not reached it, so he begins to acquire the station and perfect it according to what he knows that he lacks in the result. He seeks to know the cause and finds that he himself has left what he should do, but he has no knowledge of that. He comes across a prophetic Tradition or a sign of the Book of God Almighty which he had failed to act by. He acts according to that and the results of the station are valid for him. This is in the position of the one who misses some of the formal prayer of the leader. (223)

45.3.3. *The Uneasiness of Abu Yazid about the Lamp*

This is like Abu Yazid al-Bistami. One night the lamp made him uneasy while his state was scrupulousness. He said to his companions, "I have an odd feeling about the lamp." They said: "Our master, we once borrowed a long-necked bottle from the vegetable-man to carry some oil in. We carried it twice." He said: "Acquaint the vegetable-man about it and give him satisfaction." They did so, and the odd feeling vanished. One day he said to his companions, "My heart is missing, so search the house." They found a bunch of grapes. He said: "Our house has become the house of vegetable-mongers." They gave it away as charity and he found his heart. (223)

45.3.4. The Gazelle of Abu Madyan

It happened to our Shaykh Abu Madyan when his moment was divestment and lack of hoarding. He forgot that he had a dinar in his pocket. He used to often go away alone to Jabal al-Kawakib. There was a gazelle which used to come to him and give him milk. That was his nourishment. When he came to the mountain, the gazelle came to him. He needed food, so he stretched his hand to it as he usually did, in order to drink from its milk. It fled from him and butted him with its horns. Whenever he stretched out his hand to it, it fled from him. He thought about the cause of that and remembered the dinar. He took it out of his pocket and threw it away in a place where he could not find it. Then the gazelle came to him and was friendly with him and gave him its milk. (224)

When a man comes in and the leader has already gone down to bowing, some people say that when he catches the leader when he has not lifted his head from bowing and bows with him, he has caught the cycle and does not have to make it up. These people disagree about the precondition for that one who enters the formal prayer. Does he say two recitations of "God is Greater"—the recitation of "God is Greater" after which everything but the formal prayer is forbidden (*takbir al-ihram*) and a the recitation of "God is Greater" for bowing, or is he simply allowed to the "God is Greater" of bowing? If he is allowed it, is it a precondition that he intend the recitation of "God is Greater" after which everything but the formal prayer is forbidden by it or not? (225)

45.4. Someone Following the Leader When He Has Missed Some of the Formal Prayer with the Leader (imam) [of the Formal Prayer]

Some of them say that the single recitation of "God is Greater" is enough if he intends the recitation of "God is Greater" after which everything but the formal prayer is forbidden by it. Some people say that there must be two recitations of "God is Greater." Some people say that one recitation of "God is Greater" is allowed, even if he does not intend the recitation of "God is Greater" after which everything but the formal prayer is forbidden by it. As for the second statement, some people believe that when the leader comes up, he has missed it if he does not catch him standing. That is what Abu Hurayra said. The third statement is that when the one who enters the formal prayer comes to the last row and some of the people have not come up although the leader has come up, he has caught it. That is because each of them are leaders to one another. (226)

My position in that is that the one who takes the linguistic bowing into consideration is the one who says that he catches it when he is bowing. The one who considers the bowing in the divine law (and it is standing, bowing and prostration), says that he does not catch it unless he catches him standing while reciting "God is Greater" and when he enters the formal prayer, that is, this one who enters the formal prayer. It is better to consider the bowing of the divine law although the divine law also called bowing bowing as it is linguistically. When the sign: "*Then glorify with the name of thy Lord, The Sublime*" (56:74), was revealed, the Prophet said: "Put it in your bowing." He meant at the time of bowing. (227)

In general, it is a question which should be investigated. Everyone considers it according to what his proof gives him after he was led to it by his strenuous endeavor. Our school in this question has not been completely expressed since I fear that it would be lengthy. We do not make people worship God by our perception. It is a principle specific to me which I have been given by my proof. (228)

The leader of those who know God is The Truly Real— glory be to Him! He descends to them by His gentleness which is hidden by the attributes of humanity: joy in them, laughter for them, smiling when they come forward to Him desiring His intimate conversation in His house. "My servant! My servant! If you wander from Me, I call you to Me by state (and this refers to entering the moment of the formal prayer by words and it refers to the call to formal prayer). My servant! If you rebel against Me, I veil you and so I veil you from the eyes of the one I have appointed to carry out My limits on you and those like you. I did not punish you. I show My love for you by blessings. You draw your error to you after generosity. My generosity wipes out its traces. I have called you to come forward to My blessings. If you return to Me, I will accept you in spite of what you have done. Who does that with you in spite of the fact that He is the High, independent of you while you are in need of Him except Me?" (229)

45.4.1. The Hidden Kindness of God in Being Described by Human Qualities

This descent from God is in the position of bowing from the servant. When the one who performs the formal prayer does not catch the like of this from God, as he has not heard God say in his formal prayer, "My servant has praised Me, My servant has lauded Me, My servant has glorified Me, and My servant has entrusted to Me" with his own hearing, not by faith, the servant needs his Master and loves Him. He recognizes that God only descends to him by this descent through a secret which is hidden in him. Therefore the servant disconnects Him from all that He sends down to him. He says: "Glory be to Thee! There is nothing like Thee!" (230)

This is why the servant is commanded to disconnect in His bowing to counter by that the descent of God to him with that which we have mentioned since God performs the formal prayer blessing on us. He places us in three ranks in His formal prayer on us. One rank is that He makes us in His formal prayer on us like the ground on which we perform the formal prayer. The second is that He performs the formal prayer on us without formal prayer on the dead. The third is like the formal prayer of the Prophet. Each type has a specific group with a specific state. (231)

45.4.2. The Disconnection of the Servant and the Descent of the Truly Real

He—glory be to Him! mentions that He performs the formal prayer on us. He said: "*He it is Who gives blessings to you and His angels that He may bring you out of the shadows into the light.*" (33:43) He joined Himself and His angels in the formal prayer on the Prophet. "*Truly God and His angels give blessings to the Prophet.*" (33:56) He commanded that it be returned. He said: "*And invoke blessings for them; truly thy supplicating will bring a sense of rest to them.*" (9:103) How wondrous is the Quran for the one who reflects on its signs and remembers! (232)

When God performs the formal prayer on him, the servant must be like a corpse before Him at the funeral without movement or claim. He is in the *qibla* of his Lord. The bowing of the servant coincides with God's descent to him with the like of His words: "*Say: Each does according to his same manner.*" (17:84) He has caught the bowing. Whoever does not have the descent of God coincide with his bowing in this divine descent by the name The Generous to him, has not caught the bowing—either linguistically or in the divine law. (233)-(234)

45.4.3. God Undertakes the Best Interests of His Servants

Its interpretation regarding catching it standing before he goes into bowing, that is, before he bows, is that God undertakes the welfare of His servants and He looks at them when He establishes them. He stands over every self by what it has earned by the source of mercy. He provides for them and is good to them while they assign Him partners and disbelieve. He calls them while they turn away from Him and turn to their passion which they take as a god which they accept. (235)

45.4.4. The Greatest divine Descent

It is like that in prostration in the school of the one who thinks that the bowing is designated by the divine law is standing from His standing, bowing, from His tenderness for His servants by His name The Tender as we mentioned, and the divine prostration. It is the greatest divine descent in which God Himself descends to the stage of His servant. It is His words, "I was sick and you did not visit Me. I was hungry and you did not feed Me. I was thirsty and you did not let me drink." There is nothing greater than this divine descent. (236)

Then He explained that as so-and-so being ill, so-and-so being hungry, and so-and-so being thirsty. He put Himself in their stages in their stage and related that to Himself by referring to Himself with these states. (237)

45.4.5. The divine Cycle and the Prescribed Cycle

Whoever catches all of that from God in His formal prayer, has caught the divine bowing since God is his Leader. The servant receives that with what befits these divine blessings: thankfulness by praise through the attributes of negative qualities, disconnection, true greatness and pride, height, immensity and might. This is the prescribed bowing. (238)

The dispute in this question derives from the disagreement among the scholars about whether to take part of what is indicated by the names or all of it. Part of bowing is called bowing as all of it with all of its parts is called a bowing. This is as is said about the command of the Prophet to wash the penis. Whoever washes the end of his penis has done it since the name "penis" applies to it. Linguistically, when someone has washed the end of his penis, it is said that he has washed his penis, even if he has not washed all of it. This is like washing the name "hand." (239)

When the one is following the leader forgets to follow the leader in bowing until he prostrates, some people say that if he does not catch bowing with him, he has missed the bowing and must make it up. Some people say that he repeats the bowing if he can in order to complete the bowing before the leader stands up for the second bowing. Some people say that he follows him and repeats the bowing as long as the leader has not come up from bowing in the second bowing. (240)

These different statements, in my opinion, are based on what they understand from the words of the Prophet: "The leader was appointed to be followed." They do not disagree about the Tradition. Is it a condition of the one following that his action accompany the action of the leader or not? Is this a precondition in all three parts of the prescribed bowing (standing, bowing and prostration) or not? It is a condition for part of it? They do not disagree about the one who is following and is doing one part of the bowing while the Leader is doing another part. However, there is disagreement about it. (241)

If man is precise about this Tradition with other well-known Traditions about this question, it is clear to him that every statement in this question which we have related has a connection. All they have said is legal, even if they disagree. Praise be to God who gave ample scope in this matter! (242)

45.5. When Someone Following the Leader (*imam*) Performs What He Missed of the Formal Prayer with the Leader

45.5.1. The One Following Forgetting to Follow the Leader [of the Formal Prayer] when Bowing Forward [in the Formal Prayer]

The servant forgets to follow God in what He commands him or forbids him or in the proper manners of thankfulness which he must have with Him when presented with His blessings and beauty. That causes the invalidity of the knowledge which he missed and what he obtained in his Self-disclosure is according to that amount which he missed. My companions disagree in this question according to what we mentioned. (243)

Some people say that when you miss one glance from God in your moment while you witnessed Him immediately before that in the moment when you recognized Him by taste, what you missed in that glance is more than what you obtained before your moment. I will mention the reason for that. (244)

The reason for that is that each glance from the servant to God in His Self-disclosure to him contains the recognition of every glance and its pleasure before it and increases that by what the reality of the glance of the moment gives him. When the servants forgets what God commanded him, he has missed much good and he must make up what he missed in order to obtain this knowledge. They fall into a great deal of error in this since they have no awareness. That is because when the one who follows the leader misses something with the leader, what he catches is the beginning of his formal prayer, and he completes it according to what the obligatory formal prayer has. In our view, no one is "making up" the formal prayer since *qada* means "performing." This is a sound view. (245)

As for the error of our companions, the glances of Self-disclosure which preceded this glance in the moment here are based on the principle of following this glance. Every glance is the ruler in its moment. Where is the action of the thing in its kingdom in relation to its action in the kingdom of another? Understand! (246)

45.6. Catching Something by the Principle of Inclusion and by the Principle of Witnessing

Some of our companions say that this Self-disclosure which he is in contains what he missed and what he obtained, so he repeats because of what he has caught and obtains much good in it. That which we believe is what we have mentioned. Catching the thing is by the principle of inclusion. It is not like catching it by the principle of explicitness and seeing with the eye. The one who is the ruler of the moment is a detailed visual catching which has a specific taste. The other contains a comprehensive catching which is not visual. It has a taste which is distinct from his taste in his moment. (247)

Where is the vision of the one who has Moses' inheritance among us? It is part of the niche of Muhammad from the Muhammadan vision, from the sincere Muhammadan, even though it contains the vision of Moses. Here it follows and something else is in the time of its power. The heirs differ in excellence in the inheritance according to their ranks. Some heirs obtain all of the property. There is the heir who gets a half, a fourth, an eighth, a third, a sixth, etc. (248)

45.7. The One Who Tastes Honey Itself and the One Who Tastes It in an Apple Drink

When someone joins both perceptions (lit. catchings), each perception is in its station and is not equivalent nor like the perception of one without the other. He is the one who tastes honey by itself and then tastes it in an apple drink. He has perceived its taste in two states. He finds a difference between the two tastes without a doubt. Where is its valuation as honey in relation to its valuation as drink or apple drink? (249)

45.8 When someone following the leader (*imam*) performs what he missed of the formal prayer with the leader (*imam*), is it missed or performing in the View of the religious scholars?

If you said: "When someone who follows performs what he missed of the formal prayer making it up or performing it as it appears?" we reply that the answer is that the divine law has confirmed three schools in it. One school is that what he does after the greetings of the leader is *qada* and that what he does with the leader is not the beginning of his formal prayer. The next school is that what he does after the greeting of the leader is performing the formal prayer and that which he does with the leader is the beginning of his formal prayer. That is my position. The third school makes a distinction between words and actions. By words, they mean recitation. He makes up the words and performs the actions. (250)

If the one of the first school (that is the school of *qada*) catches one bowing of the the evening formal prayer-formal prayer, he stands up when the leader says the greetings to perform two bowings. He recites the Opening Chapter and a chapter in them and does not sit between them. In the second school, he stands up for one cycle in which he recites the Opening Chapter and a chapter aloud. Then he sits and rises for another cycle in which he recites the Opening Chapter silently. In the third school, he rises for a cycle in which he recites the Opening Chapter and another chapter, and then he sits and rises for another cycle in when he recites the Opening Chapter and another chapter. (251)

These three schools are related in a Tradition. The Tradition says: "Pray what you catch and complete what you missed." *Qada* demands that what you caught is the end of your formal prayer. Whoever makes use of both versions of the Tradition and combines *qada* and performing, says that he makes up words and performs actions as we have already clarified. (252)

45.9. Authority of the divine name Which Is the Ruler of the Moment

Whoever considers that authority belongs to the divine name which is the ruler of the moment and its master, thinks that it is the that name which rules that entire formal prayer from first to last, both for the leader and the follower. He is performing it without any doubt. That name is not removed of its authority in the moment by the greeting of the leader. It continues until everyone under the authority of the leader recites the *taslim* and is separated. That state from that name accompanies the one who has missed whatever he missed of it, even if he only catches the last sitting in the formal prayer. (253)

The one who considers that authority belongs to the name which grants bowing, which is not the same as the name which grants standing and recitation (and every movement in the formal prayer has a particular divine name, even if it is shared with another name or other divine names), says that it is *qada*. (254)

45.10. The Judgment of the Sharing of the names in the Formal Prayer

The one who considers the principle of sharing between the names in the formal prayer and that each name has a portion in it, says that he performs such-and-such and makes up such-and-such, that is, he takes the gnoses which such-and-such a name gives him and the knowledges which another name gives him. The gnostics distinguish things in that by tasting. (255)

"By the heaven of the returning rain, by the earth splitting open, it is indeed a decisive word. It is not jest" (86:11-14). The one who is ignorant of matters is not like the one who perceives. Listen then, and be entirely present! You might be among the people of obtainment and then you will be among the successful. (256)

46. On the Mysteries of the Prostration of Forgetfulness

46.1. Introduction

Religious scholars disagree about the prostration of forgetfulness and whether it is obligatory or *sunna*. Some say that it is *sunna*. Some say that it is obligatory although it is not a precondition for the validity of the formal prayer. Malik makes it a distinction between the prostration of forgetfulness for actions, and the prostration of forgetfulness for words and between adding and omission. He says that the prostration of forgetfulness which is for omitted actions is obligatory and that it is one of the preconditions of the formal prayer. (257)

46.1.1. Faith, Investigation and Unveiling

The cause of forgetfulness is doubt or forgetting while it is a certainty which is desired. Only the one who is *"on a clear sign from his Lord"* (cf. 11:7) worships God. The purest, most just and strongest of them is the faith which the believer in his Lord finds in himself which he cannot repel. Less than that in strength and purity is that faith which is based on logical proofs. If unveiling is related to the believer or the one who speculates, there is no doubt it is stronger than each of the two on its own. (258)

Forgetfulness does not enter the formal prayer of the one who is like this. The one who only speculates has forgetfulness enter his formal prayer. It is the same with the wavering believer. The prostration of forgetfulness is an obligation for him. That is because he reverts to looking at himself, his poverty, his possibility, and his incapacity by which he has a proof of his Object of worship, His utter independence, His necessary existence and effective power. That knowledge is to spite Satan who casts doubt to him in his formal prayer or worship. (259)

46.1.2. The Formal Prayer Is Conversation with God and Witnessing Him

The formal prayer is conversation with God and witnessing Him. He is told: "Worship God as if you were seeing Him," and "God is in the direction of the formal prayer of the one who performs the formal prayer." Then he turns to Him in his formal prayer and limits Him in his *qibla* as he is told to do. However, he declares Him free of having a peer or being encompassed. This is like the person who stands looking at Him and speaking with Him in his *qibla*. He has forgotten that the divinity must encompass him and be free from limitation. This is what the divine law says: "*There is not like Him anything.*" (42:11) (260)

The one who has this state must prostrate for his forgetfulness. He rejects that connection, delusion, and conception of himself. This is the prostration, and he says: "Glory be to my Lord, the Most High" three times—once for his senses, the second for his imagination, and the third time for his intellect. He disconnects Him from being perceived by his senses and so limited, or being limited by his imagination or being limited by his intellect. That is to spite Satan. (261)

46.2. The Places for the Prostration of Forgetfulness

Some say that its place is always before the greeting of the formal prayer (*salam*). Some people say that it is always after the greeting. Some people say that if it is due to an omission, it is before the greeting, and if it is for addition to it, it is after the greeting. Some people say that he prostrates before the greeting in the places in which the Messenger of God prostrated after the greeting. If there is a prostration for anything other than these places, he prostrates before the greeting. Some people say that the prostration of forgetfulness is only in these five places in which the Messenger of God prostrated. Outside of that, if it is obligatory, he does it, and if it is recommended, he does not have to do anything. (262)

That which I say and believe is that you prostrate in the places in which the Messenger of God prostrated. You prostrate before the greetings for that for which he prostrated before the greeting, and you prostrate after the greeting for that for which he prostrated after the greeting. As for other things which the one who performs the formal prayer forgets, he can choose. If he likes, he can prostrate before the greeting, and if he likes, he can prostrate for it after the greeting. (263)

46.2.1. Seeing God Before Everything

God Almighty says: "*To God belongs the command before and after.*" (30:4). If he puts looking at God before looking at himself in what he has forgotten in it, he is like the one who prostrates before the greetings. This is the station of the Siddiq (Abu Bakr). "I have not seen anything but that I saw God after it." (264)

46.2.2. Seeing God After Everything

If he puts looking at himself before looking at his Lord as the Prophet said: "Whoever knows himself knows his Lord," he is like the one who prostrates after the greeting. It is the station of the one who says: "I have not seen anything but that I saw God after it." It is the station of the people with logical proofs of the existence of the Maker. He says: "I have not seen anything but that it was a proof of God for me." He is always turning about in proofs. (265)

46.2.3. *The Intellect, Imagination and the divine law*

As for adding and omission, that belongs to the intellect and what it omits in respect of its reflection from its knowledge of its Lord which cannot be independently perceived outside of what the lawgiver described. The intellect is not led to that attribute which the Majesty of God demands. It moves him on, both absolutely and in meaning. As for adding, the imagination does not apply limitation and restriction to its Lord without believing in the disconnection in that very thing in which he limits and restricts him. This is the forgetfulness of adding and that is the forgetfulness of omission. God says: *"There is nothing like Him. He is The Hearing, The Seeing."* (42:11) In this sign, *"There is nothing like Him"* is the proof of the intellect, and *"He is The Hearing, The Seeing"* is the proof of hearing. This combines the two forms of evidence: the evidence of the intellect and the evidence of hearing. (266)

46.2.4. *The Five Places Where the Messenger of God Prostrated*

As for the places in which the Messenger of God prostrated, they are five:

1. He prostrated because of doubt.
2. He stood up after two bowings without sitting, and prostrated because of it.
3. He recited the greetings after two bowings and did the prostration.
4. He recited the greeting after three bows, and then prostrated.
5. He performed the formal prayer of five bows, and then prostrated because of it. (267)

People disagree about whether the prostration is for adding or omission or if it is for forgetfulness. Some say that it is for forgetfulness and some say that it is for the omission and adding. The latter is my position. He does one prostration for his forgetfulness, and the second prostration is for the omission or increase. It completes the omission. Adding is good: *"Light upon light."* (24:35) (268)

46.3. The Words and Actions for Which People Say You Must Perform the Prostration of Forgetfulness

Scholars agree that the prostration is performed for the *sunan* of the formal prayer. It is not done for obligatory parts or recommended parts. If the one praying forgets recommended things in the formal prayer, they do not think that he has to do anything as long as it is not more than one. This is like what Malik thought. He thought that the prostration was not obligatory for forgetting one recitation of "God is Greater," but it was obligatory for more than that. As for the obligatory parts, they can only be taken care of by doing them and mending it when forgetting them is not something which obliges him to repeat the entire formal prayer over again. As for the prostration of forgetfulness for adding, it occurs when you add to obligatory parts and practices of the Prophet (*sunan*). There is no dispute between them about it (269)

All that the divine law scholars have said about it is recommended—and that is desirable. What is other than this is *sunna* or obligatory. They say that the desirable action is recommended, and there is some dispute over stressing the command to perform it. This is connected to the states of that worship. This is held to such an extent that some of them think that if certain *Sunan* are intentionally omitted (if that is an action) or are intentionally done (if it is something to leave out), then its principle in the wrong action is the principle of the obligatory act. For instance, this would be if someone always left out the odd number or the two bows before dawn. He would be doing a wrong action. (270)

As for the middle sitting, they agree that he does the prostration of forgetfulness if he omits out. They disagree about whether the middle sitting is obligatory or *sunna*. They disagree about whether or not the leader goes back if his attention is called to it. If he goes back, when can he go back? Most people say that he can go back as long as he has not stood upright. Some people say he can go back as long as he has not begun the cycle for which he stood up. Some people say he can go back if he has only left the ground the amount of a hand-span. If he goes back with those who do not think he can go back, most say that his formal prayer is allowed. Some people say that it is invalid. (271)

46.4. Presence in All Acts of Worship: Formal, Customary (*sunna*) and Recommended

The obligations of worship are presence with God when beginning these acts. The *sunan* of worship are the presence of the obligated person in them inasmuch as he is obligated. In desired actions, presence is his annihilation in them when God takes over their principles in all of the actions. When the obligations are forgotten, the worship is not valid and it can only mended by what is forgotten, not by the prostration of forgetfulness. The meaning of the interpretation of the prostration of forgetfulness has been made clear to you. The one who forgets the sunan does the prostration of forgetfulness for them. If he forgets desired parts, he can choose. If he likes, he can prostrate, and if he so wishes, he can not prostrate. (272)

As far as the middle sitting is concerned, we have already discussed its interpretation in one section with the last prostration. As for doing the prostration of forgetfulness for it, the first prostration is for his forgetfulness, and the second is for the omission, and the sitting mends it. It is like the obligatory parts which are mended by being done and not by the prostration of forgetfulness. (273)

46.5. The Description of the Prostration of Forgetfulness

Some people say that if it is after the greeting, he recites *tashahhud* in it and recites the *taslim*. Some people say that if it is before the greeting, he only does *tashahhud* for it and the greeting of the formal prayer is its greeting. Some people who think that it is before for omission and afterwards for adding, say that he does not do the *tashahhud* for what is before the greeting. It is confirmed that the Prophet did the prostration of forgetfulness after the greeting. The *tashahhud* in forgetfulness is not confirmed, even if it is related. (274)

46.5.1. The Greeting of "Peace" of the Formal Prayer and the Circumambulation of Arrival for the Person Performing the *Qiran*

As for before the greeting, the greeting from the formal prayer and the *tashahhud* do not need to be repeated. It is like circumambulation and searching (between Safa and Marwa). That is the circumambulation of arrival for the one who is doing *qiran* since life demands circumambulation and searching. The pilgrimage demands the like of that in the school of the one who thinks that one circumambulation and one search is sufficient in that. The one who does not think that, and thinks that two searches and two circumambulations are obligatory, thinks that there is *tashahhud* and greeting. The one who says this does not think that it is valid to make a distinction between increase and omission. (275)

Similarly, the one with the first position does not think it valid to say that the prostration after the greeting occurs to spite Satan in that since it is given to the prostration of forgetfulness rather than any other actions of the formal prayer since he was ordered to prostrate and did not prostrate. The forgetfulness which overcame him came from Satan. It can only be mended by an attribute which Satan does not have if he comes near the servant when he has that attribute. Therefore the prostration of forgetfulness was prescribed for him. It is confirmed in a Tradition that when a man prostrates, Satan retires weeping and says: "The son of Adam was commanded to prostrate and he has prostrated. He has the

Garden. I was commanded to prostrate and I refused, so I have the Fire." (276)

46.5.2. *While He Is in Prostration, the Human Being is Protected from Satan*

When man is prostrating he is protected from Satan. Satan does not come near him. If Satan had come near him in the prostration of his forgetfulness, he would have forgotten while he was prostrating that prostration, and the business would be continuous. This is why there is nothing in the divine law for the one who forgets in the prostration of forgetfulness. If that occurred, it would not be from Satan. If it is not from Satan, it is not to spite Satan unless the forgetfulness is his doing. This forgetfulness must be the work of Satan. Its cause is that the one who performs the formal prayer slips from his worship. When he lets it slip, that is forgetfulness. (277)

46.5.3. *The Causes of the Absence from Worship in Someone Who Performs the Formal Prayer*

The causes of this absence which comes from the intellect in the case of some who is performing the formal prayer in any part of the formal prayer are numerous. Some causes originate with Satan. One of them is when he is overcome by seeing what is demanded by a sign of the Book of God about Unity, one of the rulings of the religion, the Garden or the Fire, or what one of them requires. If it comes from Satan, the prostration of forgetfulness is to spite him. It spites him because it is prostration and because his whisperings had no effect on him since what he forgot is mended by the prostration. (278)

For this reason, it is recommended for everyone who performs the formal prayer to perform the prostration of forgetfulness after every formal prayer since man must lose a moment in the formal prayer when he is performing it, or more. That is to spite Satan. It is the school Tirmidhi al-Hakim. I saw a group of the Zaydis who stated that in respect to those following the leader. I saw that they used to do that and I thought that it was good that they did that. Even if the goals are different, it is to spite Satan in any case. (279)

46.5.4. *The Disagreement of Scholars on Its Description*

Ibn al-Mundhir said that the scholars disagree about this question, and they have six opinions regarding that. Some say that he does *tashahhud* in it and no *taslim*. This is what Anas, Hasan and Ata say. Some say that there is *tashahhud* and *taslim* in it. I say that both are right, but I also say that there must be *tashahhud* and *taslim* in it unless the prostration is before the greeting. Then the *tashahhud* and *taslim* of the formal prayer are enough, and the forgetfulness does not need *tashahhud* and *taslim*. They are linked. If it is after the greeting, then there is *tashahhud* and *taslim*. (280)

Some say that there is *tashahhud* and not *taslim*. That is the position of Hakam, Hammad and Nakhai. Some say there is *taslim* and not *tashahhud*. It is the position of Ibn Sirin. Some say that if he likes, he performs *tashahhud* and *taslim*, and if he likes, he does not do it. Ata said he does not. Some say that if he prostrates before the greeting, he does not perform the *tashahhud*, and if he prostrates after the greeting, there is *tashahhud*. That is what Ibn Hanbal said. Ibn al-Mundhir said that it is established that the Prophet recited four "God is Greater" in it and that he recited the greetings. One must look into the establishment of *tashahhud*. (281)

46.6. The One Who Must Perform the Prostration of Forgetfulness

Scholars agree that the leader and the one performing the formal prayer alone perform the prostration of forgetfulness. They disagree about whether someone following an leader and forgets prostrates or not? Most say that he does not have to prostrate and the leader takes the responsibility from him. Makhul says that the follower must prostrate for his forgetfulness. That is my position. We do not think that the lawgiver made any distinction between the leader and the follower when he mentioned the prostration of forgetfulness. He mentioned the one who performs the formal prayer and did not specify any particular state. (282)

46.6. The One Who Must Perform the Prostration of Forgetfulness

No one takes on the burden of another and no self compensates for another self at all. Every self is a pledge for what it has earned. If you investigate this meaning by unveiling, you will know that leader does not assume the responsibility of the follower. Makhul put the collyrium of exactness on his eye in this question and his inner eye was clear. God gives success. There is no Lord but Him. (283)

46.7. When does the follower prostrate when he has missed some of the formal prayer and the leader (*imam*) must do the prostration of forgetfulness?

Scholars disagree about the person who is a follower who misses some of the formal prayer with the leader must do the prostration of forgetfulness. When does the follower prostrate? Some say that he prostrates with the leader and then makes up what he owes, whether he is before or after the greeting. Some say that he makes it up and then prostrates. Some say that when the prostration is before the *taslim*, he prostrates with him, and when it is after the *taslim*, he does then after he has made up what he owes. Some say that he does them with the leader and then does them a second time after *qada*. (284)

I say that either the one following the leader knows what the leader forgot or he does not know. If he does not know and the leader prostrates before the greeting, then he does them with him, and stands up to make up what he owes after the greeting of the leader. If the leader prostrates them after the greeting, he does not follow him. He performs what he does and does not have to prostrate for the forgetfulness of the leader. If he does prostrate after *qada*, that is a more cautious approach, and it is recommended for everyone who performs the formal prayer to perform them after his *qada* in every formal prayer always after the greeting, whether he is performing the formal prayer alone or behind a leader. (285)

If the follower knows about the forgetfulness of the leader, his forgetfulness was either in what the follower missed or in what he did with him in the formal prayer. If it is in what he missed, he does not follow him in the prostration, even if he prostrates before the greeting. If he knows that the forgetfulness of the leader was in that part of the formal prayer which he caught with him, he follows him if he prostrates before the greeting. If he prostrates after the greeting, he makes up what he missed and then prostrates. This is unless the forgetfulness of the leader is in that which the Messenger of God forgot in that part of the formal prayer which he caught with him. Then he follows the leader in his prostration before or after the greeting, and then he makes up what he owes. (286)

46.8. The Leadership of the Messenger Is Not Removed after His Death

The leader must be followed as long as he is called "leader." When the name "leader" leaves him, it is not necessary to follow him. The leadership of the Messenger is not removed. We must follow him, and God will necessarily love the one who follows him. There is no doubt of that. God says: "*Surely in the Messenger of God there has been for you a good, fair example.*" (33:21) It was said to him, "*Say: If you have been loving God, then follow me and God will love you.*" (3:31) When God loves His servant, He is all of his faculties and limbs. He only acts by his faculties and limbs, so he only acts by God. His action is protected in his movements and stillnesses. (287)

46.8.1. There Is No Condition or Quality in the Responsible Person Outside the Jurisdiction of the divine law

Then you should know that since he is thus described, the obligation of the responsible person leaves him either completely or by a temporary condition according to the jurisprudents. We do not think that it is like this. There is no state or quality in the responsible person which is outside the judgment of the divine law. If one is overcome by the state, madness, forgetfulness, sleep, or has not yet reached puberty, all these things come under the authority of the divine law. There is a principle set down for every one with a state of description— either by a general principle or one of the rules of the divine law because there must be a rule of the divine law for the one with that state. There is only the responsible person, so the obligation is not removed. (288)

These are the people about whom the jurisprudents say the authority of the divine law has been removed from them. It has not been removed from them. The divine law allows the person to act in what his nature demands, like the animal, and there is nothing held against him in that. How then can it be said that the authority of the divine law has been removed from him? The divine law has judged that he is allowed to act like that, just as the man of intellect and age is allowed to do certain things which are permitted him. Judgment in things belongs to the God, not to the intellect. The divine law is the judgment of God in things. There is nothing outside of the judgment of God. This is the view of the people of God because they are present with God in every breath. (289)

46.8.2. The Judgment of the divine law Connected to Individuals are Based on States

Even if the judgments of the divine law are connected to individuals, they are based on states. The individual is not called upon to do anything except according to the state which he has. It is because of that state that he is told to do what he is told to do. It is not because of the individual. The individual remains while the states change. The ruling of the divine law on the individual changes with the change of state. The state of childhood, unconsciousness, madness, being overcome by the state, annihilation, intoxication, and illness, each has rules within the divine law as is the case with the state of manhood, consciousness, health, going-on, sobriety, and not being overpowered by the state. They all have rulings in the divine law, so the judgment of the divine law applies to all states when you understand that God enters into the existence of individuals. (290)

46.9. Saying, "Glory be to God" and Clapping the Hands by Those Following the Leader (*Imam*) [of the Formal Prayer] When the Leader Forgets

Some people say that both men and women say "Glory be to God." Others say that "Glory be to God" is for men and women clap. That is what I say and believe by the Tradition which is related about that. (291)

46.9.1. Humanity Is a Quality Which Both Men and Women Have

Whoever considers humanity relevant, connects men and women together as the Messenger of God connected them with men in perfection. Whoever takes masculinity and femininity into consideration along with the words of God Almighty: "*And men have a degree over them (f),*" (2:228), and that the active dominates the passive, makes a distinction between men and women. He says that men say, "Glory be to God" and women clap. (292)

A woman's words may provoke natural lust, especially if there is abjectness and submission in her words and the listener who has "a sickness in his heart" imagines that she is a woman. God forbade women to be abject when He says: "*Be not soft in your saying so that he should be desirous in whose heart is a sickness, but say a saying of one who is moral.*" (33:32) This sign contains the permission for women to speak to men in a particular manner. (293)

46.9.2. The Gnostic Is Always with God in His Conversation

There is no doubt that the one who performs the formal prayer is in a state of conversation with his Lord. When a woman says: "Glory be to God!" natural imaginary inclination for her encroaches upon him. He is not safe from it when she claps, so how then is it with speech? Here the gnostic has that which he considers with God in his intimate conversation. He either speaks with his intellect or with his ego and nature. He acts according to his strength. If he is strong and sound, he is not worried about that by which intimate conversation occurs. Therefore, men and women are equal. If he recognizes that some of his ego remains and that there is illness in it, he makes a distinction between his intellect and nature until it is pure. That is how the people of God look at themselves. (294)

46.10. The Prostration of Forgetfulness for the Place of Doubt

Scholars disagree about the one who doubts in his formal prayer and does not know whether he has performed the formal prayer one, two, three, or four. Some scholars says that he builds on certainty, and that is the least amount, and he is not allowed to investigate it. Some say that if it is at the beginning, he is not allowed to investigate it. Some say that if it is at the beginning, his formal prayer is invalid, and if he repeats that, he analyzes it and acts upon what he thinks is probable, and then he does the prostration after the greeting. Some people say that he does not have to do anything if he doubts—he does not go back to certainty or investigate it. He simply must do the prostration if he has doubts. My position in this question is the last statement. However, if he builds on certainty, that is more prudent. (295)

46.10.1. *Judgment Belongs to the Master of the Moment*

When man recognize the first thought, he relies on it. Doubt is vacillation between two more things without giving preference to one. Probability involves inclination by preferring one of the two doubtful matters without being decisive. He can only resort to certainty and what he thinks likely. Authority belongs to the master of the moment, which is doubt. (296)

As one must be cautious in what lacks of his worship, he must be careful about adding. It is prescribed and God has not given him permission to increase it. The one who doubts is called upon to prostrate. If the one who builds on certainty removes the doubt, then his position is that of the one who does not doubt and we are safe in increase in that act of worship. The one who prescribed that action is the one who prescribed the prostration. The prostration is not demanded of the one who is certain or the one who is fairly sure. (297)

46.10.2. *Doubt in the Proofs of Hearing and Intellect*

Whoever doubts his intellect's proof in gnosis of his Lord and doubts the proof he hears which is contrary to the proof of his intellect in gnosis of his Lord, does not trust either proof because he does not prefer either of them. He cannot remove the truthfulness of the transmitted Tradition which is contradicted by his intellect's proof in his knowledge about the incomparability which the Majesty of God demands in the argument of the intellect. He cannot get rid of it since he believes that whatever God describes Himself with is necessary for Him for the believer if the transmitted text brings it like that. Thus he must have what the prophetic Tradition definitely brings, and so the two proofs are in opposition to one another. He cannot prefer one of them or join them together. (298)

He is the one who doubts, and so he must perform the prostration of forgetfulness since he has forgotten to act by belief without looking at both proofs. He frees the place (which is the heart) and empties it, and then adorns it with sincere self-direction: this is the prostration which is described by the two opposites. The prostration is the servant of nearness to God and the place of distance from Satan. (299)

The one who has doubt while he is prostrating has an uncertainty. By his action which is based on belief, the one with this description must consider his description in his heart, and he knows by God what he did not know and the doubt is removed from him since that knowledge gives him one of two things. He can join both proofs or he can prefer one by finding out the invalidity of that which is contrary to belief in one of the proofs and finding the doubt which conflict necessitates. God Almighty says: "*So be Godfearing of God (*here by the prostration of forgetfulness*) and God teaches you (*here by joining the two conflicting proofs, preferring one, or making one of the proofs invalid*)*." (2:282) (300)

47 Those Formal Prayers That Are Individual Obligations and Those That Are Not

47.1. Those Formal Prayers Are Individual Obligations and Those Which Are Not Individual Obligations

Know that some formal prayers are obligations for every individual. We have already discussed them in this chapter. There are also those which are not individual obligations. Some of them are *sunna*, some are general obligations, and some are voluntary. (301)

I believe that only the five formal prayers are obligatory. All other formal prayers must be called voluntary as the Messenger of God so called them in the Tradition related in the Tradition of the bedouin. When the bedouin said: "Messenger of God, do I have to do anything more?" he said: "No, unless you do it voluntarily." I think that he probably meant: "No, unless you do a formal prayer voluntarily. Then it is obligatory for you as the formal prayers are." He said: "Do I have to do anything more?" He meant: "Has God obliged me to do anything more?" Like the vow, when you voluntarily start an formal prayer, God obliges you to do as you have obliged yourself to do it. (302)

This voluntary prayer in the divine law has different states which lead to a difference in giving them different names so that you can recognize them. I consider their total to be ten: the odd number, the two cycles before the morning formal prayer, supererogatory prayers, greeting the mosque, the night formal prayers of Ramadan, the eclipse formal prayer, the formal prayer for rain, the two Festival ritual prayers, and the prostration of recitation of the Quran for the one who calls it a formal prayer. When we have finished with these ten and their interpretations, we will deal with the funeral formal prayer, the *istikhara*, and other things which are called "formal prayer" in the divine law and which do not have bowing, formal prayer, the sacred state, or *taslim*. This is like the prayer on the Prophet which the divine law commands and the wisdom of that. (303)

47.1. The Formal and Voluntary Formal Prayers and Servanthood by Compulsion and by Choice

The formal prayer demands servanthood. Since the formal prayer is divided into two sections as we have stated—what is an individual obligation and what is not an obligation. So servanthood is divided into two divisions—servanthood by compulsion (by which I pray the individual obligations) and servanthood by choice. By it, we perform all the other formal prayers which are not individual obligations. God Almighty called it supererogatory and the Messenger of God called it voluntary. God Almighty says: "*And keep vigil with it in the night for an unexpected gift for thee.*" (17:79) (304)

One of the righteous stated that no one has a definite supererogatory prayer except the Messenger of God. Supererogatory prayers are only valid for the one who has perfected his obligations. If any perfection is lacking in his formal prayers, then what he does voluntarily completes it. If there are voluntary prayers beyond that, then they can be called supererogatory. God has only testified to that for His Messenger. He commanded him and said: *And keep vigil with it in the night for an unexpected gift for thee.*" (17:79) (305)

God Almighty says in a sound Tradition: "The servant continues to draw near Me with supererogatory actions." He called whatever is beyond the formal prayer "supererogatory actions." The Messenger of God said to the bedouin to teach him the basis of Islam. After he had mentioned the formal prayers, he said: "Do I have to do anything more?" He said: "No, not unless you do it voluntarily." He called whatever is beyond the formal prayers "voluntary." (306)

47.2. The Formal Is Servanthood by Compulsion and the Voluntary Is by Choice

The formal prayer is servanthood by compulsion because rebellion is verified by doing it or leaving it. Whatever else is servanthood by choice. However, he chooses to begin it. When he begins it, we think that the rules of servanthood by compulsion bind him. That is necessary. He does not leave their jurisdiction until he finishes that act of worship. When he said to him, "Do I have to do anything more?" this is why he said to him, "No, (that is, God has not obliged you to start anything more than what I have mentioned), not unless you do it voluntarily." If you start the like of what God desires for you, do it voluntarily and enter into it, then you are obliged to complete it as the individual obligations must be fulfilled. This is the meaning of "No, not unless you do it voluntarily." You must do what you oblige yourself to do. This includes the vow and things like it. God Almighty says: "*Do not make your actions worthless.*" (47:33) (307)

47.3. The Wisdom of the Ten Voluntary Prayers

The odd number belongs to recognition of God in all things. The two cycles of the morning formal prayer belongs to thankfulness for rising at night to do what He has given him success and from the sleeper for rising to perform the obligation of the morning formal prayer. Entering the mosque is to greet the King in His house. Night formal prayers in

Ramadan are since Ramadan is one of the names of God, and one must rise at the mention of the King. He says: "*A Day when humanity will stand up for the Lord of the worlds*" (83:6). The eclipse ritual prayer is for the manifestation which gives fear. (308)

The Messenger of God was asked about the eclipse. He said: "God does not give a manifestation to anything but that it causes fear." It is what the eye sees of the change in the sun or the moon, even though they do not change in themselves. God displayed to the eye what the sun and the moon contain of fear of God in that time in the form of the disappearance of light. In the moon eclipse, it is by the natural veil of the ego, and in the solar eclipse, it is by the veil of the intellect. (309)

The rain formal prayer is asking for mercy. The Festival ritual prayers are the repetition of Self-disclosure. The prostration of recitation in the Quran is humility for the word of God. For that reason, He commanded silence and listening. The formal prayer over the dead servant who took God as a Guardian and represented Him in whatever property He gave him in thankfulness for what He entrusted him with which was denied to the one to whom it was said: "*And spend out of what He has made you ones who were successors in it.*" (57:7) He brings it out of their hands without any choice on their part. God Almighty says: "*As for what is bad, it goes forth not but scantily.*" (7:58) (310)

'Those who take God as a Guardian" [cf. 73:9] become corpses before Him. This is why He gives them the attribute of absolute purity and it is purity. He commanded us to wash the corpse in order to combine the two purities. He is in the *qibla* of the one who performs the formal prayer over him, between him and God. He is speaking to God in him for him. The one who performs the formal prayer is in purity and God is the Absolutely Pure, and the corpse is between God and the one who performs the formal prayer over him. He must be pure. His purity is in meaning and only the people of unveiling are aware of it. Therefore, He commanded the people of the divine law to wash the corpse in the outward principle so that the one who has no unveiling will be certain of his purity. I will give its interpretation in its proper section, God Almighty willing. (311)

The *istikhara* is to specify what God chooses for this servant in action and not doing so that he is on a clear sign from his Lord as God Almighty says: "*Is then he who has been with a clear portent from his Lord?*" (11:17) This is the benefit of the *istikhara*. I will put it in its section, God willing. We will mention what we have stipulated, section by section, God willing, to acquaint people with the objectives of gnostics in their acts of worship which are distinct from those of the common people, even though they share with them in the general business which embraces all people who are over obligation. God gives success. There is no Lord with Him. (312)

48 On the Mysteries of the Odd Cycle Prayer

48.1. Introduction

Abu Dawud related from Abu Ayyub al-Ansari that the Prophet said: "The odd number is a duty for every Muslim. Whoever wants to do it with three cycles may do so, and whoever wants to do it with one may do so." Abu Dawud related that the Messenger of God used to do the odd number with seven, nine and five cycles. The common Tradition about the odd number of the Prophet is that which is related by Abd Allah ibn Qays. He asked Ayisha how many bows the Messenger of God did in the odd number. She said: "He would perform the odd number with four and three, six and three, eight and three, and ten and three. He would never do it with less than seven or more than thirteen bows." (313)

Nasai transmitted from Ibn Umar that the Messenger of God said: "The the evening formal prayer is the the odd number of the daytime formal prayers, so perform the odd number of the night formal prayers." (314)

48.1.1. People's Disagreement About the Odd Cycle Prayer (witr))

People disagree about the odd number and whether it is mandatory or *sunna*. Some say that it is obligatory (*wajib*) and the one who says this states that the obligatory is between the customary-obligation and the *sunna*. Some say that it is a confirmed *sunna*, and we have already discussed its principle. We still must discuss the description, its time, raising the hands (*qunut*) in it, and performing it while mounted. We will first mention some of the tradition which command it in order to make clear to you its obligatory nature or the absence of that obligatory nature. (315)

48.1.2. The Traditions (ahadith) Indicating the Formal Nature of the Odd Cycle Prayer (witr)

Part of that is what Abu Dawud transmitted from Kharijah ibn Hudhafah. He said: "The Messenger of God came out to us and said: "God, The Mighty and Majestic has given you a formal prayer which is better than the finest camels. He has appointed it for you between the night formal prayer and morning." This includes the odd number and other formal prayers beside the odd number. This Tradition is from the transmission of Abd Allah ibn Rashid from Abd Allah ibn Abi Murra.

Only this Tradition has been heard from him. Neither of them are considered competent authorities and they are hardly seen. Abd Allah ibn Abi Murra related it from Kharijah. It is not known whether he heard it from Kharijah. (316)

When Tirmidhi mentioned this Tradition with this transmission, he said that it is rare Tradition. Daraqutni transmitted it from the Tradition of Nadr ibn Abd al-Rahman from Ikrima from Ibn Abbas that the Prophet mentioned this Tradition and said: "God has given you a formal prayer, and it is the odd number." Nadr is considered by all to be weak. He was considered weak by Bukhari, Ibn Hanbal, Abu Hatim, Abu Zuhra, and Nasai. Ibn Main said about it: "The transmission from him is not allowed." It is also related from Azarami, and Azarami is to be passed over. It is related by way of Hajjaj ibn Arta, who is weak. Abu Jafar al-Tahawi related it from the Tradition of Nuaym ibn Hammad who is weak. (317)

Then there is the Tradition of Bazzar from Abd Allah ibn Masud that the Prophet said: "The odd number is duty for every Muslim," its transmission contains Jabir al-Jufi and Abu Mashar al-Madini and others. All of them are weak. (318)

Then there is the Tradition of Abu Dawud about that. It comes from Ubayd Allah ibn Abd Allah al-Ataki from Abd Allah ibn Burayda from his father. He said: "I heard the Messenger of God say: 'The odd number is a duty. Whoever does not perform the odd number is not one of us. The odd number is a duty. Whoever does not perform the odd number is not one of us. The odd number is a duty. Whoever does not perform the odd number is not one of us." Yahya ibn Main considers Ubayd Allah to be trustworthy. Abu Hatim said that it is a sound Tradition. (319)

There is also the Tradition of Abu Ahmad ibn Adi from the Tradition of Abu Junnab. It is: "Three are obligatory for me but voluntary for you." One of those which he mentioned was the odd number. Abu Junnab used to forge Traditions. There is the Tradition of Bazzar from Ibn Abbas that the Prophet said: "I am commanded to perform the two cycles before the morning formal prayer and the odd number, but it is not obligatory for you." Jabir al-Jufi is in its chain of transmission and he is weak. Al-Daraqutni transmitted it from the Tradition of Abd Allah ibn Muhriz from the transmission of Anas. Ibn Muhriz is passed over. (320)

Abu Dawud mentioned the Tradition of Ali from the Prophet, "People of the Quran! Perform the odd number! God is the odd (*witr*) and He loves the odd (*witr*)." We have already discussed the interpretation of its principle in the section on the formal prayers which are obligatory for individuals and the formal prayer which are not individual obligations It is the section before this. (321)

48.2. The Description of the Odd Cycle Prayer (*witr*)

Some of them recommend performing the odd number with three bows separated by greetings. Some do not separate them by the greeting. Some perform the odd number with one bow. Some perform the odd number with five and only sit in the last one. Some perform the odd number with seven, nine, eleven and thirteen. That is the maximum which is related about the odd number prayers of the Prophet. (322)

48.2.1. The Odd Cycle Prayer (witr) of the Formal Prayers of Night and Day

We have already explained its interpretation inasmuch as the evening formal prayer is the odd number ritual prayer of the day and He commanded the odd number of the night formal prayer in order to make evenness in worship sound since worship is contrary to *tawhid* for it demands the worshiper and the Worshiped. The worshiper is not the Worshiped since a thing is not humbled to itself. This is why the formal prayer is divided into two parts between the Lord and the servant. When He made the evening formal prayer the odd number of the day prayer (and the formal prayer is worship). Oneness became jealous when it heard that oddness accompanies worship. Therefore, it prescribed the odd number of the night-formal prayers in order to make the odd number of the day formal prayers even. It took its revenge on the odd number of the day formal prayers by the odd number of the night ritual prayers. This is why revenge is called "odd number." It is the goal of revenge. (323)

48.2.2. The Interpretation of the Description of the Odd Cycle Prayer (witr)

If he performs the odd number ritual prayer with three bows, that comes from His words, "*So whoever committed aggression against you, commit aggression against him likewise as he committed aggression against you.*" (2:194). Whoever performs the odd number ritual prayer with one bow, it is like his words, "There is only retaliation by iron." Whoever makes a separation in the three by the greeting, considers that there is only retaliation by iron and he takes the principle of unity into consideration. Whoever does not make a separation, observes the Unity of God. Whoever performs the odd number ritual prayer with one bow, his ritual prayer is unique. Whoever performs the odd number ritual prayer with three, it is the unity of divinity. Whoever performs the odd number ritual prayer with five bows, it is the unity of the heart. Whoever performs the odd number ritual prayer with seven bows, it is the unity of the attributes. (324)

Whoever performs the odd number ritual prayer with nine bows has combined all three: the unity of the essence, the unity of the attributes, and the unity of the actions. Whoever performs the odd number ritual prayer with eleven, it is the unity of the believer. Whoever performs the odd number ritual prayer with thirteen, it is the unity of the Messenger. There is no goal after the Message. It is the end. After it, one can only refer to prophethood because there is no doubt that the source of the servant is manifest there. (325)

Part of the *sunna* is to precede the odd with the even. The reason for that is that the odd is not commanded to do the odd. If he had been commanded to do it, he would have been commanded the even. He is commanded the odd. The one who has evenness established for him is told, "Make it odd." The odd is what is desired of the servant. The Messenger of God only did the odd number ritual prayer after the even number formal prayer. God Almighty says: "*By the even number and the odd number.*" (89:3) (326)

48.2.3. Evenness and Oddness

We have already stated that evenness is the reality of the servant since oddness is only appropriate for God in respect of His essence and the unity of His rank, that is, the rank of divinity is only for God without partner. There are two types of servanthood. There is servanthood by compulsion, which is manifest in the performance of obligations, and there is servanthood by choice which appears when you perform the voluntary acts. The Messenger of God only performed the odd number ritual prayer after the even as a supererogatory act. (327)

However, he said that the evening formal prayer is the odd number of the day formal prayers and the odd number ritual prayer is prescribed for the oddness of the night formal prayers. Part of the day formal prayers are obligatory and part are supererogatory. We know that there was at least one person who did not perform supererogatory prayers—like Dumam ibn Thalaba al-Sadi. He did perform the formal prayers in the day. It may be that the odd number makes the night formal prayer odd when he does one or more cycles as long as he does not sit. The supererogatory does not have the strength of the formal prayer. The obligatory by its own strength makes the day prayer odd. The the evening formal prayer should be three bows. He sits after two bows and then stands up for the third one. (328)

There was a prohibition related against performing the odd number ritual prayer at night like the the evening formal prayer so that there will not be any confusion between the obligatory and the supererogatory. Whoever performs the odd number ritual prayer with three, five or seven, and wants to make the obligatory odd, only sits at the end of his formal prayer so that it is not like the formal prayer. When he does not sit, it stands in the station of the oddness of the evening formal prayer with its strength even though there is sitting because of the strength of the obligatory. The odd number is strong when it is more than one bow since he only sits by the strength of unity. (329)

48.3. The Time of the Odd Cycle Prayer

The scholars agree about part of its time, and that is from after the night formal prayer until dawn. They disagree about part of it, and there are five statements about it. Some say that it is allowed after the morning formal prayer. Some say that it is permitted as long as he has not performed the morning formal prayer. Some say that he performs it after the morning formal prayer. Some say that he can perform it even if the sun has risen. Some say that he performs it the next night. These statements were related by Abu Bakr Ibrahim ibn al-Mundhir in the *Book of the Looking into the Dispute*. (330)

My position is that it is allowed after sunrise. That is the position of Abu Thawr and Awzai. The Messenger of God made the evening formal prayer the odd number of the day formal prayers even though it is performed after sunset. It is like that with the odd number ritual prayer of the night. If a man does not perform it at night, he has abandoned the *sunna*. He then performs it after sunrise and it makes his night formal prayers odd, even if it happens in the day. This is as the the evening formal prayer makes the day formal prayers even, although it happens at night. (331)

48.3.1. The Odd Cycle Prayer (witr) Is Not Limited

The odd numbered ritual prayer is not limited by moments, even though it appears in moments. If it had been limited, it would not be valid that it be unique. Limitation is the opposite of freedom. I have already made it clear to you in this book in the section on time that the moment is a non-existent matter. It has no existence at all. The odd numbered ritual prayer is a recognized existent matter. How can the existent thing be limited by the non-existent so that it produces this effect in it? It is more proper to relate the effect to the existent matter according to every one who has intellect. Since the moment does not limit the odd number ritual prayer, he can perform it whenever he likes. It is better that he apply himself to performing it before dawn. It is better to follow the *sunna* in acts of worship. (332)

That which we are discussing are the interpretations given by the realities, so understand that. It is as we have interpreted the odd number ritual prayer as revenge which occurs from the odd number of the the evening formal prayer inasmuch as it is worship. The quest for revenge is not limited by time. Whenever he obtains what he seeks, he takes revenge on it without any actual limitation by time. All aspects of the interpretations are not limited by time. (333)

48.3.2. *The Raising of the Hands in the Odd Cycle Prayer*

We have already discussed and commented on the expressions used in the raising of the hands in supplication during the formal prayer (*qunut*) of the odd number ritual prayer in the section on raising of the hands in supplication during the formal prayer. People disagree about it. Some people say that you do raise your hands in supplication during the odd numbered ritual prayer and some people forbid it. Some people say that it is permitted in the first half of Ramadan, and some people say that it is in the last part of Ramadan. Some people say that it is permitted in all of Ramadan. I say that all of that is permitted. Whoever does any of that has a proof, but this is not the place for it. (334)

48.3.3. *The Gnosis of the Odd Cycle Prayer (witr) and Essential Unitary Oneness*

Since the odd numbered ritual prayer is only valid from the even—either obligatory or *sunna,* it does not have the strength of the essential oneness of unity which does not result from the even. It is not generated in the self of the gnostic by looking at: "Whoever knows himself knows his Lord." This is the recognition of oddness. It is not recognition of essential unity. (335)

Raising the hands in supplication while standing during the formal prayer is supplication, imploring, and humble seeking. It is what the odd numbered ritual prayer has from the effect of the even before it from which this recognition of oddness results. Supplication is specified. God called His servants to this. He said: "*I answer the call of one who calls when he calls to Me.*" (2:186) And He said: "*God calls to the Garden and forgiveness*" (2:221), and He said: "*God calls to the Abode of Peace.*" (10:25) He described Himself with supplication/calling. He is the odd number—glory be to Him! So the odd numbered ritual prayer demands raising the hands in supplication while standing in the odd numbered ritual prayer. (336)

Therefore, when the servant performs the odd numbered formal prayer, he should raise his hands in supplication while standing in the odd numbered ritual prayer, especially in Ramadan. Ramadan is one of the names of God Almighty. Therefore supplication is confirmed in the odd numbered formal prayer of Ramadan more than any of the other months. Know that! (337)

48.4. [Recitation of] the Odd Cycle Prayer While Mounted

Some of them forbid that because they think that it is obligatory and connect it to the *fard* formal prayers by analogy. The jurisprudents agree that the formal prayers are not permitted while mounted. Most people allow the odd numbered formal prayer mounted since the Tradition is well-established regarding that, and that is my position. (338)

48.4.1. The Formal Prayer Is Divided Between the Servant and His Lord

The formal prayer which is divided between God and the servant is not in the actions. It is rather in the recitation of the Opening Chapter of the Quran by the one who performs the formal prayer—and what has the same meaning in the words of the human being in the formal prayer according to the People of God. Therefore, the odd numbered ritual prayer while mounted is permitted. He is performing the formal prayer. Whoever considers the incomparability of God, The Majestic, in every action in the formal prayer and its interpretation about what is suitable for God in that, says that the odd numbered ritual prayer is not allowed while mounted because one of the preconditions of the validity of the formal prayer falls away when the mount walks and turns to a direction other than direction of the formal prayer. (339)

48.4.2. The Prophet Was All Face With No Back of Face

If this is contrary to the odd numbered ritual prayer of the Prophet while mounted. When it turned, you must know that the Prophet was all face without any back of the head. The Prophet said: "I see you from behind my back." Seeing is confirmed by his state and station so "faceness" is confirmed for him. He mentioned "behind" and "back" because of his humanness. They do not see as he sees. They see his back. (340)

48.4.3. Ibn Arabi Inheriting from God in Faceness

The heirs of the Prophet are in this station. I had it when I was performing the formal prayer with the people at the Azhar Mosque in Fez. When I entered the *mihrab*, my essence became all one eye. I saw in all directions as I saw in front of me. The one who left and the one who came in were not hidden from me, nor was any of the group in the formal prayer. It would happen that someone who had caught a cycle of the formal prayer with me would forget. When I uttered the greeting and turned my face towards the group for supplication, I would see that man making up what he missed. He left out a cycle and I said to him: "You have missed out such-and-such, and he completed the formal prayer and remembered. These things and these states are only recognized by the one who has tasted them. Whoever has this states faces the direction of the formal prayer wherever he is. I myself has tasted it. It is only appropriate for the one who has this state to perform the formal prayer mounted. (341)

48.4.4. *The Face of God Is in the qibla for the Person Who Performs the Formal Prayer*

I saw that one of the people who held a literalist position said that the odd numbered ritual prayer is only allowed on the female riding-camel and cannot be on another mount—a donkey, a male-camel, or a horse. Only the odd numbered ritual prayer can be done mounted. When the Messenger of God performed the odd numbered ritual prayer mounted, wherever the animal turned, the *qibla* was before him, as we have confirmed. Whoever has the like of this state, has the words of God confirmed for him in his formal prayer and in all of his actions: "*Wherever you turn, there is the Countenance of God*" (2:115). For the one who performs the formal prayer, the face of God is in his direction of the formal prayer. It indicates that the one whose state is like this and sees direction of the formal prayer in the direction behind him with his eye, he is the one who performs the formal prayer to the direction of the formal prayer. (342)

48.5. The One Who Goes to Sleep After the Odd Cycle Prayer (*witr*) and Then Gets Up to Pray During the Night

Some say that he performs the formal prayer of one blow to make his odd numbered formal prayer even, and then performs the formal prayer what he likes and performs the odd numbered ritual prayer. Some say that he does not make the odd numbered ritual prayer even. The odd numbered ritual prayer is not made even by these bows, and he is doing a supererogatory prayer of one bow which is not the odd numbered ritual prayer. It is not prescribed, and so it is something which God has not given permission for. The odd numbered formal prayer is variously considered as confirmed *sunna* or obligatory. Where is the supererogatory in relation to the confirmed *Sunan* or formal prayer? The ruling here belongs to the divine law. The Prophet said: "There are not two odd numbered ritual prayers in the night." Whoever takes the intelligible meaning into consideration, says that this one bow makes the bow of the odd numbered ritual prayer even. There is no doubt that it is better to follow the *Sunna*. (343)

48.5.1. *The divine Presence Does Not Demand Repetition*

The odd numbered ritual prayer is not repeated. The divine presence does not demand repetition because it has boundlessness. "God is Vast,

The Knowing." Knowledge is an attribute of comprehension and capacity is connected to it. A name is derived from it and a name is derived from knowledge, and you must know that. "There are not two odd numbered ritual prayers in the night." (344)

48.5.2. The Unity of God, the Unity of the Creature and the Unity of Rank

The Oneness of God is not made even by the oneness of every created thing. Everything must have oneness. It is by oneness that everything recognizes the Oneness of its Creator. That is the sign which God has in everything which indicates His oneness. That is what Abu 'l-Atahiyya referred to when he said:

> He has a sign in everything which indicates that He is One.

Nothing can have two onenesses, so the odd numbered ritual prayer is not made even when the one who slept after the odd numbered ritual prayer gets up to perform the formal prayer. (345)

Whoever takes into consideration the Oneness of the divinity and relates it to the Oneness of The Essence, which is described by divinity (for the divinity of rank is only understood with the oneness of the one who has this rank), says that when someone gets up in the night and wants to perform a ritual supplication when he went to sleep after the odd numbered ritual prayer, he adds a bow to that bow which he slept after (and it is his odd numbered ritual prayer) in order to make it even. Then he performs the formal prayer as many bows after that as he likes, two by two. When he fears that the morning formal prayer is approaching, he performs the odd numbered ritual prayer with one bow. Each position among the scholars has a particular interpretation which allows him what he believes in that. (346)

49 The Two Cycles of Dawn Before the Morning Formal Prayer

49.1. Introduction

The two bows of the morning before the morning formal prayer are in the position of the two bows before the evening formal prayer. In the time of the Messenger of God when the Companions heard the call to formal prayer for the evening formal prayer, they would hurry to perform these two bows before the Prophet came out according to the Tradition of Abd Allah ibn Mughaffal. Muslim mentioned it in his collection of Traditions. The Messenger of God would come out to them and he did not disapprove of it. The Prophet said: "There is a formal prayer between every pair of calls to formal prayer." He meant the call to formal prayer and the declaration to perform the formal prayer since there is no doubt that it is a call to formal prayer. (347)

Only the one who has made his religion healthy keeps to the two bows before the evening formal prayer unless the declaration to perform the formal prayer forestalls him. When the declaration to perform the formal prayer is recited, there is no formal prayer except for the one for which the declaration is given. That is a *sunna* which is left and shut off. I have not seen any of the jurisprudents of our time who kept to it except for Yusuf ibn Ibrahim al-Shafii al-Kurdi. God gave him success in that. (348)

49.1.1. The Prayer of the Saints (awliya) Who Return

There is a reward in these two bows before the evening formal prayer which none but God knows. God has a special Self-disclosure and knowledge of the time between the call and the declaration to perform the formal prayer. Whoever consigns with Him in that moment is singled out for an immense business. It is as we said about the transmitted Tradition which unveiling verifies. The Messenger of God said: "There is an formal prayer between every pair of calls to formal prayer." He is referring to call to formal prayer and the declaration to perform the formal prayer. He called both the call to formal prayer because it gives notice that the formal prayer is established and the leader is present. This is like when the sun and moon are called "a pair of suns" in Arabic, or Abu Bakr and Umar are called the "two Umars." (349)

This is the formal prayer of the saints (friends of God) who return to God in repentance. In the beginning, people kept to performing that a lot. That was because of divine success. The supererogatory prayer is servanthood by choice and the obligatory is servanthood by compulsion. Servanthood by compulsion needs complete presence of recognition of the manners, majesty and incomparability necessary for the Worshiped Master. Servanthood by choice departs from that—like self-discipline and withdrawal in retreat. When the servant comes to the obligatory from the supererogatory it is not like coming to it from the permitted action because that which he was in before he came to it must have an effect on his thought. This is why one keeps to these two bows. (350)

49.2. The Supererogatory Before the Obligation Is Like Charity (*Sadaqa*) Before Conversation

The two bows of dawn are like that. The supererogatory before the obligatory is charity from a person for himself. God says: "*When you consulted with the Messenger, put charity forward in advance of your conversing privately.*" (58:12) So what then do you think of the conversation of God? It is firmer still and even more obligatory. It is agreed that the principle of the two bows of dawn is *sunna*. The Prophet made them up after sunrise when he slept through the the morning formal prayer until sunrise. He performed them and then performed the morning formal prayer. We do not consider that to be *qada* (making up). He performed it at its time as he performed the morning formal prayer at its time. That is the time of the formal prayer for the one who was asleep or forgot. It is not called *qada* in the technical language of the jurisprudents. (351)

49.3. The Recitation in the Two Cycles of Dawn

Some of them recommend reciting only the Opening Chapter of the Quran in them. Some scholars say that there is no harm if he adds another short chapter to recite in the two bows of dawn. That which I believe is that if he is brief in them and quick in perfection, nothing is specified. The Opening Chapter is necessary. It is the source of the formal prayer within the formal prayer. Whoever does not recite it in his formal prayer has not performed the formal prayer. The *Sunna* relates that you should perform them well, even if the time is very short. (352)

49.3.1. The Two Cycles of Dawn Prayer Have the Doubt of Compulsory Servanthood

The reason that quickness in them is part of the *sunna* is because of the

Tradition related which states that the amount of time God will reckon all of His servants on the Day of Rising is that of the two bows of dawn. He made them quick as a mercy to his community, In general, it is a formal prayer, and its principle is that of the formal prayer and that which is not one of formal prayers. Even if it is servanthood by choice, the two bows of dawn have a certain resemblance to servanthood of compulsion because of obligatory parts which the supererogatory contains. (353)

49.3.2. The Position of the Servant in the Supererogatory

In the supererogatory prayers and other formal prayers which are not obligatory, the servant is in the position of a servant who has been partially freed or he is in the position of the servant. These have a certain breath of freedom which is not possessed by the servant who does not have this state. The *sunan* of the supererogatory is the state of servanthood. The supererogatory which is not *sunna,* that is, it is not something which the Prophet always did or specified should be done, is in the position of the servant who has been partially freed, and he is a servant inasmuch as part of him remains which has not been freed. In servanthood this state is between necessary servanthood and servanthood by choice. It is like the *sunan* between the obligatory and the supererogatory. (354)

49.3.3. The Opening Chapter (Surah al-Fatihah) of the Book is "That which is Enough" (al-Kafiya)

As for the one who thinks that only the Opening Chapter is recited in it, that is because it is "that which is Enough." By reciting it, his formal prayer is valid. As for the one who adds another chapter after the Opening Chapter, it is in order to know the stage which he obtains from this because this chapter is the rank. Nabigha said:

Have you not seen that God has given you rank?
    You see every king wavering before it.
You are a sun while the kings are stars.
    When the sun rises, not a single star appears. (355)

49.3.4. The Signs (Ayat) of the Chapters of the Quran and Proof of the Gnosis of Human Beings

The chapters of the Quran are their ranks. As each chapter has signs, so each station that anyone has with God has proofs, and the clearest of them is gnosis of God. It is confirmed in expressing it plainly. This proof is the master of the proofs as the sign al-Kursi (2:255) is the master of the signs of the Quran. It is Quran since the servant and the Master are joined in the formal prayer, and it is discernment in which the servant is distinct from the Lord by what he particularly has in recitation in the formal prayer. (356)

49.3.5. The Position of the Slave in Relation to his Lord in the Opening Chapter (Surah al-Fatiha)

God makes it clear in the Opening Chapter what the rank of the servant is. The formal prayer only takes place by it. It acquaints him with his rank with his Lord. It is a stage which is divided between the servant and the Lord, as is confirmed. The servant must recite the chapter after the Opening Chapter without any previous deliberation about what chapter he will recite or what sign from a chapter or chapters. If he deliberates about specifying what he will recite after the Opening Chapter, it lessens the knowledge of the one who wants to comprehend the face of The Real in his stage with God. That comes with the first thought. (357)

When the one who is praying finishes the recitation of the Opening Chapter of the Quran, he recites "*So recite of the Quran as much as was easy*" (73:20) and what God makes flow on his tongue without choosing a particular sign or hesitating. He waits for whatever chapter God establishes him in or whatever sign of whatever chapter God makes flow on his tongue if he does not complete the recitation of the chapter. By that, the one who is present with knowledge and careful watching knows his rank with God in that moment. He obtains it from the recitation of the Opening Chapter of the Quran from the portion which he has of it and the portion of his Lord. It is repayment for the praise of his Lord in it while the asking is by the chapter which he recites. If he finishes it, there is no doubt that he has the entire rank. If he lacks some of it, his portion of it is according to what he lacks, that is, according to what he lacks of that rank. The *sunna* is to complete the chapter according to the sound Tradition. On the Day of Rising, the reciter of the Quran will be told: "Recite and rise. You rank is with the last sign you recite."

O man! Choose for yourself and listen to Me!
The proof will shine clearly for you!" (358)

49.4. The Description of the Recitation In It

Some scholars recommend that it be silent, and some recommend that it be aloud. Some say that he can choose. That which I believe is that since no text has come about it, he can stop at the point where he hears his own recitation and no one else hears his recitation. This is a state which is between silent and aloud. It befits the moment of this formal prayer. Its moment is a moment of inter space between night and day. It is not night so that he should recite aloud, and it is not day so that he should recite silently. If it had not been for a text regarding the recitation in the obligatory the morning formal prayer formal prayer which states that it is aloud, there would have been the same principle in it. (359)

The evening formal prayer is an excellent formal prayer! It joins what is aloud by what it contains of night and what is silent by what it contains of day. It is like the one who is asleep in time. The sleeper is in a place of inter space. The sleeper sees battle cries, shrieks, and great things in his sleep while the one who is at his side does not know what this sleeper is in. (360)

It is better to deal with the moment with this sort of recitation since it is in harmony with it. By this sort of recitation, he distinguishes between it and the recitation of the the morning formal prayer and it is distinct from the obligatory. Distinguishing ranks and removing confusion in things is part of wisdom. In spite of this, I think that he can choose. (361)

49.4.1. Interpretation of the Silent and Audible Recitation in the Evening Formal and Dawn Prayer

That which he says aloud is connected to the night formal prayer since night is as long as the sun has not risen in common usage or the divine law. That which facilitates it is that dawn is part of the day in which the faster is told to refrain from eating. That is not taken into consideration in the evening formal prayer. He calls it "night" when He says: "*Fulfill the formal fasting until night.*" (2:187) It is up to the divine law to interpret one meaning with two interpretations in two moments or from two aspects. It is said in commentary on His words "*. . . and the oven boils*" (11:40, 23:27), that He means the light of dawn. It is well-known in the Arabic language. When the oven boils and appears, the servant should be performing the two bows of dawn as God Almighty says: "*Voices will be hushed for The Merciful so thou shalt hear nothing but a murmuring*" (20:108) (362)

49.4.2. The Manifestation of the Merciful for Livelihood and Stillness

The rising of dawn is a manifestation of mercy for livelihood as nightfall is for stillness. God Almighty says: "*And it is out of His mercy that He has assigned for you the nighttime and the daytime that you may rest in it and that you may be looking for His grace*" (28:73) since the day generally contains movements in livelihood, supporting the self, the interests of creation, taking care of business, display of professions, fixing products in their form and making their form excellent. It is a divine manifestation of mercy to this world. For this reason, we recommend being silent so that he can hear himself, "*. . . and you only hear a murmuring,*" that is, a soft voice fearful of God, with humility and manners with God. (363)

Audible recitation is prescribed in the morning formal prayer in this manifestation because he is commanded by an obligatory command from God to speak. He speaks because of a divine Command. If he omits it, he rebels if that is intentional according to what he is prescribed to do. It is as God Almighty says about this obligation in this manifestation which we mentioned regarding the like of this day: "*On a Day when the Spirit and the angels will stand up ranged in rows, they will not assert themselves but he whom the Merciful gave permission.*" (78:38) He spoke the truth and the permission came and it is specific that he speak aloud. The supererogatory ritual prayer does not have this rank in this manifestation. You only hear a whispering in the supererogatory. Therefore, there is a difference between the command and what is chosen. God is The Guide. (364)

49.5. When Someone Goes to the Mosque Without Having Prayed the Two Cycles of the Dawn Prayer and Finds that the Declaration to Perform the Formal Prayer Has Been Given or Finds the Leader Performing the Formal Prayer)

Some people permit that he perform the formal prayers in the mosque while the leader is performing them. Some people say that he cannot perform them at all in this state, and that is my position. Some people say that he is either outside of the mosque or inside of the mosque. If he enters the mosque, he cannot perform these two bows. If he does not enter it, the people of this position disagree about the one who is outside the mosque and has heard the declaration to perform the formal prayer or has seen the leader and the people performing it. Some say that if he is not afraid of missing the leader by doing that, he performs the formal prayer the two bows. If he is afraid that he will miss the formal prayer, he does not perform them, joins the leader in the formal prayer and then makes them up after sunrise. Another says that he can perform it outside of the mosque as long as he thinks that he will catch one bow of the the morning formal prayer with the leader. (365)

49.5.1. The Moment Belongs to the Formal Prayer

Dry ablution is invalid when water can be found and the person is able to use it. There is no doubt that whatever is more than the obligatory is supererogatory, whether it is stressed or not. There is no doubt that the obligatory is more stressed than it. The moment belongs to the formal prayer when the declaration to perform the formal prayer has been given and then the supererogatory must be deferred. Increase on something can only occur after that thing itself is obtained. Increase is allowed by the existence of something which already exists and can be added to. That is the formal prayer, and it is the basis in the imposition. It is like that in the heart of the matter. (366)

It is the formal prayer which is prescribed and he does a wrong action if he leaves it. The supererogatory comes after it has been established. Otherwise it would be false that it is increase. When it is increase, and the matter before it is established so that it adds to it, then the name "increase" is valid for it. It is better to observe the bases, and it is better to join the formal prayer with the leader when he sees him and hears the declaration to perform the formal prayer than to perform the two bows of dawn. (367)

The Messenger of God said that it was an error and displayed dislike towards the one who did that. He said to the one who performed the formal prayer when the declaration to perform the formal prayer had been given for the morning formal prayer: "Are you performing four bows for the morning formal prayer?" He repeated it to him to show his dislike for that action. This is the source of allowing it even though it is disliked. The Prophet did not order him to stop or leave it. Had it been forbidden, he would not have let him continue it. He confirmed that it is an action in the divine law which is not made invalid. God said: *"Render not untrue your charities."* (2:264) He did not return to it after he knew that the divine law disliked it and it is disliked for him to start it. (368)

49.6. The Time for Making Up the Two Cycles of the Dawn Prayer

Some say that he makes them up after the the morning formal prayer, and that is my position. Some say that he makes them up after sunrise. There is some disagreement among the people who say this. Some give it a time which is not very wide and some make it a wide time and say that the can make it up from sunrise to noon. It is not make up after noon. Some say that it is recommended to make it up and some say that it is good. (369)

49.6.1. When the Time of the Right of God is Missed, It Is Not Limited by Time

Every right of God is obligatory or desirable. When he misses its time, it is not limited by a time for the divine law did not limit it. He can make it up when he likes as long as he does not die unless that it is due to forgetfulness. Then he performs it and that is its moment. There is no *qada* in the case of sleep or forgetfulness. (370)

49.7. Lying Down After the Two Cycles of the Dawn Prayer

Some people say that it is obligatory and that is my position since it is established that the Messenger of God. Some people say that it is *Sunna*. Some people think that it is recommended. Some people do not think that it is done. (371)

49.7.1. The Religious Scholars in the Time of Ibn Arabi

It is evident for those people of Tradition who recognize the divine law of God, but not the jurisprudents who imitate the people who have undertaken strenuous endeavor to understand an issue of the divine law like the jurisprudents of today. They have no knowledge of the Quran or the *sunna* although they have memorized Quran. If they see in it what which is contrary to the position of their shaykh, they do not pay attention to it nor act by it. They do not recite in order to obtain knowledge, and they rely on the position of their leader which is contrary to this sign and Tradition. They will have no excuse in that in the presence of God. On the Day of Rising, the first one to declare himself free of them will be their leader. They will not be able to prove that he told people, "Imitate me and follow me." That is one of the prerogatives of the Messenger. (372)

If they say: "God has commanded us to follow them when He says: *'So ask the People of Remembrance if you have not been knowing.'*" (16:43) We asked them and they gave us an opinion," then our reply to them is: "We ask them so that they can convey to us the judgment of God in matters, not their own opinion. He said: 'the people of remembrance'. They are the people of the Quran, for the remembrance is the Quran." If, when we recite the Quran, we find the judgment contrary to his opinion, it is specifically incumbent upon us to take the Quran or the Tradition and leave the words of that leader unless that leader transmits a sign or Tradition to us and then we act according to the sign or Tradition since we do not recognize the language and what the principle demands. If we have knowledge of that, then we are equal with them. (373)

49.7.2. The Person Who Does Not Lie Down after the Dawn Prayer Is a Rebel

It is established in a sound Tradition that the Messenger of God would lie down after the two bows of dawn. It is also established in a sound Tradition from Abu Hurayra that the command to lie down is for everyone who performs the ritual prayer of two bows of dawn. I believe that the one who abandons lying down is a rebel. It is necessary to lie down, and he must do it even if he is making it up. The *fa* entails following. Some of the later strivers among the people of the outward and literal text who have memorized Quran have stated that the the morning formal prayer is not valid when he performs the ritual prayer of the two bows of dawn and does not lie down. But if he does not perform the two bows of dawn, then he considers his formal prayer valid. (374)

49.7.3. Lying Down is Prescribed to Distinguish the customary (sunna) from the Formal (fard)

Lying down after the two bows of dawn and before the the morning formal prayer is because of the dislike connected to the obligated person. After dawn, he only performs the two bows of the dawn ritual prayer and then the morning formal prayer. It resembles the formal prayer, so he must lie down between it and the the morning formal prayer in order to make the *Sunna* distinct from the obligatory. He rises for the formal prayer after lying down so that it is known that it is separate from the two bows of dawn. Otherwise, it might be confused with a formal prayer of four bows. This is why the Messenger of God said to the one who performed it while the caller to formal prayer was reciting the declaration to perform the formal prayer, "Are you performing four bows for the morning formal prayer?" It is recommended to make a division between it and the morning formal prayer by something that the one who is present will recognize and therefore know that it is separate from the morning formal prayer. (375)

49.7.4. Lying Down Is Prescribed by the Action and Command of the Prophet

The Prophet prescribed lying down and as an action and command. He did it and commanded it. The one who is opposed to following the command of the Messenger of God in that and imitating him has no proof. God said: "*You have a good model in the Messenger of God for whoever hopes for God and the Last Day*" (33:21). Look then at the level of the one who does not imitate what is contrary to it. (376)

50 On the Mysteries of the Supererogatory Prayer

50.1. Introduction

Some say that it is two, and that you recite the greeting after two bows, day or night. Some say that you can choose. If you like, you can do two, three, four, six, eight and what you like. Some make a distinction between the day formal prayers and say that he can do four if he likes, and the night prayer and say that he does them two by two. (377)

In other formal prayers but not the odd numbered ritual prayer, I say that he can choose between reciting the greetings after two (which is better), especially in the night formal prayer, and he can perform four in the day formal prayer if he likes—especially the four before the noon formal prayer. He can do six or eight if he likes, and whatever he likes in that. As for three, five and seven in the supererogatory prayers, that is in the odd numbered ritual prayer. Nothing has come in the divine law stipulating a single bow in anything except the odd numbered ritual prayer. He does have a choice. If he likes, he does not recite the greeting and then sits after every two bows up to the third, fifth, and seventh. If he only sits in the last one of the even ones, then he rises for one. If he likes, he can sit only after the last odd numbered bow. He delays the greeting in all cases until the odd numbered ritual prayer. (378)

50.1.1. Divine Law in Voluntary Prayers Is Based on Choice

What is prescribed about them is based on choice. Choice has no amount specified in it. The divine law has not related any prohibition or command in that to restrict what occurs in that of the actions of the Prophet. It is better to follow the *sunna,* even if that is permitted for the one who does it. We prefer following and imitation to innovation, even if it is a good one. (379)

50.1.2. Innovation Is a Sort of Mastery and Advancement

Virtue lies in following. Following is more fitting for the servant and more appropriate to his rank than innovation from himself. There is a sort of mastery and advancement in innovation and making customs. Had it not been that the Messenger of God was obliged to make a *sunna,* he would not have made it. The Prophet said: "Leave me what I have left you." He disliked questions and denounced them. No one except him is obliged to make *sunna*. Had man busied himself with observing the *Sunan* and formal prayers, he would have been immersed in his moments and he would have had no time to initiate *sunan*. How far off the mark man is with his leadership from his politics! (380)

50.1.3. The Number of the Customary (sunna) Prayers

That which one relies on are the *Sunan* which are mentioned and what is established. Part of what the Prophet did includes the two bows of dawn, four bows at the beginning of the day, four bows before the noon formal prayer, four bows after the noon formal prayer, four bows before the afternoon formal prayer, two bows before the evening formal prayer, six bows after the evening formal prayer, and thirteen bows in the night, one of which was the odd numbered ritual prayer, and four bows after the Friday congregational formal prayer. Whatever is beyond this is good upon good, *light upon light*. If he performs the formal prayer of six bows before the noon formal prayer, he joins his action and what is specified for him. That is four bows. That is better. (381)

50.2. The Formal Prayer Is the Best Subject and It Is Excellent to Have a Lot of Good

People have different schools in this. We have only mentioned what we have chosen which comes from the text or action or general tradition. The formal prayer is the best subject and it is excellent to do a lot of good. That which we mentioned about its excellence and being long in its actions and reflecting on its recitation and remembrance takes as much time as the one who does a lot of bowing making it light. (382)

That which we believe is better and which I learned from our Shaykhs among the people of God is that it is related that when the Prophet stood up to perform ritual prayer at night, he performed the ritual prayer of two bows and made them long and excellent. His bowing was nearly as long as his standing, and his rising from bowing was nearly as long as his bowing, and his prostration was like that. So his formal prayer was very nearly equal. The root is bowing. The actions in the formal prayer in rising and lowering is in the relationship to bowing in the moment from shortness or length. Part of the *sunna* is that the first bow is longer than the second. All is shorter than that which is before it, and it is like that in the formal prayers, so know that! (383)

51 On the Mysteries of the Night Prayers in the Month of Ramadan

It is established that the Messenger of God said: "If someone performs the formal prayer in the night during Ramadan out of faith and seeking its reward with God, He will forgive him his wrong actions." It is desirable, and it is called the *tarawih* and the *ashfa* (evens) because it is performed as ritual prayer two bows by two. They disagree about the number of bows which people perform at night in Ramadan. There is choice allowed in that since there is no text on it. Some people choose twenty bows not including the odd numbered ritual prayer. Some like thirty-six bows and the odd numbered ritual prayer of three bows. That is the old method which was done at the beginning. (384)

I say that there is no specific number in it. If there were, it would be imperative to follow it. Following the Messenger of God is that it is confirmed that he did not add more than the thirteen bows with the odd numbered ritual prayer except in Ramadan, and not at any other time. However, he did make them long and excellent. This is what you choose in order to join between the night formal prayers in Ramadan and following the Messenger of God. God says: "*You have a good model in the Messenger of God.*" (33:21) (385)

51.1. Ramadan is One of the names of God

Ramadan is one of the names of God Almighty. Performing ritual prayer at night in this month is for the sake of the name because the obligation to stand for Him came when He said: "*A Day when humanity will stand up for the Lord of the worlds.*" (83:6) Ramadan is His name, glory be to Him! So the gnostic stays up in it to esteem this name which is particular to this noble month. The gnostic brings this to mind in his staying up. (386)

This month has some of the attributes of God which others do not have. This is the obligation for the servants of God to fast. It is an eternal attribute in which man is disconnected from food, drink, intercourse and slander. These are all divine attributes with which the servant is described when he is fasting. When night comes, the servant stands before God by His attributes which he had in the day. It is obligatory for him to rise at the time of breaking the fast so he knows that he is a poor nourished servant who does not really possess this disconnection and that it is only an accidental matter which he has and which calls his attention to taking on the attributes of God in His disconnection from the rule of nature. (387)

51.2. Every Action of the Son of Adam Is His Except for Formal Fasting

This is why God Almighty informed us in Tradition that the fast is His while every action of the son of Adam belongs to the son of Adam. He said: "Disconnection from food, drink, and intercourse is Mine, not yours, My servant, because I am Self-subsistent. I do not need anyone to protect My existence for Me. You need someone to protect your existence for you. That is Me. I appointed nourishment for you and I made you need it to inform you that I am the One who guards your existence for you to prove your need to you. (388)

51.3. God's Independence and the Servant's Need

"Yet in spite of this poverty and need, you overstep the bounds, are haughty, proud, and self-important. You say to the one who is like you: '*I am your lofty lord*' (17:24), and '*I knew not of any god for you other than me*' (28:38), and 'I and I and I'. You are not ashamed in that by your exposure through your hunger, thirst, urine, excrement, pain by heat and cold, and accidental pains. Son of Adam! I have hurt you with three hurts: poverty, sickness and death. Then in spite of that you rush off!" (389)

So the night formal prayers in Ramadan are standing in God. Whoever is described by God, has his adverb, God encompasses everything. This is the meaning of that adverbial quality. He cannot be outside of Him. When He encompasses you in Ramadan, it is an encompassment of honor and disconnection since He made it obligatory for you in necessary servanthood to be described by that which is appropriate for Him and not for you. This is disconnection from food and intercourse with women for the entire day. That is half of the life of your existence. Then you face the night and leave your lordness which is disconnected from food and intercourse for your servanthood by breaking the fast. All is Ramadan. (390)

51.4. Formal Fasting, Like Formal Prayer, Is Divided Between the Servant and His Lord

You are in Ramadan as you are in the formal prayer when He says: "I have divided the formal prayer into two halves between Me and My servant. Half of it is Mine and half of it is for My servant." He has also divided Ramadan between Him and His servant into two halves: half is His (and it is His words, "Fasting is Mine") and it is the day, and half belongs to the servant, and it is the night, the time of his fast-breaking. It is said that the formal prayer is light and it is said that fasting is a glowing light. The glow is light. God Almighty says: *"It is He Who made the sun an illumination"* (10:5) and He says: *"He made the sun as a light-giving lamp."* (71:16) It is prescribed to stand up for the formal prayer in the night in Ramadan and it is desirable because of the relationship between the fast and the formal prayer in the division of light. By his formal prayer, he should make his night like his day of fasting. He is unified with Him in the day and in the night. He is unified with him as we said:

If our resolutions are sound, we are unified in secrets. (391)

51.5. The Soundness of Resolutions and Unification of Secrets

Intention is a precondition for the night formal prayer. In fasting with God, we are as Bilqis was about her throne. "I*t is as though it were it."* (27:42) It was it. Her ignorance made her use the *kaf* (like) of resemblance. This is like man's ignorance. He says,"I am fasting." How can the nourished one be fasting? How far from the mark! God says: "The fast is Mine, not yours." He removed the claim of fasting from him as the resemblance of the throne to her throne was removed from Bilqis. After that she knew that it was that very throne. This is what we mean by:

"If our resolutions are sound, we are unified in secrets." (392)

51.6. Unification Is the Soundness of the Ascription to Each of Those Unified

If you were to say, "The faster is man," you would speak the truth. If you were to say, "Fasting belongs to God, and not to man," you would speak the truth. Unification has no meaning except by the soundness of the relationship to every one of those unified while each of them is distinct from each other in the source of unification. He is he and he is not Him as we said in something which we composed on this meaning in a state which overcame me:

I am not I, and I am not Him. Who am I and who is He? -
Him!
O He! Say: "Me!" O "I am Him" You are Him!
No, and I is not I, and He is not Him
If it had been Him, our eyes would not have looked at Him

by Him.
There is not other than us in existence—I and Him, and Him and Him.
Whoever is ours by us for us is as His for Him by Him.
The two joys of the faster: in his natural nourishment and spiritual nourishment (393)

51.7. The Two Joys of the Person Fasting: In His Natural Nourishment and Spiritual Nourishment

In what we related, we saw that God sent down His encounter in the rank of fast-breaking. He said that the person fasting has two joys. He has a joy when he breaks his fast because it is the food of his nature. It is the food of the veil since the One who gives nourishment is God Almighty. He has a joy when he meets his Lord, and that it is the real nourishment by which he goes on. He gave these two joys to the one who fasts in the veil and in the removal of the veil. We wrote some poetry about the nobility of the loaf since it is our normal food and has a circular form: and that is the best shape. We particularly mentioned the loaf instead of anything else by which we are nourished. We spoke about those of the unisign whom God subjects to it and and the quest of all their cares to reach it. There is no doubt that every animal, rather every existent, seeks its food. We said: (394)

51.8. The Loaf Is the Veil on The Guardian (*al-Muhayman*) and the Subtle (*al-Latif*)

The loaf is the veil on al-Muhayman (The Guardian) and *al-Latif* (The Subtle, Kind)
When you see that rapid journey,
  that journey is in search of the loaf
Because God made it a veil on His names,
  the Protector and the Latif.
The commerce of offspring is by it and for it
  as well as the spirits of the subtle and the dense,
And the subjugation of the elements and the earth,
  and the formation of minerals in the caves,
And the moving of trained ships
  by the waves of the sea and the gale-winds.
The foliage of the rainy season crosses the desert,
  and the ostriches vie for it with a harsh journey.

Part of the the honor of the loaf is that
my Lord swore by it for both lowly and noble.
Creation clamors for it if they lack it for a moment,
by the permission of the One, the Compassionate
Creator.
They pray and fast for it, and make the blood of the
unbelievers lawful for it as well as the pure earth.
Birds flock to it as well as cattle.
The strong and the weak run to it.
Without a doubt that which they run to,
and the minor and the major reason,
Is the meaning.
When we look at it in reflection, like the letters,
It is the generosity in which there is no doubt.
O my yearning for that beautiful generosity!
I ransomed you from a loaf in which there lies a secret
clearly evident in the old and the rare.
Say to those who reject my sound words:
the exquisite meaning is hidden, unseen by you.
Has not God made it like the vision of HIm
in spite of them? (395)

51.9. Praying During the Night of Ramadan and Performing the Formal Fast in the Day

The attribute by which the one who performs the formal prayer stands in his formal prayer in Ramadan is the noblest of attributes because of the nobility of the name for the nobility of the time. God puts his praying at night in Ramadan in the same station as his fasting by day except in the formal prayer. It is a mercy to His servant and a lightening. This is why the Messenger of God refrained from performing it with his Companions so that it would not become an obligation for them. They might not be able to do it. Had it been obligatory for them, they would not have applied themselves to it with such zeal nor prepared for it in the same way. (396)

Then those who applied themselves to it collectively would perform it as something unfortunate and lessen it. Only a few would remember God in it and complete its bowing and prostration, and they would not recite it properly. The one who made it a *sunna* to join together behind one reciter did not do so according to what the people of today follow of distinction between those who give sermons, jurisprudents and leaders of the mosques. In reference to formal prayers like theirs, the Messenger of God told the man, "Go back and pray. You have not performed the formal prayer." (397)

Whoever resolves to perform the prescribed night formal prayers in Ramadan which is desirable should stand as the Prophet prescribed the formal prayer: with tranquillity, fear, gravity and reflecting on what he recites. If not, it is better for him to leave it. It is better to perform the formal prayer at the beginning of the night as the Messenger of God performed the formal prayer for two or three nights. The mosque is better for it than the house, as opposed to the rest of the supererogatory prayers. The Messenger of God left the mosque and entered his house to perform it as a mercy to his community. If he had made it obligatory for them, they would have been incapable of it or become lazy. As God Almighty says: "*We have not sent thee but as a mercy for the worlds,*" (21:107), and He said: "*. . . and to the ones who believe, gentle, compassionate.*" (9:128) The formal prayer is two bows after two bows as has come in the Tradition that the night formal prayer is two by two. (398)

52 On the Mysteries of the Eclipse Ritual Prayer

52.1 Introduction

It is agreed that the eclipse ritual prayer is *sunna* and that it is done in a group. They disagree about its description, recitation in it, the types in which it is permitted, and whether or not the sermon is one of its preconditions. Is the lunar eclipse the same as the solar eclipse in that? (399)

52.1.1. The Disagreement on the Description of the Eclipse Formal Prayer

Different transmissions have come about the Messenger of God. Some are well-established and some are not. Every transmission has someone who supports it. The formal prayer is permitted to anyone who performs it based on any transmission. He can choose between ten bowings twice, eight bowings twice, six bowings twice, and four bowings twice. If he likes, he can perform it two bows and two bows as is done in the supererogatory prayers until the sun is clear. If he likes, he can make supplication to God Almighty with humble supplication and fear until the sun clears. When it clears, then he should perform two bows of thankfulness to God Almighty and depart. (400)

I prefer acting by this variant because of what it contains of respect for the divine Presence and mercy to the praying community. Since they are overpowered by heedlessness and idleness, they do not fulfill the conditions of presence and manners which the formal prayer demands. The one who performs the formal prayer may hate it while not aware of it, or this worship may become burdensome for him and he will become bored with it. That is why we think that the transmission of supplication without the formal prayer is better. It is the most cautious version in respect of them. (401)

Ala ibn Ziyad used to perform it. When the eclipse had cleared, then he would prostrate. If not, he would remain standing until he bowed a second time. When he raised his head from bowing, he would look at it. If it had cleared, he would prostrate. If not, he continued standing until he bowed again, and so on until the sun was clear. (402)

52.1.2. *The Eclipse Is a Day by Which God Makes His Slaves Fear*

The eclipse is one of the Signs of God by which He instills fear into His servants. When it occurs, the *sunna* is that people hurry in terror to seek refuge in the formal prayer. This is like all the signs which provoke fear: like the earthquake, intense darkness and intense winds which are out of the ordinary. The Messenger of God was asked about the eclipse. He said: "When God gives a manifestation to something, He is feared." The Tradition is not established by means of transmission, but it is sound in meaning. (403)

We think that the Self-disclosure is always there. However, people's ignorance leads them to say (or it is said to them) something like this. Their knowledge is non-existent, so the normal pattern is broken. This is that one knows a special quality, for instance, the breaking of the normal pattern in hearing the glorification of the pebbles. The pebbles are always glorifying. There is no doubt that selves are only provoked and made to tremble by the signs which break the normal patterns. (404)

52.1.3. *Normal and Abnormal divine Signs*

There are divine Signs in normal things and divine Signs in abnormal things. The Quran has brought many of the normal Signs when He says: "and one of His Signs" and "among His Signs." He mentions normal things and says: "There are Signs in that." However, the common people do not take note of the passage of normal things. They are overcome by heedlessness and lack of presence. The cause of the solar and lunar eclipses is well-known. That which is not well-known is that it comes from a divine Self-disclosure. That is only recognized by the Messenger or a gnostic with unveiling. (405)

God made the eclipse a Sign of what He wants to provoke in phenomenal beings in the elemental world and in the world in which the eclipse appears and in the time in which it appears. It may be eclipsed at night and then it will have no effect with us. The event is also according to the zodiacal sign in which the eclipse occurs. It is a definite knowledge, that is, knowledge of the occurrence of the eclipse. There is no knowledge about what God will cause in it or during it. The eclipse occurs in one place more than another and in one place rather than in another place. It begins in one place while it does not begin in another place. It is based on the state. This is all known by those who have knowledge of it. It refers to well-known determined movements according to the people of this science. (406)

52.1.4. *The Cause of Eclipses and Their Times*

The solar eclipse is caused by the moon when it imposes itself on the sun. According to how much of it imposes itself on the sun, that amount of the sun vanishes from our eyes. That shadow which we see on the sun is from the body of the moon. It may veil all of it and then the atmosphere will become dark and the eyes will see the body of the moon. Common people imagine that that which they see is the sun itself. The sun is normally luminous in its essence and will remain so until the time when God wishes to roll it up. That is why those who know the motion of the planets know the time of the eclipse and the amount that it will be eclipsed. That only takes place at the end of the Arab month. The moon at the time is encircled and being burned by the rays. Reckoning gives us what will lead to its placing itself in front of the sun, and so there is no doubt that the eclipse occurs. (407)

It is like that with the lunar eclipse. The shadow of the earth comes between it and the sun. The eclipse occurs in that place according to how much of it comes between them. This is why it is known and there is a very limited range of error in that. If it had not been that the business is like this, it would not have been known. (408)

52.1.5. Incidental Matters, Customs, and Firm Roots

Events which occur by accident are only known when God teaches them by the tongue of whomever He wills among His servants. In our opinion, they are not accidents in what God has ordered in that since "*He revealed in each heaven its command.*" (41:12) Matters proceed according to their roots. They are established and not unsettled. He teaches them the sciences of those roots. They are customary and God is the One who has set them down. They are not logical. That does not naturally disappear, and thus it is permitted to break the normal pattern in it. It is like that with every subject until God disrupts that root. God has the will to do that and: "*To God belongs the command before and after.*" (30:4) (409)

That is why it is not said in respect of the astronomer that it is a science since the roots on which it is based come from divine execution and the ordering of One who is The Knowing, The Wise which normally continues. That is not intrinsic to them. That which is set up can be removed. The One who established it fixed it for a specific set term, and we have no knowledge of that. There is no time which we are in but that He can change the matters which He fixed in it. If that does not take place, it is only by the will of the One who fixed it, not by itself. (410)

That which is like this cannot be said to occur according to a definite knowledge. If it occurs, that which is in the One who fixed it is only known by two aspects: either He informs what is in Himself and speaks the truth, or it is after the manifestation of thing, and so it is known that were it not in the One who established it, it would not have taken place.

The One who made it take place is God Almighty. The knower is the believer who says about the like of this: "God has made the order continue and made it travel in the stages as He determined, and the normal pattern is not broken in it. This business which we mentioned must then occur." This is why the knowledge of the astronomer as well as whatever is like it is rejected as being part of the portion of the Messengers and others. (411)

52.1.6. The Eclipse of the Moon and the Sun and the Veil of the Intellect and the Self

Since the light of the moon is derived from the sun, it is like the soul since it takes the light of belief and unveiling from God. When the soul is complete and perfect and it can validly have Self-disclosures in the confrontation (that is the night of the full moon), it may turn to its nature and then the darkness of its nature will appear in it. That darkness will come between it and its divine logical light of belief as the shadow of the earth comes between the moon which is in the place of the self and the light of the sun. It is veiled from the divine Light of belief according to how much it looks at its nature. That is its eclipse, and this is the lunar eclipse. (412)

As for the solar eclipse, it is the eclipse of the intellect. God created it so that he can understand what it takes from God. Then the soul, which is in the position of the moon, comes between it and God Almighty in respect of what it takes from Him from His name, Light—Glory be to Him!—inasmuch as it is related to the earth since He says: *"He is God in the heavens and the earth"* (6:3) and *"And it is He Who is in the heaven, God, and on the earth, God."* (43:84) (413)

The intellect wants to take from God some of the knowledge of what He made exist in the earth from God. Then the soul comes between it and the knowledge of what He made exist in the earth because of its appetites. Then the intellect does not look at Him in what He caused in it. The earth designates the world of the body. The intellect is veiled by the veil of the animal appetite soul. That is the position of the solar eclipse. The eyes of those who look who are in that parallel do not perceive it. The intellect misses knowledge of God according to how much it is veiled from Him by the world of bodies. (414)

This is why God has set down for us that we turn to His conversation which is called the eclipse prayer. He also called for supplication to remove that veil. The veil is ignorance. He also called for it afterwards in the state which demands perfection. This is why the eclipse only occurs in perfection in both luminous bodies on the night of the full moon which is its perfection in taking from the face which is closest to us. The eclipse of the moon occurs in the twenty-eighth day of the moon's passage in all the stages of its orbit. (415)

52.1.7. The Jurisdiction of the Eclipse in the Earth and in the Soul (*nafs*)

Then it comes to its end and wants to face the sun from the other side in order to take back from it in perfection in the world of spirits, as it took from it in the fourteenth day in the world of bodies so that the blessings of its light will overflow to the eyes of those who look. The sun is occupied with giving light to the moon in the world of the spirits, the celestial world, in order to help its quest and honor it for coming forward to its presence. The eclipse is by that help. (416)

This is why eclipses only have an effect in the earth in the places in which the eclipse appears. As for the places in which the eclipse does not appear, it has no jurisdiction which appears in them nor any effect, that is, God has not done anything there in the world of phenomenal beings which He does in the manifestation of the eclipse. There is no actor except God. Matters are by the determination of The Almighty, The Knowing. It is the work of The Wise. When reckoning accords that the sun will be eclipsed at night, that eclipse had no jurisdiction in the outward earth since the eclipse does not appear in it. It is like that with the jurisdiction of the lunar eclipse. (417)

52.1.8. Those Who Are Constantly in Eclipse

It is also like that with the outward and inward part of man. The eclipse may occur in actions, that is, in the knowledge which demands acting by prescribed rules. It may also occur in knowledges which are connected to the inward and which have no jurisdiction in the outward. They have an effect in the place to which they are connected, either in the knowledge of the action or in the knowledge which does not demand action. According to what occurs, it becomes specifically incumbent upon the one who has a state like this to make humble supplication to God. (418)

The striver in understanding an issue in the divine law who errs is in the position of the eclipse which is not seen by the one before whom the eclipse occurs. There is no burden of wrong action on him and he is rewarded. If a text appears to him and he then abandons it in favor of his own opinion or evident analogy in his claim, then he has no excuse with God. He commits a wrong action. This is the outward eclipse which has an established effect among the scientists who know the rules of the motions of the planets. The greatest amount of this is what goes on with the imitating jurisprudents to whom they said: "Do not imitate us. Follow the Tradition if it reaches you and it is contrary to our judgment. The Tradition is our position, even if we only judge something by a proof which appears to us to be a proof in our reflection. We are only obliged to do that. However, if you follow us, you are obliged to ask us." (419)

At every moment of the same event, the judgment of the striver may change. For this reason, when Malik was asked about an event, he said: "Has it occurred?" If it was said: "No," he said: "I have no opinion." If it was said: "Yes," he gave an opinion in that moment by what his proof accorded him. The imitators among the jurisprudents in our time refuse to fulfill the reality of their imitation of their leaders by following the Tradition which their leader commanded them to do. They imitate him in the judgment while something exists which is contrary to it. They rebel against God when He says: "*And whatever the Messenger gives you, take it.*" (59:7) They rebel against the Messenger when he said: "Follow me." He only said that by a command of his Lord—glory be to Him! They rebel against their Leader when he said: "Take the Tradition when it reaches you and strike the wall with my words." (420)

52.1.9. The Formal Prayer of the Eclipse

These people are in a constant eclipse. It will remain over them until the Day of Rising. They are not with God nor with His Messenger nor their leader. They are quit of God, His Messenger, and their leader. They have no proof with God. So see then with whom these will be gathered! (421)

The ritual prayer commanded during the eclipse is for conversation with God to remove the darkness of the soul and the darkness of nature as we say, "*Guide us on the straight path, the path of those Thou hast blessed* (and they are the people of lights), *not of those against whom there is anger* (like the people of the darkness of nature) *nor those who are misguided* (like the people of the darkness of the soul)." God comes between us and that which eclipses our intellects and selves. He makes us all lights. That is for us and whoever follows us. He is The Rich and can do that. (422)

52.1.10. The Symbolism of the Cycles (rakat) in the Eclipse Formal Prayer

As for the interpretation of the two bows, you must know that the two bows are the outward and inward of the human being, or his intellect and his nature, his meaning and his letters, his visible and his unseen. (423)

As for ten, it is disconnecting his Creator in the two bows from before, after, all, part, above, below, right, left, in front, behind. This disconnection of God returns to him. It is one of his actions. He has it since this action returns all these principles to Him. He has no "before." There was only God and God is not described by beforeness. He has no "after." He goes on by God's going on and there is no after. He has no "all." He is not divided into parts or encircled in respect of his subtle nature. Whoever has no "all" in his essence, has no part. Whoever is not described by these attributes, has no directions. Man only has directions in respect of the form of his body and its structure. It is by his physical structure that the six directions are manifested. He is the source of the directions. There is no direction from itself. (424)

As for the interpretation of the eight in two, eight is the essence and the attributes. The essence of being is unseen, and its attributes are in the one essence. The lights of its attributes rise in its attributes. It is the words of God Almighty: "I am his hearing and his sight," and he mentioned his limbs. No source occurs but that it has an outward and an inward. "Whoever knows himself knows his Lord." The business is like that in the inward. In the outward, no source occurs but that it appears on the person, and the truth is within the cavity of being but is not as the accident occurs in the place of the adverb in what encloses it. (425)

As for the interpretation of six in two, it is His words, "*Wherever you turn to after that, then there is the Countenance of God*" (2:115), and "*Truly God is One Who Embraces, Knowing.*" (426)

As for the interpretation of four in two, it is His words, "*After that I will approach them from before them and from behind them and from their right and from their left.*" (7:17) On every road by he comes by, there is a pure angel there with an unsheathed sword in his hand. If he comes upon one of the gnostics, there is no angel there to guard him. He is an elixir, and Satan is stopped from whatever direction he comes against him. His heart is pure gold, and so any Satan who comes is one of the losers. (427)

52.2. Recitation of the Eclipse Formal Prayer

Scholars disagree about recitation in it and whether it is silent or out loud. Some say that it is recited silently, and some say that it is recited out loud. (428)

52.2.1. Eclipse of the Soul (nafs) and Eclipse of the Intellect

If the eclipse is of the soul, he recites silently in his conversation and remembers God in himself. If the eclipse is in his intellect, he recited aloud. That is his quest for clear proofs. In them is the outward proof which is near to the source in which the men of intellect share inasmuch as they are people of reflection, speculation and proof. The others are the people of unveiling and a Self-disclosure resulting from their spiritual strength for discipline. This is discipline of character, retreats, striving, and long conversation. (429)

52.2.2. The Luminous Structure is Outside the Jurisdiction of the Elements

Entreaty to God Almighty is prescribed in it. This is the interpretation of the long recitation in the eclipse ritual prayer. It is related that he stood in it for the length of the second chapter *Surah al-baqarah*. The second standing was maybe half of that. The third was half of the second and so on in the fourth and fifth standings. The reason for that is that the world of spirits is not tired by standing. Boredom does not touch them because their structure is luminous and it is outside of the jurisdiction of the elements. (430)

52.2.3. *Elemental Structure Leads to Far and Near Changes*

As for the organic structure which is based on the elements, it is subject to on immediate and distant changes. That is designated as fatigue and exhaustion. As one descends from the mineral to the plant to the animal to man, so the exhaustion is greater in the last stage which is man. Fatigue is more general and can quickly depart. It can be an illusion. There is no doubt that illusions play with the intellects as actions play with the names. (431)

52.3. The Time in Which the Eclipse Formal Prayer Is Performed

Scholars disagree about the moment in which the eclipse ritual prayer should be performed. Some say that it can be performed the formal prayer at all times in which the formal prayer is forbidden and which the formal prayer is not forbidden. Some say that it is not performed the formal prayer in the moments in which the formal prayer is forbidden. Some say that it is performed the formal prayer in the moment in which the supererogatory prayer is performed. Some say that it can only be performed from noon to midday. (432)

52.3.1. *The Eclipse Formal Prayer Follows States*

As the eclipse is not specified for any particular time, so the formal prayer for it is not specified for any particular time because the formal prayer follows states. It is established that we are commanded to perform that formal prayer because of it and there is no particular time which is specified. It is a commanded formal prayer as opposed to the supererogatory prayer which is not commanded. If we apply the formal prayer to supplication, we can make supplication in the time in which it is forbidden to pray and we can pray in it in other times. This is my position. (433)

52.4. The Sermon of the Eclipse Formal Prayer

The divine law scholars disagree about that. Some say that the sermon is one of the preconditions. Some say that there is no sermon in the eclipse ritual prayer. I think that it is recommended for the leader to address the people in order to remind and warn them. The eclipse is of the Signs by which God provokes fear in His servants. (434)

52.4.1. The Sermon Is Exhortation and Reminding

The sermon is exhortation and reminding. The Sign is an impetus and reminding. The eclipse is a Sign which provokes fear. The relationship occurs, so we prefer the side of the one who says that the sermon is a precondition. It is affirmed that the Prophet reminded people on that day after the formal prayer was finished. (435)

52.5. The Lunar Eclipse

Some say that he performs the ritual prayer for the lunar eclipse in a group just like the solar eclipse. Some say that he does not perform it in a group. The one who holds this position recommends that it be performed singly two bows by two bows like all supererogatory prayers. That which I believe is that it is better to perform it in a group if possible. (436)

52.5.1. The Lunar Eclipse Is of the Soul (nafs) and the Soul (nafs) Contends for Lordship

Since the moon is the cause of the eclipse of the sun, the lunar eclipse is then like a punishment for its eclipsing the sun. The lunar eclipse therefore contains two signs, and it is better to perform it in a group. The intercession of the group has more esteem than the sanctity of a single person. Therefore, it should be more certain that one should gather for it than to gather for the solar eclipse. The lunar eclipse refers to the self as we have already stated. The self is always competing for lordship as opposed to the intellect. Its wrong action is greater and its state is more perilous. It is better for the intercessors to gather in the intercession than to come singly. (437)

Some consider that eclipses designate fear as we related in the Tradition that it is an impetus for the one who performs the formal prayer to have fear. God says: "*Surely the ones who believe have prospered, those, they who in their formal prayers are ones who are humble.*" (23:1-2). He said: "*It* (that is, the formal prayer) is *arduous but for the ones who are humble, those who bear in mind that truly they will be ones who encounter their Lord and that truly they to Him will be ones who return.*" (2:45) Everyone has fear according to his knowledge of his Lord. His knowledge of his Lord is according to His Self-disclosure to him. (438)

53 On the Mysteries of the Prayer Asking for Rain

53.1. Introduction

Some people say that there is a formal prayer for the sake of asking for rain. Some people say that there is no formal prayer for it. The proof belongs to the one who performs the ritual prayer that there is a formal prayer. The one who does not mention anything has no proof against the one who mentions it. It is affirmed that the Prophet went out with the people to ask for rain. He performed the two bows with them with the recitation aloud. Then he resigned his cloak, raised his hands and asked for rain, and faced the direction of formal prayer. Scholars agree about going out to ask for rain, leaving the city, and supplication to God Almighty to send down rain. It is a *sunna* which was made by the Messenger of God, may God bless him and grant him peace. They disagree about the formal prayer in asking for rain as we have already mentioned. (439)

53.1.1. The Interpretation of All We Have Mentioned

I say that the formal prayer is not a precondition for the validity of the rain formal prayer. They also say that the sermon is part of its *sunna*. It is established that the Prophet performed the formal prayer for it and gave a sermon. Is the sermon before or after the ritual prayer? Those who say that there is a ritual prayer agree that its recitation is out loud. They disagree about the recitation of "God is Greater" in it and whether it is like the recitation of "God is Greater" is like that of the festival formal prayer or like the recitation of "God is Greater" of the daily formal prayers. (440)

Part of the *sunna* in asking for rain is to face the *qibla* standing and reversing the cloak. They agree about this, but they disagree about how the cloak is resigned. Some people say that it is turned from top to bottom. Some people say that it is turned from right to left and from left to right. I say that he should join all three qualities: top to bottom, right to left, and inside out. (441)

53.1.2. The Interpretation of the Rain Formal Prayer

They disagree about when he changes his cloak. Some people think that it is when he finishes the sermon. Some people say that it is after he has started the supplication. It is asking for a change of state by state. They also disagree about the time that one goes out to it. It is said that it is time of the festival formal prayers and some say that it is at noon. Abu Dawud related that the Prophet went out to the rain ritual prayer when the edge of the sun appeared. (442)

53.1.3. The Rain Formal Prayer Is Asking for Drink for Himself, Others or Both

The rain-formal prayer is asking for drink. He may ask for water for himself or for others or for both of them according to the circumstances. As for the people of God who are singled out and who are distracted from themselves by Him while He has made them recognize that if they stay, they are with Him, and He is with them, and if they travel, they travel by Him to Him. These ones are not concerned about whatever stage God puts them in since it is God that they see in every state. If they live in this world, they live by Him. If they are moved to the world to come, they move to Him. They are not affected by the existence or absence of means. These people do not ask for rain for themselves since they know that life is attached to them. They are strongly in need of it and it is in need of them. (443)

The benefit of the rain ritual prayer is to make the life of this world continue. When those who know God ask for rain, it is to seek increase in knowledge of God as God says to His Prophet: "*Say: Lord, increase me in knowledge.*" (20:114) This supplication is the source of the rain ritual prayer. (444)

Then the Prophet asked his Lord to send down rain. Those who know God do not ask for rain for themselves, they ask for rain for others who do not recognize God as they do by asking on His attribute when He says in sound Tradition, "My servant, I ask you for water and you did not let Me drink." He says: "How could I give Thee water when Thou art the Lord of the worlds?" He says: "So-and-so asked you for water and you did not give it to him." (445)

This Lord asked His servant for water for His servant, not for Himself. He is exalted above needs. The rain ritual prayer of the Prophet and those who know God is like that. They do it for others. They are the tongues of those who are veiled by the life of this world from life's connection to them since they are characterized by the divine rain ritual prayer. (446)

53.1.4. The Faqir Is the One Who Has No Need that He Owns

The mystic with realization is the one who has no specified need nor that he owns that need since he knows that he is the source of the need. The need does not limit him. The world needs God absolutely without limitation as He—glory be to Him—is absolutely The Rich and The Independent of the world without limitation in respect of His Essence. They counter an essence by an essence, and they ascribe to every essence that which its reality grants. How excellent is what is prescribed in the call and the declaration to formal prayer in the words, "Come to formal prayer." He did not say "to (*ila,* in the direction of)." He bound it by the end. When someone is with you, he is not your goal. (447)

You do not say that "Come" is a word of advancing. Advancing only comes from one who is turned away. Everyone who is turned away is absent. Some say that when the servant realizes by God, he is the Seer and the Seen, the Witnesser and Witnessed. So the source of the servant vanishes and only the Lord remains. God wanted His servant to see the source of His servanthood so that He can acquaint his with the blessings which He has given him and no one else. He does not recognize that until he returns to himself and sees his source while he sees his Lord. That does not occur in any of his acts of worship except for the formal prayer. He said: "I have divided the formal prayer between Me and My servant." (448)

53.1.5. The Servant's Portion of the Formal Prayer

For His portion in the formal prayer, the one who performs the formal prayer must perform it since that portion of the formal prayer which belongs to the servant cannot belong to God. He says to him, "Come to formal prayer," that is, advance to the formal prayer for the sake of the portion which is singled out for you in it. When he turns away, he turns away from himself, not from his Lord because the knowledge of God accords him that. He said: "Come forward to your formal prayer in order to see Me and see yourself. You will recognize what is yours and what is Mine. *"And We empowered his dominion and gave him wisdom and decisiveness in argument."* (38:20). You will see what you are in. This is why He did not use "in the direction of" for it would lead to allowing absence. The business in itself is not like that. (449)

When God asks His servant for water, then the servant is more entitled. When God represents His servant when He asks His servant for water to give to His servant, then the servant had better ask his Lord for water to give to drink to His servant. It is better to represent his like for God since *"there is not anything like Him."* (42:11) Part of good manners with God is the rain formal prayer for others. (450)

53.1.6. The One With the State and the One with Knowledge

The people of states are veiled from sound knowledge by the state.

When one with a state does not have his manners preserved, he is not punished for bad manners since his tongue is the tongue of the state. The one with knowledge is punished for the least thing because he appears in the world by the form of The Real. What a difference there is between the one who appears in existence by his Lord and the one who is manifested by his state! What a distance between the two stations! How far between the two stages! The one who sees knowledge is just. The one who sees the state is poor and in need of someone to purify him in his state, and it is only the one with knowledge who will purify him. (451)

Since knowledge is this rare, then testimony about character is prescribed in the judgment of the divine law on the basis of probability. He says: "I suppose, I think" because not everyone knows what the true stage of that praised person is with God. "No one is commended in front of God." Since the person with a state needs testimonial by probability, he is even more in need of the one with knowledge. So both him and the one who attests to his good character are in need of the one with knowledge. Knowledge reveals itself and appears. The state is obscure and it needs evidence to strengthen it since it is too weak to be connected to the level of perfection. The one with a state seeks knowledge while the one with knowledge does not seek the state. What man of intellect would seek to leave clarity for obscurity? If you understand what we confirmed is specifically incumbent on you in the rain ritual prayer, then begin it. (452)

53.2. Going Out to the Rain Formal Prayer

53.2.1. Presence with God in What Is Mandatory

The rain formal prayer has two states. One state is when the leader is doing something mandatory and then someone asks him to perform the rain ritual prayer. He asks for rain in the very state he is in without any alteration or leaving it, formal prayer or change of form. He calls on God and makes supplication for that. His state is like the one who is present with God in what He makes mandatory for him. Then something occurs to him which would lead him to asking for a matter and that asking does not affect the obligation in which he is engaged. It may be prescribed in it like our question. (453)

Do you not see that the Prophet told the one who performs the formal prayer to say when he sits between the two prostrations, "O God! Forgive me, have mercy on me, provide for me and mend me." He is told to seek provision in the formal prayer. Asking for rain is seeking provision. The one who has this state does not go outside the city nor change his form. He is in the best state and has the best form because the best business is to fulfill the obligations. (454)

A bedouin came to the Messenger of God by the door of the mosque while the Messenger of God was on the *minbar* giving the Friday congregational prayer sermon. He complained to him about the drought and asked him to ask God for rain. He asked his Lord for rain while he was on the *minbar* in his sermon. He did not change his state or delay it for another moment. (455)

53.2.2. The One Compelled by Need Will Have His Formal Prayer Answered Without Doubt

The other state is when the servant is not engaged in performing something mandatory and sees what will lead him to seek from his Lord for himself or for others which requires of a new preparation in a particular form. Then he prepares for that matter and performs something mandatory before Him so that it will be based on the principle of servanthood of compulsion. The one who is forced and compelled has his supplication answered without a doubt. (456)

The servant is like that when he is performing something mandatory. He wants to ask for rain, so he goes out to the place of ritual prayer, gathers the people, and performs the two bows. It is servanthood by choice to begin that formal prayer. Performing what is contains of standing, bowing, prostration, and sitting is servanthood by compulsion. In the supererogatory prayer, whatever bowing, prostration, and all that is obligatory in the formal prayer by the divine law is obligatory for him. (457)

When he makes supplication after servanthood of compulsion, then he deserves to be answered. That particular form contains raising the hands, changing the cloak, facing the direction of formal prayer, humble supplication to God and asking on behalf of those in need of that, whoever they may be. Because of what we have just mentioned, there is a dispute concerning going out to the rain ritual prayer. The Messenger of God went outside of Medina and asked for rain with a ritual prayer and a sermon. (458)

53.2.3. Going Out of the Limitation of Means to the Open Space of *tajrid*

The interpretation of going outside the city is that man abandons reliance on means for the station of divestment and open space so that there is no veil of a roof or anything else between him and the sky which is the direction of formal prayer of his supplication. It is leaving the world of his outward while the world of his inward is a state of need for its Lord. This is by the intention to take on the character of his Lord in that or by the intention of mercy to himself or others or by joining all of that. (459)

53.3. The Interpretation of the Time When He Goes Out

53.3.1. The Self-disclosure of The Real to the Heart of the Servant Resembles the Sun

He can go out from the time when the edge of the sun begins to appear until noon. That is when God gives a Self-disclosure to the heart of the servant which is like the sun because of the intensity of clarity, removal of doubt, and unveiling of ranks and degrees and what they have so that he knows and sees where he puts his feet so that he will not fall, miss the way or be harmed by ruinous thoughts or the whisperings of satan. The sun removes every darkness and releases every care. When it rises, the people of means begin to seek their livelihood. The one who asks for rain is seeking livelihood. (460)

The servant continues to entreat God for himself when the shadow is drawing in from sunrise to noon so that he seeks things from God by his Lord, not by himself. His attention is drawn to that by the contracting of the shadow until noon. Then he gets the need which he has asked for. Part of the business of the one with this state is that when he obtains what he needs, it is given to the one who needs it and its shadow is contracted. God takes from His servant in veiling so that he will remain with himself in giving to him when he asks for what he himself needs. He shows himself bit by bit as the shadow extends and appears when the sun descends up until sunset. (461)

When it is veiled from him, he remains with himself devoted to himself and preoccupied with what he has acquired. It is designated as night formal prayer. He is united to his nest and his people gather at his table with what he has acquired in the day. This is why he goes out to the place of formal prayer from sunrise. "When the Prophet went out for the rain ritual prayer, he went out when the edge of the sun had appeared." That is how we interpret its aptness and correspondence. (462)

53.4. The Interpretation of the Rain Formal Prayer The Straight Path Is the Path of the Prophets

God prescribed supplication in the formal prayer when He said: "*Guide us on the straight path.*" The rain ritual prayer is a specific supplication. God wanted that supplication to be in a particular conversation in which he asks to obtain his portion of meaning of guidance to the Straight Path, the path of the Prophets whom God has guided who are careful in seeking the first, which contains the true happiness in it which is particular to the people of God. After that, they ask for rain in seeking what is general to all of the sensory provision which is a precondition for all animals and all people: obedient and rebel, fortunate and wretched. (463)

He begins with the formal prayer in order to knock on the door of Self-disclosure and answer to supplication in what is near to God. Seeking provision comes after that and it is implied that the unbeliever will be provided for by the concern for the believer and the rebel by the concern for the obedient. This is why the formal prayer is prescribed in the rain ritual prayer. (464)

53.5. Servanthood by Choice and Servanthood by Compulsion

Servanthood by choice before servanthood by compulsion is preparation, calling present, adorning the place and getting ready. Servanthood by choice after necessary servanthood is thankfulness, joy and good news for obtaining the necessary servanthood. The first is in the position of the supererogatory formal prayers before the formal prayers and the second is in the position of the supererogatory prayers after performing the formal prayers. When the Messenger of God was given the good news that God had forgiven him his past and future wrong actions, he performed supererogatory prayers until his feet were swollen. When he was asked about that, he said: "Am I not a grateful servant? (465)

53.5.1. Worship of Thankfulness

The worship of thankfulness is a worship which is neglected. That is why God Almighty says: *"Few of My servants are grateful."* (34:13) All that people have of the worship of thankfulness for blessing is to say: *"Praise be to God and thanks be to God."* It is a phrase which contains no burden. The People of God had actions with the bodies and turning to Him by spiritual strength like this phrase. God says: *"House of David, work in thankfulness"* (34:13). He did not say: "Say." The community of Muhammad is more entitled to this description than any other community since *"let there be a community from among you who calls to good"* (3:104). (466)

53.6. The Recitation of "God is Greater" In It

53.6.1. The Rain Formal Prayer Resemblances to the Festival Formal Prayer

Some of them liken it to the festival formal prayer. The first is *Id al-fitr,* the festival formal prayer marking the end of the month of Ramadan which is leaving the state of obligatory fasting. Obligatory fasting corresponds to drought. The person performing the formal prayer is thirsty as the earth is thirsty in a drought. The *Id al-adha* , the festival formal prayer marking the day that Prophet Abraham was willing to sacrifice his son is at the time of the pilgrimage. The ten days of pilgrimage are days of leaving adornment and so the one who takes on the sacred state is told to abandon adornment. It is prescribed for the one who wants to sacrifice that from the time when the new moon of the month of Dhu-l-Hijja appears, he does not cut his nails or his hair. (467)

It is only by flowers that the earth is adorned. There are only flowers through rain. These are states which demand lack of adornment. It is like the dry earth which has no adornment as it has no flowers because of the lack of rain. Therefore the rain formal prayer is like the two festival formal prayers. He recites the "God is Greater" in it as he does them in the festival formal prayers. (468)

53.6.2. The State of the Servant in the Sacred State (ihram) and the State of the Dry Earth

Whoever considers the rain formal prayer to be a practice of the Prophet (*sunan*), supererogatory, and formal does not add anything to the usual "God is Greater." That is better. The state of asking for rain is one state. It does not have different types. The goal is to have rain descend. He does not add anything to the recitation of "God is Greater" after which everything but the formal prayer is forbidden because there is not a state which demands the recitation of "God is Greater" beyond the recitation of "God is Greater" after which everything but the formal prayer is forbidden. (469)

The person who performs the rain formal prayer is forbidden by the recitation of "God is Greater" after which everything but the formal prayer is forbidden all the appetites which the soul enjoys. He has need of his Lord in that state. In the same way, the earth is forbidden by the water by which it has its life, adornment and breath. The state of the servant in the sacred state corresponds to the state of the earth in what it is denied of fertility. (470)

53.7. The Interpretation of the Sermon (*khutba*) in the Rain Formal Prayer

53.7.1. The One Who Prays Praises God as He Deserves

The sermon is praise of God as He deserves. So God gives him what he deserves. He praises Him again for what issues from Him. That is thankfulness for the blessing he receives. The one who performs the formal prayer praises God as He deserves and because of what he has from Him. It is the portion which God has of the formal prayer. Thus there must be a sermon in the rain ritual prayer. (471)

53.7.2. The Formal Prayer Is Praise of God

Whoever thinks that the formal prayer is praise of God says that the goal is achieved and the sermon is unnecessary. It is better to increase praise of God than to restrict it to one state. The sermon contains praise and remembrance. Remembrance benefits the believers, and there is no doubt that the rain ritual prayer is asking for benefit. (472)

53.8. The Interpretation about When the Sermon (khutba) Is Given

53.8.1. As it is customary (sunna), it is better for it to resemble the customary (sunna) than to resemble the formal

As it is *sunna*, it is better for it to resemble the *sunna* than to resemble the obligatory. It is related that the Prophet said: "Do not perform the odd numbered ritual prayer like the evening formal prayer." He disliked for one to perform the odd numbered ritual prayer three when he performed it in the same form as the the evening formal prayer. It is better to make the rain ritual prayer like the festival formal prayers, and he gives the sermon after the formal prayer unless there is an explicit text stating that the Prophet gave the sermon before the formal prayer. If there is a text to that effect, then there is no resemblance to the *sunna* or the obligation. It is a root in itself upon which analogy is made by the one who allows analogy in the religion of God.

53.8.2. It Is Better for the Sermon (khutba) in the Rain Formal Prayer to Be After the Formal Prayer

In the festival formal prayer, the sermon is given after the formal prayer. The sermon is meant to remind and teach them although they do not stand. Most of them depart at the end of the formal prayer. It is better to give the sermon at the end of the rain ritual prayer because they do not depart until the leader has performed the ritual prayer for them to receive rain, and they came out to ask for rain. The sermon comes after the ritual prayer and after the supplication for rain. People do not leave, and the goal of the sermon is obtained. (474)

53.8.3. Abd al-Malik ibn Marwan Was the First to Give a Sermon (khutba) on the Festival Before the Formal Prayer

Have you not seen how Abd al-Malik b. Marwan gave the sermon at the festival formal prayer before the the performing of the prayer began? People spoke to him in the assembly and rebuked him for doing that. The Prophet only gave a sermon in the two festival formal prayers after the prayer. Abd al-Malik retorted, "What was there has been abandoned." He meant that people had abandoned sitting down for the sermon. (475)

The Companions did not leave the festival formal prayer until the Messenger of God had given the sermon. It is better to follow the *sunna*, even if the leader remains on his own because nothing more than following is binding and there is no justification. When man finishes conversation with his Lord in his formal prayer, he praises God in himself in whatever he goes to. That continues to such an extent that he is with God in all his states. When he does that, it is the in the position of the sermon after the formal prayer. He continues to be occupied with God in every state. God gives success. There is no Lord but Him. (476)

53.9. The Interpretation of the Recitation Done Aloud

53.9.1. Rain is Mercy from Allah

The one who performs the formal prayer recites aloud in the rain ritual prayer so that those behind him will hear it and reflect on its signs and be distracted from the whisperings they are subject to by pondering the meanings of the Quran and they will apply themselves to one of the reasons which demands the descent of rain since they are performing an obligation when they obey the command of God. He says: "*And when the Quran is recited, it is to be listened to and pay heed so that perhaps you would find mercy.*" (7:204) (477)

53.9.2. The Actions in Which One Has Hopes of God's Answer Are Deemed to Be Mandatory

Rain is part of the Mercy of God, and they have only come out to seek it from God. He has promised it to the one who listens to the Quran. The ruling of the actions in which one has hopes of God's answer is that of the mandatory. If the leader mentions his Lord in an assembly (which is the group) aloud in the formal prayer or his supplication, God will mention him in a better assembly than theirs [a Tradition]. In that assembly, there may be someone who asks God Almighty to fulfill the need for which this leader and the group turn to Him. They receive rain by the supplication of that angel. (478)

53.9.3. Mercy Precedes Knowledge Since People Are in Need of It

The angels say, "*Our Lord! Thou hast encompassed everything in mercy and in knowledge.*" (40:7) Mercy preceded knowledge since His servants are in need it and have manners with God . . ." God made it precede knowledge in giving. He said: "*We had given mercy from Us and We had taught him knowledge which proceeds from Our Presence.*" (18:65) (479)

It is related that God said to His servants: "Call on Me with a tongue by which you do not rebel against Me." It is the tongue of those like me among the rebels, so how will it be when it is on the tongue of the angels "*. . . harsh, severe who do not disobey whatever God commands them and they accomplish what they are commanded.*" (66:6) It is better to recite aloud in it.

The Messenger of God recited aloud in the rain ritual prayer. (480)

53.10. The Interpretation of Changing the Cloak

53.10.1. Introduction

It indicates changing the state which has brought them out: from drought to fertility and from the state of difficult life to ease. That comes from a good sign. This is as the people of the city come out to seek rain and change from the state of arrogance, insolence, and ungratefulness for blessings, to the state of repentance, spiritual poverty, and manifestation of loss and neediness. They seek change by change. The tongue of actions is more eloquent than the tongue of words. (481)

53.10.2. Changing the Cloak Indicates Changing the State

By that action, they say, "Our Lord, we have been guided to Thee and we have returned from our opposition to Thee. Being blessed is by the blessing. When we had fertility with arrogance, that resulted in drought and scarcity for us. We hope for Thy generosity if Thou hast obliged us to have poverty, abasement, neediness, and fear and fertility." The thing is only confronted by its opposite so that it results in it. (482)

53.10.3. In the State of Gratitude, the Grateful Needs What He Does Not Have

If you were to say, "God Almighty says: '*If you gave thanks, I will increase blessings*'" (14:7), we say that the thankful one in the state of his thankfulness is the same as in his need for what he does not have. That is increase which is added to the blessing which he has. It is an inward blessing, and it is the repentance which God gives him inwardly and outwardly. It is a blessing which demands thankfulness. Thankfulness demands increase. The blessing covers him outwardly by the descent of rain and inwardly by praise for God for the blessing which He has given them: (483)

Thankfulness for the blessing of my Lord is
    another blessing
from Him to me. This is why thankfulness is demanded by
My poverty and need of Him. I have nothing but blessings
    from God. He sends them one after the other.
He is Rich, and my spiritual poverty is a favor
    which is manifested from Him upon me.
Therefore, I have obtained splendor and glory.
Poverty is my boast, and my power over existence
    is by poverty. I do not know and I do not know. (484)

53.10.4. The Commerce of the Truthful Successful Ones

Do you not see that the merchant who possesses such abundant wealth and great blessing that if his wealth been divided between him, his family, his children, and his followers for all their lives, it would have been enough for them and there would have been some left over? In spite of this, he endangers himself and his property by traveling on the sea and fearful roads in quest of increase in dirhams. What impels him to leave his family and makes it easy for him to part from his home and children, summons him and makes him need to travel through these dangers? It is only the illusion of obtaining this dirham over what he has. He may well destroy himself and his property through drowning, robbery or captivity. It is certain that he is involved in an illusory matter which he may or may not obtain. (485)

When someone with this state wants to trade and his poverty drives him out, he must travel and his intention moves to another intention. He looks in the direction where he intends to travel and knows that God has caused His servants to fulfill each other's needs. He says: "Such-and-such a land needs such-and-such," and he mentions the goods which the people of that land desire. (486)

He says: "Lord! If I and others sit down and do not carry this thing to them which they need, then we will cause trouble them with exhaustion and they will leave their children in order to reach us to obtain what they need. We prefer to tire ourselves rather than having them tire themselves. We will carry what they need to them." The exhaustion which he obtains from increase of dirhams is by this intention. Such is the commerce of the truthful merchants about whom the Messenger of God said in a sound Tradition, "The truthful merchant will be gathered on the Day of Rising with the Prophets, the truthful and the martyrs." See how excellent this ascription is according to this Tradition! (487)

The Prophet and the Prophets, peace be upon them, brought from what the servants of God need which contains their happiness. They are repaid with a full wage for that. This is the state of the merchant for the one who understands. God Almighty says: "*Will I point you to a transaction that will rescue you from a painful punishment*" (61:10)? He obtains hardship by that by leaving his homeland by emigration to the land of Islam. See how remarkable the words of prophethood are! (488)

53.10.5. The Merchant Is the One Who Sells on Credit with a Set Term

This is all part of changing states. This is why the one who performs the rain ritual prayer changes his cloak. The one who does not agree with this view, which contains sound gnosis and the complete reward, is brought out by what brings people out today: the lack of spiritual poverty which makes him rise to seek that illusory increase which may or not be obtained in spite of the wealth by which he is rich, if he is rich. If he is not rich by himself in what he has and fears for his property and poverty, he is driven to increase and endangers his life and his property. He is blind to the knowledge that this traveler and his property are as we have mentioned. This imaginary poverty rouses him and comes between him and his family, children and loved ones. He is completely happy and overjoyed by that journey since he imagines that he will obtain profit. (489)

The state of the thankful one and his need to seek increase is better. Increase is definite and profit is illusory. God is truthful in His reports. The thankful one who has this real increase by his thankfulness is in his family and does not leave his homeland, his family or his children. He does not provoke himself or expose himself to perils or tire out his body. If he had given all his property as charity, then he is like a merchant who sells for a delayed term. It is stored up for him and he will find it with God on the day of his poverty and need. God must bring his provision by which he lives as well as his children's provision. It is as Luqman said: "*O my son! Truly even if it be the weight of a grain of a mustard seed and though it be in a rock or in the heavens or in or on the earth God will bring it. Truly God is Subtle, Aware.*" (31:16) (490)

This is a merchant for sells for a delayed term. Its term is the time of the Rising. That is when the term arrives. My brother, this is the wisdom of changing the cloak. (491)

53.11. The Interpretation of How the Cloak is Changed

It has three ranks. The man of knowledge combines all of them when he wants to leave the disagreement between the divine law scholars. He puts it inside out, its top to its bottom and bottom to top, and the one on his right to the one on his left and the one on his left to the one on his right. All of that stresses the indication to change the state which they have. (492)

53.11.1. The Effect of the Outer on the Inner and Vice Versa

As for the interpretation of the inside and outside of the cloak, it is the effects of his outward actions on his inward (that is, his heart and what these actions produce) and the praiseworthy inward actions also appear outwardly through action. This is like the intention to give charity and then he gives charity, or he intends to do a good action and then does it. What he has inwardly appears outwardly through action. (493)

"When you conceal the secret, God dresses it in its cloak." When you do a right action, that produces in yourself and your heart the love and desire to begin another action, especially if that action in this world results in knowledge in yourself as the Prophet said: "If someone acts by what he knows, God will bequeath him a knowledge which he did not know." God Almighty says: *"If you are Godfearing of God, He will assign you a Criterion between right and wrong."* (8:29) (494)

53.11.2. Joining the Upper World to the Lower and Vice Versa

As for changing the top and bottom of the cloak, it is joining the upper world to the lower world in subjugation, and joining the lower world to the upper world in purification and declaring absolutely pure. The upper descends as a mercy to the lower, and the lower rises out of concern to the rank of the upper in relationship to God Almighty and need of Him. As God turns to the highest of existent things in value (and it is the divine Pen and the First Intellect by what He gave it of knowledge and happiness), so He turns to the lowest of existent things in value, the most wretched and the basest of them in station with God by the same definition. (495)

53.11.3. There Is No Single Essence (jawhar) But That It is Connected to a divine Reality

In respect of His Essence, there is no rivalry in God since He is not described by the whole so that the part could be specified in Him. There is no single essence in the entire world, high and low, except that it is connected to a divine Reality. There is no rivalry in this most precious protected Presence. He sits on His Highest Throne. "If you had let down a rope, it would have fallen on God" [a Tradition]. (496)

Four angels gathered around the Kaba: one descended from the heaven, one rose from the low earth, the third came from the East and the fourth from the West. Each of them asked the other: "Where have you come from?" All of them said: "From God." (497)

One of our shaykhs related a Tradition to us the chain of transmission of which reached back to the Prophet. The Messenger of God said: "God is in the heaven as He is on the earth. The Higher Assembly seeks Him as you seek Him." The worlds are equal in seeking, but the disparity between them is known. (498)

53.11.4. Historical Memories and Knowledges by Tasting

It happened that I had a taste in this witnessing. That was when I was carrying something which was very despicable in the eyes of people. My position did not make it necessary. It had a very foul smell of salt fish. My companions imagined that I was carrying it to undertake the struggle against my ego since my position in their eyes was too high to carry something like that. They said to my Shaykh: "So-and-so is not deficient in his striving." He said: "Let us ask him what his intention is in carrying that." (499)

The Shaykh questioned me in the presence of the group and told me what they had said to him. I told them: "You are wrong in your interpretation about me. By God, I did not intend any of that. I saw that in spite of the height of His value, God has not disconnected Himself from creating the like of this so that I should disconnect myself from carrying it." The Shaykh thanked me and the companions were amazed. It is a part of this topic. God is my honor when I carry it. It is like the power in bringing its source into existence. The gnostics do not distinguish between the high and the low. This is the change of the smell of the mouth of the person who is fasting. It is more fragrant than the scent of musk with God. Where is the smell perceived from the two scents? (500)

Do not see any preference in things unless it is by their connection to divine Realities. If this is the way you look, you will not demean anything in this world. Do not gauge God and do not impute it to yourself. Take things according to what their realities accord. (501)

53.11.5. The Manifestation of the Believer in the World to Come by the Bliss of the Unbeliever in This World and Vice Versa

As for changing what is on the right to the left and vice versa, its interpretation is that the attributes of the happy in supplication, humility and abasement (and they are the people of the right in this world) move to the people of the left in the world to come. It is as if the happy take it from them in this world. (502)

God Almighty says about the happy: "*Those, they who in their formal prayers are ones who are humble*" (23:2) and "*ones who are humble toward God.*" (3:199) He said about throwing back the attribute on them: "*they fear a Day when the hearts will go to and fro and their sight.*" (24:37) He said about those who are wretched in the world to come: "*Ones who are humbled by a sense of humility looking on with secretive glances.*" (42:45) He said: "*Faces on that Day will be ones that are humbled, ones that work and ones that are fatigued, roasting in a hot fire.*" (88:2). (503)

The other change is that the happy servant in the world to come is described by what the wretched servant is described with in this world: wealth, property and power. The believer will moves to that in the world to come and the unbeliever moves from it in the world to come. The believer manifests the blessing of the wretched unbeliever in this world, and the unbeliever who is blessed in this world is manifested in the world to come by the attribute of wretchedness and despair which the believer had in this world. This is the interpretation of the right and the left in changing the cloak. (504)

53.12. The Interpretation of Changing the Cloak

53.12.1. *The Human Being in the State of Looking to His Lord*

Is the cloak changed at the beginning of the sermon in the rain ritual prayer or after he has started the sermon? Know that the interpretation of changing the cloak at the beginning of the sermon is that man is in the state of looking to his Lord by his Lord. At the beginning of the sermon, he looks to his Lord by himself. It is when He says at the beginning of the formal prayer: "My servant has praised Me." If the person who is praying had been in a state of annihilation by seeing his Lord at the time of the praise, then God Almighty would be praising himself on the tongue of His servant. Then "My servant has praised Me" would not be true from all aspects. God—glory be to Him!—speaks the truth when He says: "My servant has praised Me." Therefore, the servant must see himself when he praises his Lord. It is truthfulness. (505)

53.12.2. *Praise of the Lord by the Lord in a State of the Annihilation of Knowledge and Witnessing of the Customary (sunna)*

As for the one who says that it is after the sermon has started, it is when the servant says: "*Thee alone we worship and Thee alone we ask for help.*" At the beginning of the sermon he praises his Lord by his Lord from himself. He praises Him by His words. When discourse occurs, it is his praise of his Lord and he moves from that state in that moment. This is the interpretation of specifying whether the cloak is changed at the beginning of the sermon or after the sermon has already started. (506)

53.13. The Interpretation of Facing the *Qibla*

53.13.1. *Supplication from Someone Who Is Poor and Supplication from Someone Who Is Rich*

Whoever is all face, faces his Lord by his essence. The Messenger of God saw behind him as he saw in front of him. He was all face. The one who asks his Lord for rain should face his Lord with his entire essence. There is no part of him, sensory or ideational, outward or inward, but that it is poor and in need of the mercy of God to obtain His blessings or make His blessing continue for him. (507)

This is why God answers the supplication of person in desperate need. The one who is in desperate need is the one who calls on his Lord manifesting need of Him. People are only denied the answer from God when they call on Him since they are calling on Him from richness when they turn to secondary means. They are unaware of that and it results in lack of sincerity. The one who is in dire need is guaranteed the answer. He is sincere, and the sincere one does not turn to anything except that to which he is directing himself. (508)

53.13.2. Fakh al-Din Razi In Prison

Rashid al-Farghani informed me that his shaykh, Fakhr al-Din ibn Khatib al-Rayy, the scholar of his age, was arrested by the Sultan. The Sultan had decided to kill him and he did not have any intercessor who was acceptable to him. He said: "I wanted to concentrate my spiritual strength on God in my affair so that He would save me from the hands of the Sultan since all means were cut off for me and I despaired of all except God. That was not sincere for me because of the logical doubts which came to me about the affirmation of God in whom I believed until I concentrated my spiritual strength and my entire being on the God in whom the common people believe. I discarded my proofs and speculation from myself and I did not find any doubt in me which would lessen my faith. I was sincere in turning to Him with my entire being, and I called on Him in sincerity. Morning came and God relieved me and released me from prison. This is the interpretation of facing the direction of formal prayer. That indicates acceptance. (509)

53.14. The Interpretation of Standing During the Supplication Actions Are Divided Between the Active and Passive According to the Reality

Standing during the supplication in the rain ritual prayer corresponds to God's establishing His servants in what they need. It is the quest for provision for the descent of rain on which they rely. They rejoice in the words of God: "*Men are supporters of women*" (4:34). All selves are in the station of femaleness for the one who understands. The rank of every passive is the rank of the female, and there is only the passive. (510)

Action is divided into the active and the passive in reality. Part of the active is power and part of the passive is acceptance of power in it. Here is a sincere which contains: "*I answer the call of one who calls when he calls to Me so they should respond to Me.*" (2:186) (511)

The one by whom God arranges provision is the one who assigns the one who is provided for by means of him. Therefore it is prescribed that we stand in the supplication in the rain ritual prayer. It is as if he were saying by the state of his standing before his Lord: "Provide for us with that with which we will support our family in what you send down of abundant rain to us. It is the reason for the existence of that on which we base ourselves: 'Thou hast power over everything.'" (512)

53.15. The Interpretation of the Supplication with Worship (*Ibada*)

The supplication is the brain of the worship. The limbs have strength by the brain. Similarly, supplication is the brain of worship and the worship of worshippers is strong by means of it. "Those who are too arrogant for My worship (worship here being the same as supplication) will enter hellfire abject." It is distance from God. Hellfire is called that because of the great distance of its bottom. (513)

53.15.1. The Hands Are the Place of Taking and Giving

The hands are the place of taking and giving. It is by them that he takes and gives. They hold what they take and extend what they give. The servant raises his outstretched hands so that God can place in them the blessings for which he asks. If he raises them and places his palms towards the earth, his raising them testifies to the height and elevation of the hands of my Lord which is the upper hand. His hands are spread out to spend as he likes. (514)

The one who asks has his palms towards the earth in the rain ritual prayer, that is, send down on us good and blessing from Thy hands which will fill out poverty and need which is attached to means. It is uniquely Thine. He closes them by what Thou hast sent down of rain for them. (515)

53.15.2. The Two Cycles of the Rain Formal Prayer: Their Outer and Inner Blessing

This and its likes is the interpretation of the rain ritual prayer and the states of its people and the fact that it is a ritual prayer of two bows. It is the words of God: "He *has lavished on you His divine blessing, that which is manifest and that which is inward.*" (31:20) The first bow is for the outward blessing which fills the outward gap. The second is for the inward blessing. In it, he asks for what knowledges and gnoses and Self-disclosures which will feed the spirits and hearts. The "two hands" belong to the blessing. (516)

54 The Two Bows to Greet the Mosque

54.1. The Ruling of the Two Cycles to Greet the Mosque

54.1.1. The Ruling of the Two Cycles to Greet the Mosque with the Legal Scholars

Divine law scholars disagree about the two bows for the one who enters the mosque. Some say that it is *sunna* and some say that it is obligatory. That which I believe and say is that these two bows are not obligatory for the one who enters the mosque unless he intends to sit in the mosque. If he stands and does not sit, or crosses through and does not sit, then in my opinion he can choose. If he likes, he can do them, and if he likes, he does not do them. There is nothing held against him. If he sits and does not perform them, that is a wrong action. This is unless he enters he enters in a time in which the formal prayer is forbidden or he is not in a state of purity. (517)

54.2. Entering the Mosque in a Time in Which Supererogatory Prayer Is Forbidden

The one who enters the mosque either does so at a time when supererogatory prayers are permitted or at a time when they are they are forbidden. If he enters at a time when they are forbidden, he does not perform them. Some people might imagine that the command to greet the mosque conflicts with the Tradition forbidding the formal prayer at certain times. (518)

54.3. The Prohibition and Extent of Its Conflict with a Firm Command

Know that the forbidden is not in conflict with the command established with the jurisprudents. We have looked into that when the prohibition is established and the command is established. The Messenger of God gave us a command when he forbade us by a command to obey the prohibition absolutely and without specification. You avoid every prohibited thing included under the principle of that prohibition. The Messenger of God said in the established command in this Tradition:

"When you are commanded to do something, do as much as you are able." (519)

He commanded us to perform the ritual prayer when we enter the mosque and forbade us to perform it at certain times. We acquire the established prohibition in respect to the one who cannot do what he is commanded to do in this state because of the existence of the prohibition. The ability falls away in the divine law as it falls away logically. The Messenger of God did not say: "Do it as much as you are able" as an ability in the divine law or a logical capacity. It must be general. He says that the general prohibition stopped me from performing all that this command contains regarding times, so I cannot do this formal prayer at this time which is specifically forbidden in the divine law. Know that! (520)

54.4. The Mosque Is the House of God and the Footstool of His Self-disclosure

The mosque is the House of God, and the Footstool is His Self-disclosure for the one who wants to speak with Him. Whoever comes to Him in His house must greet Him as He has commanded him to greet Him. The Messenger of God taught us how to greet the house of our Lord. He says: *"The Light is lit in houses God gave permission to be lifted up and that His Name be remembered in it. Glorifying Him in the first part of the day and the eventide are men."* '(24:36-37) Abd Allah ibn Umar said: "If I had been a glorifier, I would have done it in full," that is, done supererogatory prayers. The glorification of the forenoon is the forenoon prayer. (521)

When we enter the mosque, we greet those who are present in it of the Higher Assembly by saying: "Peace be upon you" if there are any people there: man, woman or child. If there is no one there called 'human', the one who enters may be one of those from whose eye God has removed the customary covering of the veil. He perceives the intelligent souls in it of jinn and angels. He greets them as he greets the human beings he finds there. (522)

If he is not one of the people who are unveiled to those who are in it, he should say: "Peace be upon us and upon the virtuous servants of God." He means everyone who acts right for God among His servants in all that is other-than-God. That word reaches every righteous servant of God in the heaven and the earth. He does not say: "Peace be upon God." God is Peace. (523)

54.5. The Greeting of the Mosque and the Greeting of Foreign Kings

He should perform two bows before his Lord, The Mighty, The

Majestic. He puts God Almighty in his direction of formal prayer. By what it contains of bowing and prostration, that formal prayer is like the greeting which is given to foreign kings when people come to them and they appear to their populace. We have already mentioned the interpretation of the states of bowing, standing, sitting and prostration. Those two bows are the prostration of greeting. (524)

If he enters at a time which is not a time for formal prayer, that is, in the moments in which the formal prayer is forbidden, when he enters the mosque, he stands before his Lord, humble, abased, watchful, obeying the command of his Master in his prohibition against doing the formal prayer at this time as He forbids him to say: "Peace be upon God" in his greeting the formal prayer. (525)

If his Master orders him to sit in His house, then he performs the two bows out of thankfulness to God for that since his Master ordered him to sit with Him in His house. Those two bows at that time are bows for thankfulness to God. Whoever bows before siting down and does not intend to sit while it is a time of formal prayer, those two bows are a greeting to God for coming to Him in His house. (526)

Any gnostic among the people of God observes that he is coming to God in His house and the thought of limitation by moments does not occur to him, his bowing is the bowing of greeting for entering. In the case of someone who has a state of constant presence with God and conversation with Him in every state, that is not a greeting. It is two bows of thankfulness to God Almighty since He made him among those who are fearfully aware when he entered the mosque since He said that the mosque is the house of everyone who is fearfully aware. He ascribed it to those of His servants who are fearfully aware, as is ascribed to God. (527)

55 On the Mysteries of the Prostration of Recitation

55.1. Introduction

Divine law scholars disagree about the prostration of recitation and whether it is obligatory or *sunna*. Some people say that it is obligatory and some people say that it is *sunna* and not obligatory. (528)

55.1.2. The One Who Recites the Quran Consigns with God

The Messenger of God reported in the well-established Tradition that God Almighty said: "I have divided the formal prayer into two portions between Me and My servant." In the division, He only mentioned the recitation of the Opening Chapter and did not turn to the form of standing, bowing, prostration, and sitting. He only mentioned the Opening Chapter of the recitation from the Quran from the servant of God Almighty and what it contains of the recitation of the Opening chapter. This tradition is our proof of the obligation of reciting the Opening chapter for the one who performs the formal prayer. We say that the reciter is conversing with God Almighty by the attributes which are particular to God and those of them which are particular to the servant by realized unveiling in all of the Quran which is called the Word of God. (529)

55.1.2. We Prostrate Where the Messenger of God Prostrated

There is a sign which is particular to the presence of God, so it belongs purely to God. There is a sign which is particular to the presence of the servant, so it belongs purely to the servant. There is a sign in which partnership occurs, so it is between God and His servant. Action in that is like action in the prescribed Opening Chapter. There are places in the Word of God Almighty which demand that the one who is reciting prostrate in them. The Prophet made it clear to us where we prostrate and where we do not prostrate. It has certain preconditions: purity, the moment for prostration and facing the direction of formal prayer. The details of all that will follow. (530)

We prostrate where the Messenger of God prostrated, and we leave what he left, even if the words are a command which demands prostration. We do not prostrate because the Prophet only prescribed prostration in certain specific places which he specified for it by word and action. We do not exceed them nor add to them. There is a well-known dispute about their number. The prostration which is prescribed outside of recitation has already been mentioned: like prostration when you see portents, the prostration of thankfulness, or other things. We will mention the number of firm places of prostration which come in the Quran, and we will include the one who disagrees about them. Know that the prostrations of the Mighty Quran are from eleven to fifteen. Some of them come by the form of Tradition and some come in the actual command to prostrate. (531)

55.2. Concerning the Prostrations in the Mighty Quran

55.2.1. The 1st Prostration: Surat al-Araf (Chapter 7)

The 1st prostration of that occurs in *Surah al-araf* at the end of it. The *araf* or Rampart is a wall which is located between the Garden and the Fire. The inside of it has mercy, and it is that which is next to the Garden, and the outside of it is punishment, and it is that which is next to the Fire. There are men on it whose good and bad deeds are equal. One scale of the balance does not outweigh the other. Their scales are neither heavy nor light. God has not balanced in the balance of any of them the words, "There is no god but God." There is no evil deed equal to it except idol worship. As idol worship and unity are not joined together in the heart of the same person, so it only enters the balance for the one with scrolls for another reason which we mention in this book or which we have mentioned in the Chapter of Rising. (532)-(533)

As for the end of this chapter, it is the words of God Almighty, "*And when the Quran is recited, it is to be listened to and pay heed.*" (7:204) This sign which was sent down about recitation in the formal prayer and prostration is one of the pillars of the formal prayer. He sealed this sura by mentioning the angels and their prostration to God. He described them and said: "Those who are with your Lord (and they are the near angels) are not arrogant, too proud for His worship. (He says that they are abased and humble to Him) They glorify Him." They disconnect Him from attributes which are not fitting for Him. That is what they draw near Him with in the way of abasement and humility. (534)

55.2.2. The Prostration of the Angels Close to God

In this sign God confirms their truthfulness when they said: "We glorify Thy praise and proclaim Thee pure." God related about them that which they had related about themselves. "And they prostrate to Him." He described them as prostrating to Him with these above-mentioned states. God Almighty said when He mentioned the Prophets, peace be upon them, to Muhammad that He had given them the Book, wisdom, and prophethood. He said: *"Those are they whom God has guided. So imitate their guidance."* (6:90). They are men like him, so what do you think then about those angels who do not rebel against God when He commands them and do what they are commanded? *"And to God prostrates whatever is in the heavens and the earth, willingly or unwillingly, and their shade in the first part of the day and at eventide."* (66:6) What guidance is greater than that by which God Almighty has guided the angels? (535)

When the reciter recites this prostration, he does so in order to follow the prostration of the Higher Assembly and to be guided by them. Whoever prostrates in it and does not have a breath of what the angels obtain in their prostration in respect to their particular angelicness has not prostrated in it. It is like that in every Quran which has come. (536)

55.2.3. The Prostration of the People of the Ramparts

The people of the Rampart see the places of the Rising and that the Messenger of God prostrates in it when he asks his Lord to open the gate of intercession. It is out of exaltation of God, awe, and honor. They hear God say: *"On a Day the great calamity will be uncovered."* (68:42) In another business, the Arabs say, "War bared its leg" when fighting is fierce and the battle is bitter and the situation grave. Then they know that it is a place of prostration. When they are called to prostrate there, the people of the ramparts prostrate to obedience to the command of God. The scale of their good deeds becomes heavier due to this prostration, and so they are happy since it is a prostration of obligation prescribed in that place by divine command. Then they enter the Garden. (537)

55.3. The 2nd Prostration: It is the prostration of the shadows in the mornings and evenings along with the general prostration

This is the prostration of *Surah al-rad* (Chapter 13). It is when God Almighty says: *"And to God prostrates whatever is in the heavens and the earth, willingly or unwillingly, and their shade in the first part of the day and at eventide."* (13:15) The shadows of the spirits are their bodies. God Almighty tells us that whoever is in the heavens—and they are the high ones—and whoever is in the earth—and they are the low, the world of bodies which are based on elemental structure—prostrate to Him willingly (for the spirits in respect to their knowledge and station and bodies in respect to their essences and source) and unwillingly (in the spirits in respect to their essences and in bodies in respect to their leadership and advancing themselves ahead of their fellow men). This is a prostration of information. (538)

55.3.1. The Perfect Human Being Is Human Angel and Angelic Human

The servant must confirm the truthfulness of what God has said about those whom He mentions. He is among the people of the earth by his body and among the people of the heavens by his intellect. He is a human angel and angelic human. He prostrates willingly to his Lord and unwillingly from his limitation in respect to a particular attribute which his knowledge does not demand, even if his prostration is a prostration of essence in the heart of the matter. If he is not aware of that, he does it as worship and that saves him. (539)

55.3.2. The Stretching of the Shadows Morning and Evening

He mentioned the mornings and the evenings by the extension of the shadows at these times. He makes their extension prostration. This is in the morning and it shrinks returning to its root from which it was sent out and fearing burning for itself. It is as if it was restricted to its essence. In the evenings, it extends and grows longer by increase by manifesting the blessings of God which He has lavished on it. The mornings and the evenings are among the times in which it is forbidden to pray. The principle of prostration at those times is outside of the principle of the supererogatory prayer which is made up. The reciter is told to prostrate in this sign. He is rewarded from the gate of the one who confirms that his Lord tells the truth in His report. (540)

55.3.3. The Prostration of Following the Guide and the Prostration of Confirmation by Realization

The prostration of the Ramparts is a prostration to follow the guidance of the angels. This prostration is confirmation by realization. (541)

55.4. The 3rd Prostration: The Prostration of the Higher and Lower Worlds in the State of Abasement and Fear

55.4.1. The Prostration to God Out of Thankfulness

The 3rd prostration is the prostration of the higher and lower worlds in the station of abasement and fear. It is where He says: "*They accomplish what they are commanded.*" (16:50) He mentioned the angels and the shadow. They prostrate in the rampart by choice because of what the majesty of God demands. Here God, The Mighty, praised them because they do what they are commanded. They prostrate out of thankfulness to God since God praised them for doing what they are commanded. They prostrated out of thankfulness to God since He praised them for giving them success in obeying His commands. (542)

55.4.2. *Prostrating to God Out of Desire*

The servant prostrates since he desires to be among those whom God praises as He praised His angels. For the servant it is a prostration of abasement and humility. He says that his shadow (with the pronoun) casts a shadow in His shadow-referring to the created thing. We said that bodies are the shadows of the arwah. They only move when the spirits move them with an essential movement (543)

55.4.3. *Prostrating to God Out of Humility and Humbleness*

He said: "*To the right and to the left, ones who prostrate to God. And they are ones who are in a state of lowliness.*" (16:48) It is a prostration of abasement and humility. Whoever prostrates this prostration and does not see the prostration of his shadow on the right when the Self-disclosure occurs to him on the left or the prostration of his shadow on the left when the Self-disclosure is on the right, has not acquired any effect in the world of phenomenal being. Effects in the presence of the sources are easy in existence. What the people of strength and the right manifest is only in their effect in their effect in phenomenal being. This is one of the special properties of this prostration. (544)

55.5. The 4th Prostration: The Prostration of Those Who Know the Knowledge of Secrets and Tastes Which God Has Entrusted in their Words: It Is a Prostration of Submission, Weeping and Humility The Quran Is True in Its Sending Down and Its Revelation

The 4th prostration, the prostration of those who know the knowledge of secrets and spiritual tastes which God has entrusted in their words: it is a prostration of submission, weeping and humility. "*And We sent it forth with The Truth and it came down with the Truth and We sent it not to thee but as one who gives good tidings and as a warner. And it is a Recitation. We have separated it in order that thou mayest recite it to humanity at intervals. And We have sent it down a sending successively down.*" (17:105) He says that We sent it down with the truth "so that you can judge between people in that about which they dispute" concerning the truth. "With the truth it has come down." "We only sent you" to speak to the one on whom it was sent in order to clarify everything "as a bearer of good news," and you give good news to some people of mercy from Him, pleasure, and gardens for them in which there is abiding blessing, and to give good news to other people of a painful punishment. "And as a warner" to inform the one to whom you give good news and by what you give good news. (545)

55.5.1. The Quran Is Clear Signs in Revealed Chapters

The Quran is clear signs in revealed chapters. "A Quran (a comprehensive word which gathers many different things) which We have divided (separated into clear signs in revealed chapters) for you to recite (gather it and you gather it for the people) to people at intervals (unhurriedly in deliberate recitation)." "We sent it down" which obliges him to respect the speech of the one whose value is not known. "They do not value God with His proper value." (546)

"Say: (O Prophet!) believe in it (accept it) or do not believe in it (or reject it and do not accept it). Those who were give the knowledge (the Signs which give certainty and tranquillity in things) before it (of those who preceded him) when it is recited to them (following its signs one by one by the relationship between one sign and another), they fall down on their faces prostrating." They fall on their faces, bowing, humble. Prostration is bowing. When the camel prostrates, it bows so that it can be ridden. "*They say, 'Glory be to our Lord* (His promise is true and His words are true)! *Our Lord's promise is fulfilled*." As He made the promise, it is applied to good and evil. The threat is for evil in particular. The promise in good is from God and it must exist. The threat may be overlooked and passed over. It is part of the attribute of the generous with the Arabs. The Arabs praise their masters and great ones with it. Their poet said:

If I threaten or promise him, my threat is forgotten
and my promise is carried out. (547)

55.5.2. Prostration of Self-disclosure

The prostration of Self-disclosure is, "And they fall down on their faces weeping" over what has escaped them which they do not perceive. It is overlooked, it is written that it will be wiped out as long as it is in purity as it is written that it will not be wiped out. "It increases them in humility," that is, abasement and humility because the humble person only has that by a Self-disclosure. It must be either on the outward or the inward or both. This is a prostration of increase in humility. As we said: humility only comes from a divine Self-disclosure. Increase of humility indicates increase of Self-disclosure. This is called the prostration of Self-disclosure, so understand! (548)

55.6. The 5th Prostration: The Prostration of the General Blessing of the Merciful Because of Proofs

55.6.1. The Prostration of the Prophets Who Are Blessed

The fifth prostration, the prostration of the general blessing of The Merciful on account of proofs, it is the prostration of the Prophets who are blessed and it is in Chapter Mary (Chapter 19) when He says: "*When were recounted to them the signs of the Merciful they fell down, crying, ones who prostrate themselves.*" (19:58) It is the prostration of the Prophets to the One who has blessed them. This is the weeping of joy and happiness and the signs of acceptance and pleasure. God connected this prostration to the Signs of The Merciful. Mercy does not demand force and might. It demands gentleness and divine kindness. They weep for joy because of the good names which God has given them about these Signs. The form is that of weeping since tears flow, but the tears are tears of joy, not tears of distress, grief and sorrow, because the station of the name of The Merciful does not demand that. (549)

55.6.2. The Delight of Abu Yazid and Blood Rushing from His Eyes

In this chapter when He said: "*On the Day when We will assemble the ones who are Godfearing to The Merciful*" (19:85), Abu Yazid rejoiced and blood rushed from his eyes until he struck the *minbar* and said: "How remarkable! How can the one who sits with Him be gathered to Him!" God says: "I sit with the one who remembers Me." The one who is conscious of God remembers God with wariness. Then he is gathered to The Merciful, and it is the station of security from the caution which he is in. He rejoices at that and is happy. Abu Yazid's tears were tears of joy at how he will be gathered to Him when others will be gathered to the well. (550)

55.6.3. The Connection of the Punishment to the name, the Merciful

He says in this chapter, quoting Abraham the Friend, "*I fear that a punishment should afflict thee from The Merciful.*" (19:45) He connected punishment to the name The Merciful. It is not demanded outwardly here. Know that he indicates the name which his father was connected to in that state. There is no doubt that he was with The Merciful since he had well-being, good provision, and health. (551)

55.6.4. The Mercy of the Doctor

The other meaning in this name with context of the punishment is like the mercy of the doctor to the one who has gangrene. He punishes him by amputating the limb with gangrene as a mercy to him so that he will live. Part of His Mercy is establishing limits in this world so that they will have purity in the world to come. It is like that in every abode if you look with the eye of realization, so know that! (552)

55.6.5. Seeing Bliss in Punishment

Whoever prostrates this Quran and does not see the blessing in punishment has not prostrated it as the poet said:

I want you, and I do not want you for the reward.
I want you for the punishment.
I obtained my every wish from it except pleasure.
My ecstasy is by punishment. (553)

Rabia al-Adawiyya hit her head on the edge of a wall and it bled. People asked her: "Don't you feel the pain?" She said: "My preoccupation with approving what He Will in whatever happens has distracted me from feeling what you see in the state." (554)

55.7. The 6th Prostration: The Prostration of the Will and the Prostration of the Command

The 6th prostration is the prostration of the will and the prostration of the command. It is the prostration of the minerals and plants with the prostration of the will, and the animals and some men. The inhabitants of the spheres and the elements prostrate in witnessing and in interpretation. (555)

God Almighty said: "*Hast thou not considered that to God prostrates to Him whoever is in the heavens and whoever is in and on the earth and the sun and the moon and the stars, the mountains, the trees and the moving creatures, and many of humanity. And many on whom the punishment will be realized, and He whom God despises, then there is none who honors him. Truly God accomplishes whatever He wills.*" (22:18) God—glory be to Him!—mentioned everything in this sign, and He only mentioned something referring to a part in people. He said: "many men." He made that part of His will. (556)

The servant sets out to prostrate in this sign so that he will be among the many who prostrate to God, not the many who deserve punishment. When this servant sees that God Almighty has given him success in prostrating and has not come between him and prostration, he knows that he is among the people of concern who are connected to the "who" whose prostration is not divisible among those who are in the heavens and who are in the earth, and the sun in its setting and the moon when it is invisible, and the stars in their descents and the mountains in their dwelling, and the trees in their resting on their trunks and the beasts in their subjugation and some people who have witnessing. (557)

Whoever among the people of God performs this prostration and does not see every world in it which we mentioned and sees the prostration of part of it from its whole and the one who has some of him which does not prostrate has not prostrated. (558)

55.8. The 7th Prostration: The Prostration of Success and Salvation

55.8.1. The Ascription of Going-on and Enduring

The 7th prostration is that of success and salvation. It is the prostration of success and belief coming from humility, abasement and need. It is at the end of Chapter The Pilgrimage when He says: "*O those who have believed! Bow down and prostrate yourselves, and worship your Lord, and accomplish good so that perhaps you would prosper.*" (22:77). This is the prostration of success and it is going-on, victory and rescue. (559)

He does good by hastening to prostrate when he hears this sign recited because of his belief since God called the believers in this sign and commanded them to prostrate. It is connected to the angels inasmuch as they do what they are commanded. The servant prostrates and has success. (560)

It is a prostration which is disputed. When one prostrates and does not recognize the relationship of divine going-on and continuation and does not distinguish between the one who goes on by his going-on and the one who goes on because he is made to go on and wins (for he is distinguished from his Sign by the one who withdraws, succeeds, and is rescued in that to which he flees and says he is firm in some matters and in others by success), he has not prostrated this prostration. (561)

55.9. The 8th Prostration

55.9.1. The Difference Between Knowledge and Experience Is the Knowledge of Tasting

The 8th prostration is that of differentiation. This is the prostration of aversion and rejection among the people who admit. God Almighty said: "*And when it was said to them: Prostrate yourselves to The Merciful, they said: And what is The Merciful? Will we prostrate ourselves to what thou hast commanded us? And it increased aversion in them.*" (25:60) when they are told, "*Prostrate to The Merciful.*" The believer prostrates when it is recited in order to be distinguished by it from the unbeliever who rejects His name The Merciful. This is called the prostration of distinction. God says: "*And be separated on this Day, O ones who sin!*" (36:59). (562)

The distinction occurs between those who deny the name The Merciful and those who recognize it on the Day of Rising by this prostration which they do during the recitation. (563)

This name increases them in aversion because they are ignorant of it. That is why they said: "What is The Merciful?" by way of inquiry. This is a prostration of blessing, not a prostration of force. (564)

The unbelievers erred when they thought that The Merciful was contrary to imposition of responsibility. They thought that the command to prostrate was obligation. One must prostrate to the One who has this name The Merciful, due to the intensity of the mercy which it contains. If he had mentioned Him with the name that demands force, the unbeliever might have hurried to prostrate out of fear. (565)

This is like what happened with the proud among the leaders during the Age of Ignorance with the Messenger of God. He said to him, "Muhammad, recite to me some of what you have brought so that I can hear it." He recited to him: *"HaMim, the prostration."* When he reached the words of God Almighty: *"But if they turned aside then say: I have warned you of a thunderbolt like the thunderbolt of Ad and Thamud.'"* (41:13) They were Arabs, and their story was well-known in the Hijaz. When he heard this sign, he trembled violently due to the intensity of what he heard and his recognition of it. He said: "These are the words of The Compeller." (566)

The only thing that increased them in aversion was the connection of obligation to the name The Merciful. When someone rebels against The Merciful, He pardons him and overlooks and so he was not obligated in the beginning. If the ignorant man had known that His command to prostrate to The Merciful was not contrary to obligation, but is contrary to punishment and increases good payment, he would set out to that as the believer sets out. (567)

Whoever prostrates this prostration and does not distinguish between knowledge and experience (which is the knowledge of spiritual tastes), part of it is His words: *"We will try your reports."* (47:31) (568)

55.10. The 9th Prostration: The Prostration of the Oneness (*Tawhid*) of Immensity

The 9th prostration is the prostration of unity of immensity. It is the prostration of the "hidden secret" from the "certain news." There is disagreement about the place of this prostration in this chapter (Chapter the Ant, Chapter 27). It is said that it is when He says: "Lord of the Mighty Throne." This is the prostration of the unity of immensity if he prostrates in "great" and if he prostrates when he says: *"So they prostrate themselves not to God Who brings out what is hidden in the heavens and the earth and knows what you conceal and what you speak openly."* (27:25). This is a prostration of preponderance. (569)

55.10.1. Prostration to the Knower of the Secret and Public

He says that they were prostrating to the sun and they believed that it knew what they spoke aloud. It is better to prostrate to the One who knows what *"they conceal and what they say aloud."* They were prostrating to the sun since it brings out what the earth has hidden of plants through its heat. God said to them, "You must prostrate to the One who brings forth what is hidden in the heavens (and it is what appears of the stars after their setting and hiddenness and then they appear by rising from that hiddenness) and in the earth (and it is what it brings forth of plants)." The sun does not have that. Its appearance conceals the stars which are in the heavens. (570)

It is better to prostrate to God than to prostrate to the sun. Its principle with God is like the principle of the stars in regard to setting and rising. Its rising is from the hiddenness from which God brought it forth in the sky like the rest of the stars. This is a prostration of preponderance. The proof here in the presence of God is superior to the proof of the divinity of the sun when they take it as a god as we have mentioned. (571)

Whoever performs this prostration and does not understand the language of the beasts or know the language of the birds and has not overcome all the stars and letters of speech and does not enjoy them as he enjoys buxom girls, has not prostrated. (572)

55.11. The 10th Prostration: The Prostration of the Intellect

The 10th prostration is the prostration of the intellect. It is the prostration of remembrance by glorification and humility from recorded proofs. It is a prostration of intellect and perception. This is the prostration of "*Alif-Lam-Mim, The sending-down*" which is after Surah Luqman. "*Only those believe in Our signs who, when they were reminded of them, fall down, ones who prostrate themselves and glorify the praise of their Lord and they grow not arrogant.*" (32:15) (573)

"Indeed" is a particle of determination and the indefinite. He says: the one who verifies that Our Signs are Signs establishes proofs by them which indicate Our existence and the truthfulness of Our Message. It is not from the spiritual strength of the self when it are concentrated. They are those "who, when they are reminded of them," and remembrance only comes only from definite knowledge or forgetfulness from a man of intellect. (574)

55.11.1. The Signs of God Are Proofs of His Existence

The Signs of God are proof of His existence. "Those with intelligence remember." He says that they were perceived by logical speculation that they are proofs of what we have established them on. When they are reminded of them, they fall on their faces, that is, obtain recognition of their essences. They disconnect their Lord by what He disconnects

Himself within the *sunna* of His Messengers. Knowledge does not allow them arrogance in that. (575)

55.11.2. What Intellect Gives and What Belief Gives

Whoever prostrates this prostration and does not understand the perceptions of his intellect and does not distinguish between what he knows by speculation and what he knows by his belief, disconnects his Lord by belief and not intellect. He takes knowledge and belief where he finds it and does not pay any attention to how he reached it. The person of intellect recognizes people by the truth. The person without intellect recognizes the truth by the people. This is the greatest of the errors of speculation. The meaning which is included in the expression which the speaker intends is clarification of a matter which is sought in the truth. The ignorant man accepts it from the Messenger when he brings it. He thinks that it is impossible and rejects it from the heir and the friend of God when they bring it. Had he accepted knowledge for itself, he would have been among those who remember. (576)

55.11.3. The Three Categories of People in Acceptance of the Quran

There are three categories of people in acceptance of the Quran. God Almighty says in respect to what He revealed the Quran that the Messenger of God addresses it to three classes of people. It is conveyed to a group who hear its letters while they believe that they are from God and that is all they recognize. Another group have them recited to them so that they might reflect on its signs and know that the one who brought them did not bring them from himself, and that it is from the One Who sent him. It is recited to another group to remind the people of intelligence of what they knew before, that is, what they brought which the normal evidence would consider impossible. It is very difficult to perceive, and it is the core of the proofs. They are the people of unveiling, gatheredness and existence. Whoever does not acquire what we have mentioned in his prostration has not prostrated. (577)

55.12. The 11th Prostration: The Prostration of Thankfulness and the Prostration of Repentance

The 11th prostration is the prostration of thankfulness and the prostration of repentance. It is a prostration of thankfulness in the presence of lights. For the one who does it, it is a prostration of repentance which is not from a misdeed. It is not one of the definite places of prostration. This is the prostration in *Surah sad* when He says: "*And David thought that We had tried him and he asked for forgiveness of his Lord and fell down as one who bows down penitent."* (38:24) He prostrates it both in repentance and thankfulness. (578)

Thought has its own category. He says: "David thought that We had tested him." Linguistically, *fitna* means putting to the test. The Arabs say, "I tested the silver in the fire." He definitely seeks being veiled from his Lord. The pattern of *istifal* (*istighfar*—asking forgiveness) conveys emphasis. He falls down in humility and returns to God in what he seeks from Him, not by his power or strength. This is a proof that he has some power to veil himself. He does not do that. He returns to God in that. (579)

The statement of God supports this: *"And follow not your desire"* (38:26). If it had not been in his power to judge by it in what he wants, he would not have been forbidden and We would have taken care of his need when he referred to Us in it. We veiled him from others in Our presence. He has no knowledge of its value, although We granted him the vicegerency from Us in judging Our servants, arbitration and disposal of them. (580)

Then He said: *"He has a near place with Us"* from what he has from Us, none of which derives from phenomenal beings and other, *"and a fair resort"* and a good final seal, meaning it is witnessed, since the good and excellence come from beauty, altruism (*ihsan*). It is the station of witnessing which discloses the realities for what they are. The Messenger of God explained this to Gabriel as we have mentioned. (581)

55.12.1. The Prostration of Prophet David and the Prostration of Prophet Muhammad

The one who prostrates this prostration prostrates the prostration of repentance. There is some disagreement about the prostration. When a man prostrates and does not find in it what Prophet David found of divine Nearness and knows the end of the business, by what he will be sealed, and the end of his station and stage with his Lord in the world to come, then he has not prostrated. (582)

This then is the prostration of Prophet David. If he prostrates it with the prostration of the Messenger of God and does not find increase in all his states in every state which is proper to it regarding knowledge and action in every abode by what is proper to that abode, increases in the abode are according to what is set down for them, (then he has not prostrated). (583)

55.12.2. The Day of Judgment (din) Is the Day of This World and the Day of the World to Come

This world is the abode of obligation and action. The world to come is the abode of repayment. This world is also the abode of repayment for the one who has understanding from God. When the Messenger of God was forgiven all his wrong actions, past and future, he increased His worship of his Lord and stood until his feet were swollen out of thankfulness to God for that. This is the servant's repayment of forgiveness. This is the abode of repayment. (584)

The Day of Judgment is the Day of this world and the world to come. Implementing the punishment is repayment. The people of wretchedness are repaid for the noble character by which they acted in this world through the blessings which they receive until they move to the world to come. They have already plucked the fruit of their good in this world. Had this world not also been the abode of repayment, that would not have been the case. Whoever does not receive the like of this knowledge in his prostration has not prostrated. (585)

55.13. The 12th Prostration: The Prostration of the Precondition or of Activeness and Love

The 12th prostration is the prostration of the precondition or of activeness and love. It is the prostration of striving and expending effort in what the Majesty of God demands of exaltation and enjoying it. It is in *"HaMim, the prostration,"* (Chapter 41) and there is some disagreement about its prostration. Some say that it is when He says: *"If it is He you have been worshipping."* (41:37) Whoever prostrates there makes it a prostration of a precondition. Whoever prostrates when He says: *"Never grow weary"* (41:38) makes it a prostration of a precondition. Whoever prostrates when He says: *"Never grow weary"* makes it a prostration of energy and love. (586)

55.13.1. The Sun Worshippers

Since creation has need of the night in which to rest, and they take it as a garment between them and the eyes of those who look. They need the day in which to work to acquire their food. They see the sun, and there is day when it rises and night when it sets, and so they ascribe the existence of the day and night to it. They worship it, and so they are sun-worshippers. (587)

55.13.2. Ibn Arabi Staying with a Greek Scholar

We saw many sun worshippers in Greece. I stayed with one of their scholars and asked him, "Why do you associate the worship of the sun with the worship of God?" He replied: "We do not worship the sun inasmuch as it is the sun. God forbid! God is one God. Our men of knowledge looked at the benefits which this great luminous body has in the world and enumerated the benefits which God has connected to it. They recognized that if it had not had an importance from God, He would not have entrusted it to these matters. We seek nearness to Him by exaltation so that we will have a good intermediary with God for our purification. In our opinion, the sun is a poor servant of God Almighty. By it, God shows concern." This is what he said to me while we were sitting at his table as his guest. (588)

55.13.3. The Light of the Moon Is Derived from the Light of the Sun

God Almighty says in this prostration, "*Of His Signs* (and the pronoun refers to God) *are the nighttime and the daytime*." (41:37) "Even if they are produced by the sun. They are not part of their Signs. They are part of My Signs." Then He said: "and the sun and the moon." He informed us that God can wipe out the sign of the moon, so that its light has no authority in the eye except at night. Its light lent to it is a reflection of the light of the sun. It acts like a mirror for it. The light which the moon gives you belongs to the sun. It is only a conductor, because it is obliterated. (589)

He made the Sign of the day visible, and it is its light which is outwardly manifest to the eye. He made the rising and setting belong to the one who reckons by the sun so that he will know the divisions of his year and so that the one who reckons by the moon will know the number of years and the reckoning. God says about the new moons: "*Announce to humanity the pilgrimage to Mecca*." (22:27) (590)

55.13.4. Prostration Is Made to the Creator of the Sun and Moon

He tells them that if you worship the sun and the moon for this reason, I created these signs as proofs of Me, so prostrate to God who created them. He put them all together— night and day, and the sun and the moon—in the plural feminine pronoun, [*khalaqahunna*, "He created them."] and the feminine rather than the masculine is used here, since day, night, sun and moon are passive, not active. It is a clear likeness for the one who has intellect. (591)

Their plural (*hunna*) is the plural of someone feminine with understanding, and that calls attention to the lack that the feminine has a lesser degree than the masculine. He did not say that He created them (masc. plural) or elevate their value by applying the masculine to them. The Arabs make the masculine dominate the feminine linguistically. You say, "Zayd and the Fatimas left (masc. pl.)" and you do not say, "they left (fem. pl.)". God is the one who created them, and it is better for you to worship Him than them because the rank of the active is above the rank of the passive. God is better and more entitled to be worshiped than that which is imperfect in two ways:—it is a creature and it is feminine. (592)

55.13.5. Those Among the Angels Who Know God

In regard to those among the angels who know God, He said: *"Then those who are with thy Lord (*those who know God among the angels who are below the sphere of the moon*) glorify Him during the nighttime and daytime."* (41:38) They have more knowledge of God than you. If you are going to take any of these as a god, that would be better to prostrate to the angels than you since you know that they have more knowledge. They prostrate to God without weariness or growing tired. (593)

55.14. The 13th Prostration: Admonition to Those Who Are Heedless of God

The 13th prostration is an admonition to those who are heedless of God. It is the prostration of delight and amusement to warn those who are heedless of God. It is the prostration at the end of the Chapter of the Star (53:62). There is some dispute about this prostration. Its prostration is connected to a divine Command and abasement and poverty because "those who treat life as a game" are those who amuse themselves. God tells them: If you are the people of song, then sing the Quran. It is better for you. *"Prostrate to God and worship Him."* (53:62) (594)

55.14.1. Reciting the Quran Is Part of the What Is Customary (Sunna)

Singing the Quran is part of the *Sunna*. It is related in a Tradition, "God has not listened to anything in a manner like his listening to a Prophet chanting (reciting) the Quran." He said that God did not listen to anything as He listened to it. The Messenger of God said: "The one who does not chant the Quran is not one of us." He made this chanting part of the *sunna*. It is the dialect of Himyar. They say: "Chant for us," for *"ghani"* at the time of their harvest so that they will have energy for work. (595)

When the Arabs heard the Quran, they sang in such a way that they would not listen to the Quran. God reports that they said: *"Hear not this, the Quran, but talk idly about it while it is being recited so that perhaps you would prevail"* (41:26), as is done today by those scholars to whom God has not given success. When they hear the what the people of God say about what secrets God has given them, they say: "This is drivel and boasting." The ones who are excessive say: "This is disbelief." If they had been asked about the meaning of what they heard, they would not recognize it. (596)

55.14.2. The Promise and Threat of the Quran

God says: "Are you then amazed at this discourse?" The 'discourse' is the Quran and how it admonishes, promises and warns them. Do you wonder greatly at how the like of this has come to him while it has not been sent down on your important people? This is what they said: "*Why was this, the Quran, not sent down to some eminent man of the two towns?*" (43:31) (597)

"*And do you laugh*"—when it is presented. They are the ones whose ignorance We mentioned: they only recognize the truth by men—"treating life as a game?"—meaning 'amusing yourselves.' "Do not do it. Do not be proud. Be humble to God. These are His words which I have conveyed to you. Abase yourselves when they are sent down. In the Quran, is there not a threat which will make one weep, as well as what makes one laugh and amazed from joy at the vastness of God's mercy and His kindness to His servants. (598)

"And do you not weep?" There is a fearful threat in the Quran which will make one weep blood instead of tears when one reflects on its signs "while you treat life as a game." All of this is in the Quran. "How then do you turn away from it?" The place of this world is the place of caution, especially when death goes back and forth among you with the selves. You do not reflect about where you are going, where you are travelling, and where you will alight. This world is not the abode of security. The man of knowledge with wisdom is the one who acts in every place according to what it deserves. (599)

55.15. The 14th Prostration: The Prostration of Gatheredness and Existence

The fourteenth prostration is that of gatheredness and existence. It is the prostration of gatheredness and existence. Whoever prostrates the prostration of The Chapter of the Star, and it does not result in knowledge of the tunes and music of the joyful spheres so that he sees that the voices of everything with a voice are flutes from God's flutes in the world, and see Prophet David in this unveiling, and sees that the voices and letters speak every wondrous meaning so that the unshakable mountains shake from rapture and the one who has lost her child laughs from joy and happiness, has not prostrated it. (600)

This other prostration is in Chapter 84: "*When heaven is rent asunder.*" There is disagreement about it. Abu Hurayrah prostrated it behind the Messenger of God. He prostrated in it when He said: "When the Quran is recited to them, they prostrate not?" (84:21) (601)

55.15.1. The Oneness of Divinity, Oneness of Multiplicity and Essential Oneness

This is a prostration of gatheredness because it is prostration at the Quran. Gatheredness allows multiplicity, and multiplicity can be with likes and others. Even if unity belongs to God Almighty, the unity of the divinity (that is, *la ilaha illa Lah*) is definite and the unity of multiplicity in respect to His Most Beautiful names. As for the Truly Real, one does not speak of "all" or "part" about Him in respect to what He has in Himself. We can say about one of us: "I saw Zayd himself: all of him," since there is a possibility that you might have only seen his face and not the rest of him. The stress by "all" grants that you saw all of him. Had it not been for the existence of multiplicity in him, you would not have said all of him. (602)

55.15.2. The Quran Brings Together the Attributes of God

When he hears the Quran which combines the attributes of God which refer to disconnection and proclaiming Him holy and pure, how can the one who hears not remember its whole? He prostrates to the One who has all of the attributes of disconnection. (603)

Whoever prostrates in this chapter and does not understand the knowledge of products and what pregnant things conceal in their wombs, the types of pregnant beings in the world like the earth, clouds, women, and all female creatures, and the meanings which books bear in their letters (since they are among pregnant things) and does not understand to refer it to the place from which it came and see the form of its state with his eyes and the end since he takes an oath by what he definitely sees, has not prostrated. (604)

55.16. The 15th Prostration: The Prostration of the First Intellect

The 15th prostration is the prostration of the First Intellect. It is a prostration of teaching by witnessing and returning to God. This is the prostration of The Chapter of The Blood Clot when He says: *"Truly obey him not but prostrate thyself to God and be near to Him."* (96:19) (605)

It is a prostration of seeking nearness to God Almighty. It comes after the words of obstacle and barrier. That is when He says "No indeed" when he brings him from the one who does not accept God and the Last Day. His Lord says to him: "Prostrate and draw near" since you are preserved from that to which he calls you and you are safe from the disaster of that. (606)

55.17. The Time of the Prostration of Recitation

Some people forbid prostration during the times in which it is forbidden to perform the formal prayer. Some people allow prostration after the the afternoon formal prayer and the the morning formal prayer as long as the sun is not near to rising or setting. (607)

I say that the prostration can be at any time since the prohibition is connected to the formal prayer. Prostration which is part of the formal prayer in the divine law is not only in the formal prayer. In the same way, he can recite the Opening Chapter at any time, although its recitation in the formal prayer is part of the formal prayer. (608)

55.17.1. Prostration in Nearness

Prostration is an act of nearness of recognition and disconnection by what God deserves of height and elevation far beyond the attributes of things in-time. The like of this is not limited by one thing more than another. It is an immense relationship and exaltation for all times and all moments. Similarly, the servant should consign with his Lord by his recitation of His Mighty Book at every moment. He is praised for that and he is rewarded with God, The Mighty, The Majestic. (609)

55.18. The One to Whom the Ruling of the Prostration Applies

The scholars agree that the ruling of the prostration applies to the one who recites: he prostrates whether he is doing the formal prayer or outside of it. They disagree about the one who hears it. Some say that he must prostrate. Some say that he must prostrate if two conditions exist: the first is that the reciter prostrates and the second is that he has sat down to listen to the Quran and that the one reciting is one of those who are fit to be an leader for listening. Some of them said that the listener prostrates by the prostration of the one reciting, even if the reciter is not fit to be an leader, if he has sat down to listen to him. (610)

I do not think that either of them have to prostrate, and we dislike for them to do that. (611)

55.18.1. Sahl al-Tustari and the Prostration of the Heart

Prostration is obligatory for the heart. When it prostrates, it never comes up as opposed to the prostration of the face. This occurred to Sahl ibn Abd Allah when he first entered this path. He saw that his heart had prostrated and waited for it to come up. It did not come up and he remained in bewilderment. He kept asking the shaykhs of the path about this event, but he did not find anyone who recognized it. They are the people of thankfulness, and they speak from realized taste. (612)

He was told, "There is a greatly respected Shaykh in Abadan. If you go to him, you may find that he has knowledge about that which you are asking about." He traveled to Abadan because of this event. When he came to him, he greeted him and said: "Shaykh! Does the heart prostrate?" The Shaykh said to him: "Shaykh! Does the heart prostrate?" The Shaykh said to him, "Forever." He found his cure and clung to serving him. (613)

55.18.2. The Sufi Path and the Prostration of the Heart

This Path revolves around this prostration of the heart. When a person obtains the state of witnessing with the eye, he is perfect and his gnosis and protection speaks. Satan has no way to get at him. In respect to the friend of God, this protection is called *"hifdh."* In respect to the Prophet and the Messenger, it is called *isma*. This is so that there is a distinction between the saint or friend of God and the Prophet because of their manners with the Prophets and the Messengers who are singled out with the name *isma*. (614)

55.18.3. The Difference Between the hifdh (?) of the Saints (awliya) and the names (isma) of the Prophets

Nonetheless I will clarify the difference between the two. The Prophets have protection from Satan outwardly and inwardly. They are protected by God in all of their movements. That is because God has set them up for people. They have conversation with God. The Prophets who are sent are protected from the permitted action in respect to themselves because they enact laws by their actions and words. When they do something permitted, they bring it to the divine law so that they are followed. They informs their followers of the specific divine judgement in it. This is mandatory for them in order to make clear to people what was revealed to them. God Almighty says: *"O Messenger! State what was sent forth to thee from thy Lord; for if thou wert not to accomplish it, then thou wilt not have stated His message. And God will save thee from the harm of humanity."* (5:67) The heirs have an ample portion of this conveying. (615)

The saint is protected from what Satan intends when he casts into the heart of the saint what God Will that he cast. It up-ends his source and moves him in a direction which is pleasing to God. He obtains an immense station with God by that. Had it not been that Satan craved rebellion, he would not have returned to this saint again. He sees that what he brought him with which he desired to put him far from prostration actually increased him in nearness and happiness. The Prophets are protected from having Satan cast at them. This is the difference between *isma* and *hifdh*. (616)

55.18.4. The Knowledge Which Self-disclosure Gives to the Heart of the Saint

They assigned *hifdh* to the saint out of good manners with the Prophet. Satan has no way to get at that hearts of some of the saints because of the knowledge which divine Self-disclosure has given to their hearts. God Almighty said: *"And kept safe from every emboldened Satan*

(37:7). That type of satan is the greatest of the satans. He cannot cast anything at a person except that which is proper to his station. (617)

He comes to the saint but he can only cast acts of obedience at him, alter them and move him from one act of obedience to another one which is higher. The saint does not see any effect in it from the impulse of the soul. He sets out to do it and the rebellious Satan is content to take this from him because of his ignorance. If the saint had been based on a clear Sign from his Lord in that, that would have been better. Satan cannot diminish the knowledge of the divine Self-disclosure by any aspect. This is why the Messenger of God said about his Satan (that is, his delegated companion) that God had helped him against him and so he surrendered and obeyed him. He only commands him to do good. (618)

55.18.5. Knowledge of God from Logical Reflection

This is different from the one who has knowledge of God by means of logical speculation and proofs. Satan casts doubt to him about his proofs in order to confuse him and to make him go back to the place of speculation so that he will die without knowledge of his Lord—or with doubt, or confusion, or will be at a standstill. (619)

The saint has knowledge by Self-disclosure, so he has an inner eye which is protected from doubt. Satan (and I mean the satans among men and *jinn*) has no way to come to the heart of the one who has knowledge of divine Self-disclosure. Only those among the saints whose hearts have prostrated possess this. Satan only withdraws from man while he is prostrating outwardly and inwardly. If the heart of the saint does not prostrate, he is not protected. (620)

55.18.6. The Clear Sign of the Lord and the Reciting Witness

This is a very fine and immense question in the paths of the people of God. Only certain individuals acquire it by the might of their existence. They are those who are on *"a clear portent from his Lord."* (11:17)The clear sign is the Self-disclosure of God Almighty. That clear sign is recited by a just witness from the servant, which is the prostration of the heart. When the clear Sign of the Lord is joined with the reciting witness, the heart is preserved and protected. Such a person: "calls creation to God with an inner eye." (621)

In this station the path of the people has causes in which the people become bewildered. This is as Abu Yazid said: "I called creation to God for many years. Then I returned to Him and found that they had preceded me." It was said to him in this station, "Does the gnostic rebel?" He said: *"And the command of God has been a measured measure."* (33:38) This is utter good manners since he did not reply yes or no. This came from the perfection of his state, knowledge, and good manners, may God be pleased with him and his likes! (622)

55.19. The Description of the Prostration

Some people say that he says the recitation of "God is Greater" when he lowers himself and when he rises. Some people say that he does not recite "God is Greater" unless the prostration is in the formal prayer when he goes down and comes up. (623)

I say that he recites "God is Greater," even if it is not related nor is it disputed. (624)

55.19.1. The Recitation of "God is Greater" (Allah akbar) (takbir) of God for the Prostration is Praised

Saying "God is Greater" for the prostration is praiseworthy in any state. It is disconnection. The servant must give the tongue its portion of this prostration, and that is only by articulating "God is Greater" and each of his limbs prostrates by its reality. (625)

55.20. Formal Purity for the Prostration

Some say that he does not prostrate unless he is in a state of purity. Some say that he prostrates, even if he is not in a state of purity. I say that it is better and more excellent in purity. The Prophet performed dry ablution to return the greeting. He said: "I do not like to mention God unless I am in purity." (626)

55.20.1. Purity of the Heart and Purity of the Limbs

The purity of the heart is a precondition for the validity of prostration to God inasmuch as it prostrates. The purity of the limbs at the moment of prostration is intelligible by way of meaning. At the moment of prostration, they are not used for anything else as opposed to the heart. For this reason, when the heart of the servant prostrates, it never rises. The limbs in the state of the prostration outside of the formal prayer are used in a worship which does not have a precondition of using water or earth. It is better and more excellent, however, if he is in a state of purity. Abd Allah ibn Umar, may God be pleased with him, used to prostrate for recitation when he was not in a state of purity. (627)

55.21. Prostration Towards the Direction of Formal Prayer

Scholars disagree about the prostration of the recitation towards *qibla*. Some say that he can prostrate in the recitation in any direction which he is facing, but it is better to face the direction of formal prayer. Some say that he must face the direction of formal prayer. (628)

I say that he can prostrate in any direction. God says: *"Wherever you turn, there is the Countenance of God"* (2:115). If he can face the *qibla*, it is better because it joins the outward and the inward. (629)

55.21.1. God is the qibla of the Hearts

God is exalted above limitation, and He is the *qibla* of the hearts. *"Wherever you turn, there is the Countenance of God"* (2:115) is an incomparable reality. There is no dispute about it among the people of God. When the servant prostrates to God, he has prostrated to the *qibla*. God encompasses everything. Directions do not limit Him. "Where" does not contain Him. By source, He is in every source, and that belongs only to Him. There is nothing in existence described by that except Him. (630)

Those who prostrate join the two *qiblas* as He joined two formations in His creation by the two hands. The one who accepts limitation is limited. The one who accepts absolute freedom from limitation is absolutely free. Each is given its due *"Our Lord is He Who gave everything its creation."* (20:50) (631)

The festival ritual prayer is repetition of witnessing of what appears one on me of existence.

When that which is from Him appears to us,
  we have our desires by it in every festival.
My festival is from my existence on the day of existence
  and He blesses me by it without increase.
I proclaim Him great seven times, and then five
  from the nearness which is limited by the jugular vein.
I seek from Him what my essence
  gives of new clothes for that day.
If I had spoken by the source of my being,
  I would have distinguished the desired from the desirer.
But I occupy myself with it
  when I allude to a state in falling and rising.
By it, I speak with Him in every state
  and He veils me by the pleasure of increase.
He lifted His veil from the source of my essence,
  so the risings made me independent of my existence.
My purity is by the water of His life.
  Whoever does not find water, performs dry ablution with earth.
The source of my dry ablution is my return by my essence
  to no-witnessing in witnessing. (632)

56 On the Mysteries of the Two Festival Formal Prayers

56.1. Introduction

56.1.1. The Formal Prayer on the Two Festivals Is Customary (sunna) Without the Call to Formal Prayer or the Declaration of the Call to Formal Prayer

The two festival formal prayers are *sunna* without the call to or declaration to perform the ritual prayer. They are two days of joy. The festival marking the end of the month of Ramadan is for his joy at breaking his fast, so he hurries to the formal prayer in order to meet his Lord. The one who performs the formal prayer consigns with his Lord. The Messenger of God said: "The person who performs the obligatory fast has two joys: a joy when he breaks his fast and a joy when he meets his Lord." He wants to hasten obtaining the two joys, so the formal prayer of the *id al-fitr* is prescribed for him. It is forbidden for him to fast on that day so that he can be rewarded in his breaking the fast with the reward of the obligations in necessary worship. The reward has great value. (633)

The formal prayer of the festival *id al-adha* is like that in respect of the fasting on the Day of Arafah for the one who fasted. It is a desirable fast for the one who is not at Arafah. It is forbidden for him to fast on the Day of the sacrifice (*adha*) so that he might receive the reward of the obligatory, and it is one of the greatest rewards. (634)

56.1.2. The Day of the Festival Is the Day of Adornment

The festival is a day of adornment and occupation with states of the soul in eating, drinking and consorting. It is prescribed for the one who is not on the pilgrimage that day to begin his day with the formal prayer by conversation with his Lord so as to protect his entire day. The formal prayer on that day at the beginning of the day is like the intention in the formal prayer. As the intention preserves this worship for him, even if it is accompanied by heedlessness during the formal prayer, the intention will mend that for him. By its existence, it is connected to the perfection of the formal prayer. Its principle flow throughout the entire formal prayer, even if the one who performs the formal prayer is heedless. Similarly, the formal prayer on the day of the festival is in the position of the intention. The day is in the position of the formal prayer. (635)

Whatever amusement, diversion and permitted action a person does in that day is contained within the protection of the formal prayer until the end of the day. This is why it is called the festival formal prayer. It returns to him in every action which he does and is permitted with a reward that the one who is praying has in the state of the formal prayer, even if he is heedless, because of the soundness of his intention. (636)

56.1.3. It Is Forbidden to Perform the Formal Fast on the Day of the Festival

This is why it is forbidden for him to fast on it. It is like the recitation of "God is Greater" after which everything but the formal prayer is forbidden, and it is counter to the intention of fasting in the state of the obligatory fast. When he breaks the fast, he performs an obligatory action as he performed an obligatory action during his obligatory fast in Ramadan. All the permitted actions he does that day are like the *Sunan* of the formal prayer within the formal prayer and all the obligations on the day in all acts of worship are in the position of the pillars of the formal prayer. (637)

56.1.4. A Person's State in the Festival

The state of the servant in all of these actions on the two days of the festival is the state of the one doing the formal prayer. This is why we said that it is called the 'id formal prayer. This is different from what is said by the one who is not from our path and has not drunk our drink. He calls it that because it recurs every year. But the five formal prayers recur every day and they are not called the festival formal prayers. This is not necessary, but it is a general statement. (638)

If it is said that it is because the day of the festival is connected to adornment, we say that that adornment is prescribed in every formal prayer. God says: "*Take your adornment in every mosque*" (7:31) for the believers among the children of Adam. When breaking the fast recurs as a obligatory act of worship, it is called festival, and what is permitted reverts to what is obligatory. (639)

56.2. On that about Which Most Scholars Agree

It is recommended to perform a full bath this day before going out to the formal prayer. There is no disagreement about it being recommended and excellent. The *Sunna* is to omit the call to and the declaration to perform the formal prayer, except for what Muawiya did according to what was mentioned by Abu Umar ibn Abd al-Barr in the soundest of statements about that. It is also *Sunna* to have the formal prayer before the sermon on this day except for what Uthman ibn Affan, may God be pleased with him, did. Abd al-Malik ibn Marwan, may God have mercy on him, also did that by deduction and strenuous endeavor. He based that on what he understood that the Prophet intended by the sermon. (640)

They agree that nothing is specified for the recitation in the two festival formal prayers. However, it is recommended to recite "The Most High" (Chapter 87) in the first and the "The Enveloper" (Chapter 88) in the second, or Surat Qaf (Chapter 50) in the first, and al-Qamar (Chapter 54) in the second in order to imitate the Messenger of God. (641)

56.2.1. Outer and Inner Purity for the Servant

The full bath is general purification. Purification is cleaning. He should put on excellent clothes outwardly and that is outward attire. Inwardly, he puts on the garment of consciousness of God. What is meant by consciousness of God here is that by which man fears to uncover his fault (*awra*, genitals) or the pain of hot and cold. It is a better garment than outward clothes. (642)

56.2.2. The Presence of the Heart With God Dispenses with the Need for the Call

There are many reasons for going out this day to the place of formal prayer for the young and old. Part of what is prescribed of the remembrance of God which accompanies those who go out is that the ruling of the call to and declaration to perform the formal prayer fall away. They are an announcement to warn those who are heedless. Preparation is already present. The presence of the heart with God has no need of the announcement of The King about His visit which is in the position of the call to and declaration to perform the formal prayer for listening. (643)

56.2.3. What Muawiya Originated in the Festival Prayer

That which Muawiya did was to observe the rare. He warns the heedless since he is not far from neglecting the formal prayer because of the playing which he sees which he can enjoy. At the time of the Messenger of God people were ready to go to any length to see him. Their relief was in seeing him. He was the leader so nothing distracted them from waiting attentively for him on that day. Therefore, neither the call to nor the declaration to perform the formal prayer was prescribed. (644)

56.2.4. What Caliph Uthman Did in the Festival

As for putting the formal prayer before the sermon, the servant is conversing with his Lord in the formal prayer. During the sermon, he is conveying to the people the reminder which descended to him during his conversation. Therefore, it is better to put the formal prayer before the sermon. It is *sunna*. When Uthman ibn Affan saw that the people were splitting up after they had finished the formal prayer and that they were not sitting down to listen to the sermon, he put the sermon first considering that this state of the formal prayer is like the Friday congregational prayer. He understood that the Prophet meant for those who were present to listen to the sermon. When they split up and left, the sermon did not occur as it has been prescribed, and therefore he put it first so that they would have the reward of listening. (645)

If Uthman ibn Affan, may God be pleased with him, had understood something else from the Prophet he would not have done this and used strenuous endeavor to understand an issue of the divine law. The Prophet (did not say anything to prevent that. Circumstances have an effect on the rules for the one who affirms the circumstance. Circumstances vary according to the difference of the one who looks into them. (646)

This is especially the case since the Prophet said: "Perform the formal prayer as you saw me perform it." During the pilgrimage, he said: "Take your practices from me." If the Prophet had in mind the festival formal prayer with the sermon as he considered the pilgrimage and the formal prayer, he would have spoken about it as he spoke about the like of this. This is like what Muawiya did. He was the scribe of the Messenger of God and he was his uncle in-law, the "Uncle of the Believers." (647)

56.2.5. There Is No Way to Disparage the Companions

We must think well of them, may God be pleased with all of them! There is no way to defame any of them. If some of them spoke against one another, they could do that. There is no way for us to delve into that about which they quarreled. They were people of knowledge and people who engaged in strenuous endeavor to understand an issue of the divine law. They had a new contract with prophethood. They are rewarded for all that issued from by their strenuous endeavor, whether it is right or wrong. (648)

56.2.7. There Is Nothing Specified for the Recitation of the Festival Formal Prayer

As for specifying something in the recitation, no discussion about that has come from the Messenger of God even if he recited a certain chapter in some of the festivals which has been transmitted to us in individual Traditions. It is confirmed in the Quran that there is nothing specific in the recitation of the formal prayer when He says: "*Recite what is easy of the Quran,*" and "*And God places not a burden on any person beyond what He has given him."* (65:7) It is what he remembers at the moment of the formal prayer. All of the Quran is good and the one who recites it consigns with his Lord by His own words. If he recites that particular chapter, he has joined what is easy and action by what the Prophet did. It is very excellent and recommended. It is set down for us to take him as a model, and it is neither obligatory nor *Sunna*. (649)

56.3. The Recitation of "God is Greater" (*Allahu akbar*) (*takbir*) in the Two Festival Formal Prayers

Some people say that after the recitation of "God is Greater" after which everything but the formal prayer is forbidden and the recitation, he recites "God is Greater" seven times in the first cycle (and it is said with the recitation of "God is Greater" after which everything but the formal prayer is forbidden, and after the recitation of "God is Greater" of rising for the second cycle, he recites "God is Greater" five times. Others say that in the first after the recitation of "God is Greater" after which everything but the formal prayer is forbidden and before the recitation, he recites "God is Greater" three times, and in the second cycle, he recites "God is Greater" three times after the recitation and then recites "God is Greater" for bowing. Abu Bakr ibn Ibrahim ibn al-Mundhir related twelve different statements about the recitation of "God is Greater." (650)

56.3.1. The name id (festival) Accords Repetition of the Recitation of "God is Greater" (Allahu akbar)

Increasing the number of recitations of "God is Greater" in the two festival formal prayers over the recitation of "God is Greater" known in the five formal prayers is allowed by an additional matter which is given by the name festival. It comes from "*'awda* (return)." The recitation of "God is Greater" recurs because it is the festival formal prayer. The true greatness and pride of God Almighty recurs before recitation so that the conversation will be from an exaltation which is stressed and established because repetition stresses the confirmation of the thing which is stressed for its sake. This is because of the name festival since the names have an authority and an immense rank. Adam was honored above the angels by them. (651)

56.3.2. The Festival is the Day of Rejoicing, Adornment and Joy

The name festival gives the recurrence of the recitation of "God is Greater" because of the authority which it has in this place and after the recitation in the school of the one who thinks that it is for the sake of bowing in the festival formal prayer. The reason for that is that the festival is a day of joy, adornment and happiness, and in it people are overwhelmed in seeking their portions of blessing. The divine law supports them in that by making the fast forbidden on that day. It is prescribed for them to amuse themselves and adorn themselves on this day. (652)

On this day, the Abyssinians sported in the mosque of the Messenger of God while he was standing looking at them, and Ayisha, may God be pleased with her, was behind him. On this day, two singing-girls entered the house of the Messenger of God. They sang in the house of the Messenger of God while the Messenger of God was listening. When Abu Bakr al-Siddiq, may God have mercy on him, came in, he wanted to stop them. The Messenger of God told him: "Leave them alone, Abu Bakr, this is a festival day." (653)

56.3.3. The Multiple Recitations of "God is Greater" (Allahu akbar) (takbir) Is for His Due Majesty

Since this day is a day of happiness of the people, God set down that the recitation of "God is Greater" be multiplied in the formal prayer so that the hearts of His servants will be firm in the greatness and immensity which God deserves. This is so that the they will not be distracted from observing the right of God Almighty by performing formal prayers in the course of the day: that is, the noon and afternoon formal prayers and the other formal prayers. God Almighty said: *"The remembrance of God is Greater"* (29:45), that is, in authority. (654)

56.3.4. The Three Worlds and Seven Recitations of "God is Greater" (Allahu akbar) (takbir) of the Soul

Whoever thinks that there are three recitations of "God is Greater," it is for his three worlds. Each world has a recitation of "God is Greater" in each cycle. Whoever thinks that there are seven considers His attributes. There is a recitation of "God is Greater" for each attribute. The servant is described with the seven attributes with which God has described Himself. He proclaims Him great, for the relationship of these attributes to God is not like their relationship to the servant. He says: "God is Greater," that is, from that in every attribute. (655)

56.3.5. The Essence and the Four Attributes

When he recites "God is Greater" five times in the festival formal prayer, he looks at the essence and the four attributes which the world needs from God inasmuch as He is described by them and by them it is established that He is God. He proclaims Him great by one recitation of "God is Greater" for His Essence since *"There is nothing like Him."* He proclaims Him great by the four for these four attributes as he proclaimed

Him great in the seven since there is no resemblance in the relationship. You must know that! (656)

56.3.6. There Is Nothing in Our Hands Which Is Ascribed to Us

As for raising the hands in it, it indicates that we have nothing in our hands which is ascribed to us. As for the one who does not raise his hands in them and is content to only raise them for the recitation of "God is Greater" after which everything but the formal prayer is forbidden, he thinks that the formal prayer is nearer to tranquillity. He does not raise them because movement generally muddles and so he devotes himself only to remembrance of God by the recitation of "God is Greater" and does not think about his hands in order to raise them. That might divide his thoughts. Every gnostic takes a certain matter into consideration and acts according to what God brings to him in it. (657)

56.4. Doing Supererogatory Prayers Before and After the Festival Formal Prayer

Some say that there are no supererogatory prayers before or after it, and some say the opposite of that. Some say that there is no supererogatory prayers before it, but he can do supererogatory prayers after it. I say that the place to which he is going for the festival formal prayer is a mosque in principle like all mosques, then the principle of the one who comes to it is the principle of the one who comes to a mosque. Whoever thinks that the mosque must be greeted must do supererogatory prayers as he commands the two cycles for entering the mosque. If it is in an open place which is not a mosque, he can choose. If he likes, he does supererogatory prayers, and if he likes, he does not do them. (658)

56.4.1. The Permitted Action in the Festival Formal Prayer Becomes Like the Formal and Recommended Action in the Reward

What is meant in this say is that doing what is permitted is like doing what is obligatory and recommended as opposed which is not the case with actions on other days. The only supererogatory prayer which he does in the festival formal prayer. He does the formal prayers when their times come. (659)

56.4.2. The Human Being Is Summoned to Joy and Happiness on the Festival

The human being's activity on that day is in matters which bring him near and are commended and in the obligatory. Whoever is in a matter which is recommended and connected to a moment, that matter must have authority inasmuch as that specific recommended action has authority in the moment. It is more entitled to it. Therefore, he does not perform supererogatory prayers. He is recommended to amuse himself, rejoice, and adorn himself on that day. Another recommended matter contrary to that does not come into it. (660)

56.4.3. The Action of the Wise Judge in Cases

When its time departs, then he can hasten to all recommended matters. What was recommended for him on that day reverts to being allowed on other days. This is the action of the person of wisdom and justice in affairs. Your self has a right over you. Amusement, diversion, and delight on this day is part of the right of the self. Do not wrong yourself. If you did, you would be like the one who spent the entire night in formal prayer and did not sleep. If you have any astuteness at all, I have alerted and awakened you. (661)

57 On the Mysteries of the Funeral Prayer

57.1. Introduction

57.1.1. The Formal Prayer for the Dead Is Intercession for the Dead

The formal prayer for the dead is intercession with his Lord on the part of the one who performs the formal prayer on him. Intercession is only for the one on whose behalf God is pleased to allow intercession. God is not pleased to allow it for any of His servants except the rebels among the people of unity, whether that is by proof or belief. This is why we are told to instruct the dead so that the intercessor will have knowledge of the unity of the One with whom he intercedes and the end of the intercessor since the name, The Compassionate, has knowledge of unity when the call reaches Him and agrees to accept it. (662)

57.1.2. Intercession for Rebels Who Have Not Been Reached by the Call

The unifier to whom the call has not reached will not enter the Fire. Intercession is only for the rebels whom the call has reached. Some of them believe. Some of them have faith which stops at this person in respect of what he brought since he relies on something great which should not be altered. He needs a proof which will prove the truthfulness of his call in what he conveys from God. This person stops because God has not provided him with necessary knowledge by the truthfulness of the call of this Messenger. (663)

57.1.3. The Clear Signs of the Truthfulness of the Call of the Messenger

God Almighty says: "*Nor would We be ones who punish until We have raised up a Messenger,*" (17:15), that is, We send him with the clear Signs of the truthfulness of his claim. God Almighty informed us that He supported the Messengers with clear Signs to absolve man from himself. Belief is a light which God flings into the heart of whomever of His servants He wills. When it is added to the light of knowledge, it is: "*Light upon light.*" First we will speak about the state of the dead person over whom we pray, what is obligatory for him, and what is obligatory for us in preparing him according to the description which the lawgiver has commanded. (664)

57.2. Instructing the Dead

57.2.1. The First Situation of the Instruction

There is instruction when he is near death and the terror is great and the station is terrible. It is the moment of temptation which is the temptation of life by what is unveiled to the dying man when the cover is lifted from his eyes. He sees what those who are present do not see. His ancestors take on form for him in forms which he recognizes, but these are Satan who have taken their forms with the best dress and the best form. They tell him that they have only reached what they have of excellence because they died as idolaters, associating partners with God. (665)

The believers who are present with him at that moment must instruct him with the testimony of unity and acquaint him with the form of this temptation so that he will be alerted to that and will die a Muslim, a unifying believer. When he utters the testimony of unity and moves his tongue with it or its light appears from his heart when he remembers it, then the angels of mercy take charge of him and drive away that satanic form which had been present with him. (666)

57.2.2. The Second Situation of the Instruction

There is a second situation of instruction. He must instruct him when he goes into his grave and is covered with earth because of the questioning of the grave. There are two angels with a horrible appearance, and they question regarding the Messenger of God using words which show absolutely no respect or reverence for the Messenger of God. They ask him, "What do you say about this man?" This is the temptation of death from which we seek refuge. (667)

57.2.3. Seeking Refuge from the Trial of Life and the Trial of Death

As for the seeking refuge of the Prophets, peace be upon them, from it, they will be questioned about the one who was sent to them, and that is Gabriel, peace be upon him, as we will be questioned about the Messenger of God. The Prophet sought refuge in the *tashahhud* of the formal prayer from the temptation of life and death since he knew that the Prophets will be tested in death as the believers are tested. He commanded the believers to seek refuge from that in the formal prayer. In the formal prayer, the human being is in the station of nearness to God by speaking with Him. Therefore, he asks Him for unveiling. (668)

57.3. Placing the Dead Facing the *Qibla*

One of the conditions recommended for the family of the dying person is to face the person toward the direction of formal prayer when he is near death. If he is on his back, his feet should face the direction of formal prayer. If he is on his side, his face should face the *qibla*. (669)

57.4. Hastening to Bury the Dead

57.4.1. Hastening the Dead to Happiness and the Living Removing Evil

It is recommended to hasten to intern him and to take him swiftly to his grave. If he is happy, you are hurrying him to his good. If he is wretched, it is an evil which you take off your necks. The dead person looks into happiness and sees the one who is carrying him is removing evil from him. This haste is for the sake of the dead person and that haste is for the sake of the bearer. (670)

57.4.2. Observing the Dead in Happiness

Explanation has come in the divine law about haste in this manner so that he knows that God has only obligated His servants for the sake of good. It is not to obtain evil through that. In respect to the wretched one, he said: "Hurry up with the funeral. It is an evil which you will take off your necks." In respect of the happy one, he said: "Hurry up with him. It is good that you are taking him to." How subtle and kind is the judgment of the Prophet! (671)

57.4.3. Haste Is from Satan Except in Three Things

It is related that haste is from Satan except in three matters. One of them is preparation of the dead. Part of its preparation is to hasten to bury him. If the dead person is happy, he speaks while he is being carried on his bier, saying: "Take me ahead! Take me ahead!" If he is wretched, he says: "Where are you taking me!" Every living creature except for the *jinn* and men hear that. (672)

57.5. Washing the Dead

57.5.1. Washing the Dead and Purification for the Formal Prayer

The living must also wash the dead. It is like the purification for the formal prayer. The living is called upon to do that. People disagree about its principle. Some say that it is a general *Sunna*. Some say that it is obligatory by a command which has come down when the Prophet said: "Wash her three or four times." He said about the man who died in the sacred state for the pilgrimage: "Wash him." There is no doubt that this is the form of command. If it is accompanied by a particular state which brings it out as teaching the description of the full bath, it is made a *Sunna*. The one who thinks that it contains a command and the description says that it is obligatory. (673)

57.5.2. Death Is Ignorance and Knowledge is Life

The interpretation of the ignorant man is the dead and death is ignorance, so that the man of knowledge must teach the ignorant because whoever deems the ignorant to be ignorant does not know that the questioning is obligatory for him in what he does not know. It is therefore a specific duty for the man of knowledge to teach him if he does not know the judgement of the divine law in his movements. He must "ask the people of remembrance." When he does not do that, he has rebelled. He teaches him what he is specifically obliged to teach him. That is his purification. This, in short, is the interpretation of washing the dead. (674)

57.6. The Dead Who Must Be Washed

As for the dead who must be washed, they agree that one washes the dead person and the person has been slain when he has not been killed in a battle fighting against the unbelievers. They disagree about the martyr killed in the war against the unbelievers, about washing the idolater, and about washing the one to whom the name martyr is applied, and about the one who was killed by an idolater outside of battle. Some say that all of these are washed. Some say that they are not washed. (675)

57.6.1. Washing Is Worship and Cleanliness

Some say that the full bath is an act of worship which brings a reward to the one who is washed, and so he says that the idolater is not to be washed. Some think that washing is cleaning and so he says that the idolater should be washed. The Prophet commanded that those who were killed at the Battle of Uhud be buried in their clothes and not washed. (676)

57.6.2. The Martyr Is Not Washed

Whoever thinks that the martyr is not washed because the name of martyrdom is applied to him, says that the one whom the Prophet has stated is a martyr is not washed. Some think and understand that the Prophet meant a state. The martyr who is not washed is the one who is killed in battle while fighting those who cover over the truth. He says that all others should be washed. (677)

57.6.3. The Interpretation of this: the Martyr Is Alive and Provided For

The one who is killed in the way of God while in a battle fighting against those who cover over the truth *"is living with their Lord. . . provided for."* (3:169) We are commanded to wash the dead. It is not said that he is dead and he is not reckoned to be dead. He is alive by a true divine report from that which *". . . falsehood approaches it not from before it nor from behind it."* (41:42) (678)

57.6.4. Removing Sight from Perceiving the Life of the Martyr

God has taken our sight away from perceiving many things as He has taken our sight away from perceiving the glorification of the plants, animals, inanimate objects, and everything. God Almighty says: "*And assume not those who were slain in the way of God to be lifeless. Nay! They are living with their Lord. They are provided for.*" (3:169) God Almighty said: "*And say not about those who were slain in the way of God: They are lifeless. Nay! They are living, except you are not aware*" (2:154) of their life as the dead person is alive when he is questioned. We see him but we are not aware. We know absolutely that he is being questioned. Only the one who has intelligence can be questioned. The one who is intelligent is the one who is described with life. We are forbidden to say that they are dead. He told us that they alive, but we are not aware. The like of this has not come concerning the one who is not killed in the way of God. He is dead. If he is a martyr or alive like him, we have not been informed about that. The martyr is present with God. This is why He said: "*with their Lord.*" (679)

57.6.5. The Corpse Is Washed and Purified in Order to Be Present With His Lord

The dead person is washed and purified in order to be present with his Lord in purity. He will meet Him in the inter space after death in the prescribed purity. This martyr is present with his Lord by martyrdom alone with his being slain in the way of God. He is not washed. He is with his Lord. (680)

He is the one who says that there are means in which he relies and trusts. He believes that God only does something by them, not in them. That is because he lacks knowledge since his self is weak and his faith unsettled as he is unsteady about the truth of God's promise of provision which He allots to His servants. He says: "*By the Lord of the heaven and the earth. It is truly The Truth just as you yourselves speak.*" (51:23). (681)

5.7. The Interpretation of Washing the Polytheist

57.7.1. Explicit and Hidden Polytheism

This is a sort of explicit idol worship. It is not hidden because nature dominates him in that to which he is accustomed. One of them said to rebuke the one whose faith was unsteady:

> You are satisfied with a moneychanger as a guarantor
> even if he is a polytheist,
> and yet you are not content with your Lord as a guarantor! (682)

57.7.2. The Purification of the Heart of the Dead Person with Certainty

Those with knowledge of God must purify the heart of this dead person and wash it with certainty and tranquillity until it is clean. The idolater must be washed. Some say that the like of this idolater does not have his trust in provision lessened. He says that he is unsteady by nature since God has not specified moment or amount for him. (683)

57.7.3. God Has Connected Those Who Gain Means to Means by His Wisdom

Know that by His wisdom, God has connected those who gain means to means. That agitation is not because the one who trusts doubts about God and fears that he may not provide for him. That agitation is human agitation and the sensation of pain of loss and lack of patience. God has informed him that He will provide for him, and He must do so, whether he is an unbeliever or a believer, because he is alive. God Almighty says: *"And there is no moving creature on earth but its provision is due from God,"* (11:6), but He has not told him when or from where. He has not specified the time or the means. He informed him that the self will not die until its provision is completed. (684)

57.7.4. Death Is Anxiety for the Believer, Gnostic and Unbeliever

When the normal means by which he obtains by which he obtains provision are lacking, he does not know whether it is finished and his time has come or not. He is anxious and upset about death. Death is a source of anxiety for the believer because of the evil he has done, and for the gnostic since life is from God when he comes to it, and for the unbeliever since he will lose the things to which he is accustomed. The form of fear is the same but the reasons are different.

Whoever does not die by the sword will die by something else.

The means vary, but the disease is the same. (685)

57.7.5. Seeking Refuge from Hunger and Illness

If he is not anxious about his provision in the knowledge of God, he is in agitation because he does not know the moment when his provision will reach him, as we have already said: when the means are cut off. He is fearful when that lasts for a long time and the pangs of hunger occur. Need leads him to have doubt in it when the person can easily have doubts in its presence because of his self-importance. The Messenger of

God sought refuge from hunger and said that it is an evil bedfellow. It is an affliction from God, and the one who has it has need of patience. He does not know whether or not God will provide him with steadfastness in that. Very few of God's servants are provided with steadfastness in affliction. This is why medicine is prescribed. It is to calm the self and the weakness of nature by relying on means to acquire imaginary health. That is to frequently visit the doctor. (686)

57.7.6. The Causes of Affliction and Good News for the Steadfast

God Almighty said: "*We will certainly try you with something of fear and hunger and diminution of wealth and lives and fruits.*" (2:155-157) All of these are means of affliction by which God tests His servants so that He knows those who are patient among them as He told us. He knows who among them are patient and those who are not. He said: "Give good news to the patiently steadfast" in that by which We tested them. (687)

57.7.7. The Attribute of the Steadfast

Then part of His bounty and mercy is that He has described us as "*the patiently steadfast*" so that we travel their path and are described by their attributes when disasters and calamities occur by which God tests His servants. He said in describing the patiently steadfast, "Who, when they are struck by an affliction, say: 'We belong to God and to Him we return,'" meaning when it is lifted from them. Then He told us about what the one who is like this. He said: "*Those who, when an affliction lighted on them, they said: Truly we belong to God and truly we are ones who return to Him. Those are they on whom blessings will be sent from their Lord and mercy; and those, they are the ones who are truly guided.*" (2:156-157) Matters are clear for them for what they really are. (688)

57.7.8. Washing the Polytheist (mushrik) Who Has Hidden Polytheism (shirk)

Whoever thinks this, says that the idolater is not washed, that is, this idolater because his belief in the unity of God is sound. He is not purified since he is a believer. You must wash and purify the one who is weak in belief and certainty in relying on what God desires when he cuts off means for him. (689)

57.8. Concerning Who Washes and Is Washed

Scholars agree, may God be pleased with them, that a man washes a man and a woman washes a woman, There is no disagreement between them regarding that when she dies. (690)

57.8.1. Disparity in Ranks of the Perfect

The one who is also perfect in rank is seen by the one who said: "*The Messengers. We have given advantage, some of them over others.*" (2:253) He said: "We have preferred some Prophets over others" although they all have the degree of prophethood. (691)

When the perfect one sees a matter in another perfect one which needs to be purified, he purifies him of it, and that other perfect one must follow him in that and not disdain that. The Messenger of God said about Prophet Moses the one who spoke directly to God, "If Moses had been alive, he would have had to follow me." (692)

57.8.2. Judgment Belongs to the Master of the Moment

The reason for that is that although perfection exists, authority belongs to the master of the moment. He is the abrogating principle and is alive. The abrogated principle is dead. The moment has power. Had the master of the moment been lacking in the degree of perfection, he would still have had power over the perfect. How then is it with the perfect one? Had he been alive, he would have purified himself. If what he lacked had been unveiled to him, he would have worked to obtain it. It is like that with the principle of the one who lacks the degree of perfection in the path. (693)

57.8.3. The Disciple (murid) Washes the Disciple (murid)

A disciple should wash another disciple if something occurs from him which must be washed. The other should accept it from him. God has said about those: "*But those who have believed and the ones who have acted in accord with morality, and have counseled one another to The Truth, and have counseled each other to endure patiently.*" (103:3). He commanded us to help one another in dutiful obedience and fearful awareness, and forbade us to help one another in wrong action and enmity. (694)

57.8.4. The One With Appetite and the One With Doubt

The one whose appetite overcomes him in nature and the one whose doubt overcomes his intellect are veiled from their judgment in them because the one with doubt imagines that it is a proof in itself, and the one with appetite imagines that it is really in God. When the one who has knowledge of this—even if he does not have perfection, and these two are more perfect than him or they both have perfection—does indeed know that question, he must purify him of this doubt since the one who has is described as being dead in it since he has no knowledge of it. It is the same with the one who has appetite. (695)

If that doubt is in the battleground of the war of logical speculation and strenuous endeavor in seeking proofs and it overcomes him, he is slain by it, and in the heart of the matter, it was in the way of God at the hand of an idolater. He only intended good. He was acting in the way of God. The doubt shares the same form as the form, and so he is alive and is not described as dead. It is not obligatory to wash the living who knows that what he is in is doubt. (696)

57.8.5. The One Who Engages in Strenuous Endeavor to Understand an Issue Cannot Judge Against Another Who Does This

The person who exercises strenuous endeavor to reason an issue of the divine law cannot judge against another person who has undertaken the strenuous endeavor. The divine law has confirmed the judgment of both, as is the case with the one who thinks that the attributes of God are connected to His Essence by the judgments which those relationships must have and the other one who thinks that the attributes of God are extra matters to The Essence of God. They agree that God is The Alive, The Knowing, The Powerful, The Transforming, The Hearing, The Seeing, The Speaking. This is in dogma. That derives from examination and strenuous endeavor to reason an issue of the divine law. He is dead and killed with the one who rejects the one with doubt. He is alive with himself and with his Lord. The one with proof must not be washed, even if he is wrong. (697)

It is like that with matters involving speculation. For instance, when the Shafii is a judge, he cannot reject the testimony of the Hanafi if he is upright, although he believes that date wine is permissible, and he will impose the punishment on him when the Hanafi drinks it since he is a judge who thinks that it is forbidden by the proof, and so he must impose the punishment on him. It is like that with the Hanafi who is a judge. He sees that the Shafii has married his illegitimate daughter. He testifies in his presence and he does not reject his testimony since he is just and he separates him from his wife who is his illegitimate daughter inasmuch as he is a judge with authority. He is the master of the moment. (698)

57.8.6. Judgment Belongs to God Who Has Confirmed the Judgment of the One Who Engages in Strenuous Endeavor to Understand an Issue

This is in the position of the martyr who is not washed although we see from his senses that his spirit has left his body like all those who are killed. The judgment belongs to God and no one else. The ruling of the person who has used strenuous endeavor to reason an issue is confirmed, so we cannot remove the judgment of his reasoning. That would be to remove the judgment of God in respect to him. (699)

The underlying principle of this topic is that the perfect accepts what the imperfect points out in a question about which he has more knowledge. There is the Tradition about the fertilization of the date-palms to his Companions: "You know the needs of your world better." He referred to what he had said. Similarly, the Prophet referred to what they said on the Day of Badr about camping near the water. (700)

57.9. When a Woman Dies Among Men and a Man Dies Among the Woman When They Are Not With Their Spouses

Scholars, may God be pleased with them, disagree about a man who dies among women and a woman who dies among men when they are not with their spouses. There are three positions about that. Some say that each of them washes the other. Some say that they perform dry ablution and do not wash them. Some say that they neither perform the full bath or dry ablution. (701)

I say that each of them washes the other behind a cloth which is over the dead person if it is a relative, or it is done behind a covering which is set up between the dead person and the one washing him. The form of washing is to pour water on him without extending the hand to any of the limbs. If it is a relative, then he must avoid extending the hand to the genitals. It is enough to pour water on them with a barrier, and that is necessary. This is what I believe in the like of this question. (702)

57.9.1. Death in Interpretation in the Sufi Order

The interpretation from the point of view of this Path is that death is doubt which occurs to this person in speculation as death occurs to the living or natural appetite which rules him and blinds him. It brings him doubt. He sees his Lord in things, so there is no dispute that he is dead with the group, whether he is perfect or imperfect, lacking in the degree of perfection. (703)

57.9.2. The Rebellion of Adam

God says about the perfect: "*And Adam rebelled against his Lord and he erred.*" (20:121) That is, he feared. He had eaten through use of his interpretation and he had thought that he was right and had not infringed upon that which was sacred in the heart of the matter. The prohibition was connected to drawing near, not to eating, and so his interpretation was reinforced. He spoke about the perfect "Angels, harsh, severe who do not disobey whatever God commands them and they accomplish what they are commanded." (66:6) Divine jealously compelled them today: *"Wilt Thou be one who makes on it someone who will make corruption in and on it?"* He said: *"Truly I know what you know not."* (2:30) (704)

The rank of the one who is not perfect is well-known. The imperfect may be a disciple before the perfect and under his authority and obedience like a married couple. He is like one of the community with his Prophet who is sent to him. (705)

57.9.3. The Perfect Gnostic With His Disciple

This is how this perfect gnostic is with his disciple. The perfect may die in a question which he does not know while the disciple knows it. The Shaykh sees it from the disciple as he said in the two Traditions before this. This is how the state of the disciples is with the shaykhs. The shaykhs are only ahead of them in certain matters which are desirable to follow. (706)

The disciple may be a disciple of another shaykh and the man among the people may belong to another Prophet in the time which was before the time of the Messenger of God. If this question which this imperfect person is ignorant about is part of what is connected to the general path inasmuch as it is a path to God, then someone other than his shaykh can purify him of it by what he makes clear to him in it. He should accept it if he desires success and has a claim in the path. (707)

If this question about which he is ignorant is not general, but rather is particular in respect to the station of the shaykh, even if it is imperfection with this other shaykh, he should not restrain that disciple from that question. Similarly, the person using strenuous endeavor to reason an issue should not turn another person like himself to a judgment which his proof has not accorded him. The follower of a person who uses strenuous endeavor to reason an issue should not be the follower of another person's reasoning from the question in which he follows his leader when he says to him: "This is the judgment of God. (708)

57.9.4. Purification of the Disciple (murid) by Other Than His Shaykh

If it is a general question which would lessen unity or prophethood, then he can purify him of that, whether or not that disciple is under his authority. The form of his full bath and purification which he must do is that he makes him recognize the face of the truth in the question. He does not care whether he accepts it or not. It is like washing the corpse. If he is a place which accepts washing, then he benefits by it. If he is not a place or is not worthy to accept washing—and he means worthiness by place—and washes him, it is like washing the idolater who does not benefit from it. The living has performed what he was obliged to do. (709)

It is only obligatory for the one who calls to God to convey. God says:

"What is with the Messenger is not but the delivering of the message and God knows whatever you show and whatever you keep back." (5:99) He has not obliged him to create acceptance and guidance in the one who listens. Whoever knows that there is a lack of acceptance says that they do not wash one another. If that question is in beliefs, he says that there is a full bath. If it is in the branches of judgments, he says that there is dry ablution. The place of dry ablution of the two people are not the private parts. The face and the palms of a woman are not private parts. He can perform dry ablution for her, and she can do it for him when he dies. (710)

Such is the general rule of the divine law. The hearing of the disciple is not dependent upon any of the people of legal opinion. The disciple takes it from every shaykh, and the shaykh takes it from every disciple because judgment does not belong to either of them. It belongs to God as opposed to recommended and permitted things in discipline and striving. The disciple cannot leave the judgment of his shaykh in that. (711)

57.10. Washing the Relative Who Has Died

Some scholars disagree about the relative. One says that a man can wash a woman and that woman can wash a man. Another says that neither of them can wash the other. Another says that a woman can wash a man, but a man cannot wash a woman. The distinction in our position has already been discussed. (712)

57.10.1. The Perfect and Imperfect of the People of the Divine Law

The relatives are all people of the divine law. The man is the perfect one who is the one who is wise in action and knowledge. He combines the outward and the inward. The imperfect are the jurisprudents who know and do not act, and speak of the outward while they do not recognize the inward. It is as God Almighty says: *"They know only that which is manifest in this present life. And of the world to come they are ones who are heedless."* (30:7) (713)

57.10.2. Doubt and Appetite in Creed and Rulings

When a relative falls into doubt or appetite from perfection or imperfection, and if it concerns creeds, then each of them washes the other, that is, acquaints him with the aspect of soundness in that, whether the one who knows that is imperfect or perfect. If it concerns rulings, neither of them washes the other. It is a judgment confirmed in the divine law, whether he is perfect or imperfect. (714)

57.10.3. *The Imperfect Washes the Perfect*

For the one who thinks that a woman can wash a man, it is the imperfect washing the perfect. The imperfect can purify the perfect when he realizes that the perfect has fallen into a doubt. He must do so. It is like when the jurisprudent sees that the gnostic has slipped and done something which is forbidden in the divine law about which there is no disagreement. He can reproach him for it. The gnostic has more knowledge about what he has done. If it is as the jurisprudent has informed him, it is specifically incumbent for him to accept that purification by repentance and returning from it. If he is sound in the inward matter and the jurisprudent has judged by the form and does not know the inward matter, the jurisprudent has then done what is obliged to do. The imperfect washes the perfect. (715)

57.10.4. *Sometimes the Imperfect Does Not Wash the Perfect*

The perfect does not wash the imperfect in the like of this question. The perfect discloses the innocence of the person from what is ascribed to him which would necessitate the imposition of the punishment. The imperfect judge rules that the punishment be carried out on him. The perfect man cannot reject the judgement of the religious scholar in that question because he knows the innocence of the person against whom the punishment is directed. In the like of this, the perfect cannot refute the imperfect. (716)

57.10.5. *A Man Does Not Wash a Woman*

Similarly a man cannot wash a woman when she dies since she is a private part. The Prophet spoke about the woman who had cursed her husband in the *lian* divorce and lied; he knew that, but God has decreed the *lian*. However, in reality, the man spoke the truth and the woman was lying. The Prophet said: "If it had been up to me . . ." The affair belongs to that, so he abandoned his unveiling and knowledge for the outward judgment. (717)

57.11. A Husband Washing His Wife or a Wife Washing Her Husband

They agree that a woman can wash her husband. They disagree about a man washing his wife. Some say that he can wash her and some say that he cannot wash her. (718)

57.11.1. *The Disciple (murid) and His Shaykh, and the Shaykh and His Disciple (murid)*

When the disciple of the shaykh sees that the shaykh has done something which the Path with the shaykh does not demand, the disciple must inform the shaykh about that since it is possible that he has been forgetful in that. He cannot remain silent about it. When the shaykh sees that the disciple has performed an act of obedience according to his position which is an act of rebellion in the position of the shaykh although the divine law rules that it is sound in respect to the one who does it and that has come from strenuous endeavor, then the shaykh, the perfect one, should not reject that even if he recognizes that the person who has undertaken the strenuous endeavor or the follower has erred in his reasoning. Therefore, a man does not wash his wife if she dies. (719)

57.11.2. The Imitating Disciple and the One Who Strenuously Endeavors to Understand an Issue

The one who believes that he washes her says in the interpretation that the shaykh must acquaint the disciple, who is imperfect, that the person who used strenuous endeavor has erred in that matter. This is the definition of his washing. The disciple who follows the person who used strenuous endeavor must return to the words of his shaykh, If the disciple is a person who uses strenuous endeavor to reason an issue of the divine law, he is forbidden to return to the words of the shaykh in that question unless the words of the shaykh are in the position of the one who opposes the system of proof. Then the words of the shaykh are stronger than the proof of the person who used strenuous endeavor, and so the person who uses strenuous endeavor must return to the words of his shaykh. That is his reasoning, that is, his return by preferring the proof which the shaykh has over the proof which he has since he transmitter may have lied or there might be an error in his analogy since the truthfulness of the shaykh has an effect in himself in that. (720)

57.12. A Divorced woman and the Formal Bath

They agree that an irrevocably divorced woman does not wash her husband. They disagree about the woman singly divorced who can be taken back. Some say that she can wash him and some say that she cannot wash him. (721)

57.12.1. The Disciple (murid) Cannot Rebuke his Shaykh

The disciple may entirely leave the judgment of the Shaykh. He cannot rebuke his Shaykh. If he does, it is not accepted from him. He is in a state of suspicion because of his desertion. He is imperfect, so how can he purify the perfect while he is still in a state of imperfection? (722)

57.12.2. The Disciple (murid) Withdrawing from His Shaykh on Account of an Error

If the disciple withdraws from the Shaykh out of shame before him because of an error which he has done or some slackness on his part, that is like the divorce which can be revoked. The principle of respect for the shaykh inside the disciple is still there, even if he withdraws from him or the shaykh makes him emigrate out of good manners for him. (723)

57.12.3. In the Moment of Error the Disciple (murid) Needs His Shaykh

A shaykh met one of his disciple who had erred and was ashamed to be with the shaykh and therefore left him. When he met him, he was ashamed and the disciple took a path than that of the shaykh, but then the shaykh overtook him and grabbed him. He said: "My son, do not keep the company of the one who wants to see you as being protected. The shaykh is needed in moments like this." So he removed the shame which had afflicted him and he returned to his service. Then the disciple is in the position of the divorced woman who can be taken back. She has not left his authority. This is the interpretation as we have already mentioned in the place in which the imperfect washes the perfect. (724)

57.13. The Judgment About the One Who Performs the Formal Bath (*ghusl*)

Some people say that the one who washes the dead person must perform a full bath. Some people say that the one who washes the dead person does not have to perform the full bath. (725)

57.13.1. Instruction and Purification with the divine Presence

When the man of knowledge teaches someone else and purifies him of ignorance by what knowledge he receives, he may teach by his Lord, that is, he is present with God. God is the teacher as He says: "*The Merciful taught the Quran*" (55:1-2), so he does not have to perform a full bath. God is the One who washes that ignorant person of his ignorance by what God teaches him by the tongue of this shaykh. (726)

57.13.2. Teaching Another by Oneself

If the washer teaches him by himself and while he is teaching him withdraws from seeing that his Lord is the One who teaches him by his tongue at that moment, then he must have a full bath because of that heedlessness which came between him and presence with his Lord in that teaching. (727)

57.14. The Description of Washing

Part of that is whether or not the corpse's shirt is removed from him when he is washed. Some say that he removes his garment while he covers his private parts. Some say that he is washed in his shirt. (728)

57.14.1. Logical Doubt and Natural Appetite

The one with doubt or the one who is overcome by natural appetite, even if it is allowed, is described as dead. If the washer can show him the truth from his doubt itself or his appetite, he is like the one who washes the corpse in his shirt and does not remove it from him. If he can only show it to him by removing that doubt because of his incapacity, he is like the one who removes the garment of the corpse when he washes him. (729)

57.15. Performing Formal Ablution (*wudu*) on Behalf of the Corpse While He Is Being Washed

Some people believe that ablution is done on behalf of the corpse, and some people think that ablution is not done for him. Some people say that it is excellent if ablution is done for him. (730)

57.15.1. Formal Ablution (wudu) in the Formal Bath (ghusl) Is Special Purification Within General Purification

Ablution in the full bath is special purification within general purification. If the question demands that some of the world of the person is like an error which issues from his limbs, then he washes those particular limbs with the purification that they deserve—like the eye, the ear, the hand, the foot, and the tongue. (731)

57.15.2. Faith in General Washing

Faith is general washing. He combines the purification of the limbs in particular with ablution and faith, which is general purification. That is necessary. There is no dispute about the full bath, but there is dispute about ablution. It is better to combine both types of worship if that is feasible rather than simply performing the more general one. (732)

57.16. The Set Number for the Washing

Some scholars say that it is obligatory, and some say that it is not obligatory, so know that. (733)

57.16.1. Everything Has Its Measure with God

What brings about purification from this doubt when it is without specification or a specific time for it to occur? Some say that the number is obligatory. He says that we are commanded to take on the qualities of God. God says: "*everything has its measure with Him*" (13:8), and it is the number of times. "*We only send it down in a known measure*" (15:21), and He sends it down in a measure as He likes. (734)

57.16.2. The Formal Bath (ghusl) of the Prophet with a sa and His Formal Ablution with a mudd

The Prophet said that the one who performed ablution more than three times had acted badly, been excessive and done wrong. He made the number of times from one to three. He disliked extravagance in the use of water in the full bath and ablution. The Messenger of God performed the full bath with a *sa* of water, and ablution with a *mudd*. (735)

57.17. Those Who Make the Number Formal

They disagree on it. Some of them oblige any odd number. Some of them oblige only three. Some of them limit the minimum amount in that and do not limit the maximum. He says that it is not less than three. Some of them limit the maximum and say that it does not exceed seven. Some of them recommend the odd and do not make any limit in it. (736)

57.17.1. The Odd Number in Washing Is Formal Because It is Worship

As for the odd number in the full bath, it is obligatory because it is worship. Part of its condition is presence with God in it. He is the Odd. The washing must be an odd number in principle and state. That is from one to seven. If it is more, it is extravagance when purification occurs by it. That is his oddness in washing according to what occurs to him in the state of washing. It is the seven attributes or matrices. The people of speculation have argued about them when debating divine Qualities. They are: life, knowledge, power, will, speech, hearing, and seeing. (737)

57.17.2. Washing the Attributes of the Servant with the Attributes of the Lord

The servant is described by all these attributes. It is reported that God said in respect of the one who draws near by supererogatory acts, that God is his hearing, his sight, etc. The relationship of these created attributes are changed to the servant by God. He hears by God, sees by Him, knows by Him, has power by Him, lives by Him, wills by Him, and speaks by Him. He has washed his attributes by His Lord, and he is pure made absolutely pure by His attributes. (738)

57.17.3. Wash the Dead the Like of This Washing

This is the number of times of washing the dead from one to seven according to what is more or less. This covers all of the dispute which occurs in the even and the odd, few and many, making a limit and not making a limit, so reflect on it! Wash your dead with this sort of washing! The perfect with the imperfect is like the man of intellect and belief with the man of intellect alone or belief or alone. (739)

57.18. Impurity Which Issues from the Belly of the Corpse After the Washing

Impurity may come out of the belly of the dead person after he has been washed. Some say that the washing is repeated. Some say that the washing is not repeated. Those who say that it is repeated, disagree about the number of times up to seven. They agree that it is not more than seven. (740)

57.18.1. Fresh Doubt After Purification from It

Doubt may come after purity is obtained by the speed of its removal from its imagination since his conception is weak. Then the teaching is repeated to him seven times. If that overcomes him, he is like the one overcome by incontinence and emission of wind. The teaching is not repeated to him. He will not accept its constancy. (741)

57.18.2. Seven Is the Limit of Perfection in divine Knowledge

We agree about seven because it is the end of perfection in divine Knowledge inasmuch as He is God. This is why God connected wisdom in the existence of effects in the elemental world to the path of the seven planets in the twelve constellations. He made seven travellers and we know that it is in the end of perfection of existence. (742)

57.18.3. Twelve Is the Limit of the Ranks of Number

He made the perfection of the path lie in the twelve so that the limit of the ranks of numbers. It is from one to nine, then tens, hundreds, thousands. This is twelve and it occurs in and goes on without end without increase. It is like that with the path of the seven in the twelve constellations. "That is the determination of The Mighty, The Knowing" (41:21). (743)

57.19. Pressing the Corpse's Abdomen

They disagree about pressing on the belly of the dead person before washing him. Some think that it is done and some do not think that it is done. (744)

57.19.1. The Great Tasting the Small in His State

Pressing is the great testing the small in his state. Does he have a doubt in what he fears will detract from his purity when the great purifies him or not? This is so he calls him with insight into him that he has a doubt which he fears will manifest itself at another moment. The teacher protects himself at the beginning before he gets involved so that exhaustion will occur and be great. (745)

57.20. The Shroud

Shrouding the dead is like the clothes of the one who performs the formal prayer. He is only performed the formal prayer over when he is shrouded. It is like the formal prayer on the mat and the cloth which comes between him and the earth because he is in the place of your prostration. If you had prostrated, it is like that on which one performs the formal prayer. (1)

57.20.1. Shrouding the Man and the Woman

As for the woman, the order of her shrouding is that the washer first covers her loins with a loin-cloth which is wrapped around a person's waist. Then there is the full shirt, and then the head-covering, and that is what is wrapped around her head. Then comes the wrapper and then there is another garment which covers all. The Messenger of God gave to Layla al-Thaqafiyya when she washed Umm Kulthum, the daughter of the Messenger of God. He handed her garment after garment and told her to do that which we have mentioned. This is the *sunna* in shrouding the woman. (2)

57.20.2. The Shrouding of the Messenger of God

As for shrouding the man, we have no text describing it except that when the Messenger of God died, he was shrouded in three white garments of Sahuli cloth and none of them was a shirt or a turban. This is according to those of his Companions who were present. It has not reached us that any of them or anyone from whom they conveyed rejected that or disputed it. It says in the words of the transmitter that there was no shirt or turban. That may be an outward probability. There is no doubt that the text about three garments is from the transmitter. An odd number is recommended is shrouding. (3)

57.20.3. Shrouding the Man and Woman

Some people think that the man is shrouded in three garments and the woman in five garments. He takes what we have just mentioned. Some say that the minimum of a man's shroud is two garments, but the *sunna* is three garments, and the minimum for a woman is three garments while the *sunna* is five garments. Some people do not think that there is any limit in that, but it is recommended that it be an odd number. The

Messenger of God said that the man who died in pilgrim sanctity should be shrouded in two garments. (4)

57.20.4. The Aim in Shrouding

The aim of shrouding is to conceal the dead person from the eyes. When Musab ibn Umayr was killed on the Day of Uhud, he was shrouded in the single garment he was wearing. It was a short cloak which did not completely cover him. The Messenger of God ordered that his head be covered with it and he placed something over his face so that it was veiled from the eyes. (5)

57.20.5. *The Human Being Was Created from Earth*

Since man is created of earth, when one of the people of God who has presence with God sees earth, he remembers that from which he was created. They look at the words of God Almighty, "*Our Lord is He Who gave everything its creation then He guided it.*" (20:50) That is, on the Day of Rising. (6)

57.20.6. The One Who is Praying Is Conversing with His Lord

The one who is praying is conversing with his Lord. When the one who performs the formal prayer stands in his intimate conversation and there is nothing between him and the earth and he sees the earth with his eyes, it may remind him of his formation and that from which he was created and its humiliation and abasement. God made the earth utterly abased in abasement by this structure. The poet said:

> Blows by the edge of the sword, the market of their
> butter-man.
> When they do no exist, you are unfruitful.

He uses the structure *faul* (*dhalul*, abased) for stress. There is nothing more abased than the one on whom the abased walk. We and all creatures walk on it and we are servants, that is, abased. (7)

The one who performs the formal prayer might be distracted by looking into himself and that from which he was created away from the intimate conversation with his Lord in what he recites of His words. He is absent to what he says to God and what God says to him. It is very bad manners on the part of the reciter. It is better to have a partition. The one who performs the formal prayer is forbidden to face a man like him in his *qibla* or to make him his object in front of the person performing the formal prayer. So he should put it to his right or left brow. All of this is so that it does occupy the position of an idol, by divine jealousy. They used to fashion idols in the form of men. He commanded him to cover the dead person because the dead person is in front of the one who is praying. The one who is praying is speaking with God in his *qibla*, interceding for this dead person. Its interpretation will come in the formal prayer over the corpse, God Almighty willing. (8)

57.21. *Walking with the Bier*

Walking with the bier is like hurrying to the formal prayer. Some of them said that it is *Sunna* to walk ahead of it. Others said that it is better to walk behind it. That which I believe is that a man walks behind the bier before the formal prayer over him, and he puts him in front of him as he puts him in the formal prayer. After the formal prayer, he walks in front of it to serve it, going ahead of it to its halting-place which is the grave since he thinks well of God and that God has accepted intercession for him during the formal prayer. The grave has one of the meadows of the Garden. (9)

God has recommended that His servant have good opinion of Him and He says: "I am with My servant's opinion of Me, so let him think well of Me." It is related that God was asked: "Who is the most beloved to Thee, Prophet Jesus or John, peace be upon them?" God Almighty said to the asker: "The one with the best opinion of Me." That is, Prophet Jesus. Fear dominated Prophet John. (10)

57.21.1. *The Angels Walk with the Bier as Long as There Is No Shouting*

It is better that he not ride out of good behavior with the angels. The angels walk with the funeral as long as it is not accompanied by crying out. If there is crying out with it, then the angels leave it. Then you can choose between riding and walking. The dead person on the bier is like the person who is carried on the litter. Our companion, Abu-l-Mutawakkil, saw a bier which was being carried with a dead man on it. He pointed at it and said:

> He still carries us while mankind carries him. How
> remarkable!
> A carrier who is carried! (11)

57.21.2. *The Interpretation of Walking in Front of the Bier*

Going in front of the bier is because the one who is walking intercedes for the person with God. He goes ahead to be alone with God about him. The intercessor does not know whether his intercession will be accepted or not unless he reaches the grave and arrives forgiven by the generosity of God who accepts the request of the intercessor. If he is among those forgiven before that, the one who walks ahead of him is one of those who announce that he is coming to whoever went ahead of him to his halting place, which is his grave. He is like the chamberlain before him who shows respect for him. The people of unveiling see all of that. (12)

57.21.3. The Interpretation of the One Who Walks Behind the Bier

As for the one who walks behind him, he thinks that he should have him before him as he was in front of him in the formal prayer over him since he considers himself in relation to that. Death is terror. There is an angel with him. When the Prophet saw a Jew's funeral, he stood up. They told him: "It is a Jew's funeral." He said: "Isn't there an angel with him?" Another time he said: "Death is terror!" Another time he said: "Isn't it a soul?" Each statement has a certain aspect. "Isn't it a soul?" is the most hopeful of the statements for the man of intelligence. He stands up with the angel. (13)

57.21.4. The Angels Are Generally Better than Men

In the Tradition saying that angels are better than human beings, the one who is surpassed rises for the excellent one according to us, and the one who thinks that the angels are generally better than men. This is like what the Messenger of God said to me in a true dream in which I saw him. (14)

57.21.5. The Nobility of the Articulate Soul

As for the words of the Prophet: "Isn't it a soul?" about the Jew, that is the most hopeful part which the People of God hold fast to when they are not among the people of unveiling. Their inner eyes are illuminated by belief in the nobility of the articulate soul, even if that person is wretched since he will enter the Fire. He is like the one who is wretched here with the sicknesses of the self in regard to destruction of property, loss of position, and loss of what is important to him. This is a spiritual pain, not a sensory pain, and that is the portion of the animal ruh. However, all of this does not affect its honor. It is breathed out of the spirit which is ascribed to God by means of honoring. The root is noble. Since it was from the most noble of worlds, the Messenger of God rose for it because of its source. This informs us that all of the souls are equal in the root. (15)

57.21.6. The Universality of divine Mercy

Qushayri mentioned in his *Risalah* that one of righteous said:

"Whoever sees himself as better than Pharaoh has not recognized." He blamed him and said that he should not think that. This is one of the most tremendous questions which proclaims the universality and all-embracing nature of mercy for every soul, even if the souks fill up both abodes. They must fill both abodes as is related. God will deal with the souls as their nobility demands by a secret which is only known by the People of God. It is one of the secrets particular to them. As the limit joins them together, so the station joins them by their essence if God Almighty wills. (16)

God says about those who are wretched: *"Truly thy Lord is Achiever of what He wants."* (11:107). He did not say, "an uninterrupted punishment," as He says about those who are fortunate. He says: "O human being!" and he did not specify any particular person. The outward grants that He means the one who opposes His command and absolutely rebels against him, and does not obey Him. *"O human being! What has deluded thee as to thy generous Lord, He Who created thee, then shaped thee in proportion."* (82:6-7). (17)

He says that He brought you into existence by His generosity so the servant tells him, "O Lord, Your generosity deceived me." Some people may say that there when they reflect on it during the recitation. Then it is the reason for his repentance. It may be said in the Gathering. He may say it in Hell. It is the reason for his blessing since he only says that to Him in the moment in which he wants Him to treat him with generosity and open-handedness. His mercy preceded his wrath. "The mercy of God encompasses everything" in favor and merit. Basically all is a favor from God, glory be to Him! He has written mercy for Himself for those who are fearful of Him. The one who is fearful fears Him by His favor. He makes him a locus for righteous action. (18)

57.22. The Description of the Funeral Formal Prayer

Part of that is the number of recitations of "God is Greater." The first people disagreed about that and say that it is from three to seven, inclusive by the disagreement about effects. The Tradition is that the Prophet said that recitation of "God is Greater" in the funeral four, five, six, seven, eight times. It is also related that he did the recitation of "God is Greater" three times. When the Negus died, the Messenger of God said the recitation of "God is Greater" over him four times. It is confirmed that he did it four times until God Almighty took him to Him. (19)

57.22.1. The Interpretation of the Four Recitation of "God is Greater" of the Funeral Formal Prayer

The maximum number in the obligatory formal prayers is four. There is no bowing in the funeral-formal prayer. It is all standing. Every standing has a recitation of "God is Greater." He says that recitation of "God is Greater" four times to complete the number of the cycles of the formal prayer. (20)

The first recitation of "God is Greater" is for the recitation of "God is Greater" after which everything but the formal prayer is forbidden. He is forbidden to ask other than God Almighty for forgiveness in it for this dead person. (21)

In the second recitation of "God is Greater" He proclaims God Almighty great since He is alive and does not die: "*Every soul is one that experiences death*" (3:185) and "*everything perishes except His Countenance*" (27:88). (22)

The third recitation of "God is Greater" is for His Generosity and Mercy in accepting intercession for the one who is the object of the intercession, so He asks for him like the formal prayer on the Prophet when he died. We know that the one who asks God for the means of intercession has intercession. The Prophet did not intercede in it for the one over whom he performed the formal prayer. He asked God for the means of intercession in order to encourage his community to do that. (23)

The fourth recitation of "God is Greater" is the recitation of "God is Greater" of thankfulness since the one who performs the formal prayer has a good opinion of his Lord and assumes that He has accepted the request of the one who performs the formal prayer over him. God—glory be to Him! —has prescribed the formal prayer for the dead only to reassure us that he accepts the request of the one who performs the formal prayer for the one over whom he performs the formal prayer. God Almighty has given permission for making a request in it, and he is not allowed to think in himself that He will not accept the request of the one who asks. (24)

God Almighty says about the intercession on the Day of Rising: "*They intercede not but for him with whom He is content.*" (21:28) and He says: "*Who is there that will intercede with Him but with His permission?*" (2:255) He says: "*No intercession profits with Him but for him to whom He gives permission.*" (34:23) He gives us permission to intercede for this dead person by the formal prayer over him. Where there is no doubt, we are assured of the answer. (25)

After the recitation of "God is Greater" of thankfulness, he says the greetings of departure and taking leave of the dead person, that is, you have met peace from your Lord. This is why the Prophet said that they should refrain from mentioning the bad qualities of the dead person. At the end of his formal prayer over them, the one who says has said: "Peace be upon you." He informed that the dead person is safe from him. If he speaks badly of him after this, he is saying that he was lying when he said: "Peace be upon you." He was not safe him since he spoke badly about him after his death. He dislikes that for the dead even as God dislikes him to speak that way about the living. The living will remind him of it when he does not stop himself from doing that. That leads to him having little modesty before his Lord. (26)

57.22.2. *Raising the Hands While Reciting "God is Greater" (Allahu akbar) (takbir) Over the Dead and Crossing the Hands*

As for raising the hands in every recitation of "God is Greater" and crossing them, there is some dispute about it. There is no doubt that raising the hands announces poverty in every state of the states of recitation of "God is Greater." He says: "We have nothing in our hands. We have lifted our hands to Thee in every state. There is nothing in them and they own nothing." (27)

57.22.3. *The One Who Crosses Intercedes and the Intercessor Asks*

As for crossing them, he is one who intercedes. The intercessor asks. The request is a state of abasement and poverty for that for which he asks, whether he is asking that for himself or for someone else. In respect to the other person, the asker is his representative in asking for that for someone else. He must therefore stand in the station of abasement and need of that for which he is in need. (28)

Crossing the hands is an attribute of the abased. Its description is placing on hand over the other by holding on to the back of the hand, the wrist, and forearm. It is like taking a contract when two hands are joined: the hands of the two people making the contract. That is to say: "Thou hast taken a contract with us that we call on Thee and we make a contract with Thee for Thy generosity since Thou rescued us. Thou hast said: *"And when My servants ask thee about Me, then truly I am near. I answer the call of one who calls when he calls to Me."* (2:186) He did not say that "he calls on Me for himself or for someone else." (29)

57.22.4. *Supplication for the Dead and Intercession with God for Him*

"You have given us permission to make supplication for the dead and to intercede with Thee for him." Only the answer remains. It is realized and certain for the believer. This is why the last recitation of "God is Greater" is for thankfulness. The greeting is a greeting of departure and recognition of the peace and security which the dead person receives with God, and the mercy and restraint in not mentioning evil qualities on our part. (30)

57.23. The Recitation in the Funeral Formal Prayer

Some say that there is no recitation in the funeral formal prayer. It is only supplication. Some say that he praises God and lauds Him after the first recitation of "God is Greater," performs the formal prayer on the Prophet after the second recitation of "God is Greater," intercedes for the dead after the third recitation of "God is Greater," and says the greetings after the fourth recitation of "God is Greater." (31)

Others say that he recites the Opening Chapter of the Book after the first recitation of "God is Greater," and does that which we have mentioned in the rest of the recitation of "God is Greater." That is my position. That is because since there must be lauding and praise, it is better to do it with the words of God. The name "formal prayer" is applied to it, and it is not good to turn away from the Opening Chapter. That is the position of al-Shafii, Ahmad ibn Hanbal and Abu Dawud. (32)

57.23.1. The Perfect One Sees Himself as Dead Before God

Abu Yazid al-Bistami said: "I looked at creation and saw that they were dead. I said the recitation of "God is Greater" over them four times." One of our shaykhs said that Abu Yazid saw the world of his soul. This description belongs to the one who has no gnosis of his Lord and no recognition of Him, and it also belongs to the one who is the most perfect in gnosis of God. The perfect gnostic sees himself as dead before his Lord, The Mighty, The Majestic, since God is his hearing, his sight, his hand, and it is His tongue which is praying over him. God Almighty says: "*He it is Who gives blessings to you.*" (33:43) When God is the One who performs the formal prayer, then His words are the Quran. (33)

57.23.2. The Recitation of the Opening Chapter After the First Recitation of "God is Greater" (Allahu akbar)

The gnostics must recite the Opening Chapter of the Book. God recites it on their tongue and performs the formal prayer over them. He praises Himself by His words, and then He proclaims Himself great over this connection when He praises Himself by the tongue of His servant in the funeral-formal prayer over His servant who is before his Lord, the Almighty. The Merciful is in his direction of formal prayer, and He is the One who ask. The One who praises in The Living, The Self-subsistent. (34)

57.23.3. The Prayer for the Prophet After the Second Recitation of "God is Greater" (Allahu akbar) (takbir)

After the recitation of "God is Greater," then he blesses His Prophet who conveyed from Him. God Almighty says: "*Truly God and His angels give blessings to the Prophet.*" (33:56) Had it not been for the honor of the angels over all creatures which He joined the pronoun in "they pray" between them and God, He would have been enough for them. After that, there is no need for another proof. He presented the angels with "and" so that it is certain that the pronoun joins those who were mentioned before. (35)

Then He proclaims Himself great on the tongue of this gnostic who is performing the formal prayer. He is greater than the illusion which this divine descent gives in distinguishing the attributes between God and His servants by that which joins them and that by which they are distinguished in the ranks of preference. That illusion and give that the divine realities are distinguished from one another by the rivalry of the servants. Every servant in every state is connected to a divine reality. divine realities are relationships which are exalted above rivalry for preference. That illusion may give that the divine realities are distinguished from one another by the rivalry of the servants. Every servant in every state is connected to a divine reality. divine realities are relationships which are exalted above for rivalry for preference. This is why he does the third recitation of "God is Greater." (36)

57.23.4. Supplication for the Dead After the Third Recitation of "God is Greater"

Then after he recites and says the formal prayer on the Prophet, he begins to make supplication for the dead person from His words: *"If there had been a Recitation that would set mountains in motion with it or the earth would be cut off with it or the dead would be spoken to with it,"* (13:31), it would have been this Quran which was sent down on you, O Muhammad. Since the matter is like this and the dead person is in the principle of the inanimates since outwardly his sensory spirit has departed, his principle is that of the inanimates. (37)

God Almighty said: *"If We had sent forth this, the Quran, on a mountain, you would have seen it as one that is humbled, one that is split open from dread of God."* (59:21) He described it with fear and specified that the description by fear is the same as description by knowledge of what has been sent down on him. God Almighty says: *"Only those of His servants who dread God are knowing."* (35:28) The meaning which obliges lack of fear is the connection of the spirit to the body. Lack of fear occurred in the joining because each of them loves the other one. When they are parted, each of them returns to its Lord by His essence. Then he knows that about which he was ignorant before due to his structure. Fear accompanies him because of this knowledge. (38)

Therefore, the Quran is the first of that which he uses for supplication for the dead in the formal prayer over him and his praise of God in the formal prayer. The dead person is in the station of fear in respect to his spirit and in respect to his body. When the gnostic has gnosis, he only utters and speaks the Quran. Man must be in all of his states like the one who performs the formal prayer over the dead man in the funeral. His essence always sees the funeral before his Lord. (39)

He is always praying constantly in all states over himself by the words of his Lord by habit. The one who performs the formal prayer is always making supplication. The one over whom he performs the formal prayer is always dead and asleep. The one who sleeps by his soul is dead. The one who dies by his Lord is asleep like the sleep of the bridegroom. God represents him. We wrote about this meaning:

Sleeper! How many of you are asleep
    while you are calling!
Take note! God takes charge of you in what He calls,
    even had you slept through it.
But your heart is asleep to that
    to which He calls you and alerts you
in the world of phenomenal being
    which destroys you to that by which you died.
Look to yourself before you travel
    if something doubtful is your provision. (40)

O God! Give him an abode better than his abode, that is, the next formation. God says: "I have done it." The organic formation of this world is his abode. It is a putrid abode, full of faults and sicknesses and destruction. The winds and rains descend on it, and the passage of nights and days lays waste to it. The next formation is the abode which is exchanged for it, and the Prophet described it. He said that they do not urinate or defecate or blow their noses. He detached them from filth. This world is a place which accepts ruin and passions affect it. (41)

Then He says: "a better family than his family." He says: "I have done it." His people in this world are the people of outrage, envy, incompatibility. severance, rancor and enmity. God Almighty says about the people to which the dead person will move: "*And We will tear out any grudges from their breasts. They will be as brothers on couches, one facing the other*." (15:47) (42)

Then He say, "a wife better than his wife." How can there not be a better wife when "*they restrain their glances?*" (55:56) In their eyes, no one is better than him and he does not see any better than them. They are adorned for him and he for them. They are excellent for him and he is excellent for them, as God Almighty says about the Garden. He will make them enter the Garden and show them to them. Their beauty is for their sake. They do not smell any scent of food from them. They do not see any beauty from food from them. (43)

57.23.5. Supplication for the Dead Is Accepted

Their supplication in the formal prayer for the dead is accepted because it is a secret supplication. There is no good which they invoke for the dead person but that the angel says to this one who performs the formal prayer for good, "He has it and you have twice its like," representing the dead person and repaying the one who has said the formal prayer over him. It is a true report and true words. It is certain that both the one who performs the formal prayer and the one over whom he performs the formal prayer will obtain good. It is established by the Messenger of God that when the believer makes supplication for his brother secretly, the angel says to him, "He has it and you have twice its like." The angels report that this one making the supplication from God Almighty. The report of the angel is true and there is no lie in it. In reality, he performs the formal prayer on himself. It is a very excellent sleep between his Lord and the one who is praying over him. (44)

If the one who performs the formal prayer over him is a gnostic of his Lord, beloved with Him, it is God that is his hearing, his sight, and his tongue. It is only his Lord who performs the formal prayer. He puts the Lord in the *qibla* in the formal prayer. The dead man who is lying down is between his Lord and his Lord. How sublime is this sleep! Would that it would last forever! We ask God Almighty for that for our brothers and for us. When our time comes, let the one who performs the formal prayer over us be a servant who hearing, sight and tongue is God. We ask this for ourselves, our brothers, our children, our parents, our family, our acquaintances, and all the Muslims, men and *jinn*! Amen, by His might and generosity. (45)

Since the state of death is the state of the dead meeting his Lord and joining with him, he gathers together what was divided in all the Books and scrolls which were revealed. He specified the Opening Chapter from Quran since it is divided between God and His servant by divine report. The divine law called it "formal prayer." He said: "I have divided the formal prayer into two parts between Me and My servant." He specifically mentioned the Opening chapter rather than any of the other chapters of the Quran. He specified its recitation in every aspect of the formal prayer over the dead since it contains praise and supplication. (46)

57.23.6. What Praise is Greater Than "the Merciful, the Compassionate"

Every intercessor must praise the one with whom he intercedes by what befits the The Merciful, The Compassionate. It is praise which is praiseworthy in itself. It is established in sound tradition from the Messenger of God: "There is nothing that God loves more than to be praised." God Almighty has described His servants, the believers, as praisers. He blamed and cursed the one who censures the presence of God and ascribes to Him that which is improper, like poverty and tight-fistedness since the Jews said that God's hand is tied. That indicates tight-fistedness. God says that they were liars when he says: *"His hands are ones that are stretched out: He spends how He wills."* (5:64). Generosity covers both of His hands. "Do not despair of the spirit of God." For us, this is one of the most hopeful signs recited to us. (47)

The intercessor is specifically enjoined to praise his Lord without a doubt. Intercession can be accepted with the permission to do it. There is nothing to stop acceptance. It is related in sound tradition that when the Messenger of God wants to intercede on the Day of Rising, he will first praise God before the intercession with praises that he will not know until that day. That place will demands that by its state. Praise of the One with whom he intercedes is according to the crimes of those for whom He intercedes. He therefore puts praise of God before his intercession according to the noble qualities which that place demands. The place of the Rising has not been seen today and it has not yet occurred. This is why he will not know them until that time. (48)

57.24. The Salutations (*salam*) in the Funeral Formal Prayer

People disagree about whether it is one or two salams. Most people say that it is one salam. One group say that there are two salams. They also disagree about whether the salam will be aloud or not. (49)

My position, and that which I say is that the principle of the greeting in the funeral ritual prayer for the leader and the one following the leader is the same as the principle of the salam in the normal formal prayer, even if he is alone. (50)

57.24.1. The Intercessor Is in the Presence of the One With Whom He Intercedes

When the one who intercedes is in the presence of the One with whom he intercedes and the object of his intercession is between him and his Lord, so he specifies the one for whom he intercedes, as the intercessor calls to mind an event which occasions the intercession by mentioning it with the One with whom he intercedes, then the presence of the one with wrong action before him is in the station of the event which he calls to mind by mentioning it. Had the wrongdoer not been present, he would have been in a state of withdrawal from all that is other than his Lord by his turning to Him. When he finishes his intercession, he returns to those present of men, angels, and believing jinn. He greets them as he does in the formal prayer. It is good news from God for the dead. It is as if he had said to them: "There is only safety for him and you." God has accepted the intercession because of the permission which we confirmed. (51)

57.24.2. The Dead Person Is Happy about the Prayer for Him

Whoever says that if the dead person is among the people over whom the formal prayer is said and the formal prayer is said over him and that intercession is not accepted, he has no good at all. By God, no! That person is happy without a doubt, even if his wrong actions were as numerous as the sand, and pebbles, and earth. As for the one singled out by God with that, he is forgiven. As for the one who is singled out for injustices to the servants, God will put things right between His servants on the Day of Rising. In any case, there must be good, even if it comes after a certain time. (52)

When the one who intercedes with God in his formal prayer performs the formal prayer over the dead, he must not single out a specific wrong action. He must be general in mentioning all that is considered to be an evil which comes between him and his happiness. He should ask God to forgive his evils in general and to acknowledge all the evils of the dead person even if the one who performs the formal prayer does not make that universal. If God wills, He will completely overlook all, and if He wills, He will deal with the dead according to the intercession of the intercessor. (53)

This is why the one who performs the formal prayer over the dead must ask God to save him from the punishment, not to have him enter the Garden, since there is not a third abode. There is only the Garden and the Fire. That is if he only asks to enter the Garden and nothing else. God will accept his request. However, he may see great terrors on the way. This is why the intercession of the one who performs the formal prayer should be in order that God rescue the one over whom he is praying from what will come between him and well-being and that which accompanies it. That is more beneficial for the dead person. When he does that, the announcement of peace in the formal prayer is valid, that is, he has encountered peace and safety from all that he dislikes. (54)

57.25. The Place Where the Leader (*Imam*) Stands When He Performs the Funeral Formal Prayer for the Dead Person

They disagree about where the leader stands during the funeral formal prayer. One group says that he stands at the waist, whether it is a man or a woman. Some people say that he stands at head of a man and at the waist of a woman. Some say that he stands at the chest of both of them. Some people say that he can stand where he likes, and that there is no particular rule in that. That is my position. (55)

57.25.1. The Aim of the One Who Prays for the Dead

Imagination and illusion have power. The goal of the one who performs the formal prayer is to ask God Almighty. He speaks with Him about this dead person and calls the dead present before him, so he is not concerned about where he stands in relationship to him. Hesitation about that splits his thought about the aim of this, especially when the dead person is a woman. When the leader stands at her waist, he imagines that he is veiling her from those who are behind him. He has not veiled her from himself, so that illusion weakens his presence with God in respect to her. (56)

57.25.2. The Heart Which Faces The Real

In reality, the part of man which faces God is his heart. The heart of the one who performs the formal prayer in this fashion is scattered and he calls to mind that which he should not call to mind by his illusion. This is bad manners in intercession, and whoever is like this is not an intercessor. It is more fitting to call the one who performs the formal prayer like this "dead" than the dead person himself because of his bad adab with God, with death, and with the dead person!. (57)

The one who performs the formal prayer should not call to mind where he stands in relationship to the dead person. He should devote all of his spiritual strength to God on whom he calls for intercession for this dead person. There is many a person who performs the formal prayer over the dead person while it is the dead person who is interceding for him! May God place us among those who intercede here and there! (58)

57.25.3. The Human Being is Obligated from His Head to His Feet

The human being is obligated from his head to his feet as well as what is between them. He is commanded not to look at that which it is not permissible for him to look at in the divine law. This is all that is particularly obligated of his head. He is commanded not to run with his feet to that which it is not lawful for him to run to, in, and from. God has made him responsible for guarding what is between the two when he acts with his hand, belly, genitals and heart. (59)

If the one who performs the formal prayer could completely cover the dead person, he would do so. He should stand wherever God inspires him to stand in relationship to the corpse. It is better to stand at his heart and chest. It employs all of the limbs to good and evil. There is not doubt that it is the best place for the one who performs the formal prayer and intercedes to stand. It puts it behind him and God singles it out. If He forgives the heart, He forgives the entire body. All of the limbs follow the heart in everything in this world and the world to come. (60)

57.25.4. The Heart Is Like a Piece of Flesh and Like Something Subtle

The Messenger of God said about it: "There is a piece of flesh in the body. When it is sound, the entire body is sound. When it is unsound, the entire body is unsound. It is the heart." Similarly, when intercession for it is accepted, it is accepted for all of the limbs. (61)

By the heart, here the divine law means the piece of flesh which is encircled by the breast. It does not mean his subtle self or intellect by the heart. There is a secret in this information for the one who understands and knows, It is only obtained by unveiling. God Almighty said: "*Truly in that is the reminder for him who had been one who has heart,*" (50:37), and He says: "*That they may meditate on its signs and those imbued with intuition may recollect.*" (38:29) He also said: "*Their hearts that are in darkness which are within their breasts.*" (22:46) This is an allusion from God about the breasts. (62)

When He speaks of soundness and unsoundness, He means this piece of flesh and what occurs to it in the body in the way of sicknesses, health and death. The heart which is this piece of flesh is the place of the animal spirit. The animal spirit spreads out from it to all of the sensory body in all that it senses and desires. This is the vapor which rises from the ventricle of the heart. The blood is sound, then the vapor is like it. Therefore the body is sound. The resign is also true. This is information which the Prophet have given us about what the matter really is. (63)

57.25.5. The Natural Elemental Body and Human latifa

It is knowledge about what the basis of the business is in this natural elemental body which is the tool of the subtle aspect of self of the responsible person when he manifests what the divine law obliges him to manifests of acts of obedience particular to the limbs. When man is not preserved in his nourishment and does not look to the soundness of his nature and animal spirit which manages the nature of his body, then the faculties are faulty and weak, and the imagination and conceptual faculty are unsound because of the unsound vapors which arise from the heart. Reflection is weak and the memory is poor. The intellect is damaged since the tools by which it perceives matters are unsound. The King acts by his ministers and subjects. It is like that when it is sound. (64)

The Prophet took the unsound root into consideration since it makes these tools unsound. When it is sound, that makes the tools sound since man can only do what he has been charged to do by his Lord when these tools are sound, upright, and safe from matters which make them unsound. That only comes from the heart. This is part of the sum of words which the Prophet was given. (65)

If he had meant the intellect by the "heart" here, he would not have gathered together the benefits which he gathered together when he meant the heart which is encircled by the breast. This is why he used the term "piece of flesh" and part. It is in order to remove any doubt so that no one can imagine that it is contrary to that and the listener will not apply it to the intellect. This is as God says: "*It is not their sight that is in darkness, but their hearts that are in darkness*" (22:46), when they are unsound and blind to the perception of that which they should perceive. The unsoundness of the inner eye to what the outward eye gives it comes from the unsoundness of the its location. The unsoundness of its place comes from the unsoundness of its animal spirit whose place is the heart. (66)

57.25.6. The One Who Prays Stands at the Breast of the Dead Person

(Therefore, the one who performs the formal prayer should stand at the breast of the dead person when he performs the formal prayer over him. This is better and more fitting for the sake of his heart which is the root in his soundness or unsoundness. 67)

57.26 The Arrangement of the Biers in the Funeral Prayer

57.26.1. The Disagreement About the Arrangement of the Biers

They disagree about the arrangement of the biers when there are both men and women over whom the formal prayer is to be performed. Some people say that the men are put next to the leader and the women next to *qibla*. Some people say that it is the resign. Some people say that he should pray over the men in one group and over the women in one group. (68)

57.26.2. Ibn Arabi's Position on the Arrangement

My position in that is that if there are two men among the dead, one of them is put next to the leader and the other is put next to direction of formal prayer and the women are put behind them. If there is only one man, he is put next to the leader, and it is better if he is put next to direction of formal prayer. There is no set rule in the divine law regarding all of this at which we can stop. We have looked to see whether we can find a rule about that in the divine law and we did not find one. (69)

57.26.3. *The Arrangement Reported from Some of the Companions*

It is related from some of the Companions that they used to put the men next to the *qibla* and the women next to the leader. When they were asked about that, they said that it was the confirmed custom of the Prophet. I think that it is the most fitting. When something like that occurs, we consider it to be part of that which is based on tradition. It is better to remain with the judgement and this is the reason for the caution of the one who makes a distinction between men and women in the formal prayer. (70)

57.26.4. *What Ibn Arabi Prefers in the Arrangement*

I prefer to put the man closest to the direction of formal prayer. When the Prophet buried those killed at Uhud, he put the most excellent closest to the *qibla*. All of them were buried in the same grave. It is better to put the more excellent closest to the *qibla* because he is nearer to God in the divine law. God knows best. (71)

57.26.5. *Women Are More Entitled to the qibla*

Women are the place for the formation of being. They are nearer to the Maker, so they are more entitled to the *qibla* than men, even if formation occurred in men once. That was only the formation of Eve from Adam. The principle belongs to that which dominates. This is especially true since opposite the formation of Eve from Adam is the formation of Jesus in Mary without any father. The general rule with the female is that they are the place of formation and so they are more entitled to the *qibla* since every child is born with proper character (*fitra*). When he is born, he comes to us. He has a new contract with his Lord as the Messenger of God said about the rain, "It has a new contract with its Lord." (72)

57.26.6. *Men Are Closer to the Leader (imam)*

Therefore men should be next to the leader. The other interpretation is that when the dead man is closest to the leader, he veils the woman from the leader. The woman is private, and it is better to have the dead man next to her than the living since the dead cannot see. Therefore women are more entitled to His female-servants and He veils them from the leader and the one who performs the formal prayer over them. (73)

57.26.7. *The Gnostic Leader (imam)*

If the leader has gnosis and knows from Himself that God is His hearing and his sight, he is not then concerned about whether the women are put in front or the men or put in front. When one is like this, it is better to put the women closest to him and the men closest to the *qibla*. It is the strongest position in interpretation because God has given form to most natural phenomenal beings through causes. Therefore, it is better to put the women next to the leader who is like that. It is an interpretation which is unquestionable. The leader who is like this is a tool. God has taken possession of his affair, "*most of humanity knows not.*" (12:21) (74)

57.26.8. The Real Does Not Accept Limitation So Nothing Is Veiled from Him and Nothing Veils Him

There are wondrous and amazing secrets in this question. Had men of intellect come upon them, they would have been amazed and bewildered, and they would have known the wisdom of God in things and the meaning of the veil of light and darkness and what defines this veil. The Truly Real does not accept any limits. Nothing is veiled from Him and nothing veils Him. If something had veiled Him, that veil would have imposed a limit on Him. He does not accept the veil and the servant cannot be veiled from God. He is veiled to a particular relationship. (75)

God Almighty says about those who act outrageously: "*They will be from their Lord on that Day ones who are alienated.*" (83:15) He related the Lord to them, and it is a relationship which they hope for and do not find since they sought after it in a direction in which it does not exist. They are like the person who intends to travel to the east and yet is walking towards the west with his body. He imagines that he is moving in the direction which is his goal. This is in the words of God Almighty, "*there would appear to them from God that with which they never reckoned*" (39:49). Then they wake up from the sleep of their heedlessness. They reach a station and alight from their mounts. They seek that which was their goal and they are told, "You parted company with it at the very first step. You have only put yourselves further away from it." They will say, "Would that we could go back!" There is no way to do that. This is why they are described as being veiled from their Lord who was their goal when they set out on a path which was not prescribed for them. (76)

57.26.9. Judgment Belongs to the divine law, Not to You

If you know that which we have interpreted, then arrange the dead according to your station and do not make any judgement. Judgment does not belong to you. It belongs to the one who gave us the divine law. If you perceive a sound established judgment in that from the Prophet by means of unveiling in that station, then act by it and do not exceed it. Stop there. "*There is only misguidance after the truth*" (10:32). (77)

57.27. The One Who Misses the Recitation of "God is Greater" (*Allahu akbar*) (*takbir*) For the Dead

They disagree about the one who misses some of the recitation of "God is Greater" over the dead in certain places. Does he enter the formal prayer with a recitation of "God is Greater" or not? Does he make up what he missed or not? If he does make it up, does he first make supplication between the recitation of "God is Greater"s or not? (78)

Some say that he says the recitation of "God is Greater" as soon as he joins the formal prayer. Some say that he waits until the leader says the recitation of "God is Greater" and then pronounces it. As for making up what he missed, some say that he makes up whatever supplication and recitation of "God is Greater"s which he missed. Some say that he makes up the recitation of "God is Greater"s which he missed in order and does not make up the supplication. (79)

57.27.1. The School of Ibn Arabi

I say that the recitation of "God is Greater" which he catches with the leader is the first recitation of "God is Greater" and then he should complete his formal prayer with its recitation of "God is Greater"s and supplication. (80)

57.27.2. The Recitation of "God is Greater" (Allahu akbar) (takbir) Is Exalting God

The recitation of "God is Greater" is exaltation of God. He should hurry to it and not wait for the leader. He should make up the recitation of "God is Greater"s which he missed in order without supplication. God Almighty says: "Whoever is distracted from asking Me by My invocation/ remembrance, I will give him better than what I give those who ask." The object of his supplication here is the dead man. By the remembrance of the one who performs the formal prayer, He gives the dead better than what He would have given him had he made supplication for him. The goal of supplication for the dead is benefit. The greatest benefit is obtained by invocation/ remembrance. (81)

Some people say that one should not pray at the grave. Some people say that only the guardian can pray at the grave when he misses the funeral-formal prayer and other people have already performed the formal prayer over the dead person. Some people say that whoever missed the funeral-formal prayer can pray at the grave. (82)

Those who say that one can pray at the grave agree that it is a precondition that he be recently buried. These disagree about the period of time in that. The maximum is a month. (83)

I say that one can pray at the grave without any limitation in the period of time. (84)

One does not pray over the dead person until he is concealed from the eyes in his shroud. There is no difference between being concealed by his shroud or concealed by his grave. It is established from the Prophet that one can pray over the dead person after he has been buried in his grave. The interpretation here is that the body is created from earth and it returns to its root. There is no difference between it when it departs from it and emerges on the face of the earth and when it is under the earth. It is part of it. (85)

That which is intended by this formal prayer is the spirit which manages the body. It taken up to its Creator. It has left the body, so there is nothing to stop one from praying over him. If the object of that formal prayer is the body rather than the spirit, it is the same whether it is above or below the earth. The Prophet did not make any distinction. Every human being returns to his root. His spirit joins the other spirits and the elemental part of his body rejoins the elements. (86)

57.27.4. The Disagreement About Praying at the Grave

Part of that is the formal prayer over someone who is one of the people of "*la ilaha illa Lah.*" Some say that they must all have the formal prayer said over them, no matter whether they are people of great wrong actions, passions and innovations. My position is the first one. Others do not allow the formal prayer over the people of great wrong actions or over the people of injustice and innovations. If the one who says this had known that the one who performs the formal prayer over the dead intercedes, it is established that the Prophet said: "I have preserved my supplication as intercession for the people of great wrong actions among my community." (87)

57.27.5. The Prayer For the People of Oneness (tawhid) in General

The Prophet said: "Pray over the one who says: 'There is no god but God.'" He did not distinguish nor specify anyone. He made a general statement when he said "whoever." It is a general indefinite noun. What we understand from these words is that one should pray over the people of tawhid, whether their tawhid comes from speculation or belief, (By belief, I mean the imitation of the Messenger) or from both speculation and belief together. (88)

The meaning of faith (*iman*) in saying '*la ilaha illa Lah*' is that the unifier says it as a prescribed act of nearness since it is prescribed for us. There is no way to attain to true recognition of it except by revelation or unveiling. It is unseen. "*God places not a burden on a soul beyond its capacity.*" (2:286) This is why the Prophet connected it to words. (89)

57.27.6. THE ONE FROM WHOM THE WORD OF ONENESS (TAWHID) IS INCONCEIVABLE OR WHO WAS NOT HEARD TO UTTER IT

One performs the formal prayer over the one who cannot possibly speak or the one who has not been heard to utter it, like the suckling child. The suckling child is connected to his parents in respect of judgment. One should pray over him. As for the one who has not been heard to utter it and is in the Abode of Islam among the Muslims and it is not known at all what judgment he had and whether or not it was Islam, is judged according to the Abode where he lives. One performs the formal prayer over him. If the concern of the Abode is connected to him to verify his Islam, then what do you think about the concern of God? The people of "*la ilaha illa Lah*" by any aspect and in every case will not remain endlessly in the Fire until they associate or make a *Sunna* of association of partners with God. Those ones will never leave the Fire. (90)

57.27.7. NOTHING RESISTS ONENESS (TAWHID)

Passions, innovations, and every wrong action does not lessen *la ila illa Lah* are not taken into consideration. Nothing can resist *tawhid* when it exists in the self of the person. Had it not been for a text which has come down concerning the idolater and the one who makes a *Sunna* of idolatry, intercession would have encompassed all who are confirmed by existence, even if they did not unify. (91)

The idolater has a sort of Unity (*tawhid*), that is, *tawhid* of the greatest divine rank. The idolater makes the associate an intercessor with God. They say: "These are our intercessors with God" as they say: "*We worship them not but that they may bring us near to God.*" (39:3). This polytheist unifies God in His immensity. The associate does not have this rank. If it had had this rank, he would not have made him an intercessor. The intercessor is not the judge. (92)

57.27.8. THE PUNISHMENT OF THE IDOLATER ON THE DAY OF RISING

They have a whiff of *tawhid*. Because of this whiff of *tawhid*, even if they do not leave the Fire, it is unlikely that God will not give them a sort of bliss in it in the means to which pains are connected. The least amount of bliss that they might have is that He will put coolness in heat, and its opposite, which is heat, in intense cold so that each of them experiences some pleasure as they had a whiff of the breath of Unity. God created them with a nature by which they accept the bliss of these means which is not in harmony with that. "And that is not a great matter for God." (14:20) "*Truly thy Lord is Achiever of what He wants.*" (11:107) So text has come down which comes between us and the judgment which we have just mentioned. The possibility remains based on its root in this question in the divine law. It is supported by His words, "*My mercy encompasses everything*" (7:156), and His words, "My mercy preceded My wrath." (93)

57.28. The One Who Is Killed by the Leader (*Imam*) for a *Hadd* Punishment

Some people do not think that the leader should pray over him. Some people think that the leader should pray over him. That is my position. (94)

57.28.1. Killing for Someone Killed Is Purification of Meaning

The one who washes is not barred from praying over the one he has washed. The leader is the washer here. This killing is a purification of meaning for the one slain. It expiates. There is a tradition related regarding that. The leader should pray over him since his purification is unquestionable. (95)

57.28.2. Should the leader (imam) pray for someone who dies while a hadd is yet to be imposed on him?

The wonder about the position of the person who forbids for the leader to pray over him while he is present with him is that if the one who is subject to the punishment had died before it was inflicted, then the leader would still pray over him although he is certain that he was liable for this punishment which he deserves. His self was not pure. His affair is left up to God. If he likes, He will punish him for it, and if he likes, He will pardon him. Traditions have come about that. (96)

57.28.3. Carrying Out the hadd in This World Is Expiation in the World to Come

It is more appropriate if the leader performs the formal prayer over him after he has killed him for a punishment. He is like the one who washes him. The only meaning for carrying out the punishments on the believers in this world is to remove that from them in the world to come as opposed to the one who is killed for the political reason or in disbelief (unless it is for a punishment). (97)

57.29. On Suicide: Does one pray for him or not?

Some people say that the formal prayer is said over him, and some people say the formal prayer is not said over him. I say that it is the first. (98)

57.29.1. Permission to Pray for the Dead Is Permission to Intercede for Him

Since God gave permission for intercession by the formal prayer over the dead, we know that He is pleased with that and that the request for him is accepted. He informed us that the one who kills himself will be in the Fire forever without end and that the Garden is forbidden him. There has not been related to us any prohibition against praying over the suicide. The believers must pray over the suicide by this possibility. God might accept the intercession of the one who performs the formal prayer over him, especially when there are sound traditions and roots which demand that he leave the Fire while the tradition which has been related says that he will be in the Fire forever and is barred from leaving it. (99)

57.29.2. Death Is a Cause for Meeting God

The wisdom indicated in this question lies in the words of God Almighty: "My servant has hastened his self to Me and so I have forbidden him the Garden." There is an indication and a reality in it. The indication is: *"They are ones who take the lead from them."* (23:61) and *"Race towards forgiveness from your Lord,"* (57:21) and "whoever comes near Me a hand-breath, I come near him an arm-length." Death is a cause for meeting God. During his life, man is travelling and traversing stages by his breaths until he meets his Lord. He has given him a specific limit but he has hastened the meeting. He has set out to him before reaching that limit. That is a cause which has no effect in meeting Him. (100)

If it comes out of yearning to meet God, He meets him by lifting the veil at the beginning. He says: "I have forbidden him the Garden. The Garden is the covering." That is to say, "I have forbidden him from being veiled from Me. He has hastened himself to Me." He did not specify that in detail, so it can be applied to the aspect of the tradition of the believer since it is supported by the basic principles. That is more fitting. (101)

57.29.3. Belief Has Strong Authority in the Believer

The Prophet spoke about the one who kills himself with an iron object, poisons himself, or throws himself off a mountain. He did not say "among the believers" or anyone else in the tradition. Therefore the possibility occurs. When a possibility occurs, we consult the basic roots. We see then that belief has strong authority. When it is present, he cannot be in the fire forever without end. We know absolutely that the Prophet related that about the idolaters and how they will be punished forever. He said that: "the one who kills himself with iron will have his iron in his hand plunging it into his belly in the fire of hell forever." That is to say, this is a type of punishment whose authority is in the fire. It is like that with the one who drinks poison and kills himself. He will drink it in the fire of hell forever. This is a type of punishment with which this unbeliever is punished. It is related that: "whoever commits suicide with something will be punished by it." (102)

57.29.4. Legal Proofs Are Derived from Various Perspectives

As for the believer, far be it that anything resist belief in the unity of God! It is necessary that the text is about the idolater, even if the Prophet did not specify him in that Tradition. The proofs of the divine law are taken from many directions and are put together in order to strengthen each other since the believers in relationship to one another resemble a building in which the parts support one another. Belief in one thing strengthens belief in something else, and so each part of it strengthens the rest. The people of the Garden will see their Lord with a vision of bliss after they enter the Garden as has been related in the Tradition about the visit. "When people take their places in the Garden, they will be summoned to the Vision." (103)

57.29.5. The Person Who Commits Suicide Thinks God Is More Merciful Than His Current Situation

God may single out this person who has hastened himself to Him and therefore committed suicide. He says: "I have forbidden him the Garden before he meets Me." The one who kills himself may want to advance the Vision and then enter the Garden. The one who kills himself thinks that God is more merciful to him than his present situations which obliges him to hasten. If it had not been that he imagined that there would be rest from punishment with God from his present punishment, he would not have set out to Him. (104)

God says: "I am in My servant's opinion of Me, so let him think well of Me." If the one who commits suicide is a believer, he has a good opinion of his Lord. His good opinion of his Lord is that which makes him kill himself. It is more fitting to apply the words of this divine tradition to him since there is no text which states the opposite of this interpretation. If it appears in it later, then the one who looks has gone far from the confirmed roots in his view when he counters this interpretation with eternal wretchedness. If he considers it and weighs it, he will recognize what we have said. It says in sound traditions that the one who has in his heart the smallest amount of belief—less than the weight of a mustard-seed—will come out of the Fire. Only the one whom we mentioned will remain. In this tradition, God only said that He had forbidden him the Garden in particular. (105)

57.29.6. God Is Too Generous to Have Carrying Out the Threat Ascribed to Him

If we say that there must be punishment, then he is forbidden to enter the Garden without punishment like the people of major wrong actions. Therefore it is a text about the suicide and other people of major wrong actions in the principle of volition. The person with scrolls will not enter the Fire although he is among the people of major wrong actions since he only had the words: "There is no god but God." The length of his Islam is the length of his life in this world. (106)

His end is that it is certain that the threat will be carried out against the one who kills himself before he enters the Garden and he would not be forgiven. God is too generous to have carried out the threat ascribed to Him. Will is ascribed to Him. Generosity weighs heavier as one of the Arabs described even though he himself was among the people of desires:

> When I promise or threaten, I forget My threat and I fulfill My promise.

This is why there is no text in the divine law about the threat. It is related about the promise, "*So assume not that God will be one who breaks His promise.*" (14:47) The threat is only about evil. The promise is for both good and evil. (107)

57.30. The Judgment About One Who Is Killed in Battle

Some people say that there is no formal prayer said over him and he is not washed. Some people say that the formal prayer is said over him and he is not washed. (108)

57.30.1. The Martyr Is Alive With His Lord

Life is ascribed to the martyr who is killed in battle. Some think that God has taken our sight away from perceiving the life of the martyr and that he is alive and provided for, even as Zayd and Umar are alive. One does not pray over the one who is alive in this way. (109)

Some think that the prayer is supplication for him since his actions in this world have been cut off. Even if he is alive with his Lord, he does not act. This person says that the prayer should be said over him, that is, he makes supplication for him as one makes supplication for the dead since he is cut off from actions which bring one near to the degrees which are only obtained by actions doe by someone who acts for himself or by someone who represents him in his action. This is like the one who fasts on behalf of his guardian when he dies or performs the pilgrimage on his behalf when he dies or is unable to perform it. The prayer over the martyr then is in the station of this sort of action. If he had been present, his action would not have been terminated. (110)

57.31. The Rulings Concerning the Prayer for a Child

Some people say that the prayer is not said over the child unless he has cried out. Some say that the prayer is said over him if he has completed four months (in the womb) since the spirit exists after this period of time. (111)

57.31.1. God Commanded Us to Pray For the Dead

God commanded us to pray over the dead in the *Sunna*. He did not say the dead who died after previously being alive. When we see the form of the foetus, even if it is smaller than a gnat, and its limbs are formed so that we know that it is a human being (even if it is before the ruh is breathed into it), the divine law states that that form is a dead person. God Almighty says: "*You had been lifeless then He gave you life.*" (2:28) He applied the name "death" to us before He breathed the spirit. (112)

57.31.2. Nothing Forbids Praying For a Foetus

One performs the formal prayer over the foetus when it emerges and it is termed to be a miscarriage if we see its form, even if the spirit has not been breathed into its outward form. The name death is definite. Nothing forbids the prayer over him by any aspect. The Messenger of God did not say that one can only pray over the person who has died after having previously been alive. There is nothing to oppose that. If there were, the command would only refer to the one who has already been alive. The lack of transmission does not indicate the removal of the principle. It is understood from the divine law that one performs the formal prayer over the dead without any specification except that the Prophet specified that it is forbidden to pray over the unbeliever and other people which he specified said should not have the prayer said over them. The child is not included among them. (113)

57.31.3. The Child Is Prayed For and Does Not Inherit

Al-Tirmidhi mentioned that Jabir ibn Abd Allah related that the Messenger of God said: "One performs the formal prayer over the child, but he does not inherit or leave an inheritance until he utters a cry." He judged that the prayer be said over him and did not judge inheritance for him as he did for the one who died after having been alive. The tradition of al-Mughirah from the Prophet is: "One performs the formal prayer over the child." (114)

57.31.4. Did the Prophet pray for his son Ibrahim?

Some of them believe that one does not pray over the child at all.

Their proof is that the Prophet did not pray over his son Ibrahim who was eight months old. This person is counted by the fact that the Prophet did pray over his son Ibrahim. This Tradition strengthens the Tradition of al-Mughirah and Jabir. (115)

57.32. The Ruling Concerning the Children of the Enemy Who Die

It is said that their judgement is that of their parents. One does not pray over them. Some say that their judgement is that of the Muslims who have captured them. (116)

57.32.1. The Position of Ibn Arabi

My position is that when the Muslim can pray over small children who have died and who have not yet reached discrimination and intellect, he should pray over them. They are on the innate nature (*fitra*) of Islam. (117)

57.32.2. The Child is Weak and the Weak Is Always Shown Mercy

The Arabic word for "child" is derived from *tifl*. It is dew which falls from the sky in the morning and evening. It is the weakest sort of water which descends from the sky. The child in relation to adults is like the light drizzle. the downpour, the pouring rain, and other types of rain which descend. It has this weakness. The weak is always shown mercy. The pray is mercy, so one should pray over the child when he dies by every aspect. There is no meaning which allows one to abandon the prayer over him. (118)

57.33. The One Who Is Most Entitled to Lead the Funeral Formal Prayer

57.33.1. The Disagreement on Those Most Entitled to Lead the Funeral Formal Prayer

They disagree about the one most entitled to lead the funeral-prayer. It is said that it is his relative, and it is said that it is the ruler. I say that it is the ruler. It is established that the Prophet performed the formal prayer over the dead, and it is not transmitted about him at all that he took the relative into consideration or asked about him. Husayn ibn Ali had Said ibn al-As, the governor of al-Medina, lead the funeral prayer for Hasan ibn Ali. In this matter, it is better to join it to the Friday congregational prayer to the group prayer than to join it to the relative in his covering him and burying him. (119)

57.33.2. The Ruler Has Absolute Authority

The ruler has absolute authority in the general and the particular. He is stronger than the one who has power in only certain matters. He is more entitled to pray over the dead and to consign with God and intercede for the dead person. He is God's representative. God's regard for the one whom He has appointed as vicegerent is greater than His regard for the one to whom He has not given that general position in the vicegerency. His words are more acceptable to Him. He has entrusted the rule to him over those in his power. (120)

57.33.3. In Reality, The Ruler is God Almighty

In reality, the ruler is God Almighty. When one has this name established for him by the most universal aspect, the more universal is the most entitled to pray over the dead. The ruler is the one who has the authority of the moment among the divine names. He intercedes with the divine name which has appointed him for the person from the one who has the most general connection to him. That is the Merciful. "*His Mercy encompasses everything*" (7:156). (121)

57.34 The Time of the Funeral Formal Prayer

57.34.1. The Time When It Is Prohibited to Pray For or Bury the Dead

Some people say that the prayer is not said over him at the moments in which it is forbidden to perform the prayer. Some people say that the prayer is not said at sunset or sunrise. Some people say that the prayer can be said over him after the the morning formal prayer-prayer as long as it is not light and after the the afternoon formal prayer prayer as long as it is not yellow. Some people say that the prayer can be said over him at any moment, and that is my position. (122)

However, he is not to be buried at three times, even if one is allowed to say the prayer over him. This is because it is related in tradition that the dead are not buried at these times. That is sunrise, sunset and noon. (123)

57.34.2. The Prayer Is Intimate Conversation and Asking While Present

The prayer is conversation and request based on presence and witnessing. It is not limited to any moment which was not limited by the divine law. The funeral prayer is not limited. There is no prostration in it. (124)

57.34.3. Noon Is the Moment when the Fire Is Stoked

As for noon, that is the moment when the Fire is stoked. The grave is the first of the stages of the world to come. We do not say that death is the first stage since death is a state and not a stage. The grave is a stage. If he to be buried at that moment, the dead person would see the Fire being stoked. He might be overwhelmed by terror. God is Compassionate to the believer and did not allow us to bury the dead at that moment as a mercy to them. (125)

57.34.4. Sunrise and Sunset Are Times When the Unbelievers Prostrate

As for sunrise and sunset, they are the times in which the unbelievers prostrate. Hell comes forward to seize them for doing that. If the dead person were to be buried at that moment, he might see the Fire setting out to seize these groups and he would be overcome with terror when it advances supposing that it is making for him. This is like the one who is walking down a road while someone is behind him who is the object of a search. He sees a person in front of him who is aiming to seek out the one is behind him and is frightened of him by the ugliness of his countenance. This person might imagine that he is the object of this person who is coming ahead. He is not safe from the one who is coming until he actually passes him. Then he knows that he was after someone else. (126)

When the unbeliever prostrates to other-than-God, Hell sets out to seize him because it is jealous that anyone should prostrate to other-than-God. When he raises his head from prostration, it retreats by the command of God Almighty. It is possible that this prostrater might not return to the like of that and might turn in repentance. He is in the abode where repentance is accepted. This is why it does finish its advance to him. (127)

57.34.5. This World Is Not the Abode of Tranquillity For a Creature

As long as man is still alive, one hopes that the unbeliever will become Muslim and one fears that the Muslim will become an unbeliever. It is not the abode of tranquillity for a creature as long as he has not been given good news. Fear is removed with good news since the report is true. The judgement for modesty and humility remains. The fear of the one given good news and his pallor belongs to modesty, and not to fear. (128)

57.35. The Funeral Formal Prayer in the Mosque

57.35.1. The Disagreement about Whether It Is Permitted to Pray for the Dead in the Mosque

Some people permit it and some people dislike it. There is no disagreement about when the dead person is outside of the mosque and the one who is praying over him in the mosque. There is also some dispute about the prayer over the dead in the graves. I say that all of that is permitted. (129)

57.35.2. The One Who Prays Over the Bier Is Interceding

Interpretation of this: The one who performs the formal prayer over the dead is interceding. Wherever he is, he intercedes. God says: "*He is with you wherever you are.*" (57:4) We know that He is with the dead wherever he is and He is with me wherever I am. He is not limited by place. The prayer over the dead is allowed at every place without limitation. There is no place more filthy than the place of Pharaoh. The idolater is impure. In spite of that, Prophets Moses and Aaron came to him. God said to them: "*I am with both of you. I hear and I see.*" (20:46) (130)

57.35.3. Prohibition Against Bringing the Bier Into the Mosque

I used to say that one could say the prayer over the dead when they were in the mosque or elsewhere until I saw the Messenger of God in a dream. He forbade biers to enter the mosque and forbade the prayer over them (there). He forbade it, so after that, I did not pray over the dead in the mosque. The Prophet said: "Whoever has seen me, has seen me. Satan does not take my form." (131)

57.36. The Preconditions for the Funeral Prayer

57.36.1. Dry Ablution (tayammum) for the Funeral Prayer

Most of them say that purity is a precondition for it as is *qibla*. They disagree about performing the dry ablution for it when someone is afraid that he is going to miss it. Some people say that one can perform the dry ablution for it. Some people say that one cannot perform dry ablution for it and that one does not perform the funeral-prayer with dry ablution. My position is that purity is not a precondition. However, I dislike that one turn to God and mention Him without the purity of the divine law. (132)

57.26.2. God Is With the Servant in Every State

Ayisha, may God be pleased with her, said: "The Messenger of God used to remember God at all times." The business should be like that. God is with the servant in every state, especially with the believer. (133)

58 The Prayer Asking for Blessings (*Istikhara*)

58.1. The Messenger of God Taught His Companions the Prayer of Asking for Blessings

t is related that the Messenger of God "used to teach his Companions the prayer asking for blessings as he taught them a chapter of the Quran." It is related that the Prophet used to command that two cycles be performed the formal prayer for it and that thc supplication should take place after the greeting for the two cycles which he performs the formal prayer for its sake. It is recommended that he recite in the first cycle the Opening Chapter and the words of God Almighty: "*And thy Lord creates whatever He wills and chooses. Not for them had there been a choice.*" (28:68) Or *Surah al-kafirun* (Chapter 109). In the second cycle, he should recite the Opening Chapter and The Chapter of Sincerity (Chapter 112). Then he makes supplication with the supplication which has been transmitted about that after the greeting. (134)

58.2. The Prayer Asking for Blessings Is a Very Important Matter

He does an *istikhara* for every important matter which he wants to do and every need which he wishes be fulfilled. Then he begins that matter. If there is good in it for him with God, He will make its means easy for him so that he obtains it. Its end is praiseworthy. If He makes it means difficult for him and he does not obtain it easily, he does not oppose the decree and he knows that had there been good for him in it with God, its means would not have been difficult. He knows that God has chosen for him to leave it and he is not pained by that. The end of leaving it will be praised. (135)

58.3. The Prayer Asking for Blessings and the People of God

The people of God must pray this prayer of asking for blessings at a specific time which they occupy themselves with day or night in every day. When they say the supplication after the offering of salutations (*taslim*) for the two bows (*rakat*), they say in the place in which the business should be named what we will presently mention. (136)

He should say: "O God! If Thou hast that all that I move in for me and for others, and all that others move in for me and for my family, my children and what I own is good for me in my judgment and this world, and my affair, sooner or later, from this hour until the same hour of the next day, then make it easy for me, and decree it for me and gladden me by it. (137)

"If You know that all that I move in for me and for others, and all that others move in for me and for my family, my children and what I own is evil for me and for my family, my children and what I own is good for me in my judgment and this world, and my affair, sooner or later..." as will come in the supplication after this if God Almighty wills. When he does that, he will not make any movement nor will anyone move in a relationship to him except by that which has certain good in it for him in action or non-action. I myself have tested this. He should always do it every single day at a specific time which demands it and not at any other time. (138)

58.4. The Form of the Prayer Asking for Blessings

The form of the supplication of the *istikhara* is: "O God, I ask Thee for good by Thy knowledge, and I ask Thee for power by Thy power. I ask Thee for some of Thy immense overflowing favor. Thou hast power and I do not have power. Thou hast knowledge and I do not have knowledge. Thou hast knowledge of the unseen worlds. O God! If Thou knowest that this matter (and he names the business) is good for me in my judgment, my livelihood, and the end of my business (or he can say, my affair), sooner or later, then decree it for me and make it easy for me and bless me in it. If Thou knowest that this matter (and he names the business) is evil for me in my religion, my livelihood, and the end of my business (or he can say, my affair), sooner or later, then turn it from me from it, and decree good for me wherever it is, and make me pleased with it." (139)

58.5. Explanation of the Prayer Asking for Blessings by the Gnostics

When the gnostic asks his Lord for good in a specific matter or important business, when he says: "O God (*Allahumma*)" he has present in his heart, "I aim for this." Will comes in here because the aim is will. He drops out the *hamza* (ʾ) and it contains with the *ha* of *Allahumma* since it is close in articulation and proximity. That shows you an immense connection. If he were to expand *Allahumma* (O God!), he would say "assure us of good," that is, direct it to use." (140)

He said: "*inni* (indeed I)." The I-ness of the thing is its reality. It indicates himself. He said: "I ask Thee for good by Thy knowledge," he says:

"O God, direct my reality to what Thy knowledge chooses for me of what has good in it for me. Thou knowest what good is right for me and I do not know if this is what I turn to in order to seek after it. Thou hast the power to bring it into existence and I have no power to accomplish that. If there is good for me in doing it and manifesting its source, Thou knowest it and decree it for me, that is, do it for me. If there is good for me in not doing it and not manifesting its source, then turn it from me since I have called it present in my thoughts and imagination. Therefore, it has a sort of existence. That is its conception in my imagination. Do not give it any power over me to manifest its source. This is the meaning of His words: "turn it from me." (141)

Then he says: "Turn me from it," that is, come between me and it. Put between me and it the veil which is between existence and non-existence so that I do not call it present and it is not present with me in source and imagination. I ask You for power by Your power because power is an attribute of bringing into existence. It is a more specific connection than knowledge. He acts by knowledge and brings into existence by power and does not act by it. He put knowledge before power because there may be good in leaving what he seeks to do and bring into existence. (142)

It is as if he were saying: "If there is good for me in obtaining what I seek to obtain, then I ask Thee for power by Thy power, that is, give me the power to obtain it." If he is one of those who say that the action is ascribed to the servant like the Mutazilites and the relationship is in his words: "By your power," (that is, by the power which Thou hast created in Thy servants.) If he is one of those who say that the action is not ascribed to the servant, his words: ". . . by Thy power" means the power of God which is His attribute, and it is related to Him by the principle of the attribute, not by the principle of creation. (143)

He says: "Thou hast power and I do not have power." This statement occurs from both groups. That is to say: "Thou hast the power to create for me the power to do it if Thou knowest that there is good for me in it. He intends to give information about the reality of negating the power of the servant. He says: "Thou hast the power to bring it into existence and let me obtain what I seek. I do not have any power with which to obtain it "since he knows that power in time cannot bring into being." It does not exceed its place. (144)

Then he says: "Make me pleased with it," that is, give me joy and happiness by obtaining it or not obtaining it for the sake of what Thou choosest for me in what Thou already knowest. Decree good for me wherever it is, Thou hast more knowledge of the places, times and states in which there is good for me rather than others. Thou hast knowledge of the unseen worlds. Thou hast what is hidden from us about that. I do not know it. (145)

Then it is to let you know that knowledge of the affair does not include seeing it. This indicates that the relationship of your seeing things is not the relationship of your knowledge of them. The relationship of knowledge is connected to the visible world and the unseen. Every thing which is seen is known in whatever is visible of it. Not everything which is known is seen. It is not related at all in the divine law that God sees the Unseen worlds. It is related that He 'knows' the Unseen worlds. This is why He has described Himself with vision, saying: "*Does he not know that God sees*" (96:14)? He described Himself with sight and knowledge. He made the relationships distinct and distinguished them from each other so that he knows what is between them. (146)

(Since it is not conceivable that there be anything unseen in respect of God, we know that the unseen is a relative matter since it is hidden from us. When he says: "Thy art the Knower of the unseen worlds," it is as if he were saying: "What is hidden from us." It is like that in the visible world and the unseen. It is what is hidden from us and what we do not see while He sees it. Seeing the thing does not necessitate knowledge of its definition and reality. Knowledge of the thing necessitates knowledge of its definition and reality whether it is non-existent or existent. If not, one does not know it. 147)

All things are seen by God in the state of their non-existence. If that had not been the case, He would not have singled out some of them to come into existence rather than others. Pure non-existence is that in which there are no source-forms. There is no distinction of seeing in it as opposed to the non-existence of possibles. Knowledge is to distinguish things from each other. Separating things from each other is designated as seeing them and specifying them, that is, he sees them with his eye. If they are described as non-existent, they are not non-existent for God, The Real, in respect to His knowledge of them. (148)

This is like the man who is an inventor. He imagines things in the form in which he wants to invent them and then he brings that forth and manifests its source. So the thing is described by particular existence while, when it was non-existent, it was described by existence in respect of mental existence in respect to us and the existence of knowledge in respect to God. Things are therefore manifested in reality from one existence to another existence, from the existence of knowledge to specific existence. What is impossible is the pure non-existence which does not have distinct sources in it. (149)

This is the meaning of some of what the supplication of the *istikhara* contains. When he says: "Make it easy for me," he is referring to the means which are the signs and proofs of obtaining the goal. (150)

59 Regarding What Is Connected to the Formal Prayer

59.1. Introduction

59.1.1. The Ascription of the Formal Prayer to God

Establishing the formal prayer is manifesting its structure in its most complete form. Its form varies according to the one to whom it is ascribed. When it is ascribed to God, it has a different form than when it is related to other-than-God: men, jinn or other creatures. God forms it with a perfect formation. This is why He said: "*My Mercy encompasses everything*" (33:42) since the prayer is ascribed to Him when He said: "*He is the One who performs the formal prayer over you*" (33:43) as His Mercy to His servants. We will discuss that. (151)

59.1.2. The Ascription of Formal Prayer to Angels and Others

The formal prayer is also ascribed to the angel. He brings it forth and performs it completely, that is, manifests it and he only manifests a complete prayer. The prayer of the angel is only complete in formation and form. It is like that with every prayer which is related to the inanimates and plants and animals except for the jinn and men. Their prayer might be complete or it might not be complete. First we will discuss the prayer of God. (152)

59.2. The Formal Prayer of God and the Angels

God Almighty says: "*He it is Who gives blessings to you and His angels*" (33:43) in general. He said: "*Truly God and His angels give blessings to the Prophet*" (33:56) in particular with a particular prayer. The pronoun in "they pray" joins God and the angels. The angels cannot be attached to God's prayer on His servant. They do not exceed their rank. In this prayer, God descends to the prayer of the angels for the sake of the plural pronoun. God's prayer on the Prophet is in the station of the prayer of the angels on the Prophet. (153)

59.2.1. The Distinction of the Prophet Having Their Prayer for Him

This is different from His words, "*He it is Who gives blessings to you.*" (33:43) Here He only brought the angels after that which we have just mentioned. He separated His prayer on us and the prayer of the angels when He said: "over you." Here He only brought the angels after that which we have just mentioned. He separated His prayer on us and the prayer of the angels when He said: "over you." Then He said: "to bring you out." He used the singular with bringing out and He did not use the plural pronoun which joins God and the angels in the prayer on the believers as He did when He said: "they pray on the Prophet." The Prophet is distinct from other men by a rank which none but him has been given, that is, that which we have mentioned to you. (154)

So it contains all of us, and the Prophet is among us when He says: "*He it is Who gives blessings to you.*" (33:43) He put himself in the singular in that. Then He said: "and His angels." He put the angels in the singular in the prayer over the servants. One of the servants is the Prophet. Therefore, all of creation has the unity of the prayer from God and the unity of the prayer from the angels. He singled out the Prophet alone in what He told us about him when He used the plural in an all-encompassing prayer which is shared by God and the angels. He said: "*God and His angels give blessings to the Prophet*" (33:56). It is well-known that the formal prayer performed with a group is not the formal prayer performed by the one who is by himself. These two states are distinct from each other. The Prophet won this prayer. (155)

Then He commanded us to supplicate on him, in this all-encompassing formal prayer. That is when we say the supplicate on him, God is our tongue as has come in a Tradition. Then the supplication which we are commanded to do is valid. The supplication of the angels is like that in this station which joins them and God in the supplication. The supplication of the angels is like that in this station which joins them and God in the supplication on the Prophet. He is their articulation in that supplication. (156)

The honor of the Prophet over all mankind in this rank is confirmed. It is an unquestionable honor which exists. If anyone is equal to him, we have no recognition of that fact. That is a possible honor. He specified that he has excellence which the one who is not singled out does not possess. Even if he performed the formal prayer on him like this in the same way and we do not have any information about it, his excellence is still established in every case. (157)

After God Almighty said: "He is the One who performs the formal prayer on you," He said: "O you who believe." He did not say whether it is belief in existence or unity. It could be in existence which is more general since it is more universal in mercy. He said to them, "Remember God often (in every state) and glorify Him" (that is, supplicate to Him. Ibn Umar said: "Had I been a glorifier, I would have completed it." He meant that he would have performed the formal prayer, the full prayer (not the short prayer) in the morning and the evening." He joined all of the five prayers in this sign. ""*So glory be to God at the time of the evening hour and at the time when it comes to be in the morning. To HIm be the Praise in the heavens and the earth and in the evening and at the time of noon.*" (30:17-18) (158)

As for the determination of words, when He said this, and commanded us to remember and to perform the formal prayer, He said: "*He is the One who blesses you.*" (33:43) He informed us that He performs the formal prayer over us. Two things are understood from this: one is that He performs the formal prayer over us and therefore, we must remember and praise Him. So we pray to Him morning and evening. That is the food of the intellects and the spirits as the food of the body in these moments is in His words: "*They will have their provision in them in the early morning at dawn and evening.*" (19:62) He provides for every creature according to what its reality demands. The food of the spirits lies in glorification. They are told, "Glorify Him," that is, pray to Him at these moments and remember Him in every state. He limited glorification, but He did not limit invocation/remembrance to any time. Therefore we know that glorification is a particular invocation which is connected to these moments. (159)

The other thing is that when you perform the formal prayer and remember God, He performs the formal prayer on you. Our prayer and remembrance of Him between the two formal prayers is from God Almighty. He performs the formal prayer on us. We pray to Him and He performs the formal prayer on us. From His first prayer on us, we pray to Him. From His second prayer on us comes our happiness, for we pluck the fruit of our prayer to Him and our remembrance. (160)

Then He says that "His angels" also pray over you with what is prescribed for them in that. That is His words: "Those who carry the Throne and all those around it who glorify the praises of their Lord and believe in Him and ask for forgiveness for those who have believed say: Our Lord! Thou hast encompassed everything in mercy and in knowledge. So forgive those who have repented and have followed Thy way and guard them from the punishment of hellfire. "*Our Lord! And cause them to enter the Gardens of Eden which Thou hast promised them, those who were in accord with morality, among their fathers and their wives and their offspring. Truly Thou, Thou art The Almighty, The Wise. And guard them from the evil deeds. And whomever Thou hast guarded from the evil deeds on that Day, surely Thou hast had mercy on him. And that is the winning the sublime triumph!*" (40:7-9) All of that are the words of the angels. The prayer of the angels over us is like our prayer over the dead. It is the same for the one who has intelligence. (161)

Then He says: "to bring them out" with the *lam* ("to") of causation "from the darkness to the light." It begins from Him, and is a favor, and it is because of the supplication of the angels. It is that which we have mentioned. This is why He said: "and the angels." It is their words, "Shield them from evil actions." Evil actions are darkness. He brings some of them out of the darkness of ignorance to the light of knowledge, from the darkness of opposition to the light of harmony, from the darkness of misguidance to the light of guidance, from the darkness of idolatry to the light of unity, from the darkness of the veil to the light of Self-disclosure, and from the darkness of wretchedness and exhaustion to the light of felicity and rest. (162)

Then He says: "He is Merciful to the believers," that is, He shows mercy to the those who affirm since they believed in His existence which is more general than belief in Unity. After that, belief in divine existence ascends in degrees. All in which belief is obligatory is arranged in ranks. Then He said: *"Their greeting, on the day when they shall meet Him will be 'Peace!'"* (33:44) When the meeting takes place, he will be given the good news of peace and safety. He will never be wretched after that meeting. God has people who meet Him in the life of this world and they are given the good news of peace. Then there is the one who meets He when he dies. Then there is the one who meets Him when he rises from the grave. Then there is the one who meets Him in the divisions of the places of the Rising, and that is most of them. Some of them will meet Him after they have entered the Fire and been punished in it. When the meeting occurs, God will greet him with "Peace!" They will not be wretched after that meeting. This is why He stipulated peace in the meeting without specifying any particular time since the ranks vary in meeting Him. The last to meet Him will be the one who simply believes that He exists. He said: "the believers" without limiting it. Therefore we do not limit it. (163)

He says: "He has prepared a generous wage for them." Every wage is according to the amount of belief. The least of them is the reward of the one who believes in the existence of God as God. This ascends in degrees to the one who has the greatest belief. God's prayer is His mercy to His creation. This is why He says: *"He is merciful to the believers,"* and He says: *"The Merciful turned His attention to the Throne."* (20:5). The Throne is what encircles all of his Kingdom which exists. *"My mercy encompasses everything."* (7:156) His Throne encompasses everything as well as the Fire and whatever is in it. Mercy flows in every existent thing. The prayer of God is upon every existent thing. (164)

Creation consists of imaginary forms which God moves and from which God speaks. They are directed and the rules of power flow in them. They are effaced in the very source of their archetypes and they are non-existent in the state of their existence. Those ones are the silent-speaking, and the dead-alive, like the life of the martyrs.

The intellect witnesses what the eye does not see. (165)

Establishing the divine prayer is universal mercy to His creatures. It itself is created. God Almighty says: *"He gave everything its creation"* (20:50). Mercy is something. He created and made universal. It is like that with the prayer of the angels. It is complete in form. They make supplication for those who turn in repentance as we have mentioned. They also said: *"And guard them from the evil deeds."* (40:9) That was also general. Every matter is included in the prayer of the angels: for the disobedient and obedient in all types of acts of obedience and rebellion. (166)

59.3. The Prayer of People and Jinn

As for the prayer of men and *jinn*, it is the word of God Almighty: *"Those who perform the formal prayer."* (5:55). Establishing the good news of it is that it is related to them with the meaning of mercy as it is related to the angels, and with the meaning of supplication, mercy and completing the recitation of "God is Greater," standing, bowing, prostration and sitting as is related in a Tradition. (167)

Whoever completes its bowing and prostration and what is prescribed in it, even if he is in a group which demands the group prayer and following the leader, has completed its form. If he lacks something of it, it is according to what he lacks of it. God will not accept it incomplete. He adds some prayers to others. If there are a hundred prayers and there is something lacking in them, some of them will complete the others and they will come to God complete. Therefore, for instance, a hundred prayers might become eighty prayers, or fifty, or ten, or more or less than that. That is what the prayer of *jinn* and men is like. (168)

59.4. The Prayer of the Higher and the Lower World and What Is Between Them

God Almighty says: "Do you not see that to God prostrates whoever is in the heavens and whoever is in the earth and the birds spreading out their wings. Each (that is, of these)—He knows its prayer [and the pronoun can refer to God in His words: "His prayer," that is, God's prayer on it by existence itself and His mercy to it in that (24:41). (169)

The pronoun in "and its glorification," can refer to His glorification in all, that is, whatever is used to glorify your Lord is His prayer. God has described Himself with the prayer and He has not described Himself with glorification. This general sign covers the higher and lower worlds and whatever is between them. (170)

59.5. Some of the Secrets of Gnosis of God and Other Ranks

59.5.1. The Setting Up of Secondary Means and Their Mutual Dependence

Part of the jealousy of God is that any creature have a favor another creature. The favor belongs to God. He did not create any creature but that He gave a creature power over it by a certain aspect. If one creature wants to pride himself over another creature by what comes from that creature to him, he bows his head, submitting to what comes to him from that other creature. That does not occur to the gnostics, like the Prophets and the Messengers and the perfect among those with knowledge of God, because they recognize the realities of matters and that which God has connected to the world and what His majesty deserves which should be His alone and in which He has no partner. God set up means and assigned matters to one another. (171)

59.5.2. The Prophet's Acknowledgement of the Help of the Helpers

The Prophet said to the Helpers when he mentioned that God had guided them to Him, "If you like, you could say, 'We found you an outcast and gave you shelter, weak and we helped you.'" He mentioned what was from them in respect to Him and that God had the power to help him without any cause. However, he does what wisdom demands by what he is molded on since God created him in His form. He said to His Messenger: "*And invoke blessings for them; truly thy supplicating will bring a sense of rest to them.*" (9:103). (172)

59.5.3. God Is the One Who Blesses His Servants with All That They Possess

This is glory, power, and a favor which is exposed to the risk of fault and sickness. God protected His Prophet from that. He placed a remedy opposite this fault as it is also a remedy for what has a remedy. God Almighty says: "*O those who have believed! Give your blessings to him and blessings of peace and invoke peace for him.*" (33:56) If we pride ourselves with the prayer on him by way of favor, we find that he performed the formal prayer on us when he was commanded to do that. If it is conceivable in logical possibility that he does a favor by his prayer on us, our prayer on him prevents him from remembering this, although he is the greatest master. God—glory be to Him!—did not leave him any favor to bestow on His creation since He is the One who bestows blessing and favor on His servants by all they have and all that comes from them in fulfilling the contracts of God. (173)

So occupy yourself with what I have pointed out to you. It is one of the secrets of gnosis of God and recognition of the ranks of what is other-than-God if you possess intelligence. (174)

59.6. Some of the Secrets of Declaration to Perform the Formal Prayer (*Iqama*)

59.6.1. The Connection of the Declaration to Perform the Formal Prayer (Iqama) to Time and Place

Know that God has connected the formal prayer to certain times. These are the moments in which the formal prayers are performed. God Almighty says: "*Truly the formal prayer has been —for the ones who believe— a timed prescription.*" (4:103) He connected it to places, and these are the mosques. God Almighty said: "*The Light is lit in houses God gave permission to be lifted up* [that is, God has commanded to be raised up so as to distinguish the houses related to God from the houses related to creatures] *and that His Name be remembered in it* [with the call to and declaration to perform the formal prayer, recitation, invocation, and exhortation]." (24:36-37) (175)

Glorifying (praying to) Him in them (that is, since God has commanded them to pray in them) in the mornings and evening are men (He did not mention women because 'men' includes women. Eve is a part of Adam. He was content to mention men without women as a mark of honor to men and to point out that women are connected to men. Here He called women men since they are not denied the rank of perfection. They can be perfect just as men can be perfect. It is established in tradition that Maryam and Asiya, the wife of Pharaoh, were perfect. "who are not distracted by trade or selling." (176)

59.6.2. Men Whom Neither Trade Nor Selling Distracts

Trade is used for both buying and selling. Selling is only selling. He praised them for trade, which is buying and selling in anything which God has commanded trade. God Almighty says: "*Will I point you to a transaction that will rescue you from a painful punishment? You believe in God and His Messenger and struggle in the way of God with your wealth and your lives. That is better for you if you would know.* " (61:10-11) (177)

He said about selling: "*Truly God has bought from the ones who believe themselves and their properties for the Garden is theirs!*" (9:111) That is the price. He made it the price in the Tradition about the two adversaries, the wronger and the wronged. When God puts things right between His creatures on the Day of Rising, God will order the wronged person to lift his head. He will look at *Illiyun* and such beauty that he will be dazzled by it. He will say, "O Lord! What Prophet is this for? What martyr is this for?" God Almighty will say, "It is for the one who gives Me the price." He will say, "And who possesses the price of this?" He says: "You do—when you forgive this brother of yours." He will say, "Lord, I have forgiven him." He will say, "Take your brother by the hand and enter the Garden." When the Messenger of God related this Tradition, he would recite: "*So be Godfearing of God and make things right among you,*" (8:1), adding: "*God will put things right among you. . .*" on the Day of Rising. (178)

59.6.3. The Believer Is Praised in the Quran for Trade and Selling

The believer is praised in the Quran for trade and selling what he has the power to sell. God did not explicitly state that he buys. Trade is barter and taking a price. Selling is selling what he owns. Buying is purchasing what you do not have. In the Quran, He has only described as buying in the Quran the one to whose wrong action God has testified: "*Those are they who bought fallacy for guidance and punishment for forgiveness.*" (2:175) He said: "*Truly those who exchange the compact of God and their sworn oaths for a little price.*" (3:77) (179)

The reason that God has not described the believer as buying is that God created him and gave him possession of all that God had created in His earth which is his dwelling-place and situation. He said: "*It is He Who created for you all that is in and on the earth.*" (2:29) All that is on the earth is his property, so there is nothing for him to buy. He denied him access to misguidance which is an attribute of non-existence. God did not command us to follow it. He brought us out of non-existence to existence, so we do not seek what will bring us out of it. This is exactly because He created us to worship Him. If we purchase misguidance with guidance, then we have chosen non-existence over existence, and the false over the truth for which He created us. Therefore He did not describe the believer as buying. (180)

59.6.3. The Clever Believer Sells the Permitted for the Formal

That to which God has given him possession is what is allowed for him and what is obligatory for him. He does not sell or dispense of the obligatory things. He can sell the class of permitted things for obligatory ones. This is why he can sell that which he is permitted to sell. The clever and intelligent believer looks at his moment and sees that it has the principle of something which is allowed. He says: "I have no profit in this property. This world is the abode of trade. Therefore we will sell this permitted thing for an obligatory thing. That is better for me and then I will not lose my moment." (181)

He is relaxing with his brothers and says: "O Lord! I want to sell this permitted thing for something obligatory!" God says to him: "That is up to you." Therefore he sells the relaxation which he has for what that place accords in the way of beauty and excellence which indicates God. He reflects about the beauty of God's creation, its perfection and excellence. His joy is more complete and his heart has greater happiness. He is not in the permitted at all since he had sold it for this obligatory thing. God took selling into consideration. He did not consider buying at all in respect of the believer. The believer owns the robe of permission and the robe of obligation. He possesses both of them. Removing it is called selling, and putting on the garment of the obligatory is not called buying. He owns it, its mount, and its baggage. Man does not purchase what he already owns. (182)

God denied misguidance to His creation. Then those who preferred misguidance to guidance purchased misguidance. They did not own it by the guidance which God had put in their possession. *"Their trade was not to be bettered nor had they been ones who were truly guided"* (2:16) in that purchase because God has not prescribed buying for His servants. (183)

59.6.4. Those Whom Nothing Distracts from God

Then God says: *"Men whom . . . . trade nor trading diverts from the remembrance of God"* (24:37) when they hear the caller to the formal prayer in this House calling to God, He is the Doorman. He says: "Come to the formal prayer," and they turn towards intimate conversation with their Lord. He gives them a Self-disclosure at the front of His house, which is the *qibla,* for "God is in the *qibla* of the servant." (184)

The people of God then abandon their selling and trade in this world for this remembrance when they hear it. "And to perform the prayer," that is, complete its structure when they do so by excellently following the leader, and excellent bowing and prostration, and what it contains of the 'remembrance of God' which is the greatest thing in it as God Almighty informs us. He says: *"Truly the formal prayer prohibits depravity and that which was immoral"* (29:45) because of the recitation of "God is Greater" after which everything but the formal prayer is forbidden . It forbids him to act in anything except the formal prayer for as long as he is in the formal prayer. That recitation of "God is Greater" stops him from indecency and wrongdoing. He abandons them. Therefore, he has the reward of the one who performs the command of God and obeys Him, and the reward of the one who desists from the things which God has forbidden in the formal prayer itself, even if he did not intend to do them. (185)

59.6.5. The Prayer Precludes Indecency and the Wrongdoing

See how noble the formal prayer is! See what this wondrous question gives us! That is that when man is acting in something obligatory, he has the reward of the one who acts in the obligatory. His occupation with that obligatory things includes lack of occupation with that which he is forbidden to do in the way of indecency and wrongdoing. Therefore, he has the reward of the one who intends to not do something indecent or wrongful. Most people abandon what they have in this respect due to their lack of presence when they first prepare. Had it not been that the business was like that, there would not have been any benefit when He says: "The formal prayer precludes indecency and wrongdoing." (186)

The formal prayer is the servant's action. By his formal prayer, he is one of those forbidden indecency and wrongdoing, even if he does not speak. He has the reward of two acts of worship: he has the reward of the prayer which is worship, and the reward of forbidding indecency which is also worship. Very few of our companions put their mind to observing these things in their acts of worship in the divine recognition which has come on the tongue of the lawgiver in the Book and the *Sunna*. (187)

59.6.6. "The Remembrance of God (dhikr) Is Greater"

Then He says: "*The remembrance of God is Greater*" (29:45), that is, in it. It is the greatest of its actions. The formal prayer contains both words and actions. He said that the remembrance of God in the formal prayer is the greatest of the states of the formal prayer. Not all of the words of the prayer are remembrance. There is also supplication. God made a distinction between remembrance and supplication. He said: "Whoever is distracted by My remembrance from asking Me. . ." That is supplication. The remembrance here is not remembrance which is outside of the formal prayer so that it would predominate the prayer. It is the remembrance which is the prayer. This comes from the connection of the formal prayer to the place and state. (188)

59.6.7. The One Who Commands Another to Piety and Forgets Himself

One of the states of establishing the formal prayer is the one who commands others to consciousness of God while he forgets himself. God rebuked the one who is like this and categorizes him as someone who has no intellect. He said: "*You command humanity to virtuous conduct and you yourselves forget while you recount the Book? Will you not then be reasonable?*" (2:44) Goodness (*birr*) is one of the states of the formal prayer. The Messenger of God said: "The formal prayer establishes piety and tranquillity." (189)

Then He commanded the one who is like this to "seek help with steadfastness and the formal prayer," that is, with steadfastness in the formal prayer. He devotes himself entirely to it. God says: "*Command thy people to the formal prayer and persevere in it.*" (20:132) (190)

He says: "while you recite the Book." In it, you will find His words: "*It is most troublesome, repugnant to God.*" After He says: " *That you say what you accomplish not.*" (61:3). This is the state of the one who commands others to obedience while he forgets himself. "Don't you understand?" Don't you have intellects with which to see how ugly that which you have is? (191)

59.6.8. Humility to God Only Comes from divine Self--disclosure (tajalli)

Then He mentioned humility with the formal prayer and said: "*And truly it is arduous but for the ones who are humble.*" (2:45) Humility to God comes only from divine Self-disclosure. The formal prayer is conversation. There must be a Self-disclosure if you see that he is humble. If he is not humble in his formal prayer, he has not performed the formal prayer. The Messenger of God considered divine Self-disclosure a reason to be a for the existence of humility in the heart, especially in the formal prayer. The Self-disclosure of most people is either by presence—and that is for certain individuals—or by calling present in the imagination. That is the case with most of the elite. God is in the *qibla* of the one who performs the formal prayer. (192)

As for the humility of the great who are connected to the Highest Assembly, their humility comes from a real Self-disclosure. "They are constant in their formal prayer," even if they eat, drink, have intercourse, or trade. When they are in a state like this, God has commanded them to seek help by the formal prayer and steadfastness in it. The one who performs the formal prayer consigns with his Lord. When the servant is constantly with his Lord in the place of conversation, he must have modesty in the presence of God. He cannot command anyone to dutifulness while he forgets himself. He must begin with himself. (193)

59.6.9. Piety (birr) is Beauty (ihsan) and Good

Piety is doing the best (*ihsan*) and doing good. Part of that is that if he needs a morsel, he eats it. If he sees someone else who needs it and their need is on the same level, he gives that to the other person and forgets himself. His Lord said to him, "Begin with yourself." He prescribed that for him even in supplication. When he makes supplication to God on someone's behalf. it is better for him to begin with himself. (194)

The food of the spirits is acts of obedience. This heedless person with little modesty before God stands and commands someone else to dutifulness while he himself is acting shamelessly and forgetting himself. He does not command himself to do that. He is like the person who feeds someone else while he leaves himself although he is in utter need of that food. His own self is more of an obligation for him than the other one. I will make the reason for that clear to you, if God Almighty wills. (195)

59.7. Good Actions Are Charity for the Soul

That is because all acts of good are charity for the souls, no matter what good it is—sensory or spiritual. The believer must act in that as his Lord has set down, not according to his own passion. Then he has fallen from that sublime degree to something below it among the common believers. If he is one of the gnostics, then he is a rebel. (196)

59.7.1. The First One in Need of Charity Is the Soul of the Servant

When man gives his charity, the first one to receive it should be himself before every other self in need. He gives charity to the needy. If he passes by the first one in need, that comes from his passion, and is not for God. God told him, "Begin with yourself." That is the first to receive it among the people of need. In *ihsan*, it is prescribed for him to begin with the nearest neighbor. If he then prefers the more distant neighbor to the nearer while they are equal in need, then he has followed his passion and he has not stopped at the limits prescribed by his Lord. This applies to all the actions of piety and goodness. The cause of that is heedlessness of God Almighty. The servant is commanded to have the attribute which puts him present with God. That is the formal prayer. (197)

59.8. The Effect of the Formal Prayer on the State

59.8.1. Affliction Does Not Enter into Thankfulness Nor Steadfastness into Blessing

Part of the effect of the formal prayer on the state is found in the words of God to the believers: "*So remember Me and I will remember you. And give thanks to Me and be not ungrateful!*" (2:152). He commanded them to practice remembrance and thankfulness. He also commanded them to seek help in that with steadfastness and the formal prayer. He informed them that God is with those who are steadfast in it and in every hardship with which God is pleased to charge His servants. This is because steadfastness is one of the stations whose preconditions are hardships, disliked things, and afflictions, both sensory and spiritual. He put steadfastness here in that which we have just mentioned. It balances His words, "Be thankful to Me and do not be ungrateful to Me." Affliction does not enter into thankfulness nor steadfastness into blessing as might be thought by someone who possesses no recognition of the realities of things. (198)

59.8.2. Steadfastness in the Formal Prayer Produces Remembrance of God (dhikr) and Thankfulness

Here is the formal prayer and steadfastness in it entails constancy, firmness, and devoting the self to it. It has an effect in the form of remembrance and thankfulness. Steadfastness here is His words: "*And command thy people to the formal prayer and to maintain patience in it.*" (20:132) That is why He mentioned steadfastness with the formal prayer. As steadfastness in remembrance, thankfulness in remembrance, and thankfulness have an effect, so steadfastness produces the same effect in the formal prayer. The formal prayer, inasmuch as there is steadfastness in it, produces remembrance and thankfulness inasmuch as it is the formal prayer. (199)

That is because the prayer is conversation between God and His servant. When the servant speaks to His Lord, it is more fitting that he speak to Him with His words which He has stipulated be used to consign with Him. That is the recitation of the Quran in the states of the formal prayer in standing (and it is the recitation of the Opening Chapter and what is easy of His words with it), bowing (and it is His words: "*Blessed be the Name of thy Lord Possessor of The Majesty and The Splendor.*" (55:78) in his bowing since he mentions his Lord in his formal prayer with His words which were sent down), and in prostration (when he says: "Glory be to my Lord the Most High," since His words came down: "*Glorify the Name of thy Lord, The Lofty.*" (87:1) The Messenger of God said: "Put it in your prostration." (200)

59.8.3. The Opening Chapter Combines Remembrance and Thankfulness

God commands us to remember Him and to thank Him. The Opening Chapter combines both remembrance and thankfulness. That is what the one who performs the formal prayer recites when he is standing. The thankfulness in it is His words: "Praise be to God, the Lord of the worlds." That is the same as remembrance and thankfulness with all that he mentions in it and in the entire prayer. His remembrance of God and thankfulness in the prayer is greater and more excellent than His remembrance and thankfulness outside the prayer. The prayer is the best place of worship. This prayer produces this excellence in remembrance. It comes back to the one who remembers. (201)

59.8.4. The Remembrance Which Comes in the Quran

Whoever wants to remember God Almighty and to thank Him both verbally and through action should perform the formal prayer and remember Him with every remembrance which has been sent down in the Quran, and not in anything else. By that, he intends the remembrance and supplication which is in the Quran so that it removes any liability from himself. Whoever remembers Him with His own words removes any liability from himself in what is related to God in that remembrance. He is reciting His words in his remembrance. (202)

He utters whatever glorifications are in the Quran, whatever praises are in the Quran, and whatever supplications are in the Quran. There is harmony between the remembrance of the servant by the Quran since it is the word of God and God's remembrance of him when He says: "I will remember you." God remembers the one who remembers Him. His remembrance is His words and therefore there is a correspondence between the two remembrances. When he remembers Him with a remembrance which he invents, that correspondence between the words of God when He remembers the servant and the remembrance of the servant does not exist. Here the servant does not remember him by what has come in the Quran and does not intend to do that. Even if he happens to use just the same expression, that was not his intention. (203)

Then this remembrance by the Quran comes in the formal prayer, and so it is better in the sight of God to connect it to the mandatory forms of remembrance. The servant is commanded to recite the Opening Chapter in the formal prayer. This is why it is considered obligatory by those scholars who make it obligatory. Similarly, the servant is commanded to glorify in bowing and prostration with what has been sent down in the Quran. The Prophet said: "Put it in your prostration." He commanded. (204)

The one who performs the formal prayer is commanded to glorify God three times or more in his bowing as God has commanded him to do three times or more in his prostration. That is the least amount, and it is possible that the command makes it obligatory. That is why one of the scholars, Ishaq ibn Ibrahim ibn Rahawayh, thought that it was obligatory and that the formal prayer of the person who did not glorify three times in his bowing and prostration was not allowable. (205)

59.8.5. Seeking Help in the Remembrance of God (dhikr) and Thankfulness by the Formal Prayer and Steadfastness

God Almighty says: "*And pray for help with patience and formal prayer. And truly it is arduous but for the ones who are humble.*" (2:45) If it had not been that God taught him that the formal prayer was a specific duty for the servant, He would not have commanded him to do it. He put the formal prayer in the same position as Himself. God says to the servant: "We ask you for help," that is, in Your worship. He made the servant seek help by his Lord and commanded him to seek help in his remembrance and thankfulness by the prayer. Therefore He put the formal prayer in the same position as Himself in helping the servant in remembrance and thankfulness. (206)

59.8.6. The One Begins the Formal Prayer Is Enmeshed with The Real

Friend of God! The state, attribute, movement and action which God has sent down about the greatest of things is enough for you! It is the remembrance of God which is put in the same position as Himself? It is as if whoever enters the prayer is enmeshed with The Real. The Real is Light, and this is why He said that the prayer is light. He put it in the same position as Himself. The Prophet said: "The coolness of my eye is in the formal prayer." It is that by which it rejoices in vision and contemplation. The one who performs the formal prayer is enmeshed with The Real in the formal prayer. He sees Him and consigns with Him. Therefore the prayer combines these three states. (207)

It is like that when He says in this sign: "*And give thanks to Me.*" (2:152) You can say: "I thanked Him." Or "I was thankful to Him." "I thanked Him" states that He Himself is thanked. "I was thankful to Him" has two aspects. One is the same as "I thanked Him" and the other is that thankfulness is for His sake. When thankfulness is for His sake, God says: "Thank the one whom I entrusted with blessing among My servants for My sake." Thanking him for the cause is the same as thanking him for God. He thanks him because of His command. Here the one with the blessing represents his Lord. Obeying the representative is obeying the one who appointed him. "*Whoever obeys the Messenger has surely obeyed God.*" (4:80) This is why God says: "Be thankful to Me," and not "thank Me." That covers both states. (208)

In both cases He says: "Seek help in that by steadfastness and the formal prayer" as He commanded help in that which necessitates thankfulness. That is acting well with blessings. He says: "Help one another to dutifulness (which is acting well with blessings) and fearful awareness." Make that a protection. It is in harmony with the formal prayer. The formal prayer is protection from the indecency and wrongdoing as long as the servant is enmeshed in it. God has called Himself the Protector, and the formal prayer is protection. The servant is enmeshed with the formal prayer and it is protection from that which we mentioned. God is the Protector! (209)

See how noble the state of the formal prayer is for the one who looks and can perceive! The happy one is the one who applies himself to it, perseveres in it and is constant in it. Part of its honor is that God only attached the threat to the one who neglects it, and not to the one who is forgetful in it. He said: "*So woe to ones who formally pray, ones who are inattentive to their formal prayers.*" (107:4-5) He did not say, "in their formal prayers." The servant in his formal prayer is between conversation and witnessing. He may neglect his conversation by his absorption in his witnessing, and he may neglect his witnessing by his absorption in his conversation about His words which he uses to consign with Him. (210)

59.8.7. Doubt in the Formal Prayer Which Is Mended by the Prostration of Forgetfulness

The words of God tell about the attributes of disconnection and praise which He must have, and they provide information about what is connected to phenomenal beings in the way of rules, tales, stories, promise and threat. Someone's mind might wander about thinking of phenomenal beings since the words indicate them when he is commanded to reflect on his recitation. He might abandon himself to that phenomenal being since he sees it and then his mind might move from phenomenal being might from being something mentioned in the Quran to the being itself. It is no longer that which is mentioned in the Quran according to the limits in which He informed him about it. (211)

When that happens, this is called doubt for him in his formal prayer and he does not know how much he has performed the formal prayer. Then he must prostrate the two prostrations of forgetfulness in order to spite Satan and to mend the lack by them and add preponderance by praying them. His formal prayer is multiplied and his reward is multiplied. That occurs both in the obligatory and the supererogatory prayer. God has not threatened the one who forgets in his formal prayer with something disliked. Whoever has taken note of that which we have mentioned and alluded to perceives the bounty and mercy of God to His servants. People are heedless about that. The only ones who recognize the nobility of acts of worship are "the servants of God over whom Satan has neither power nor proof." May God place us and you and those who are steadfast, pray, outstrip and do not pray for His favor, but yet are granted favor. (212)

59.9. The Different Types of the Formal Prayer and the Prayer for the Prophet

59.9.1. The Different Types of Formal Prayer and the Different States of the One Who Prays

The principle of the supplication on the Prophet varies according to the different states of the one who utters it since the one who utters the formal prayer is a creature and performs the formal prayer for him. It varies according to the difference of the object of the prayer when the One who performs the formal prayer is God Almighty. As for the first, it is well-known that man is a place of change and that his states vary. Thus his formal prayer varies with the difference of his states. We have already discussed the different states of those who pray in this chapter, like the formal prayer of the sick person and the formal prayer of the person in fear. We have also discussed the differences of the state of the one who performs the formal prayer for the sake of that: like the eclipse ritual prayer and the rain ritual prayer. (213)

59.9.2. The Difference According to the Object of the Formal Prayer

As for its difference according to the object of the formal prayer, it is like God's prayer on His servants. God Almighty says: "*Truly God and His angels give blessings to the Prophet. O those who have believed! Give your blessings to him and blessings of peace and invoke peace for him.*" (33:56) The believers asked the Messenger of God how to perform the formal prayer that God had commanded them to pray on him. The Messenger of God said: "Say, 'O God, bless Muhammad and the family of Muhammad as Thou hast blessed Abraham and the family of Prophet Abraham,'" that is, like Thy prayer on Abraham and the family of Abraham. This shows you that the divine prayer varies according to the different states of those who are the object of the prayer and their stations with God. (214)

59.9.3. The Excellence of Abraham

This Tradition shows the excellence of Abraham over the Messenger of God because he wanted the prayer on him to be like that of Abraham. Know that God commanded us to bless the Messenger of God, but He did not command us to bless his family in the Quran. The Messenger of God taught us to bless him with the prayer on the family. The Prophet did not seek the same prayer as that on Abraham (in respect to them as individuals. divine concern for the Messenger of God is more complete since he was given matters no Prophet before him was given—not Abraham or anyone else. That comes from the supplication of God Almighty on him. How then can he seek the prayer from God on him like His prayer on Abraham in respect to him himself? God willing, I will clarify what is meant by that. (215)

59.9.4. The Family of Muhammad: Constant Prophethood and Severed Prophethood

This is because the supplication for a person is made on his behalf in respect of himself and in respect of what is related to other than him. The supplication in respect of what is related to other than him is the general supplication for the group. The group does not have the same principle as the single individual. (216)

Know that in Arabic, the family of a man are his elite who are near to him. The elite of the Prophets and their family are the the righteous, the people with knowledge of God, the believers. (217)

We know that the family of Abraham had Prophets and Messengers of God, but the rank of prophethood and the message has been removed from the visible world. There is no Prophet after the Messenger of God in his community for whom God will make a divine law different from the divine law of Muhammad. There is no Messenger after him. The rank has not been denied or prevented inasmuch as it does not give a divine law, especially since the Prophet said about the one who had memorized the Quran, "Prophethood is contained between his sides." Or as the Prophet said regarding true dreams: "They are a part of prophethood." He described some of his community and said that they had obtained the station, even though they do not have a different divine law than his divine law. (218)

We know that the Prophet told us that Prophet Jesus will descend among us as a just judge. He will break the crosses and kills the pigs. We have no doubts at all that he is the Messenger of God and His Prophet. He will descend, and there is no doubt at all that he has the rank of prophethood with God, but he will not have the rank of giving divine law when he descends. The Prophet said: "There is no Prophet or Messenger after me," and so we know that prophethood and the message has been cut off. Giving divine law is meant by this. (219)

Since prophethood is the noblest and some perfect rank, it is attained by those of His servants whom God chooses. We know that giving-divine law is a non-essential matter in prophethood since Jesus will descend among us as a judge without giving a divine law. There is no doubt that he is a Prophet. The rank of prophethood is hidden in creation since the divine law is no longer given. (220)

It is known that there were Prophets and Messengers among the family of Abraham who came after him, like Isaac, Jacob, Joseph, and whatever Prophets and Messengers are descended from them. They brought outward divine law which indicates that they have the rank of prophethood with God. The Messenger of God wanted to connect the rank of prophethood with God to his community: they are his family, the righteous with knowledge, even if they do not give divine law. However, they still have a sort of divine law giving within his divine law. He said: "Say: 'O God! Bless Muhammad and the family of Muhammad (that is, bless him in respect to the family he has) as Thou hast blessed Prophet Abraham and the family of Abraham,'" that is, inasmuch as Thou hast given the family of Abraham prophethood as a mark of honor to Abraham. Their prophethood was manifest by giving divine law. "You have decreed that there is no divine law after me, so bless me and my family by giving the rank of prophethood with Thee, even if they do not make divine law. (221)

Part of the perfection of the Messenger of God is that he joined his family to the Prophets in rank. It is more than what Abraham has, since his divine law will not be abrogated. The divine law of Abraham and those after him were partially abrogated. They abrogated one another. (222)

The Messenger of God only taught us the prayer on him in this form of revelation from God and by what God showed him. That supplication is answered. Therefore, we definitely know that there are people in this community who are connected to the rank of the Prophets in prophethood with God, not in giving divine law. This is why the Messenger of God clarified and stressed the fact when he said: "There is no Messenger or Prophet after me." He confirmed the message in respect to giving divine law. (223)

God honored His Messenger since He made his family witnesses over the communities of the Prophets as He made the Prophets witnesses over their communities. Then He singled out this community, that is, the men of knowledge in it, when He prescribed strenuous endeavor for them in judgements and he confirmed the judgement which their strenuous endeavors reaches, their worship according to it, and the worship of those who follow them in it. This is like the judgment of the divine law of the Prophets and their followers. No Prophet is like this community if he is not a Prophet by revelation sent down. God made the revelation of the men of knowledge of this community lie in their strenuous endeavors as He said to His Prophet "*so that thou shalt give judgment between humanity by what God has caused thee to see.*" (4:105) The person who so strives only judges by what God shows him in his strenuous endeavor. These are certain whiffs of giving divine law, but it is not the same as giving divine law. (224)

"The family of Muhammad" who are the believers of his community, the men of knowledge, have the rank of prophethood with God. It will appear in the world to come, and it has no authority in this world except for the amount of prescribed strenuous endeavor. They only perform strenuous endeavor in the religion and judgments by a command sent down directly from God. If it happens that one of the people of the House has this sort of knowledge and strenuous endeavor, and have this rank, like Hasan, Husayn, Jafar Sadiq and other people of the House, then they combine family (*al*) and kinship (*ahl*). (225)

You should not imagine that the family of Muhammad are simply the people of his immediate kin. This is not what the term means among the Arabs. God Almighty says: *"Go to the family of Pharaoh."* That is, to his elite. In this way "family" is only related in this way to the one who has great value in this world and the world to come. This is why we are told, "Say: 'O God! Bless Muhammad and the family of Muhammad (that is, bless him in respect to the family he has) as Thou hast blessed Prophet Abraham and the family of Abraham,'" that is, in respect to that which we have mentioned, not in respect to the individuals themselves instead of the group. It is an formal prayer in respect of the group. We mentioned it because it was before the time of the formal prayer on the Messenger of God. (226)

So the Messenger of God confirmed that he is the master of people on the Day of Rising. When one is like this with God, how can the prayer on him be like the prayer on Prophet Abraham in respect to the individuals themselves? Only that which we mentioned remains. (227)

This question comes from a divine event which occurred to us. God has praise and favor. It is related that the Prophet said: "The men of knowledge of this community are like the Prophets of other communities." One variant has: "the Prophets of the tribe of Israel." The chain of transmission of this Tradition is not firm. However, we have related it in order to put the listeners at ease, since the men of knowledge of this community are joined in rank with the Prophets. (228)

59.9.5. Those Who Are Not Prophets But Whom the Prophets Envy

The Prophet said that on the Day of Rising, "People who are not Prophets or witnesses will have a staired pulpits set up for them on the Day of Rising." Here he means the Messengers when he says "witnesses." They are witnesses for their communities. By this group, we do not mean those we mentioned. They envy them for what they have of rest, and lack of sorrow and fear in that place. The Prophets, Messengers, and men of knowledge of this community, the righteous heirs with the ranks of the Prophets are fearful and alarmed for their communities. (229)

Those do not have communities or followers. They are entrusted with themselves as the Prophets are entrusted with themselves. They have neither communities or followers for whom they fear. Fear is removed from them on that day for themselves and others as God Almighty says: *"The greatest terror shall not grieve them,"* that is, for themselves and others among the Prophets and men of knowledge. However, the Prophets and men of knowledge fear for their communities and followers. This is the source of their envy for them in that place of standing. When they enter the Garden and their places are specified and their ranks are clear, Illiyun will appear to those with intelligence. (230)

This is a very important question and it has immense value. We have not seen anyone before us who directed themselves to it or said anything about it as occurred with to us in this event, unless that has not reached us. God has hidden ones among His servants who are only recognized by Him. "God speaks the truth and guides to the path." (231)

I have explained for you that the prayer of God on His servants varies according to their states. May God place among those most esteemed by Him and not come between us and our servanthood! (232)

The summary of what we have mentioned is that the one who performs the formal prayer it should say: "O God, bless Muhammad by Thy placing his family Prophets and Messengers in rank with Thee, and bless the family of Muhammad as Thou hast blessed the family of Abraham by what Thou hast given them of giving-divine law and Revelation. He gave them tradition, so some of them transmit tradition, and Thou hast prescribed strenuous endeavor to understand a legal issue for them and confirmed its judgement in the divine law." They resemble the Prophets in that. Examine what we have indicated to you in this question and you will truly see the truth. (233)

APPENDIX A
AL-GHAZZALI'S "MYSTERIES OF THE POOR RATE" FROM HIS *THE ALCHEMY OF HAPPINESS* TRANSLATED BY JAY R. CROOK (MUHAMMAD NUR)

CONCERNING OBLIGATORY PURITY

Know that God, *may He be praised and exalted,* says: *Truly God loves the repentant and those who are pure.*[307] (Q. 2:222) God loves the pure. The Messenger (S) said: *Purity is half of faith*. He also said: *Islam is based upon cleanliness*. Therefore, do not suppose that all of the virtue and importance of purification refers (just) to the body and clothing and the use of water; rather, purity has four levels:

THE FIRST LEVEL is the purification of the inmost secret of the soul from everything other than God Most High. As He says: *Say 'God' and then leave them*. (Q. 6:91)[308] The point of this is that when one is empty of all but God Most High, one may become occupied with and immersed in God Most High. This is the true realization of the phrase There is no god but God. This is the degree of the faith of the truly righteous.[309] Being cleansed of other-than-God[310] is one half of faith. Until one is cleansed of other-than-God, one cannot be adorned with the remembrance of God Most High.

THE SECOND LEVEL is the purification of the external aspect of the soul from such foul traits as envy, pride, hypocrisy, greed, enmity, frivolousness, etc., in order to be adorned with pure and approved characteristics, such as humility, contentment, repentance, patience, fear, hope, love, etc. This is the degree of the faith of the devout. Being cleansed of blameworthy characteristics is half of faith.

THE THIRD LEVEL is the purification of the limbs and parts of the body from sins such as backbiting, lying, eating forbidden things, treachery, looking upon unrelated persons of the opposite sex,[311] etc., so that one may be adorned with courtesy and obedience in all matters. This is the degree of the faith of ascetics. Keeping one's parts clean of all forbidden things is half of faith.

THE FOURTH LEVEL is keeping the body and clothing free of impurities so that all of the body may be adorned with bowing and prostration and the fundamentals of formal prayer. This is the degree of Islamic purity; for the behavioral difference between Muslims and unbelievers is in this prayer. This purity too is half of faith.

Therefore, in this manner it may be understood that at all of the levels of faith, purity is one half. By the rule that half or more is the thing, (the

Messenger) said: *Islam is established upon cleanliness.* Then, this purity of body and clothing, which all pay attention to and strive for, is the lowest degree of the purities. However, because this is easier and the carnal self also partakes of it—for cleanliness is pleasant, and the self is at ease in it, and all persons can see it and thereby know of one's purity—it is for this reason easier upon the people. However, the carnal self has no profit in the purification of the soul from envy, pride, hypocrisy, and love of the world and the purification of the body from sin and evil. The eyes of people do not fall upon it—for it is visible to God, and not to mankind, and for this reason not everyone shows an interest in it.

EXCURSUS: UNDER WHAT CONDITIONS IS PRECAUTION LAWFUL?

This obligatory purification (of the body), although it is of the lowest degree, has much virtue, too, but on the condition that its rules are observed and that anxious distraction and excess do not affect it. When it reaches the limit of anxiety and excessiveness, it becomes repugnant and disliked, and it may become an offense. The precautions which the Sufis practice such as wearing footgear,[312] wrapping the head with one's drawers (so that the head and face not be dirtied), requiring absolutely pure water, keeping a water pot so that no one puts his hand in it[313]—all of these are good, but they should not complain about anyone among the religious jurisprudents who does not observe these things, except under certain conditions. Moreover, it is not for Sufis to complain at all about jurisprudents and others who do not take such (extra) precautions, for these precautions are good, but with six conditions:

THE FIRST CONDITION is that because of the time they take, they keep one from worthier matters. For example, if one is prevented by the time consumed with these precautions from learning some knowledge, if one has the ability to do so, or meditating upon something so that an increase (of available time) leads to an insight, or working to provide for one's family or oneself, so that one will not have to beg from another or consume things which people should not, one should not occupy oneself with these (extra) precautions, for the other (obligations) are more important than the (extra) precautions of purity. It is for this reason that the Companions of the Prophet never engaged in such precautions. They were busy with earnest striving in God's way, seeking knowledge, and matters more important than those (precautions). That was why they went barefooted, performed their prayers upon the earth, sat on the ground, and wiped their hands after eating on the soles of their feet. They were not wary of the sweat of beasts of burden, for they made a greater effort to purify the soul rather than the body. So, if a person is of this nature, the Sufis should not complain of him. However, it is not fitting for a person who, out of laziness, does not observe these precautions to complain of those who observe them, for observing them is superior to not observing them.

THE SECOND CONDITION is that one keep oneself from hypocrisy and frivolity in this, for whoever observes these precautions proclaims from head to toe: "I am an ascetic because I keep myself so pure." An avidity is born in him so that he fears lest he fall in the opinion of the people. He must examine himself in this and place his feet on the earth before people, travel the path of leniency, and make his preparations of precaution in private.[314] If his self struggles in this, he realizes that the calamity of hypocrisy has infected him. In this case, it is obligatory upon him that he travel the path of leniency, walk with naked feet, sit upon the earth, pray upon the bare earth, and cease the precautions. For hypocrisy is forbidden and the precautions are a recommended practice.[315] As he cannot avoid the forbidden except by ceasing to practice the precautions, it is obligatory upon him to abandon them.

THE THIRD CONDITION is to follow the way of leniency sometimes, but not turn away from the precautions incumbent upon oneself, just as the Messenger (S) purified himself with the water pot of a polytheist. 'Umar (R) purified himself with the pitcher of a Christian woman. Most of the time, they performed their prayers upon the earth and they honored more those who slept upon the ground with nothing between them and the bare earth. Then, as one separates oneself from their conduct and deems it inappropriate, and one's self does not permit one to conform to their (customs); that is sufficient proof that the self has found an eagerness for this precaution. (In this situation), it is important that one refrain from this.

THE FOURTH CONDITION is that one should abstain from any precaution which annoys the hearts of Muslims, for vexing the hearts of Muslims is forbidden, while abandoning the precaution is not; as when a person extends his hand to take one's hand in greeting or in embrace—and that person's hand is sweaty—it is forbidden to withhold one's hand. Rather, a good nature and an approach that delight the soul of a Muslim in such a situation are more blessed and superior than a thousand precautions. In the same way, if a person steps upon one's prayer-rug, uses one's water pot for purification, or drinks water from one's jug, it is not appropriate to forbid him and show displeasure; for when the Messenger (S) requested water from Zamzam, 'Abbas (R) said: "Many have put their hands in that water and muddied it. Let me find a special pail and draw water for thee." He replied: "No, I prefer the blessing of the hands of the Muslims."

Most of these ignorant ascetics[316] do not know of these subtleties and pull back from a person who does not follow the precautions, injuring his feelings. It may happen that they will speak sharply to their (own) fathers, mothers, brothers, or friends if they touch their water pots or clothing. All of this is forbidden! How could it be lawful to insult people, which is forbidden, because of a precaution, which is not obligatory? Most of those who do this, being afflicted with arrogance, consider it a rare opportunity to withdraw from someone in this way in order to annoy him and to display their own purity and magnificence! They call others "those who have non-smelling noses,"[317] while the Companions used to accept them gently.

If a person just uses stones in cleansing himself (after passing urine or a bowel movement),[318] they consider this act itself a great sin! All of this is from the meanness of their character and a proof of their internal impurity. It is a religious obligation to purify oneself of this meanness, for all such things are causes for destruction, while refraining from the precautions is not a cause for destruction.

THE FIFTH CONDITION is to observe those very precautions in eating, dressing, and speaking which are more important. When one refrains from that which is more important, it is a proof that one is cautious out of self-adornment or out of habit; just as the person who eats something unclean when hunger does not compel him and then will not perform the obligatory prayers until he has washed his hands and mouth. He does not know this much, that the eating of whatever is unclean is forbidden! If it is unclean, why does he eat it unnecessarily? If it is not unclean, why does he wash his hands? Why does he pray on a cloth upon which illiterates may have sat? Why does he eat the food prepared in the homes of the common folk? Precaution about the purity of the morsel is more important, yet most of these people eat food prepared in the homes of merchants and Turks and perform their prayers on their cloths. This is not the sign of candor in this matter.

THE SIXTH CONDITION is that these precautions not be executed with forbidden or abominable things, such as in exceeding the three times in performing one's purification; the fourth time is prohibited in order that the process not be prolonged while Muslims are waiting for him, for this is not fitting.[319] Nor (is it fitting) to use an excessive amount of water, or to delay a prayer after the beginning of its time, or to be the imam[320] and keep the congregation waiting, or to promise a Muslim something and then delay in fulfilling it, or because it is the time for him to engage in business and (not doing so) will cause loss to his family— all such things are unlawful, because these precautions are not obligatory—

or to spread a prayer rug on the floor of the mosque so that no one may touch his clothing.[321] In this (last) there are three abominations: first, he has occupied a part of the mosque of the Muslims, whereas he has a right to no more space than he needs for himself; second, the prayer line may be interrupted, whereas the Practice of the Prophet is that the congregation stand shoulder to shoulder; and third, he avoids the Muslims the way he would avoid dogs or some other pollution. This is not fitting. There are many abominations that ignorant ascetics commit by way of precaution, but they do not know it.

EXCURSUS: THE KINDS OF EXTERNAL PURIFICATION

Not that thou hast learned that external purification is separate from internal purification, and that internal purification of is of three kinds: first, the purification of the limbs of sins; second, the purification of the soul from bad characteristics; and third, the purification of the heart of all that there is save God; know that there are also three kinds of external purification:

THE FIRST KIND is the purification from unclean things. Know that all physical things that God Most High has created are clean except a drink that induces drunkenness—a little or a lot of it is a pollution. All animals are clean except the dog and the pig. All dead animals are unclean except for four: humans, fish, locusts, and everything in which blood does not flow such as flies, bees, scorpions, and worms which (accidentally) fall into food. Everything inside an animal that becomes transmuted or altered[322] is unclean, except that which engenders the animal, such as semen, the eggs of a fowl, and the silkworm. Everything that is not altered, such as sweat and tears, is clean.

Anything unclean invalidates formal prayers except five things for which there is leniency because of difficulties: first, an uncleanness which remains after cleaning oneself with three stones, on condition that it be restricted to its own place.[323] Second, mud on a roadway—even if one definitely sees an impurity in it, but in an amount that one cannot prevent—is excused, unless one should fall into it, or an animal should kick up filth upon one's clothing—this is rare and not excused. Third, filth which reaches footgear, in an amount that it is not possible to avoid, is excused; if one is to perform formal prayer while wearing the footgear, then one rubs the footgear in the earth.[324] Fourth, the blood of lice on thy clothing or the clothing of someone else that thou art wearing, whether a little or a lot, is excused, even if one has sweat on it. And fifth, blood which is secreted from small pimples or pustules, of which the human skin is not devoid, and in the same way, the light fluid that seeps out of such small sores, except in the case that they be large and of pus, resembling a boil, and (this) is rare. It must be washed away. If a trace of it remains after washing, we hope that it will be excused. However, if a person has been cupped or injured, the blood must be washed off. Then, if there is a trace of it (on his person) and some danger in its being washed, then he should (not pray at that time) and perform the make-up prayers (at some other time). This excuse is unusual.

EXCURSUS: [THE KINDS OF][325] CLEAN AND UNCLEAN WATER

If water passes over something unclean one time, except for the filth of a dog, it is clean,[326] unless the impurity itself still remains. In that case, it must be washed until it disappears. If it has been washed and well-rubbed, but there still remains a stain or odor, (nonetheless) it is clean.

All water created by God is clean and cleansing,[327] except in the case of four kinds of water: first, water which has been used one time to remove an impurity resulting from defilement[328] is clean, but does not cleanse; second, that which has been used to remove some unclean filth is neither clean nor cleansing; third, that which is less than 250 manns[329] in quantity, but into which some impurity has fallen, even if its appearance is not altered, is unclean according to the school of Shafi'i (R); however, if the amount of water exceeds 250 manns, so long as it is not altered in appearance by some impurity falling into it, it is clean; fourth, the water is clean in which some clean substance can be observed, such as saffron, soap, or alkali ashes, thereby changing its taste, smell, or color; but it is not cleansing. However, if the change is slight, then it is (also) cleansing.

THE SECOND KIND is the purification from causes of defilement. In this, there are five matters to be learned: the rules of conduct concerning elimination,[330] cleansing after an easing of nature,[331] the lesser ablution,[332] the greater ablution and the dry ablution.[333]

THE MANNER OF ELIMINATION

One should be in a deserted place away from the eyes of others. If possible, it should be (done) behind a wall. The privates should not be uncovered prior to sitting. One should not face the sun or the moon. The direction of prayer should not be behind one, nor should one face the direction of prayer, unless there is a wall before him. In that case, it is lawful, but it is to be preferred to have the direction of prayer to one's left or right. One should not ease nature in a place where people assemble. One should not urinate standing in water and one should not defecate beneath a fruit-bearing tree. One should not defecate or urinate in any hole. One should not urinate against the wind or on hard earth to avoid being splattered. One should not urinate standing up except out of necessity. One should not urinate where people perform their ablutions or bathe. When sitting, one should incline to the left. When one enters the place of purification,[334] one should lead with the left foot; when one comes out, one should lead with the right foot. (While there), one should not possess anything with the name of God written upon it. One should not go bareheaded to the toilet. When one enters, one should say: *I seek refuge with God from the noxious, impure filth of the sender of evil, the accursed Satan*; and when coming out, one should say: *Praise be to God Who has taken away from me that which troubles me and leaves with me that which benefits me.*

THE MANNER OF CLEANSING ONESELF

One must have at hand three stones or clods of earth before elimination. When one finishes, one should take one in the left hand and place it on a place (of the body) where there are no excreta and then move it to the place of impurity. One should rub it in around in such a way in order to remove the excreta and not spread it. If, after the use of three stones, the area is not clean, one should use two more, so that it will be an odd number. Then, one should take a larger stone with the right hand and the penis with the left hand and touch the stone with the penis three times, or touch the penis on a wall in three places. One should use the left hand to move it, not the right hand. If one is content with that, it is enough. However, it is to be preferred that one combine the stones and water.

If one is to use water, one should rise from that place and go to another place so that the water does not drip on it. One should pour water with the right hand and rub with the left hand until one knows from the palm of the hand that nothing remains. Knowing that it is now clean, one should not use a lot of water or (use it) forcefully so that the water may go inside. Rather, when performing the cleansing, one should allow oneself to relax. Whatever is not reached by the water with this much is from inside and the rule of impurity does not apply to that lest one give way to anxiety (about this).

The same is true of the cleansing (of the penis) after urination. One should bring the hand down under the penis three times and shake it three times, walk back three steps, and cough three times. One should not trouble oneself more than this, lest anxiety assail one. If one has performed this (cleansing), whenever one supposes that some wetness has appeared after cleansing oneself after elimination, one should throw some water on one's underdrawers and say to himself that that wetness was from water; the Messenger (S) commanded this because of anxious promptings.

When completing the cleansing after elimination, one should wipe the hands on a wall or the ground. Then one should wash them until no odor remains. At the time of cleansing after elimination, one should say: *O God, purify my heart of hypocrisy and protect my privates from vile deeds.*

THE MANNER OF THE LESSER ABLUTION

After completing the cleansing, one should use a toothbrush.[335] One should start from the right and above, then (brush) to the left and below. Then (one should brush) the inside surfaces of the teeth in the same order. After that, one should also brush the tongue and the palate. One should know that using a toothbrush is important. In the Traditions, it is said: "One formal prayer having used a toothbrush is the equal of seventy prayers without having used one." One should state an Intention when brushing: "I clean the guardians[336] of the remembrance of God."

Just as after elimination one does not omit performing the lesser ablution, which was the Practice of the Messenger (S), one should never perform the lesser ablution without using a toothbrush. If one is not performing the lesser ablution, but knows that there has been some change in one's mouth—for reason of sleep, or keeping the mouth closed for a long time, or eating something with a strong odor—it is the Practice of the Prophet to brush one's teeth.

When finished with that, one sits upon and elevated place facing the direction of prayer and says: I*n the name of God the, the Merciful, the Compassionate, I see refuge with Thee from the goadings of the devils and I seek refuge with Thee, my Lord, from their being present (with me).* (Q. 23:97-98) Then, one should wash one's hands three times and say: *O God, I beseech Thee for prosperity and blessing, and I seek refuge with Thee from misfortune and destruction.* Then, one recites the intention for the lawfulness[337] of formal prayer, or the intention for the removal of impurity, delaying the declaration of intention until the time of washing the mouth three times. Then one throws water into the mouth, unless one is fasting, and one says: *O God, help me to remember Thee and thank Thee and to read Thy Book.* Then one sniffs water into the nostrils three times and says: *O God, let me smell the perfume of the Garden and be satisfied with me.*

Next, one washes one's face three times and says: *O God, brighten my face with Thy light on the day Thou shalt brighten the faces of Thy saints.* Water should touch every hair that is on it to its root, except the hairs of a beard and mustache[338] that are very thick and dense. One should pass water over the beard and mustache and run the (wet) fingers through the hair.

This is called "combing." Whatever is on the sides of the face from the top of the ear to the temples is the limit of the face. One should insert the finger into the corner of the eyes to remove whatever is in the corner of the eye of collyrium[339] and the like.

After that, one washes the right arm three times up to the middle of the upper arm—as close as possible to under the upper arm is preferred—and says: O God, give me my book (of deeds) in my right hand and make my reckoning easy. Then one does the same with the left hand and moves rings so that water goes under them, and says: O God, truly I see refuge with Thee (against) Thy giving me my book in my left hand or from behind my back.

Then one wets both hands and places the spread fingertips together and brings them over the head from the front of the scalp to the nape of the neck, then back again to the starting point so that both surfaces of the hair are moistened; this is once. One does this three times so that all of the head is wiped, and says: *O God, cover me with The mercy and send down of Thy blessings upon me and shade me beneath Thy Throne on the day when nothing will shade me save Thy shadow.* Then one wipes the ears thrice, inserting the fingers into the cavities of the ears and bringing the thumbs down behind the ears, and says: *O God, make me one of those who listen to the Word and follow the best of it. Then one wipes the all of the neck and says: O God, free my neck from the fire and I seek refuge with Thee from the chains and fetters.*

Then one washes the right foot three times to the middle of the calf and runs the fingers with the little finger of the left hand under (the foot), beginning with the little toes of the right foot and ending with the little toe of the left foot, and says *O God, make my feet firm on the Bridge on the day when feet slip from it. One washes the left foot in the same way and says: O God, I seek refuge with Thee lest my foot slip on the Bridge on the day the feet of the hypocrites will slip.*

After completing (these things), one says: I testify that there is no god but God, the One; He has no partner; and I testify that Muhammad is His Servant and His Messenger. O God, make me one of the repenters and make me one of the purified and made me one of Thy righteous servants.

One who does not know Arabic should be instructed in the meaning of these words, so that he may know what he is saying. In the Traditions, it is related that when anyone in a state of purity remembers God Most High, all of his parts become purified from the sins and the errors he has committed. If he does not mention God, nothing is purified except that which was touched by water.

One should perform the ablutions before each formal prayer, even if nothing has occurred to cause one to lose the state of purity, for it is related in the Traditions: "Whoever renews his purity, God Most High renews his faith for him." When one has purified oneself correctly, one must know that one has cleansed that which is seen by the people, but that which God Most High sees is the soul. When one has not cleansed it with the repentance of disagreeable traits, one is like the person who will host the king and cleans the outer door but leaves dirty the court and the dais where the king will sit.

EXCURSUS: SIX THINGS DISLIKED IN THE LESSER ABLUTION

Know that in the lesser ablution six things are disliked: talking, striking the face with the hands,[340] shaking the wet hands (so that water scatters from them), performing the ablution with water which has been warmed in a water pot, wasting water, and performing the acts more than three times each.

However, drying the face with the intention to prevent dirt from settling on it or not doing that so that more of the traces of worship remain upon it have both been reported and both are permissible when that is the intention, and both have merit. It is preferred that one use an earthen vessel when purifying oneself, for it is more humble than a (metallic) ewer or bowl.

THE MANNER OF THE GREATER ABLUTION

Whoever has sexual intercourse or a discharge of semen, either asleep or awake, must perform the greater ablution. It is one's obligation to wash the entire body and that the water reach the roots of the hair, and that one declare the intention to remove the state of impurity.[341]

The Practice of the Prophet is that one first utters: In the name of God. Then, one washes the hands thrice after which one washes clean all impurities from the body. Next, one performs the lesser ablution as described above, with all of the Practices of the Prophet—one should delay in washing the feet until the last when one is leaving the bath.[342] So, one should throw water[343] on the right side (of the body) three times and on the left side three times. One should rub every place the hands can reach. One should try to wash any spots of the body that are (pressed) together,[344] as this is a religious obligation. One should refrain from handling the genitalia.

THE MANNER OF THE DRY ABLUTION

Know that whoever cannot obtain water, or does not have a sufficient quantity for himself and his comrades to drink, or the way to the water is obstructed by a wild beast, or there is a person there that one fears, or—if the water is someone else's property—that person will not sell it except at an exorbitant price, or one has a wound which water might affect and endanger one's life or prolong illness; (such a person) must wait until the time of the obligatory prayer, then look for a place where the earth is clean. Then, he strikes the earth with his two hands so that the dust rises and with his fingers together. Then he recites the intention of permission.[345] Then, he wipes all of his face with both hands, not taking pains lest the dust enter into the hair.

Then, he removes his rings and strikes the earth again with his hands, fingers spread apart. Then, he places the back of the fingers of his right hand on the bottom of the fingers of his left hand. Then, he puts the fingers of his left hand on his right forearm. Then, he rubs the palm of the left hand on the left forearm. Then, he rubs the left thumb over the right thumb. Then, he does the same to the left hand with the right hand. Then, he rubs both palms together. Then, he rubs the fingers between each other. If this is done in one stroke, it is sufficient. If one cannot do this, it is permissible to do more so that the dust may reach all parts of the hand. With such a dry ablution, one may perform the obligatory prayer and as many voluntary prayers as one wishes. However, to perform another obligatory prayer, one must perform another dry ablution.

THE THIRD KIND is the purification from bodily dirt. This is of two types:

THE FIRST TYPE is dirt such as that which is found among the hairs of the head, beard, or mustache. It must be gotten rid of with a comb, water, and the clay of the bathhouse.[346] The Messenger (S) never parted with his comb, either on a journey or at home. It is a Practice of the Prophet to keep oneself clean of such dirt. Another is the dirt that accumulates in the corner of the eye. One should remove it when performing the lesser ablution. Another is in the ear. When one emerges from the bath one should take care of this. Also, there is that which is in the nose and the plaque on the teeth. They can be removed by brushing with a toothbrush, rinsing, and sniffing. Too, that which accumulates on the knuckles or the back of the foot and heel and that which is under the nails, or any other dirt on the body (should be removed). Getting rid of all such things is the Practice of the Prophet.

Know that if such dirt remains, purification is not nullified; the dirt does not impede the water from the skin, except if there is a lot under the fingernails, an abnormal amount. In that case, it is an impediment.

Cleansing oneself from such dirt with hot water and clay in the bath is a Practice of the Prophet.

EXCURSUS: CONDUCT IN THE BATHHOUSE

Whoever enters a bathhouse four things are obligatory,[347] and there are ten Practices of the Prophet:

TWO OF THE OBLIGATIONS concern the private parts: (1) One should cover the (male) body from the navel to the knee from the sight (of others). (2) One should watch the hand of the servant, for handling is a greater impropriety[348] than seeing. And two concern the private parts of others: (3) One should refrain from looking at the private parts of others. If someone uncovers his privates, one should caution him. There is no fear, for, if one does not, one is in rebellion (against God), and whoever does not do this leaves the bath in a state of rebellion. A story about this is told of Umar (R): One day he was sitting in the bath. He was facing the wall with something bound about his eyes.[349] This is also incumbent upon women. (4) Eating bread in the bathhouse is prohibited, except for some manifest reason.

AS FOR THE PRACTICES OF THE PROPHET, they are: (1) reciting an intention that "I do this so that I will be adorned for prayer, not for the eyes of people." (2) One should pay the bathhousekeeper in advance so that he may be pleased with one's pouring out of water and know what he is being given. (3) Then, one should enter with the left foot and one should say upon entering: *In the name of God, the Merciful, the Compassionate; I seek refuge with God from the noxious, impure filth of the sender of evil, the accursed Satan.* This is because the bath is the place of Satan. (4) Then, one should endeavor to go at a time when the bathhouse is empty or at a time when it is relatively empty. (5) One should not enter the caldarium[350] hurriedly to sweat a lot. (6) Upon entering, one should wash both hands immediately. One should not waste water; one should use a quantity that will not displease the bathhousekeeper. (7) Upon entering, one should not greet with "Peace" (salām), but if some one grasps thy hand,[351] one should not be concerned. If some one greets him, he should reply: *May God safeguard thee,* but should not speak much. (8) If one recites the Quran, one should do so softly and not raise one's voice. But if one utters the "seeking refuge,"[352] it may be done in a loud voice. (9) One should not enter the bathhouse at the time of the sunset obligatory formal prayer and when the sun is going down. One should not go to the bathhouse between the time of the sunset obligatory formal prayer and the obligatory formal prayer before going to sleep, for that is the time of the circulating of Satan. (10) When entering the caldarium, remember the fires of hell. One should remain there an hour or more to know what the prison of hell will be like.

Indeed, if one is intelligent, when looking at anything, one remembers the Hereafter. When one sees darkness, one sees the gloom of the grave. When one sees a snake, one remembers the snakes of hell. When one sees something dreadful, one remembers Munkar and Nakir[353] and the guardians of hell. When one hears a harsh sound, one remembers the blast of the Trumpet (announcing the Day of Judgment). When one sees rejection and acceptance in some business, one is reminded of the rejection and acceptance of the Hereafter. These are the lawful Practices of the Prophet.

From the medical point of view, it is said that employing lime once a month is beneficial. When one is about to leave, throwing cold water on the feet prevents gout and headaches. One should not pour cold water on the head. When leaving the bathhouse in summer, one should sleep; that is better for one than a medicinal draught.

THE SECOND TYPE is of a different kind. It is the cleanliness from the refuse of the body. There are seven of these:

First: The hair on the head. Shaving (the head) is preferred and cleaner, except for nobles.[354] However, partial shaving and leaving hair in different places, as is the custom of soldiers, is disliked and has been interdicted.

Second: Keeping the mustache level with the (line of the upper) lip is a Practice of the Prophet. Letting it lengthen to below that line is interdicted.

Third: Plucking out of he hair in the armpits every forty days is a Practice of the Prophet. If one becomes accustomed to this in the beginning, it is easy; if one is not accustomed to this, shaving is preferred so as not to give oneself trouble.

Fourth: It is a Practice of the Prophet to remove the pubic hair with lime or by shaving. This should be done at least once every forty days.

Fifth: It is cutting the nails so that dirt does not accumulate under them. However, if there is dirt under them, purification is not invalidated, since the Messenger (S), having seen such dirt on the hands of some people, ordered them to cut their nails, but not to make up their prayers. In the traditions, it is recorded that when the nails become long, they become the residence of the devil. One should begin with the superior nails, and the hand is superior to the foot, and from the right to the left. The finger that is extended (when reciting) the "Testimony" is superior to the others. That is the index finger of the right hand, so it is to be preferred to begin with that one. Then from the right side until the left side is reached. Place the hands upon each other so that they form a circle and then begin with the index finger of the right hand. One proceeds to the right little finger; then start with the little finger of the left hand and finish with the thumb of the right hand.

Sixth: It is cutting back the umbilical cord, and that is done at the time of birth.

Seventh: It is the circumcision of males and females.

EXCURSUS: THE ETIQUETTE OF THE BEARD AND MUSTACHE

It is customary to let male facial hair grow to the length of a fist and then cut it so that it does not become excessive. Ibn 'Umar[355] (R) and a party of the Followers[356] did thus. Another party said that it should be left longer. Know that ten things are disliked concerning the facial hair:

First: Dyeing the hair black. In the Traditions, it is related that this is the dyeing of the inhabitants of hell and the dyeing of the unbelievers. The first person to do this was Pharaoh. Ibn 'Abbas (R)[357] relates that the Messenger (S) said: "During the Last Days there will be a people who blacken their hair; they shall not smell the perfume of heaven." And also in the Traditions it is related: "The worst of the elderly are those who make themselves like the young, and the best of the young are those who make themselves like the elders." The reason for this prohibition is that it is a disguise with corrupt motives.

Second: Dyeing the hair red or yellow. However, it is (acceptable to) the Practice of the Prophet (as a stratagem) if warriors fighting for Islam do this so that the unfaithful will not be spurred to fight hard and look upon them as weak and old.

Third: Whitening the facial hair with sulfur so that others will think one is old and give him more respect. This is foolishness, for respect comes with knowledge and intelligence, not with age or youth. Anas Malik (R)[358] says that when the Messenger of God (S) received the command and departed,[359] there were not twenty white hairs in all of his hair.

Fourth: Removing (by cutting or plucking) white hairs from the facial hair and being ashamed of old age. This is as though one were ashamed of the light that God Most High gave him. This is ignorance.

Fifth: Plucking the hair at the onset of youth out of fancy or pride so that the face may appear hairless. This is ignorance, for God Most High has angels whose recited praying[360] is this which they say: Praise be to Him who has adorned men with beards and women with tresses.

Sixth: Dressing the facial hair with the fingernails like a pigeon's tail so that it may appear better to women and so they like him more.

Seven: Letting the hair on the head grow long with locks that fall below the earlobes, more than is approved by the righteous.

Eighth: Admiring the blackness or whiteness of one's hair, for God Most High does not like those who are conceited.

Ninth: Combing one's hair for people to see, not for observing the Practice of the Prophet.

Tenth: Leaving it in disarray in order to pretend to asceticism so that people may suppose that he does not take the trouble to comb his own hair himself.

Let this suffice concerning the rules of the purification of the body.

CONCERNING FORMAL PRAYER

Know that (obligatory) formal prayer is a pillar of Islam and the foundation of religion. It is the forerunner and master of all acts of worship. A compact is made by whoever performs these five obligations according to their conditions and at their (proper) times with God Most High that he will be in His security and protection. If he has abstained from committing any major sins, all of his other sins will be erased. The five prayers are the atonement for all of them. The Messenger (S) said: "The similitude of these five obligatory prayers is a clear channel of water which flows by the door of a person's house. Everyday he washes himself five times in that water. Is it possible that dirt would remain on him?" They said: "No, O Messenger of God." He said: "These five prayers carry away sins the way the water carries away dirt."

The Messenger (S) also said: "Formal prayer is a pillar of religion. Whoever refrains from it has destroyed his own religion." They asked (the Messenger): "What is the best of deeds?" He replied: "Performing one's (obligatory) formal prayers at their (proper) times." And he said: "The key to heaven is formal prayer." And he said: "God Most High has not imposed upon His servant anything—except His Unity—more pleasing to Him than (obligatory) prayer. If there were anything more pleasing than this, the angels would have occupied themselves with it as they do with prayer. One group is bowing, another group is prostrating, another group is standing, and another group is sitting."[361] And he said: "Whoever deliberately omits one obligatory formal prayer is an unbeliever." That is, it is close to being a fault in his belief itself, as they say: "Whoever has lost his water in the desert has lost his life." That is, he has reached (a place) close to (his) destruction and has fallen into (mortal) danger. And he said: "The first thing that is examined on the Day of Resurrection is (a person's record of) formal prayer. If it is complete and according to rule, it is accepted; then according to that his other deeds are accepted as they are; but if (the record of formal prayer) is deficient, then he is driven away despite all of his other works.

And the Messenger (S) said: "The formal prayer of whoever purifies himself well and performs them at the proper times, and bows and prostrates himself properly, and whose soul is humble and modest, goes to the Throne white and shining and says: 'May God Most High watch over thee as thou hast watched over me.' And the formal prayers of whoever does not perform his obligatory formal prayers at the correct time, is lax in his purification, and careless in his bowing and prostrating, and does not perform them in submission and humility, goes to heaven black and dark and says: 'May God Most High make thee wasted, just as thou hast wasted me,' so that God Most High wills that his formal prayer be wrapped about him like a ragged garment and that he be driven out." And the Messenger (S) also said: "The worst of thieves is he who steals a formal prayer."

THE MANNER OF THE OUTWARD ASPECT OF FORMAL PRAYER[362]

Know that the outward aspect of prayer is like (its physical) body. It has a true nature and a secret that is the spirit (**rūḥ**) of formal prayer. We shall first expound the external aspect of formal prayer.

The first is that after the purification of the body and clothing and the covering of the privates, one stands on a clean place facing the direction of prayer. The feet should be placed the distance of four fingers apart.[363] The back should be straight and the head inclined forward. The eyes should be fixed on a spot not further away than the place of prostration.[364] When standing erect, one should recite: Say, I seek refuge with the Lord of mankind. (Q. 114:1)[365] One should concentrate one's thoughts on keeping the devil away from oneself.

THE CALL TO ASSEMBLE FOR PRAYER, THE CALL TO ASSEMBLE IN RANKS FOR THE COMMENCEMENT OF OBLIGATORY PRAYER, AND THE DECLARATION OF THE INTENTION

Then, if there is someone who is possible for one to follow,[366] the call to assemble[367] is proclaimed loudly. If not, then one limits oneself to the call to assemble in ranks.[368] The Intention[369] is recited in one's heart. One says to the heart, for example: 'I perform the obligatory noon formal prayer for God Most High.'

THE MAGNIFICATION:[370]

When the meaning of those words has become present in the heart, one lifts one's hands to a point near the ears, so that the fingertips are level with the tops of the ears, the thumbs are level with the earlobes, and the palms in line (vertically) with his shoulders. When one has assumed this stance, one says: God is Greater.[371] Then, one places one's hands, one upon the other, above one's navel and below one's chest. The right hand is on top of the left hand. The finger of Testimony[372] and the middle finger are extended over the left forearm, while the other fingers are circles around the forearm. The hands should not drop down (to the sides after pronouncing the Magnification) and then be brought back towards the chest; rather, they should be placed on the chest (directly from the position by the ears), for that is more correct. Between the two positions, one should not move the hands about, neither forward nor to the sides.

One should not exaggerate in pronouncing the Magnification, so that the u after All[h is noticeable or the a after the b in akbar sounds like broad.[373] Such things are the work of those influenced by devilish insinuations and the ignorant. Pronounce these words during formal prayer in the same way that thou wouldst pronounce them when speaking ordinarily outside of prayer, without ostentation and exaggeration.

THE RECITATION: When the hands are placed upon each other, one should say: *God is greater (than all) in greatness; praise be to God in plenitude; praise God in the morning and the evening. Then one recites: I have turned my face towards...*[374] *Then one says: Praise be to Thee, O God, and with Thy praise and may The name be blessed and Thy majesty exalted; there is no god other than Thee;* so that all schools (of religious jurisprudence) and all narratives (of Traditions) may be brought to together.[375] *Then one says: I seek refuge with God from the accursed Satan; verily God is the All-Hearing, the All-Knowing and In the name of God, the Merciful, the Compassionate.*

THE PRAISE AND THE CHAPTER: After this one recites "The Praise,"[376] observing the prolongations of vowels and the doubled consonants.[377] One should not exaggerate in articulating the letters so that they become confused. Observe the difference between (the letters) Ḍād and Ẓā; however, if one cannot, it is acceptable.[378] When completing the recitation (of this chapter), one should say 'Amen' (*āmīn*), not as though it is the last word of the chapter, but a little separate from it. Then another chapter is recited or whatever one wishes of the Quran. In the first two bows of the dawn, sunset, and evening prayers, they are to be recited aloud, except when one is following an imam.[379]

THE BOW. After pronouncing a Magnification, one bows,[380] but not immediately upon finishing the recitation of the Quranic verses. One raises one's hands during this Magnification as before. One prolongs the Magnification until one reaches the end of the bow and then one's hands are placed on the knees. The fingers, spread apart, are in line with the direction of prayer. The hands are not removed from the knees; rather, one keeps them straight. One's back and head are straight, like a plank, so that one's entire figure is like the letter *Lām*.[381] The elbows extend beyond one's sides and the upper arms do not touch the sides. However, a woman keeps her upper arms against her sides.[382] While remaining in this position, one says three times: Glory be to my Lord, the Mighty, and with His praise. If there is no imam, it is better that one say this seven or ten times.

Then one straightens up from the bow and—without folding the hands—one says: *God listens to those who praise Him. Then one rests while standing and says: Our Lord! All praise is Thine in the fullness of the heavens and in the fullness of the earth and in the fullness of all other things that Thou may wish.*

In the second bow of the dawn prayer, it is a requirement to recite the "Declaration of Obedience to the Will of God."[383]

THE PROSTRATION: Then, one pronounces a Magnification and prostrates oneself,[384] so that everything touches the earth to make one as near to it as possible: first the knees, then the hands, then the forehead and the nose. The hands are placed on the ground in line with the ears, the fingers together. The forearms lie on the ground, but there is a space between the upper arms and the sides, and (between) the belly and the thighs. Women bring these parts together.

Then, one says three times: *Glory be to my Lord, the Highest, and with His praise.* If one is not following an imam, it is better to increase the number. Then, one pronounces the Magnification and rises from the prostration and sits back on one's left leg, placing the hands on the thighs, and says: *Lord! Forgive me and have mercy upon me; provide for me and guide me; reward me, protect me, and excuse me.* Then, one performs another prostration. After that, one sits back, but lightly, and pronounces the Magnification. Then, one stands and performs the next bow in the manner of the first, saying: I seek refuge with God before reciting the Praise.[385]

THE TESTIMONY OF FAITH: Now, when one has finished the second bow, one sits for the Testimony—sitting upon the left leg, as between the two prostrations with the hands on the thighs, but here the fingers of the right hand are curled, except the finger of Testimony[386] which is omitted.[387] At the time of reciting the Testimony, it is extended at the point when one says *illāllāh (except God),* not when one says lā ilāha (There is no god). It is permissible for the thumb to be omitted also. The second

Testimony is performed in the same manner, however both legs are out from under to the right. The left buttock is on the ground.[388]

In the first Testimony, one rises after saying: *O God, bless Muhammad and the people of Muhammad,* but in the second Testimony, one continues to the end of the well-known prayer.[389] Then one says: Peace be upon you and the mercy of God, turning the head to the right so that someone looking from behind him sees his face in profile. Then one pronounces the second "Peace" to the left in the same way. With these two greetings, he makes his Intention of leaving the prayer and the Intention of the greeting those present and the angels.[390]

EXCURSUS: SOME DISAGREEABLE ACTIONS DURING FORMAL PRAYER:

Beginning a prayer when one is hungry, thirsty, angry, feels the need to urinate or defecate, or with any mental preoccupation which prevents humility; extending the legs close together; raising one leg; sitting on the ankles during the prostration; sitting on both buttocks; bringing the knees to the chest; inserting the hands inside clothing; holding clothing when prostrating; tightening the underdrawers, releasing the hands; looking from side to side; cracking the knuckles; scratching the body; yawning; playing with the hair of the mustache or beard; smoothing the ground just before prostration; blowing on the ground at the time of prostration; interlocking the fingers; and leaning back against something. In summary, the eyes, hands, and all body parts must be according to the rules of etiquette and the nature of formal prayer in order for the prayer to be fulfilled and fit to be a provision for the Hereafter. However, of all that has been said above, the religious obligations are no more than twelve things: the first Magnification, the standing, the recitation of "The Opening," the bow and the resting during it, the standing erect from the bow, the prostration and the resting during it, the raising of the body from the prostration, the sitting for the last Testimony, the blessing upon the Messenger, the sitting during that, and the salutation.

Doing this much makes a valid prayer, with the meaning that the sword will spare him;[391] however, the acceptance of the prayer is not certain.[392] It is as though a slave girl without ears, nose, hands and feet were sent to a king; she is alive, but it is by no means certain that she will be an acceptable gift.

DISCLOSING THE TRUE NATURE AND SPIRIT OF FORMAL PRAYER

Know that what we have said above was about the body and outward aspect of formal prayer. This form has a true nature, which is its spirit. And know that for every act of the acts of prayer and for every phrase of its phrases there is another—unique—spirit. Without the real spirit, it is as though the formal prayer were a dead person, a body without life. If the basis is present, but the actions and rules are not observed fully, it is like a blind person with his ears and nose cut off. If the actions are there, but the spirit and true nature are not in them, it is as though it has eyes, but not the power of sight, and has ears, but not the power of hearing.

The basis of the spirit of formal prayer is humility and the presence of the soul during the entire formal prayer; for the purpose of formal prayer is to direct the soul to God Most High and the renewal of the remembrance (of God) through awe and glorification. *As God Most High said: Establish worship for My remembrance.* (Q. 20:14) And the Messenger (S) said: "There are many who get nothing from formal prayer other than trouble and fatigue. This is because they are performing the formal prayer with their bodies and neglecting (the participation of) their souls." He also said: "There are many who pray; but, of their prayers, only a sixth or a tenth is recorded. The amount recorded is the part of each person's prayer in which his soul is present." And he said: "Pray each prayer as though thou wert saying farewell to some one"; that is, as though thou wert saying farewell to thine own passions with this prayer; rather, as though thou wert saying goodbye to everything other than God Most High and devoting thyself entirely to the formal prayer. This is why 'Ayishah[393] (R) used to say: "The Messenger (S) used to talk with us and we with him. When it was time for the obligatory formal prayer, he would say: 'We have never known each other and ye have never known me'; this was from the devotion he had to God Most High." And the Messenger (S) said: "God Most High does not look at the formal prayer of him whose soul is not in his prayer."

When Abraham the Friend (of God)[394] (A) used to pray, the agitation of his soul could be heard at a distance of two miles. When 'Ali (R)[395] desired to perform his prayers, he trembled and the color of his face changed. He would say: "The time has come for the trust[396] which the seven heavens and the earth could not bear when it was shown to them."

Sufyan Thawri[397] (R) says: "Every prayer in which my soul is not present is not a correct prayer." Hasan of Basrah[398] used to say: "Every prayer in which the soul is not present is closer to punishment." Mu'adh (bin) Jabal[399] (R) says: "Whoever looks purposely to the right or left to see who is standing there has not prayer."

Even though Abu Hanifah[400] (R) and Shafi'i[401] (R) and most of the theologians (R) have said that prayer is valid if at the time of the Magnification the soul is disburdened, they issued this legal opinion[402] out of necessity, lest negligence overwhelm the people. The correct meaning of (that opinion) is that the sword is removed from their necks.[403] However, only that amount (of prayer) in which the soul is present is fit to be provision for the Hereafter. In all, there is hope that the condition of a person whose soul is only present at the time of the Magnification will be better than that of him who does not perform the obligatory prayers at all; yet, there is also the fear that his condition will be worse, because a person who presents himself for service negligently may be judged more harshly than one who does not perform his prayers at all. It was for this that Hasan of Basrah (R) used to say: "This prayer is closer to punishment." Indeed, in the Traditions it is related: "Anyone whose praying does not restrain him from vile deeds and abominations has no result from it, save distancing himself from God Most High."

So, after all of this, thou hast learned that a complete formal prayer is that in which the spirit is present in its every part. (A formal prayer) in which it is not present except upon hearing the Magnification, is nothing more than a death gasp; though alive, there is nothing in but a (single) breath.

DISCLOSING THE TRUE NATURE OF THE SPIRIT OF THE ACTS OF FORMAL PRAYER

Know that the first thing that reaches thee is the Call to Prayer. When thou hearest it, thou must attach thyself to it in thy soul and cease any other activity thou mayest be performing, for that is what the elders did. When they heard the call to prayer, he who was a blacksmith with his hammer raised in the air would lay it down. He who was a shoemaker, if he was driving his awl, would leave it where it was. They would jump up from their places, reminded by this caller of the summons on the Day of Resurrection. They knew that whoever hurries at this time to answer that summons will not be met by anything at the Resurrection except glad tidings. If it be in this way that thou look upon this summoner, with thine own soul full of joy and eagerness, know that thou wilt be received in the same by that Summoner.

THE PURIFICATION: The secret of the purification is that thou knowest that the cleanliness of the clothing and the skin is the cleanliness of the sheathe. The spirit of this purification is the cleanliness of the soul through repentance, regret, and the avoidance of disagreeable habits; that is what God Most High looks at. The place of the true nature of formal prayer is the soul, but the body is the place of the form of formal prayer.

COVERING THE PRIVATE PARTS: The meaning of this is that thou coverest from the eyes of people those parts of thine outer form that are unseemly. Its spirit and secret is that thou coverest all that is unseemly of thine inner being from the gaze of God Most High and that thou knowest that nothing can be concealed from Him except that which thou cleansest from within. And, that is cleansed when thou hast regret for the past and determine not to return to that, for: One who repents of his sins is as one who has not sinned. Repentance turns sins into trivialities. If thou canst, veil thy privates in shame, fear, and abashment and stand before God Most High broken-hearted and abashed, like a run-away slave who stands with an ashamed heart before his own master and does not raise his head out of his own disgrace.

TURNING TO THE DIRECTION OF PRAYER:[404] The (external) meaning of this is that one turns his physical face from all other directions to one direction. The secret of this is that one turns the countenance of the soul from all that is in the two worlds[405] to focus upon God Most High and to become of one nature. Just as the physical direction of formal prayer is one, so the direction of formal prayer of the soul is one, and that is God Most High. When the soul flows through the valley of thoughts, it is as though the physical face were turning from side to side. As this is not the manner of formal prayer, (distracted thoughts) are not the true nature of formal prayer. In regard to this, the Messenger (S) said: "Whoever stands in formal prayer and his mind, his face, and his soul, all three, are with God Most High, that servant (of God) returns from formal prayer as though on that day he had been newly born from his mother; that is, he is cleansed of all sins."

So, know truly that just as by turning the physical face away from the direction of formal prayer, the form of the prayer is nullified, so turning the face of the soul from God Most High by carrying other thoughts (to the formal prayer) nullifies the true nature of the spirit of formal prayer. Moreover, the soul takes priority, for the external is the sheathe of the internal. What is important is that which is within the sheathe; the sheathe has little value.

THE STANDING: Externally, this is that the body stands with lowered head, like a servant, before God Most High. Its secret is that the soul has ceased all movement and is prepared for service in the way of glorification and contrition. At this time, one must remember one's position before God Most High at the Resurrection. At that time, all of one's secrets will be revealed and paraded before one. One knows, too, that at this time all of one's secrets are plainly visible to God Most High. He sees everything that is in one's soul or that was in it, and one knows that He is informed of one's interior and exterior.

How strange it is that a righteous person, when someone is observing him to see how he performs his prayer, moves his limbs according to rule and does not look from side to side. He is ashamed to be seen or noticed hurrying in his prayer by someone else, yet (though) he knows that God Most High observes him, he is not ashamed before Him! What ignorance is greater than this that he be careful to pray according to rule in front of a helpless servant who has nothing, yet does not fear the eye of the King of Kings and relaxes his conduct before Him?

It was for this that Abu Hurayrah[406] (R) asked: "O Messenger of God, how should one be modest before God Most High?" He replied: "Just as a righteous person is modest before his own family."

It is for reason of this glorification (of God) that when a group of the Companions (R) were quietly at prayer, birds would not fly away from them. The birds thought that the people were statues. All of the limbs of whoever accepts the greatness of God Most High in his soul and realizes that He is watching him are submissive. And regarding this, when the Messenger (S) saw a person stroking his beard during prayer, he said: "If there were humility in his soul, his hand would also have been like his soul."

BOWING AND PROSTRATION: Know that it is, externally, the humbling of the body; the purpose of their secret is the humbling of the soul so that one may understand that putting the face on the ground—the placing of the most precious of one's body parts on the dirt, which is the lowliest of things—is so that one may know that one's origin is from earth and one's return will be to it. One shows pride appropriate to one's origin in order to understand one's own unworthiness and helplessness. In the same way, there is for every act a true nature and a secret; if one neglects them, nothing redounds to him from his acts save the outer form.

DISCLOSING THE TRUE NATURE OF THE RECITATION (OF THE QURAN) AND REMEMBRANCES (OF GOD) IN FORMAL PRAYER

Know that every word that must be uttered during prayer has a truth that must be understood. The speaker must be of a character to be truly sincere. For example: the meaning of *Allāhu Akbar* is "God is Greater." If one does not know this meaning, he is ignorant; if he knows it, but there is something in his soul greater than God Most High, he is not truthful. It will be said to him: "These words are the truth, but thou art speaking lies." Whenever something else is obeyed more than God Most High, that thing is greater to him, his object of worship, and his "god"[407] which he serves. As God Most High says: *Hast thou seen him who takes his low desires for his god*? (Q. 25:43)

And when he said: *I have turned my face towards Him Who created the heavens and the earth,* if at that moment his soul was concerned with something else, then his statement was a lie. When the first words in the conversation with God Most High is a lie, the danger is obvious. And, when he said: *as a true believer and as a Muslim,* he claimed to be a Muslim. But the Messenger (S) said: "A Muslim is he from whose hands and tongue the Muslims are safe." He must possess these qualities or seek to become like that.

When he says: *Praise be to God,* he must renew the blessing of God Most High in his soul, and his soul must be turned into total gratitude, for this is the word of gratitude, and gratitude is in the soul.

And when he says: *Thee do we worship and Thee do we beseech for help,* the truth of sincerity must be renewed in his soul.

When he says: *Guide us,* his soul must take on the qualities of supplication and lamentation, begging for guidance. Every word in praise and the declaration (that *there is no god but God*), and in the recitation (of verses from the Quran) must be thus, as he knows. His soul is transformed into those qualities; but the exposition of that would be lengthy. If there is to be a portion of the true nature of the formal prayer (for the one praying), it must be like that. If not, one has contented oneself with a meaningless form.

DISCLOSING THE REMEDY FOR THE SOUL SO THAT IT WILL BECOME PRESENT (IN PRAYER)

Know that there are two causes for the heedlessness of the soul during prayer; one is external, and the other internal:

(EXTERNAL) As for that which is external (heedlessness), it is that one prays in a place where one sees and hears, and one's soul becomes distracted by that, for the soul is the follower of the eye and the ear. The remedy for this is that one should pray in a place where one cannot hear anything. If the place is in darkness, so much the better—or one can close the eyes. Most devotees have constructed a small dark room for worship; for in a large place the soul is more (easily) distracted. Ibn 'Umar (R) whenever he prayed, removed his sword, books, and every garment from in front of him lest his eye would fall on them.

(INTERNAL) The second cause is internal: it is scattered thoughts and memories. This is more difficult and harder, and is of two kinds:

One comes from some activity that for a time is preoccupying the soul. The tactic for that is to complete the work first in order to make the soul free (of the preoccupation) and then perform the prayer. For this, the Messenger (S) said: "*When dinner is ready at the same time as the evening prayer, first eat the dinner*." In the same way, if some one has something to say, let him say it before (praying) so that his soul may be empty of that thought.

The other kind is the thinking about a work that cannot be completed in an hour, or the scattered thoughts that normally overwhelm the soul. The remedy for this is to keep the soul focused on the meaning of the remembrances and (the verses of) the Quran one is reciting and to think about their meaning in order to drive away the other thoughts. This quiets the worries and, if it does not conquer them, the appetite for them will not be so strong. However, if the appetite is strong, thinking about it will not be overcome in this way. The solution is to take a purge to eradicate the source of the illness. This purge is the abandonment of that thing about which one is concerned in order to escape from it. If this is not possible, one will never be freed from these thoughts and one's prayer will always be mixed with the whisperings of the self.

He is like the person who sits under a tree and does not wish to listen to the chirping of the sparrows in it. He seizes a stick in his hand and drives them away, but they quickly return. If he wants to be free of them, the solution is to cut down the tree; for as long as the tree remains, the sparrows will flock to it. In the same way, as long as the appetite for some matter occupies his soul, scattered thoughts will necessarily stay with him.

It was for this that when the Messenger (S) was brought a fine robe with beautiful designs on it as a gift and his eye fell upon the pattern during prayer, he returned the robe to the owner as soon as the prayer was over and put his old clothing back on. And, new straps were put on his slippers. His eye fell on the straps during prayer; they were fine. So, he ordered that they be taken off and the old straps put back on. Another time, brand new slippers were made for him. He found them beautiful. So he prostrated himself and said: "I have humbled myself, *O God, may He be exalted and glorified, so that tomorrow Thou dost not take me as Thine enemy for that glance*." He took them off and gave them to the first needy person he saw.

Once Talhah[408] (R) was performing his prayer in his own datepalm garden. He saw a beautiful bird that was flying among the palms but could not find a way out. His soul became concerned (about the bird) and he lost count of the number of bows he had performed. Later, he went to the Messenger (S) and complained about his soul, and he gave the palm garden away in charity as the expiation (for that lapse).

The forefathers did many things like that and knew the remedy for (achieving) the presence of the soul. In short, if remembrance of God

Most High has not overcome the soul before prayer, it will not be present during the formal prayer. Thoughts that have been admitted to the soul to the extent that they occur during prayer will not leave the soul. Whenever one wants to pray with the presence of the soul, he must treat the soul outside of prayer so that it is empty (of worldly concerns). This is accomplished by always keeping the concerns of the world at a distance from oneself and being satisfied with the world according to one's needs. And the purpose, too, of this satisfaction (of needs) is the freedom for worship. If this not be the case, the soul will not be present, except in a few prayers. One must increase the supererogatory prayers[409] and prepare the soul to the point that it will be present for, say, four bows of prayer; for supererogatory prayers compensate for the obligatory.

DISCLOSING THE PRACTICES OF THE PROPHET OF CONGREGATIONAL FORMAL PRAYER

The Messenger (S) said: "One formal prayer with the congregation is like twenty-seven formal prayers alone." And he said: "Whoever performs the evening obligatory formal prayer with a congregation is a though he had spent half the night in formal prayer and supplication. Whoever performs the dawn obligatory formal prayer with a congregation is as though he spent the entire night in formal prayer and supplication." And he said: "For whoever performs obligatory formal prayer with the congregation continuously for forty days so as not to miss the first Magnification, two patents of innocence are written: one from hypocrisy and the other from hellfire." It was for this reason that whenever some one from among the forefathers missed the first Magnification, he mourned for three days. If he missed an obligatory formal congregational prayer, (he mourned) for seven days.

Sa'id Musayyib[410] says: "I have heard the call to the dawn obligatory formal prayer for twenty years; it has never happened that I was not in the mosque before that." Many religious scholars have said: "It is not right for a person who has no excuse to perform an obligatory formal prayer alone." Therefore, it is most important to regard congregational formal prayer highly and to observe the rules of conduct for leading the formal prayer and for following the imam.

The first is that no one should be made the imam except with willing agreement of the people who make him thus. One must be careful that he is not disliked. When he is asked (to lead the formal prayer), he should not refuse without an excuse, for the merit of being the imam is great, greater than that of the summoner to prayer.[411] He must take care about the purification of his garments and observe the times of obligatory formal prayers and commence them at the beginning of its time period,[412] not waiting for the congregation. The merit of the prayer at the beginning of its time period is great. When two of the Companions were present, they did not wait for a third. At a funeral prayer, when there were four persons present, they did not wait for a fifth. One day the Messenger(S) was delayed, and they did not wait for him. 'Abdurrahman 'Awf went forward (to lead the prayer). When the Messenger (S) arrived, one bow had been completed. When the prayer was over, they were anxious (about the Prophet's reaction to this), but the Messenger (S) said: "Ye have done well. Always do thus."

Leading the prayer should be performed purely for God, and the imam should not accept any payment. The Magnification should not be pronounced until the lines are straight. He should raise his voice when pronouncing the Magnifications and then recite the Intention of Imamate in order to receive its spiritual reward. If he does not, the congregational prayer is valid, but the spiritual reward for leading the congregation does not redound to him.

He should recite the Quran loudly in jahri[413] prayers and observe three silent pauses: First: after pronouncing the Magnification, while he is reciting: I turn my face...,[414] and the congregation is preparing for the recitation of the Opening; second: after reciting the Opening, he should pause so that the slower members of the congregation may complete their recitations of it; and third: after reciting the other passage from the Quran, he should pause long enough so that the Magnification will be separate from the Quranic recitation. The members of the congregation do not recite anything after the Opening, unless they are too far away to hear the recitation of the imam. He performs the bows and prostrations unhurriedly and does not utter the praise more than three times.

Anas[415] (R) says: "No one was more unhurried or more complete in prayer than the Messenger (S)." The Practice of the Prophet is that prayer not be prolonged, as there may be persons in the congregation who are weak or have some business to attend to. The congregation must move after the imam does, not at the same time. They do not press their foreheads to the ground in the prostration before the imam has done so. They do not begin their bow until the imam has reached the limit of his, for this is (the meaning of) following the imam. If one deliberately precedes the imam, one's prayer is nullified. After the salutations (at the end of prayer), (the imam) should not sit long before saying: O God, Thou art the Peace, Peace is from Thee, Thou hast given blessings, O Lord of Majesty and Veneration.

Then (the imam) rises slowly and faces the people and offers supplications. The people should not turn their faces away from him, for that is disliked.

DISCLOSING THE MERIT OF THE FRIDAY CONGREGATIONAL FORMAL PRAYER

Know that Friday is a great day and its merit is enormous. It is the festival of the believers. The Messenger (S) said: "Whoever does not attend three Friday prayers without excuse has discarded Islam and his soul is tarnished."

In the Traditions, it is related that on every Friday God Most High liberates six hundred thousand servants from hell. The Messenger (S) said: "Every day (the heat of) hell flares up at the time of decline of the sun, except on Friday. On that day, it does not flare up." And he said: "Whoever dies on a Friday receives the reward of a martyr and is exempted from the torment of the grave."

THE CONDITIONS OF FRIDAY CONGREGATIONAL FORMAL PRAYER

Know that just as there are conditions for other formal prayers, so there are (additional) conditions for the Friday congregational prayer. There are six additional special conditions:

The first condition is time. If the imam should utter the final salutations after the time for the afternoon obligatory formal prayer has begun, the prayer is lost and should be completed as though it were the noon obligatory formal prayer.

The second condition is place. This formal prayer is not convened in the desert or among tents. Instead, it must be held in a city or a village in which there are at least forty adult, sane, and free men resident. If it is not held in a mosque, is it valid.

The third condition is number. It is not correct to hold the Friday congregational obligatory formal prayer unless forty free, legally competent residents are present. If fewer than this number are present, either in the sermon or in the obligatory formal prayer, it would appear to be invalid.

The fourth condition is the congregation. If the each of the people performs formal prayer alone, it is not correct. However, if a person comes in time for the last bow, his formal prayer is valid, even if he is alone in the second bow.[416] If he arrives too late for the second bow, then he recites the Intention for the noon obligatory formal prayer.[417]

The fifth condition is that one has not performed another Friday congregational formal prayer,[418] for it is not lawful to perform two such prayers in the same city, except if the situation is that the prayer (area) is filled to capacity or performing the prayer in it is difficult. If one cannot (pray there) and performs a second Friday formal prayer, it is valid if the first Magnification has been uttered before.

The sixth condition is that there be two sermons before the formal prayer; both are obligatory. Sitting between the two sermons is obligatory (upon the imam) and standing during the sermons is obligatory (upon the imam). During the first sermon, four things are obligatory: *Praising God*—saying Praise be God is enough; blessing the Messenger (S); advising piety—*I counsel the servants of God to devote themselves to God is sufficient*; and to recite at least one verse from the Quran. There are the same obligations in the second sermon, but instead of a verse from the Quran, a supplication is offered.

Know that this obligatory (Friday congregational) formal prayer is not required of women, slaves, children, and travelers. It is lawful not to attend for reason of mud, rain, and sickness—so that the illness may not spread—but it is preferred that such a person perform the obligatory noon prayer after the congregation has dispersed from the obligatory Friday prayer.

THE (TEN) RULES OF ETIQUETTE AT THE FRIDAY PRAYER

Know that there are ten Practices of the Messenger, and people should observe (these) rules of etiquette:

THE FIRST ETIQUETTE: Greeting Friday on Thursday with thy soul; preparing such things as white clothing, taking care of other activities beforehand so that one may betake himself to the mosque early; sitting quietly after the afternoon prayer on Thursday in praise and seeking forgiveness—for the virtue of this hour is very great and is (more) excellent in comparison with that hour on Friday. It has also been said that lying with one's wife is a practice of the Prophet so that she too will need to perform the greater ablution (bath), both (husband and wife), on Friday.

THE SECOND ETIQUETTE: One should perform the greater ablution the early morning if one wishes to go the mosque early; if not, it is preferred to delay. The Messenger (S) ordered the Friday bath, a definite order to the point where some of religious scholars have supposed that it is a divinely imposed obligation. The people of Madinah, when they wanted to speak harshly to someone, would say: "Thou art worse than a person who does not bathe on Friday." If someone is in a state of ritual impurity, when he has performed the greater ablution for that, it is preferred that he recite the intention to perform the Friday bath and again throw water over himself. However, if he declares both intentions[419] together, (one bath) will suffice and he will obtain the reward of the Friday bath.

THE THIRD ETIQUETTE: One should go to the mosque well-turned out, clean, and in a good state. Cleanliness is that one should remove (unwanted) hair, pare the nails, and trim the mustache. If one has gone to the bath earlier and done these things, that will suffice. Well-turned out is that one wears clean white clothing—for God Most High likes white clothing—applies some pleasant fragrance, with the intention of showing respect to the mosque and for the obligatory formal prayer, so that no unpleasant odor may emit from his person to disturb others and cause them to talk about him.

THE FOURTH ETIQUETTE: Going to the mosque early, for its merit is great. In the old days, they used to repair to the mosque in the early morning carrying lamps. The roads were so crowded that it was difficult to walk. Ibn Mas'ud,[420] may God have mercy upon him, went on a path and found that three men had gotten (to the mosque) before he had. He rebuked himself and said: "Thou art in the fourth degree! What will be the outcome for thee?"

They used to say that the first innovation that appeared in Islam was the omission of the practices of the Messenger. How is it that while Jews and Christians go early to synagogues and churches on Saturday and Sunday, Muslims are laggards on Friday, which is their day?

The Messenger (S) has said: "For the person who goes at the first hour on this day to the mosque, it is as though he has sacrificed a camel. If he goes at the second hour, it is as though he has sacrificed a cow; at the third hour, a sheep; at the fourth hour, a chicken; at the fifth hour, an egg. If he goes at the time the imam is ascending the pulpit, the angels who were recording these sacrifices roll up their scrolls and become attentive to the sermon. Whoever arrives at this time has the reward of the obligatory prayer, but nothing else."

FIFTH (ETIQUETTE): Not to climb over people if one is late, for it is related in the Traditions that should a person do that, at the Resurrection, they will make a bridge of him for the people to pass over. The Messenger (S) saw someone doing this. When the prayer was completed, he asked the man: "Why didst thou not participate in the obligatory prayer?" He said: "O Messenger of God, I am here with thee." The Messenger said: "I saw thee crawling over the congregation." That is to say, for a person who does thus it is as though he had not attended the prayer. However, if there be an empty place in the first row, it is lawful to aim for that first, for the fault is those who left the first row incomplete.

THE SIXTH ETIQUETTE: One should not pass in front of a person performing his prayer. When one sits by a wall or column, one should sit close to it so that there is no passage in front of him, for it is forbidden to pass in front of someone who is praying. In the Traditions, it is related: "If dust is raised so that the breeze blows it at him, it is better than passing in front of one who is praying."

THE SEVENTH ETIQUETTE: One should seek (to pray in) the first rank. If one is not able to, howsoever closer to it the better, for its merit is great, unless there are soldiers in the front rank wearing silk clothing, or the black clothing of the preacher is silken, or his sword is of gold, or some other prohibited thing. In that case, the farther away one is the better, for it is not appropriate to choose a place where there is some prohibited thing.

THE EIGHTH ETIQUETTE: When the preacher comes out, one should not talk and should attend to the replies (to the phrases) of the summoner to assemble for formal prayer. then pay attention to the sermon. If someone speaks, one should silence him with a gesture, not with words, for the Messenger (S) said: "Whoever says 'Be quiet!' during the sermon, or 'Listen!' speaks idly; whoever speaks idly at this time has not attended the Friday congregational prayer."

If one is seated far away and cannot hear the sermon, he still must remain silent, nor should he sit anyplace where people are talking. He should not perform any formal prayer at that time, except the Greeting to the Mosque.[421]

THE NINTH ETIQUETTE: After one prays, one should recite "the Praise" seven times,[422] "*Say, He is the One God*"[423] seven times. He should also recite the two "I seek refuge"s,[424] for in the non-Prophetic Traditions,[425] it is written: "They are like a refuge from Satan from one Friday to the next." Then one should say: "*O God! O Free From Want (Ghan\)! O Praised One! O Inceptor! O Restorer! O Merciful! O Friend! Bestow upon me from what is lawful to Thee rather than what is unlawful, and in obedience to Thee rather than from Thy punishment, and from Thy grace rather than from anyone other than Thee!*" It is said: "Whoever persists in this invocation, his sustenance will appear from a place from which he had no hope and will become free of needing (the help) of others."

After this, one performs six bows of formal prayer, the Practice of the Prophet, for this is the number which has been ascribed to the Messenger (S).

THE TENTH ETIQUETTE: One should remain in the mosque until the time for the afternoon prayer has come. It is even more meritorious to sit in the mosque until the sunset prayer. It is said: "This has the reward of the Greater and Lesser Pilgrimage."[426] And if one is not able to do this and returns home, he should remember God Most High until that time,[427] and not neglect this while Friday lasts, lest he be deprived of its grace.

THE (SEVEN) RULES FOR FRIDAY

One should strive for seven virtues throughout all of this day:

The FIRST rule is to attend an edifying assembly in the early morning and to avoid storytellers and circles of gossipers. One should repair to the assembly of a person whose speech and conduct do not excite love for the world, but rather invite one to the Hereafter. Any talk which is not like that is not an assembly for edification. However, if it is (an edifying assembly), there is a Tradition that states: "Attending one such assembly is more meritorious than a thousand bows of formal prayer."

SECOND: During this day, there is a precious and noble hour. In the Traditions is related: "Whoever makes a request during this hour, it is granted." There is a dispute about which hour is meant: Is it the time of the rising of the sun or its declining?[428] Is it sunset or is at the time of the call to formal prayer? Is it the moment the preacher ascends the pulpit, or the time when congregation assembles in ranks for formal prayer? Is it the time of the afternoon obligatory formal prayer? The truth is that its exact time is unknown and ambiguous, like the Night of Power.[429] We revealed it on the Night of Power. Ah, what will convey unto thee what the Night of Power is? The night of Power is better than a thousand months! The angels and the Spirit descend therein by permission of their Lord with all decrees. Peace, until the rising of the Therefore, one must be alert for it throughout the day and never stop remembering (God) and worshipping (Him).

THIRD: During this day one should send many blessings upon the Messenger (S), for he said: "The sins of eighty years are forgiven for him who sends blessings upon me eighty times." They asked him: 'O Messenger of God, how should we send these blessings?" He said: 'O God, bless Muhammad and bless the people of Muhammad with a blessing that is acceptable to Thee and rendered for his truth! Grant him the means and the merit. Send him to the praiseworthy place Thou hast promised him. Reward him on our behalf that which is best of what Thou dost reward a prophet on behalf of his people. Bless all of his brothers from among the righteous prophets, O Most Merciful of the Merciful!' It is said: "Whoever repeats this on Friday seven times will receive the intercession of the Messenger (S); it is assured." If one says only "O God, bless Muhammad and the people of Muhammad," it is enough.

FOURTH: One should read the Quran much during this day. One should read The Chapter of the Cave;[430] its merit is mentioned in the Traditions. The ascetics of the forefathers used to recite The Chapter of the Unity[431] a thousand times on Friday and bless (the Prophet) a thousand times and say a thousand times: "Glory be to God! Praise be to God!

There is no god but God and God is greater."

FIFTH: On this day one should perform more (formal) prayers. In the Traditions, it is related: "Whoever goes to the mosque should immediately perform a four-bow prayer. In each bow, he should recite the Opening once and *Say: He is God, the One!*[432] fifty times. Such a one will not depart from this world without having been shown his place in heaven or having it shown to someone else who will inform him of it."[433]

It is recommended that on this day one recite the following four chapters in these four bows: *The Cattle, The Cave, Ta Ha, and Ya Sin.*[434] If one cannot do this, then one should recite: *The Prostration, Luqman, Smoke, and The Sovereignty.*[435]

Ibn 'Abbas (R) never omitted the formal prayer of praise[436] on Friday; this formal prayer is well known. It is preferred that one pray until noon.[437] After that, one should attend some edifying assembly until the time of the afternoon prayer, and after that, engage in praise and seeking forgiveness until the sunset prayer.

SIXTH: One should not neglect giving alms on this day, even if it is nothing more than a piece of bread; for the merit of almsgiving on this day is increased, but any beggar who begs at the time of the sermon should be stopped. It is unseemly to give something to such a person.

SEVENTH: In general, one must, this day of the week, regard the Hereafter with certainty. One should devote the whole day to good works, and do the work of the world on other days. For God Most High says: *And when the prayer is ended, then disperse throughout the land and seek of God's grace.* (Q. 62:10) Anas (R) says: "This does not mean buying and selling and the business of the world; rather, it is the seeking of knowledge, visiting brethren and the ill, accompanying the (funeral) cortege, and acts such as these."

DISCUSSION: Know that what is absolutely necessary about formal prayer has been said. Other matters should be asked as the occasion arises, for they cannot be discussed in a book of this kind. However, there are many devilish insinuations in one's Intention to perform the prayer. They should be remarked upon here.

Know that these insinuations occur to a person who has some flaw in his mind, or is a melancholic, or is ignorant of the Religious Law and does not know the significance of the Intention. Thine intention is the desire that turns thy face to the direction of formal prayer. It inspires thee to rise to thy feet and follow its command. It is as though someone says to thee: "Such-and-such a learned scholar has come! Stand up for him and venerate him!" Thou dost not say to thyself: "I have formed the Intention to stand on my feet in respect for such a person and at the command of such-and-such a person." Instead, thou standest up immediately and the intention is in thy soul, without thy saying the words in thy soul or with thy tongue. All that thou sayest to the soul is talking to thyself, not the declaration of Intention, for the intention is that eagerness which appears in the soul and impels thee (to act).

Moreover, thou must know what the command is: that it is for the performance of the noon prayer or the afternoon prayer. When the soul is not neglectful of this, thou sayest *God is Greater*! If it is negligent, thou remindest thyself. Do not suppose that the meaning of the performance of a divine command and the noon obligatory formal prayer are collected at once in the soul in detail; because they are near to each other, they (only) seem to be collected. This is sufficient, for if some one says to thee: "Art thou performing the obligatory noon formal prayer?" thou sayest: "Yes." At the moment thou sayest "yes," the general meanings of this are in thy soul, not the details.

So thy speaking to thyself—as a reminder—is the same as the question of that person, and "God is Greater" takes the place of thy saying "yes." Anything more than that is an enquiry which will distract thy soul and the prayer. Thou must take it easy. If thou hast done this much, in the proper manner, know that the prayer is valid, for the Intention of prayer is like the intention of all acts. For this reason, during the time of the Messenger (S), none of the Companions (R) were ever disturbed with reservations about the declaration of the Intention, for they knew that the matter was easier (than that). As for that person who does not know this, it is out of his ignorance.

Endnotes

307 " pure" : the word used here, *mutaṭahhirīn*, refers to the state of purity called *ṭahārat* which has the specialized meaning of being purified (by *wuḍūʾ* or *ghusl*) and in a state to perform certain religious obligations such as formal prayer (*namāz*) and the reading the Quran.

308 In the Quran, the sentence is completed thus: Say ' God' and leave them to their wallowing as they play.

309 " truly righteous" : *ṣiddīqān.*

310 " other-than-God" : *ghayr Ḥaqq.*

311 " relationship/ ; *maḥram.*

312 " footgear" (*jūrāb*): the Persian so translated can refer to boots, socks, or stockings; in other words, something on the feet. In modern Persian, it tends to refer to socks and stockings, things made of cloth, with separate words for shoes, boots, sandals, and the like.

313 So as to eliminate the possibility of pollution of the water. The water pot is used for making ablutions and for cleansing oneself after natural bodily functions.

314 Ghazzali is not condemning excessive caution exhibited by many of the pious in following the expanded minutiae of the laws of purity, but he is pointing out that they can be impractical for ordinary folk in their daily lives and furthermore, can ensnare the practitioner in the vices of pride and contempt and ultimately hypocrisy with respect to those unable to devote so much time or resources to these things. Instead of making a public display of these preparations, he advises that such precautions be taken in private.

315 Hypocrisy is forbidden (*ḥarām*) by God' s law. Violations of the Practice of the Prophet are at a lower level of gravity.

316 " ignorant ascetics" : literally " ignorant reciters of the Quran" (*qurrāʾān-i jāḥil*). " Reciters of the Quran" (*qurrāʾān*): the pious and holy; ascetics. While reading of the Quran is of course praiseworthy and an act of great piety, the term is also used perjoratively to refer to those make a show of it. There is often a suggestion of the taint of professional piety about them in literature.

317 This word, *bi-khushm* or *bi-khashm*, has prompted lengthy notes in both AA and HK. Among the varied proposals, it may mean

a person whose sense of smell does not function or " something resembling some filth" (Dr. Minawi). Steingass suggests for khasham " offensive smell of the nose from polypus, ozena."

318 Cleansing oneself with stones in the absence of water is permissible, but should be repeated with water whenever it is available.

319 When performing the obligatory ablutions for prayer (*wuḍūʾ*), one washes the hands, mouth, face, etc. One washing is obligatory (*farḍ*), the usual Practice of the Prophet (*sunna*) is three times. Ghazzali implies that washing in excess of this is ostentation and profligacy.

320 " *imām*" : the leader of a congregational formal prayer.

321 By spreading prayer rug, he creates a space about himself to prevent physical contact with others.

322 Everything that is altered, for example, by the digestive processes in the gut of an animal.

323 When water is unavailable to clean oneself after bowel movements and urinating, stones may be used. Since this is not as efficient a method, it may happen that some impurity may remain. After using three stones for this purpose, the requirements are fulfilled, but in the event an impurity has fallen upon another place, such as the leg or thigh, this must be removed before performing the formal prayers.

324 That is, to clean the footgear as much as is possible.

325 From the AA text.

326 It should be remembered that Ghazzali is discussing the cleanness and uncleanness of water from the point of view of its suitability for use in washing and bathing for prayer, reading the Quran, etc.; not from the point of view of modern ideas about sanitation or potability.

327 " clean and cleansing" : clean water does not create a state of impurity. Cleansing water is clean and can be used to ablutions, etc.

328 " defilement" (*ḥadath*) means any act or event which causes one to lose the state of purity necessary for prayer, etc., such as urinating, bowel movements, or the emission of semen. The remedies for this are first washing. After the washing it would be necessary to perform an ablution, either the lesser (*wuḍūʾ*) or the greater (*ghusl*), depending upon the cause, in order to perform prayer, read the

Quran, etc.

329 mann: various values are given for the weight of a mann. There are forty sers in a mann. Because the weight of a ser varies in different countries and periods, it is difficult to give an exact calculation. Ghazzali' s mann, depending upon the weight of the ser, was probably between 40 and 84 lbs. (Steingass)

330 " elimination" (*qaḍā-yi ḥājat*) here means " the elimination of bodily wastes."

331 " cleansing after an easing of nature" : *istinjā*.

332 " lesser ablution" : *wuḍū*.

333 " dry ablution" : *tayammum*.

334 " the place of purification" (*ṭahārat-jāy*): a euphemism for toilet.

335 " toothbrush" : The Arabic (and Persian) is *miswāk*, a kind of toothbrush made from the twig of certain trees.

336 That is, the teeth, as they are involved in the articulation of the remembrance of God.

337 " lawfulness" (*istibāḥat*): literally, deeming something permissible.

338 " beard and mustache" : *maḥāsin* (good things), so called because they adorn the male face.

339 " collyrium" : *kuḥl*.

340 In the corresponding Arabic passage in *The Revival*, Ghazzali says: " and striking the face a striking with water" ; that is, splashing the face with water rather than washing it carefully.

341 " state of impurity" : *janābat*.

342 Ghazzali mentions this because washing the feet is the last part of the lesser ablution; however, in the greater ablution washing the body completely intervenes before the washing of the feet. It is assumed that the person bathing is in a standing position. See following Note.

343 It should be noted that Ghazzali is not describing a bath using tub or shower. The water is dipped out of some container and thrown over the body, a practice of bathing still prevalent in many parts of the world. In doing this, naturally the feet would be the last parts of the body to be washed before putting on clogs or footgear and

leaving the bathing place.

344 That is, places where parts of the body fold over each other, such as behind the ears, the armpits, the groin, behind the knees, between the toes, etc. Every external surface of the body should be washed.

345 " permission" : *istibāḥat*: see Note 337 above.

346 This clay, *gil-i garmābah*, is a special preparation of clay used for washing in bathhouses.

347 " obligatory" : *wājib*.

348 " a greater impropriety" (*farā-tar*): literally, " higher, farther up"

349 So as not to see the privates of others.

350 caldarium (*khānah-yi garm*): The hot or steam room of a bathhouse.

351 That is, shakes your hand or grasps them in both hands as a sign of friendship.

352 " seeking refuge" (*isti*[c]*ādhat*): that is, I seek refuge with God from the accursed Satan.

353 Munkar and Nakīr: the two angels (their names mean " Unknown" and " Repudiating") who visit the dead in their graves and interrogate them about their belief in the Prophet and Islam.

354 This is a sanitary recommendation. The " nobles," being more affluent, presumably had access to better sanitary facilities.

355 Ibn ' Umar: ' Abdullah bin ' Umar bin al-Khattab, Abu ' Abd al-Rahman, the popular son of the second of the Rightly Guided Caliphs, ' Umar bin al-Khattab (see Note 299). He was noted for his generosity and died at Makkah AH73/692CE at the age of 84.

356 " the Followers" (*tābi*[c]*īyān*): the generation that followed after the generation of the Companions, who were contemporaries of the Prophet (S).

357 Ibn ' Abbas: ' Abdullah bin ' Abbas bin ' Abd al-Muttalib, one of the most important of the Companions. He studied with ' Ali bin Abi Talib and was expelled from Makkah by ' Abdullah bin Zubayr. He repaired to Ta' if where he died in AH68/687-8CE.

358 Anas Malik: Anas bin Malik, Abu Hamzah al-Ansari. The " al-Ansari" indicates that he was one of the Helpers from Madinah

who gave aid to the Muslims fleeing Makkah in Hijrah. He was the Prophet' s servant, a soldier, and an important source of Traditions. He died at Basrah in AH93/711CE.

359 That is, he died.

360 " recited praying" : *tasbīḥ*.

361 That is, the angels are in the principle physical postures of the formal prayer.

362 Although the following exposition of the procedure for the service of formal prayer applies to what is broadly correct for all Muslims, there are differences among the various schools of religious jurisprudence in the details. There are also some differences between men and women in the manner of performing the formal prayers.

363 That is, the width of four fingers of the hand; the feet should be placed from about
three and one-half to four and one-half inches apart.

364 That is, where the face or forehead touches the ground or prayer rug during prostration.

365 That is, one should recite the entire last surah of the Quran that begins thus: I seek refuge with the Lord of mankind, the King of mankind, the God of mankind, from the evil of the whisperer [the devil], who whispers in the hearts of mankind, of jinn and mankind. (Q. 114:1-6)

366 That is, if there is someone possessing the necessary qualifications to lead the prayer.

367 " call to assemble" : *adhān*.

368 " call to assemble in ranks" : *iqāmah*.

369 " the Intention" : *nīyat*.

370 " Magnification" : *Takbīr*. The meaning is " God is Greater than all else."

371 " God is Greater" : *Allāhu Akbar*.

372 " the finger of Testimony" (*angusht-i shahādat*): the right forefinger.

373 That is, so that the second a in *akbar* sounds like the ā in ' father,' rather than having the correct short vowel which is more like the a in ' back.'

374 *Wajjahtu wajhī*. Ghazzali' s intention here is that one should

recite the entire verse beginning with those words. It is: Lo! I have turned my face toward Him Who created the heavens and the earth, as one by nature upright, and I am not of the polytheists. (Q. 6:79). The verse actually commences this way: *Innī wajjahtu wajhī...* It is recited when the one is standing in position for the performance of the formal prayer after the call to assemble (*iqāmah*) is completed, and immediately before the declaration of the Intention. The Intention ends with a Magnification (*takbīr = allāhu akbar*) at which the hands are raised to the level of the ears, as Ghazzali has already described above in the section on the Magnification.

375 That is, to harmonize all schools of religious law and various (sometimes conflicting) Traditions.

376 The Praise (al-Ḥamd): Familiar quotations from the Holy Quran are often referred to by their first prominent word or phrase. In this case, " the praise" is the first word of the second verse of the first chapter of the Quran, more often referred to these days as " The Opening" (*al-Fātiḥah*). When performing the formal prayers, one first recites this chapter and then follows it with another chapter or some verses from another chapter of the Quran. At a minimum, any Muslim who performs the five daily prayers recites this chapter of seven verses 17 times a day.

377 Persian pronunciation, like English, normally does not double consonants (we say " little," not " lit-tle"). In borrowed words from languages where doubled-consonants often have meaning differences—and Arabic is one such language, Persian speakers ignore them in ordinary conversation but often pronounce them in careful, formal speech. In Arabic, for example dabara means " he turned his back; it elapsed," but *dabbara* means " he planned, made arrangements, managed, etc." Not pronouncing the doubled b would drastically alter the meaning.

378 Ghazzali is referring to two of the so-called " Arabic letters" which have no equivalent in Persian pronunciation or most other languages. Indeed, Arabic is called the " language of Ḍād," supposedly because no other language in the world possesses such a sound.

379 When an *imam* is leading the prayer, only his voice is heard in these recitations.

380 The act of bowing is called rukū^{c}. Each bow is called a *rak^{c}at.*

Formal prayers are, in part, identified by the number of bows they contain.

381 " the letter *lām*" : the letter L. The similitude is apposite in English as well, because the L has a similar shape in both scripts; that is, a longer vertical and shorter horizontal stroke at the base of the vertical. The Arabic lām faces to the left, while the Latin L faces to the right. The Arabic has a greater or smaller curve at the junction, but the Latin L usually has a right angle.

382 One of the few occasions when Ghazzali points out different rules for the two sexes. It may be pointed out that in the Medieval world few women anywhere were able to read. Books were normally written with the male reader in mind. (Not many males could read either, although in the Islamic world, the literacy rate of both sexes was considerably higher than in the West of that era because of the great emphasis Islam placed upon learning to read the Quran.)

383 According to Shafi' i and others. Abu Hanifah did not require this. There are different forms of this (the Qunūt) prayer. The most common version is: O God, guide me among those whom Thou hast guided, and preserve me among those whom Thou has preserved, and befriend me among those whom Thou hast befriended, and bless me in what Thou hast granted and save me from the evil of what Thou hast ordered, for Thou dost order and no order is given contrary to Thine order. Surely, he is not disgraced whom Thou befriendest, blessed art Thou, our Lord, and highly exalted!

384 The act of prostration is called sujūd. Each individual prostration is a *sajdah*.

385 " the Praise" : that is, the first chapter of the Quran, more formally called " The Opening" (*al-Fātiḥah*). The recitation of the Opening precedes the recitation from another part of the Quran in the standing that precedes each bow of the formal prayer.

386 See Note 372 above.

387 That is, not curled.

388 The right buttock is on the left leg.

389 That is, O God, bless Muhammad and the people of Muhammad as Thou didst bless Abraham and the people of Abraham; surely Thou art Praised, Majestic. O God, give blessings to

Muhammad and the people of Muhammad as Thou didst give blessings to Abraham and the people of Abraham; surely Thou art Praised, Majestic.

390 This greeting is addressed to " you" (plural), even though one is alone, or only one other person is present. This is because the appointed angels are always present and they share in this greeting. This is also the reason for the common use of the plural in this greeting when meeting or taking leave from someone; that is, even if only one person is being greeted, the greeting is usually in the plural to include the angels. It may also be pointed out that Arabic has three numbers: singular, dual, and plural.

391 That is, that he is a Muslim and killing him is not lawful.

392 That is, it is not certain that the prayer will be acceptable to God.

393 cĀyishah: the daughter of the Abu Bakr, the first caliph, and a favorite wife of the Prophet. She survived the Prophet by many years, dying in Madinah at the age of 67 in AH 58/678. Many Traditions are related on her authority.

394 Abraham: in Arabic and the Islamic world he is known as Ibrāhim with the epithet " the friend of God" (*khalīl-ullāh*).

395 ' Ali: the Prophet' s cousin and son-in-law. He married the Prophet' s daughter Fatimah. He became the fourth caliph and was assassinated in AH 40/661CE. A man of immense personal integrity and incorruptible faith, the dispute over his accession to the caliphate led to the schism between the Sunnis and the Shiahs.

396 " the trust" (*al-amānah*), a reference to Quranic verse: Lo! We offered the trust unto the heavens and the earth and the hills, but they shrank from bearing it and were afraid of it. And man assumed it. Lo, he hath proved a tyrant and a fool! Q. 33:72)

397 Sufyan Thawri: Sufyan bin Sa' id bin Masruq, Abu ' Abdullah al-Thawri. A noted ascetic, he was also a well-known scholar, especially with regard to Tradition and the Law. He lived from about AH97/715CE to AH163/778CE. He died in Basrah.

398 Hasan of Basrah (Ḥasan al-Baṣrī): Abu Sa' id al-Hasan bin Yasar (AH23/642CE to AH110/728CE). Born in Madinah, his mother was a slave of one of the wives of the Prophet. He became the sec-

retary of the governor of Khorasan (northeastern Iran, northwestern Afghanistan, and parts of southern Central Asia). Settling in the new city of Basrah, he became famous for his piety and learning.

399 Mu' adh (bin) Jabal: Mu' adh bin Jabal bin Aws. He helped to collect the revelations contained in the Quran. The Prophet appointed him as the judge of Yemen. He died about AH18/639CE.

400 Abu Hanifah (Abū Ḥanīfah): Imam al-Nu' man bin Thabit bin Zuta Abu Hanifah. The son of a silk dealer, he was a leading scholar of Islamic law and theology and the eponymous founder of the Hanafite school of Islamic law. He earned his living as a silk dealer in his native city. He was born in Kufah in southern Iraq c. AH80ķ700 and died in a Baghdad prison in AH150/CE776, imprisoned by the Abbasid Caliph Mansur (rgd. AH136/CE754 to AH158/CE775) for refusing to accept the post of judge (qāḍī) in Kufah. A brilliant intellectual and theologian, he is the reputed founder of the Hanafi school of Islamic jurisprudence. Apparently, no authentic writings of his own are extant, but his influence on the development of Islamic law and ethics is incalculable. Today, more Muslims adhere to the Hanafite school than any other.

401 Shafi' i: Imam Muhammad bin Idris al-Shafi' i was the founder of one of the four orthodox (or Sunnite) schools of religious jurisprudence. He was born in Askalon (or nearby Gaza) in Palestine in AH150ķ767CE and died in Cairo in AH204/820CE. Unlike Abu Hanifah, he left behind a considerable body of writings.

402 " legal opinion" : *fatwā*.

403 See Note 391 above.

404 The direction of prayer is known as the qiblah. From wherever one is performing a formal prayer, it is the direction of Makkah, or more specifically, the House or Ka' bah situated in the heart of the city.

405 That is, this world and the Hereafter.

406 Abu Hurayrah: ' Abd al-Rahman bin Kakhr Abu Hurayrah. One of the Companions of the Prophet and a most important source for the Traditions. Abu Hurayrah (father of the kitten) was very fond of a kitten; hence the nickname. Because of his position in the Prophets' household, he related more Traditions than any other

individual. He died at Madinah in AH59/678CE.

407 The " god" (*ilāh*) that Ghazzali refers to is the one denied in the Testimony: " There is no god but God."

408 Talhah: Ṭalḥah bin ' Ubayd Allah al-Taymi. An early convert to Islam, he became a general and a wealthy land owner. When about 64 years old, he was killed in battle fighting against ' Ali in AH35/656CE.

409 " supererogatory prayers" : *nawāfil.*

410 Sa' id Musayyib: Sa' id bin al-Musayyib al-Qurashi al-Makhzuni. He was of the generation following the Companions called the Followers (tābiᶜīn). He was famous for his judicial decisions (fatwā) and was called the *faqīh al-fuqahā* (the jurist of the jurists) and also the Lord of the Followers (*sayyid al-tābiᶜīn*). He is quoted as saying that he would walk nights and days in search of a single Tradition. He died AH94/712CE.

411 " the summoner to prayer" : *muʾadhdhin.*

412 The day is divided into periods for each obligatory formal prayer. For example, the noon prayer begins at high noon (according to the position of the sun, not according to the clock) and lasts until mid-afternoon when the period for the afternoon prayer commences. Ghazzali says that performing obligatory formal prayers at the beginning of their portion of the day is more meritorious than later on within the limits of that period, although a prayer is equally valid when performed any time within those parameters.

413 " *jahrī* prayers" : Those prayers in which the Opening (*Al-Fātiḥah*) and the following Quranic selections are recited aloud in the first two bows, i.e., the dawn, sunset, and evening prayers.

414 Ghazzali' s intention here is that one should recite the entire verse beginning with these words.

415 Anas: Anas Malik. See Note 358.

416 The make-up bow to compensate for a missed bow or bows in a congregational prayer due to late arrival.

417 The obligatory Friday congregational prayer has two bows and is performed in lieu of the usual obligatory noon prayer of four bows. If one arrives too late to participate in the obligatory Friday congregational prayer, one should perform the four-bow noon prayer.

418 That is, on the same Friday.

419 That is, the intention to perform the greater and ablution to restore the state of purity and the intention to perform the greater ablution for Friday.

420 Ibn Mas‘ ud: ‘ Abdullah bin Mas‘ ud, a Companion of the Prophet and one of the “ illustrious ten” (*casharah mubashsharah*) who were assured of Paradise by he Prophet. He died at Madinah in AH32ḳ652CE at the age of 60.

421 The Greeting to the Mosque: a two-bow supererogatory prayer performed upon entering a mosque.

422 One should recite the first chapter of the Quran, the Opening (*Fātiḥah*) seven times.

4 23 One should recite the 112th chapter of the Quran seven times.

424 One should recite the 113th and 114th chapters of the Quran once. They both begin Say: I seek refuge with my Lord...

425 “ Traditions, non-Prophetic” : *āthār*.

426 The Greater Pilgrimage is called Ḥajj, and the Lesser is called *cUmrah*.

427 That is, the sunset obligatory formal prayer, for in the Islamic calendar, the next day (Saturday) begins at sunset, in accordance with Semitic custom, rather than at midnight as is the Western custom. Friday ends with the call to prayer for the sunset prayer, which begins Saturday.

428 That is, late afternoon.

429 The Night of Power (*shab-i qadr*): this is mentioned 97th chapter of the Quran: Lo! 433 dawn. (Q. 97:1-5) Much has been written through the centuries about the meaning and the spiritual and mystical interpretation of this chapter. There is a consensus that it is one of the last ten nights of Ramadan, probably the 25th, 27th, or 29th night. It appears to be associated with the first revelation of the Quran received by the Prophet. The revelations continued for about 23 years.

430 “ The Chapter of The Cave” (*Sūrat al-Kahf*): the 18th chapter of the Quran.

431 “ The Chapter of the Unity” (*Sūrat al-Ikhlāṣ*): the 112th chapter of the Quran. The word *ikhlāṣ* literally means “ sincerity,

loyalty, fidelity." As it comes from a root meaning " being pure, being saved from, being liberated," it can be construed to mean ' being cleansed of (polytheism, or other-than-God). Among other things, it is a refutation of the Christian doctrine of the divinity of Jesus and his fatherhood by God.

432 These are the first words of the Chapter of the Unity mentioned in the previous Note. It should be remarked that this chapter is among the shortest in the Quran, consisting of fewer than twenty words in Arabic.

433 That is, someone else will see his place in an inspired dream and inform him of it.

434 " The Cattle (al-Anᶜām), The Cave (al-Kahf), Ṭā Ḥā, and Yā Sīn" : These are the 6th, the 18th, the 20th, and the 36th chapters of the Quran respectively. The last two take their names from the Arabic letters, the like of which head several chapters. The significance of these letters is the subject of much speculation.

435 " The Prostration (al-Sajdah), Luqman, Smoke (al-Dukhān), and The Sovereignty (al- Mulk)" : these are the 32nd, the 31st, the 44th, and the 67th chapters of the Quran respectively.

436 " Formal prayer of praise" : *tasbīḥ*.

437 Noon: the text has *waqt-i zawāl* which is capable of several interpretations. Literally, it means ' the time of the decline' ; that is, the point where the sun starts to decline from its zenith in the sky, which is the true noon. (This is not necessarily the same as noon according to modern time zones.) The period referred to by Ghazzali is the forenoon.

General Index

Index to Quranic Verses

Books in English by or about Ibn al-Arabi

ALONE WITH THE ALONE: CREATIVE IMAGINATION IN THE SUFISM OF IBN ARABI Henry Corbin (A), Ralph Manheim (T) pp 454 "Henry Corbin's works are the best guide to the visionary tradition.... Corbin, like Scholem and Jonas, is remembered as a scholar of genius. He was uniquely equipped not only to recover Iranian Sufism for the West, but also to defend the principal Western traditions of esoteric spirituality."-- Introduction by Harold Bloom

In this book, which features a powerful new preface by Harold Bloom, Henry Corbin brings us to the very core of this movement with a penetrating analysis of Ibn 'Arabi's life and doctrines. Corbin begins with a kind of spiritual topography of the twelfth century, emphasizing the differences between exoteric and esoteric forms of Islam. He also relates Islamic mysticism to mystical thought in the West. The remainder of the book is devoted to two complementary essays: on "Sympathy and Theosophy" and "Creative Imagination and Creative Prayer." A section of notes and appendices includes original translations of numerous Sufi treatises.

Harold Bloom's preface links Sufi mysticism with Shakespeare's visionary dramas and high tragedies, such as The Tempest and Hamlet. These works, he writes, intermix the empirical world with a transcendent element. Bloom shows us that this Shakespearean cosmos is analogous to Corbin's "Imaginal Realm" of the Sufis, the place of soul or souls.

IBN ARABI: A MOVEMENT OF SUFI SPIRITUALITY IN THE MODERN WORLD Suha Taji-Farouki (A) pp 490 "A marvellous book ... historically and ethnographically well informed, with equally well-informed use of theory - handled with very considerable sensitivity - and lucidly written." Paul Heelas, author of The New Age Movement and The Spiritual Revolution "Empathetic in approach and immensely well-documented, this is an exemplary work. Its great importance for akbarian studies is its discussion of the way in which Ibn 'Arabi's teachings have been received and transformed in the modern world." Michel Chodkiewicz, author of *Seal of the Saints* and *An Ocean Without Shore* "A masterful and multifaceted study. This important book opens out to provide a much-needed critique of the sociology of Islam in the age of globalization." Victoria Rowe Holbrook, author of *The Unreadable Shores of Love and Beauty and Love* "The primary reference work on Beshara will be this thoughtful, intelligent and immensely well-researched book. We can learn a great deal from it." Peter Young, Principal of the Beshara School of Intensive Esoteric Education

CONTEMPLATION OF THE HOLY MYSTERIES: THE MASHAHID AL-ASRAR OF IBN ARABI IBN ARABI (A), Cecilia Twinch (T), Pablo Beneito (T) pp 136 A major work of mystical literature, this account focuses on 14 visions in the form of dramatic conversations with the divine, interspersed with dazzling visionary episodes regarding the nature of existence, humans' relationship with reality, and the way to achieve true happiness. The introduction presents a resume of Ibn Arabi's life and examines in detail the style and symbolism of the contemplations. Presented for the first time in English, this work is a superb example of Ibn Arabi's inimitable style and deep perception.

DIVINE GOVERNANCE OF THE HUMAN KINGDOM:INCLUDING WHAT THE SEEKER NEEDS AND THE ONE ALONE Ibn Arabi (A), al-Jerrahi al-Halveti (T) pp 300 A powerful but little known work, this volume contains three mystical texts. *Al-tadbirat*, the largest, is a fascinating treatise on the divine design and management of the world, and the central role the human model plays in the creative and governing process. The other two are *Kitab kunh ma la budda minhu lil-murid* (or, *What the Seeker Needs*), a brief guide for those want to follow the Sufi path, and *Kitab al-ahadiyyah* (or, *The One Alone*), an esoteric essay on transcendental unity.

DIVINE SAYINGS: 101 HADITH QUDSI: THE MISHKAT AL-ANWAR OF IBN ARABI by Muhyiddin Ibn 'Arabi (A) Stephen Hirtenstein and Martin Notcutt (T) pp 120
Much of the early scholarship on Ibn Arabi focused on his contributions to the intellectual sciences, especially metaphysics and spiritual psychology. Only gradually have scholars come to acknowledge the extent of his immersion in the transmitted sciences such as Quran and jurisprudence. As for the Traditions, it is difficult to overestimate the importance that he gives to the field. One must always keep in mind that his goal was to make the fullness of Muhammadan sanctity more accessible, that is, the whole range of spiritual perfections realized by Muhammad in act, word, and inner reality. As he says in a typical passage, 'Our vision of God in the Muhammadan form through the Muhammadan vision is the most complete vision that there may be. So we never cease encouraging people to achieve it, both orally and in this book' (*Futuhat* IV 184). In many ways it is the Traditions, Muhammad's own words, that provide seekers with the most immediate access to the Muhammadan form. Stephen Hirtenstein and Martin Notcutt have produced in *Divine Sayings* a beautifully translated version of Ibn Arabi's best known collection of Traditions, based not only on the published Arabic text but also several important manuscripts, with full scholarly apparatus. They have done a great service to all those who would like to gaze upon the Muhammadan form though the eyes of al-Shaykh al-Akbar. - William C. Chittick, Stony Brook University.

This classic collection (and first critical edition) of 101 memorable *Divine Sayings* related by the Prophet, translated in full for the first time in English, is not just an indispensable key to the teachings of Ibn Arabi and the wider traditions of Islamic spirituality. These short sayings are also a simple, direct, immediately accessible summary of the most universal spiritual lessons: The all-encompassing primacy of God's Love and Compassion; the corresponding human tasks of attentiveness, perseverance, and true service; the practical centrality of purified intention and constant remembrance—and the interaction of all those elements at each stage along our spiritual path. - James W. Morris, University of Exeter. Anqa Publishing.

THE FOUR PILLARS OF SPIRITUAL TRANSFORMATION: THE ADORNMENT OF THE SPIRITUALLY TRANSFORMED (*Hilyat al-abdal*) Muhyiddin Ibn Arabi (A), Stephen Hirtenstein (T) pp 80 "One of Ibn Arabi's most accessible and widely studied works, the *Hilyat al-abdal*, highlights the practical foundation of spiritual discipline underlying all of his metaphysical and theological writings." —Professor James Winston Morris, Boston College

IBN ARABI William C. Chittick (A) pp 160
Muhyi ad-Din Ibn Arabi (1165 - 1240) was an outstanding Spanish-born mystic and one of the most prolific writers in Islamic history. He made major contributions to the fields of Quran commentary, jurisprudence, theology, philosophy, cosmology, and spiritual psychology, and he was also a great poet of love. Although he is known as the first spokesman for 'the oneness of being', his real focus was the diverse modalities of human perfection. He marks a transition in Sufism in practical instructions on healing the heart and aphorisms on the divine mysteries to an equal stress on the theoretical issues that had long been the topic of philosophy and theology.

IBN AL-ARABI'S BARZAKH: THE CONCEPT OF THE LIMIT AND THE RELATIONSHIP BETWEEN GOD AND THE WORLD Salman H. Bashier (A) pp 206

IBN ARABI - TIME AND COSMOLOGY Mohamed Haj Yousef (A) pp 254 This book is the first comprehensive attempt to explain Ibn 'Arabī's distinctive view of time and its role in the process of creating the cosmos and its relation with the Creator. By comparing this original view with modern theories of physics and cosmology, Mohamed Haj Yousef constructs a new cosmological model that may deepen and extend our understanding of the world, while potentially solving some of the drawbacks in the current models such as the historical Zeno's paradoxes of motion and the recent Einstein-Podolsky-Rosen paradox (EPR) that underlines the discrepancies between Quantum Mechanics and Relativity.

IBN ARABI AND MODERN THOUGHT: THE HISTORY OF TAKING METAPHYSICS SERIOUSLY Peter Coates (A) pp 214 These penetrating metaphysical and spiritual teachings cross the divides of culture and time, providing unexpectedly modern insight.

IBN ARABI IN THE LATER ISLAMIC TRADITION: THE MAKING OF A POLEMICAL IMAGE IN MEDIEVAL ISLAM Alexander D. Knysh (A) pp 449 This book examines the fierce theological controversy over the great Muslim mystical thinker Ibn Arabi (1165-1242). Even during his lifetime, Ibn Arabi's conformity with the letter of the Muslim dogma was called into doubt by many scholars who were suspicious of the monistic (unitive) tendencies of his metaphysical teaching, of his claims to be the Prophet's successor and restorer of the true meaning of the Islamic revelation, and of his allegorical interpretation of the Quran. Following Ibn Arabi's death, these misgivings grew into an outright condemnation of his teachings by a number of influential thirteenth through fifteenth century theologians who portrayed him as a dangerous heretic bent on undermining the foundations of Islamic faith and communal life. In response to these grave accusations, Ibn Arabi's advocates praised him as the greatest saint of Islam who was unjustly slandered by the bigoted and narrow-minded critics.

As time went on, these conflicting images of the mystical thinker became rallying points for various political and scholarly factions vying for lucrative religious and administrative posts and ideological denomination. In thoroughly analyzing the heated debates around Ibn Arabi's ideas throughout the three centuries following his death, this study brings out discursive strategies and arguments employed by the polemicists, the hidden agendas they pursued, and the reasons for the striking longevity of the issue in Islamic literature up to the present day. On the theoretical level, this book reassesses the validity of such common dichotomies as orthodoxy versus heresy, mainstream versus mystical interpretations of Islam, and communalism versus individualism as well as other issues related to the history of Islamic thought.

IBN AL-ARABI ON THE MYSTERIES OF BEARING WITNESS TO THE ONENESS OF GOD AND PROPHETHOOD OF MUHAMMAD pp 396 from Chapter 67 of the *Futuhat al-Makkiyya* translated by Aisha Bewley. The master of Islamic spirituality describes the first of the five pillars of Islam by not only disclosing its mysteries but detailing the rulings of the divine law as well.

IBN AL-ARABI ON THE MYSTERIES OF PURIFICATION AND THE FORMAL PRAYER pp 730 from Chapters 68 and 69 of the *Futuhat al-Makkiyya* translated by Aisha Bewley. Ibn al-Arabi delves into the mysteries of the Islamic practices of purification and the formal prayer. In exhaustive detail he explains possible issues that may arise from the point of view of the divine law as well.

IBN AL-ARABI ON THE MYSTERIES OF THE PURIFYING ALMS pp 280 from Chapter 70 of the *Futuhat al-Makkiyya* translated by Aisha Bewley. Ibn al-Arabi explains the mysteries of the Islamic practice of the purifying alms in a way no other scholar ever has. He opens up doors of intuition to the astute reader.

IBN AL-ARABI ON THE MYSTERIES OF FASTING pp 292 from Chapter 71 of the *Futuhat al-Makkiyya* translated by Aisha Bewley. Ibn al-Arabi relates mysteries of fasting from the gnostic (*irfani*) perspective while at the same time following the divine law in every detail.

IBN AL-ARABI ON THE MYSTERIES OF PILGRIMAGE pp 326 from Chapter 72 of the *Futuhat al-Makkiyya* translated by Aisha Bewley. Every detail that a pilgrim would want to know about the mysteries of the pilgrimage in addition to the divine law rulings is contained in this volume.

IBN ARABI: THE TREE OF BEING Shaykh Tosun Bayrak (A) pp 255

IBN ARABI: THE VOYAGE OF NO RETURN Claude Addas (A) pp 134 This is a concise introduction to the life and thought of Ibn 'Arabi, who is considered as the 'Greatest of Sufi Masters'. Written by the author of a best-selling biography of Ibn Arabi, *Ibn Arabi: The Voyage of No Return* traces the major events of Ibn Arabi's life: his conversion to Sufism; his travels around Andalusia and the Maghreb; his meetings with the saints of his time; his journey to Mecca; his travels in Egypt, Palestine, Mesopotamia, Anatolia and Syria; his most important books. The events of Ibn Arabi's 'inner voyage', however, are far more spectacular than those of his outer life and are here presented directly from the many autobiographical sections found in his writings. Through her detailed analysis of Ibn Arabi's works and her profound understanding of his ideas, Claude Addas gives us a comprehensive insight into the major doctrines of this most influential of Sufi, masters: the doctrine of prophethood and sainthood, of inheritance from the prophets, of the 'imaginal world', of the 'unicity of Being', of the 'Seal of the Saints', and many others. Addas also introduces the main disciples of Ibn Arabi down to the nineteenth century and traces both his unequalled influence on the course of Sufism and the controversies that still surround him till today. *Ibn Arabi: The Voyage of No Return* is essential reading for anyone interested in Islamic mysticism and is a genuine contribution to scholarship in this field.

IMAGINAL WORLDS: IBN AL-ARABI AND THE PROBLEM OF RELIGIOUS DIVERSITY William C. Chittick (A) pp 220

ISLAM AND THE LIVING LAW: THE IBN AL-ARABI APPROACH Eric Winkel (A) pp 128 Ibn Al Arabi, the mystic scholar of the 13th century, highlights the ambiguities of language and the polysemantic, multi-faceted text of the Quran. With Al Arabi's help, Winkel expounds how narrowly religion is interpreted by most scholars. Al Arabi disturbs the comfort of man-made religion by his reflections on language, and Winkel's book takes up the same challenge.

JOURNEY TO THE LORD OF POWER: A SUFI MANUAL ON RETREAT Ibn Arabi (A), Abd al-Kerim al-Jili (Commentary), Rabia Terry Harris (T) pp 128 This is the first English translation of a 12th-century Sufi text dealing with spiritual ascent. Ibn Arabi's writings have influenced both Muslim and Christian traditions.

KERNEL OF THE KERNEL Muhyi al-Din Muhammad ibn Ali Ibn al-Arabi (A) pp 50

MECCAN REVELATIONS OF IBN ARABI, VOLUMES I AND II Edited and translations by Michel Chodkiewicz and William Chittick pp384 **MECCAN REVELATIONS OF IBN ARABI, VOLUME II** Edited by Michel Chodkiewicz (E) pp 270 Perhaps no mystic in the history of the world has delved as deeply into the inner knowledge that informs our being as did Ibn 'Arabi. He was born into the cultural and religious crucible of Andalusian Spain in 1165, a place and time in which Muslim, Jewish and Christian scholars learned from each other and from the Greek classics that were then being translated and circulated. Drawing from the most advanced philosophical and metaphysical thinking of his time and from his extensive knowledge of the religion of Islam, Ibn 'Arabi created an extraordinary mystical theology that essentially sprang from his own spiritual realization. Because of the advanced nature of his teachings he has been known for 800 years as the Sheikh al-Akbar, or the Greatest Master.

Because of the subtlety of his language and complexity of his thought, access to Ibn 'Arabi has always been difficult and translation daunting. Previously only short extracts were available in English. This volume, is the second of our acclaimed translation of Les Illuminations de la Mecque, and contains more of the "Greatest Shaykh's" wisdom for the first time in English, on such issues as the gnostic and the sacred law, the mystic properties of Quranic letters, the secrets of Forgiveness and the attainment of Divine Nearness.
This great book soars beyond time, culture and any particular form of religion. Describing what is fundamental to our humanity, it is astonishingly universal. Finally readers in the West have an entree into one of the most important, profound works of world literature.

MUHYIDDIN IBN 'ARABI - A COMMEMORATIVE VOLUME Edited by Michael Tiernan pp 380 This unique volume celebrates the 750th anniversary of the death of one of the world's mystical giants, Muhyiddin Ibn Arabi, known throughout the Muslim world simply as the Shaykh al-akbar (the greatest teacher). This text brings together, for the first time, works by eminent scholars and students of the Shaykh from many different countries.

MYSTICAL ASTROLOGY ACCORDING TO IBN 'ARABI Titus Burckhardt (A), Keith Critchlow (F), Bulent Rauf (T) pp 64 A unique work, providing the underlying spiritual principles (from the point of view of one of the greatest Sufi masters who ever lived) lacking in most modern books of astrology. It will complement and deepen anyone's personal library or collection of works on astrology.

PERFECT HARMONY (CALLIGRAPHER'S NOTEBOOKS) Ibn 'Arabi (A), Hassan Massoudy (I) pp 64 Among the other three volumes in Shambhala's series is Perfect Harmony: Sufi Poetry of Ibn Arabi, which pairs the poetry of the 13th-century Sufi mystic with contemporary calligraphy by Hassan Massoudy. In a moving afterword, Massoudy explains how he became involved in calligraphy as a child, and how his work is inspired by poetry.

PRAYER FOR SPIRITUAL ELEVATION AND PROTECTION Muhyiddin Ibn Arabi (A), Suha Taji-Farouki (T) pp 150 "The importance of having a stable text with full vocalization based upon the best manuscripts is evident. But the author's careful study of the chains of transmission and the detailed information about the recitation of the prayer in the contemporary world are also of the highest interest." Prof Michel Chodkiewicz

QUEST FOR THE RED SULPHUR: THE LIFE OF IBN 'ARABI QUEST FOR THE RED SULPHUR: THE LIFE OF IBN 'ARABI Claude Addas (A), Peter Kingsley (T) pp 347 The first serious biography of the most influential figure in the history of Islamic mysticism. It is based on an enormous amount of documentary evidence...In his voluminous writings Ibn Arabi recounted his visionary experiences, his journeys, real and imaginary, and his meetings with other mystics, both alive and dead.

Quest for the Red Sulphur: The Life of Ibn Arabi is undoubtedly a landmark in Ibn Arabi studies. Until the publication of this book, anyone who wanted to learn about the life of Ibn Arabi has had little choice of material to work from. This major study by Claude Addas is based on a detailed analysis of a whole range of Ibn Arabi's own writings as well as a vast amount of secondary literature in both Arabic and Persian. The result is the first-ever attempt to reconstruct what proves to have been a double itinerary: on the hand the journey that took Ibn Arabi from his native Andalusia to Damascus—and on the other hand, the 'Night Journey' which carried him along the paths of asceticism and prayer to the ultimate stage of revelation

RINGSTONES OF WISDOM (FUSUS AL-HIKAM) Ibn al-Arabi (A) Caner K. Dagli (T) pp 352 *The Ringstones of Wisdom* is one of the most influential and controversial books of Islamic civilization. This relatively brief but far-reaching text covers topics such as creation. prayer, the relationship with God with the world, and the interpretation of dreams.

SEAL OF THE SAINTS. PROPHETHOOD AND SAINTHOOD IN THE DOCTRINE OF IBN ARABI Michel Chodkiewicz (A), Liadain Sherrard (T) pp 192 This is by far the best available explanation of the central importance of sanctity for understanding both the practical and the theoretical teachings of Sufism. - William Chittick; An extraordinarily good book about an extremely difficult thinker...Chodkiewicz not only knows the texts remarkably well, but also avoids and rejects certain errors of perspective common among other scholars. TLS

SELF-DISCLOSURE OF GOD: PRINCIPLES OF IBN AL-'ARABI'S COSMOLOGY William C. Chittick (A) pp 483 *The Self-Disclosure of God* continues the author's investigations of the world view of Ibn al-Arabi, the greatest theoretician of Sufism and the "seal of the Muhammadan saints." The book is divided into three parts, dealing with the relation between God and the cosmos, the structure of the cosmos, and the nature of the human soul. A long introduction orients the reader and discusses a few of the difficulties faced by Ibn al-Arabi's interpreters. Like Chittick's earlier work, *The Sufi Path of Knowledge*, this book is based primarily on Ibn al-Arabi's monumental work, *al-Futuhat al-makkiyya "The Meccan Openings."* More than one hundred chapters and subsections are translated, not to mention shorter passages that help put the longer discussions in context. There are detailed indexes of sources, Koranic verses, and hadiths. The book's index of technical terminology will be an indispensable reference for all those wishing to delve more deeply into the use of language in Islamic thought in general and Sufism in particular.

SEVEN DAYS OF THE HEART Pablo Beneito (A), Ibn Arabi (Author), Stephen Hirtenstein (T) pp 182 *The Seven Days of the Heart* is a collection of prayers for the nights and days of the week by one of the world's greatest mystics, Muhyiddin Ibn Arabi (1165-1240). This is the first time these extraordinary and beautiful prayers have been translated into English. There are fourteen prayers, full of the most astounding expressions of contemplation and devotion to God. This is a unique spiritual masterpiece, made available for the first time to English-speaking readers.

STATIONS OF DESIRE: LOVE ELEGIES FROM IBN 'ARABI AND NEW POEMS Michael Sells (A) pp 136 Islamic poetry is enjoying an influx of readers in English, but poems by such Sufi saints as Rumi and Ibn Arabi have suffered from terrible translations. Sells, who has proven his talents in the highly regarded anthology Early Islamic Mysticism (1996), is confident enough to include some of his own poems, inspired by Ibn Arabi's love elegies, alongside his versions of the master's work, and his deftly wrought, spare verses are quite good in their own right. But Ibn Arabi is the star here, and these translations show the twelfth-century Muslim mystic at his very best. This is truly beautiful love poetry, and the oft-posed question of whether the beloved in it is God or a human quickly becomes irrelevant. Furthermore, by invoking the Beloved in both genders, Ibn Arabi invokes love that transcends gender and identity, and flies in the face of the stereotype of Islam as inherently sexist. Love for God and romantic love each is, as Ibn Arabi writes, "a garden among the flames." Truly a collection to be treasured. John Green

SUFI METAPHYSICS AND QURANIC PROPHETS: IBN 'ARABI'S THOUGHT AND METHOD IN THE FUSUS AL-HIKAM Ronald L. Nettler (A) pp 160 The *Fusus al-Hikam* is acknowledged to be a summary statement of the sufi metaphysics of the "Greatest Master", Ibn Arabi (d.1240). It is also recognized that the *Fusus* is a work of great complexity both in its ideas and its style; and, over the centuries, numerous commentaries have been written on it. Each of the chapters of the *Fusus* is dedicated to a Quran prophet with whom a particular "wisdom" is associated. In *Sufi Metaphysics and Quranic Prophets*: Ibn Arabi's Thought and Method in the *Fusus al-Hikam*, Ronald Nettler examines ten chapters from the *Fusus* which exemplify the ideas, method and perspective of the entire work. Concentrating on a detailed analysis of the text, the author brings out the profound connection and integration of scripture and metaphysics in the world-view of Ibn Arabi. Sufi Metaphysics and Quranic Prophets serves not only as an explication of Ibn Arabi's thought in the *Fusus*, but is also a great aid in the overall understanding of Ibn Arabi's theology.

SUFI PATH OF KNOWLEDGE William C. Chittick (A) pp 478
Translations of Ibn Arabi from the *Meccan Revelations*.

SUFIS OF ANDALUSIA: THE RUH AL-QUDS AND AL-DURAT FAKHIRAH M IBN 'ARABI (A) pp 173 This work was originally published in 1971. Muhyiddin Ibn Arabi was one of the greatest mystics whose influence was pervasive and profound. *Sufis of Andalusia* consists of biographical sketches of some of the contemplatives and spiritual masters among whom Ibn Arabi spent his early years.

SUFISM AND TAOISM: A COMPARATIVE STUDY OF KEY PHILOSOPHICAL CONCEPTS Toshihiko Izutsu (A) pp 493 In this deeply learned work, Toshihiko Izutsu compares the metaphysical and mystical thought-systems of Sufism and Taoism and discovers that, although historically unrelated, the two share features and patterns which prove fruitful for a transhistorical dialogue. His original and suggestive approach opens new doors in the study of comparative philosophy and mysticism.

Izutsu begins with Ibn Arabi, analyzing and isolating the major ontological concepts of this most challenging of Islamic thinkers. Then, in the second part of the book, Izutsu turns his attention to an analysis of parallel concepts of two great Taoist thinkers, Lao-tzu and Chuang-tzu. Only after laying bare the fundamental structure of each world view does Izutsu embark, in the final section of the book, upon a comparative analysis. Only thus, he argues, can he be sure to avoid easy and superficial comparisons. Izutsu maintains that both the Sufi and Taoist world views are based on two pivots--the Absolute Man and the Perfect Man--with a whole system of oncological thought being developed between these two pivots. Izutsu discusses similarities in these ontological systems and advances the hypothesis that certain patterns of mystical and metaphysical thought may be shared even by systems with no apparent historical connection.

This second edition of Sufism and Taoism is the first published in the United States. The original edition, published in English and in Japan, was prized by the few English-speaking scholars who knew of it as a model in the field of comparative philosophy. Making available in English much new material on both sides of its comparison, Sufism and Taoism richly fulfills Izutsu's motivating desire "to open a new vista in the domain of comparative philosophy."

TARJUMAN AL-ASHWAQ Muhyiddin Ibn Al-Arabi (A) pp 155
The *Tarjuman al-Ashwaq* or *Interpreter of Desires* by Ibn Arabi is acknowledged as one of the major works in Sufi literature.

THE REFLECTIVE HEART: DISCOVERING SPIRITUAL INTELLIGENCE IN IBN ARABI'S MECCAN ILLUMINATIONS James Winston Morris (A) pp 424 For centuries Ibn Arabi has been considered the "Greatest Master" of Islamic spiritual teaching, but Western readers have only recently had access to his greatest writings. This introduction to Ibn Arabi's *Meccan Illuminations* highlights the mysticism and realization of Sufi spiritual life, providing an intellectually penetrating look without requiring specialized knowledge. The development of several key themes and modes of reflection in Ibn Arabi's spiritual teachings are explored as are the gradually unfolding meanings that distinguish this important classical text of Sufi practice.

TWENTY-NINE PAGES: INTRODUCTION TO IBN 'ARABI'S "METAPHYSICS OF UNITY" A.E. Affifi (A) pp 80

UNIVERSAL TREE AND THE FOUR BIRDS (MYSTICAL

TREATISES OF MUHYIDDIN IBN ARABI) Muhyiddin Ibn Arabi (A), Angela Jaffray (T) pp 135 "In the history of monotheistic spirituality, in particular its Western, Abrahamic branch incorporating Judaism, Christianity, and Islam, there is really no one, from taproot to topmost leaf tip, like Muhyiddin Ibn Arabi. This short, lyrical and evocative book, with a conceptual spine strong as tensile steel, makes a rich perspective palpably real to the reader through the eloquence of its imagery and the uniqueness of its author's unforgettable voice."

UNIVERSAL TREE AND THE FOUR BIRDS THE SPIRITUAL LIFE AND THOUGHTS OF IBN AL-ARABI
Stephen Hirtenstein (A) pp 256 "By far the simplest and most heart-warming rendition of Ibn Arabi and his teachings that I have come across. A wonderful contribution to the integration of spirituality in our modern scientific thinking by making Ibn Arabi accessible to the popular mind." -- Amit Goswami, professor of Physics, University of Oregon, author of The Self-Aware Universe

CPSIA information can be obtained
at www.ICGtesting.com
Printed in the USA
JSHW050755290622
27548JS00005B/79

9 781567 447750